ROLLING THUNDER AGAINST THE RISING SUN

ROLLING THUNDER AGAINST THE RISING SUN

The Combat History of U.S. Army Tank Battalions in the Pacific in World War II

Gene Eric Salecker

STACKPOLE
BOOKS

To my brothers—
Alan, Gary, Paul, and Greg.
I love you all so very much.

Published by
STACKPOLE BOOKS
5067 Ritter Road
Mechanicsburg, PA 17055
www.stackpolebooks.com

Cover design by Tracy Patterson

Printed in the United States of America

10 9 8 7 6 5 4 3 2 1

FIRST EDITION

Library of Congress Cataloging-in-Publication Data

Salecker, Gene Eric, 1957–
 Rolling thunder against the Rising Sun : the combat history of U.S. Army tank battalions in the Pacific in World War II / Gene Eric Salecker. — 1st ed.
  p. cm.
 Includes bibliographical references and index.
 ISBN-13: 978-0-8117-0314-7
 ISBN-10: 0-8117-0314-2
 1. World War, 1939–1945—Campaigns—Oceania. 2. World War, 1939–1945—Tank warfare. 3. United States. Army—History—World War, 1939–1945. I. Title.
D767.9.S36 2008
940.54'26—dc22
                                                                    2007036632

TABLE OF CONTENTS

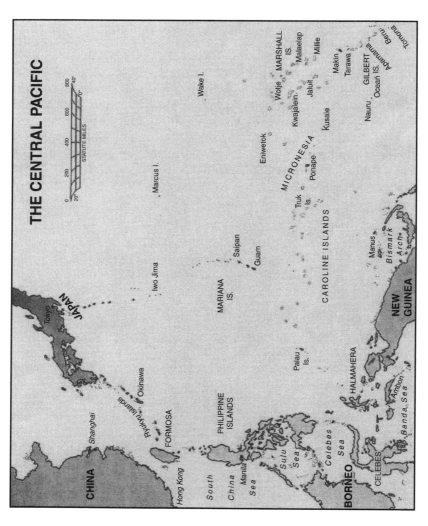

The Central Pacific

CHAPTER ONE

Baptism of Fire

Five M3 Stuart light tanks of Company B, 192nd Tank Battalion (Light) rumbled out of the Philippine village of Rosario on the main island of Luzon late on the morning of December 22, 1941, heading west toward the coastal road skirting Lingayen Gulf. Brig. Gen. James R. N. Weaver, the Provisional Tank Group commander, in charge of both the 192nd and 194th Tank Battalions had been informed that a large Japanese landing party had come ashore earlier that morning and was moving south toward the coastal village of Damortis, six miles to the west. Since the 194th TB, plus Company D of the 192nd TB, had been sent south to protect the area below Manila, General Weaver called upon the tanks of the remaining three companies of the 192nd TB, Companies A, B and C, to stop the Japanese thrust from the Lingayen area.[1]

2nd Lt. Ben R. Morin, commanding officer of Company B, 192nd TB, was in the lead tank. Originally, Gen. Jonathan M. Wainwright, commander of the Northern Luzon Force of Filipino and American troops, had asked for a full "company of [fifteen] tanks" but because of a shortage of gasoline, only five tanks were sent forward. Pvt. Lester I. Tenenberg (Company B, 192nd TB) wrote, "As our company prepared for our assault on the enemy, we found to our dismay that only enough fuel for five tanks had been delivered to our bivouac area from post ordinance. After carefully calculating the number of gallons needed for the assault and the return, or possible continued fighting or withdrawal, our commanding officer [General Weaver] ordered only five tanks to attack the Japanese forces at once."[2]

Upon reaching Damortis, Lieutenant Morin discovered that the invading Japanese were still to the north, closer to the landing beaches. Reports received from Filipino troops in the area suggested that the Japanese had not yet landed their tanks and/or artillery. Believing these reports, General Wainwright ordered Weaver's tanks to lead the counterattack and go all the way up the coast road.[3]

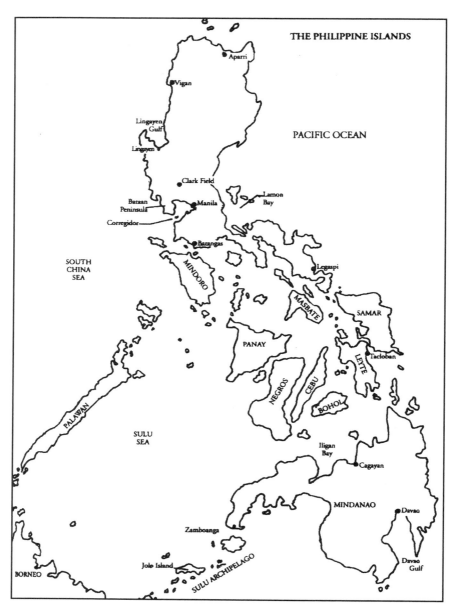

The Philippine Islands

"General Wainwright . . . knew nothing about the deployment and use of tanks in warfare," wrote Private Tenenberg, "but ordered our tank company to lead an attack on the Japanese forces believed to be in the area." Without time for reconnaissance, General Weaver and the 192nd TB went on the offensive believing they were facing only a handful of Japanese infantry.[4]

As the five tanks continued north along the coast road, Lieutenant Morin decided it was time to fire a trial round with his 37mm cannon. When he did so, the cannon jammed and locked in recoil.

Col. James H. Leach, a tank commander stationed in Hawaii, had run into the same problem. He wrote, "[We] were able to test fire the 37mm gun on some of the tanks. . . . We discovered to our dismay that several of the 37s would not return to battery for a second shot. When the gun went into recoil, the gun shield dropped just enough to bind the tube. . . . Later, we enlarged the hole in the gun shield." Unfortunately, Lieutenant Morin did not have time to fix his cannon. With only four .30 caliber Browning machine guns (one in a coaxial position mounted alongside the cannon and fired by the gunner; two stationary, forward-firing sponson-mounted guns located directly above the left and right tracks fired remotely by the driver; and a chassis mounted swivel gun on the right side of the hull fired by the assistant driver) Morin continued on.[5]

Since the coastal road was so narrow, the five tanks traveled single file at fifteen miles per hour. Suddenly they came upon the first hostile troops they had ever seen. Walking down the road was an equally surprised column of Japanese soldiers, who quickly dove into the ditches, firing their rifles as they did. Unable to fire the jammed 37mm cannon, Morin's crew opened fire with the coaxial turret machine gun, while his driver, Pvt. Louis Zelis, began to weave the tank from side to side, remotely firing the stationary sponson-mounted guns down one ditch and then the other.[6]

About two miles south of Agoo, as the tanks rounded a bend, they ran into a Japanese roadblock consisting of enemy infantry, tanks, and antitank guns. Lt. Emmett F. Gibson (Company B, 192nd TB) later wrote, "There was nothing in the experience of Morin and his crew to prepare them for such a bath of death as this." Almost instantly Lieutenant Morin's tank was hit by a round from a Japanese tank or anti-tank gun. The unexpected shot sprang the driver's door hatch in front of Private Zelis, exposing him to incoming small arms fire. Seconds later, a second shot hit in almost the exact same spot, clipping the open hatch and leaving it dangling over the edge of the hull. With rifle fire plinking off the tank, Lieutenant Morin signaled Private Zelis to pull the vehicle out of the line of fire.[7]

While the other American tanks in line chewed up the enemy infantry with machine-gun and cannon fire, Morin's tank came to a stop. Almost immediately, an 8.5-ton Japanese Type 95 Ha-Go light tank rushed forward and straight at the halted 13.5-ton Stuart. Although U.S. tankers had been told that the Japanese had not yet landed their tanks, the appearance of this Japanese light tank indicated how wrong the reports were. Sitting completely still, the M3 Stuart was a sitting duck and the Japanese tank struck it full force on the left drive sprocket. Quickly, Private Zelis threw the Stuart into reverse and pulled back up onto the road. Throwing the M3 into forward again, Zelis discovered the left drive sprocket was badly damaged and instead of going forward, the tank swung to the left and onto a dry, hard rice paddy.[8]

As the Stuart spun to the left, the tank's right side was exposed to heavy enemy fire. Shells struck the hull and, as the tank continued to turn, the right rear.

Having only light, one-inch armor on the sides and rear, a Japanese shell tore through the iron plating around the engine compartment and demolished the battery case, causing the Stuart to come to a complete stop between fifty and seventy-five yards from the road. The radio and electronically-controlled sponson side guns went dead and the engine caught fire, pouring smoke into the fighting compartment. Not knowing what the smoke was, Lieutenant Morin ordered his crew to don their gas masks while Private Zelis climbed from his driver's seat and extinguished the blaze. Although the fire was out, the heat inside the tank was unbearable.[9]

While Lieutenant Morin's tank was being battered, the four following tanks were having trouble of their own. The second tank, commanded by Staff Sgt. Albert T. Edwards, also took heavy incoming fire but managed to return the fire with its 37mm cannon and .30 caliber machine guns. As the crew watched in horror, their light caliber cannon rounds glanced off the enemy tanks without doing any appreciable damage. Unlike the Stuart tank, which had perpendicular surfaces and took the brunt of the enemy shells head-on, the Japanese tanks had sloping sides that deflected the American rounds. Although some historians believe the American rounds missed the enemy tanks because of their low silhouette, the Type 95 Ha-Go tank stood seven feet two inches high, only thirteen inches shorter than the M3 Stuart tank. It was the angled, sloping surfaces of the Japanese tanks that saved them from the rounds of the American tanks, not the "low silhouette."[10]

Additionally, the American tankers quickly discovered another deficiency with the construction of their Stuarts. The plates making up the hull were riveted

192nd or 194th TB M3 under attack by Japanese soldiers. MACARTHUR MEMORIAL

together, not welded. When enemy shells hit the rivet heads, the rivets tore away and ricocheted around the fighting compartment. More than one American tanker would be wounded by these deadly, stinging missiles.[11]

As the fighting at the Japanese roadblock continued, PFC Henry J. Deckert, the gunner in Sergeant Edwards' tank, cleaned out an enemy machine-gun nest with his turret-mounted coaxial machine gun. Rated as a cook, Deckert had successfully lobbied for a job as a tanker and quickly had proven his worth. Seconds later, however, an armor-piercing shell tore through the turret and decapitated Deckert, making him the first American tanker to be killed in a tank-versus-tank fight in World War II.[12]

The same shell that killed Private Deckert passed out the rear of the tank and through the engine compartment. Although the shell passed clear through the engine, the tough little Stuart kept running. When Sergeant Edwards spotted Lieutenant Morin's tank sitting dead in the dry rice paddy with smoke pouring from the engine compartment, he believed Morin and his crew were dead. With Deckert decapitated and a huge hole in his engine, Edwards ordered his driver to turn around and head for safety.[13]

The crews of the other three tanks also thought Lieutenant Morin's crew was already dead, so they too turned around and fled the Japanese roadblock. All of the American tanks had sustained some damage, including one tank that had its oil system completely disabled and another that had a shell go through its main drive. Still, the reliable Stuarts were able to race back to Rosario. Private Tenenberg commented about the dependability of the Stuart: "How [Sergeant Edward's] tank continued moving is beyond me, but the motor kept running, and the tank made it all the way back to our bivouac area. Only when it got there did it stop, immobilized." Although mechanics worked on all four tanks for hours, they eventually gave up the ghost. General Weaver recalled, "All four tanks [eventually] had to be towed out [of Rosario] and all were lost later in the day by bombing or mishaps during salvage."[14]

Unknown to the others, Lieutenant Morin and his crew were still alive inside their smoking tank. Shortly after the other four American tanks withdrew, the Japanese finally stopped shooting and four Type 95 Ha-Go light tanks came straight toward the disabled Stuart. Unwilling to subject his crew to additional injury, Lieutenant Morin threw open his commander's hatch and came out with his hands up, becoming the first American tanker to be captured in World War II.[15] As each crewman climbed out of the tank, he must have wondered how he had gotten into such a mess.

Company B of the 192nd Tank Battalion had originally been the 33rd Tank Company, a National Guard unit from Maywood, Illinois. After World War I, the United States War Department had questioned the feasibility of tanks, deciding they should only be used to help the advance of infantry. A Provisional Tank Brigade, consisting of several National Guard tank companies wholly subordinate to the infantry, was established under the National Defense Act of 1920. In actuality, however, the Provisional Tank Brigade never came into existence. Instead of organizing the independent tank companies into a single fighting force, the units were split apart, with the different companies being assigned to different infantry divisions.[16]

Tank supporters believed the companies should be consolidated and operated separately from the infantry, arguing that foot soldiers would slow the tanks down and take away their advantage of speed and mobility. The tankers lobbied the War Department to form a totally independent branch of the Army, similar to the infantry, cavalry or artillery. Instead, the War Department compromised. Although most of the tanks would still belong to the National Guard tank companies and be subordinate to the infantry, a handful were turned over to the cavalry to form the 7th Cavalry Brigade (Mechanized).[17]

In spite of the constant nudging by tank enthusiasts, the War Department refused to budge any further until September 1939, when a highly mobile force of German tanks crashed across the German-Polish border and overran Poland in only eighteen days. Suddenly the effectiveness of an independent armored unit had been horrifically demonstrated. Surprised by the ease and swiftness of the attack, the U.S. War Department considered the establishment of some form of independent armored unit. In April 1940, General-in-Chief George C. Marshall pitted the infantry and their tanks against the 7th Cavalry Brigade at the Louisiana maneuvers. Although badly outnumbered, the mobile use of the cavalry tanks beat the sluggish use of the infantry tanks hands down. After that, General Marshall seriously began considering the establishment of an independent armored arm of the service.[18]

Then, in May 1940, after the German blitzkrieg easily overran Belgium, Luxembourg, and France, the War Department decided it was time to act. On July 10, the 7th Cavalry Brigade and the Provisional Tank Brigade were combined to form a new independent arm of the Army, the U.S. Armored Force, consisting of two armored divisions formed from existing elements of the infantry, cavalry, and artillery. Five days later, the first independent tank battalion was created. Separate from the two new divisions, the independent battalion was designated a general headquarters (GHQ) tank battalion and came under the direct control of Army Headquarters. As a small, self-contained armored unit, the independent tank battalion could be attached to any infantry regiment that needed heavy firepower.[19]

On September 1, 1940, orders went out to establish four additional separate GHQ tank battalions. Pursuant to a presidential order dated November 16, 1940, the first unit, the 192nd GHQ Tank Battalion, was inducted into active service on November 25 with the U.S. Army for one year of duty. Taken from the existing National Guard units, the new battalion was formed from the 32nd Tank Company, from Janesville, Wisconsin, (now Company A, 192nd TB); the 33rd Tank Company, from Maywood, Illinois, (Company B, 192nd TB); the 37th Tank Company, from Port Clinton, Ohio, (Company C, 192nd TB); and the 38th Tank Company, from Harrodsburg, Kentucky (Company D, 192nd TB). Once under Federal control, the companies were ordered to report to Fort Knox, Kentucky, for training as a unit.[20]

Upon arrival in mid-December, the tankers discovered the Army was not yet ready for them. Sgt. Morgan French (Company D, 192nd TB) noted, "They put us in tents for a while, because they were building all new barracks at Fort Knox at that particular time. And what really made it so bad, it was wintertime and it got real cold."[21] While the men waited for the buildings to be completed, their ranks were filled by men who had been drafted into Federal service. "From the new men coming in under [the] Selective Service system, we were able to hand-pick the men we wanted to fill us up to battalion strength," wrote Lt. Alvin C. Poweleit, the assistant battalion surgeon. "The new recruits were carefully replaced in the tank companies of their state, Wisconsin selectees in Company A, Illinois in Company B, Ohio in Company C, and Kentucky in Company D." Although Poweleit felt that the new recruits were "extremely good men," Sergeant French had a differing opinion:

> I tell you, it was really something to see these young men coming down from the lower parts of Kentucky; some of their hair was down to their shoulders and some of the uniforms didn't fit them, some of them had World War I uniforms issued to them!

In addition to the four line companies, a Headquarters Company was formed. Cpl. Robert J. Stewart (Company A, 192nd TB) from Janesville, Wisconsin, wrote, "When we got down to Fort Knox they made the Headquarters Company. It was the company that had to do with supplies; one part of the Headquarters Company was in charge of food and the other was in charge of the vehicles, maintenance on the tanks and the trucks, things like that." To form the Headquarters Company, men were taken from each of the four line companies. "So that was our first split of some of the original guys from Janesville," Stewart added. "They were no longer members of Company A, but Headquarters Company. Not that it mattered a whole lot of difference, because our whole battalion was a small battalion, and still like a family."[22]

While the 192nd TB was being trained in Kentucky, the other three GHQ tank battalions were coming together elsewhere. In January 1941 the 193rd TB was brought into Federal service at Fort Benning, Georgia, and a month later the 191st TB was federalized at Fort George G. Meade, Maryland. The last battalion, the 194th TB, came under Federal jurisdiction on March 12, 1941 at Fort Lewis, Washington, and for some reason consisted of only three companies. The 34th Tank Company from Brainerd, Minnesota, became Company A, 194th TB; the 35th Tank Company, from St. Joseph, Missouri, became Company B, 194th TB; and the 40th Tank Company, from Salinas, California, became Company C, 194th TB.[23]

Like the 192nd TB, the 194th TB discovered the Army was ill-prepared for their arrival. "We arrived at Fort Lewis on February 22, 1941," wrote Maj. Ernest B. Miller, commanding officer of the battalion. "A wild scramble ensued. We worked night and day. Housing was not yet completed. A Headquarters and Headquarters Company [194th TB] had to be organized . . . [and] proper uniforms were not available nor could the Quartermaster furnish them." And, like the 192nd TB at Fort Knox, the ranks of the 194th TB had to be filled by the draft. "Early in April,

1941," Miller wrote, "we received draftees to fill the battalion to war strength. They came to us all the way from the Middle West to the Pacific Coast."[24]

As the 194th TB began its training, it ran into big problems. "Up to the latter part of July, we had only eight tanks—the 'Mae West' type (double turret)—1937 vintage, and just about worn out," wrote Miller. "Our maintenance crews worked like slaves to keep them running. . . . The latter part of July, we received a few more tanks. They were single turret jobs, also of 1937 vintage, but reconditioned."[25]

Since the Army was ill prepared to equip both the 192nd and the 194th TBs, each outfit began its training with old M2A2 double turret "Mae West" National Guard tanks. Recalled Lieutenant Poweleit, "When we arrived at Fort Knox, each tank company had two tanks which had been issued to them two or three years prior to reporting to active duty. These tanks comprised our entire armor." To build up their inventory, the tankers from the 192nd TB had to improvise. "[T]he only way we could get a tank would be to take what had been salvaged by some other unit," wrote Poweleit. "We made frequent visits to the salvage yard. . . . By drawing from the ordnance replacement parts, we reassembled enough tanks so that we [soon] had almost a full complement of tanks."[26]

Because of the lack of equipment, the new tank units were forced to improvise during some of their training exercises. "[W]e did some mock training with broomsticks and tin cans," Lieutenant Poweleit remembered, "but this was limited. . . . This part was overplayed in some of the information that was put out prior to World War II." At Fort Lewis, the 194th TB improvised in another way. "Two-by-four frames were constructed of approximately the same size as the crew compartment of the tank," Major Miller wrote, "inside of which men were placed to learn tank signals and coordination. . . . [We] used our imagination."[27]

Being National Guard units, the tankers had been required to train with regular Army troops two weeks out of every year. Sergeant French remembered, "We were under the supervision of the regular Army and went through maneuvers with units of the regular Army. So, if we goofed up they would correct us. . . . [W]e had sixty-six men in a company, and all of them were pretty well trained in whatever their job was. Tank driver, tank commander, crewman, radio operator, and all that."[28]

Because of this training, the tankers developed skills and tactics that might have been lacking if left on their own. When the men from the 192nd and 194th TBs arrived at Fort Knox and Fort Lewis, respectively, they were reasonably familiar with Army doctrine and routine. Additionally, because they were old National Guard units, they had a mixture of talent in their units. Lieutenant Poweleit recalled:

One of the things we did have that was an asset to us, was the fact that we had an unlimited number of men with very good mechanical ability. Many of them were mechanics in civilian life, working in garages and other types of skilled trades. . . . [Some] had experience in operating equipment, such as bulldozers and all types of tractors, and knew how to take care of equipment and how to repair it. Of course, we sent as many men as we could to the armored school at Fort Knox which was being started at that particular time.[29]

In July, the 194th TB was notified that it was to participate in large-scale maneuvers around Fort Lewis. Although Major Miller welcomed the exercise, he disliked the way his tanks were to be used. He reported, "The directive stated that the tanks of the 194th would be split up so as to give both sides tank units. . . . I immediately replied with a carefully worded letter, pointing out that it was totally against Armored Forces doctrines to split tank units; that they should function as a complete and composite battalion." He ended his letter by, "calling attention to the necessity of allowing the 194th to participate as one team, for which they were created, and to gain the benefits of an enviable training phase, which they had had no opportunity to participate in before."[30]

Instead of rejoining the 194th TB, the War Department broke the battalion up even further. With diplomatic relations strained between Japan and the United States, the War Department decided in August 1941, to send an Army task force to Alaska, including one company from the 194th TB. Although Major Miller fought the move, he eventually selected Company B. And, to make matters worse, Company B was to be given most of the tanks the 194th TB had on hand.

Then, just when it appeared as though things had hit rock bottom, Major Miller was informed that his two remaining companies were being sent to the Philippine Islands to bolster American and Filipino forces already there. Although Miller was told that the 194th TB "may have to come off the boat fighting," the unit was not restored to full strength—Company B still went to Alaska. The 194th TB would be going to the Philippines with only two under-strength companies.[31]

In preparation for the move, Companies A and C gave their vintage, out-of-date tanks to the fledgling 191st and 193rd TBs. Thirty-seven brand new M3 Stuart light tanks, along with about a dozen halftracks, would be waiting for the 194th TB at the San Francisco dock.[32] Although the new tanks would be an improvement, the men were given no time to train with them. Both the men and the new tanks were to be loaded immediately onto a ship. Any familiarization would have to take place in the Philippines.

Major Miller and his staff went to San Francisco ahead of the unit and discovered that the ship taking them to the Philippines was the USS *President Coolidge,* a converted luxury liner. Wrote Miller, "[We] measured the space allotted for tanks and found we could load them all if the turrets of nineteen were taken off. This would render them unfit for combat for many hours after arrival at our destination." Fortunately for the 194th TB, the 17th Ordnance Company was also embarking on the *President Coolidge.* "They were familiar with the M3 tank," Miller recalled. "It was agreed that they would furnish the detail to strip the nineteen turrets and also, to help load the tanks. This was a relief to me. Our people had never seen the M3 and I had been wondering how we could accomplish the almost impossible."[33]

When the men of the 194th TB finally arrived in San Francisco and began assisting the men from the 17th Ordnance Company, problems arose with the port authorities. "All of the tanks had some aviation gasoline in the gas tanks," wrote Major Miller. "One of the [port] regulations stated that all gasoline must be removed from vehicles. Aviation gasoline is high test and very dangerous." Although the port authorities initially refused to let the tanks onto the *President Coolidge* with gas in them, pressure from the Army and the expediency of time eventually won out and the vehicles were put on board.[34]

At 9:00 P.M. on September 8, 1941, the *President Coolidge* steamed out of San Francisco. Almost immediately the 194th TB ran into more troubles. The radial-type airplane engine on the M3 Stuart required it to be started and turned over daily so the cylinders would not freeze up. On the first day out, a few crews went down into the hold where the tanks were stored and started the engines. "The fumes nearly knocked out some of the men," a maintenance officer reported, "There's no way for those fumes to escape and there's danger of an explosion!" In spite of the regulations, the engines were never started again. Major Miller wrote, "Numerous inspections were made but that was all."[35]

In Kentucky, the 192nd TB was informed in late August it was to participate in army maneuvers near Camp Polk, Louisiana. The 1941 Louisiana maneuvers were destined to be one of the largest mock wars in history, waged across much of Louisiana. On September 15, more than 400,000 participants, including the tankers from the 192nd TB, began battling it out in western Louisiana. One side, given the two new armored divisions and the 192nd TB, attempted to mass its armor and break through the "enemy" lines. Although the overall attacks failed, the Army general staff liked what they saw. Private Tenenberg recalled, "Our battalion, the only National Guard unit attached to the 1st Armored Division, performed at an extraordinary pace. It seemed we did everything right. Under the watchful eyes of the army's special investigative team, which included Gen. George S. Patton, . . . our battalion was declared the finest tank unit of all those on maneuvers. In effect, we won the war games."[36]

Sergeant French agreed with Private Tenenberg. "We went through [the] Louisiana maneuvers really thinking everything was screwed up, but come to find out General Patton picked us out [as] being the best tank battalion." Sergeant French was surprised by the selection because "tanks were breaking down, and all this." Noted French, "[I]n my mind I was thinking things were screwed up, but I was just one little section, but . . . according to the umpires, our battalion was superior over all the rest of the units down there."[37]

While the 192nd TB was still engaged in the Louisiana maneuvers, the *President Coolidge,* with the 194th TB aboard, steamed into Manila Bay. On September 26, while the tanks, halftracks, and other heavy equipment were being unloaded by civilian longshoremen, the tankers were bussed to Fort Stotsenburg, sixty miles northwest of Manila, and adjacent to Clark Airfield, the main bomber field in the Philippines. Upon arrival at their new base, the men were informed that they would be living in tents until barracks could be constructed. In typical army fashion, the Fort Stotsenburg authorities had been notified of the intended arrival of the 194th TB only a few days before.[38]

The next day, the thirty-seven new M3 tanks were unloaded from the *President Coolidge* and put back together. At 9:00 P.M., with darkness enveloping them, the tankers started the sixty-mile trip to Fort Stotsenburg. Major Miller recalled the move:

> Travel was on the left-hand side of the road in the Philippines. We were not used to that as yet. Tanks are hard enough to handle in the daytime without adding darkness, and unfamiliar driving regulations, to the ordeal. Filipinos had never seen a tank before. . . . Visualize, if you can, tank drivers straining, twisting, dodging, sounding their sirens—60 miles of it—amid the screechings of children darting suddenly in the path of the oncoming tanks, curious Filipinos blocking the way, dogs yapping, oncoming traffic including both automobiles and carabao carts—constantly having to remember to drive on the "wrong" side of the road— visualize, and you will have some idea of that trip.[39]

Add to all this the fact that almost all of the drivers had never driven an M3 Stuart tank before!

Throughout the next few weeks, Major Miller fought a losing battle to obtain essential supplies for his outfit. "It was not until about November 1st, more than thirty days after we had arrived, that we were able to procure gasoline to run the tanks!" Miller bitterly wrote. "Our tanks were equipped with 37mm guns which had never been fired. We requested recuperating oil and ammunition so as to test fire these guns and also to train the men. . . . The request was flatly turned down! The first firing of our 37mm guns was done when the Japanese were actually in sight!"

Another problem occurred with the shortwave radios issued to the battalion. The radios were not standard issue and were not designed for use in tanks. In order to install the radios, the men had to remove the driver's side sponson, or chassis, machine gun. This left a huge hole where the machine gun should have been. When Major Miller made a request to have pieces of metal welded over the holes, the request was routinely denied. He could "make no modifications on the M3 tank without proper authority of the Ordnance Department."[40]

In spite of the lack of proper equipment and gasoline, the tankers began attending schools on the nomenclature and function of the Stuart light tank. If they could not drive and fire their new tanks, they could at least discover how they operated. Additionally, the 194th TB sent jeep patrols into the areas north of Fort Stotsenburg and Clark Field to map the roads and familiarize themselves with the terrain.[41]

Back in Louisiana, the 192nd TB received secret orders around October 6 telling them that they were going to the Philippines. While most of the men felt that their selection was based upon their excellent showing at the Louisiana Maneuvers, historian Donald A. Schutt noted another, more important reason. He wrote:

> The principal reason behind the decision to send the 192d . . . was simply that as a General Headquarters tank battalion it had been created for just such an exigency.
>
> All along, armor leaders had feared that their newly created Armored Force would be stripped of personnel to provide the needed manpower at a moment when they were trying to establish and train independent armored divisions. . . . The call up of the National Guard companies to fill the GHQ battalions solved the problem. Any future possibility of breaking up armored divisions was now lessened considerably.[42]

Private Tenenberg agreed. "Actually," he wrote, "unbeknownst to us, we had been selected weeks [before the Louisiana maneuvers] as the tank group to fill Gen. Douglas MacArthur's plan for defending the Philippine Islands."[43]

Like the 194th TB, the 192nd TB got new M3 Stuart light tanks before it left the United States. "[W]e transferred all our old tanks to other units," Lieutenant Poweleit remembered. "We were given top priority to draw a full complement of both tanks and halftracks, all new guns, all men equipped throughout. . . . [I]n order to get new tanks we had to have them pulled away from units [scattered] all over the United States." Noted Private Tenenberg, "The 192d Tank Battalion was . . . issued brand-new tanks, so new that no one knew how to operate them. And because we needed so many, they were commandeered from other units. . . . All of our old tanks were traded to the tank units that were staying in the States. The new tanks accompanied us to the Philippines."[44]

Unfortunately, in some cases, some of the Stuarts were no better than the tanks they were leaving behind. "Many had about ninety-six hours of running time on [their engines]," noted historian Schutt, "and in accord with maintenance policies were due for a complete overhaul at one hundred hours. The term 'new' as applied to these M3s meant only that they were the latest models." Because the Stuarts were new to the men, the tankers were unfamiliar with its 37mm cannon. On the old M2A2 Mae West tank the largest weapon was a .50-caliber machine gun.[45]

Near the end of October the 192nd TB, under the command of Maj. Theodore F. Wickord from Maywood, Illinois, took its seventy-one "new" tanks, about thirty halftracks, and the rest of its equipment and boarded a train for San Francisco. On October 27, 1941, the men filed aboard the government steamship *Hugh L. Scott*, (formerly the luxury liner *President Pierce*), along with a couple of Air Corps units. Private Tenenberg recalled, "When the government converted the ship to a troop carrier, it dispensed with the luxury accommodations. Most of the men slept on hammocks, three deep, in the hold of the ship."[46]

The ship left San Francisco on October 28 and steamed into Manila Bay at 8:00 A.M. on Thursday, November 20. "We arrived in the Philippines on November 20, 1941," wrote Private Tenenberg, "the newly proclaimed Thanksgiving Day, nicknamed 'Franksgiving Day' because President Franklin D. Roosevelt moved it [ahead] one week to allow for more shopping days between Thanksgiving and Christmas." Taken by train to Fort Stotsenburg, the men from the 192nd TB enjoyed a Thanksgiving meal with their fellow tankers from the 194th TB. While most of the men managed to get a turkey dinner with all of the trimmings, Private Tenenberg only got hot dogs, while Pvt. Abel F. Ortega, a Mexican-American replacement from San Antonio, Texas, had to scrounge for a piece of bread with gravy on it. "That was my Thanksgiving dinner for 1941," he recalled.[47]

Like the 194th TB, the men of the 192nd were surprised to discover they would be living in Army tents at Fort Stotsenburg. "The tremendous buildup in the Philippines of both men and equipment, over such a short period of time, caused a severe housing shortage and required hundreds of us to live in tents on the perimeter of Clark Field," wrote Private Tenenberg. "This 'tent city' arose overnight, with thirty or more tents in an area that only days before was a parade ground. Each tent was more like a tent-house, about twenty feet square, with wooden floor and wooden supports. The canvas that was stretched over the basic form had a door and two window openings on each side. Six men were assigned to each tent."[48]

Over the next few days the 192nd TB tankers tried to acquaint themselves with life in the Philippines and get their equipment ready for the future. Sergeant French recalled, "[W]e worked like nothing you ever seen, day and night, Saturdays and Sundays and everything else, getting our equipment together because we had to mount all the machine guns and all the radios and get everything in our tanks." Much of the equipment and weapons were covered with a heavy grease called cosmoline to prevent it from rusting in the salty sea air. To remove the cosmoline, the men had to drop the thickly covered pieces into boiling water and wait until the grease melted off. Then, the pieces had to be stripped, dried, oiled, and reassembled. As Lieutenant Poweleit recalled, "The cleaning of this equipment occupied the tank battalion up until December 7."[49]

While the enlisted men worked, Major Wickord and his officers were briefed by Major Miller of the 194th TB on General MacArthur's plan to defend the Philippines. Code-named "War Plan Orange 3" or WPO-3, the plan called for the Filipino and American troops to halt any Japanese invasion at the water's edge. If that failed, the defenders were to make "retrograde movements involving delaying actions, holding up of the enemy, while advancing as far as possible."

Finally, if all else failed, the Filipino and American troops were to withdraw into the Bataan Peninsula on the west central coast of Luzon and fight a delaying action until reinforcements and supplies arrived from the United States or Hawaii. General MacArthur estimated he could hold Bataan for at least six months, during which time he would surely be reinforced. In order to make WPO-3 a success, however, the United States had to protect the vital sea lanes to Hawaii by holding on to the important islands of Guam and Wake, and to protect the Navy ships at Pearl Harbor. The loss of any one element might spell doom for the defenders of the Philippines.[50]

In spite of all of the recent signs of aggression by Japan, however, General MacArthur and his advisors did not believe that the Japanese would launch an invasion of the Philippines before April 1942. As men, material, tanks, and airplanes slowly arrived in the Philippines, the confidence of MacArthur and his generals increased. Having more than 31,000 trained American and Filipino soldiers on hand, along with 35 B-17 Flying Fortress heavy bombers (the largest collection outside of the continental United States), more than 250 additional airplanes of all types, 2 tank battalions, and about 100,000 Filipino militia, MacArthur was confident he could repel any Japanese invasion at the beachhead. Becoming overconfident, MacArthur modified WPO-3 and its successor, RAINBOW-5 (essentially the same as WPO-3) and abandoned the idea of falling back to the Bataan peninsula. Figuring he could stop anything that the Japanese could throw at him, he scrapped the idea of building up a stockpile of ammunition, gasoline and supplies on the Bataan peninsula ahead of time. His Filipino and American forces were expected to stop the invaders at the waterfront, and Douglas MacArthur was confident it could be done.[51]

CHAPTER TWO

War

On November 26, in order to equalize the strength of the two tank battalions, Company D, 192nd TB was transferred to the 194th TB to make up for the loss of Company B, 194th TB, which had been sent to Alaska. Wrote Major Miller, the commanding officer of the 194th, "There was no chance whatever to train this company as a part of our outfit. It was like a football team—getting ready to call signals at the start of the game only to find that a strange, new face had appeared in the backfield." Subsequently, each battalion now consisted of a headquarters company and three tank companies, each possessing fifty-four tanks and twenty-three halftracks. Additionally, by the end of the month, the two tank battalions were formed into the 1st Provisional Tank Group, under the command of James Weaver, (then a colonel) which became a separate tactical unit in General MacArthur's U.S. Army Forces in the Far East (USAFFE). Rounding out the Provisional Tank Group was the 17th Ordnance Company.[1]

In spite of how it looked on paper, the Filipino and American defenders on Luzon were ill prepared for the expected fight. Noted Lieutenant Poweleit, "For my own observations, the preparedness of Luzon was very poor and it would have been easy to take. It seemed as if no one gave a damn what happened."[2]

When Colonel Weaver tried to train and prepare his tankers for the expected hostilities, he found that his requests for additional ammunition and gasoline were denied. Likewise, the 192nd TB was denied additional gas and ammunition for training purposes. General Weaver noted, "Accordingly tank operation was not accomplished to familiarize the personnel—35 percent new to any kinds of tanks, all new to the M3 tank with its antiaircraft gun, fixed guns in sponsons fired by remote control by the driver, and most important, with the new main battery—the 37 mm gun."[3] Added Private Tenenberg, "[W]e asked for the use of a firing range so that we could become familiar with the weapons mounted on our new tanks. This request was . . . denied."[4]

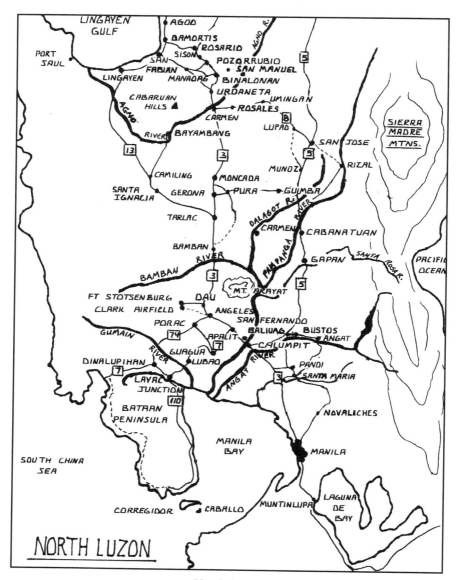

North Luzon

Near the end of November, due to information gleaned from intercepted Japanese dispatches, the forces around Clark Field held two full-scale alert exercises. Fortunately, Major Miller of the 194th TB had already worked out a plan. "The plan," he wrote, "was worked out with the tanks taking station on and around Clark Field, primarily to repel any airborne troops with which we might be faced."[5]

When Lieutenant Poweleit, the battalion surgeon for the 192nd TB, realized the tanks would be situated next to the runways, which were likely targets for Japanese bombs, he suggested that the men should be allowed to dig bomb trenches. As he later recalled, his request was greeted with "loud laughter and glib remarks."[6]

Beginning in early December, the men spent the daylight hours on half alert, camouflaging all 108 Stuart tanks and about 46 halftracks. At night, both the 192nd and the 194th were placed on full alert while the searchlights of Clark Field swept the blackened sky for enemy planes. On December 5, orders were finally received to distribute ammunition to the tanks. Noted Major Miller:

It was then that an ugly rumor was confirmed. The various ammunition available for our 37mm tank guns was armor piercing shells. No high explosive shells were to be had! . . . Armor piercing shells are merely large bullets . . . capable of piercing certain thicknesses of armor plate. This is of little or no use against personnel. High explosive shells burst on contact, exploding shell fragments over a wide area. This type of shell was nonexistent in the Philippines. We would be compelled to depend entirely on our machine guns against enemy personnel.[7]

Additionally, Sgt. Forrest Knox (Company A,192nd TB) ran into problems with the machine-gun ammunition. "We realized we didn't have any ammo loaded [in belts]," he wrote, "and when they couldn't find the machine-gun belt loader they told us to load the damn stuff by hand." Recalled Corporal Stewart, "[O]ur thumbs got raw pushing [the bullets] in."[8]

Monday, December 8, 1941, (December 7 in Hawaii), the tankers awoke to the news over their transistor radios that Japanese planes had attacked Pearl Harbor. "When you have planned on war, the announcement is something like an anti-climax," wrote Major Miller. Cpl. Bernard T. Fitzpatrick (Company A, 194th TB) wrote, "I could not believe the announcement. . . . Most of the men could not believe that the Japanese would be so foolish. We assumed that the attack had been easily brushed aside. After all, Pearl Harbor was so well armed." Noted Private Tenenberg, "Everyone was on edge, because we did not know what was happening and, more important, we were still totally confused as to how to operate our tanks and their new cannons." Immediately the men were put on full alert and ordered to get their tanks and equipment ready.[9]

Since many of the tanks of the 192nd TB still had a layer of cosmoline in their cannon barrels, Sergeant Knox was ordered to get rid of the protective grease. With only one rammer staff in the entire battalion, Knox improvised by cutting a piece of bamboo and wiring a chunk of burlap to the end. "An absolute no-no in the Army—the one thing you never do," he wrote, "is wash a barrel with gasoline, because it removes the oil, permitting the barrel to rust. By God, I cleaned seventeen cannons that morning. Just zip, zip with a bucket of gasoline and my piece of burlap. Each tank commander yelled at me, but I told them I was cleaning out the cosmoline so they could fire the cannons. It was up to those jack-asses to put the oil back in so they wouldn't rust."[10]

While Sergeant Knox was cleaning gun barrels, other men were still busy loading belts of ammunition. "We were busy all morning long, loading those machine gun belts," stated Corporal Stewart. "We had one little loader that you cranked by hand, and it would push these .50-caliber shells into the belt as it went by but that wasn't getting the job done fast enough, so we had a whole bunch of guys loading these by hand." While the men worked, they watched the activities at Clark Field. "We were encamped within a block or two of Clark Field," Stewart added. "Well, all morning long the B-17s were flying over, taking off and circling around and coming back and landing. We thought, 'Good Lord, we don't have a thing to fear; these planes are really out there keeping track of what's going on.'"[11]

Although word of the Pearl Harbor attack had reached the Philippines around 4:00 A.M. Philippines time, General MacArthur and his staff took no offensive action. Although nineteen B-17 Flying Fortresses were stationed at Clark Field on December 8, the heavy bombers did not take to the skies until 10:00 A.M., and then only as a precautionary move to get them off the ground and out of harm's way. Although General MacArthur's B-17s were the most formidable aerial strike force outside of the United States, the general and his staff felt that although Japan had committed an overt act of war against the United States, they had made no such move against the Commonwealth of the Philippines.[12]

Even after 10:00 A.M., when it was reported that a flight of Japanese planes was spotted heading toward Clark Field, and after the B-17s had taken to the air, MacArthur failed to attack. Unwilling to draw the Philippines into an unwanted war, MacArthur told his B-17s to circle the area and await further orders.[13]

Company B/192nd Tank M3 tank on Luzon, late 1941 or early 1942. PROVISO EAST WEBSITE

Around 11:00 A.M., when the reported flight of Japanese planes failed to arrive, the B-17s were recalled to Clark Field to refuel and bomb-up for a strike against the Japanese island of Formosa. General MacArthur had finally decided to go on the offensive. By noon all of the heavy bombers except two were back on the ground. A half hour later, most of the pilots were attending a briefing on the upcoming raid while most of their crews were eating a midday meal. At the same time, the tankers were given their meals. Although some of the men from the 192nd TB went to the Fort Stotsenburg mess hall, the 194th TB tankers were ordered to "stand by their vehicles." Lunch would be brought to them.[14]

Sergeant French, who was driving a motorcycle as a messenger for the 192nd TB, recalled, "We was in the mess hall up there eating chow, . . . and I'd just got through eating . . . [when] somebody said, 'Oh, look at them Navy bombers!' We was all looking at them, it was beautiful flying up there in formation. There was about fifty some-odd of them, as well as I can recall. And about [the] time we looked at them real good, we heard some making a whistling, hissing sound, [and saw bombs] falling. [A]bout the next thing we seen was buildings, people, airplanes, and everything else going up in the sky because they was . . . bombing Clark Field." At exactly 12:40 P.M.. on December 8, 1941, fifty-three Japanese bombers, flying in two perfect V's, began dropping their bombs on Clark Field.

Private Ortega recalled the morning attack:

[S]ince I was new to the organization they put me on guard duty guarding the tanks and the halftracks while everybody else ran across the airfield to go eat. . . . A little fella from Oklahoma and myself were . . . guarding the tanks when we heard this small roar and it got louder and louder and we didn't know where it was coming from. Finally, we looked up in the sky and that's when we saw these bombers coming over Clark. . . . [W]e thought they were American bombers. See, we were so young, 21, 22 years old.

Private Ortega and the Oklahoma tanker watched the unidentified airplanes for a few seconds before they realized what was going on. "All of a sudden I heard swishes, and swish, swish; swish, swish, all over the place," Ortega recalled. "That was the bombs coming down. . . . It was an experience that I'll never forget. They was unloading these large, huge bombs. The shrapnel was flying all over the place, zinging through the palm trees, and the banana trees, [and] the tall grass."[15]

At the 194th TB command post near Clark Field, Major Miller also heard the roar of the approaching planes. "The roar was like the deep growl of many powerful beasts—snarling as one. It was unmistakable." Like the others, he thought the planes were U.S. Navy bombers. "Then they dropped their load of bombs," he wrote, "bombs that glistened in the sunlight—bombs that fell with determined aim to land on field installations and our grounded airplanes, lined up like ducks on a pond! Bombs! Hundreds of them!" Sergeant French was still at the Fort Stotsenburg mess hall and watched the bombers carpet the area. "It seemed like they concentrated their bombing right on that mess hall," he recalled. "Then the bombs trail[ed] off down into the maintenance buildings and the aircraft, and then down the runway and that area."[16]

Lined up alongside the main runway, the stationary B-17s were easy targets for the falling bombs. Sergeant Knox was eating beside his tank when the bombs struck. He recalled, "The guy with me and I popped inside a tank and closed the turret. We're sitting in there and this guy says, 'What do we do now?' 'Well,' I said, 'I don't think we do anything.' 'We can't stay here,' he replied. I said, 'Sure we can.'" Although some tankers fired at the high-flying bombers, the majority figured that the safest thing was to button themselves up inside their tanks or find a safe place to hide and wait for the bombers to finish their run.[17]

"We had just got there, you know, two weeks before the war started, we hadn't even dug any foxholes, any kind of a shelter to protect ourselves," recalled Private Ortega. "So the guys were hidden under trucks, under tanks, wherever they could find a place." After only a few minutes the bombers flew off. The pattern bombing hit almost every building on the base, setting many on fire. An oil dump behind Clark's huge hangar buildings had been hit, sending a huge column of thick black smoke rising into the sky. Sergeant French had jumped on his motorcycle during the bombing and was driving toward the motor pool at Clark Field when the oil dump exploded. "That was the awfulest [sic] explosion and fire and smoke," he remembered. "I laid the motorcycle down and got in a ditch. . . . [It] was so smoky and dusty that I had to put on my gas mask. . . . [That] was about the scardest [sic] I ever was in my life that day!"[18]

In spite of the pasting that Clark Field took, only one tanker was killed. PFC Robert H. Brooks (Company D, 192nd TB, now attached to the 194th TB) was caught on the wrong side of the runway when the bombs began falling. Sergeant French recalled, "The young man was my halftrack driver. He was over at the tank talking to some of the crew, [when the bombers] came in there and started bombing and he run [sic] across the airfield trying to get back to his halftrack and that's when a bomb fell behind him. . . . I think it almost blowed [sic] his head off and blowed off one of his arms. He never knew what hit him." Although Private Brooks, the first American tanker killed in World War II, was a light-skinned African American, only a few people in the battalion knew it. At a time when the U.S. Army was still very much segregated, it was better to leave such things unknown.[19]

About ten minutes after the bombers flew away, just as the inhabitants of Clark Field and Fort Stotsenburg were beginning to feel safe, a swarm of thirty-four Japanese Zero fighter planes arrived.[20]

"Immediately after this bombing raid then the fighter planes came in and started strafing the heck out of everything," reported Sergeant French. This attack however, was met with some resistance by many of the tankers. PFC Roy Diaz (Company C, 194th TB) recalled:

My buddy and I set up a .50-caliber machine gun right out in [a] rice paddy [beside the runway]. I worked it around and said, 'When we get one coming in real close, you feed this thing. I'm going to knock him down.' About then here comes this darn Zero, no more than 500 feet away. I'm about to touch my .50 off when this tank officer starts screaming. 'Don't fire. You'll give our position away.' He's in a tank and we're out there in the wide-open rice paddy. I don't know what position we'd give away. We didn't have a position. Anyway, this Zero came over and we watched him. He was so close I saw that the pilot wore a white scarf. I could have knocked him down with a shotgun.[21]

Private Ortega was still beside the command halftrack when the Zeros started coming over. "I had a .50-caliber machine gun on my halftrack so I let 'em have it," he stated. "I could see the planes as they came through the clouds, and the dark [smoke], strafing, and I would shoot at 'em. 'Course, I couldn't tell whether I hit 'em because of the dark smoke swirling in the air."[22]

Sergeant Knox, who had buttoned up inside his tank, wrote, "After a while I decided to have a look and I tipped the hatch back. I had no more than got out of there when the Zeros started coming. I grabbed the machine gun, jerked the pin from the mount, and yelled for a box of ammo. Once I hooked it on the side, flipped the lid, and worked the bolt one more time to get a round in the chamber, I was ready to go." As Knox stood on the deck of his tank and readied the small .30-caliber anti-aircraft gun mounted behind the turret, the Zero fighters zipped overhead. "I said, 'For heaven sakes!' I'd never been trained for antiaircraft fire and the .30s had no AA sights. They called it an 'anti-aircraft' mount, but it was like a lot of things the Army did. Once they wrote the name on it, that was what it became. Ridiculous!"

As the Japanese fighters zipped past, Sergeant Knox opened up with his machine gun. "I was firing so much that the empty ammo cases kept building up on the deck [of the tank]," he wrote. "As I was trying to depress the breach down into the open hatch, in order to get enough elevation on the barrel, I had to lean over and my feet would slip on the empty casings. I'd start to go nose down into the turret. To push myself up I'd have to let go of the gun. I don't think I hit anything. They never bothered to explain how far you had to lead an aircraft in order to hit it. I found out later. But at this particular time, when it should have been duck soup because they were so close, I was missing them by fifty feet."[23]

Sgt. Zenon Bardowski (Company B, 192nd TB) was riding shotgun in a halftrack when the high-altitude bombers appeared. Immediately, Bardowski instructed the driver, Pvt. Frank Goldstein, to seek cover under the trees. Sergeant Bardowski's son, Steve, recalled, "At this point they started opening up on [the bombers], which was kind of worthless because they were real high. My dad told his driver, 'I can't get a decent shot, Goldie. Pull out so I can get a better shot.'" When Bardowski's halftrack pulled out onto the runway, Sgt. James P. Bashleben, nearby in another halftrack, followed suit. "Bashleben's .50 [caliber machine gun] jammed, it wouldn't fire," Steve Bardowski continued, "but my father was able to keep up the fire . . . and a Zero came down [and] my dad unloaded a whole belt at

Company B/192nd TB on Bataan Peninsula, early 1942. Standing on the far left is Sgt. Zenon Bardowski. PHOTO COURTESY STEVE BARDOWSKI

him. He'd fired a .50 before but obviously never in action and he succeeded in bringing the aircraft down."[24]

Sgt. Zenon Bardowski became the first man in the U.S. Armored Force to shoot down an enemy plane in combat during World War II. For his heroic action, Bardowski received a Bronze Star.[25]

At almost the same time, Pvt. Earl G. Smith (Company D,192nd TB, attached to the 194th TB) became the second tanker to down an enemy airplane. Major Miller, his commanding officer, wrote, "One of the members of Company D could not contain himself. Forgetting that he might be exposing our ground positions in the case of airborne landings, he manned the .30-caliber machine gun, mounted on the turret of his tank. He brought down a fighter plane." Only nine Japanese Zeros were lost during the Clark Field attack, two shot down by the tankers of the Provisional Tank Group.[26]

After forty-five minutes, the Zeroes flew away and the defenders of Clark Field and Fort Stotsenburg climbed out of their hiding places. All around the tankers and airmen was devastation and ruin. Lieutenant Poweleit wrote, "The field's hangars and quarters were a total wreck. Eighteen [actually seventeen] B-17s were irreparably damaged, along with the other planes. Dead bodies were lying all over. . . . Explosions and fires continued for five or six hours after the raid. Clark Field was in shambles." Although a total of 227 soldiers, airmen and civilians had been killed at Fort Stotsenburg and Clark Field, the Provisional Tank Group had lost only Private Brooks. Among the 400 or more injured personnel, only "a few" came from the tank group.[27]

Fortunately, none of the tanks or halftracks had been severely damaged, although a few had been hit by flying shrapnel. The camouflaged, concealed positions had kept the vehicles well hidden from the Japanese pilots, who were more intent on going after the many American airplanes parked out in the open. Additionally, the thick black smoke from the oil dump fire blowing back over the Fort Stotsenburg tent area had kept the tanker base somewhat concealed from Japanese strafers.[28]

As the tankers viewed the devastation around them, many were shocked that America had been caught so unaware. "It is difficult to analyze the feelings one has, during and after such a bombing," Major Miller wrote. "The first reaction is one of almost complete disbelief, disbelief that we could be caught in such a deplorable and helpless condition. . . . The next reaction . . . was hope. Hope that things were not as bad as they seemed. Hope, that now [that] we were baptized with fire and blood, the veil would be lifted—and vision would be clear and in the right direction!" Major Miller, and all of the other tankers, were hoping General MacArthur and his staff would finally take the Japanese threat seriously and act accordingly.[29]

Throughout the rest of December 8, the men of the twin tank battalions sat in their tanks and halftracks and guarded against further attack by enemy airplanes or paratroopers.[30]

At dawn, Colonel Weaver moved parts of his two tank battalions to new positions in order to defend a larger area from enemy attack. While all of the tanks remained around Clark Field, the officers and service personnel from both battalions were moved north and south of Clark Field to guard flat areas that the Japanese might use as parachute drop zones.[31]

A little after 9:30 A.M. on December 10, the Japanese bombers returned to Clark Field. Noted Lieutenant Poweleit, "They dropped bombs and strafed, but the damage had already been done." Added Private Tenenberg, "[The] attacks left more dead and injured, but we had so few airworthy aircraft that our equipment losses were minimal." That same day, the Japanese landed 2,000 troops near Aparri, on the north coast of Luzon, and another 2,000 at Vigan, on the northwest coast. Although the landings were opposed by the few remaining American fighter planes and B-17s, both landings came off without a hitch. By the evening of December 10, the Japanese had consolidated each beachhead and had 4,000 battle-ready troops ashore.[32]

Throughout the next few days the Japanese pushed outward from their beachheads and captured several Filipino airfields. Utilizing the captured runways, the Japanese soon gained air superiority over northern Luzon. Next, the Imperial soldiers began pushing southward along Luzon's west coast, toward the town of Lingayen at the base of Lingayen Gulf.[33]

Around 8:30 A.M. on December 12, six Japanese bombers came in at a low altitude and dropped their bombs on Clark Field and Fort Stotsenburg again. Perhaps because the planes were so low, many of the tankers and Air Force personnel opened up on the Japanese with anything they had. Major Miller had just finished taking his first shower in four days when the planes appeared. "Foolish as it sounds," he wrote, "I picked up my .45-caliber pistol and stood on the back steps of our quarters, shooting at the planes until the gun was empty." When the attack was over, Major Miller heard laughter from all around him. "It came from . . . some of the men who were in shallow foxholes, nearby," he wrote, "and then I realized that [I] was standing nude, firing at planes with a .45 pistol!"[34]

That same day, another force of Japanese troops landed at Legaspi, on the east side of the long southern tail of Luzon. Coming ashore virtually unopposed, more than 3,000 Japanese soldiers and marines began moving north toward Manila, about 150 miles away. With this sudden threat from below, General MacArthur, whose headquarters was in Manila, moved quickly to oppose it.[35]

In mid-afternoon, Major Miller was told that the 194th TB, the most experienced of the two tank battalions in the Philippines, would be moving to join the Southern Luzon Force protecting the southern approach to Manila. Almost immediately, Miller ordered his battalion into motion.[36]

A slow, drizzly rain fell throughout the night of December 12 and into the next day, as the 194th TB (still including Company D, 192nd TB) left its bivouac area around Clark Field. A total of 162 vehicles, including fifty-four Stuart tanks, nineteen halftracks, and dozens of trucks, jeeps, reconnaissance cars and motorcycles started south down Highway 3. "We had to move without lights, down the one highway toward Manila," Major Miller wrote. "The strain on drivers and vehicles, particularly tanks, is severe enough in daylight driving. To drive at night, without lights, in a continuous rain, and against other traffic is enough to give anyone a severe case of extreme jitters."[37]

Traveling inside a tank, Corporal Fitzpatrick recalled, "The move was difficult because all traffic in the Philippines drove on the left-hand side of the road. We were driving under blackout conditions, with only the faintest blue-green light from the painted-over headlights. That eerie glow was swallowed up by the mist and drizzle three feet from the front of the vehicles."[38]

Corporal Fitzpatrick continued with his description of the move:

> There were a few minor accidents as tanks and trucks slipped into ditches or made a wrong turn and wandered off in the darkness toward Bataan. One tank overturned, but luckily no one was hurt on that long night.[39]

Major Miller, in charge of the move, added, "The drivers and their reliefs were worn out mentally and physically and were almost nervous wrecks. It should be remembered that the tanks and halftracks had no windshields . . . [and] everyone was wet to the skin."[40]

By sunup, the tankers had reached the Calumpit Bridge area, about thirty miles northwest of Manila. After resting there for two days, while someone in charge tried to decide what to do with the tanks, the entire group was set in motion again. After passing through Manila, the tankers took up position in a pro-tected grove of mango trees near the barrio of Muntinlupa, about fifteen miles southeast of Manila.[41]

While the 194th TB was moving south, the 192nd TB tanks, still stationed around Clark Field, were subjected to frequent Japanese air attacks. Pvt. Edward DeGroot (Company A, 192nd TB) remembered the attacks on Clark Field and how he dealt with them. "After the initial bombing [on December 8] they used to run bombs up every day," he said. "I'd kinda go to safety—we'd jump in the tank. Even if it got a direct hit it wouldn't do any damage." Lieutenant Gibson added, "Enemy bombers and bombs became as much a part of the daily life . . . as dodg-ing traffic had been back home. We never really grew to like them, of course, but unless we were right underneath, we didn't pay much attention to them. . . . We learned that we weren't going to be killed every time a bomber came over."[42]

Below Manila, the 194th TB was consolidating its position at Muntinlupa. On December 15, Major Miller moved Company C a bit farther south to a strong defensive line along Tagaytay Ridge, a 2,000-foot high embankment a few miles behind the west coast beaches. Noted a historian of Company C, 194th TB, "The company remained in this area from December 15 to the 24th. During this time they ran reconnaissance and patrol, [and] hunted presumed fifth columnists who were flashing mirrors by day and setting off flares at night near our ammo dumps [to signal Japanese planes]. No one was captured but after shooting up some sus-pected native huts, the suspicious activities ceased."[43]

After gaining air superiority, the Japanese finally launched their main inva-sion of Luzon. On the night of December 21, eighty-five transport ships, carrying 43,110 battle-hardened veterans of the 14th Army fresh from the fighting in China, and between eighty and one hundred Type 97 Chi-Ha medium and Type 95 Ha-Go light tanks of the 4th and 7th Tank Regiments, dropped anchor in Lingayen Gulf. At 11:00 P.M., a newly promoted Lieutenant Colonel Wickord received word to move his 192nd TB north toward Lingayen Gulf.[44]

Within a short time, the tanks and halftracks of Company B were traveling north up Highway 3. Plans had been made for the vehicles to be refueled at Gerona, a small hamlet about thirty-five miles north of Dau, and again at the coastal village of Bauang, another eighty-five miles farther north. However, when the column reached Gerona, mass confusion ensued. Nobody in Gerona had been informed the tanks were coming so nobody was ready when they arrived.[45]

Back at Clark Field, Companies A and C finally got into motion around 3:00 A.M. on December 22. Left behind were the officers and service personnel of both companies, and the men, vehicles, and tanks of Headquarters Company. It was their job to continue to guard Clark Field against a Japanese parachute invasion.[46]

As Companies A and C moved north up Highway 3, they ran into the same kind of problems that had plagued the 194th TB during its night move south. The men were unfamiliar with the road and had to travel through darkness with blacked-out headlights. As historian Donald Schutt wrote, "Sharp curves, narrow bridges, and bombed portions of the highway posed serious obstacles."[47]

Around 7:00 A.M., the tank column finally reached its initial assembly area near Binalonan village, about seventy miles north of Clark Field, and fifteen miles from Lingayen Gulf. Farther north, around the village of Rosario, Company B was preparing to go into action.[48]

Even without receiving fuel in Gerona, the Company B tanks and halftracks had continued north up Highway 3. By the time they reached Rosario, however, the men discovered they were fearfully low on gas. While the tankers waited and wondered what to do next, Generals Wainwright and Weaver arrived to assess the situation.

While the 192nd TB tanks were clawing their way northward, Imperial Japanese soldiers had begun storming ashore unopposed at three locations along Lingayen Gulf. Before the morning was over, the Japanese held a beachhead fifteen miles long and their infantry and armor were pushing south toward the town of Damortis.[49]

Without full knowledge of the situation, General Wainwright ordered General Weaver to send out a "company of tanks" to assist the 11th Philippine Division, which had been told to hold back the invaders. With enough gas for only five tanks, General Weaver could send only Lieutenant Morin's platoon of Stuarts, which eventually ran into a Japanese roadblock just south of Agoo (see Chapter One). The first tank-versus-tank battle for the Americans in World War II had gone against them.

CHAPTER THREE

War Plan Orange-3

Shortly after the four surviving tanks of Lieutenant Morin's platoon returned to Rosario, General Weaver arrived with word there was "increasing violence" from enemy activity around Damortis. He had news that the men of the 26th Philippine Cavalry were in dire need of tanks. Climbing into a command half-track, Weaver decided to see for himself what it was like around Damortis.[1]

Just short of Damortis, General Weaver's halftrack was forced to the side of the road by Japanese planes. For two hours, Weaver and his crew were pinned down by the attacking planes until, finally, his driver jolted the halftrack into the roadway and raced east toward Rosario, drawing the "unabated attention of hostile planes" almost the entire way.[2]

While General Weaver was pinned down outside Damortis, Colonel Wickord and Companies A and C of the192nd TB had arrived at Rosario. Bringing along a small cache of gasoline, the remaining tanks of Company B finally were refueled. When General Weaver eventually returned to Rosario he ordered Company C to rush to the aid of the Philippine cavalry, whereupon the commanding officer, Capt. Robert S. Sorenson, "fainted and went all to pieces." Unable to rely on Sorenson, Wickord stripped him of command and sent him to the rear.[3]

With a new commanding officer, Company C moved out toward Damortis. As the tanks rumbled west, they noticed dead cavalry horses littering the road. "The 26th Philippine Cavalry . . . was heavily engaged that first day," reported Lieutenant Gibson. "Bombs drove the horses wild. They became unmanageable, plunging in frantic circles, galloping in terror into the teeth of the Jap fire, or tossing their riders at critical points of the battle."[4] It was readily apparent that the use of horses in modern warfare had come to a disastrous end.

Around 7:00 P.M., Company C found the Philippine cavalrymen atop a small hill just east of Damortis. Taking positions around the hill and beside the roadway, the tankers added their firepower to that of the cavalrymen. What happened next has never been fully explained and created a minor controversy between the tankers and the Philippine Cavalry.

Historians backing the 26th Cavalry report the tankers had orders to fall back from the forward position at 8:00 P.M. no matter what. So, when eight o'clock arrived, Company C pulled out and left the cavalry high and dry. On the other hand, historians backing the tankers report that Company C waited for the cavalrymen to move off the hill.[5]

The truth probably lies somewhere in between. It appears as though the 26th Philippine Cavalry began to pull back from its hillside positions as soon as the tanks arrived. Then, at 8:00 P.M., thinking the cavalrymen were all gone, the Stuarts pulled off the hill and headed back toward Rosario. When the tankers caught up with the retreating cavalry, they did not stop to act as a rear guard but drove right through to Rosario.

As the cavalrymen continued to withdraw, another group of tanks approached them from behind. In the darkness, the 26th Philippine Cavalry could not see the tanks clearly and thought they were more tanks from Company C. Unfortunately, the tanks were Japanese and began firing wildly into the startled cavalrymen. Horses and riders panicked and rushed down the highway toward Rosario. Fortunately, as one of the Japanese tanks was crossing over a wooden bridge, a cavalry officer set the tank on fire, which in turn destroyed the bridge and halted any further pursuit for the night.[6]

After Company C reached Rosario, it linked back up with Companies A and B and eventually the entire battalion pulled back eighteen miles to the hamlet of Urdaneta. Left behind were the four badly damaged tanks from Lieutenant Morin's platoon. A short while later, the Japanese attacked Rosario from the northwest and pushed the hard-pressed cavalrymen out of the town.[7]

The next day, December 23, while the 192nd TB strengthened its position at Urdaneta, General Wainwright received permission from General MacArthur to pull his entire command back behind the Agno River, about five miles south of the hamlet. Realizing his northern force could not defend the broad plain of central Luzon, General MacArthur reissued War Plan Orange-3, the plan to concentrate everything on the Bataan Peninsula. In order to buy time for the army to concentrate however, General Wainwright's northern force would have to delay the Japanese long enough for the Allied troops in the south to reach Bataan. If Wainwright failed, the southern force would be cut off and left to rot on the vine.[8]

On the morning of Christmas Eve, the Japanese came on again, locking horns with the tenacious 26th Cavalry. While the Filipino cavalrymen were fighting a delaying action, the rest of General Wainwright's force moved south across the Agno. To try to slow the Japanese pursuit, the retreating army began laying makeshift land mines along the road. Unfortunately, Capt. Walter H. Wright, commanding officer of Company A, 192nd TB, was mortally wounded while laying one of the mines. With the death of Captain Wright, the capture of Lieutenant Morin, and the dismissal of Captain Sorenson, the 192nd TB had now lost all three of its original company commanders.[9]

While the Japanese from Lingayen Gulf were pushing southward, 7,000 Japanese soldiers made a surprise landing at Lamon Bay, about seventy-five miles southeast of Manila. With Manila now caught in a vice, General MacArthur moved to keep the enemy from closing the vice before all his American and Filipino troops on southern Luzon could reach the Bataan Peninsula. In order to help keep his road networks in northern Luzon open, MacArthur ordered some of his units on southern Luzon, including the 194th TB, to move north and help bolster Wainwright's porous defensive line behind the Agno River.[10]

At 11:00 A.M., Major Miller received orders to leave one of his tank companies (seventeen tanks) with the Southern Luzon Force and take his other two to Carmen, on the Agno River. While Company C stayed behind to hold Tagaytay Ridge, Company A, 194th TB and Company D, 192nd TB (which was still attached to the 194th) began heading north. Corporal Fitzpatrick, with Company A, recalled, "Again we were off to an area that we had not been able to scout, and we had neither proper maps nor guides. . . . As we passed back through Manila, each platoon stopped, and men were sent to get maps from the local gas stations. My tank had a Standard Oil map. It covered the main highways but of course was no help with the back roads or trails."[11]

In spite of their lack of proper maps, both companies reached the Agno River by 7:00 P.M. and soon were in position west of Carmen. Noted Corporal Fitzpatrick, "The commanders of Company A and Company D . . . guided us into positions on the curving south bank of the river. We were strung out to cover a front of about twenty-five miles."[12]

The defensive line established behind the Agno River was known as D-2. (Defensive position D-1 had been set up in front of the Agno River and offered less protection, since a major river separated the defenders from the Bataan Peninsula.) About dusk on December 24 the tanks of the 192nd TB began pulling back from Urdaneta to the opposite side of the Agno. Although Companies A and C crossed safely, Company B was delayed for some reason and before it could safely reach the Carmen bridge, the span was destroyed by Japanese bombers. Undaunted, the tankers turned their vehicles west and headed twenty miles downriver to Bayambang and the only remaining bridge over the Agno.

Unfortunately, no direct route connected the two river towns. Surrounded by darkness, the tankers forced their way down small dirt roads and narrow paths, losing only one tank in the process when it threw a track and flipped over into a ditch. Although Company B ran into a smattering of enemy troops, it managed to avoid the main body of Japanese troops and eventually reached a highway leading toward Bayambang.

Turning south, the twelve tanks finally crossed the Agno River at 10:20 A.M. Christmas morning but did not reach Carmen until almost noon. Once there, the exhausted tankers joined the rest of the 192nd TB on the east side of town, helping to protect a sixteen-mile stretch of riverbank. On the west side of Carmen, Company A, 194th TB and the attached Company D, 192nd TB spread out to protect a twenty-five-mile stretch of the river.[13]

The Japanese continued with their heavy air attacks on Christmas Day but as Lieutenant Poweleit reported, "the spirit of Christmas was with us." He wrote, "A number of trees in our area were filled with fireflies, which glowed like Christmas trees. The tropical evening was lovely, the moon was bright, the evening fragrant with the strange scent of tropical flowers. We sang a few Christmas songs and went to bed early." Wrote Corporal Fitzpatrick, "About noon some trucks came up the road. . . . [The truck crews] yelled Christmas greetings and passed down hot Christmas dinners. They had cooked in Tarlac and tracked us down to deliver our last full Christmas dinner for a long, long time."[14]

The tanks of the 192nd TB, covering the D-2 line west of Carmen, were spread out over a vast area, "with individual tanks at most of the critical points—some only in radio contact." Likewise, the tanks of the 194th TB were also spread

194th TB M3 Stuart on Bataan, late 1941 or early 1942. US ARMY

mighty thin. In fact, the tanks and halftracks of Company D, 192nd TB were positioned at the far west end of the D-2 line, separated from everyone else by a stretch of dense jungle. "There was no contact with the western element except by radio," recalled Major Miller.[15]

Early on the morning of December 26, the Japanese attempted to cross the Agno River at several different locations but were thrown back by heavy fire from the tanks and infantry. "It was in this action, just west of Carmen, that the absence of high-explosive shells, for our 37mm guns, was felt," noted Major Miller. "While armor-piercing ammunition did help materially in knocking out observed gun positions of the enemy, it was of little good for use against enemy personnel." Still, Miller estimated that his 194th TB killed more than 500 Japanese soldiers.[16]

Farther to the east, along the 192nd TB front, 1st Sgt. Roger Heilig (of Company B) was standing guard at a river crossing when he noticed several shadowy figures attempting to cross. At first he assumed they were Filipino soldiers left behind in the retreat from the D-1 line, but then realized "there were NO Filipino soldiers across the river!" Grabbing a Thompson submachine gun, Heilig threw himself on the river bank and opened fire. "Japanese from the other bank opened fire on him with their mortars," reported Lieutenant Gibson, "but Heilig held his post. He must have wiped out thirty of the enemy soldiers as they waded across the stream. He and his Tommy gun stayed there until additional forces came up; and the Japs made no crossing there."[17]

After failing in their attempts to cross the river, the Japanese decided to soften the D-2 line with mortar and artillery fire. Lacking any mortars or artillery of their own, the Americans could respond only with the few 75mm guns mounted in the backs of special M3 armored personnel carriers (halftracks) known as self-propelled mounts or SPMs. As Major Miller recalled, "[These halftracks] would dash in between the tanks, and deliver a few shells at the Japs, and then seek a new location. The result was, that the 'spot' [the halftrack had just vacated] would receive undivided attention from Jap artillery and mortars. It was one hell of a mess!"[18]

After working over the D-2 line with their artillery and mortars, the Japanese came on again. This time, the Imperial soldiers attacking beyond the east side of Carmen managed to lodge a bridgehead opposite the 26th Philippine Cavalry, forcing the cavalrymen to pull back to save themselves. With the withdrawal of the cavalry, the entire right side of the D-2 line suddenly collapsed. After attempts to reestablish a new defensive line just below Carmen failed, the Allied commanders made the decision to pull everybody back about another twenty miles to the D-3 line, which ran from the mountains west of Santa Ignacia on the far left, through the villages of Gerona and Guimba, to the mountains east of San Jose on the far right.[19]

Through a mix-up in orders and in the confusion of the retreat, the 192nd TB received orders from an infantry general to pull back to the D-3 line. Spread out to the west, the 194th TB was forgotten and received no orders. Once again, the misunderstanding of who was to command and give orders to the General

192nd or 194th TB M3 armored personnel carrier (halftrack) Self-Propelled Mounts (SPM) on Luzon, late 1941 or early 1942. MICHAEL GREEN COLLECTION

Headquarters Tank Battalion was coming back to haunt the tankers. "Whether or not the 192nd should have taken their orders from [the infantry general], or waited for General Weaver, which they were under orders to do, is beside the point," commented Major Miller. By dusk on December 26, the 194th TB had been "left alone on the entire front—and didn't know it."[20]

While most of the 192nd TB tanks and halftracks raced south through Carmen, one platoon of Company A tanks stayed behind to act as a rear guard. After a short while, when the others were safely away, the five tanks raced west along the riverbank, entering Carmen from the east. At the same time, a group of Japanese soldiers entered from the north. A sharp firefight broke out between the tanks and the infantry but the tanks managed to keep moving and reach Highway 3. Quickly turning south, the platoon raced across the bridges below Carmen only minutes before they were destroyed by the retreating army.[21]

Immediately west of town, the tankers of Company A, 194th TB had no idea the Japanese were occupying Carmen. Near 9:30 P.M. the Japanese rolled a few antitank guns into the center of town and established a roadblock on Highway 3. At about the same time, Capt. Ed Burke, in command of Company A, 194th, made a reconnaissance toward Carmen. As he neared the village, he was fired on and badly wounded by unseen Japanese soldiers. (He was captured the next morning.) Lt. Harold Costigan, a platoon commander from Company A, witnessed the shooting and immediately "ordered the tanks to open fire with their machine guns." Realizing the Japanese had entered Carmen, Costigan radioed the other tanks in his platoon to follow him, and headed east into Carmen before the Japanese could close off Highway 3.

The five tanks raced along in column through the darkness, firing all of their guns, when suddenly they came upon the Japanese roadblock. Coming in from the west, Costigan and his men had to make a sharp right turn to get onto Highway 3. "They slammed through a probably incomplete Japanese roadblock and drove into town and turned south on Route 3 in a rain of fire," wrote Corporal Fitzpatrick. "One tank missed the corner and blazed through the intersection down the road three miles to Rosales, where he could turn south on another road, which he had all to himself."[22]

In the brief firefight, a thermite grenade landed on the flat rear deck of one of the tanks and in a short time burned through the thin armor plating and dropped into an ammunition tray. Instantly, the crew bailed out and was picked up by the following tank. "By this time," noted Major Miller, "the ammunition inside the tank was exploding and the aviation gasoline had caught fire. It was an inferno in less time than it takes to tell it." In all, Lieutenant Costigan's platoon lost two tanks and three men. "The other three [tanks] were badly hit," reported General Weaver, "but were regassed, repaired and sent back to [fight]."[23]

As the 192nd TB and Lieutenant Costigan's platoon from Company A, 194th TB made their way south down Highway 3, Major Miller, who thought the rest of his 194th TB tankers had been told to retreat, set up an improvised roadblock about six miles south of Carmen. Keeping two tanks and a halftrack from his Headquarters Company, and one of the tanks from Lieutenant Costigan's platoon, he sent all of the other fleeing tanks and personnel south toward the D-3 line. Eventually, an SPM halftrack with a 75mm gun arrived after escaping across country and was quickly added to his improvised roadblock.[24]

Near 11:00 P.M., an American general in command of the Philippine troops west of Carmen asked Major Miller if he could hold the roadblock long enough for him to put his men on two waiting trains and hurry them south to the D-3 line. The general figured the two trains would pass over Highway 3 at Moncada, about five miles farther south, about 4:00 A.M. The general was hoping Miller and his small force could keep the Japanese at bay until the two trains had passed.[25]

Agreeing to do his best, Miller and his men waited in silence until 2:50 A.M. when they suddenly heard the approach of a motorized column. "We had laid our guns in fixed positions, so that the entire highway, including ditches, was completely covered at several angles," reported Miller. When the Japanese column came close enough, the Americans opened fire. "Our 75mm gun opened up and at that close range, it practically swept the road," Miller continued. "All the tanks and the halftrack fired steadily for about fifteen minutes." After that time, Major Miller feared his position would be outflanked and gave orders to abandon the roadblock. "We [then] proceeded slowly and reached the railroad crossing about ten minutes before the two trainloads of Philippine Army [troops] came through. There was no [further] enemy action."

After the two trains had passed, Major Miller and the others withdrew farther south, reaching the D-3 line around 8:30 A.M., December 27. A few minutes later, Filipino engineers effectively destroyed the bridges between Moncada and the new line.[26]

To the west of Carmen, the rest of Company A, 194th TB and the whole of Company D, 192nd TB knew nothing of the exploits of Lieutenant Costigan's tanks and the sharp firefight at Miller's roadblock. "[B]ack at the river we knew only that firing had broken out [in Carmen]," recalled Corporal Fitzpatrick. "Then all was quiet, and we waited in the darkness. . . . We waited all night. It was still quiet in the morning. I heard a rooster crowing near Carmen." Near mid-morning on December 27, Capt. Jack Altman, the commanding officer of Company D, 192nd TB, made a routine reconnaissance toward Carmen and drew heavy enemy fire. In an instant he knew he and the other stranded tankers were in trouble.

"At this point in our uncertainty and confusion," wrote Corporal Fitzpatrick, "Captain Altman took command of the seven remaining tanks of Company A as well as his own [nine] tank crews in Company D. He did not issue hard-and-fast orders, but he said we should head south across some cane fields to a carabao-cart trail that he hoped would parallel Route 3, so we might get ahead of the Japanese and rejoin our own battalion." Recalled Captain Altman, "I found I couldn't get through on the road. The Japs had mined it—and they were too strong for me to smash through." Added Lieutenant Gibson, "If [Altman] couldn't go ahead, if the road was denied to him, he'd try to go around."[27]

Quickly Altman headed his column west toward a narrow carabao-cart trail. He was hoping to find a railroad track that cut through the jungle and would lead the tankers back to Highway 3. "It was a slow process and almost impossible without guides," commented Major Miller. Wrote Corporal Fitzpatrick, "[We] went single file through the fields, jolting up and over the low earth banks between fields, until we found the carabao-cart trail and made our way south." Although the column had several brushes with the enemy and had to ford a number of small jungle streams, they kept moving. In the confusion, one of the tanks became separated from the others and continued west. Eventually the crew abandoned their vehicle and joined up with Philippine guerrillas.[28]

"Altman and his tankers kept going and eventually found the railroad," reported Major Miller. "They took the grade southeasterly until it brought them to Highway 3. There was much rejoicing and they proceeded south to Moncada." Added Corporal Fitzpatrick, "We opened up the tanks and headed for the bridge across the river at Moncada." Unfortunately, by the time the men reached Moncada the two bridges over the river had already been blown.[29]

"I asked [the other tankers] what they wanted to do," recalled Captain Altman. "I was worried about the tanks, and I said it would be a damned shame to let the Japs get them. The boys thought so, too. So we burned them!" In orderly fashion, the men destroyed their tanks and halftracks by "shooting into successive tanks with the 37mm, a grenade in the engine compartment, or a can of gasoline." One platoon leader, however, could not bring himself to destroy his tanks and instructed his men to only pull the wiring and rheostats. He was hoping to eventually salvage the vehicles. Instead, the Japanese managed to get the moderately damaged tanks running again and eventually turned them against the Americans.[30]

Having destroyed their tanks, Altman and his men, some of which were slightly wounded, turned toward the river. "Darkness had fallen by the time we left the fifteen tanks and began to cross the river, partly swimming and partly crawling on the fallen bridge girders," recalled Corporal Fitzpatrick. "Men who could swim especially well towed the wounded across. I wasn't wounded, but I couldn't swim. I borrowed three canteens and emptied them, and with my own canteen they served as a life preserver."[31]

Although every man made it safely across, they were still far north of the D-3 line. "There were snakes, and rocks; precipices and choking vegetation to worry about," wrote Lieutenant Gibson. "There was a Jap army between them and home." In spite of the apparent dangers, at 1:00 A.M. on December 27, Captain Altman and his men finally reached the D-3 line. "Eighty men started that epic struggle," noted Gibson, "and eighty men were still on their feet when they reached safety."[32] However, another sixteen tanks had been lost to a simple breakdown in communications.

South of Manila, Company C, 194th TB was still helping hold a defensive line against the Japanese coming up from Lamon Bay. On December 26, Lt. Robert F. Needham and his 2nd Platoon tanks were ordered by an American major in charge of Philippine infantrymen to take his five tanks and reconnoiter a road in his sector. Although Lieutenant Needham first wanted to make a reconnaissance, the infantry major assured him "that the Japanese had nothing but small arms in front of us."[33]

The five 2nd Platoon Stuarts moved out in column down the narrow mountain road with Lieutenant Needham in the lead. As Needham's tank disappeared around a bend, the driver of the second tank, commanded of Staff Sgt. Emil S. Morello, temporarily lost visual contact and stepped on the accelerator to close the gap. At that very instant a Japanese antitank gun fired. Only the quick acceleration of Morello's tank saved it from becoming a casualty of war.[34]

Seconds later, the air was filled with antitank and small-arms fire. A shell hit Lieutenant Needham's tank, mortally wounding Needham and PFC Robert Bales. "They got it around the first bend," commented Private Diaz. "Never had a chance. Not a chance. The Japs had antitank guns hidden off the side of the road. Needham got it in the turret. The first shell cut him right in half." The Japanese shell severed Lieutenant Needham's leg and disabled the American tank, causing it to plunge off the road into a rice paddy.[35]

Sergeant Morello, in the second tank, quickly realized the Stuarts could not turn around on the narrow road so he ordered the other tanks to follow him. Dashing madly forward, with cannon and machine guns blazing, the four Stuarts bolted ahead toward a Japanese roadblock made of felled trees. Additionally, the Japanese had fires built around the roadblock and were throwing green wood on top of the fire to create a thick smoke screen.[36]

Barreling through the smoke, Sergeant Morello's driver did not hesitate but crashed through the roadblock. Directly behind the felled trees was a 77mm anti-tank gun and crew. Again, the driver did not hesitate. The light Stuart smashed into the gun and kept going, followed closely by the other three tanks. Once past the roadblock, the four American tanks sped along, firing at anything that moved. For about a quarter of a mile they barreled past numerous enemy gun positions and machine-gun nests until finally they reached a wide spot in the road. As Major Miller explained, "The tank commander [Morello] had made up his mind that the only way out was the way they came in." Turning around, the four tanks started back down the narrow road, shooting at more enemy positions and over-running more enemy troops.

As the tanks neared the spot of the initial roadblock, an anti-tank round slammed into Morello's tank and knocked off the idler sprocket. Some of the rivets holding the tank together sheared off and ricocheted around inside the tank, seriously wounding Pvt. Eddie DiBenedetti in the neck. Without the idler sprocket, Morello's tank slid off the road and into a surrounding rice paddy. Almost immediately Morello told his driver to shut off the engine and instructed his crew to secure all hatches and feign death.[37]

The next tank in line, commanded by Sgt. Glenn Brokaw, also took incoming fire, which killed three crewmen and seriously wounded Brokaw. In fact, all of the remaining tanks were soon put out of action, but in all of the confusion and smoke the remaining crewmembers somehow managed to escape. In total, five more American tankers had been killed and five more tanks had been lost.[38]

Inside Sergeant Morello's tank, the sergeant and his three crewmen were still feigning death. When the Japanese looked inside, they saw the splattered blood from DiBennedetti's neck wound and assumed the crew had been killed. For the next several hours, the four men remained perfectly still while Japanese soldiers swarmed all over and around the vehicle, trying unsuccessfully to pry open the hatches. Eventually the main battle line moved forward and most of the Japanese went with it.

As the day wore on, a Japanese kitchen was set up not more than twenty feet from the disabled tank and enemy troops continued to pass through the area. As the sun blazed away, Morello's crew began to suffer. Major Miller recorded, "The tank crew was exceedingly thirsty. They had no water, and the tropical sun had been beating down all day. The armor plate became almost red hot and the inside of the tank became a living hell. . . . The crew licked the sides of the tank for any moisture present."[39]

Around 3:00 A.M., December 27, Allied artillery fire unexpectedly began pounding the enemy kitchen area, destroying three Japanese trucks and demolishing the mobile kitchen. Although the fire came dangerously close, Morello's crew had to wait it out. After two hours the fire ceased and Morello discovered the Japanese were leaving. By 7:00 A.M., the area was completely quiet. Finally, Morello and his crew climbed out of the inferno of their tank and began a long trek through the jungle and over the mountains. Eventually, they ran into two more wounded survivors from their tank platoon, making it back to Manila on December 29. While Private DiBenedetti was admitted to a Manila hospital, the other escapees were eventually ferried over to the Bataan Peninsula on January 5 where they rejoined the surprised ranks of their fellow tankers. "It was a joyful reunion," Major Miller wrote, "even for men who knew they were to be on Bataan until they were killed or captured." For his actions in saving his fellow tankers, Sergeant Morello was awarded the Silver Star.[40]

CHAPTER FOUR

Into Bataan

All through December 27, the Japanese halted to consolidate their forces. That evening, the Northern Luzon Force fell back to D-4, a twenty-five-mile defensive line stretching from Tarlac on the left to Cabanatuan on the right. Wrote historian Louis Morton, "In the face of a well-trained and better-equipped enemy, [the North Luzon Force] had fulfilled its mission—to hold the Agno line until the night of 26–27 December." Determined to halt the Japanese at D-4 and allow the South Luzon Force time to retreat to the Bataan Peninsula, General Wainwright ordered, "D-4 will be held at all cost until ordered withdrawn."[1]

With the loss of so many tanks on December 26, General Weaver redistributed the remaining tanks among the companies and battalions. "They just consolidated all the tanks and more or less reissued them out to where everyone would have an equal amount," recalled Sergeant French. Afterward, the tanks were positioned with Companies B and C, 192nd TB on the right side of the D-4 Line, Company A, 192nd on the center, and Company A, 194th TB and the attached Company D, 192nd TB on the left.[2]

On December 28, General MacArthur became increasingly concerned about the railway and highway bridges at Calumpit, over the wide Pampanga River. The twin-span highway bridge was vital to troops withdrawing from southern Luzon. If the bridge was destroyed, the southern Luzon force would be cut off and trapped. In order to protect the bridge, USAFFE ordered an antiaircraft unit to set up south of Calumpit and ordered the 194th TB to hasten to Apalit, three miles northwest of the town. The next day, Major Miller moved Companies A, 194th and D, 192nd TB, twenty tanks, to Apalit. "The tank group commander told me to hold the Calumpit Bridge at any cost and to shoot anyone who attempted to blow it," wrote Miller.[3]

Once in position, Major Miller had his men collect anything that could be used on Bataan. "It now became apparent that Bataan was to become a land of want,"

Miller wrote: "Between now and January 4th, the rear echelon of the 194th Tank Battalion salvaged and moved about 12,000 gallons of aviation gasoline and about six truckloads of canned food to Bataan."[4]

Shortly after the two companies of tanks left the D-4 Line, the Japanese hit hard on the right flank, attempting to strike south down Highway 5, capture Manila and cut the Allied forces in two. Late in the afternoon, the enemy massed its infantry and tried to cross the Pampanga River to the east of Cabanatuan. While the infantry was fighting its way across the river, a column of about thirty Japanese tanks, supported by artillery fire, rushed down Highway 5 and began crossing the river opposite Cabanatuan. The Philippine defenders and Companies B and C, 192nd TB were outflanked on the right by the infantry and pounded in front by the tanks and artillery. To save their lives, the Filipinos and Americans began to pull back. Lieutenant Poweleit was south of the river and recalled, "We saw our tanks in the distance, moving southward over the flatlands."[5]

As the tanks withdrew, enemy artillery continued to fire. Noted Lieutenant Poweleit, "One of our tanks received a blow which caused it to turn over, injuring the crew." This may have been the tank commanded by Sgt. Raymond P. Mason (Company B, 192nd TB), with a three-man crew. During the retreat, Mason's tank was disabled and cut off. When the three Americans tried to surrender, the Japanese motioned for them to start running and then opened fire. Only one crewman survived.[6]

As the Japanese surged forward on the right, a group of 100 bicycle-mounted Imperial soldiers headed west to outflank the left side of the D-4 Line. Waiting for them at the Dalagot River Bridge, however, was a handful of Filipino infantry and the tanks of Company A, 192nd TB. After setting demolitions on the bridge, the Filipino infantry and one platoon of Stuarts set up a defensive line on the east side of the river and waited for the Japanese to come.

At 3:15 A.M. on December 30, the bicycle-mounted enemy neared the position. Noted Lieutenant Poweleit, "After the last bicycle had passed the tanks, they opened fire and killed the whole group. [The platoon] then ran over the Japanese with their tanks in order to get out of the area." As the Stuart tanks raced across the bridge to the west bank of the river, they left behind them eighty-two dead enemy soldiers and the handful of Filipino soldiers. Seconds later, Filipino engineers blew the bridge, stranding their fellow countrymen on the far side.[7]

When the sun came up, the Japanese advanced in full force. Without tank support, the Filipino infantry was forced to retreat and scrambled back across the river as best it could. Eventually, the soldiers took up defensive positions about 500 yards from the river, beside the other two platoons of tanks from Company A. At 2:15 P.M., the Japanese brought up an anti-tank gun which knocked out one tank and forced the others to withdraw. Noted historian Morton, "With . . . their location known to the enemy, the tanks began to pull back. Since they were not under [Filipino] control, there was no way to keep them in position."[8]

The infantry fought for more than two hours without the Stuarts before General Wainwright ordered everybody in the center to fall back to the last line of defense, the D-5 line. The earlier withdrawal of the right flank made the rest of the D-4 line untenable. Only the hard, bitter fighting in the center, at the Dalagot River Bridge, had prevented the D-4 line from collapsing entirely.[9]

By late afternoon, most of the Filipino infantry on the left flank had pulled back, destroying any bridges between them and the advancing Japanese. However, shortly after the Japanese occupied the town of Tarlac, a platoon of five Stuart tanks and two SPM halftracks broke out of the enemy-infested town and raced for the safety of the new D-5 line. The tanks were probably the platoon from Company A, 194th TB that had abandoned the Philippine infantry on the east side of the Dalagot Bridge. As the vehicles sped south, the Japanese opened fire with artillery, hitting one tank and killing the entire crew. When the crews in the remaining tanks and halftracks reached a wide stream they found all of the bridges destroyed. After a few anxious moments, the tankers abandoned their vehicles and swam across the stream.[10]

The new D-5 line used the Bamban River as a natural obstacle and stretched from the town of Bamban on the left, in front of extinct Mount Arayat in the center, to Sibul Springs on the right. As an added bonus, an impassable swamp covered most of the right flank. By far the strongest defensive line thus employed, D-5 included fire trenches, wire and stake obstacles, and cleared fields of fire. Noted historian Morton, "Plans called for a stand here until the South Luzon Force could slip behind the North Luzon Force, up Highway 3, into San Fernando."[11]

Unfortunately, on the right flank, the Filipino infantry continued to flee down Highway 5 as the Japanese massed their forces in Cabanatuan. Noted Cpl. William A. Hauser (Headquarters Company, 192nd TB), "[The] Filipino Army troops were something else. . . . Those guys would bug out and the only thing keeping the Japs back would be the tanks." With the infantry in full flight, the tanks of Company C, 192nd TB were ordered to move forward and slow the Japanese advance.[12]

Moving north and reaching the town of Baliuag late in the day on December 30, Company C discovered a narrow-gauge railroad bridge over a small river just north of town. "We knew that the bridge would be the only possible place that [the Japanese] would be able to cross," reported 1st Lt. William Gentry, "so we set up our defenses in view of the railroad bridge which was in a large rice paddy at the edge of the town." Five tanks under Lieutenant Gentry were on the south side of town, while five tanks under 2nd Lt. Marshall Kennedy (Headquarters Company, 192nd TB) were to the southeast. Remembered Corporal Hauser, "Our lieutenant [Kennedy] pulled his tank real gently into a nipa hut so that it covered him. Then he aimed his barrel out one of the windows." The other nine tanks did likewise.[13]

Early on the morning of December 31, Japanese tanks and infantry reached the railroad bridge. While the tanks halted to wait for planks to be brought forward to aid them in crossing the bridge, the foot soldiers crossed over the open ties and moved into the outskirts of town, setting up an observation post in a church steeple. Just before noon, the planking was put down and the tanks began the crossing. By late afternoon, several Japanese Type 97 Chi-Ha medium tanks had assembled in the rice paddy near the bridge. The Americans, hidden inside the huts, maintained radio silence and waited patiently for the Japanese tanks to come closer. Before they did, however, one of the tank battalion officers drove his jeep into town to see how things were going. When the Japanese lookouts in the church steeple spotted the American jeep, they became "quite excited." Spotting the waiting Japanese at the same time, the officer calmly turned his jeep around and drove away as if nothing was amiss. Recalled Lieutenant Gentry, "We waited [for him] to clear and then opened fire on the Japanese from the houses."[14]

"Our first round of fire concentrated on the collection of Japanese tanks at the end of the bridge out in the open field," continued Gentry. "We immediately pulled out from our position under the house and signaled Kennedy that we were going to drive the Japanese tanks in his direction. He held his position until the tanks came within view of his platoon and at this particular point he entered the fight, too." The tank-versus-tank battle began at 4:00 P.M. and moved back and forth through the streets of Baliuag. "We were chasing the [enemy] tanks up and down the streets of the town, under buildings and through buildings," Lieutenant Gentry recalled. Added Corporal Hauser, "About four o'clock the shit hit the fan. . . . The battle lasted a while and we kept going back and forth, up and down the streets. Once we were a couple of feet from [Lieutenant Kennedy] hidden in the shack. He got four goddamn Jap tanks."[15]

After almost two hours the ten American tanks were ordered to pull back about five miles to the southwest. "We were able to definitely establish that we had eight [Japanese] tanks out of action when we were ordered to withdraw," Lieutenant Gentry proudly noted. In addition to stopping the enemy tanks, the ten Stuarts had managed to chase the enemy infantry back across the bridge. "The only [American] casualty from the encounter," Gentry wrote, "was a sprained ankle when one of the boys attempted to get off a tank in a hurry to tell his part of the story after the fight was over."[16]

Although Company C had bloodied the Japanese at Baliuag, it had failed to totally stop their advance. When Company C pulled back, the Japanese quickly moved in again. Since Baliuag was less than twelve miles east of the Calumpit bridges, General MacArthur was fearful that the Japanese might rush farther ahead and capture the vital spans. With the Calumpit bridges in their possession, the Japanese could turn south and head toward Manila. So, even as the last of the South Luzon Force was racing north towards the bridges, MacArthur issued orders to blow both the highway and railroad bridges at Calumpit no later than 5:00 A.M., New Years Day.

South of Calumpit, Company C, 194th TB was still acting as a rear guard, slowly moving north behind the retreating soldiers and fleeing civilians. "We covered the retreat from the south all the way to Bataan," wrote Private Diaz. "Soon as the Filipino Army would move out, we'd cover for them. We'd stay there until the last officer came through, and then we'd pull back and cover the next area. Then the Filipinos would go through and we'd do it all over again."[17]

Reported a historian of Company C, 194th TB, "[T]hey made a sleepless 100-mile, night dash . . . in six hours." Along the route lay the Philippine capital of

Manila. Declared an "open city" on December 25, all armed combatants were prohibited from entering the city. However, when the tankers reached the city limits, they decided to ignore the prohibition orders and headed straight through the city.[18]

By midnight of New Years Eve, Company C, 194th TB had reached the Calumpit Bridge over the Pampanga River. While they reassembled and waited for orders to cross, they watched more than 100 empty trucks pass by in "headlong flight [away] from Manila, where there were ample supplies in the warehouses." Wrote the company historian, "Had these supplies been moved while there was still time (12/10–12/23) the U.S. and Filipino forces could conceivably have held out on Bataan and with far less suffering."

By 1:00 A.M. on New Years Day, the last of the Philippine infantry had crossed the bridge. Ninety minutes later, the tanks began to cross. As they were doing so, their sister tanks from Company C, 192nd TB rushed down from the northeast and fell into line behind waiting Stuarts. Together, the two sister companies crossed the twin span and at precisely 6:15 A.M., the Calumpit bridges were blown. Commented Corporal Fitzpatrick, "The long triple-span [sic] steel and concrete bridges had gone up, with the wide Pampanga River between us and the Japanese forces to the east."[19]

With the bridges gone, USAFFE turned its attention to the successful withdrawal of the D-5 line into the Bataan Peninsula. Troops falling back would have to pass through San Fernando, and move southwest down Highway 7 to Bataan. To secure the road, the Provisional Tank Group was moved to the town of Angeles, eight miles above San Fernando.[20]

Only Company C, 192nd remained behind near the Calumpit Bridge, spreading out in harvested rice paddies directly north of the blown spans. The tankers took up sheltered positions along the west bank and although the first enemy troops began to appear around dusk, the tanks were not bothered until shortly after midnight when the Japanese began shelling the American position with mortar fire. "At this point," reported Lieutenant Gentry, "we opened fire by setting the [harvested] rice stacks on fire and gave them small-arm machine gunning."

Aided by the light from the burning stacks, the tankers blasted away with their 37mm cannon. "In fact," noted Lieutenant Gentry, "we were down to the point where we were shooting a single Japanese with a single round of 37mm ammunition." Around 2:00 A.M. on January 2, with Company C running low on ammunition, the tanks were ordered to withdraw. "We pulled back under orders to San Fernando," Gentry wrote, "where we refueled and filled up with ammunition."[21]

North of Angeles, the Filipino defenders managed to hold the D-5 line against stiffening Japanese pressure throughout the whole of New Years Day. When night fell, the infantrymen withdrew down Highway 3 to Angeles and then southwest down Highway 74 towards Bataan. That same night, the infantrymen to the east, guarding the Pampanga River crossings, were ordered back to Bataan through San Fernando. Covering the retreat from both directions were the tanks of the Provisional Tank Group.[22]

When the overall withdrawal began, all six tank companies stood firm while the infantrymen and a cavalcade of trucks, buses, and jeeps headed south toward the Bataan Peninsula. Then, around midnight, the tankers themselves began pulling back. When the tanks passed through San Fernando and turned southwest down Highway 7, they found mass confusion.[23]

"[W]e were in a line with trucks carrying Filipino Regular Army troops," recalled Sgt. William Mattson (Company A,194th TB). "Any time they heard planes or bombs they'd just jump out of their trucks and run off. This, of course, kept backing up the road. Finally I had enough, and when a Jap plane began strafing the road at Guagua and the Filipinos left their trucks, I hopped out of my half-track and got in the Filipino truck right in front of us and drove it down to Bataan." To Sergeant Mattson's surprise, the truck contained gas, ammunition, and flour. "It just happened that we had a first sergeant who'd been a bricklayer, and when he found I had driven in a truck of flour, he scrounged around some and built us an oven. Once we found the yeast, we began to have fresh bread. We were the envy of the other outfits."[24]

On the afternoon of January 2, the Japanese struck at a hastily prepared defensive line running from Porac to Guagua, pushing the Filipino defenders back about 2,000 yards. The next morning, the Filipinos tried to regain the lost line but ran into heavy fire from Japanese artillery and strafing aircraft. Calling for support, the tanks of Company C, 192nd TB went forward. "We went over in the vicinity of Porack [sic] and there the Philippine army was having considerable trouble with artillery fire," wrote Lieutenant Gentry.

The Stuarts moved into position and fired only a few rounds before the enemy artillery forced them to withdraw. A short time later, the tanks moved forward again, but after one of the gunners fired his 37mm cannon with the muzzle cover still on, exploding the barrel, the tankers feared the Japanese were using anti-tank guns and withdrew a second time. Finally, when an infantry officer and a tank sergeant agreed to walk in front of the tanks and guide them into safe positions, the tanks came up a third time.[25]

"We were soon able to find out the exact position of an [enemy] artillery battalion from a Filipino lieutenant who was returning with a straggling platoon," Lieutenant Gentry continued. "After getting his location, we immediately pulled out to see what we could do with it. When we arrived at the gun positions, we were able to get three of the guns, but the Japanese immediately pulled out and dispersed. We chased them over the area, putting trucks out of action and taking care of as much infantry that we could." In spite of the success of the tanks, the Philippine infantry was unable to retake its lost position.[26]

Early on the morning of January 3, the Japanese on the right side of the Porac-Guagua line began advancing down Highway 7. Near 9:30 A.M., when they were about 1,000 yards north of Guagua, they suddenly ran into a platoon of tanks from Company C, 194th TB. Historian John W. Whitman described the following action. "The American tankers were veterans now," he wrote, "familiar with the art of delay and withdrawal. Taking advantage of every turn in the road, ducking into concealment offered by huts and vegetation, and using their speed, the Americans flayed the Japanese as they doggedly pushed south." Around noon, when the main Japanese force arrived, Company C disengaged and withdrew beyond Guagua.[27]

The next day, January 4, a Japanese column, spearheaded by tanks, penetrated the Allied line and captured Guagua. During an attempted counterattack, which included the Stuarts from Company A, 192nd TB, a group of Philippine infantry mistook the American tanks for Japanese tanks and began firing mortars at them. Although none of the tanks were hit, the counterattack failed and Guagua remained securely in Japanese hands.[28]

Around 1:00 P.M., with the loss of Guagua, General Wainwright ordered everyone to pull back from Porac–Guagua to a new position behind the Gumain River. "This would be the last line established before retiring to Bataan," commented Colonel Miller. On the left, the troops around Porac, including Companies B and C, 192nd TB, had no trouble pulling back down Highway 74 but in the center and on the right, the quick thrust by the Japanese into Guagua threatened any retreat down Highway 7.

In the center, the Filipino soldiers and supporting tanks of Company A, 192nd TB suddenly found themselves cut off. Determined to save themselves, the infantry began a thirty-mile circuitous route away from the Japanese.[29]

After covering the withdrawal, the Company A tankers were about to pull back themselves when someone discovered an alternate path that would take them back to Highway 7. Moving by "trail and cross-country" the tankers first went south and then east to the highway. At about 3:00 P.M., despite losing three tanks, Company A, 192nd TB reached Highway 7 and shortly thereafter linked up with the tanks of the 194th TB. "They were very glad to see us and we were most happy to see them!" noted Colonel Miller.[30]

On the right side of the Porac–Guagua line, the tanks of the 194th TB (and attached Company D, 192nd TB) had begun pulling back from their positions. Reaching Highway 7 in broad daylight, they were soon fired upon by the advancing Japanese. "Hostile fire swept through us from east and north," Colonel Miller reported. "We returned the fire blindly and finally ran out of it." Farther south, the 194th TB linked up with Company A, 192nd TB, when it sent it on ahead, and then continued on, bringing up the rear of the retreating army. "Somehow," commented Corporal Fitzpatrick of the 194th TB, "we made it out of Guagua—battered but still intact."[31]

Near 4:00 P.M., the Japanese sent about 700 soldiers through some swampy ground south of Guagua to threaten the flank of the retreating Philippine defenders. Fortunately, Colonel Miller had anticipated such a move and had established two roadblocks, one to the right rear and one to the left rear. When the Japanese moved in from the right, they unexpectedly ran up against four SPM halftracks and three Stuart tanks of Company C, 194th TB. "Had the block not been in place," Miller wrote, "the Japanese would have established themselves in our rear, set up a road block of their own, and destroyed us later in the afternoon. . . . The guns of the block had been laid on ditches as well as the road. There was no escaping from that withering fire."[32]

At 7:30 P.M., the 194th TB crossed the Gumain River. Major Miller immediately placed his 194th TB and the two companies from the 192nd (Companies C and D) along the southern bank. Behind them, about a mile away, the Philippine infantry and artillery worked hard to form a new main defensive line: the Gumain River Line.[33]

Near 1:50 A.M., January 5, Japanese infantry and tanks advanced against the forward line of tanks under the glare of a full moon. "The moon came up quite late in the evening and gave us excellent visibility," Miller, who was subsequently promoted to the rank of colonel, noted. "[The Japanese] came across the open field [to our front] in bright moonlight. . . . All our guns were in operation and the slaughter was terrific." Added Pvt. William N. Kinler (Company A, 194th TB), "There was a moon and the Japs attacked. Some were wearing white shirts and they came across the field shouting. They were clearly visible and we inflicted a lot of damage."[34]

During the battle, tracer rounds from the Japanese set fire to some high grass around a few American tanks. Abandoning the relative safety of his tank, Lieutenant Petree (194th TB) jumped out of his turret, rushed forward, and began beating out the approaching flames with his coat. Although Japanese gunfire blazed all around him, Petree seemed to live a charmed life. Then, suddenly, Lieutenant Petree went down. Sometime during the attack, an enemy soldier had infiltrated the American position and had climbed a nearby tree. From his elevated position he was able to shoot Lieutenant Petree in the back. "With the help of one of my tank crew," wrote Colonel Miller, "we manned the antiaircraft machine gun on top of the turret. We fired into the tree . . . [and a] body dropped [down]." Lieutenant Petree died a week later, never knowing that his actions had earned him a Distinguished Service Cross.[35]

At about the same time, another Japanese soldier managed to get close enough to throw a thermite grenade on top of one of the defending Stuarts. When the grenade detonated, it severely injured one crewman and left the other three dazed. Seeing the danger, Staff Sgt. Henry M. Luther (Company A, 192nd TB) rushed over from another tank and drove the damaged tank to safety. For this unselfish act of bravery, Sergeant Luther received a Silver Star medal.[36]

"At about 3:00 A.M., [the Japanese] withdrew," Miller reported, "leaving masses of dead and wounded behind. It was impossible to estimate the number of Japanese casualties. From what we could see, it was tremendous." With a clear-cut victory in hand, Colonel Miller decided to pull his force back to the Gumain River line at about 5:00 A.M.[37]

"In getting the column organized, one tank went over a steep embankment in the darkness and overturned," wrote Colonel Miller. "Luckily, no one was seriously injured. We tried to rescue the tank but the grade was so steep that it was impossible. We removed the weapons, twisted the gasoline valves in the crew compartment, and shot 37mm armor-piercing bullets through the motor, setting the tank on fire." After moving back to the main line, the tanks from Companies

A and C, 194th, and A and D, 192nd TBs took up a position behind a railroad grade running perpendicular to Highway 7.[38]

Preservation of the new defensive line was essential if the Allies hoped to get all of their troops onto the Bataan Peninsula. About eight miles south of the new line lay the Culo River, which ran across the entrance of the peninsula. On the right, Highway 7 ran down to the town of Layac Junction on the north bank of the Culo River and then turned sharply west, paralleling the river. A few miles away, Highway 7 ran into Dinalupihan and junctioned with Highway 74, coming down from the left side of the Gumain River line.

The only bridge across the Culo River was at Layac Junction, where a single steel span began the start of Route 110, the only road leading south into Bataan. In order for the Filipinos and Americans on the left flank of the Gumain River line to withdraw safely, they first had to move south down Highway 74 to Dinalupihan, then east toward Layac Junction, and then south across the Culo River. All the time, the troops on the right would have to hold the advancing Japanese at bay. Finally, when the left flank troops were all across the river, the right flank would withdraw. Such a move would need precise timing and a lot of luck.[39]

Throughout January 5, the Japanese pressured the Gumain River line but never attacked in force. Squeezed into smaller and smaller defensive lines, the defenders began to overlap each other until one unit intermingled with another. Noted historian Morton, "In one section, infantry, artillery, and tanks were mixed together in complete disorder." Beginning that night, on orders from General Wainwright, the troops on the left began to withdraw. By 8:30 P.M. all of the Filipino soldiers on the left flank were across the Culo River so the foot soldiers guarding the right flank began to pull back. Just before 2:00 A.M. on January 6, the last group of the soldiers, the 26th Philippine Cavalry, crossed the Culo Bridge. The only Allied troops north of the river were the tankers of the 192nd and 194th TBs.[40]

"I waited by my tank for at least an hour before I realized I was the only man awake," recalled Sergeant Knox. Exhausted beyond belief, many of the tankers had fallen asleep while waiting for the other units to cross the river. "I ran the full length of the column and reached in and belted each driver on the head," Knox wrote. Once awake, the tankers crossed with no trouble. Wrote Colonel Miller, "It was entirely without event and we crossed the bridge, near the Layoc Junction, at about 2:00 A.M. . . . The 194th Tank Battalion was the last unit to go into Bataan."[41]

As the last tank crossed the bridge, an engineering officer assigned to detonate the bridge asked a tank commander if there were any more tanks behind him. The tanker "[swore] by all that was holy that all his tanks had crossed" and the engineer prepared to blow the span. However, since the Japanese were nowhere in sight, General Wainwright ordered the officer to wait a few more minutes to see if any straggling infantry came across. A few minutes later, a lone American tank rumbled out of the darkness and hastened across the bridge. With no other friendlies in sight, at precisely 2:05 A.M., the Culo Bridge was blown.[42]

The North Luzon Force had held up the advancing Japanese army for three weeks, making a stand at five defensive lines, and blowing up 184 bridges. Their stubborn resistance had enabled the 15,000 defenders of the South Luzon Force to withdraw through, or around, Manila and into the Bataan peninsula. Along with the island fortress of Corregidor, which guarded the entrance to Manila Bay, the naturally strong defensive position of Bataan was to be the last stronghold for the Allied troops on Luzon.[43]

CHAPTER FIVE

Bataan

A defensive line had been set up almost directly behind the Culo River at Layac Junction to stall the Japanese and give the newly arriving troops time to sort themselves out. For the first time in the Philippines, American infantrymen, soldiers of the 31st Infantry Regiment (IReg), took up positions beside Filipino scouts and soldiers. As usual, the Provisional Tank Group was close at hand, spacing themselves out along a narrow jungle trail that ran parallel to the river, with 194th TB on the left and the 192nd TB on the right. Acting as antitank weapons, the heavy guns of the SPM halftracks were sighted on possible avenues of approach by enemy tanks. At this time, Company A, 192nd TB, which had been fighting with the 194th TB, was returned to its parent battalion.[1]

The Japanese advanced against the Culo River line shortly after 10:00 A.M. on January 6 and almost immediately were hit by Philippine artillery. Within a matter of minutes an artillery duel erupted. Aided by observation planes, the longer-range Japanese guns zeroed in on the Philippine positions. When the Japanese advanced again, they struck the badly shaken and demoralized American and Filipino troops and penetrated a portion of the line. Only a spirited counterattack prevented a full rupture and managed to slow the enemy advance.

When the Japanese managed a partial breakthrough on the right side, a composite company of tanks was ordered to "move out and cover the East Coast Road." The East Coast Road was Route 110, the only highway into the peninsula. At 6:30 P.M., when the Japanese broke through a second time, Colonel Miller feared that the road south would be cut and ordered all of the remaining tanks to "assemble in column" on Route 110.[2]

By 9:00 P.M., both battalions had reached the coast road. Four hours later, the tanks and halftracks rolled into their new position on the heavily wooded northern slope of Mount Samat, eight miles below a new defensive line that stretched across the entire peninsula.[3] Here, the Americans and Filipinos were bound to make their stand. They had run out of retreating room.

The Bataan peninsula, twenty miles wide at the top and twenty-five miles long, jutted out from Luzon into Manila Bay like a sore thumb. An extension of the Zambales Mountain range (which continued down the spine of Bataan), the peninsula held two extinct volcanoes and three or four smaller mountain peaks. Heavily vegetated, Bataan was covered with jungle and small streams. Access to the area was limited to Route 110, which circled around the outside of the peninsula. On the east side, the road was called the East Road and was an all-weather, single-lane highway, but on the west, the West Road was "not as well surfaced." The only other road that could be accessed by vehicles cut across the center of the peninsula and connected Pilar in the east with Bagac in the west. All other roads were tangled jungle trails.[4]

The main defensive line for the Allies was set up close to the top of the peninsula, stretching from Mauban on the west coast, across Mount Natib in the center, to near Abucay on the east coast. Further down the peninsula, a reserve battle line was drawn roughly parallel with the western and center portion of the Pilar-Bagac road, but then turned sharply to the southeast and followed the Orion Cutoff road to the barrio of Orion, about three miles below Pilar.[5]

Because of the spine of mountains that ran down the center of Bataan, the defense of the peninsula was split into three areas. West of the spine was designated I Corps area, under the command of General Wainwright; east of the mountains was II Corps area, commanded by Brig. Gen. George M. Parker; while the southern tip, at the end of the mountain range, was service command area. Mount Samat and the bivouac area of the Provisional Tank Group was in the II Corps area and just behind the reserve battle line.[6]

After arriving at the Mount Samat area around 1:00 A.M. on January 7, 1942, the tankers were finally given a period of rest. "This was the first rest for the combat elements since December 24th," wrote Doctor Poweleit. "[We were informed that] we would have a period of rest for the men, and they certainly need it; they were half dead, half fed and ragged. Many had wounds which ordinarily would have sent them to the hospital, but the men were needed on the front."[7]

Unfortunately, at that same time the men received some bad news. Corporal Stewart recalled, "The minute we got into Bataan our rations were cut in half because we didn't have enough supplies to continue to give us what they considered a whole ration." Added Colonel Miller, "This was not too difficult at first. We served two meals a day, at 8:00 A.M. and from 4:00 to 5:00 P.M., dividing the half ration between the two. We also apportioned the food we had salvaged, into the two meals. . . . Our salvaged food helped a great deal, but not for long."[8]

In total, General MacArthur had to feed almost 110,000 people on the Bataan peninsula. When it was first decided to put War Plan Orange-3 into action on December 23, thousands of Filipino civilians headed toward Bataan. In addition to the 70,000 Filipino soldiers and 12,500 American servicemen crammed into Bataan, there were also more than 26,000 Filipino civilians.[9] With so many people,

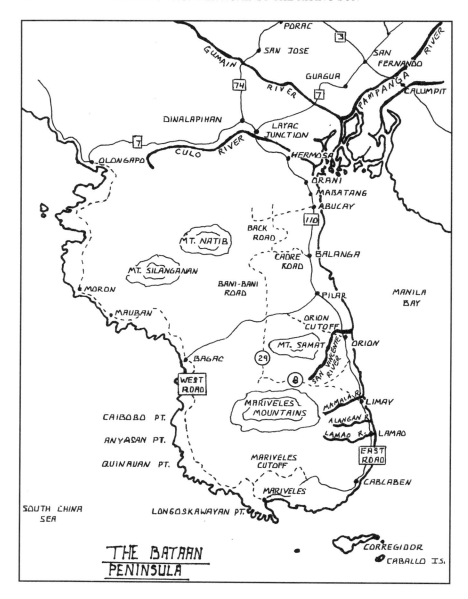

The Bataan Peninsula

and so little food, it was necessary to put everybody on half rations. However, it should not have been.

Before moving toward Bataan, Colonel Miller and the 194th TB had guarded the Calumpit Bridge. While there, the tankers had witnessed an unbelievable sight. Wrote Colonel Miller, "My men counted between 100 and 150 empty supply trucks

. . . rolling toward Bataan that should have been crammed with life-sustaining food and pertinent equipment procurable only in Manila." Supplies, ammunition, and essential parts for tanks, vehicles, and airplanes should have been delivered to Bataan the minute WPO-3 went into effect, but somebody had goofed. "What happened to the plans to evacuate the port area in Manila of pertinent supplies?" Miller criticized. "What happened to that part of the Orange Plan concerning canned meats and such in the wholesale warehouses in Manila? Why was no rice moved from the vast storages at Cabanatuan—also a part of the Orange Plan? Why was Bataan put on half rations immediately after the troops withdrew into the peninsula? The simple answer is that there was this period of indecision when foodstuffs, equipment, and other supplies should have been hauled into Bataan and were not. Hence the empty trucks."[10] No matter who was responsible, everyone was placed on half rations, and the people on Bataan suffered.

Although supplies and parts were short and the tankers tried to make necessary repairs, it was the 17th Ordnance Company (the same unit that had come to the Philippines with the 194th TB), which came up from the service command area, that really made the difference. Noted General Weaver, "The 17th Ordnance Company . . . going into high gear . . . [brought] up long-needed spare parts, tracks, motors, batteries, [and] radios from the stores on south Bataan." Added Corporal Fitzpatrick, "Spare parts were almost as scarce as food."[11]

Some thirty-six tanks had been lost during the battles of Luzon, ten from the 192nd TB and twenty-six from the 194th, so while the men were recuperating, the two units were reorganized. Instead of the pre-war complement of five tanks to a platoon and fifteen to a company (plus two for the company commanders), the tanks were redistributed so each platoon now consisted of only three tanks, or nine in each company (plus one for the company commander).[12]

On January 9, Japanese airplanes swooped in and broke the calm of the Provisional Tank Group.[13] The attack was staged in conjunction with a new push by the Japanese to capture the Bataan peninsula. Prior to the assault, the Japanese had become convinced they were facing a demoralized mob of Filipino and American soldiers. As a result, they moved roughly 15,000 battle-hardened troops out of the Philippines for an invasion of the Dutch East Indies. The veteran soldiers were replaced by 6,500 new recruits. At 3:00 P.M. on January 9, a terrific artillery barrage against the II Corps area on the right signaled the opening of the attack by the inexperienced troops.[14]

The Allied defenders managed to halt the attacks of January 9, forcing the Japanese to shift their forces toward the lightly defended center of the peninsula. Here the attacks were slowed by the rugged, mountainous jungle terrain. On January 10, General MacArthur, who had moved his headquarters from Manila to Corregidor, made his one and only visit to Bataan. Among the units that he visited were the Provisional Tank Group. Wrote Lieutenant Poweleit, "MacArthur . . . [was] cognizant of the poor condition of our men. Their thin, gaunt faces and their ragged conditions, many of them wearing dressings from previous wounds. He also realized that the half rations didn't help matters." When MacArthur asked

Poweleit why the wounded men were not in a field hospital, the doctor replied, "Who would man the tanks?" Reported Poweleit, "[MacArthur] just shook his head and said, 'I know.'"[15]

Throughout January 11 the Japanese tried unsuccessfully to break through on the right, along the East Road, while two columns slowly chopped their way through the jungle towards towering Mount Natib. By the morning of January 12, all of the Japanese columns were in position and an all-out advance was made against the entire II Corps line. While the right and center of the Allied line held, the left side, near Mount Natib, collapsed. As the penetrating Japanese advanced, they threatened to swing back east and encircle the rest of the II Corps defenders. Only a well-timed counterattack halted any further advance by the determined enemy troopers.[16]

On January 14, the Japanese struck along the west coast, stepping off from near the top of the peninsula and pushing south toward the Allied line. By January 16, they had pushed their way through the jungle to the beachside town of Moron, only a few miles above the I Corps main battle line at Mauban. With the Japanese in their front yard, the I Corps defenders called for a few tanks, and Captain Moffitt and Company C, 194th TB responded.[17]

While the tanks were leaving the rendezvous area to move to the west coast, the Japanese opposite II Corps kept driving inward until they had created a large pocket near Mount Natib. By the night of January 16 they were in a position to turn the Allied left flank and circle around behind the defenders. To counter such a move, the American 31st IReg and Filipino scouts counterattacked on January 17 and 18, reducing the pocket by half. On January 19, after a few Allied soldiers were killed by treetop snipers, General Parker called for some tanks. General Weaver refused. As he wrote, it would be "like sending an elephant to kill flies."[18]

Noted Colonel Miller:

> Evidently because of the armor plate on a tank, request after request was made that tanks be employed in hunting out snipers. When a little thought is given to the subject, one can readily see that in order to hunt snipers—the sniper, first of all, must be seen. Visibility inside of a tank is very limited, to say the least. To have complied with the request would have meant that tankers would have been compelled to get out of their tanks to find the snipers, thus making them the same kind of patrol which was already being used. The fact also remained that most of the terrain was impassable for tanks.[19]

Throughout the next few days, the Japanese shifted more and more troops toward the Mount Natib pocket. Then, at noon on January 22, the Japanese launched another attack, catching the Allies completely by surprise and threatening to envelop the infantry trying to reduce the pocket. Forced to fall back or be surrounded, the Americans and scouts pulled back. Again faced with a huge bulge in their line and the threat of being encircled and captured, USAFFE commanders began making plans to abandon the main battle line and withdraw to the reserve line behind the Bagac-Orion Cutoff Road.[20]

On January 17, after Captain Moffitt's ten tanks reached Mauban on the west coast of the peninsula, General Wainwright, who still lacked the knowledge of how to use tanks in combat, suggested "moving two or three tanks along the beach and across a coastal creek, to overrun [Japanese-held Moron]." When reconnaissance discovered that at least one Japanese antitank gun guarded the beach approach, General Weaver tried to get the plan changed. Feeling certain that the 13.5-ton Stuarts would bog down in the sand and be sitting ducks for the antitank gun, Weaver pointed out that all ten tanks would have to attack for the assault to succeed. Even then, he feared, at least three or four tanks would be lost. Realizing that he could not afford to lose *any* tanks, Wainwright withdrew his plan and conceded the loss of Moron. The tanks were then moved south to a position about five miles below Mauban.[21]

Two days later, on January 19, the Japanese pushed south from Moron. Using the same tactics as their brethren to the east, one column of soldiers started down the West Road, while another began chopping its way through the jungle. By January 21, the flanking column had passed through the I Corps line and had cut the West Road three miles below Mauban. By quickly establishing a massive roadblock, the Imperial troops threatened to entrap and eliminate the Filipino defenders of Mauban.[22]

In the wee morning hours of January 22, after the Japanese roadblock was discovered, General Wainwright called upon the ten tanks of Company C, 194th TB. By 6:00 A.M., the tanks were in position on the West Road when they suddenly received word to wait for the Philippine cavalry. They were coming up from a reserve position and had been ordered to assist the tanks. In the meantime, General Wainwright wanted one platoon of three tanks and a small force of infantry to reconnoiter the West Road. Shortly after 6:00 A.M., the small force started forward.[23]

"When [the tanks] reached the first bend in the road," Private Tenenberg wrote, "they encountered fire from an antitank gun. The commander of the lead tank fired a burst from his machine gun in the turret and followed it with a high-explosive shell from the 37mm cannon, silencing the anti-tank gun. The Japanese and their equipment were strewn all over the road, and before the tanks could advance, the crews had to clear the road."[24]

While the tankers were cleaning up their mess, the infantry started out well in advance of the tanks. When the three tanks started forward again, they went only about a quarter of a mile before the first two tanks rolled over unseen Japanese land mines. "Japs had infiltrated behind the infantry from one or both flanks," wrote Colonel Miller. "When the infantry was out of sight, the pie-pan mines were laid in the trail and covered so they could not be seen." Although none of the tankers were injured, both vehicles were disabled with broken tracks and idlers. "The crew of the remaining intact tank," added Private Tenenberg, "along with crew members from the disabled tanks, hooked cables from one tank to the other and then to the tank still in operating condition, and towed the two disabled tanks to safety."[25]

Incensed over the way the tanks had been left on their own, General Weaver sent a blistering report to USAFFE Headquarters on Corregidor. "The report severely criticized General Wainwright for allowing such asinine use of tanks," stated Colonel Miller. Even the men in the ranks knew better. Private Tenenberg wrote, "Unfortunately, once again men were being ordered into battle by non-tank officers, who knew nothing about the damage a land mine could do to the tracks of a tank." Eventually General Wainwright saw the report and, as Colonel Miller noted, "It did not improve the relations between him and the tankers, particularly so after General MacArthur left for Australia and Wainwright became the supreme commander!"[26]

Even after the Philippine cavalry arrived, the Allies were unable to eliminate the Japanese roadblock on the West Road. Over the next few days, General Wainwright tried repeatedly to reopen the road and reestablish contact with his trapped troops in Mauban, but each attempt failed. Finally, on January 25, the Mauban defenders abandoned the town and fled south along the western beach. By nightfall, Mauban and the I Corps main battle line had been abandoned. The Allied defenders quickly fell back to the reserve battle line behind the Bagac-Orion Cut-off Road. [27]

On the east side of Bataan, in the II Corps sector, plans were already underway for a withdrawal to the reserve line when I Corps troops fell back. Penetration near Mount Natib had made the II Corps main battle line untenable. The subsequent order for withdrawal called for "a progressive evacuation of the line, to be completed by daylight of the 26th." To protect the retreating army, a temporary defensive line would be established along a narrow jungle trail called the Cadre Road, halfway between the main battle line and the reserve line. As usual, the Provisional Tank Group would be a part of the rear guard.[28]

On the night of January 23–24 the artillery and service troops began pulling out of the main line and heading south. The 192nd TB was ordered to cover the withdrawal of the troops on the right and eventually withdraw down the East Road. The 194th TB, which was covering the center and left side of the main line, was told to cover the withdrawal and then retreat down a secondary road known as the Back Road. The 194th TB would have to share this narrow jungle road with all of the retreating infantry.[29]

Although the withdrawal of the artillery went off without a hitch, the retreat of the infantry was mass confusion. "The two exits were completely blocked," wrote Colonel Miller. "Bringing out the Philippine Army was like herding a flock of sheep. . . . Units intermingled with other units and became hopelessly lost in the mob. It was impossible to do anything else but keep the mass moving to the rear."

In the midst of all this confusion the Japanese army decided to attack. Striking out from around the area of Mount Natib, the Japanese were temporarily halted by the American 31st IReg and the Philippine scouts, giving the confused mob time enough to make their escape. Then, at about 1:00 A.M. on January 25, the

Americans and scouts decided they had done enough. Asked to cover their retreat was Company D, 192nd TB (which was still attached to the 194th TB).[30]
Recalled Colonel Miller:

> The moon was not yet up and it was very dark. How it was accomplished I will never know, but we succeeded in moving some tanks [and SPMs] up the road to the left flank positions. . . . The tanks fired blindly in the darkness while the [infantry] withdrew out of hostile fire to a group of Filipino buses, which had been assigned to carry them to the rear. They were on their last legs and ready to drop in their tracks, but not too far gone to utter words of thanks. The tanks returned very slowly, firing as they came and the SPMs sprayed the evacuated area with shells. Firing by both tanks and 75s had been very effective. The Japs did not follow up.[31]

Once Company D had rejoined the 194th TB, the entire regiment, including four SPMs, started south down the Back Road. "By this time the moon was up, which helped somewhat," Miller wrote, "but it still was a difficult negotiation due to the trail's intricacies." At one point, a platoon of tanks took a wrong turn and began circling back toward the Japanese before discovering their mistake. By dawn of January 25, the tanks had reached the Cadre Road and spread out along the perpendicular road as a protective screen, facing north toward the dense jungle wall. "The road was about twenty feet wide and ran east and west," Colonel Miller reported. "There was absolutely no possible chance for any field of fire except for the width of the road. Dense jungle was on both sides. Why we were ever ordered into such a position will always remain a mystery." Still, Miller established listening posts in front of his tanks and SPMs and waited for the pursuing Japanese.[32]

Along the East Road, it was broad daylight before the 192nd TB began to fall back, continuing to cover the retreat. As they did so, they found their way clogged with buses carrying the Filipino infantry. All day long, Japanese planes strafed and bombed the East Road, causing numerous casualties. Still, the column kept moving. Just after sunup on January 25, the 192nd TB reached the town of Balanga and dug in.[33]

According to an order issued by USAFFE Headquarters on January 25, it was the job of the tanks to keep the enemy at arms length until the reserve battle line could be manned. The order read:

> Tanks will execute maximum delay, staying in position and firing at visible enemy until further delay will jeopardize withdrawal. If a tank is immobilized, it will be fought until the close approach of the enemy, then destroyed; the crew previously taking positions outside and continuing the fight with the salvaged and personal weapons. Considerations of personal safety or expediency will not interfere with accomplishing the greatest possible delay.[34]

As Private Tenenberg noted, "The order was very clear: Protecting the complete and successful withdrawal of all U.S. and Filipino forces, as well as civilians, was our first order of business. Reading between the lines, the message said death was better than an early withdrawal on our part."[35]

Near 10:00 A.M., Japanese artillery began pounding Balanga. An hour later, enemy dive-bombers appeared. Sometime during the day a vital bridge just south of Balanga was destroyed, severing the intended escape route of the 192nd TB. Fortunately, however, the Japanese did not press the attack. When evening came, the tanks headed west, along the Cadre Road. Passing behind the defending vehicles of Colonel Miller's 194th TB, Colonel Wickord's 192nd TB turned south on the Bani-Bani Road and groped its way through the impenetrable darkness.[36]

Luckily, the 194th TB had spent the day in relative solitude. That night, after the 192nd TB had turned down the Bani-Bani Road, the 194th TB followed. "The night was very dark—almost pitch black," Colonel Miller recalled. As both the 192nd and the 194th TBs groped their way south along the narrow Bani-Bani Road, the tanks became strung out in a long line. "About an hour after we started, I received a radio call from the commanding officer of [Company A, 194th TB at the rear of the column]," recalled Colonel Miller. "One of his tanks had slipped off the side of a bridge in the darkness, until it hung on the very edge."

Inside the tank was Corporal Fitzpatrick. "The tank I was in ran partly off the edge of [a] bridge and became stuck," he recalled. "We piled out of the tank as it teetered on the edge and, working awkwardly in the dark and dusty night, we tried to pull it back onto the bridge with [tow] cables. The tank fell off the bridge and landed upside down under the bridge." Knowing that salvaging the tank would be impossible, the vehicle was destroyed and the men moved on.[37]

By sunup of January 26, the Provisional Tank Group was safely behind the reserve battle line. Having done an incredible job of herding a fleeing army back to a new battle line, the group was given a few days' rest and went into bivouac a few miles behind the new position.[38]

CHAPTER SIX

The Points and Pockets

While the Allied troops were falling back to the reserve battle line, the Japanese staged an amphibious move against the west coast. On the night of January 22–23, roughly 1,000 Imperial soldiers set out for Caibobo Point, a narrow strip of beach about five miles below Bagac. If the landing was successful, Bagac, the western anchor of the new reserve battle line, would be in peril from both the north and south.

The Japanese ran into trouble from the very beginning. The darkness, the waves, inadequate maps, and American PT boats scattered and confused the attackers. One group, about 600 soldiers, landed three miles south of Caibobo Point at a small outcropping called Quinauan Point. The other group, about 300 men, landed seven miles farther south at Longoskawayan Point, only 2,000 yards west of the port city of Mariveles, the only sizable city on Bataan. Wet, seasick, and disoriented, both groups stumbled ashore and slowly began moving inland.[1]

By 8:30 A.M. on January 23, the Allies had discovered the Japanese invaders. Immediately, "a mixed force of sailors, Marines, airmen, constabulary, and Philippine Army troops" was sent to contain the lodgments. By noon on January 29, the pocket at Longoskawayan Point had been eliminated and the lodgement at Quinauan Point had been contained.[2]

While the fighting was taking place, the Japanese decided to reinforce the men at Quinauan Point before they were wiped out. On the night of January 26, a force of 200 Imperial soldiers attempted another amphibious move. However, the boats got lost and came ashore 2,000 yards north of their objective, landing instead at Anyasan Point, a few miles above Quinauan Point. Early on the morning of January 27, the Allies discovered the new threat and quickly shifted enough troops from Quinauan Point to easily contain the 200 Japanese troops.[3]

Between January 27 and February 1, the Filipino and American foot soldiers pounded away at both Quinauan and Anyasan points. Unfortunately, the rough terrain of the area greatly aided the invaders. At Anyasan Point, the Japanese hid in the "canebrakes, thickets and creek bottoms"; while on Quinauan Point, they hid in the "dense forest and thick undergrowth."[4]

To the north, the Japanese had been pushing forward and on the night of January 28–29 finally found a soft spot in the I Corps reserve battle line. Pushing into the mountainous wild jungles of central Bataan, about 1,000 soldiers found a gap near the Tuol River valley. Noted historian Morton, "It is hard to imagine heavier, more nearly impenetrable or bewildered jungle then that in which [the Japanese] found themselves. . . . Visibility throughout the area is limited, often to ten or fifteen yards." Because of the terrain, the Japanese themselves became confused and split into two groups. On January 29, both groups were discovered and formed defensive positions. The smaller group, about 250 men, established a defensive perimeter, dubbed the Little Pocket, about 400 yards inside the Allied lines while the larger group, about 750 men, took up a position, called the Big Pocket, about a mile inside the lines. Almost immediately the American and Filipino defenders surrounded the two pockets.[5]

On January 31, knowing they would need tanks to eliminate the Japanese on the points and in the pockets, General Weaver was asked to send over "a battalion less a company [of tanks] to the west coast." The next morning, twenty-three tanks from Headquarters Company and Companies A and C, 192nd TB began moving toward the threatened sectors.[6]

To complicate an already confusing situation, on the night of February 1–2 the Japanese made another move to reinforce their men on Quinauan Point. This time, the Allies were forewarned when a document detailing the action was found on a dead Japanese officer. When the barges set out, they were intercepted by American PT boats and a few P-40 aircraft, and shot at by artillery and machine guns. Instead of reinforcing Quinauan Point, the reinforcements headed straight for shore and landed at Anyasan Point, reinforcing the defenders there.[7]

Around noon on February 2, four tanks from Company A, 192nd TB reached the southern tip of the Big Pocket. Although one tank soon developed accelerator trouble, the other three were selected to lead an armor/infantry attack straight north through the pocket, up a narrow jungle trail. Because of the thick vegetation the tanks would be forced to stay on the trail. Nonetheless, at 3:00 P.M., the three tanks, followed by a platoon of infantry, stepped off.[8]

"God, you couldn't see," recalled Pvt. Daniel N. Stoudt, driving the second tank in line. "Half the time I was driving I couldn't see. I actually didn't see a thing. . . . All I did was drive and shoot both [sponson-mounted] .30s just to make noise more than anything." Although the Japanese infiltrators returned fire, the tanks kept moving and drove completely through the pocket to the reserve battle line. Unfortunately, the supporting infantry could not keep up and were forced to remain on the south side of the pocket. Later, when the tanks tried a return trip, one tank rolled over a hidden land mine, blowing the belly out of the tank and knocking off one of the tracks. Fortunately, only one man was wounded and the tank was dragged back safely to friendly lines.[9]

That same afternoon, a platoon of three tanks from Company C, 192nd TB led by Lt. John Hay reached Quinauan Point. Altogether, five assaults were made by the Stuart tanks and Philippine scouts. Impeded in their progress by felled trees and thick vegetation, each assault failed. Noted historian John W. Whitman, "[The tanks] spent most of their time making short rushes into the jungle clearing a path for the infantry. The same three tanks were used continuously, and the tankers neared exhaustion in their oven-like vehicles."[10]

On February 3, Lieutenant Hays' tanks went in again. Historian Morton wrote, "Stumps and fallen trees impeded the advance of the tanks whose usefulness was further limited by the absence of proper coordination between infantry and armor, and faulty communication and control. When the [tanks and scouts] halted at 1700 [5:00 P.M., they] were not far from [their] original line of departure." Two thousand yards farther north, nine tanks from Companies A and C, 192nd were attacking Anyasan Point.[11]

There, too, thick vegetation forced the tanks to move blindly down narrow jungle paths in column. Although infantry support had been requested, the exhausted Filipino scouts remained at least 100 yards behind the tanks. Something had to go wrong. Lieutenant Poweleit recalled, "The Japanese made an attack on [Pvt. Robert] Young's tank which had gone farther than the rest. The tank hit a mine and blew a track off." When the crew tried to get out, the Japanese hit the tank with a flamethrower, killing two men and badly wounding two others.[12]

That night, the Japanese counterattacked and recovered most of the ground they had lost during the day. With the disabled tank now inside their lines, the Japanese figured the Americans would be coming back for their wounded comrades and therefore set a trap. Digging foxholes under the tank, the Imperial soldiers threw the dirt inside the tank to hide the telltale signs of foxholes from the Americans. In doing so, the piled up dirt suffocated the two wounded crewmen. Wrote Private Tenenberg, "By burying the men in the tank, the Japanese were able to plan a surprise attack on our rescue crew tank and crew. The Japanese hid in holes beneath the tank, and as soon as our rescue effort started, they began firing at us. Luckily, being under the tank did not allow them clean shots, and . . . [w]ithin minutes the [rescue] team eliminated the small Japanese contingent under it." Although the rescue crew managed to reach the disabled tank, they were unable to hook a tow cable to it and were forced to abandon it again when night fell.[13]

Over the next few days, the tanks and the Philippine scouts formed a symbiotic relationship. Although the scouts had been led to believe that the tanks, with their armor plating, were invincible, they soon discovered that the Japanese took full advantage of the limited fields of vision of the Stuarts and often ran up on the sides to place magnetic mines against their hulls. It was only through experiment and error that a working relationship was established between the tankers and the scouts. The scouts needed the tanks to knock out heavy gun emplacements and stubborn areas of resistance, and the tankers needed the scouts to keep the pesky minelayers away.[14]

Up at the Big Pocket, February 3 was another busy day for the two remaining Company A, 192nd TB Stuarts that had reached the reserve battle line. One tank and a squad of Filipino scouts advanced into the jungle until they came upon an enemy machine gun position hidden under the roots of a giant banyan tree. Because the tank had come too close to the tree before stopping, the crew could not depress their 37mm cannon low enough to get off a lethal shot. Instead, Lt. Willibald C. Bianchi, a Philippine officer, climbed atop the tank and fired the .30-caliber antiaircraft gun at the emplacement. In spite of being wounded several times, Bianchi remained in place until an antitank shell hit the tank and blew him off. As the crew scrambled out of the disabled tank, some of the scouts pulled Bianchi to safety. Lieutenant Bianchi, who survived his wounds, was later awarded the Medal of Honor.[15]

When the first tank became engaged in the firefight, the second Stuart moved up to help but got stuck on a banyan stump. Immediately, the tank came under heavy enemy fire until two scouts crawled forward and used hand grenades to destroy a Japanese machine-gun nest. Taking full advantage of the opportunity, the crew scrambled out of their disabled tank and made it safely back to the reserve line.[16]

On February 4, the one remaining tank was reinforced by a three-tank platoon from Company B, 192nd TB. Although all four tanks and the Filipino infantry spent the whole day trying to reduce the Big Pocket, they made little progress. As historian Morton wrote, "It was evident that a coordinated and stronger offensive than any yet made would be required for victory."[17]

At Anyasan Point, after the loss of Private Young's tank, riflemen were instructed to stick closer to each tank. Wrote Sergeant Knox from Company A, "The infantry followed right behind the tanks as we fired and crept forward. Everything was killed in the spider holes and foxholes as we passed over them with grenade and rifle fire."[18]

At Quinauan Point, Lieutenant Hays' three sturdy tanks were reinforced on February 4 with two more tanks (probably from Headquarters Company, 192nd TB). A radio control halftrack also arrived to help coordinate everything. With infantry support carrying handheld walkie-talkie radios, the tanks soon started another advance. Historian Whitman described the attack:

> The tanks, their sirens wailing, were the deciding factor now. The once-thick concealing vegetation had been shot away, allowing the tanks to see and maneuver. Guided by radio, they moved forward firing at targets spotted by nearby infantrymen. They shot apart Japanese positions or crushed them with their 13-ton weight.[19]

The tanks and infantry pushed the Japanese back until they were less than fifty yards from the cliffs overlooking the South China Sea. Faced with annihilation, many Japanese committed suicide by jumping off the cliff while others tried to scramble down the rocks. Greeting the few live Japanese that reached the beach was a fusillade of American and Filipino small arms fire.[20]

Surveying the area after the battle, Lieutenant Poweleit wrote, "This morning, Quinauan Point was cleared. . . . Our tanks did a bang-up job. Viewing the battlefield was pretty ghastly. Bodies were bloated, rotted and covered with flies and maggots."[21] The fight for Quinauan Point had lasted fifteen days and had left 600 Japanese dead. For the Allies, the cost was 500 dead or wounded.[22]

On February 5 and 6, the eight remaining tanks at Anyasan Point continued their attacks. Wrote Sergeant Knox, "Each day the tanks went into the pocket spread out on a single front. Most of the time we were hub to hub, maybe ten feet or less between vehicles. The combined fire of all machine guns and cannons was fierce. The brush lay right down and would straighten back up as the fire slackened. We gradually cut down all the trees and brush about the size of a football field." Unfortunately, the acquisition of ground was not permanent. Noted Sergeant Knox, "Each night the Japs pushed back and each day we recovered the same ground."[23]

Sergeant Knox also recalled the effect all the shooting had on the machine guns. He wrote, "Some of the machine-gun barrels I replaced had the rifling wore right out of them. . . . We were burning eight to ten thousand rounds [of ammunition] a day in our tanks. Supply officers screamed like mad. We were way over our allotment." The fierceness of the American attack was summed up in a message sent out by one of the Japanese commanders on Anyasan Point. "The battalion is being attacked by superior enemy tanks and artillery," he radioed, "and we are fighting a bitter battle. The battalion is about to die gloriously."[24]

In the Big Pocket area, the three tanks of Company B, 192nd and the remaining tank from Company A, 192nd continued their assaults. Headhunting pygmy Igorate tribesmen from the mountains of northern Luzon, who hated the Japanese, helped the tankers. "[T]here was these little black natives, little pygmies" recalled Private Ortega. "And they helped in the war effort, too. They did a lot of sabotaging. They would hide, you could never find them."[25]

To help the tankers, the Igorates walked in front of the tanks and pointed out enemy bunkers and foxholes. After a few of the Igorates were wounded, however, the tankers let the pygmies ride on the tops of the tanks, where they were able to sight the enemy and direct the tank commander by pounding on either side of the turret with a stick.[26]

On February 6, as the four tanks operating around the Big Pocket were pushing down a narrow trail with Lieutenant Winger in the lead, a Japanese soldier suddenly doused Winger's M3 Stuart with a flamethrower, temporarily blinding the crew. Confused and unable to see, the driver tried to get the tank away from the flamethrower but instead got it stuck on something. No matter what the driver did, the tank would not move. In a heartbeat he called for help.[27]

Sergeant Bardowski, who had been trailing behind in the second tank, sprang into immediate action. "[M]y dad swiveled the turret towards the [flamethrower]," said Steve Bardowski, "and the M3 had a shoulder stock on the 37mm . . . and on either side you had pistol grips with triggers, one fired the 37mm, the other fired the .30-caliber, the coaxial. Under pressure, and understandably so because he'd never seen a flamethrower . . . he squeezed both at once and the 37mm . . . apparently hit the fuel tank of the flamethrower and blew it up."

"So Dad ordered his driver to pull up behind [Winger's tank] and even in those days the tanks had towing cables, front and rear," continued Steve Bardowski. "Under fire, he dismounted, climbed down from the turret, climbed down in front, unhooked the cables, ran to the back of Lieutenant Winger's tank and went to hook it up to pull it off, and when he got there, all he had in his hand was the hook. While he was crossing the little bit of open ground [between the two tanks] the enemy fire shot the cable away."

Undaunted, Bardowski ran around to the rear of his tank. "[He] took the cables from the rear and dragged them up to the front, again still under fire," Steve Bardowski continued. "[He] hooked the end to his front pintels and then hooked the running end to Lieutenant Winger's tank, remounted and pulled it free." Miraculously, Sergeant Bardowski was never hit by the high volume of enemy fire directed at him.[28]

For Sergeant Bardowski, the heroics were not yet over. After unhooking his tank from Lieutenant Winger's, he continued his assault against the Japanese positions. When he spotted a 47mm antitank gun blocking the road in front of him, he told his driver to keep going. Then, Bardowski fired a 37mm cannon round straight through the protective gun shield of the antitank gun. "[The tank round] apparently hit the ready ammo or a round about to be loaded or maybe the round in the breach," Steve Bardowski recalled. "The gun exploded [and the Stuart] crushed it. That killed the crew and they got through."

Steve Bardowski continued, "[U]nbeknownst to them, they had [also] run over a Nambu light machine-gun nest beside [the antitank gun]. In the [tropical] heat, by the time they got back to the bivouac area, the entrails and odd bits and pieces of Japanese soldiers had putrefied." Complaints from Bardowski's fellow tankers eventually forced Sergeant Bardowski to take his tank into a nearby river and wash it off. For Sgt. Zenon Bardowski's actions on February 6, he was awarded a Bronze Star medal.[29]

Apparently, according to historian Whitman, the gore and blood that covered Bardowski's tank was not limited to that vehicle alone. Noted Whitman, "American tankers had the disagreeable job of scraping pieces of Japanese out of their tank treads, wheels and sprockets. In desperation, they threw sand against the tank hulls to reduce the stench."[30]

During the fighting that morning, Lieutenant Winger was mortally wounded by friendly fire. Once Winger's tank was out of harm's way, the crew scrambled out and headed toward the Allied line. As the tankers came through the foliage, an inexperienced Filipino soldier opened fire with a Browning automatic rifle, wounding Lieutenant Winger in the belly and legs. "He was carried into a collecting station," recalled Doctor Poweleit. "He had a number of holes in his large bowel and looked very bad. He wanted to know if we were going to cut his legs off. I assured him we would not. He died during surgery—a great loss."[31]

On the night of February 6–7, the Japanese north of the I Corps sector decided to try to break through to the Big Pocket. By nightfall, the attackers had forced a huge bulge 600 yards deep inside the reserve battle line, subsequently called the Upper Pocket. In an attempt to contain the drive, most of the Allied troops and armor that had previously been employed against Quinauan Point were quickly shifted to the area.[32]

Near the end of the first week in February, I Corps commanders finally realized that the repeated, uncoordinated attacks against the pockets were going nowhere fast. Instead, the commanders decided to concentrate on one pocket at a time. So at 9:00 A.M. on February 7, the available Filipino infantry and a few tanks from the 192nd TB began pushing in on the Little Pocket from all sides.[33]

During the attack, one of the Stuarts was set on fire by a Japanese hand grenade, trapping the crew. Sgt. John Olin Hopple (Headquarters Company, 192nd TB), who had been a member of Lieutenant Winger's crew on February 6, was in a nearby tank and knew first-hand the horrors of fire. Leaping from his new tank with a fire extinguisher, he put out the flames and saved the crew. For his unselfish bravery, Hopple was awarded a Distinguished Service Cross.[34]

On February 8, after an unsuccessful Japanese amphibious attempt to rescue the trapped troops at Anyasan Point, the Filipino scouts and the American tanks pushed in again on the half-starved invaders. "[That] day we made considerable progress at Anyasan," noted Lieutenant Poweleit. "We only suffered a few wounded that day. Tank action was over at Anyasan and fighting was mostly mopping up."[35]

At both Anyasan Point and the Little Pocket, the Filipino and American forces made great strides on February 8, pushing the invaders into smaller and smaller pockets. That night, the Japanese made one final amphibious move to rescue their trapped brethren on Anyasan Point but failed miserably. The few remaining Japanese soldiers on Anyasan were on their own.[36]

Over the next few days, from February 9 through February 11, the Filipino soldiers continued to make great gains on the Point. On February 12, about 200 half-starved, half-crazed Japanese attempted a break out from the Point, surprising and overrunning two Filipino command posts before being stopped. On February 13, the Philippine scouts moved in and killed the last of the invaders. The battle of the Points was over. At Anyasan Point, the Allies lost 170 men killed and wounded. The Japanese lost almost 900, all of them killed. Noted Lieutenant Poweleit, "[Between Anyasan and Quinauan Points] there were 1,156 killed. I walked over the battlefield. It was horrid, but I realized that grass would soon grow over this place and cover its offensiveness."[37]

To the north, on the night of February 8, the Japanese in the Little Pocket somehow managed to slip through the Allied encirclement and flee north toward their own lines. When the Filipino infantry and American tankers moved forward on February 9, they found only dead bodies, discarded equipment, and a few

Japanese snipers. While passing through the area, Sergeant Hopple was shot by an enemy sniper. He died three days later at a Bataan hospital.[38]

With the Little Pocket gone, the Allies began shifting forces to the Big Pocket. Perhaps realizing their fate, the Japanese in the Big Pocket attempted a massive breakout to the north on the night of February 10. Meeting stiff resistance, the breakout failed miserably.

The next day, the Filipino infantry and scouts renewed their attacks. By 10:00 A.M., they had secured the entire length of Trail 7. As they did so, they came across one of the Stuart tanks that had been lost earlier and discovered the machine guns were still operational and loaded with ammunition. Climbing inside, the infantry used the tank as a stationary pillbox and raked the surrounding jungle with .30-caliber machine-gun fire.[39]

That evening, the Japanese made one final desperate attempt to escape the Big Pocket. Passing quietly through the jungle, 600 Japanese, including 100 badly wounded, somehow found a gap in the Allied lines and pulled out of the pocket. On the morning of February 12, when the Filipinos and Americans renewed their attack, they found the Big Pocket devoid of any living Japanese. Recalled Lieutenant Poweleit, "We counted 550 Japanese bodies in varying degrees of putrefaction."[40]

After fleeing the Big Pocket, the 600 Japanese quietly made their way north. On February 15, after moving through the jungle for four continuous days, 377 living skeletons finally reached their own lines. These were the sole survivors of the 1,000 Japanese soldiers who had been trapped inside the Big and Little Pockets. More than 600 Japanese soldiers had been lost to American or Filipino gunfire or the deadly Bataan jungle.[41]

On February 12, after the Japanese were gone from the Big Pocket, I Corps commanders began shifting troops to the Upper Pocket. Among the units moved were the 192nd TB and the Igorate pygmies. Once again, the Igorates rode atop the tanks and directed their movements and gunfire. Noted historian Morton, "Hoisted to the top of the tanks where they were exposed to the fire of the enemy, these courageous tribesmen from North Luzon chopped away the entangling foliage with their bolos and served as eyes for the American tankers. From their position atop the tanks they fired at the enemy with pistols while guiding the drivers with sticks."[42]

On February 14 the Upper Pocket salient had been reduced by one half. The next day, the pocket was reduced by half again. By February 16, the remaining Japanese had been squeezed into an area no bigger than a football field. On February 17, the Filipino infantry finally pushed the invaders back across the original reserve battle line, thereby reducing the pocket to zero. For all intents and purposes the Battle for the Pockets was over. Including the Battle of the Points, the Japanese had lost more than 2,000 men since January 22, almost all of them killed. The few who survived were in no shape to continue the fight. On February 17, the entire Japanese Army pulled back from the reserve battle line and moved into the old Mauban–Abucay line to reinforce and regroup. Without even realizing it, the Allies had scored the first victory in the battle for Bataan.[43]

CHAPTER SEVEN

Siege and Suffering

L ong before the Japanese Army pulled back from the Allied reserve battle line, their commanders had been considering such a move. Having expected to take the Bataan peninsula with one quick push, the commanders decided to pull back and regroup when the campaign dragged on and thousands of men were being lost.[1]

The Allies had no way of knowing the Japanese were gone and waited for the enemy to renew the attack. After a while, patrols went out and discovered the Japanese had pulled back. "The enemy has definitely recoiled," General MacArthur wrote. "His attitude is so passive as to discount any immediate threat of attack."[2]

With the Japanese gone, the weary defenders turned to a more immediate need—hunger. Doctor Poweleit had been monitoring the food intake of the tankers and recorded his observations in his diary:

January 9—We were on half-rations, but by the time the food arrived it was one-third rations.

January 14—Our men were rapidly deteriorating physically, due to lack of food.

January 15—We were issued carabao meat. Many men refused to eat it and gave it away. I told them they should be damn glad to get this food but they laughed. The health of the few who ate this meat was greatly improved the next day.

January 21—Our men are beginning to show signs of malnutrition.

February 11—Our men were suffering from malnutrition and vitamin deficiency. They are hardly able to work on the tanks to maintain them.

March 9—I reported to General Weaver that in the 192nd alone about half of our men were unable to do a good day's work. A similar situation existed in the 194th Tank Battalion. The overall weight loss for the Provisional Tank Group was thirty-five to forty pounds. The rations that our men were given were little better than a fourth of what a person should normally have.[3]

Whenever possible, the men tried to supplement their ration with whatever they could. "Our food was very scarce," noted Sergeant French. "We was eating rice, carabao, if they could find one someplace and kill it. . . . We killed iguanas. . . . We shot monkeys, snakes, anything else that would live. We ate monkeys, dogs, we ate anything that was more or less eatable. We used to go up in the mountains and get the poor old Filipinos' chickens. Bananas that we could find, mangos, papayas, cashews, we learned to eat the hearts out of banana trees and we learned a lot of things how to survive by doing these things."[4]

Although Private Ortega and his friends were starving, they drew the line when it came to eating monkeys. "We thought maybe that was food," recalled Private Ortega, "but after he was skinned and we hung it up it looked so much like a human being that we just forgot it." Wrote Corporal Fitzpatrick, "At first to me, [monkey] seemed too much like eating a child, but towards the end I ate any bit I could get my hands on."[5]

As the months went on, and starvation grew, nothing was sacred. "[W]e ate all the cavalry horses of all of the Philippine cavalry," remembered Private Ortega. Recalled Private DeGroot years later, "The horse and mule meat tasted like the finest steaks I have today."[6]

Company D, 192nd TB, had come from Harrodsburg, Kentucky and, as Colonel Miller explained, "[They] had the Kentuckian's deep love for horses. Whether they actually knew that part of their miserable ration was horse meat stew, I do not know. In all honesty, I do not believe the majority did. . . . After the horse meat disappeared, and it was generally known that it was horse meat, some of the Kentuckians said they did not know it, and if they had, they would never have eaten it. Knowing them as I did, I am thoroughly convinced they meant what they said!"[7]

Other animals that became the main ingredient of stews were any type of lizard, especially iguanas. "There were small and large lizards—some four to five feet long—which were caught when possible and used for food," wrote Colonel Miller. Added Private DeGroot, "[T]he iguana was a white meat, and I thought it . . . well, when you're starving . . . I thought it was okay."[8]

"If a GI was lucky," remembered Private Tenenberg, "he could wrangle an invitation aboard the [USS] *Canopus* for an evening meal." Tied up at the Mariveles docks at the southern tip of Bataan, the submarine tender *Canopus* supplied ammunition, gasoline, and most importantly, food to all of the submarines in the Philippines area. Discovering that the crew was eager to obtain captured Japanese souvenirs, Tenenberg and his buddies brought back Japanese flags, rifles, swords, and all sorts of equipment from the abandoned battlefields. "The first night we had roast beef, all the trimmings and chocolate cake with ice cream. The following night we had the special fried chicken, once again with all the trimmings, and cherry pie a la mode." Added Tenenberg, "An old saying goes, 'The Navy eats well.' How true, how true."[9]

With a lack of food, the men's immune systems deteriorated and they became more susceptible to a myriad of tropical diseases. "[My father had] malaria, beriberi, wet beriberi . . . whatever came along, he caught," said Steve Bardowski. Reported Colonel Miller, "The men were up and down with malaria, dysentery, diarrhea, and dengue fever—and malnutrition was setting in." Added Private Tenenberg, "So many men were sick with dengue fever and malaria, that we had to set up emergency dispensaries in the field because many of the sick could not be moved to the base hospital [in Mariveles]."[10]

By the end of February, all of tankers were physically weakened. "Morale and mental attitudes were of the best but physique was declining rapidly," noted Colonel Miller. "Malnutrition made itself quite evident. Men would become dizzy, with black spots appearing before their eyes. The majority had contracted all of the diseases heretofore mentioned. Malaria was very persistent."[11]

Doctor Poweleit was perhaps in the best position to see the long-term effects of the starvation diet. In the middle of January he found a scale and weighed the men. He wrote, "Nearly all were down fifteen to twenty pounds." Six weeks later, he weighed the men again, noting that "the average man had lost about thirty or forty pounds."[12]

The tankers were not alone in their misery, however. Every soldier on Bataan went through the same suffering. "By April 1, one thousand men a day entered our hospital wards with one or more disabling sicknesses," wrote Private Tenenberg. "Two days later, our medics estimated that between 75 and 80 percent of our frontline troops were ill."[13] Yet, the "Battling Bastards of Bataan," as the defenders started calling themselves, had to fight on. Their very lives and freedom depended on it.

In addition to the shortages of food and medicine, there was also a lack of gasoline. When the Allies first entered the peninsula, the supply of gasoline was considered "adequate for several months if strict economy was practiced." During the first two weeks however, gasoline was being eaten up by the trucks, jeeps, artillery tractors, halftracks, tanks and every other motor vehicle at the rate of 14,000 gallons a day. Historian Morton wrote, "Ultimately the consumption of gasoline was reduced to 4,000, then 3,000 gallons daily."[14]

In addition to the quantity of gas, the tankers were also worried about the quality. "92-octane gas, the lowest rating gas that the tanks could use for safe operation, was no longer available," wrote Private Tenenberg. "Putting gas with an octane rating of 85 into our tanks meant that we could not be sure how our engines would respond under extreme circumstances." The 194th TB had been able to salvage 12,000 gallons of the 92-octane gas from the Luzon supply dumps to use solely in the tanks, but before long, even that began to disappear.[15]

In spite of the shortage of gasoline, the 17th Ordnance Company, which was still attached to the Provisional Tank Group, struggled to keep the tanks in operating condition. The battles of the points and pockets had played hell on the outside of the tanks. Wrote historian Whitman, "The effect of enemy fire and jungle vegetation was such that the outside of some tanks were entirely stripped of headlights, sirens, and fenders."[16] Working with the few spare parts that they had, the ordnance men somehow managed to put the tanks back together again and keep their engines running.

Additionally, the 17th Ordnance Company tried to compensate for the lack of antipersonnel shells which had plagued the tankers from Day One. "[B]ecause we were no longer in direct contact with Japanese armored vehicles, our ordnance department converted our 37mm armor-piercing shells into high-explosive shells," reported Private Tenenberg. Although most of the tankers were glad to see the change, a few, like Sergeant Bardowski, had become adept at killing Japanese with the armor-piercing rounds. "I liked aiming with the four-power telescope and see a Jap and press the trigger and watch that 37mm with a tracer go through him," Sergeant Bardowski said. "That was good hunting."[17]

Another shortage plaguing most of the Bataan defenders was a lack of clothing. However, this did not seem to affect the tankers too much. Working inside a hot tank in a tropical climate forced most of the tankers to work in the bare minimum. Steve Bardowski remembered his father saying that "most of the time [the tankers] just wore a pair of, like the Navy swim shorts and boondocker shoes, that's all they wore." Although the tankers had been issued one-piece coveralls, most of the men did not wear them. "They had them," Steve Bardowski said, "but it was just too hot. They wore as little as humanly possible."[18]

With so little clothing, life inside the cramped confines of a tank could be interesting. "Inside the tank it was hot and it was awful," said Private Ortega. Stripped to shorts and shoes, Ortega said that the gunners had to be careful of the empty shell casings. "[W]hen they would fire," he said, "the empty shell casings were hot and they'd burn them." Noted historian Whitman, "Hot cannon and machine-gun cartridges bounced off bare skin and raised blisters. After a time it was easy to identify a veteran tanker. He was the one with bruised and burned skin."[19]

With the withdrawal of the Japanese from the entire reserve battle line, the Provisional Tank Group assumed a supporting role. The 192nd TB, which had been shifted to I Corps sector, remained on the western side of Bataan and continued to help General Wainwright. Because of the dense jungle terrain and a lack of gasoline, the tankers were forced to patrol the area on foot, something to which they were not accustomed.[20]

The 194th TB remained on the eastern side of Bataan. Noted Colonel Miller, "We were to provide front line support for II Corps and also provide beach defense on Manila Bay, from the front line southward to Cabcaben [on the southeast tip of Bataan]." Like the tankers of the 192nd TB, much of the patrolling was done on foot.[21]

Although the battered and diseased Japanese had no plans to start a major offensive until more reinforcements were brought in, they nevertheless kept the Allied defenders on constant alert. "Periodically, the Japs would get out on Manila Bay at night and fire artillery pieces, from landing barges, at our beach installations," wrote Colonel Miller. "Damage was slight, but not to our nerves."[22]

In spite of some frayed nerves, the morale of the Provisional Tank Group—and almost all personnel on Bataan—was still high. After repelling the Japanese attacks and amphibious invasions, morale soared. The men in the trenches actually wanted to go on the offensive and take the fight to the enemy, but headquarters wisely ruled against it. As historian Morton wrote, "Troops on the defensive in a static situation required less food, less gasoline, less ammunition, and less of all other supplies than those who chose to attack." Since MacArthur had failed to adequately stockpile supplies on Bataan, the men dug deeper and waited for the Japanese to come to them.[23]

On March 12, morale dropped when word reached the troops that General MacArthur had left Corregidor for Australia. "We heard it by rumor at first," wrote Colonel Miller, "which was soon confirmed by official orders. The reaction among officers and men, was at first somewhat bitter, but after time had been taken out for a little reasoning, Bataan defenders on the whole, did not retain the bitterness. They realized that the order, without doubt, had been issued by the President for the good of the war effort. . . . There were some who held their bitterness . . . but the vast majority did not."[24]

Lieutenant Poweleit agreed with Colonel Miller. He wrote, "Several men were upset by [MacArthur leaving]; however, most of them felt he could do a better job in another area, like Australia."[25] Still, it was more what MacArthur said, and not what he did, that angered the men.

Back on January 15, when the Japanese attacks were at their height, General MacArthur had issued a message claiming "Help is on the way from the United States." The message stated, "Thousands of troops and hundreds of planes are being dispatched" to Bataan. He called for the defenders to "hold until these reinforcements arrive." The message ended by stating, "our supplies are ample; a determined defense will defeat the enemy's attack." Two months later, MacArthur was on his way to Australia.[26]

The fact MacArthur had issued such a statement and then fled to Australia angered many. The troops knew MacArthur had been late in implementing War Plan Orange-3 and had failed to stockpile supplies on Bataan. They knew that while MacArthur was going to Australia they were facing annihilation. "Some of the guys got pretty bitter when they found out that Doug had escaped to Australia," wrote Corporal Stewart. "I was led to believe that General MacArthur was the greatest tactician in the whole world, I thought he could do no wrong. But he was actually responsible for not picking up on the details. First of all, he should have known that an army lives on its stomach. But he thought we should fight to the death. Stand right up there on the front line, throw your chest out there and let it happen. Let them shoot you down. That was more or less his way of doing things."[27]

When MacArthur left and the reinforcements never materialized, Stewart felt justifiably angry. "Yeah it was a disappointment, it was the same feeling as if I were a little kid expecting Santa Claus and Santa Claus never came. That was the letdown that we got."[28]

Private Ortega, who was captured on Bataan and later sent to Japan aboard one of the infamous "Hell Ships," was equally critical. He said, "[W]e don't think much of MacArthur. He left us there by ourselves. He sent a sheet out, and we read it, it said hold on, I'll be back, I'll bring you back thousands of planes and thousands of this, and thousands of that. . . . [A]ll the ships were sunk [at Pearl Harbor], I don't know how he was gonna get everything over to us, but he promised us all that help. Of course, it came in 1944 but we were already in Japan by that time."[29]

When General MacArthur left for Australia, General Wainwright became the overall commander in the Philippines. With Wainwright's promotion, Maj. Gen. Edward P. King was given command of the men on Bataan, which consisted of roughly 60,000 Filipino troops, 8,000 Philippine scouts, and 12,500 American servicemen. General Parker remained in command of the II Corps sector on the east side of Bataan, while General Jones, now a major general, took over Wainwright's I Corps sector on the west side.[30]

The change in commanders meant little to the men in the ranks. During the lull in the fighting, the men continued to improve their defenses and add to their training. Because of all of the problems between the tanks and the infantry during the retreat to Bataan and afterward, infantry commanders were given a series of lectures in the proper use of tanks. Noted General Weaver, "A comprehensive instruction by battalion was instituted by the armored troops amongst the Philippine Army troops, and a high degree of cooperation and coordination effected in plans and operations."[31]

Wrote historian Schutt, "One reason for [the problems between tanks and infantry] may have been Tank Group's attachment to USAFFE for control and direction. In this role, the tanks supported [the infantry] but never came under their control. If this did not create resentment in lower level commanders, it certainly did at higher levels where General Weaver and General Wainwright frequently disagreed about [the] use of the tanks." The comprehensive instruction was meant to help bridge the chasm between tanks and infantry. Added Schutt, "Through USAFFE publications, [Weaver] sent circulars outlining the essentials of tank-infantry teamwork to all unit headquarters. These bulletins especially emphasized the great importance of infantry accompanying each tank advance and that tanks were not to be used as pillboxes or left forward without infantry protection."[32]

At the beginning of April, 1942, the training suddenly came to an abrupt end. The Japanese were on the move again.

CHAPTER EIGHT

Surrender

Although the Japanese Air Force continued to harass the Bataan defenders throughout February and March, they stepped up their air campaign during the first few days of April. At the same time, Japanese infantry began probing the reserve battle line. "Small but fierce localized [infantry] attacks were being staged on the II Corps line," wrote Colonel Miller. "They were repelled but casualties were heavy. We knew that the Jap was trying to find the right spot in our line for an all-out offensive against us."[1]

On Good Friday, April 3, the reinforced Japanese began bombarding the extreme left side of the II Corps line. At 3:00 P.M., Japanese tanks and infantry attacked over the mountainous terrain, driving a 1,000-yard deep wedge near Mount Samat. Immediately, General King called upon his reserves, including the 194th TB.[2]

The Japanese began April 4 with another massive bombardment, causing a few of the starved and fatigued Filipino infantry units to break for the rear. As the Japanese pushed south down Trail 29, the 41st Philippine Infantry Division [PDiv], on the right, shifted farther right. By pulling to the west, the 41st PDiv opened up Trail 29 and isolated itself from the rest of II Corps.[3]

As the Japanese pushed south down Trail 29, their tanks turned east and assaulted the flank of the troops in front of Mount Samat, easily brushing them aside. By the end of the day, the Allied forces had abandoned the threatened flank and fled eastward, toward the center of the II Corps sector, further isolating the 41st PDiv. In an effort to save the Filipinos, Colonel Miller was ordered to furnish a company of tanks to help out in a planned rescue. "I designated Company C [194th TB], and shortly after dark started out with them on the trek," Miller reported. General Parker was hoping to begin his counterattack with the tanks and the 45th Philippine Scouts at 6:00 A.M. on April 6.[4]

The Japanese began Easter Sunday, April 5, with another heavy bombardment, followed by another drive eastward against the left flank of II Corps. Although Filipino artillery managed to stall the Japanese all morning, by 1:00 P.M. the attackers had captured Mount Samat and outflanked the Philippine guns. Threatened with capture, the Filipino artillery fell back and opened a wider gap in the Allied line.[5]

With the retreat of hundreds of Filipino soldiers, the narrow mountain trails that Colonel Miller's tanks were using to get into position for the rescue attempt were clogged. Unable to advance, Miller had to wait until almost midnight on April 5–6 before putting his eight tanks into motion again. "A good share of the way," he recalled, "we had to almost literally bring our men up and either lift [Filipino] vehicles off the trail or shove them off with tanks. In addition, our tanks were in very bad shape. We coaxed, cussed, and hauled."

Somehow, the tanks reached the jumping-off point at 6:10 A.M. on April 6, only ten minutes behind the proposed starting time, but discovered that the infantry, the 45th Philippine Scouts, had already moved out. Hastening up Trail 29, the tanks quickly caught up with the scouts but advanced only a short distance before an advance patrol ran into a strong Japanese roadblock. Two hours later, after a mortar was brought up and dropped five rounds onto the startled Japanese defenders, the scouts overran the position. Unfortunately, the unexpected delay at the roadblock and hastily laid Japanese landmines delayed the advance so much that the column was stopped by nightfall about a mile short of the stranded 41st PDiv.[6]

While the rescue column was pushing north, the Japanese on the western flank of II Corps were pushing east. With pressure along the entire flank, and with hundreds of Filipino infantrymen streaming to the rear, the decision was made at 3:00 P.M. to abandon the area and fall back to a new position behind the San Vincente River, which ran at a diagonal angle to the old line. By nightfall, Japanese tanks and infantry had pushed 7,000 yards south of the original reserve battle line.[7]

When the reserve battle line collapsed, the scouts and tankers were told to abandon their rescue mission and move back down Trail 29 to its termination at a T-junction at East–West Trail 8. Once there, they were to move east along Trail 8 and reestablish contact with II Corps. At the same time, another group of Philippine infantry would drive west on Trail 8 until the two forces met. Although tired and hungry, the scouts and tankers started south immediately.[8]

When the rescue force withdrew, the 41st PDiv finally abandoned its isolated position and fled west over the spine of the Mariveles Mountains into I Corps area.[9] While this was taking place, the 45th Scouts and Company C, 194th TB reached the T-junction. While one battalion of scouts, supported by two tanks, started east on Trail 8 about 1:00 A.M. on April 7 to link up with the new group of Filipino infantry sent to meet them, the rest of the relief column waited at the road junction to protect the only avenue of retreat available if the eastern route was already cut—the road west into I Corps.[10]

"[The] two tanks were placed at the head of the column," reported Colonel Miller. "Scouts were out in front, on foot, to act as 'feelers.'" Near 2:30 A.M., the tanks were approaching a bend in the mountain trail when the scouts discovered a

Japanese ambush. An instant later, an enemy antitank round slammed into the turret of the lead tank, commanded by Lt. Frank E. Riley. The shell just missed Riley's head but burst his left eardrum. Aided by bright moonlight, the Japanese hit the Stuart with four more armor-piercing rounds, disabling the tank and injuring Riley's foot and sending metal shards into the eyes of his driver. While machine gun bullets bounced off the sides of the tank, Riley and his crew fired one shell at the roadblock and then scrambled out of the tank and fled to safety.[11]

The second tank had stopped directly behind Riley's in a bit of a depression, which evidently saved it from the antitank fire. "At least one, and perhaps more, Jap shells hit the top and bounced off," reported Colonel Miller. As the Filipino scouts laid down a covering fire, the second tank retreated around the bend in the trail. "[The fire of the scouts] is the only thing that saved us," wrote Miller.[12]

With one tank disabled and a few men injured, the reconnaissance force stalled. At daylight, when it was determined that the task force was not strong enough to break through the roadblock and link up with the Filipino infantry fighting through from the east (which never actually occurred), the reconnaissance force was ordered back. By 8:00 A.M., the small group was back at the junction of Trails 29 and 8.[13] As it turned out, it was fortunate the second group had stayed behind.

While the reconnaissance force had been gone, a small group of scouts, supported by two more tanks, moved back north up Trail 29 for about 1,000 yards to watch for advancing Japanese. Sometime during the early morning hours, a wild firefight began. Holding on stubbornly, the small group did not back away from the enemy until word was received that the reconnaissance force had come back to the trail junction.[14]

As the American tanks and Filipino scouts gathered again at the T-junction, a few enemy tanks suddenly appeared and made a frontal assault. Quickly, the American Stuarts destroyed two of the enemy tanks and sent the others scurrying for cover. Using the seven remaining Stuart tanks as a rear guard, the relief column began withdrawing to the west, toward I Corps. Although the men and tanks were bombed and strafed, the Japanese ground troops did not pursue and by 6:00 P.M. the entire group was in I Corps territory. Once there, the seven tanks of Company C, 194th TB were attached to the 192nd TB and along with the entire I Corps fell back to the Binuangan River, about halfway between the reserve battle line and the end of the peninsula. The collapse of II Corps on the right had made the I Corps reserve line untenable.[15]

In the II Corps area on April 7, a few Filipino troops had taken up a defensive position behind the diagonal San Vincente River. Near 7:00 A.M. the Japanese opened up a heavy mortar and artillery bombardment and a few hours later pushed forward with their infantry. Unable to hold back the pressure, the center of the San Vincente line suddenly collapsed.[16]

As the Filipino infantry fled to the rear, the tanks of Company D, 192nd TB tried to protect them. "Tanks came up to try to assist us in the wide open daylight," wrote one of the infantrymen. "But it was futile. They were bombed. I saw tanks

turned upside down, blasted, and burned." Still, the tankers bought the fleeing Filipino soldiers a few minutes of time before they too turned around and fled south.[17]

A bit to the north, near the east coast town of Orion, a few II Corps defenders, including the tanks of Company A, 194th TB and a few from Company D,
192nd TB, were still holding onto an original section of the reserve battle line.
Although the Japanese continually tried to push armor down the East Road, the
tanks and infantry held out. When the center of the San Vincente line gave way,
however, the units at Orion were suddenly threatened with envelopment and were
forced to make a hasty retreat. With the Stuart tanks once again acting as a rear
guard, the men and vehicles raced to the safety of a new defensive position about
one mile to the south, behind the Mamala River.[18]

By nightfall on April 7 the Allies were trying to reform new defensive lines
on both sides of the Bataan peninsula. On the west side, in I Corps area, the
defenders were trying to form a new line behind the Binuangan River, hoping to
anchor their left flank to the China Sea and their right to the Mariveles Mountains.
In the II Corps area, a defensive line had been set up behind the Mamala River.[19]

Almost before the Mamala line could be established, however, orders went
out for everyone to fall back another 4,000 yards to the Alangan River. Wrote historian Morton, "The story of the last two days of the defense of Bataan is one of
progressive disintegration and final collapse. Lines were formed and abandoned
before they could be fully occupied. . . . Orders were issued and revoked because
they were impossible of execution. Stragglers poured to the rear in increasingly
large numbers until they clogged all roads and disrupted all movement forward.
Units disappeared into the jungle never to be heard from again. In two days an
army evaporated into thin air."[20]

At 11:00 A.M. on April 8, Japanese planes bombed the Alangan River line. At
the start of the bombing, about 2,500 men were holding the line but by 3:00 P.M.,
hundreds of Filipino troops had fled from the far right side of the line. "Only the
tanks and the remaining 75mm guns (SPM) [of the 194th TB] stood in the way of
the advancing Japanese," wrote Morton. Though they made every effort to organize a holding position, they, too, were forced to pull back. The East Road, which
the Japanese had carefully avoided since their disastrous assault in early January,
now lay open."[21]

By 5:00 P.M. the situation was critical. Communication between Bataan headquarters and the front line was almost nonexistent. The only form of communication was the tank radio network, but only those commanders close enough to
tanks or halftracks knew what was going on. As darkness fell, the 194th TB tanks
and SPMs followed the retreating infantry and moved to a new line behind the
Lamao River. "At [the] Lamao [River] we stood exhausted by our tanks and halftracks under the banyan trees," remembered Corporal Fitzpatrick. "Hungry and
edgy, we watched in silence the tide of gaunt and worn men." The defenders were
running out of geography. A retreat from the Lamao would push the Americans
and Filipinos off of the peninsula. As the moon rose in the sky on April 8, the Battling Bastards of Bataan dug in along their last line of defense.[22]

Near 7:00 P.M., word was received that the Japanese may already have out-flanked the left side of the new line, so a few 194th TB tanks and SPMs, and a brigade of coast artillery troops, were rushed to a position southwest of Cabcaben to stop the breakthrough. Earlier, perhaps in anticipation of such a problem, Company A, 192nd TB, which was on the west side of the peninsula in I Corps territory, was ordered to move east over the southern end of the East–West Road to aid the crumbling II Corps.[23]

The eight tanks of Company A reached the Mariveles cutoff without difficulty and then moved onto the cutoff road to avoid the traffic jam in town. Once past the town, the tanks filed onto the East Road and ran into a flood of refugees. Although they pushed onward and drew close to Cabcaben, they soon discovered that a promised cache of gasoline had been confiscated by the SPM halftracks. Low on fuel, and facing a jam of people, the tanks turned around and went back to Caibobo Point on the east side of Bataan. Remembered Private DeGroot, "On the night of April 8th, everything was in chaos. They had us get in our tanks and go [around] and see if we could stem the tide. We did go up and around the other side of the peninsula, for maybe five or six miles, but the roads were so crowded with people we had to turn around and go back; there was no way of handling it. It was a sad night."[24]

While Company A was in motion, Navy personnel in Mariveles destroyed everything of military value. The siege of Bataan was nearing an end and everybody knew it. "That night," recalled Lieutenant Poweleit, "we blew up the ammunition dump. The explosions rocked the peninsula." At 6:30 P.M., General King told General Weaver to be prepared to demolish all of his tanks and equipment if he received the code word "CRASH." In turn, Weaver passed the information along to Colonels Wickord and Miller. Within a few minutes, the news had been passed along to the men.[25]

"After four months of fighting the enemy, of being on short rations, and of surviving everything from malaria to gunshot wounds with little or no medical treatment, we heard the news," wrote Private Tenenberg, "The Japanese had finally cracked our last defense. We were now only about two miles from the water's edge with no place to go and without the means to fight. We were going to surrender." Under the circumstances, most everyone realized that it was the only thing to. "Fighting for another day would only mean thousands more would die," added Tenenberg. "Surrender was the only way to save as many men and women as possible."[26]

Some men, however, disagreed. Sergeant Bardowski called his platoon together and informed them of the surrender rumor. "I want to fight, I hate the fuckin' Japs, I don't want to surrender," he said. "Let's see if we can get to Corregidor." Bardowski led three tanks and a halftrack down to Mariveles and maneuvered through the panicked citizenry and demoralized soldiers that crowded the city streets. At the Mariveles wharf Bardowski approached a chief petty officer that was hurriedly readying a Navy barge for movement to Corregidor. When he asked the officer if his tanks and men could get a ride out to the island, the officer informed Bardowski that he had strict orders not to take any tanks to Corregidor. Unable to take the tanks, Bardowski and his men then began destroying their vehicles by dropping hand grenades into the engine and crew compartments.

When finished, the eighteen tankers walked back to the Navy barge and Bardowski asked, "Hey sailor, how 'bout takin' me and my boys out to Corregidor?" When the petty officer replied that he had no orders to evacuate tankers, Bardowski shifted his Thompson sub-machine gun to a more ready position. "Well," Bardowski said, "there have to be some exceptions to the rules." Knowing full well that Bardowski meant what he said, the petty officer replied, "Welcome aboard, Army." Noted historian Whitman, "Had [the chief petty officer] not taken the platoon, Bardowski probably would have shot him—he was tired of playing games."[27]

In the late afternoon, the 194th TB received orders to consolidate forces near Tank Group Headquarters outside of Mariveles by daylight on April 9. At dark, Colonel Miller and his headquarters group started toward Mariveles. "We picked up Company D [192nd TB] and put them in the column," he wrote. "Military police stopped us several kilometers north of our destination. They stated that existing dumps of munitions were to be blown up in a short time and all traffic was to be halted during the operation."[28]

As the tankers waited and listened to the distant explosions, they suddenly felt the earth shake under them. At approximately 9:30 P.M. on April 8, a strong earthquake rocked the island of Luzon. "Even Mother Nature seemed to be turning against us," wrote Colonel Miller. In Mariveles itself, Lieutenant Poweleit noted, "[The ground] shook and shook (like a dog shaking water off his back) but finally stopped. An earthquake had followed the ammunition explosions."[29]

Near 11:50 P.M., the 17th Ordnance Company, which was still attached to the Provisional Tank Group, received orders to begin destroying all of its equipment. "In the 17th Ordnance Company," wrote historian Whitman, "mechanics placed hand grenades around vehicle engines and detonated them. Tanks under repair were likewise immobilized. Men resorted to sledge hammers to smash radios and arc-welding gear. Weapons were broken and burned." Anything and everything that could be used by the Japanese was being destroyed.[30]

Near 3:30 A.M. on April 9, General King realized the jig was up. Intent on surrendering the men on Bataan before they could suffer another day of unrelenting attacks, he sent out two junior staff officers to negotiate a surrender. At 5:30 A.M., the surrender team's vehicle crossed into enemy territory and while the staff officers looked for a Japanese officer, General Weaver ordered the systematic destruction of all of the equipment of both tank battalions.[31]

Having been eyewitnesses to the complete collapse of II Corps, the men of the 194th TB had been expecting as much. "[Colonel Miller] led us aside from our tanks and halftracks and trucks to a clear space in the shade of some acacia trees," recalled Corporal Fitzpatrick. "The men quietly gathered, most sitting on the grass, some leaning against trees. Colonel Miller faced us and told us formally what we already knew: we were surrendering."[32]

Private Falconer admitted, "When the order came to surrender it was a great relief to me. I should have been very wary, very fearful, but I wasn't. I thought it was a beautiful day. We found some abandoned trucks and some food. I had, right then, one of the best meals I've ever eaten in my life. I had creamed peas on toast. While we waited for the Japanese we sang songs."[33]

Other members of the 194th TB were not so jovial. "It was terrible," noted Sergeant French. "I felt like committing suicide, but I didn't, I couldn't, I couldn't do it. . . . [Y]ou know, it was awful. It was just, it was just disgusting."[34]

Upon orders from Colonel Miller, the men began destroying their equipment. Wrote Sergeant French, "[We] burned up our trucks and jeeps, and buried all our ammunition, all our machine guns, put them in the foxhole and covered them up." Added Colonel Miller, "We placed our vehicles in segregated areas, broke off the gasoline valves in the crew compartments of the tanks so as to flood them with the aviation gasoline, and set fire to the interior. We also fired 37mm armor-piercing shells into the tank and truck motors. Gasoline was dumped into the cabs and bodies of the trucks. The armor plate on the tanks was subjected to such intense heat that it was made useless except for scrap iron. There was not much left of our vehicles. Small arms and machine guns were completely stripped. Parts were tossed into the blazing vehicles, gun barrels were bent around trees, and stocks of rifles and Tommy guns were broken. We tossed the remains far out into the jungle."[35]

Attached to the 194th TB, the crews of the SPM halftracks also set about destroying their vehicles. Wrote historian Whitman, "In the self-propelled artillery battalions, the 75mm guns mounted on the half-tracks were rigged for destruction. Gunners removed piston-rod coupler keys, loaded the guns, and closed the breeches. They attached long lanyards, and when they fired the guns, both the guns and the half-track were completely wrecked."[36]

The 192nd TB, stationed on the west side of the peninsula, had missed witnessing the destruction of II Corps. Company B, 192nd TB was quartered near the base of the peninsula and reacted accordingly when word of the impending surrender arrived. "Our captain called us over while we were there on Bataan, in the jungle there, and he lined us all up," said Private Ortega. "He told us that we had surrendered, that our army had surrendered. . . . Of course, that made us real sad, you know, when we heard the news." Private Tenenberg, also of Company B, recalled, "We troops felt let down, even betrayed. If we had been supplied with enough ammunition and guns, troops and equipment, and food and medical supplies, we believed that we would have been able to repel the Japanese. Instead, we were facing a degrading surrender and the brutality that was surely to go along with it." Then, like the 194th TB, Company B, 192nd TB began destroying its tanks and equipment.[37]

"First," wrote Private Tenenberg, "we lined up the tanks one behind the other and then fired rounds of 37mm shells from one tank into the engine and body of the tank in front. Then we threw away our guns and ammunition." Private Ortega recalled what he did to the halftrack that he drove. "So I went back and destroyed as much of the halftrack as I could, especially the motor. I'd take a sledgehammer and I'd break and bust everything that I could. We threw the machine gun parts all over the jungle there. We'd tear it apart and throw the parts all over the place so [the Japanese] couldn't find it and put it back together."[38]

When he was through, Private Ortega got down on his knees in front of the dashboard and prayed. Years later, he still recalled his words, "I said, 'God, I don't want to die . . . I'm too young to die,' I told him. I was twenty-two years old. 'I've just started to live,' I said, 'but if you give me my life and let me live through whatever is expected in the coming times, I will serve my fellow soldiers. I will do all I can to help them, that we both together may come out of this alive.'" Then Ortega began to cry. "I cried, ya know, not because I was afraid or scared, I just wanted to get it all out. And when I did, when I cried, all of that came out of me . . . I felt great, I'd done all I was suppose to do." Admitted Private Tenenberg, "There was not a dry eye among us."[39]

Farther up the west side of the peninsula, far away from the collapse of II Corps, the rest of the 192nd TB was just as shocked by the surrender news. Private Hauser wrote, "We all thought that with full fuel tanks and full ammunition belts we would try a breakout. We had no idea, even remote, that the commanding general would surrender. I for one was more scared of surrendering than trying to fight in a breakout." Many of the other men agreed and it was only after being threatened with court-martial that the rest of the 192nd TB began destroying their vehicles and weapons.[40]

Headquarters Company, 192nd TB somehow received orders not to burn their equipment. Instead, the two tank crews disabled their tanks by destroying the machine guns and throwing the 37mm cannon breech blocks away. Likewise, the half-track crews poured dirt into their gas tanks, drained out all the oil, and then raced their engines until the pistons seized up.[41]

A bit farther north, near Caibobo Point, where Companies A and C of the 192nd TB were encamped, the men had no restrictions on the destruction of their equipment. Tank crews simply drove their tanks into the jungle, opened the engine compartments, cut the fuel lines and tossed in matches. Simultaneously, other men destroyed the small arms by taking them apart and throwing the parts away or burying them. A few men, however, still believed that a last-ditch effort might take place, so they hid a few machine guns and some ammunition in the jungle.[42]

In spite of the best efforts of both tank battalions, the Japanese somehow managed to find or put together eleven American tanks after the fall of Bataan. Consequently, at least one of the tanks was used in the subsequent invasion of Corregidor.[43]

After all the tanks and equipment had been destroyed, a few tankers decided to follow the path of Sergeant Bardowski and go to Corregidor. Around noon, Sergeant French and about twenty maintenance men from Company D, 192nd TB made their way down to the coast. "[W]e went on around and we found a big yacht in a cove," French recalled. "Everybody was in such a rush, a scramble, it wouldn't run and nobody took any time to try to fix it. We wasn't in no rush. There wasn't no use being in a hurry." Taking their time, the mechanics soon discovered that the problem lay in the ignition system. "Somebody had goofed up the ignition wiring on it," French went on. "We worked it over and bypassed the ignition switch and fired up them big old engines on that thing. 'Oh man, we in business!'"

By the time the ignition was repaired, the Japanese had moved into the area. Sergeant French went on, "By the time we got ready to pull offshore late in the afternoon, oh, I'd say about three o'clock in the afternoon, there were great big cliffs, high cliffs up here see, and the Japanese was up there. They was firing at us with small arms. . . . It was pretty far up. We loaded that thing up and about seventy-five people loaded on that thing and went across the bay from Mariveles to Corregidor."[44]

In an act more reminiscent of Sergeant Bardowski, Private Goldstein and a few other tankers from Company B, 192nd TB attempted to commandeer a Filipino boat. Since the approaches to Corregidor were mined, the boat captain refused to take the tankers to the island. Pointing his .45 caliber pistol at the captain, Private Goldstein convinced the mariner that it would be in his best interest to take the men to Corregidor. Leaving after dark, Goldstein was able to signal Corregidor with a flashlight and get the correct coordinates to safely guide the boat through the minefields.[45]

For the men who remained on Bataan, the end came soon enough. After General King's representatives finally located the Japanese officials, they came back to get the general. At 9:00 A.M., General King met with the Japanese commander, Lt. Gen. Masaharu Homma. Although King informed Homma he was responsible only for the men on Bataan, the Japanese commander insisted that King surrender all of the Allied troops throughout the Philippines. Wrote historian Rutherford, "In the end it was agreed that if the troops on Bataan wished to surrender they would have to do so individually. At 1230 King agreed to surrender unconditionally himself to save his men."

The surrender of General King marked the beginning of the end for the soldiers on Bataan. Whether they knew they were surrendering as mere individuals or not was a moot point. More than 76,000 Allied soldiers, including 12,000 American soldiers, were about to become prisoners of war in the largest capitulation of American forces in the history of the United States.[46]

In the bivouac area of the 194th TB, April 9 was a quiet day. After destroying their vehicles, the men just sat down and waited. "We took all the food we had in our outfit and divided it equally among all our personnel," recalled Colonel Miller. "We had more to eat that day than we had had on any occasion since the start of the war."[47]

"That afternoon," recalled Corporal Fitzpatrick, "we bathed in a nearby stream. Clothes were issued from each company's supply truck. I was fortunate to receive a new pair of well-fitting shoes." Near 7:00 A.M. on April 10, the first Japanese soldiers marched into the bivouac area of the 194th TB. Private Falconer recalled their appearance. "The first Japs we saw were bone tired. They marched right past us. One Jap private was so exhausted that he stumbled and fell in front of us Americans. A Jap officer gave some command, two riflemen came up, picked up the fallen soldier, took him off the road where we couldn't see him. Then we heard a shot and the two Japs returned alone."[48]

The appearance of the first Japanese soldiers in the bivouac area of the 192nd TB was a bit more harrowing. The tankers were still sound asleep when they were abruptly awakened by loud voices shouting in Japanese. "The Japs had come for us," noted Private Tenenberg. "They stormed our area carrying handguns and machine guns; they were ready for business. My knees began shaking, my hands felt cold and clammy, and sweat broke out on my neck and forehead. We were all scared beyond anything imaginable." While some enemy soldiers were kind to the tankers and asked politely for cigarettes, others were more brutal. "These rough soldiers did not ask for a thing," continued Tenenberg, "they just took whatever they wanted. They ransacked our bodies and our sleeping area." A number of resistant tankers were beaten by the conquering Japanese, including Private Tenenberg.

Sometime in the afternoon, the tankers were told to head south down the West Road towards Mariveles. A large number managed to climb aboard army trucks that had been purposely spared from destruction, but many more were forced to walk. Miraculously, some of the men believed that they were to be shipped home to San Francisco in exchange for Japanese prisoners-of-war.[49]

On the east side of Mariveles, in the bivouac area of the 194th TB, the men waited more than twelve hours before the Japanese began to move them. At around 7:00 P.M., the men were formed into a column and marched out of camp. "In the column were the 194th Tank Battalion, [Company D] of the 192nd Tank Battalion, Air Corps personnel, and other casual troops," recalled Colonel Miller. Although the men had expected to be sent to Mariveles to be placed aboard trucks for transport to prisoner-of-war camps in central Luzon, the column headed north, away from the city. Marching up the East Road, the column reached the barrio of Limay around noon on April 11. "As far as the 194th Tank Battalion is concerned and those other elements with us," wrote Miller, "Limay was the start of the [Bataan] Death March."[50]

Back at Mariveles, the men from the 192nd TB were also starting the march. After discovering they were not being sent home to San Francisco, the men were taken from their trucks and told to march north up the East Road. At 6:00 A.M. on April 11, the tankers of the 192nd TB started the long Bataan Death March.[51]

The island of Corregidor, at the mouth of Manila Bay, held out for another four weeks, finally surrendering on May 6. Men from the two tank battalions, such as Sergeant Bardowski and his platoon from the 192nd TB and Sergeant French and his maintenance section from the 194th TB, discovered that their escape to "the Rock" had only prolonged the suffering. Fortunately, though, the 15,000 men (and some Army nurses) on Corregidor, including about 2,000 who had fled from Bataan, were spared the horrors of the Bataan Death March. More than 70,000 men began the infamous march up the East Road and by the time it was over perhaps 10,000 men, mostly Filipino soldiers, had perished, many brutally beaten to death. Ill-prepared to handle such large numbers of prisoners, Japanese logistics broke down completely. Without enough vehicles to transport the men, or enough food or water to nourish them, the prisoners suffered horribly.[52]

For the men of the 192nd and 194th Tank Battalions, the war was over. Yet, although they were captives of the Japanese they could feel proud of their accomplishments. "The timetable for a total Philippine victory had been established by the Japanese high command in Tokyo," wrote Private Tenenberg, who noted that victory was supposed to be completed by January 22, 1942. "The defensive and strategic action, the determination, and the fighting skills of the U.S. and Philippine forces on Bataan, gave the United States an extra seventy-six days, from January 22 to April 9, to fortify Australia and to provide the Allies with a base of operations within the Pacific theater." Added Lieutenant Poweleit, "The 192nd Tank Battalion [and the 194th Tank Battalion] as part of the Provisional Tank Group interfered with the Japanese timetable and Australia was saved."[53]

In spite of their lack of training and late arrival in the Philippines, and in spite of problems with command and fuel and ammunition, the Provisional Tank Group had fought superbly. The 192nd and 194th TBs had provided continuous rear-guard defense during the long withdrawal into the Bataan peninsula and, once there, had provided the necessary firepower to help repel several major Japanese thrusts. In recognition of the fine work performed by the two tank battalions and the 17th Ordnance Company, Gen. George C. Marshall, the Army chief of staff, cited all three units for "outstanding performance of duty in action during the defense of the Philippines."

Wrote General Marshall, "In the course of withdrawal into Bataan, [Provisional Tank Group] units were constantly in the field covering the supporting four divisions of the North Luzon Forces and two of the South Luzon Forces. . . . This unit contributed most vitally in all stages and under extraordinary handicaps to the protection of the operations and successful withdrawal. Its units were the last out of both North and South Luzon and the last into the Bataan peninsula on 7 January 1942."[54]

In further recognition, Marshall wrote, "[T]his group was charged with the support of the I and II Philippine Corps, the cordon defense of the coasts of Bataan and the defense of the three major landing fields. . . . Under constant air attack these units, despite heavy losses in men and materiel, maintained a magnificent defense and through their ability, courage and devotion to duty contributed in large measure to the prolonged defense of the Bataan peninsula." Added General Weaver, "[The] service rendered by the troops of this armored force was as grilling in its continuity, severity, and exactions as any rendered in either war by any arm."[55]

Although the 192nd and 194th TBs lost only a few men in battle, literally hundreds died at the hands of the Japanese. Noted Lieutenant Poweleit, "Of the various companies of the 194th, two-thirds of the enlisted personnel died in combat, prison camps, work details or drowned when their prison ships were bombed or torpedoed by the Americans in the attempt made by the Japanese to take them to Japan." Similar statistics could be applied to the 192nd TB.[56]

With the fall of Bataan, two Army tank battalions ceased to exist. But there were many more on the way.

CHAPTER NINE

Reinforcements and Turnabout

While the Philippines were under attack, the United States strengthened its armored force in the Hawaiian Islands. The only tank unit present in Hawaii prior to December 7, 1941, was the 11th Tank Company, stationed at Schofield Barracks on Oahu. Realizing that a single company of antiquated M2A2 Mae West light tanks would be of little help against an anticipated Japanese invasion, the War Department decided to send the 193rd Tank Battalion, another unit composed of old National Guard tank companies, to Hawaii.

Like the 192nd and 194th TBs, the 193rd TB came into existence on September 1, 1940, when existing National Guard tank companies were formed into GHQ tank battalions. The 193rd TB was formed from the 30th Tank Company (TCo) from Forsyth, Georgia (now Company A); the 31st TCo from Ozark, Alabama (Company B); the 36th TCo of Houston, Texas (Company C); and the 45th TCo out of Denver, Colorado (Company D).[1]

The 193rd TB was at Fort Benning, Georgia, on December 7, 1941, when the Japanese attacked Pearl Harbor. "Nine days later," recalled Staff Sgt. James H. Leach, "the 193rd tankers, re-equipped with maneuver-worn M3 [Stuart] light tanks repossessed from the 2nd Armored Division, were on a troop train headed west to San Francisco's Angel Island."[2]

"Ready for combat we were not," said Sergeant Leach. "For example, only two other noncommissioned officers and myself, plus a private first class volunteer from the 2nd Armored Division, were the only tankers in our company who had ever fired the tank's 37mm gun, much less trained on it." To help familiarize themselves with the new weapons, the officers set up "an 'on tank' training program while on the rolling train." As Sergeant Leach wrote, "We moved our crews over the flat cars to our tanks for a crash familiarization course on the tank and the 37mm gun." By December 22, the 193rd TB had reached Angel Island and five days later, ready or not, the battalion was placed aboard the *President Taylor.* Along with three other transports and a few Navy escorts, they set out for a "secret destination."[3]

While steaming west across the Pacific, the 193rd TB did some more work with their new tanks. "Eight tanks were lashed on the deck where their 37mm guns were free for action and gun crews were kept on them on a 24-hour basis," noted the battalion historian. "Instructions on the 37mm gun were given to all personnel." Unfortunately, the tankers soon encountered the same recoil problems that had plagued the tank crews in the Philippines. Noted Sergeant Leach, "We discovered to our dismay that several of the 37s would not return to battery for a second shot. When the gun went into recoil, the gun shield dropped just enough to bind the tube, preventing its return to battery—and to think we were en route to war." Like the Philippine tankers, the 193rd TB tank crews ended up jerry-rigging the guns. "Later, we enlarged the hole in the gun shield, but," as Leach admitted, "this was an ordnance job."[4]

On January 7, the convoy docked at Honolulu Harbor, Oahu, Hawaii Territory. After disembarking without difficulty, the men were transported by train to Schofield Barracks and were eventually placed in barracks buildings previously occupied by the 11th TCo. Wrote the 193rd TB historian, "[The 11th Tank Company] had taken to the field immediately after the Japanese attack on Oahu on December 7th 1941." While the 11th TCo continued to guard the beaches, the 193rd TB settled into a routine of training and work.[5]

While the Bataan defenders were still holding out, the 193rd TB expected to be sent to the Philippines. However, the War Department already had decided to write off the Philippines and instead kept the 193rd in Hawaii. Still, other tank units were already on their way across the Pacific.

On January 23, 1942, the 754th Tank Battalion, as part of Task Force 6814, left New York for the Pacific. The 754th TB did not come from consolidated National Guard tank companies but instead had been constituted in December 1940 in the Regular Army as the 74th Tank Battalion (Medium). Five months later, on May 8, 1941, the unit was re-designated the 754th TB (Medium). Activated on June 1 at Pine Camp in Watertown, New York, near Lake Ontario, most of the men came from New England, New York, New Jersey, Pennsylvania, and Ohio.[6]

For seven months the 754th TB remained at Pine Camp, going through "intensive training and preparation for things to come." However, like the battalions before them, the 754th TB lacked the proper vehicles for training. Noted a battalion historian, "although it had been designated a medium tank battalion, the only full-tracked vehicles it had for training purposes were known as infantry combat cars, vintage 1930s." In spite of this handicap, the battalion continued to train its personnel, even taking part in a number of field exercises in the surrounding area.

On December 7, the men had just completed a ninety-odd mile trip through snow and freezing cold to Auburn, New York, when word was received that the Japanese had attacked Pearl Harbor. Almost immediately, the 754th TB was ordered back to camp. "The return to camp was by forced march," wrote one battalion historian, "departing the city of Auburn with first light, traveling over snow-covered icy roads, arriving at the post in a blinding blizzard late that night. . . . Little did its personnel surmise that the unit would shortly be moving from the frigid environs of northern New York to the 'alluring' palm fringed tropical islands of the south Pacific."

On December 29 the unit was redesignated a light tank battalion, which meant little since it still had no tanks of any kind. Then, shortly after New Year's Day, the men of the 754th TB braved the cold to load their scout cars and halftracks onto flatcars. "Undoubtedly," commented the historian, "many will remember those subzero days and nights, pulling maintenance checks on vehicles, preparing weapons for shipment and, [the] crating of all those other supplies essential to a tank battalion." On January 17, 1942, the battalion began moving to the Brooklyn Army Base and were placed aboard SS *John Erikson.* On January 23, the *John Erikson* and seven other ships, escorted by a handful of Navy warships and designated Task Force 6814, slipped out of New York harbor.

Leaving from New York, almost everyone assumed that the ships were headed for Europe, but when the convoy turned south the rumor began to spread that they were headed for the Pacific. "Here it was," the 754th TB historian recalled, "a unit trained for winter combat and so outfitted heading for the tropics. Destination, the Philippine Islands? The answer to this question will never be known. Possibly due to the misfortunes of war and the reverses suffered in the Philippine Islands the convoy . . . continued to the southwest." On February 27, the ships steamed into Melbourne Harbor in Australia, thirty-six days after leaving New York. Task Force 6814 was the first major U.S. Army operation in the southwest Pacific.[7]

Once in Australia, the troops were temporarily housed in the town of Ballarat, seventy-five miles inland, until the first week of March when they were put back on board the *John Erikson* and taken east to New Caledonia. On March 18, after a short delay with engine trouble, the *John Erikson* brought the 754th TB into Noumea Harbor where the tankers immediately had their first taste of "combat."[8]

"What disillusionment," wrote a battalion historian, "no sooner did we settle down than the battle began—'The Battle of Mosquito Hollow.' Mosquitoes to the right, mosquitoes to the left, mosquitoes all around. One couldn't see the tiny winged monsters because of the dark, but they made their presence known." Unable to remain near the dock area for long, the 754th TB was eventually moved to the center of the island, to the small village of St. Vincent. "What a relief," commented the historian, "the area was free from mosquitoes."[9]

Selected to safeguard the island, two American infantry regiments that had been a part of Task Force 6814 spread out around the island while the 754th TB, now equipped with M3 Stuart tanks, went into reserve. Noted an infantry historian, "The 754th Tank Battalion, one of the first tank battalions sent to the south Pacific, was . . . designated as a reserve force, a powerful combat arm, which could be dispatched quickly to either regimental sector in the event of an emergency." Added a second infantry historian, "The 754th Tank Battalion at St. Vincent was held as a striking force to be thrown in wherever needed." Unknown at the time, however, the island of New Caledonia would never be threatened by the Japanese and the 754th TB would spend more than a year of quiet guard duty.[10]

David C. Dumbeck, (Headquarters Company, 754th TB) recalled, "New Caledonia was a beautiful land owned by the French. The northern part . . . had mountains with streams of clear, cool water running down them and were covered with big timber. It reminded me of our western states. There were also many acres of flat, level country to the south." A primitive island, New Caledonia had only one major highway which was soon "chewed up" by the constant training exercises of the tanks. As a consequence, the 754th TB was ordered to build a new road. Recalled the battalion historian, "Using the most primitive of methods . . . and back-breaking manpower, trees were felled, bridges were built, and road surfaces graded where necessary." Before long, the 754th TB had constructed a first-class road across the entire length of the island.[11]

The 754th TB stayed on New Caledonia for seventeen months and used the time wisely. "For the first time since activation," noted the 754th TB historian, "the battalion was at full strength in men and equipment and this period became one of intensive training in tank tactics from platoon to battalion level. It was here that the battalion was welded into a tough, well-knit armored fighting unit." When on March 12, 1942, the different infantry and support units on New Caledonia were designated the "Americal Division," from the combination of the words America and New Caledonia, the 754th TB became part of the new unit. Eight months later, however, when the Americal Division reinforced Guadalcanal, the 754th TB stayed behind and became a part of the First Island Command.[12] In the meantime, the War Department continued to build up its presence in the Pacific.

In late 1940, shortly after the existing National Guard tank companies were formed into the four independent tank battalions, the War Department had decided to create additional independent tank battalions. Realizing that certain situations might dictate the use of a single battalion rather then an entire division, and not wanting to have to borrow a battalion from one of the existing Army tank divisions, the Army had created ten new independent tank battalions.

The 71st through the 80th independent tank battalions were created in December 1940. A few months later however, the designations were changed to the 751st through the 760th. (Thus, as mentioned above, the 74th TB became the 754th TB). In March 1942, with the United States now engaged in a second world war, the decision was made to add three more independent battalions, designated the 761st through 763rd. While the 761st TB was constituted on the American mainland and eventually would go to Europe, the 762nd and 763rd TBs were constituted in Hawaii.[13]

Utilizing personnel and equipment from both the 11th Tank Company and the 193rd TB, both the 762nd TB (Light) and the 763rd TB (Light) were activated on April 23 at Schofield Army Barracks. Many of the men that made up the cadre of the two new units had been in the National Guard tank companies before the war. William E. Bonnell (Company B, 763rd TB) recalled his earlier training:

> When I first went in the service it was in a Guard unit. We had light tanks with no weapons. When we went in the field we had a broomstick as a tank gun.

Eventually sent to Hawaii, Bonnell became a member of the 763rd TB and went through intensive training on the M3 Stuart light tank. However, it would be more than two years before he or anyone else in either the 762nd or the 763rd TBs saw combat.[14]

While the few new Pacific tank battalions were being activated and trained, the Japanese were pushing steadily across the Pacific. By the end of April 1942, the Japanese had captured the Philippines and most of the islands north of Australia. Japanese troops also had invaded Burma and the northern half of the Solomon Islands chain, and had landed troops along the northern shore of New Guinea. In less than five months, Japan had managed to construct a wide defensive perimeter around their home islands and had moved into position to threaten Australia.[15]

Quickly, American servicemen were forwarded to Hawaii, Australia, New Caledonia and a half dozen other islands along the vital air and sea lanes that were being used to ferry supplies and material to Australia.[16] At the same time, the American military commanders waited and watched, looking for an opening to strike back at Japan. In mid-April 1942, the Americans found an opening. On April 18, Lt. Col. James H. Doolittle and sixteen B-25 twin-engine bombers made a surprise air raid on Tokyo and several other Japanese cities. Coming at a time when the Japanese war machine seemed virtually unstoppable, the attack was a great shock to Japan.[17]

Although the Doolittle raid caused little material damage, it greatly boosted American morale and humiliated the Japanese military. In an attempt to push their defensive perimeter farther away from their home islands, the Japanese made two fatal mistakes. The first came at the battle of the Coral Sea (May 7–8) when the Japanese were stopped in their attempt to capture Port Moresby, New Guinea, just north of Australia. The second mistake came a month later at the battle of Midway (June 4–7). Suffering their most devastating defeat of the war, the Japanese were stopped from capturing strategically placed Midway Island and suffered the loss of four aircraft carriers and hundreds of men and planes.[18]

Although defeated at Coral Sea and Midway, Japan continued to try to capture the Solomon Islands and all of New Guinea. On July 3, the Japanese moved onto Guadalcanal Island in the Solomons and began constructing an airfield. Later that same month, Imperial troops landed on the north shore of New Guinea and began pushing their way over the Owen Stanley Mountains toward Port Moresby. While Adm. Chester W. Nimitz, in charge of the Pacific area, sent the 1st Marine

Division (MarDiv) against the Japanese on Guadalcanal, General MacArthur, in charge of the southwest Pacific area, sent American and Australian soldiers against the Japanese coming over the mountains. On January 3, 1943, after months of maneuvering through some of the worst jungle terrain in the world, the Allied troops defeated the Japanese and captured Buna.[19]

Although the Allies had managed to wrestle heavy artillery through the jungles of New Guinea to use against the Japanese, and the Australians had managed to bring up a few light tanks, the Americans had used no tanks in this first Allied land victory in the Pacific war.[20] But there would be many more opportunities to come.

American Marine Corps and Army units fought the Japanese on Guadalcanal for six long months. Dozens of land battles, more than a hundred air raids, and several naval engagements took place between August 1942 and early February 1943 before the Japanese finally decided they could not retake the island and abandoned Guadalcanal completely.[21]

Although the Americal Division from New Caledonia fought on Guadalcanal from mid-October until February 1943, the 754th TB was left behind in New Caledonia. Their presence, however, was sorely missed. Noted an Army historian:

> One type of fire support—tanks—did not play a major role on Guadal-canal. Although the few [Marine Corps] tanks present occasionally proved valuable in reducing enemy bunkers, neither Marine nor Army forces had enough tanks on the island to mount sizable tank-infantry assaults. Nor did the terrain of Guadalcanal permit the maneuver of armored columns. Army commanders and troops would have to find more level battlefields to learn armor-infantry coordination.[22]

Guadalcanal had been a long, drawn-out affair, but combined with the Allied victory in New Guinea it meant that the Japanese threat to Australia and the vital sea and air lanes was over. It also meant that the momentum now belonged to the Allies.

Perhaps feeling that the war in the Pacific had finally swung in their favor, the War Department created two new tank battalions in Hawaii in early 1943. On January 20, the 766th TB (Light) and the 767th TB (Light) both were constituted in the Regular Army. Two weeks later, on February 8, both battalions were activated at Schofield Barracks. Issued M3 light tanks, the two new battalions began training for their day in combat.[23]

In the spring and early summer of 1943, America maintained momentum and rolled up a string of important victories. In March, American planes intercepted a convoy heading toward New Guinea and inflicted considerable damage in the battle of the Bismarck Sea. In April, American planes shot down a Japanese bomber carrying Adm. Isoroku Yamamoto, the architect of the attack on Pearl Harbor and Japan's main strategist on the Pacific war. In May, United States troops landed on Attu Island in the Aleutian Islands of Alaska and soon defeated Japanese soldiers who had invaded the island a year before.[24]

In mid-summer, the United States began Operation Cartwheel—the isolation of the strong Japanese naval and air force base at Rabaul on the northern tip of New Britain Island in the Bismarck Archipelago. While forces under General MacArthur moved west along the northern coast of New Guinea, toward the Huon Peninsula, troops under Adm. William F. Halsey invaded New Georgia Island in the northern Solomons. Although the Japanese fought back bravely, the Allies prevailed. By the end of September, both the Huon Peninsula and New Georgia Island were in Allied hands.[25]

Once again, Army tanks were absent from the two offensives. Marine Corps tanks saw action on New Georgia Island but in the rapid move up the New Guinea coast, through dense jungle and swampy terrain, American tanks were never used. In the spring and summer of 1943, all the Pacific American tankers were busy training for the fight they knew was coming.

On August 6, Companies A and C, 754th TB, plus the medical detachment and a detachment from Headquarters and Service Company, moved from New Caledonia to Guadalcanal. Although the tankers would be used to help guard the vital airfields on Guadalcanal, the primary purpose of the move was to give the men an opportunity to train in a jungle environment with their new M3A1 Stuart tanks. "New tactics had to be developed for the use of tanks in this type terrain and so began another intensive training period," wrote the 754th TB historian. "This under the most exhausting conditions, excessive heat, and many times very little sleep. Everything we had learned about armored tactics and had practiced in the States and on New Caledonia were of no use to the battalion here in the jungle."

The historian added, "[The] primary purpose was to test the feasibility of tank use in jungle warfare, develop new tactics and acclimate the troops to the weather and terrain." Working side-by-side with the newly-formed 3rd Marine Division, and later with the 37th Infantry Division (IDiv), the men of the 754th TB slowly developed new tactics for cooperation between infantry and tanks. "It was here," concluded a 754th TB historian, "that new tactics were developed which were to assist us immeasurably at a later date when the battalion was actively engaged in combat."[26]

At about the same time, in the United States, several more independent tank battalions that would see service in the Pacific were being created. To maintain the initiative, the War Department realized that it would need massive amounts of men and materiel to defeat Japan. Even though the War Department was still dedicated to a Germany-first attitude, it realized that major offensive movements in the Pacific were about to take place and dozens more infantry divisions and tank battalions would be needed.

On September 10, 1943, at Camp Bowie, Texas, the 706th TB (Medium) was constituted from a reorganization of the 4th Armored Division. Ten days later, four more battalions were raised from a reorganization of existing armored divisions. At North Camp Polk, Louisiana, the 710th TB (Medium) and the 775th TB (Medium) came into existence with a reorganization of the 4th and 8th Armored

Divisions, respectively. At Camp Barkeley, Texas, the 713th TB (Medium) was formed after a reorganization of the 11th Armored Division, and at Camp Chaffee, Arkansas, the 716th TB (Medium) was constituted as a result of a reorganization of the 14th Armored Division. Two weeks later, on October 9, another unit, the 711th TB (Medium), came into being when the 9th Armored Division was reorganized at the Desert Training Center in California.[27]

A series of changes in the tables of organization in the fall and early winter of 1943 affected each of the new battalions. Noted historians Mary Lee Stubbs and Stanley Russel Connor, "The 1943 tables of organization eliminated the light and medium battalions and called for a single type of tank battalion composed of one light tank company, three medium tank companies, and headquarters and service companies. This distribution gave the battalion a striking force in its medium companies and a reconnoitering, exploiting, and covering force in its light company." Added historian Rich Anderson, "[Each medium tank battalion] had four lettered companies (A-C and D, which was a light tank company), a service company, and an H&H [Headquarters and Headquarters] company with a HQ, a mortar platoon, a reconnaissance platoon, and an assault gun platoon."[28]

Each of the three medium tank companies in an individual tank battalion had seventeen regular medium tanks and one medium tank equipped with a 105mm cannon. Each medium tank contained a crew of five. The battalion's single light tank company had seventeen light tanks, each with a crew of four. Additionally, each tank battalion had a headquarters company with two regular medium command tanks in its headquarters section and three 105mm assault tanks in its assault gun platoon. In all, a typical tank battalion had fifty-three regular medium tanks, seventeen light tanks, and six 105mm assault tanks.[29]

Training for the new battalions got under way almost immediately. The 706th TB was at Camp Bowie and went through a typical routine. The battalion historian recalled, "Miniature ranges were set up by each company prior to forthcoming training in tank gunnery and much stress was placed on snappy drill and school of the soldier. . . . M4A3 tanks . . . were loaned by units of the 4th Armored Division for our training."[30]

The M4 medium tank, nicknamed the "General Sherman" or just "Sherman," became one of the most recognized tanks in the world and the workhorse of the U.S. Army and Marine Corps. Outnumbered in production only by the Russian T34 tank, the M4 Sherman series eventually numbered almost 47,000. Noted one tank historian, "Its numbers, reliability, and ease of handling and maintenance were the great strengths of the M4 family, and the basic reasons for its success as a combat tank."[31]

The first two models of Sherman tanks were built on the chassis of the existing M3 medium tank (see Chapter Ten) but later on, a more suitable cast steel chassis was made. All of the Shermans had a fully traversing cast steel turret and, for the most part, carried a 75mm cannon. (Although the M4 assault gun tanks carried a 105mm gun.) For additional armament, the Sherman carried a coaxial

.30-caliber machine gun mounted alongside the cannon, a .30-caliber machine gun in a ball mount on the right side of the hull, and a .50-caliber anti-aircraft machine gun mounted on the turret roof.

Weighing almost thirty tons, all models of the M4 Sherman had two-inch frontal armor, and one-and-one-half inch side and rear armor. The turret had three inches of armor up front, and two inches on the sides and rear. The weakest spot on the tank was the half inch of armor at the rear floor, and the biggest drawback was its overall height, sitting eleven feet one inch off the ground.[32]

To run the M4 efficiently, the Sherman needed a crew of five. Two men rode in the hull front: the driver on the left and the assistant driver/bow gunner on the right. Inside the turret were three men. The commander sat on the right side of the cannon with the turret gunner directly in front and a little below him. Directly to the left of the commander, on the opposite side of the cannon breech, was the cannon loader. Hatches were provided above the two men in the hull but there was only one hatch in the turret roof, directly above the tank commander. In case of an emergency, it was extremely difficult for all three men in the turret to get out of the tank in a hurry.[33]

The first two models of Sherman tanks, the M4 and M4A1, used a Continental 9-cylinder radial aircraft gasoline engine, which, like the engine in the M3 Stuart light tank, needed to be cranked over before starting. In December 1941, the next model, the M4A2, received two GMC diesel engines. In January 1942, the M4A3 came off the assembly line powered by the new Ford GAA V-8 tank engine. Easy to maintain and operate, the M4A3 model became the workhorse for the U.S. Army in World War II.

The M4A1 was the first model in production and had a cast steel hull with distinctive rounded edges. Perhaps having learned a deadly lesson from riveted construction, no rivets were used on any of the turrets or hulls of the Sherman tanks. At the time, the M4A1 hull was the largest one-piece steel casting ever made.[34] The M4A2 model that followed had a welded hull with a sharp, angular front glacis plate. Due to the M4A2's finicky diesel engines, the Army refused to use the tank for overseas service so most of the M4A2s ended up with the Marine Corps or in the hands of the American allies.[35]

The third model to go into production, the M4, had an early run with a welded hull and then in 1943 switched to a composite hull that featured a cast front and a welded rear. The M4A3 model, the next in line, used only the fully welded hull but had a new cast steel chassis. In late-production versions of both the M4 and M4A3 models, a hatch was put into the top turret over the cannon loader, making it much easier for the three men inside the turret to get out in an emergency.[36]

Just as quickly as the different M4 Sherman tanks rolled out of the manufacturing plants, they were shipped off to the new tank battalions being formed in the States or sent overseas to some of the existing tank battalions where the war in the Pacific was heating up.[37]

CHAPTER TEN

Taking Makin

In July 1943, while the offensives on New Georgia and New Guinea were taking place, the Joint Chiefs of Staff began eyeing some of the islands in the central Pacific along Japan's outer defensive perimeter. Capture of these islands would not only crack the perimeter, but also further relieve the pressure on the air and sea routes to Australia. Among the islands under scrutiny were the Ellis Islands and the Gilbert Islands. In August, after it was discovered that the Ellis Islands were devoid of Japanese, American servicemen rushed ashore and quickly built a number of small airfields. Shortly thereafter, bombers began using these airfields to soften up the next targets: Tarawa Atoll, in the Gilberts; and Nauru Island, 390 miles west of the Gilberts. The invasions of both islands were scheduled for November 20.[1]

The most important island in Tarawa Atoll was Betio, which was to be seized by the 2nd Marine Division. Nauru Island was to be seized by the 27th IDiv from Hawaii, aided by tanks of the 193rd TB, the first tank unit rushed to Oahu after the attack on Pearl Harbor. The capture of Nauru would be the first offensive action for the Army in the central Pacific, so both the 27th IDiv and the 193rd TB began amphibious training on the shores of Oahu.[2]

By the time training started for Operation Galvanic, as it was being called, Companies A and B of the 193rd TB had been issued M3 medium tanks, popularly called General Lee or Lee tanks. The third company, Company C, still retained the light Stuart tank. The M3 Lee was the first successful medium tank employed by the United States, but by mid-1942 it was outdated by the more reliable and more fundamentally sound M4 Sherman. Weighing almost 31 tons, the M3 Lee sported two cannon: a sponson-mounted 75mm gun on the right side of the hull (which traversed only 30 degrees side-to-side), and a 37mm cannon mounted in a top turret. Additionally, the M3 Lee carried a .30-caliber coaxial machine gun alongside the 37mm gun, a .30-caliber antiaircraft gun attached to the turret, and two .30-caliber machine guns fixed on the left side of the hull.[3]

193rd TB M3 Lee tank used on Butaritari Island, Makin Atoll. US ARMY

A crew of seven was needed to operate the M3 Lee: three in the turret and four in the hull. Inside the turret was the tank commander in the left rear, the 37mm gunner just in front of the commander, and the 37mm loader in the right center. On the right front side of the hull sat the 75mm gunner and his loader while the driver sat in the front center with the radio operator directly behind him.[4] Although obsolete by the time of the Nauru operation, the M3 was still a reliable tank and in the hands of a well-trained crew could do plenty of damage.

Training for the amphibious operation at Nauru began on September 5, 1943, when two Lee tanks from Company A participated in a landing barge drill. However, when the two tanks crawled aboard the wooden LCVP barges (landing craft vehicle, personnel) they proved to be too heavy. Immediately a request went out for LCMs (landing craft mechanized), capable of carrying a medium-size tank. Two weeks later, after enough LCMs arrived, the amphibious training began in earnest.[5]

In late September, the 193rd TB was attached to the 27th IDiv, with the tankers taking orders from infantry commanders. This situation, where a single independent tank battalion was attached to an infantry division, was exactly why the independent tank battalions had been created.[6] Unfortunately, however, the time allotted to form a close working relationship between the two units was not enough. Wrote a War Department historian, "Time was . . . insufficient for infantry and tank crews to achieve adequate effectiveness in cooperation before the actual operation began. Communications between crews inside the tanks and infantrymen outside them was an unsolved problem; another was the method by which infantry officers could bring tanks directly into support." As the infantrymen and tankers worked to iron out these troubles, another problem arose.[7]

On September 28, the invasion of Nauru was changed to Butaritari Island in Makin Atoll, 150 miles north of Tarawa Atoll. Navy planners had decided that Nauru Island was too far west of Tarawa for ships and planes from one task force to support the other in an emergency. After careful consideration, the target was switched to Butaritari, which would leave the two naval forces within easy reach of each other.[8]

The switch from Nauru to Butaritari made little difference to the men in the ranks, but Maj. Gen. Ralph C. Smith, commander of the 27th IDiv, was worried the shallow reefs surrounding Butaritari might cause trouble for his landing craft. Smith figured the only way to quickly secure the beachhead was to bring his first wave ashore in LVT (landing vehicle, tracked) amphibious tractors, or amtracs, capable of climbing over the reef.

Since the Marines were using all available amtracs for the Tarawa invasion, Smith could procure only one amtrac for training while he waited for another fifty to arrive from San Diego. In the meantime, he discovered that none of his infantrymen knew how to drive a tracked vehicle, so he had to get a detachment of tankers from Headquarters Company, 193rd TB to crew the amtracs. On October 15, the crews began training on the single amtrac and then on October 30, exactly three weeks before the invasion date, when the fifty new amtracs arrived, training began in earnest.[9]

On November 5, three LSTs (landing ship, tank) carrying the amtracs with their 193rd TB crews and the initial assault troops left Pearl Harbor with a destroyer escort. Five days later, six various transport ships loaded with infantry and support equipment, and the tankers and Stuart light tanks of Company C and the M3 Lee medium tanks of Company A (both 193rd TB) left Pearl Harbor in the escort of three destroyers.[10]

Makin Atoll in the central Pacific is triangular in shape. The northern side is a concave coral reef, stretching seventeen miles. The western edge consists of a much straighter reef, measuring fourteen miles from end to end, but is broken in spots, leaving access into an inner lagoon. Two long, flat, narrow islands, Butaritari and Kuma, stretch from the southern end of the fourteen-mile reef northeast toward the eastern tip of the concave reef. Butaritari Island, measuring thirteen miles long and less than one mile wide, looks like a long, bending ribbon widening out slightly to a T on the far-western end. In 1943, the island was covered with coconut trees and taro pits which were used by the natives in growing edible taro plants, making Butaritari Island a terrible place to drive a tank.[11]

For some time, the Japanese had used Butaritari as a seaplane base. Four wharves reached out into the lagoon. The main line of defense was concentrated between the first and third wharves. At either end of this main area, the Japanese had cut wide clearings and constructed jagged tank barriers. Each barrier was about six feet deep and about fourteen feet wide. On either end of the barrier, where it was too wet to dig, the Japanese had constructed a coconut log fence measuring four and a half feet high. A crossfire of rifle pits, machine gun nests, and pillboxes provided mutual support in the main defense area.[12]

The invasion of Butaritari Island called for the infantry to land at two separate points. Red Beach was on the western end of the island, on top of the T, while Yellow Beach was on the lagoon side, in the center of the main defense area. Two battalions from the 27th IDiv and two platoons of light tanks from Company C,

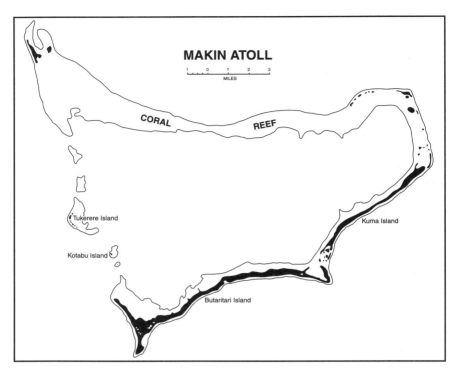

Makin Atoll

193rd TB would land on Red Beach at approximately 8:30 A.M. The Red Beach invaders were expected to secure the wide western end of the island and then advance eastward, drawing the attention of the Japanese toward them. Two hours later, the second landing force, consisting of one battalion of infantry, the medium tanks of Company A, 193rd TB, and a platoon of light tanks from Company C, would land on Yellow Beach, right in the heart of the main Japanese defense area. Although he was taking a risk by dividing his attack force, General Smith was certain that the 27th IDiv and the attached 193rd TB could capture Makin Atoll without much trouble.[13]

A little after 6:00 A.M. on November 20, 1943, U.S. Navy ships and planes began pounding Red Beach. At 8:15 A.M., the amphibious tractors headed for the beach. Five minutes later, the first wave of infantry-laden LCVP barges and LCMs carrying the light tanks of Company C, 193rd TB and a handful of infantry headed for shore. 2nd Lt. Murray C. Engle, 1st Platoon leader, recalled, "When [the] line of departure was reached and [the LCMs] started moving in, the tanks were buttoned up with the exception of the tank commander's turret lid. The tank commander kept his lid open and observed the beach through field glasses, to see if any last minute changes in plan of attack were necessary. About one hundred yards from shore the tanks were completely buttoned up, and ready to leave the LCM."[14]

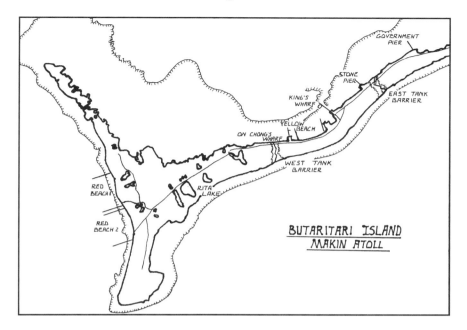

Butaritari Island (Makin Atoll)

The amtracs had no trouble clambering over the coral reef, but a few of the LCVPs and LCMs got hung up while still forty feet from shore. Instantly, the infantrymen plunged into chest deep water and began wading toward the beach, but the tanks had to wait until the handful of infantry that were in the LCMs were clear

193rd TB M3 Lee tank on Butaritari Island, Makin Atoll. US ARMY

193rd TB M3A1 drives off Red Beach on Butaritari Island, Makin Atoll, on November 20, 1943 to hunt for snipers. The tank still carries the fording trunk.
US NAVY

before they could exit the barge. Lieutenant Engle in Stuart Tank No. 40 complained, "Infantry riding in LCM with tanks apparently haven't been sufficiently impressed with the idea of getting out of the way of the tanks in coming off the barges. Both in practice runs and in our actual landing tanks had to wait on the infantry to get out of the way to avoid running over them. The infantry had a tendency to immediately hit the ground upon landing and if they had been under fire, I'm afraid it would have been much worse."[15]

Surprisingly, Red Beach remained relatively quiet as the Americans came ashore. Meeting only a smattering of rifle and machine-gun fire, the infantry quickly moved inland while the 1st and 2nd Platoon tanks of Company C, 193rd TB rumbled cautiously over the huge coral boulders toward two pre-arranged assembly areas.[16]

As the 1st Platoon Stuarts began to concentrate in their assembly area, the crews refused to take orders from infantry officers. Complained an Army historian, "[The tanks] were initially held up by their refusal to receive commands except through their own company officers, and then by the difficulties of terrain. Although they came in before 0900, they were of no assistance to the infantry . . . until late in the day." In all, it took three hours for all five 1st Platoon tanks to link up and another two hours to reach the infantry, which had moved about 1,300 yards eastward down a coral road that traversed the length of the island.[17]

After finally getting all five of his tanks ashore, Lieutenant Engle and his 1st Platoon started eastward. He wrote, "[We] then moved in column formation down the main road to catch up with the [infantry]. As there was no engineer equipment

193rd TB M3A1 with a fording trunk moves off Red Beach on Butaritari Island, Makin Atoll, on November 20, 1943. US ARMY

available, tank crews had to fill in shell craters with logs, rocks, etc. to enable them to get through. Finally about 1400 [2:00 P.M.] the tanks caught up with [the infantry]." The foot soldiers had stopped behind an imaginary line that ran across the island just north and east of Rita Lake, the largest of several shallow ponds on the west end of Butaritari. When the five tanks arrived, however, they were ordered to

Company C/193rd—VA TB 1st Platoon leader, 2nd Lt. Murray C. Engle's M3A1 Tank No. 40 stuck in a hole on Butaritari Island, Makin Atoll, November 20, 1943. US ARMY

A tanker attempts to extricate Company C/193rd TB 1st Platoon leader, 2nd Lt. Murray C. Engle's M3A1 Tank No. 40 from a shell hole on Butaritari Island, Makin Atoll, November 20, 1943. US ARMY

move farther east along the narrow roadway to see what was out ahead. With Lieutenant Engle in the lead, the tanks moved out.

"We were fired on by snipers and machine guns," commented Tech 4 Frank C. Kulaga, the driver of Stuart Tank No. 41. "Our gunner knocked out a machine gun which had been firing on tank No. 40 [with Lieutenant Engle]. We then advanced about 200 yards where tank No. 40 ran into a shell hole and had to be towed out." Explained an Army historian, "The highway at that point was a causeway [between two ponds] off which other tanks could not move to bypass the first. Hence, the lead tank had to be towed off and the shell hole filled before the column could proceed."

Since each shell hole in the road had to be filled in before the tanks could proceed, forward progress was extremely slow. Then, after going only 300 yards, the tanks began drawing heavy fire. Lieutenant Engle halted his tanks and called for infantry support, but was told to push on and try to link up with the troops on Yellow Beach.

As the five tanks pushed farther east, Japanese resistance began to slacken. By 4:00 P.M., they were within sight of the east tank barrier. "When about three hundred yards from [the] tank trap, [American] medium tanks were sighted," reported Lieutenant Engle, "we moved up and met them." Although infantrymen from both Red and Yellow Beach had made an earlier link-up along the ocean shore, the junction between the M3 Stuart light tanks of Company C and the M3 Lee medium tanks of Company A was the first link on the lagoon side.[18]

Both sides of the T end of Butaritari were found to be devoid of Japanese defenders and by 12:40 P.M. both areas were declared secure. Since the Red Beach assault was going so smoothly, the invasion of Yellow Beach was set in motion. At 9:52 A.M., infantry-laden amtracs and LCMs carrying the Stuart light tanks of the 3rd Platoon, Company C, 193rd TB and the Lee medium tanks of Company A, 193rd TB passed through a break in the atoll and moved into the lagoon. As the assault waves started forward, a pall of thick black smoke from burning fuel dumps that had been hit by the preliminary naval bombardment filled the air.[19]

When the amtracs and LCM barges were 500 yards from shore, a deadly Japanese crossfire suddenly erupted from the two wharves on either side of the landing beach and from two half-sunken ships in the lagoon. Sgt. Wilbur R. Johnson's medium No. 8 was in a LCM on the far right edge of the invasion wave. He wrote, "On my right was two old enemy hulks that were laying out and to the right of Onchong's [sic] Wharf. I cleared my 37mm gun by firing on these hulks, I also put several bursts of machine gun fire on the wharf where enemy guns could be seen."[20]

Although the amtracs had no trouble reaching the beach, most of the LCMs bottomed out when they were still 200 yards from shore. As the mediums rumbled down the LCM ramps and into the cloudy, churned-up surf, a couple of them ran into trouble. Medium No. 4, commanded by Capt. Robert S. Brown, commander of Company A, sank into an unseen shell hole while medium No. 17, commanded by Sgt. Jean O. Newby, did likewise. Sergeant Newby reported:

> We left the barge, went forward about 25 yards and hit a shell hole. We got out of that and went about 15 yards more and hit another. The water was about 7 feet deep and our tank drowned out. The tank immediately filled with smoke. . . . The crew dismounted right there with great speed through the right sponson door. I remained inside the tank. As soon as the crew got out of the tank they were machine gunned from shore and with more speed they came back inside the tank.[21]

Two medium tanks and one light tank were lost to unseen shell holes but thirteen mediums and three light tanks made it to shore. Once on dry land, however, the tanks ran into new problems. Medium No. 6, commanded by Lt. Col. Harmon L. Edmundson, commanding officer of the 193rd TB, had trouble getting off the beach because of the thick black smoke from the burning fuel dumps and medium No. 20, commanded by Sgt. Henry F. Knetter, got hung up on a tree stump in the bottom of a taro pit. Although temporarily stalled, Sergeant Knetter recalled, "I fired nearly a hundred rounds of .30 cal. at a bunch of Japs running toward the west on the ocean side. Hung as we were no other gun could be fired."[22]

Once ashore, the mission of the medium tanks was to head straight across the island to the ocean shore. Once the island was cut in two, the mediums were to split into platoons and head east and west, toward the two tank barriers. Unfortunately for the tankers, the land between Yellow Beach and the ocean was covered with taro pits. As medium No. 11 was heading south, it ran into one of the pits and overturned.[23]

The first tank to reach the southern shore was medium No. 15 under Sgt. James C. Toole. "When I reached the ocean side I saw I was alone," he reported, "so I went back to the [Yellow Beach] and got with tank No. 14 [under S/Sgt. Roger H. Smarr]. We then proceeded back to the ocean side, shooting pillboxes and places the enemy might be." Unfortunately, Sergeant Smarr's driver dumped medium No.14 into a shell hole and it took him an hour and a half to get out. All the while, medium No. 15 stayed around to provide cover fire.

By the time medium No. 14 got out of the shell hole, mediums No. 13 and No. 16 had come up and the four tanks pressed southward. "When we reached the ocean side of the island we ran into enemy fire that was coming from a pillbox and from the trees," Staff Sergeant Smarr noted. "We fired 75mm [rounds] into the pill box and was [later] told by the infantry that we had killed ten Japs along the beach." Having reached the ocean, the four tanks turned east and headed for the southern end of the east tank barrier.[24]

Back near Yellow Beach, medium No. 20 with Sergeant Knetter remained stuck on the stump until medium No. 6 with Colonel Edmundson, and mediums No. 10 and No. 19, came up and towed it free. However, when the four tanks started south toward the ocean shore, No. 20 ran over another stump and became stuck again. With time of the essence, the other three pressed on.[25]

Mediums Nos. 6, 10 and 19 reached the south shore and were joined by No. 8 and No. 9. At 12:30 P.M., an infantry company near the ocean end of the west tank barrier put out a call for tank support. "Then we started to the western tank barrier," wrote Sgt. Frank M. Greco of medium No. 10, "and Colonel Edmundson gave me orders to knock out machine-gun nests and pillboxes. We proceeded to knock them out. We had infantry with us, and worked with them knocking out any obstacles that were in our way."[26]

The tanks and the infantry continued pressing westward along the ocean side, knocking out Japanese strong points wherever found. Wrote Sgt. Louis J. Spenyovics of medium No. 9, "Near the tank trap we ran into several machine gun nests. Our 37mm gun put them out of action. We used 75mm HE [high explosive] and machine guns also." By 1:30 P.M. the tanks had broken the Japanese defenses closest to the ocean and the infantry moved over the southern end of the west tank barrier. Continuing westward, the infantry eventually ran into soldiers moving east from Red Beach. The first link-up between the two beachheads was made around 3:00 P.M.[27]

While the infantry from Yellow Beach was advancing westward, Colonel Edmundson moved his own tank and two other M3 medium tanks for an assault against the northern (lagoon) end of the west tank barrier. Coming up to the area where the barrier consisted of a high log wall, the three tanks blasted away until they had blown a huge hole through it. Then, after two more M3 Lee tanks came along, three tanks crossed through the gap and eventually linked up with the Stuart light tanks of the 1st Platoon, Company C, 193rd TB from Red Beach.[28]

After the three Lee tanks passed through the gap, Colonel Edmundson took a total of five tanks and made a frontal attack against the center of the west tank barrier. Spraying the area with machine-gun and cannon fire, the enemy pillboxes, machine-gun nests, and rifle pits were quickly overrun and by 4:50 P.M. the fighting in the center was over. An hour later, the entire western half of Butaritari was firmly in American hands. On the eastern half however, the battle had just begun.[29]

Near noon, after taking about an hour to consolidate their hold on Yellow Beach, the 27th IDiv soldiers turned east toward the east tank barrier. Near the base of King's Wharf, on the eastern flank of Yellow Beach, the men ran into a fortified Japanese air raid position and came to a dead halt. After a half hour of futile attempts to capture the position, the infantry called for tank support and 2nd Lt. George P. Evans brought up three Stuart light tanks from the 3rd Platoon, Company C, 193rd TB.

Moving into position, Lieutenant Evans' tanks fired 37mm high explosive shells at the shelter entrances. Recalled Evans, "The range was point blank, being, no more than 20 yards. The result was satisfactory because fire ceased from [the] shelter and from eight to ten Japs were left laying about the entrances." Aided by engineers with TNT charges, and infantry fire that cut down the Japanese as they fled, the tanks and infantry finally took the entire complex at 4:00 P.M., almost four hours after finding it.[30]

On the ocean side of Butaritari, four medium tanks under 2nd Lt. Burton V. Cline in medium No. 15 tried to advance toward the east tank barrier without infantry. Meeting very heavy resistance, and hampered by a thick growth of trees and numerous taro pits, the tanks advanced only 350 yards in three hours. At 2:30 P.M. they were ordered back to a tank park near Yellow Beach.[31]

Once back at the tank park, Lieutenant Cline's four M3 Lee medium tanks were eventually joined by eight more medium and four light tanks. Noted Lieutenant Evans, who brought over one of the light tanks, "Confusion resulted and many of our own troops fired at each other throughout the remainder of the night." Two tankers, one from Company A and one from Company C, were killed when they left their slit trenches to catch infiltrating Japanese.[32]

On the west end of the island, four light tanks from the 1st Platoon, Company C, 193rd TB, spent the night near the lagoon end of the west tank barrier. Sergeant Kulaga from Stuart No. 43 wrote, "It was pretty quiet up until the next morning, when the moon came up the snipers began firing on us and they shot our tank commander as he was getting into the tank to pull his turn on guard and [he] died instantly."[33]

Early on the morning of November 21, Capt. Charles B. Tobin, the commanding officer of Company C, 193rd TB, took control of several light Stuart tanks and began hauling skids of ammunition and fuel from Red Beach to Yellow Beach.

Since portions of the lagoon were still under Japanese fire, the Americans were stockpiling supplies on Red Beach and transporting them to Yellow Beach. Wrote Sgt. John S. Sloane, the gunner in Captain Tobin's Tank No. 38, "Several tanks were hauling skids of 75mm ammo. The rest had three (3) drums of fuel on back deck and lashed to tank turret. We got under way at 0920 and made our way along [the] coral road toward Yellow Beach and Tank Trap. From time to time shell holes made [the] going rather rough and the farther we proceeded, the more evident became the Jap snipers."[34]

As the sniping increased, the tankers fired back. "Later in the morning," recalled Sgt. Thomas W. McCain commanding Stuart No. 44, "I used the antiaircraft gun to strafe the treetops to stop [the] snipers from firing on our troops. I saw no snipers, alive or dead, but [the] infantry troops said we got some."[35]

Captain Tobin's tanks had crossed through the shattered west tank barrier with their supply skids and began angling toward Yellow Beach when Captain Tobin's skid snagged on a tree stump and snapped its tow cable. While Captain Tobin walked back toward the tank barrier to elicit help, his crew exited the tank and began working on the busted cable.

"Everything was okay momentarily," Sergeant Sloane wrote, "when firing opened on us from the left and from the direction of two old sunken hulks off Yellow Beach. We knew we were in a spot and dived under the tank for cover." Eventually, the crew climbed back into the tank just before an infantry lieutenant ran up and volunteered to operate the antiaircraft gun on the turret. "He seemed to know where to fire and I was operating the coaxial gun," recalled Sloane. "I took his lead and fired in on his target."

In the middle of this firefight, a terrible explosion suddenly rocked the tank. Sergeant Sloane explained, "The whole crew blacked out for several seconds and the tank filled with a dense smoke. Bewildered, dazed, and hurt, we evacuated the tank." Somehow, a Navy dive bomber had accidentally dropped a 2,000-pound bomb only twenty-five feet from the tank. Although no one inside the tank was seriously wounded, the infantry lieutenant was mortally wounded and two nearby infantrymen were killed. Also, Captain Tobin, who was returning to his tank, was wounded in the neck.

Additionally, the bomb blast put several holes in the suspension system of Captain Tobin's Stuart No. 38, blew off the front of the bow machine gun, and damaged the antiaircraft gun and the 37mm cannon. In spite of this damage, however, the tank engine was still operational, so Captain Tobin took No. 38 back to Red Beach for repairs.[36]

The twelve M3 medium tanks that spent the night at the Yellow Beach tank park had to wait for the Stuart light tanks from Red Beach to bring up more fuel and ammunition before they could move out. Because of the delay, the advance against the east tank barrier did not get started until 11:10 A.M. With Colonel Edmundson and six tanks assisting, the infantry began its advance along the ocean side of Butaritari. Progress was extremely slow because of the lack of roads and serviceable trails and the tanks were forced to move in single file. Then, when the lead tank, medium No. 19, threw a clutch, the entire advance came to a halt. After some time, medium No. 19 finally got out of the way and headed back to the tank park and the rest of the force moved forward again. Soon, however, the advance began running into stiff resistance. Sergeant Johnson in medium No. 8 described the advance:

> We had complete infantry support so we moved up slowly, encountering enemy rifle and machine gun fire. A few snipers were soon wiped out. Several tanks were ahead of me, so I followed and covered the last one as we moved up. . . . We encountered a machine gun on our right, so infantry moved back and we blasted it out with a 75mm HE [high explosive]. The infantry moved in there and found several dead Japs. . . . We did not advance but a few hundred yards that day.

At 4:45 P.M., the advance halted about 200 yards west of the east tank barrier. While the infantry dug in for the night, the tanks headed back to the tank park for more ammunition and fuel.[37]

On the lagoon side, the advance kicked off a little after 11:00 A.M. when Captain Brown came up with five M3 medium tanks and a handful of Stuart light tanks. After silencing a number of Japanese pillboxes, and silencing a few Japanese machine-gun emplacements in a partially submerged seaplane, the advance moved slowly east along the coral roadway. "Spent all day knocking out pillboxes and crushing them with our tank, until we were out of 37mm ammunition," wrote Sergeant Greco. By 4:30 P.M., the tank/infantry assault had moved about 1,000 yards from Yellow Beach until it was only 200 yards short of Stone Pier. With daylight fading, the infantry dug in and the tanks returned to the tank park to replenish their spent ammunition and refuel their thirsty engines.[38]

After being resupplied, a few Stuart light tanks were ordered up to the front line "to assist local security" while a number of Lee medium tanks were ordered to the south shore to help repel a rumored Japanese counterinvasion. Recalled Sergeant Smarr in medium No. 14, "We parked our tanks for the night, facing the ocean about 30 or 40 yards apart to watch for the enemy. The infantry was all around us." Added Cpl. Robert A. Viets of medium No. 16, "We stayed in the tank all night. We stayed in the tank about 18 or 20 hours without getting out."[39]

Although the Japanese invasion never materialized, the enemy harassed the front line infantrymen and Stuarts all night long. "Shortly after nightfall the enemy laid down a light mortar barrage," reported Lieutenant Evans. "It lasted a short time but our troops had apparently become 'jittery' and began tossing hand grenades at the slightest provocation. As a result one infantryman got killed and several [were] injured." Added Sgt. Guy M. Bolt in Stuart No. 52, "There we spent a very miserable night, due to enemy rifle fire and hand grenades being thrown."[40]

At 5:15 A.M. on November 22, Captain Tobin and the 1st and 2nd Platoon light tanks of Company C, 193rd TB followed a fresh battalion of 27th IDiv troops from Red Beach to the front line. For the past two days, General Smith had kept one battalion in reserve just in case they were needed to reinforce the

Marines on Tarawa. On November 20, when the 2nd MarDiv invaded Tarawa, the situation had looked bleak, but after two full days of vicious fighting, the Marines finally gained the upper hand. With his reserve battalion no longer needed on Tarawa, General Smith intended to use these fresh troops to start the final push to take Butaritari.[41]

At 7:00 A.M., American artillery began pounding the wooded area in front of the east tank barrier. An hour and a half later the shelling stopped and the fresh troops went forward. On the lagoon side, the infantrymen were assisted by Captain Tobin's two platoons of light tanks and six medium tanks that had come up from the tank park. On the ocean side, the infantrymen were accompanied by Lieutenant Lawrence's six medium tanks that had been guarding the southern shore against the rumored Japanese invasion. As each group moved eastward, Japanese resistance was almost nonexistent.[42]

By 9:20, the entire advance had moved within sight of the east tank barrier. Twenty-five minutes later, the artillery resumed firing, concentrating on the east tank barricade. At 10:10 the shelling stopped and the tanks and infantry moved forward again, fanning out across the narrow width of the island. On the lagoon side, Sergeant Greco in medium No. 10 reported, "There was no opposition except a few snipers across the tank trap. We then formed in a line formation with infantry behind us and proceeded to crush a few pillboxes and knocked down a few houses. The infantry gave us good cover."[43]

On the ocean side, Lieutenant Lawrence in medium No. 16 recalled, "Enemy activity was light, but two machine-gun nests were destroyed by the tanks. The tank barrier was very ineffective as we crossed it with no trouble. . . . [Afterwards] our progress was slowed by numerous stumps and fallen trees."

Once past the barrier, the oceanside advance slowed. Sergeant Johnson in medium No. 8 reported, "The going was tough so every tank followed to cover the leading tanks. I could see the rest of the medium tanks, also the light tanks moving up on the lagoon side. We traveled slow with the infantry spread out in a complete line across the island. We blew up several pillboxes and wiped out all machine guns." After advancing only 400 yards, however, the oceanside terrain became extremely rough, so the tanks there turned north and came up behind the vehicles on the lagoon side, traversing the main island roadway.[44]

At 10:42 A.M., the advance had moved about 300 yards east of the east tank barrier and had reached a barracks area between the main roadway and the lagoon. As the tanks stopped to shell the buildings, General Smith undertook a bold move to seal off the eastern end of Butaritari and catch the Japanese in a trap.[45]

Near 11:00 A.M., a special detachment from the 27th IDiv climbed into amtracs and shuttled across the lagoon to a spot about 4,000 yards beyond the east tank barrier. Once ashore, the detachment set up a defensive line across the narrow width of the island and prepared to act as an anvil for the sledgehammer that was pounding in from the west. As the men were digging in, however, a group of natives informed the soldiers that most of the Japanese had already passed through the area and were rushing east toward Kuma Island, off the northeast tip of Butaritari.[46]

While the shuttle move was taking place, the tanks and infantry finished their assault on the barracks buildings and then six M3 Lee medium tanks and most of the infantry resumed the advance along the island roadway. About 500 yards beyond the barracks area, the attack group came up to Government Pier, the last of the long manmade structures that reached out into the lagoon. "[W]hen we were nearing Government Wharf we saw some anti-tank guns and some pillboxes," remembered Sergeant Spenyovics in medium No. 9. "We did not see anyone around the guns, but we sprayed them with machine gun fire and 37mm HE."[47]

Continuing on, the tanks and troopers soon linked up with the special detachment of infantry that had circled around in the amtracs. At that point, the Americans realized that the Japanese had indeed slipped by and were moving down the tapering eastern end of Butaritari toward Kuma.[48]

Still hoping to catch the Japanese before they made the crossing, the tanks and infantry pushed on, but after going only 500 yards they ran into a group of 300 native refugees. "Waited one hour until all the natives were evacuated from the east," said Corporal Erickson in medium No. 6. "[We] then proceeded eastward another 300 yards, meeting very little resistance." The delay in dealing with the Butaritari natives had given the Japanese the time they needed to slip away from the pursuing Americans.

Near 5:00 P.M., as darkness fell, the American commanders called off the pursuit. As the infantry dug in, the light and medium tanks returned to the tank park to rearm and refuel. All in all, the November 22 advance had taken the Americans to within two miles of the end of the island roadway, and about four miles from the very end of Butaritari.[49]

During the night of November 22–23 the remaining Japanese on the eastern end of Butaritari made several uncoordinated attacks against the infantry line. Each attack failed. Near 6:00 A.M., Captain Tobin took his Stuart light tanks back to the front lines, with the mediums to follow. At 7:00 A.M., when the light tanks reached the infantry, Tobin was informed the Japanese had trapped a platoon of soldiers near the ocean shore. Captain Tobin immediately sent Lieutenant Evans and three tanks to the rescue.

Although Lieutenant Evans lost one tank when it got stuck in swampy terrain, the other two managed to reach the beleaguered infantrymen. Recalled Lieutenant Evans, "After reorganizing, [the infantry] followed the two tanks back into the jungle. We 'flushed' up about ten Japs and overran a machine gun. The infantry accounted for the Japs."[50]

While Lieutenant Evans was rescuing the trapped soldiers, Captain Tobin set out with three light tanks and fifty infantrymen to reconnoiter Tanimaiaki Village at the terminus of the island roadway. With the infantry clinging to the tanks, the three Stuarts hustled down the roadway until they reached the village. When no one was found at Tanimaiaki Village the infantry-laden tanks cut across a narrow inlet in the lagoon to the very eastern tip of Butaritari, which bends back upon itself toward the northwest. "We proceeded across [the] lagoon which was dry at low tide," wrote Sergeant Sloane of No. 38. "We made our way through thick jungle undergrowth which finally forced us to stop. Infantry proceeded to search area and tanks returned to main body to give report. . . . The tide was coming in fast, and we just about made it back in a foot and a half of water."[51]

Following close behind the Stuart light tanks were ten Lee mediums that hurried down the roadway to Tanimaiaki Village with infantry on their backs. After reaching the deserted village and the end of the roadway, 2nd Lt. Calvin C. Gurley dismounted from his medium No. 15 and went ahead on foot, trying to find a way to get the tanks to the far end of the island. Recalled Sgt. Quentin Sorrow in medium No. 18, "When we got to the end of the road one of the officers got out and picked a way for us to get through a narrow swamp to another part of the island." While five mediums stayed behind, the other five followed Lieutenant Gurley into the jungle.

"[We] knocked out pillboxes and snipers until we could find no more," wrote Sergeant Sorrow. Added Sergeant Smarr in medium No. 14, "[Lieutenant Gurley] also located a pillbox with seven Jap officers in it and had it blown up by one of the tanks." Before the small group reached the end of the island it was ordered back to King's Wharf where it was to begin reloading aboard the transports. For the M3 Lee tanks of Company A, 193rd TB, the battle of Makin Atoll was over. At 11:30 A.M., November 23, 1943, General Smith sent a radio message to the waiting ships, "Makin Taken." The entire operation had cost the U.S. Army 66 killed and 150 wounded. On Tarawa, the Marines and Navy had lost 939 killed and missing, and 2,085 were wounded.[52]

By the morning of November 24, all of the medium tanks, and the 1st and 3rd Platoons of light tanks were back aboard their transports. Left behind on Butaritari were the 2nd Platoon light tanks of Company C, 193rd TB, which had been tabbed for garrison duty. The 193rd TB had four men killed on Makin, two from Company A and two from Company C, and had sixteen men injured, including three officers. By the first week in December the ships were back at Pearl Harbor and the commanding officers were evaluating the operation.

The biggest concern among all involved was a lack of communication. "Decided improvement needed in communication between tank leader and infantry leader," reported Captain Tobin. Added Lieutenant Engle, "In working with infantry in the advance there is a great lack of communications between tanks and front line troops. In the tanks, vision is so limited that the crew can't pick out any targets, especially machine gun positions. The only targets easily discernible from a tank being pillboxes, bomb shelters, etc."[53]

Another concern centered on sending the tanks out without infantry support. "Tanks were exposed dangerously by being sent too far ahead of the infantry," reported Lieutenant Lawrence. "Had the enemy possessed antitank guns and other antitank weapons, we would have lost many tanks." 1st Lt. Robert E. Holmes agreed, "If any antitank defense had been used the results might have been very unsatisfactory."[54]

Overall, the tank commanders were satisfied with the performance of both the light and medium tanks. Writing about the Stuart light tanks, Captain Tobin stated, "The M3A1 tank proved both durable and maneuverable despite very adverse terrain conditions. . . . 37mm canister is excellent for removing snipers from trees." And, for the M3 Lee tanks, Lieutenant Evans noted, "The mediums were highly successful throughout the operation because of the immense fire-power they possess in their 75mm and because of their heavy armor. Time and time again a well-placed 75mm shell destroyed a pillbox or machine gun nest. . . . In my estimation the medium tanks did a stellar job."[55] And this from the com-mander of a light tank platoon!

The attacks on Tarawa and Makin atolls were clear-cut victories for the Americans and their tanks, but everyone realized it would take more victories to win the war in the Pacific.

CHAPTER ELEVEN

Closing the Solomons

While the Americans were finally going on the offensive in the central
Pacific, the drive to isolate Rabaul was moving along as scheduled. On
November 1, 1943, U.S. Marines landed at Empress Augusta Bay in the center of
Bougainville Island in a move that caught the Japanese completely by surprise.
The Japanese had built fortified airstrips on both ends of the island but had left the
center almost totally undefended. Over the next few days, while the U.S. Navy
successfully thwarted Japanese attempts to reinforce Bougainville, the Marines
consolidated their beachhead and three regiments of the Army's 37th IDiv were
brought in as reinforcements. Subsequently, the expanded beachhead was divided
into two sections, with the Marines on the east and the 37th IDiv on the west.[1]

By December 15, the Marines and soldiers had pushed their defense perimeter almost four miles out in all directions and two airstrips had been built near the
bay. At that time, the Army began bringing in the detachment of tanks from the
754th TB on nearby Guadalcanal.[2]

Weeks before, on November 7, the 754th TB, which had half its force stationed at Guadalcanal and the other at New Caledonia, was elevated from a light
tank battalion to a medium tank battalion and redesignated 754th TB (Medium).
Noted the battalion historian, "The battalion was now authorized four tank companies. Companies A, B and C were redesignated medium tank companies and
the newly created Company D, a light tank unit." While Company D was being
created on New Caledonia, the detachment on Guadalcanal, consisting of half of
Headquarters Company, and Companies A and C, began boarding LSTs for transport to Bougainville. "It was about Christmas time in 1943 when we left Guadalcanal," David Dumbeck wrote. "We celebrated the holiday early and shoved off.
We were in good spirits, as Guadalcanal was getting dull and we wanted to be
moving on. We realized another island meant being that much closer to the end of
the jungle fighting and war with the Japs."[3]

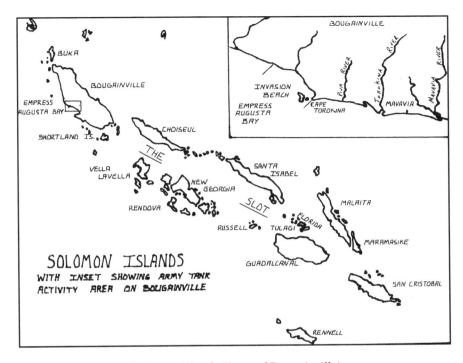

Solomon Islands (Inset of Bougainville)

Although newly designated as a medium tank battalion, the 754th TB detachment still had its Stuart light tanks. "For all we cared, they could have left the light tanks back on Guadalcanal for the natives to play with," Dumbeck commented, "as we found they were no more than a death trap if hit by a 75mm. Sure they were okay for small arms fire but a .50 caliber would dent the walls and sometimes go through." Taken into the waiting LSTs, the Stuarts and halftracks were chained to the lower deck of the flat-bottomed ships.

As the ships moved up the Slot they ran into a terrible storm. "There was a storm that lasted for three or four days on our way to Bougainville," Dumbeck recalled. "The waves came at us with the top of the wave being 100 feet high. It seemed like the ship would go right under the wave but we always rode it out on top. Water sprayed all over the deck. Our LSTs were rocking like teeter totters." In the middle of this storm, someone noticed that the blocks and chains holding the tanks and the halftracks in place were beginning to come loose. "If one of [the tanks] had come loose and really started banging back and forth," Dumbeck continued, "it probably would have went right through the wall of the ship and down to the bottom of the Pacific and I imagine we would have went right along with it." Fortunately, the warning came early enough and the chains were duly tightened.[4]

On New Year's Day, 1944, the 754th TB detachment finally reached Bougainville and began guarding the twin airstrips. Although glad to be away from the boredom of Guadalcanal, life on Bougainville proved anything but idyllic for the tankers. An unknown tanker wrote:

> Bougainville . . . is covered with a thick jungle growth, its floor a verdant garden, rich with loam and constant moisture from daily rains. . . . [A]rmy ants, spiders, unnamable and indescribable bugs fall on you. Myriad birds take flight with shrieks that set your heart to rapidly beat. Night brought on a cacophony of sound that left you spellbound, scared, unable to distinguish the sounds of night from [the] terror of night warfare. . . . [D]aily the rain added to the marshy underfooting. With the heat and humidity, clothes and shoes mildewed and rotted off your body. Your bedding was always damp. The combination of all this nature caused jungle rot and fungi to grow whenever and wherever the skin was broken.[5]

For the first time in the war, members of the 754th TB had to use their tanks in combat. Small reconnaissance patrols were sent out to familiarize the crews with the surrounding area and on occasion ran into enemy resistance. "It was now we got our first good chance to use our small tanks," wrote David Dumbeck. "We were surprised as we did pretty well with them, but only because the Japs met us with mostly small arms fire. The machine guns we had on the tanks are what mowed down the Japs." Added Dumbeck, "[W]e had some pretty wicked battles."

On one patrol, the Japanese hit Dumbeck's lead tank with an antitank gun. "We did get hit finally by either a 37mm or a 75mm that blew off a track and knocked a hole through the tank," he recalled, "but no one even got hit by it. I guess our guardian angel was looking after us. It was a miracle no one was killed."[6]

Between December 25, 1943, and January 9, 1944, the Bougainville Marines were replaced by the Americal Division from New Caledonia. On January 30, with two Army divisions now holding the entire American pocket, the 754th TB detachment got its baptism of fire. On that date, an attacking force of infantry, light tanks from Company A, the SPM halftracks of the assault gun platoon, and a newly created platoon of 81mm mortars moved out to reduce a Japanese position opposite an American outpost near the mouth of the Torokina River, on the American right flank.

Moving along the coast, the Americans ran into a series of well-concealed Japanese pillboxes with swampy ground on both sides. Unable to flank the positions, the Americans attacked head-on. Wrote historian Harry Gailey, "Unfortunately the tank crews had buttoned up in order to escape small arms fire, and the crews could not locate the pillboxes."

Noticing this, S/Sgt. Jesse Drowley of the Americal Division climbed atop a tank and used tracer fire from the tank's antiaircraft gun to show the tankers where to fire. "The tank, under constant enemy fire, continued to within 20 feet of the pillbox where Staff Sergeant Drowley received a severe bullet wound in the chest. Refusing to return for medical treatment, he remained on the tank and continued to direct its progress until the enemy box was definitely located by the crew." Wounded again, Drowley stayed with the tanks until two more pillboxes were destroyed before allowing himself to be evacuated. For his unselfish act of bravery, and for helping to save two wounded comrades earlier in the day, Drowley was awarded the Medal of Honor, the only member of the Americal Division to receive one.[7]

Summing up the American assault, the 754th TB historian wrote, "This engagement was successful in that an untold number of enemy pillboxes were reduced, heavy casualties inflicted on the enemy and the perimeter extended and straightened. This action proved that tank–infantry teams are effective in jungle combat." In their baptism of fire, the 754th TB had two men killed and twelve wounded, and lost one light Stuart tank.[8]

Near the end of January, things became rosier for the 754th TB when new M4 Sherman medium tanks began to arrive. Noted David Dumbeck, "We were never so happy as when the medium heavy tanks came." Added the battalion historian, "They looked like and were a more formidable weapon with their three-inch armor plated turret and 75mm gun. . . . Receipt of these heavier tanks proved to be another big morale booster."[9]

The 754th TB detachment spent the next few months getting accustomed to their new tanks and in spite of their size, the crews discovered the new Shermans were actually cooler than the old Stuart. "The light tanks were made of thin steel and were quick to heat up inside," recalled Dumbeck. "[T]he heavier tanks, being thicker steel never heated up until we did a lot of firing, then it got hot from the shell casings. . . . We never went into battle with our tanks wearing less than full dress, that means helmet and all. That was orders, a man could be burned real bad [from the hot casings]."[10]

About this same time, the American tankers began painting over the bright white star insignias on the sides of their tanks. Through combat, tankers had discovered that the big American star was an inviting target to Japanese antitank guns.[11]

Although the 754th tankers on Bougainville responded to an occasional call for help from the infantry, they spent most of their time protecting the twin airstrips. Army planes were now using the airstrips to bomb nearby Rabaul so the Japanese on either end of Bougainville decided to move inward to capture the airstrips. Fortunately for the Americans, this movement of the Japanese was detected and the American perimeter was ready when the enemy attacked.[12]

On March 9, the Japanese attacked the northeast corner of the American perimeter, near Hill 700, a prominent feature overlooking the beach and the twin airstrips. Although two light tanks were sent forward to assist the 37th IDiv, neither tank could climb the steep slopes of Hill 700. "It wasn't until after the infantry positions were reconsolidated that tanks were able to assist in holding the hill," reported the battalion historian. That night, two Sherman tanks from Company A were positioned so that their fire could sweep "avenues of approach leading to the crest and the infantry positions." For perhaps the first time in the Pacific, infantry telephones were given to the tankers, which provided "ground-to-tank communication . . . in directing fires down these draws." After four days of

754th TB M4 Sherman medium tanks along the Bougainville coast, March 1944.
US ARMY

fruitless effort, the Japanese attacking the northeast corner backed off. The action now shifted a few hundred yards to the west, to the center of the American line.[13]

On March 11, the Japanese had moved in close enough to spray the center of the American enclave with mortar and artillery fire. At dawn on March 12, the Japanese overran seven 37th IDiv pillboxes and made a sizable lodgment in the American lines. Although the infantry called for tanks, the request was denied because the tank commanders were fearful the tanks might be used as stationary pillboxes. At 4:00 A.M. the next day, however, when the Japanese rushed forward again, four M4 Sherman tanks from the 1st Platoon, Company C, 754th TB rumbled to the front.[14]

The 754th TB historian recalled what happened next: "Our months of training on Guadalcanal paid off. Tanks in two waves led these assaults with three medium tanks leading the way, covered by two light tanks. Interspersed with this second wave of tanks were infantry troops which supplied close support to the tanks which in turn gave cover by canister shell fire to those units leading the attack."[15]

David Dumbeck was more graphic. He wrote, "There were thousands of [Japanese] with rifles and grenades and when they got to where they thought they were sure of taking our airstrip, we moved in with infantry hiding behind our tanks and gave them all we had, hour after hour. They fell like leaves after a heavy autumn frost. There were so many dead, our tanks had no place to go without running over bodies. The tracks of our tanks were a terrible mess of human flesh that later had to be removed, serving as a reminder of the terrible battle that had ensued. There were only a handful of Jap soldiers who ran back into the jungle and escaped." He added, "We all found that if it had not been for the [medium] tanks that came in the nick of time the Japs would of ran over us as their men out-numbered us ten to one."[16]

On the morning of March 15, the Japanese attacked again and made a small penetration to the west of the old break. This time, a platoon of Shermans from Company A, 754th TB moved up to help the infantry. A historian for the 37th IDiv recalled:

> The tanks lumbered forward directed by the infantry, who designated targets with smoke grenades and tracers. The attack was most successful, the big guns on the tanks blasting the Japanese out of their holes. Those who were not blasted were forced to keep their heads and tails low, and the infantry methodically cleaned up after the tanks. Twice, the Nips tried antitank mines but the infantry picked off the suicide mine-layers before they got close. Many of the Japanese quavered at the sight of the tanks bearing down on them and rather than risk their smashing shells or squashing treads, they committed suicide.

Two days later, when the Japanese attacked the same area, another combined infantry–tank attack drove them back again.[17]

On the evening of March 23, the Japanese regrouped and attacked again. Striking the center of the American perimeter, the Japanese pierced the 37th IDiv line and made a sizable salient. At 7:25 A.M. on March 24, the 3rd Platoon Shermans of Company A, 754th TB led a counterattack against the lodgment. Taking

754th TB "Popeye III," an M3A1 Stuart light tank, on Bougainville on March 16, 1944. US ARMY

the lead, the tanks shelled the Japanese position with 75mm cannon fire and then waited as the infantry rushed forward. Wrote historian Gailey, "The attacking riflemen used smoke grenades to indicate targets for the tank gunners, who then used their big guns to blast pillboxes, banyan roots, or whatever afforded the hapless Japanese some shelter. The Shermans' .50-caliber machine guns supported the advancing infantry squads, who literally rooted out the Japanese from the banyan trees. By noon the enemy salient had been annihilated."[18]

By the end of March, the Japanese were in full retreat and the Americans were on the offensive. By early April it was apparent that Rabaul was no longer a major threat. American bombers had neutralized Rabaul and the ever-growing U.S. Navy had chased the Japanese warships toward Truk. Instead of annihilating the Japanese on Bougainville, the Americans decided to contain the Japanese on either end of the island and let them wither away on the vine.[19]

For the most part, the 754th TB saw only occasional action after the infantry pushed into the wild jungles of Bougainville. On April 8, a platoon of tanks attacked with the Americal Division, near the village of Mavavia, about 3,000 yards east of the Torokina River, and captured a number of Japanese pillboxes. On April 19, in the same area, a platoon of tanks from Company A successfully helped rescue four men from the 24th IReg, the first black American infantry regiment to see combat in World War II.[20]

Five days later, on April 24, two platoons of Sherman tanks from Company A again assisted the black soldiers. The attack force advanced almost 1,200 yards east of the Mavavia River before the tanks were halted by swampy ground. All

754th TB, Bougainville Island, March 16, 1944. "Lucky Legs II," an M4 Sherman, spearheads the advance of the infantry of Company F, 129th IReg, 37th IDiv. US ARMY

along the way, the tank–infantry teams had knocked out numerous enemy strong points and had killed an "undetermined number of enemy troops." Said the 754th TB historian, "Here again, the success of these actions was due in large part to those jungle tactics developed on the 'Canal' and the close protection furnished by supported infantry."[21]

The assault of April 24 was the last offensive action for the 754th TB Bougainville detachment. Noted the 37th IDiv historian, "The 754th Tank Battalion and its tank-fire support saved a large number of casualties and set a pattern for capabilities and limitations of tanks in jungle warfare." Although American troops stayed on Bougainville until they were replaced by Australian troops in mid-December 1944, the battle for Bougainville was over long before the Americans left. For all practical purposes the battle ended after the unsuccessful Japanese attacks in March.[22]

On June 18, the New Caledonia detachment of the 754th TB joined the forward detachment on Bougainville. "Together as a complete unit, at last!" declared the tank historian. From the end of June 1944 until the American troops left in December, the 754th TB spent its time on Bougainville recuperating and training. The men knew full well that the war was far from over.[23]

During the fall of 1943, the Army went through a series of reorganizations. In Brisbane, Australia, the 1st Cavalry Division was reorganized so that its 7th Reconnaissance Squadron became the 603rd Light Tank Company (TCo) equipped with Stuart light tanks. The 603rd TCo thus became the first Army tank unit in General MacArthur's Southwest Pacific Area after the loss of the 192nd and 194th TBs on Bataan.[24]

In the United States, another separate tank battalion that would see action in the Pacific was formed on November 11. As a result of a reorganization of the 12th Armored Division, the 44th TB (Medium) was constituted near Watertown, Tennessee. Eight days later, at Schofield Barracks, the 762nd, 763rd, 766th, and 767th TBs, all light tank battalions, were redesignated medium battalions. After the assaults on Tarawa and Makin, the Army decided that more medium tank units were needed to fight the fanatical, dug-in Japanese.[25] With much more fighting foreseen in the Pacific, the Army wanted to be prepared.

CHAPTER TWELVE

Another Crack
in the Outer Barrier

The next stepping stone toward Japan in the Central Pacific was the Marshall Islands, 565 miles northwest of Tarawa and Makin. As early as August 1943, Admiral Nimitz had suggested several reasons to seize the Marshalls. Among other things, Nimitz believed the Marshalls would "provide bases for further advance toward communication lines vital to the enemy" and that "Allied lines of communication to the south and southwest Pacific would be strengthened." After much consideration, it was decided to take Kwajalein Atoll. The target date for the invasion was January 31, 1944.[1]

Sixty miles long and twenty miles wide, Kwajalein is the largest atoll in the world. Shaped like a giant banana, the atoll consists of a series of reefs and islands around a huge lagoon of some 800 square miles. The three most important islands in the atoll are Roi and Namur, a pair of connected islands at the top of the banana, and crescent-shaped Kwajalein Island at the very bottom. While the 4th MarDiv would invade Roi–Namur, the Army's 7th IDiv would capture Kwajalein. The soldiers would be supported by the 767th TB.[2]

Constituted at Schofield Barracks in February 1943, the 767th TB had been dutifully training for its first combat. On November 5, the battalion was attached to the 7th IDiv to facilitate tank-infantry cooperation. Noted one Army historian, "[A]s soon as reports began to flow in from the Gilberts, tank and infantry officers worked in close conjunction to prevent repetition of errors committed in that operation. To improve coordination, tank companies and platoons, as nearly as possible, were trained with the infantry battalion with which they were to work." On November 20, the 767th TB (Light) was redesignated a medium tank battalion. Companies A through C would replace their light tanks with medium tanks and a new company, Company D, would be added as a light tank company.[3]

Since there were no M4 Sherman tanks in Hawaii, the men were forced to borrow eight M3 Lee medium tanks from the 193rd TB, which recently had

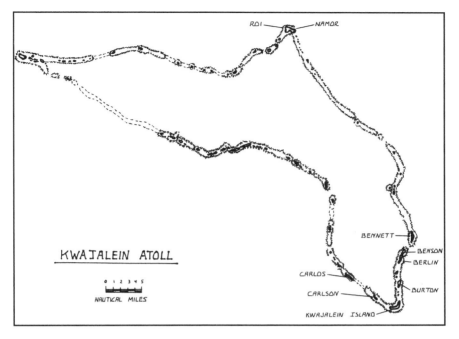

Kwajalein Atoll

returned from Makin. On December 26, with just four weeks left before the invasion, the 767th TB finally received M4A1 Sherman tanks. Immediately Companies A, B, and C began an intensive training program to familiarize themselves with the limitations and capabilities of their new Shermans.[4]

A group of M4A1 Shermans, 767th TB, landing at Kwajalein Island with fording trunks. US ARMY

Knowing that a number of tanks had been lost in underwater shell holes at Makin, the 767th TB went well beyond waterproofing their tanks. Non-oxide grease, waterproofing tape, lacquer, and in some cases, a layer of paint was applied to any surface that might leak. Huge tin intake and exhaust stacks were attached to each tank and all of the distributors, crankcases, and carburetors were ventilated by direct air lines. By the time the mechanics were through, each light and medium tank was capable of traveling through water seven feet deep.[5]

Another improvement made to the tanks as a direct result of the Gilbert operations was the attachment of an external telephone, equipped with a pressure button near the receiving end, "where the thumb will rest." On Sherman tanks, the telephone was mounted in a small box on the rear plate, directly over the left track. On the Stuart tanks, the box was placed in the center of the rear plating. When an infantryman needed to talk to the tank crew, he toggled a small switch located on the telephone mount, which in turn flashed a signal light inside the tank. When the tank stopped, the infantryman used the phone to converse with the tank commander in a "loud, slow, and very distinct" manner. Enough cord was attached to each phone to enable the infantryman to move to either side of the tank when talking or to "lay in a prone position." As noted in a confidential letter that went out to the 7th IDiv, "The enemy knows nothing of our new system. Let's keep it a secret—until it is too late to do him any good."[6]

And finally, operations on various islands had shown the need for a flame-throwing tank. Although infantry-held flamethrowers had been quite effective against enemy strong points, the infantryman carrying the device was vulnerable every time he worked his way close enough to use the weapon. Working together, Capt. Joseph L. Sohner, 767th TB operations officer, and Capt. Albert A. Todd, 767th TB maintenance officer, developed an efficient way of employing a flame-thrower in an M3 Stuart tank.[7]

Taking a standard M1A1 infantry flamethrower, Sohner and Todd cut the gun down to a shorter length so it could be fired through the hole left in the right-hand bow plate after the existing machine gun ball-mount was removed. Next, the two officers tackled the problem of the fuel tanks. The standard five-gallon infantry fuel tank gave twelve seconds of fire, which the tankers decided was not enough. By experimenting, the officers discovered that by removing the .30 caliber ammunition boxes on the right-hand floor of the tank, they had enough room for a twenty-five-gallon fuel tank. To propel the fuel, a fifteen-pound carbon dioxide cylinder from a typical fire extinguisher did nicely. Wrote Captain Sohner, "The problem of manufacture was taken to Honolulu Iron Works. The time limit for manufacture and installation was eight days. Approval for purchase was procured and the tanks were manufactured in four days." By the end of 1943, all eighteen M3A1 Stuart light tanks of Company D, 767th TB were equipped with flamethrowers.[8]

During the third week of January, after weeks of training, the invasion force began boarding transport ships. The tanks and men of the 767th TB were placed aboard three LSDs, one company on each vessel, eighteen tanks to a ship. Additionally, the eighteen flamethrowing light tanks of Company D and five M10 tank destroyers of a new assault gun platoon were divided among a few AKAs (Cargo Ship, Attack) and APAs. At twelve noon on January 22, the ships of the Southern Attack Force, carrying the 7th IDiv, reinforced, left Hawaii and headed west toward the Marshall Islands.[9]

Over the next few days, Navy planes from supporting aircraft carriers carried out a continuous bombardment of Kwajalein and nearby islands. Before sunup on January 31, small groups of infantrymen went ashore on three small islands northwest of Kwajalein and secured a passage through the outer ring of the atoll into the large lagoon.[10]

Next came the capture of two small islands codenamed "Carlson" and "Carlos." Situated two and a half and six and a half miles northwest of Kwajalein, respectively, the Army intended to use Carlson as a firebase for their artillery and Carlos as a supply depot. At 9:10 A.M., a handful of 7th IDiv soldiers and a few flamethrowing Stuart light tanks from the 2nd Platoon of Company D went ashore on both islands. With only a sprinkling of Japanese on either island, the defenders were quickly overrun and by 12:30 P.M. the American artillerists were setting up their guns on Carlson.[11]

Near 3:00 P.M., a general bombardment of Kwajalein Island began as American artillery, warships, Navy planes and Army B-24s pounded the island throughout the day and night. Wrote historian Philip A. Crowl, "The preparatory bombardment of Kwajalein Island was unprecedented in the Pacific in both volume and effectiveness."[12]

At 9:00 A.M. on February 1, the first wave of infantry-laden amtracs and new amphibian tanks headed toward the western tip of the island and Red Beaches 1 and 2. Four waves of infantry would land on each beach followed by a wave of light tanks and then a wave of mediums. On Red Beach 1, the 1st Platoon Stuarts

Company D/767th TB. M3A1 Stuart Light tanks on Carlson Island, Kwajalein Atoll on February 4, 1944. US ARMY

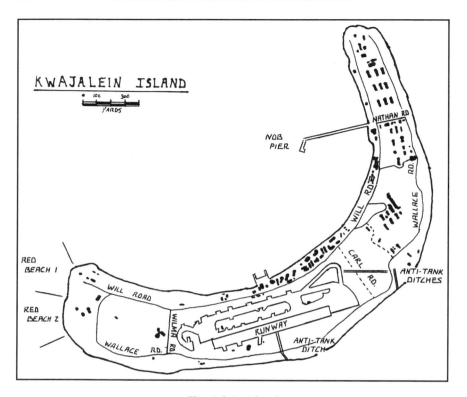

Kwajalein Island

of Company D, 767th TB would be followed by the 3rd Platoon Shermans of Company B. On Red Beach 2, the Stuarts of 3rd Platoon, Company D, would precede the Shermans of 1st Platoon, Company A.[13]

At 9:30, the first infantrymen touched shore. Seventeen minutes later the LCMs carrying the light tanks ground to a halt on the surrounding reef. In spite of the improved waterproofing, three of the six Stuart tanks on Red Beach 1 drowned out in the surf. Upon landing, it was discovered that only about half of the flame-thrower units in the tanks that reached shore were operational. Apparently, the water landings had shorted out some of the ignition systems.[14]

At 9:50, the LCMs carrying the medium tanks discharged their cargo at the reef. Two Shermans heading toward Red Beach 1 and one heading toward Red Beach 2 foundered in the surf, but the rest made it safely ashore. Within forty minutes, the tanks were moving out after the infantrymen, who were running into little enemy opposition. Unfortunately, as four Shermans of Company A from Red Beach 2 moved forward, they ran into marshy ground immediately behind the beachhead and bogged down.[15]

By 11:30, the infantry had pushed about 250 yards beyond the beaches. Moving rapidly, the infantry quickly overran what little resistance it met long before the tanks had time to deploy. At 12:05 P.M., the rest of the Company A Shermans began landing on Red Beach 2. Although one tank foundered in a large shell hole, the remaining eleven made it safely ashore, avoided the marshy ground, and eventually closed with the infantry.

On Red Beach 1, the 2nd Platoon of Company B reached shore at 2:00 P.M. without mishap. The six Shermans immediately went forward along a new road that had been hastily dug by bulldozers, and began supporting the renewed drive of the 7th IDiv. By 2:50, the infantry-tank assault, which was driving eastward along the lagoon side of Kwajalein, had penetrated another 500-plus yards to Wilma Road, one of many cross-island roads. To the south, along the ocean side, the infantry and tanks reached Wilma Road at about 2:30 P.M. and then halted to regroup for one final push before twilight.[16]

Directly beyond Wilma Road lay a Japanese airstrip. To the north lay Will Road, which ran the entire length of the island on the lagoon side and to the south lay Wallace Road, which traversed the entire length of the island on the ocean side. As early as 2:40, elements of the 184th IReg, 7th IDiv were advancing along Will Road while elements of the 32nd IReg, 7th IDiv were moving along Wallace Road. Near five o'clock, the entire advance was halted after about one-third of the airfield had been captured.[17]

With darkness rapidly approaching, all of the tanks already on the island were moved back to their respective landing beaches to replenish ammunition and fuel. At the same time, those tanks still afloat were brought ashore. When all was done, the 767th TB had ten light tanks of Company D on Kwajalein, while Companies A and B had fifteen mediums apiece and Company C had all eighteen ready for action. Additionally, the five open-turreted M10 tank destroyers from the Assault Gun Platoon, Headquarters Company, 767th TB were also ashore. Seven tanks, however, had been lost in the surf.

At 7:15 A.M. on February 2, while the eighteen Shermans of Company C remained in reserve, all of the other light and medium tanks and the five tank destroyers went forward to support the renewed infantry assaults. In reporting on the use of the flamethrowing Stuarts, Lt. Col. William G. Bray, commanding officer of the 767th TB wrote, "The light tank platoons supporting this operation were usually sent to the front-lines with the medium tank companies. . . . Flame throwers were used to ignite buildings, piles of rubbish and in a few cases, to burn out strong pillboxes. [However,] rubbish and debris hampered the light tanks in approaching close enough to most pillboxes for maximum effect of the weapon."[18]

Commenting on the M10 tank destroyers, Colonel Bray wrote, "The M10 Platoon operated with tactics almost identical to the medium tanks. As the M10 has an open turret, it was necessary to avoid trees, which might hide snipers. One submachine gunner in each vehicle was designated to be constantly alert for snipers. Many of the enemy were killed by sub-machine gunfire from the M10s. As the [cannon] gunner fired into a blockhouse, the balance of the crew got the enemy with sub-machine guns as they tried to leave the installation being fired upon."[19]

Two companies from the 184th IReg, 7th IDiv started forward with ten Shermans of Company B and four Stuarts of Company D on the lagoon side of the island. Noted Army historian Crowl:

> In the assault waves the medium tanks and infantry advanced abreast. Tanks sprayed the treetops with their .30-caliber machine gun fire, coming to a stop when it was necessary to turn their 75-mm guns against pillboxes. The standard procedure when one of these positions was encountered was for the tank to advance up to the pillbox with two or three infantrymen covering it and one tankman on the ground guiding his vehicle. The tank ordinarily then took its position so that its machine gun could cover the entrance to the pillbox while the 75-mm gun fired at the wall. Frequently while this action was taking place the infantry wave bypassed the structure and continued beating the ground ahead.

Working together, the tank-infantry assault passed beyond the airfield and by 10:40 A.M. had reached Carl Road, another cross-island roadway on the far end of the airfield.[20]

On the ocean side, the 32nd IReg, 7th IDiv started out moving parallel to Wallace Road, but almost immediately, a Japanese dual-purpose gun halted them until Navy dive-bombers knocked it out. Then, with the support of the medium tanks of Company A, and a few light tanks of Company D, the GIs pushed forward again. Within a few yards, however, the advance came up against an unexpected tank ditch running from the main runway almost to the ocean shore. While the tanks headed toward the runway to get around the ditch, the infantry kept moving until a Japanese pillbox opened up. Two moving Shermans fired at the pillbox, but when they failed to eliminate it, three Shermans turned around and rejoined the infantry. After a fifteen-minute firefight, the stubborn pillbox was finally destroyed and the three tanks headed toward the runway to catch up with their two brethren. Although a few more Japanese pockets were encountered, the 32nd IReg reached Carl Road about the same time that the 184th IReg did.[21]

As the Americans on the ocean side of Kwajalein looked out beyond Carl Road, they spotted a diagonal tank trap covered by interlocking rifle trenches and pillboxes. Fearing that the position could not be taken with only one company of medium tanks, the 32nd IReg commander called for another. Around 12:30 P.M., the tanks of Company B began moving over from the lagoon side.

When the Company B Shermans arrived, they moved in on the left side of the American line and lined up almost perpendicular to the Japanese right flank. At the same time, Company A moved up to Carl Road to fire directly into the Japanese position. Near 2:00 P.M., after a heavy preparatory bombardment by airplanes and artillery, the 32nd IReg and the tanks of Company A, 767th TB went forward.

The Americans advanced against the diagonal tank trap on a 225-yard front with the Sherman tanks in the lead, firing their .50-caliber machine guns. Once the tank trap was reached, the two companies of tankers discovered the ditch was too deep to cross, so they broke off their fire support and moved around to the right flank, heading toward Wallace Road. Once there, however, the crews discovered only a flimsy wooden bridge crossing over the tank trap. Unwilling to risk their 34-ton vehicles on the flimsy bridge, the tankers halted until they could figure out what to do next.

At this point, the entire advance ground to a halt. Without tank support the infantry could not go forward. Finally, two light and two medium tanks traveled out onto the sandy ocean beach and flanked the tank trap defenders. Coming up from behind, the tanks took the enemy by surprise and the American infantry surged forward. By using tank and infantry fire, and demolition charges set off by combat engineers, the entire Japanese strong point fell within thirty-five minutes of the tank flanking move.[22]

On the lagoon side, the 184th IReg had moved out without tank support, but after running into stiff resistance they too came to a halt. In the late afternoon, after hours of fighting, a handful of Shermans from Company B returned from the ocean side. However, after two tanks bogged down in some marshy land around Carl Road, the assault was ended for the night. At 6:30 P.M., after failing to extricate the two stuck tanks, the crews disabled the guns and evacuated the vehicles.[23]

On the ocean side, the advance ground to a halt around 6:45 P.M. and the Shermans and Stuarts retired to a bivouac area near the west end of the airstrip. About two-thirds of Kwajalein was now under American control, but there was still a lot of fighting ahead as the Japanese were squeezed into the northeastern tip of the island.[24]

At 7:00 A.M. on February 3, the medium tanks of Company A and the light tanks of the 1st Platoon, Company D moved up on the ocean side to assist the advance of the 32nd IReg, 7th IDiv. On the lagoon side, the medium tanks of Company B and the light tanks of the 3rd Platoon, Company D, moved up to help the 184th IReg, 7th IDiv.[25]

Following a ten-minute artillery bombardment, the entire line stepped off at 7:15 and advanced about 200 yards before the 32nd IReg on the ocean side came upon a collection of Japanese buildings known as the "Admiralty Area." A large concrete pillbox dominated the entrance to the area and two Sherman tanks and a platoon of engineers moved up to eliminate it. With the tanks firing their 75mm cannon and the engineers assaulting the pillbox with demolition charges, the Japanese defenders were soon chased out into the open and killed by small arms fire.[26]

Pushing through the Admiralty Area, the ocean side attackers soon found themselves following Kwajalein's crescent shape and curling northward towards the pointed tail end of the island.[27]

The initial advance of the 184th IReg had been without the aid of the B Company Shermans because of a misunderstanding between the tankers and their infantry guides. After the foot soldiers had gone only 200 yards, however, they came to a grinding halt when they ran into a concentration of Japanese pillboxes and rifle pits scattered among some wrecked buildings. Although the infantry attempted to infiltrate the area, they managed only to break themselves into small groups that became totally isolated from one another. When tank support was called, the Sherman crews discovered they could not fire into the buildings because of the scattered pockets of American infantrymen.[28]

For more than an hour the tanks had to sit idle while the infantry pulled back and reorganized. Then, around 9:45 A.M., with the tanks in the lead, the advance moved forward again. Unfortunately, this advance was no better than the last since the tanks moved out firing at targets of opportunity instead of firing at hot spots pinpointed by the infantry. When an infantry captain attempted to coordinate the movement of the tanks and infantry, he had trouble contacting the tank commander because most of the rear deck tank telephones had been shorted out by saltwater.[29]

The fighting along the lagoon side now broke down into individual firefights between small groups of GI's or individual tanks. Close to the shore, two infantrymen spotted a pair of Japanese machine guns innocently sitting out in the open beside a roadway. Fearing a trap, one of the soldiers rushed over and managed to get the attention of a medium tank commander. As the tank rumbled forward, a white flag suddenly popped up out of a ditch near the Japanese machine guns. Still fearing a trap, the tank opened fire. Reported historian Crowl, "[A] few moments later [the GI] crawled forward and found twelve dead enemy soldiers directly behind the guns in a camouflaged ditch, from which they could have fired at anyone curious enough to approach."[30]

Heavy Japanese fire continued to stall the advance along the lagoon side as the Americans tried to push their way eastward through wrecked buildings and rubble. Whenever a squad of infantrymen got pinned down, the tanks went forward to help, but with so many individual firefights going on at one time, the advance was going nowhere fast. Eventually it was decided to shift the assault around to the center of the island and assault the Japanese pocket of resistance from the south, pushing them into the lagoon. At the same time, a reserve battalion and a few tanks would continue eastward down the center of the island.[31]

By 4:00 P.M., the Americans had successfully shifted around the Japanese flank and were in position to push north. Four medium tanks of Company B and two M10 tank destroyers assisted in the push and in no time helped the infantry reach Will Road. Once the roadway was crossed, however, the tanks and infantry encountered dozens of enemy pillboxes, shelters, and gun emplacements covering the area between the roadway and the lagoon. After mortar fire was called in to soften up the area, the tanks and infantry pressed on. Near 6:00 P.M., the Japanese position collapsed and the assault team finally reached the beach.[32]

While the Japanese hot pocket was being crushed, the reserve battalion of infantry from the 184th IReg, supported by four Shermans from Company B and four Stuarts from Company D, had been pushing eastward. Once again, however, the attackers moved forward at a snail's pace. The tanks and infantry had to stop often to eliminate Japanese strong points or wait for engineers to come up and destroy enemy pillboxes and bunkers with demolition charges. By sunset, the entire lagoon-side assault had pushed only about 800 yards past its morning starting point and was well short of its objective of a cross-island road known as Nathan Road.[33]

The ocean-side assault made a little better progress as the 32nd IReg, along with the Shermans of Company A, the Stuarts of Company D and a few M10 tank destroyers followed the curve of the island toward the north. Near 2:00 P.M., the right flank, moving directly along the coast, reported it already had reached Nathan Road. (In reality, they were at a parallel road, 150 yards short of Nathan Road.) However, in the center of the island, the left flank of the 32nd IReg was running into all kinds of trouble.

Noted historian Crowl, "[The center] route lay through a maze of ruined buildings, debris, connecting trenches, and still active pillboxes, as well as shelters crowded with hiding enemy. The terrain and poor communications prevented tank-infantry cooperation, and while the tanks were reducing the enemy positions, the infantry had to work near [the tanks] rather than with them." Eventually the center group bypassed the pillboxes and debris and by 5:30 P.M. was adjacent to the right flank unit waiting behind what they thought was Nathan Road.

With darkness coming on, the entire American advance came to a halt. While the foot soldiers dug in for the night, the tanks returned to their bivouac areas. Then, around 7:00 P.M., the Japanese launched a series of uncoordinated counterattacks. Although the Japanese kept up their disjointed harassing attacks all night, they were never able to completely break the American line.[34]

While the slow advance was taking place on February 3, the 17th IReg, 7th IDiv, along with supporting units, invaded Burton Island, about three miles directly north of Kwajalein. Among all of the islands of Kwajalein Atoll, Burton Island, which measured only 1,800 yards long by 250 yards wide, was believed to contain the second-largest concentration of enemy troops. After two hours of preliminary bombardment, the infantry landed on the lagoon side of Burton at 9:35 and immediately pushed across the island toward the ocean shore. A few minutes later, the 2nd Platoon light tanks of Company D, 767th TB and six Sherman tanks from the 2nd Platoon of Company C came ashore.

As the medium tanks spread out across the entire width of the island, the crews discovered that because Burton Island was so narrow, only four tanks could work abreast as they pushed steadily northward. Working together, the tanks, infantry and a handful of engineers silenced numerous machine-gun nests, pillboxes and bunkers as the Shermans moved up first and blasted holes in the bunkers through which either the engineers tossed demolition charges or the infantry fired bazooka rockets. By nightfall, when the advance finally stopped, the Americans had captured about one-half of the island. While the infantry dug in on a defensive line across the island, the tanks pulled back to the landing beach to refuel and rearm.[35]

At 6:15 A.M. on February 4 on Kwajalein, all of the Company A Shermans, along with a platoon of B Company Shermans and a platoon of D Company Stuarts moved out of the tank bivouac area with a fresh battalion of infantry from the 32nd IReg, 7th IDiv, hoping to spearhead the final push toward the tip of the

767th TB/Company C, M4A1 Shermans on Burton Island (Kwajalein Atoll), February 4, 1944. US ARMY

island. After the February 3 advance, the remaining Japanese had been squeezed into an area measuring only 1,000 yards long by a tapering 400 yards wide. At 7:15, as the tanks and infantry moved past the maze of ruined buildings and Japanese strong points that had been bypassed the day before, they began taking heavy fire from hidden Japanese. Instead of ignoring the fire, the men and tanks turned to eliminate the pesky enemy and did not reach the front line until 10:00 A.M.[36]

On the lagoon side, the 184th IReg moved out at 7:15 A.M. without any tank support in an attempt to capture Nob Pier, the wooden structure jutting out into the lagoon. Almost immediately the advance ran into trouble as fire from a large air raid shelter halted the attackers until a few tanks from Company B rumbled up and threw a few 75mm shells into it. Then, suddenly, thirty-one Korean laborers and one Japanese soldier dashed out with their hands up. Within minutes, the prisoners were being herded to the rear under the watchful guns of a Company B tank.[37]

After this first large-scale surrender the Americans began taking more prisoners. In the center of the island, the fresh battalion of the 32nd IDiv and the tanks of the 3rd Platoon, Company B, 767th TB captured five Korean laborers in an underground shelter and then used the prisoners to persuade other laborers to surrender. In a short time, a total of thirty-three Korean workers had given themselves up.[38]

By noon, the 184th IReg and the tanks of the 1st and 2nd Platoon of Company B had reached the base of Nob Pier. Although 7th IDiv Headquarters had believed the pier would be heavily fortified, tankers and foot soldiers found the structure totally undefended. By 2:35 P.M., Nob Pier was firmly in American hands.[39]

On the ocean side, the tanks soon outdistanced the 32nd IDiv foot soldiers as the GIs fanned out across the entire tapering width of the island. When the infantry finally caught up to the tanks, the tanks and soldiers drove north until they came up against a large enemy blockhouse. Seven tanks stopped to fire cannon bursts into the structure and eliminate the position while the infantry moved around the sides and continued to root the enemy out of small spider holes. At 4:10 P.M., as the tanks and infantry were still fighting their way toward Kwajalein's northern tip, the 7th IDiv commander reported, "All organized resistance . . . has ceased." After that, most of the tanks were sent back to their bivouac areas. Unfortunately, the announcement was a bit premature.[40]

For the next three hours, the 32nd IReg continued to fight its way north over the last 150 yards of Kwajalein. Fortunately, a few 767th TB tanks had remained behind. Finally, at 7:20 P.M., the infantry reached the northern tip of Kwajalein and "all organized resistance" was finally eliminated.[41]

The assault on Burton Island continued on the morning of February 4 after a night of small, ineffective Japanese counterattacks. At 7:30 A.M., the 2nd and 3rd Platoon Shermans from Company C, 767th TB, assisted by a few flamethrowing Stuarts from Company D, moved out with the infantry close behind. Although the tank–infantry attack encountered a few areas of stubborn resistance, the entire island was in American hands by 1:37 P.M. Noted Colonel Bray, "The tank operations on Burton Island is especially interesting because of the smooth operation of the tank-infantry team. Here, the tanks moved in advance of the infantry and blasted strong points and the infantry then quickly moved in and finished all enemy resistance. This momentum was maintained to such an extent that the mission was completed in less than a day and a half."[42]

At 4:00 P.M., Colonel Bray received a message from 7th IDiv Headquarters to prepare the C Company tanks on Burton Island for another amphibious assault on two more atoll islands, specifically Berlin and Bennett Islands, still further north. At 11:00 P.M., the Shermans got back aboard their LCMs and at 10:30 A.M. the next morning, February 5, five Sherman tanks from the 1st Platoon landed on Berlin Island with a battalion of infantry. Fifteen minutes later, three Shermans from the 2nd Platoon and a battalion of infantry landed on Bennett Island.

At 11:45 A.M., when enemy resistance stiffened on Bennett Island, the Stuart tanks of the 2nd Platoon, Company D were brought ashore. Although a few dugouts gave the advancing infantry and tanks a bit of trouble, the Bennett Island defenders were soon overrun and the island was declared secure at 4:42 P.M. On Berlin Island, all resistance ended at 3:14.[43]

The final operation for the 767th TB on Kwajalein Atoll came a little while later when the Sherman tanks of the 1st Platoon of Company C preceded a platoon of infantrymen across a northern reef connecting Berlin with the next island north, Benson Island. Moving rapidly, the tank–infantry team brushed aside what few enemy defenders they found and secured the island with only one GI killed and one wounded.[44]

The assault on the southern islands of Kwajalein Atoll had cost the Americans 142 dead, two missing in action, and 845 wounded. Losses for the 767th TB were one killed by an accidental explosion, and eight wounded, mostly by sniper fire or shrapnel. Japanese losses amounted to almost 5,000 dead, and seventy-nine Japanese soldiers and 127 Korean laborers captured.[45]

Forty-five miles to the north, the 4th MarDiv had successfully captured the northern islands of Kwajalein Atoll, especially Roi and Namur Islands.[46]

The success of the Kwajalein Atoll operation proved that the Americans had learned well from the bloody assaults against Tarawa Atoll. A heavier, better concentration of ship, air and artillery fire had softened up the islands before any

American troops went ashore, and the tanks and infantry had worked together in teams to eliminate enemy pockets of resistance. Noted Colonel Bray, "We immediately adopted the formations . . . where one echelon of tanks are in front of the infantry, a second with the first line of infantry, and a third [usually the Stuart light tanks] just in rear of the advancing infantry. This formation was found to be very satisfactory."

Additionally, Colonel Bray noted with pride, "It is interesting to note out of seventy-two tanks participating in this operation, 113 ship to shore landings were made with the temporary loss of only seven tanks. This was accomplished by special care on the part of the tank crews, by superior waterproofing, foot reconnaissance guiding the tank ashore and the sincere efforts put forth by the [LCM] boat coxswain."[47]

Between February 5 and February 16, all of the tank companies were reloaded aboard their transports and sent back to Hawaii. By February 24, the 767th TB was back at Schofield Barracks. Commented the tank battalion historian, "This concluded the participation of the 767th Tank Battalion in the [Marshall Islands] in conjunction with the 7th Infantry Division. This operation resulted in the complete conquest of Kwajalein Island and islands adjacent to it in the Kwajalein Atoll—the first Japanese-owned territory to be conquered by American troops in this war."[48]

With the seemingly easy capture of Kwajalein Atoll, American commanders stepped up their plans to move farther into the Marshall Islands and capture Eniwetok Atoll, at the far northern end of the island group. The capture of Eniwetok Atoll would move American planes and ships 330 nautical miles closer to the Caroline Islands and the important Japanese naval base of Truk. On February 2, when it looked as though Kwajalein Atoll would fall without much trouble, Admiral Nimitz asked for permission to attack the northern atoll and was given the green light.[49]

On February 17, utilizing Marine Corps and Army troops, Nimitz began his invasion of Eniwetok. That same day, American carrier-based planes attacked Truk. In two days and one night of almost constant attacks, the Americans destroyed 275 Japanese planes and more than 200,000 tons of auxiliary shipping, although the Japanese had foreseen such an attack and had moved most of their combat ships out of the harbor. For all intents and purposes, Truk was rendered useless as a naval base and although the Japanese defenders on Eniwetok Atoll fought valiantly, they lacked air and sea support and after only six days the entire atoll was in American hands.[50] By the end of February 1944, Admiral Nimitz had isolated Truk and was already planning the next move that would bring him closer to Japan.

CHAPTER THIRTEEN

Isolating Rabaul

In December 1943, General MacArthur made another move to isolate Rabaul. On December 15, the 112th Cavalry Regiment (CReg) landed on the southwest tip of New Britain Island. Eleven days later, the 1st MarDiv stormed ashore at Cape Gloucester on the western tip of New Britain, and by December 29 had secured a Japanese airfield near Cape Gloucester.[1] Although Marine tanks saw action on New Britain, no Army tanks were involved.

While the New Britain invasion was in progress, MacArthur renewed his advance along the northern coast of New Guinea. Australian troops took the town of Finschhafen on the eastern tip of the Huon peninsula in early December and on January 2, 1944, the American 32nd IDiv landed at Saidor, about 100 miles west along the coast. By mid-January, the Allies were in firm control of western New Britain and the Huon Peninsula, and had secured the Vitiaz and Dampier straits between the two land masses. At the same time, MacArthur learned that the Admiralty Islands, part of the Bismarck Archipelago, were lightly defended. Lying 360 miles west of Rabaul, the capture of the Admiralties would further isolate Rabaul and provide MacArthur with a new base for further movement along the New Guinea coast.[2]

Although MacArthur had planned to invade the Admiralty Islands near the end of March, the successes of his rival, Admiral Nimitz, in the central Pacific forced him to advance his timetable by a full month. By capturing the Admiralty Islands, MacArthur was hoping to use the natural anchorage at Seeadler Harbor as a base to make his next move toward Hollandia, on the coast of far western Dutch New Guinea.[3]

Although the impending invasion had been in the works since November 1943, MacArthur's decision to launch his attack by the end of February caught everyone by surprise. Since the decision came on February 24, his staff and subordinates had only five days to prepare for the February 29 invasion.

In record time, however, the invasion fleet came together and transported the troops of the 1st Cavalry Division (CDiv) from Australia to the Admiralties. Accompanying the cavalrymen was the 603rd Tank Company, which had been in existence for only about four months and only recently had been reorganized as a medium tank unit. During the Admiralties operations however, the 603rd TCo would be using both light and medium tanks.[4]

The first of the Admiralties to be invaded was Los Negros Island. Approximately fifteen miles long and shaped like a backward letter "C," Los Negros was invaded on February 29 when elements of the 1st CDiv landed on the narrow back of the "C" and quickly overran the sole island airfield. Over the next few days, the cavalrymen consolidated their beachhead, and on March 6, three Stuart light tanks from the 603rd TCo went ashore to offer what aid they could. Because large portions of Los Negros were covered with heavy undergrowth, thick jungle vegetation, and rolling ridgelines, the tanks saw very little action. In fact, the thick, gooey clay soil of the island slowed the tanks more than did enemy fire.[5]

While Los Negros was being consolidated, the 1st CDiv turned its attention toward big Manus Island, just west of Los Negros and separated from the smaller island by only a narrow strait. On March 11, small patrols of cavalrymen easily captured two small unoccupied islands just north of Manus that were to be used as artillery bases. But on a third island, Hauwei Island, about five miles northeast of Manus, the cavalrymen ran into an unexpected ambush. After extricating them-

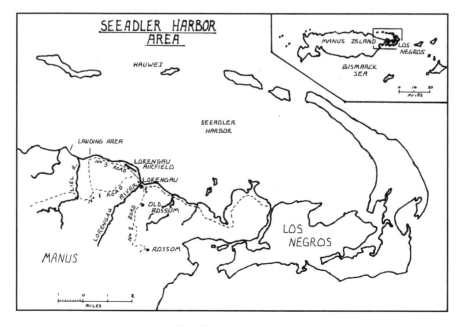

Seeadler Harbor Area

selves from the trap, the cavalrymen called for armor, and at 9:00 A.M. on March 13, a 603rd TCo M4A1 Sherman medium tank rumbled ashore for the day's advance.

At ten o'clock, the cavalrymen began advancing eastward in a line abreast across the 400-yard wide island, with the lone tank operating on the south flank. Although the Japanese possessed numerous machine guns and rifles, they lacked any antitank weapons. When the cavalrymen encountered a large enemy bunker on the south shore, the tank moved forward. Four direct shots from the 75mm gun and four well-placed mortar rounds quickly reduced the emplacement to rubble. By noon the Americans were on the eastern shore.[6]

With the three smaller islands captured, the 1st CDiv soon brought over artillery and began shelling the northern coast of Manus Island. The largest island in the Admiralties, Manus measured roughly forty-nine miles east to west by sixteen miles north to south. Heavily wooded and mountainous, the northern coast had to be secured if MacArthur was going to use Seeadler Harbor as a base for his warships.[7]

On March 15, a brigade from the 1st CDiv stormed the northern shore of Manus, landing just west of Lorengau airfield. Although the foot soldiers met little Japanese resistance, they were slowed in their advance by the clinging red mud that was made even more gooey due to recent rains. By nightfall, however, the muddied troopers had occupied a ridgeline overlooking the western end of the airstrip.[8]

The next morning, March 16, one light and two medium tanks from the 603rd TCo landed on Manus. Unable to maneuver through the clingy, slippery mud by themselves, the tanks elicited the aid of an Army bulldozer. Wrote Army historian John Miller, Jr., "The tanks had been hauled through the jungle with the aid of a D7 bulldozer which cut down grades, cleared undergrowth, and towed the tanks when they [got] stuck." When the three tanks finally reached the front, the cavalrymen moved forward, silenced a few enemy emplacements and reached an inland road known as Number 1 Road. Once there, the foot soldiers turned and began following the road eastward.[9]

One medium tank and the helpful bulldozer stayed with the cavalrymen as they advanced up Number 1 Road. Hemmed in by a heavy jungle, the tank-cavalry team had to reduce each Japanese bunker by storm once they encountered it. As the M4A1 Sherman tank moved forward and fired point-blank, the cavalrymen rushed forward and lobbed in hand grenades. By the end of the day the slow but steady advance had carried the attacking force to within 100 yards of the eastern end of Lorengau airfield.[10]

Along the coast, a squadron of cavalrymen tried to move into the area south of the airstrip, but ran into a mess of Japanese bunkers and gun emplacements. Unable to move through the thick jungle, the troopers were ordered to advance eastward down the airstrip itself and seize the eastern end. Assisting the men would be the M3A1 Stuart light tanks from the 603rd TCo.

As the cavalry troopers and tanks moved east down the airstrip they came under heavy fire from enemy bunkers south of the runway. As the cavalrymen returned fire, some of their shots inadvertently landed among a group of troopers that had managed to work their way in behind the enemy. Since the tanks were equipped with two-way radios, they knew that American troops were behind the Japanese emplacements and refused to fire, but because of their "buttoned up" condition they could not relay the information to the cavalrymen around them.[11]

Finally, after some time, the cavalry troopers behind the Japanese pulled back, even though their fire was inflicting the most damage upon the Japanese positions. Although the fire team on the runway continued the battle for a few more hours, the tanks and cavalrymen eventually backed away and left the eastern half of the airstrip in Japanese hands for the night.[12]

On March 17, fresh troopers were brought up to attack the line of Japanese pillboxes and bunkers guarding the southern edge of the airstrip. Prior to the advance, however, twenty-four 81mm mortars, two 37mm antitank guns, and the two Stuart tanks pulverized the positions. When the cavalrymen finally went forward at 10:33 A.M. they discovered that the heavy concentrated fire had "practically wiped out all enemy resistance." By 1:00 P.M., the entire Lorengau airfield had been captured and a link had been made with the troops on Number 1 Road.[13]

While the airstrip was being taken, the squadron of cavalrymen on Number 1 Road had been pushing eastward. Number 1 Road ran parallel to the coast, although further inland, until it passed beneath Lorengau airfield. It then turned sharply north to link up with Number 3 Road, which ran along the coast. As the cavalrymen moved forward, assisted by two medium tanks and a single light tank, they met little enemy resistance. Whenever a bunker complex was encountered, the cavalry troopers stepped aside and the medium tanks blasted it point-blank. The only casualty among the tanks occurred when the light tank rolled over a Japanese land mine and lost a track. By 1:00 P.M., the tanks and troopers reached the Number 3 Road junction and a linkup was made with the cavalrymen and tanks moving east from the airfield.[14]

The combined force continued eastward toward the Lorengau River and, beyond that, the village of Lorengau. Although most of the Japanese defenders on Manus had already been killed, the few retreating survivors buried antitank and antipersonnel mines all along the roadway and caused the Americans to take two hours to advance the 1,500 yards to Lorengau River. At 3:00 P.M., when the Americans finally reached the river, a reconnaissance party was fired on from a strong series of enemy bunkers on hills when it tried to cross the water. Satisfied with the day's gain, the cavalrymen and tankers dug in for the night.[15]

The next morning, March 18, the cavalrymen stormed across the river, suffering surprisingly few casualties. Although the Japanese had planted electronically controlled antipersonnel mines between the river and the hill, the mines were rendered useless when a sharp-eyed cavalryman spotted the wire and cut it. By early afternoon the cavalry assault had taken Lorengau village.[16]

While one cavalry troop was advancing toward Lorengau, another troop moved south down another island roadway, Number 2 Road, toward the village of Rossum. Since few Japanese had been around Lorengau, the Americans believed that most of the survivors had fled inland toward Rossum. After moving only a short distance, however, the troopers ran into a couple of strong Japanese road-blocks and called for armor support.

On the morning of March 20, one light tank, one bulldozer and a semi-trailer truck carrying supplies moved down Number 2 Road to assist the stalled drive. Although hampered by difficult terrain, the tanks and cavalrymen worked together and eventually knocked out the enemy roadblock. However, another 300 yards down the road, near the village of Old Rossum, the patrol ran into more bunkers and pillboxes and about 150 Japanese soldiers. Although the light tank managed to knock out two of the bunkers, several of the cavalrymen succumbed to the high heat and humidity of Manus and their commander had to ask for his unit to be replaced.

When the request was granted, the cavalrymen easily withdrew down Number 2 Road but when the tank tried backing down the narrow trail, it rolled over a Japanese landmine and lost a track. Ignoring incoming enemy fire, the bulldozer operator hooked a cable to the light tank and towed it all the way back to Lorengau. Left behind, however, was the semi-trailer truck.[17]

The next day was wasted looking for nonexistent trails around the Japanese position, so on March 22 a squadron of cavalry, accompanied by an M4A1 medium tank and a bulldozer, advanced down Number 2 Road again. This time, it was the bulldozer that hit a land mine and threw a track. After that, a mine-detecting squad led the way, inching along ever so slowly. Whenever a concentration of Japanese bunkers was found, the cavalrymen and the tank pulled back and let the American artillery on the nearby islands pummel the area. After a sufficient amount of time, the shelling stopped and the troopers and tank mopped up what was left. By 6:50 P.M., the combat patrol reached the northern edge of Old Rossum where it stopped for the night.[18]

The next morning, when the cavalrymen and a light tank tried to renew the advance, they found the roadway blocked by more mines and the abandoned semi-trailer truck, which the Japanese had set on fire. The tank was unable to advance past the burning truck, so the cavalry troopers moved on without armored support. By the end of the day, however, the soldiers had managed to silence twenty-one Japanese bunkers and advance about 200 yards south of the burning truck.

By the next morning, the burned-out truck had been removed and a 603rd TCo Sherman was able to accompany the cavalrymen on their advance. The tank, however, was not always appreciated. Noted an Army historian, "Tanks drew enemy fire, which was extremely costly to the men near the tank. In addition, there were no means of communicating with the tank commander except through the pistol port. . . . The [cavalrymen] thought the tank was more of a hindrance than a help."[19]

By nightfall, the tank–cavalry team had gained only a few hundred yards, and in six days of fighting the 1st CDiv had advanced only 2,000 yards south of Lorengau. Realizing that something had to be done to break the stalemate on Number 2

603rd TCo M4 "Sloppy Joe" at Lorengau, Manus Island, Admiralty Islands, March 24, 45. This tank destroyed a Japanese antitank gun, a radio station, and 22 Japanese pillboxes on Hauwei and Manus Islands. US NAVY

Road, a new squadron of cavalry troopers moved into the area on March 25 to relieve their exhausted comrades. At the same time, Australian planes dropped 500-pound bombs along the trail.

When the planes were finished, the American artillery fired into the Japanese positions. Then, even before the artillery was through, cavalry reinforcements and two Sherman tanks and one Stuart from the 603rd TCo started down the road. Once again, the advance was agonizingly slow, since the road had to be checked for mines. In spite of the precautions, one Sherman blew a track on a hidden mine and had to be pulled out of the way by a bulldozer before the other two tanks could proceed. Continuing forward, the remaining Sherman and the Stuart soon joined by the cavalrymen in an assault against a ridgeline infested with Japanese bunkers.

Through dogged determination, the cavalry troopers clawed their way up the ridge until they were right on top of the enemy positions. At this point the two tanks ceased firing from long range and rumbled forward to fire their cannons point-blank into the Japanese bunkers. Those positions that could not be reduced were simply buried by the bulldozer. By 5:00 P.M. all enemy resistance along the ridgeline had ceased and the cavalrymen dug in along the crest for the night. From their vantage point atop the ridge, the troopers could see there were no more Japanese bunkers. The last heavy concentration of Japanese gun emplacements along Number 2 Road had been taken.[20]

By the end of March, 1944, the Americans had full possession of the northern coast of Manus Island, all of Los Negros, and the huge anchorage of Seeadler Harbor. With the Admiralty Islands under American control, General MacArthur sought to invade New Ireland Island, which ran at a northwest–southeast diagonal above New Britain Island and Rabaul. MacArthur especially had his sights set on the Japanese base at Kavieng on the northwestern tip of New Ireland, but Adm. William "Bull" Halsey talked him out of it. With Rabaul under increasing pressure, the Japanese had already withdrawn most of their ships, planes and troops from the region. Instead of invading New Ireland, Halsey suggested isolating the position even further by taking Emirau Island, halfway between New Ireland and the Admiralties. On March 14, U.S. Marines stormed ashore on unoccupied Emirau and the Americans immediately began building an airfield and PT-boat base.[21]

With the capture of the Admiralty Islands and Emirau Island, and the earlier toehold on New Britain Island, the entire Bismarck Archipelago was now under American control. General MacArthur then began planning his next move along the New Guinea coast and eventually back to the Philippines.[22]

CHAPTER FOURTEEN

Leapfrogging the New Guinea Coast

With the increased American activity in the Pacific in early 1944, it was deemed necessary to move a few more independent tank battalions from the United States to the Pacific as soon as possible.

In early March, the 44th, 706th, and 711th TBs moved to the West Coast in preparation for their move overseas.[1]

The first to leave was the 711th TB, which departed Portland, Oregon, on the night of March 22–23 and reached Hawaii on March 29. Once there, the 711th TB began "undergoing amphibious training and tank–infantry tactics . . . with the 98th Infantry Division."[2]

The 44th TB also departed Portland on March 22–23, but its ship soon developed trouble and had to make a detour to Los Angeles. On March 27, after the repairs were completed, the ship steamed west again. Commented the battalion historian, "On this day when well out to sea our destination was announced—Finschhafen, New Guinea." On April 21, the 44th TB finally reached the eastern end of New Guinea and on May 11 the battalion landed at Finschhafen. Attached to the Sixth Army, the 44th TB joined the 603rd Tank Company as the only Army tank units in General MacArthur's southwest Pacific area of operations.[3]

The final unit to move to the Pacific was the 706th TB. Setting out from Seattle on March 28, the battalion reached Honolulu harbor on April 3, where it was eventually attached to the 77th IDiv.[4]

General MacArthur's capture of the Admiralty Islands not only isolated Rabaul but frightened the Japanese who had been assembling near Madang on the northern coast of New Guinea. Fearful that MacArthur would leapfrog behind them and cut off their line of retreat, the Madang Japanese began retreating along the coast toward Wewak, about 150 miles away.

Unknown to the Japanese, MacArthur did plan to leapfrog along the New Guinea coast and land near the village of Hollandia, about 150 miles west of

Wewak. MacArthur reasoned that a landing at Hollandia would totally isolate the Japanese defenders at Wewak and cut them off from their supply bases in the Dutch East Indies. At the same time, it would provide him with another excellent anchorage and another forward air base to cover his continuing drive toward the Philippines.[5]

American intelligence had discovered that although the Japanese were stock-piling close to 350 fighter and bomber planes at Hollandia to help cover their troops at Wewak, their land forces around Hollandia were very weak. In early March, after MacArthur received approval for an April 22 invasion of Hollandia, he began a heavy aerial bombing campaign of the area by long-range B-24 bombers and P-38 fighters. By the time of the American landings, very few Japan-ese planes were still airworthy.[6]

On April 22, the 24th and 41st Infantry Divisions landed unopposed twenty-five miles apart on either side of Hollandia, while the 163rd IReg, 41st IDiv landed without incident on Aitape, halfway between Wewak and Hollandia. The next day, the 24th and 41st divisions began moving east and west respectively, attempting to encircle Hollandia and capture three enemy airfields. Since most of the Japanese in the area were rear-echelon service personnel, they fled into the jungle and headed northwest to Sarmi, about 120 miles away.

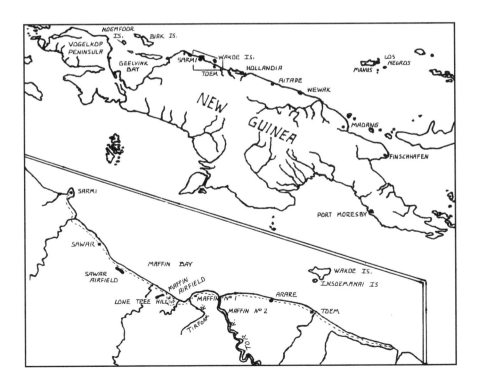

New Guinea

The two American divisions were slowed by thick jungle terrain and rain-swollen streams, but managed to encircle Hollandia and link up with each other on April 26. When they eventually overran Hollandia and the three airfields, the infantrymen found 340 wrecked Japanese aircraft, mute testimony to the harsh accuracy of the bombers and fighter planes.[7] Although the 603rd TCo was brought over from the Admiralty Islands to support the operation, the thick jungle had made it impossible to employ tanks. Fortunately, the lack of Japanese opposition made their use unnecessary.

Although MacArthur's successful leapfrog to Hollandia had trapped the Japanese along the middle of the New Guinea coast, they were far from defeated. MacArthur's next move was to consolidate his gains by moving his Australian troops west along the coast to keep pressure on the Japanese and prevent them from attacking Aitape or Hollandia before either site could be fortified. At the same time, MacArthur looked farther down the coast.[8]

MacArthur's next objectives in his northern New Guinea campaign were the Wakde Islands, three miles off the New Guinea coast and about 100 miles west of Hollandia. Additionally, MacArthur wanted to seize the settlement of Sarmi, about twenty miles west of Wakde Island. Although the Wakde Islands consisted of two islands, tiny Insoemanai and the much larger Insoemoar (which the Americans referred to as "Wakde" throughout the operation), MacArthur was interested only in the latter, which contained an excellent Japanese airfield. Part of the 41st IDiv, fresh from its unopposed captures of Hollandia and Aitape, would make the Wakde landings assisted by the 603rd TCo.[9]

As the invasion date of May 18 drew near, General MacArthur decided to add Biak Island to the mix. Located off the northwest coast of Dutch New Guinea, Biak was an island large enough to support a heavy bomber airstrip, which would be used to support Admiral Nimitz's central Pacific drive through the Marianas and Palau Islands. The date set for the Biak invasion was May 27.[10]

For the invasion of Wakde, the American commanders decided to seize a few nearby spots along the New Guinea coast to use as fire bases for their artillery and mortars. On May 17, without a hitch, the 41st IDiv stormed ashore near the settlement of Arare, about four and a half miles southwest of Wakde, and tiny Insoemanai Island, about 3,500 yards off Wakde's southern shore. By early afternoon, the artillery was set up on Arare and the mortars and heavy machine guns were in position on Insoemanai. In response, the Japanese on Wakde began firing their own machine guns and mortars at Insoemanai, which in turn drew a responding fire from the Americans.

Almost immediately, engineer units attached to the 41st IDiv began enlarging the Arare beachhead and bulldozed a road eastward to the settlement of Toem, just opposite Wakde. In mid-morning, M4A1 medium tanks of the 1st Platoon, 603rd TCo came ashore at Arare and went into bivouac. If needed, they could move to either end of the beachhead or down the new road to Toem.[11]

Wakde Island, only 3,000 yards long by 1,200 yards wide, was dominated by the Japanese airstrip, which took up almost half of the island. Although mostly

603rd TCo M4A1 Sherman tanks at Arara, New Guinea, May 17, 1944. US ARMY

flat, Wakde did have a raised knoll on a small fingerlike peninsula that jutted out from the southeastern shore. A number of coral caves were also dug into a slightly raised area in the northeastern corner of the island. Defending Wakde were 800 Japanese soldiers who had built hundreds of pillboxes, machine-gun emplacements, and two well-constructed concrete air-raid shelters.[12]

Early on the morning of May 18, 1944, Wakde was rocked by a heavy pre-invasion bombardment. Shortly after 9:00 A.M., troops from the 163rd IReg, 41st IDiv were transported from the Arare beachhead to Wakde, landing on the southern shore, near the base of the fingerlike peninsula. The Japanese resisted with a heavy concentration of machine gun and rifle fire, but the Americans would not be denied. At 9:25, as more infantry continued to arrive from the mainland, the four Sherman tanks of the 1st Platoon, 603rd TCo attempted the transfer. Unfortunately, one tank shorted out its electrical system on the Arare beach and a second rumbled off the ramp of its LCM at Wakde and disappeared into seven feet of water.[13] Before the operation was even a half hour old, the 603rd TCo had lost half its tanks.[14]

While soldiers from Company A, 163rd IReg turned southeast and cleared the peninsula, Company C moved directly north toward the center of the airstrip. Companies B and F, accompanied by the two tanks that managed to reach Wakde, pushed west toward a collection of prewar plantation houses. Coming upon three

Japanese pillboxes, the two tanks fired "intensely" and blew the emplacements "into the air." Moving in among the plantation houses, the tanks and infantry eventually cleaned out all resistance through the combined use of tank cannons and hand grenades.[15]

Leaving behind a platoon to mop up the area, the two infantry companies turned north to capture the western end of the airstrip while the two M4A1 Shermans returned to the beachhead to replenish their ammunition. After rearming, the tanks responded to a call from Company C, 163rd IReg, which had run into a number of Japanese bunkers near the center of the airstrip. A 41st IDiv historian wrote, "Now [C Company] used tank 75s to stun pillbox garrisons, then lobbed grenades into fireports, [and] shot dead any Jap who showed himself." By 11:30 Company C and the two tanks had managed to fight their way up to the airstrip.[16]

At about this time, the infantry platoon that had been mopping up the plantation area called for assistance from the two tanks. Rushing to the area, along with the men of Company A who had finished clearing out the peninsula, the tanks found the platoon stopped by a pesky enemy machine-gun nest. Noted the historian of the 41st IDiv, "It took a 30 minutes' battle around noon, with rifles, grenades, tank MGs [machine guns]—even bayonets—to clear the plantation houses." By noon, the defenders finally were eliminated and the tanks returned to the beachhead to once again replenish their ammunition.[17]

After rearming, the two tanks set out to support Company A on a drive to clear out the western end of Wakde but one tank broke down and had to be left behind. Moving along the southwestern shore, the infantry and the lone tank made good progress until they ran into three strong Japanese bunkers. With a squad of foot soldiers providing covering fire on each side of the tank, the Sherman moved to within 20 feet of the emplacements and blasted them with cannon fire. When small groups of Japanese soldiers in trenches behind the bunkers attempted to charge the tanks, the flanking squads and the tank itself cut them down. With the bunker complex area silenced, the tank and the Company A infantrymen easily cleared the rest of the western end of Wakde and then turned north. Around 1:30 P.M., they became the first American soldiers to reach the northern shore.[18]

By early afternoon, more than half of Wakde Island had been captured. Company A, 163rd IReg and the lone 603rd TCo Sherman had turned east after reaching the north shore, north of the airstrip, and had pushed almost to the center of the island. At the same time, the other three rifle companies had been working on the south side of the airstrip and had managed to eliminate all of the Japanese defenders in the center of the island. The only remaining pockets of resistance were southeast of the airstrip and in the northeastern corner of the island, among the coral caves. Near 3:45 P.M., the Americans made one last coordinated attack along the entire front.

The single Sherman tank of the 1st Platoon, 603rd TCo remained on the left flank with Company A, while two additional tanks that had been brought over from the mainland were kept in reserve. Although Company A and its supporting tank pushed all the way to within 100 yards of the east end of the airstrip, the attack by the other three rifle companies bogged down. Even after the two new tanks were called over, the GIs could advance no more than 300 yards from their starting point. When the soldiers dug in for the night, they were still 450 yards short of the east end of the airstrip.[19]

On the morning of May 19, Company A was instructed to hold its advance position north of the airstrip while the other companies attacked eastward. All three functional tanks on Wakde would now support the renewed drive. At 9:15 A.M., an hour-long mortar and artillery barrage rained down upon the Japanese. Then, at 10:15, Company C, 163rd IReg and the three medium tanks began moving east along the southern shore.

The historian for the 41st IDiv recalled:

Up the eastern slope toward the Japs marched C, with three clanking, throbbing tanks. A few Jap rifles cracked. Tank MGs began strafing . . . A Jap charged [one] tank. At first the Jap seemed bent on putting rifle bullets down the 75 barrel, then mounted the tank as if to jab [his] bayonet down an open hatch. As he topped the tank, [Lieutenant Walter] Larson and [Sergeant] Seeger gunned him down. An unarmed Jap leaped on [another] tank, but [Lieutenant Floyd] Stanfield was able to determine just what the Jap had in mind; the Jap died too soon.

[The third] tank bypassed a slit trench full of Nips. To recall the tank, a rifleman exposed himself to hammer on the turret with a gunstock. Finally, we turned the tank and brought his guns to bear on the trench, then finished the Japs off with a few grenades and rifle-fire. We slew thirteen Japs and [had] one Yank wounded.[20]

Working methodically, the tanks managed to silence each enemy strong point while the infantrymen killed any Japanese soldier who tried to escape. As the advance reached the east end of the island and swung northward, the GIs and tankers began rooting out the Japanese hiding in the shallow coral caves along the eastern beach.[21]

Meanwhile, Companies B and F (both 163rd IReg) moved across the middle of the island toward the northeast corner. After running into numerous Japanese positions, the infantry called for tanks. At 10:30, two tanks that had been helping Company C rumbled over and began blasting at the annoying enemy emplacements and at Japanese soldiers hiding among the wreckage of shattered airplanes and in foxholes covered by heavy brush. Noted historian Robert Ross Smith, "This brush was difficult for the soldiers afoot to penetrate but the tanks, spraying every likely hiding place with machine-gun fire, rapidly broke paths through." Added the 41st IDiv historian, "Our tanks crawled over huge debris piles and blazed down with MGs while we searched out what they had missed." Since every inch of the heavy brush had to be inspected for hidden enemy soldiers, the advance moved along at a snail's pace. It was not until 2:00 P.M. that Companies B and F, and the two accompanying tanks reached the eastern end of the airstrip.

By 4:00 P.M., the Americans had squeezed the Japanese into the coastal caves in a small northeastern corner of Wakde. Satisfied with the day's progress, the infantry commander had his men throw up a night defense around the pocket and then moved most of the men back toward the beachhead for their first hot meal in two days. Having fought all day long, the three Sherman tanks of the 603rd TCo pulled back to rearm and refuel and prepare for the next day's advance.[22]

At 9:00 A.M. on May 20, all four rifle companies advanced without the aid of the tanks. Noted the 41st IDiv historian, "A tank could not approach on that narrow beach, nor depress its 75 from above to shoot into the caves." The few remaining Japanese soldiers inside the coral caves were quickly buried alive by demolition charges. In just a few hours, the Japanese pocket had crumbled and Wakde Island was declared secure. At least 800 Japanese soldiers died on Wakde, while the Americans lost forty-three, none of them tankers. Wrote the 41st IDiv historian, "The tanks certainly saved us more casualties."[23]

Even while the fighting was in progress, Army engineers had begun filling in the shell craters on the Wakde airstrip. On the afternoon of May 21, the first American planes began landing on Wakde. With his new advance air base in operation, General MacArthur made his next leapfrog move along the New Guinea coast.[24]

Beginning on May 23, the Americans at Arare began moving west toward the Japanese airfields near Sarmi, sixteen miles away. Infantrymen from the independent 158th Regimental Combat Team (RCT) moved steadily forward along the coast over a narrow jungle road for about five miles before running into large numbers of Japanese soldiers who had retreated from the Arare area. As the 158th RCT tried to cross the Tirfoam River it ran into stiff resistance. Four Sherman tanks from the 1st Platoon, 603rd TCo, recently back on the mainland from Wakde, moved forward to eliminate the enemy positions but a Japanese antitank gun on the opposite side of the river damaged three tanks before it could be eliminated with return fire. After that, all four Shermans withdrew to Arare while the infantry called in artillery and mortar fire.[25]

Forging ahead, the infantry crossed the Tirfoam but advanced only one mile more before running into further resistance, this time near an eminence known as Lone Tree Hill. From May 25 through May 30 the GIs tried unsuccessfully to move around the hill and capture a nearby Japanese airfield. Noted historian Smith, "Tanks would have been of great help to [the 158th RCT], but the bridge over Tirfoam could not bear their weight, and the road west of the stream was in such disrepair that tanks probably could not have negotiated it." The Americans eventually brought two 603rd TCo tanks to the front line by shuttling them along the coast in two LCMs and then driving them inland through the jungle, but even these could not break the stalemate.[26]

Unable to break through, the Americans pulled back behind the Tirfoam and went into a defensive stance behind a perimeter that stretched twelve miles along the coast, from the Tirfoam River on the west to the village of Toem on the east. During the next week, the Japanese worked their way south of the strung-out American positions and made repeated attacks against the isolated units. Although the GIs took heavy casualties, their lines never broke. By June 5, when troops of the 6th IDiv began arriving as reinforcements, the Americans went back on the offensive.[27]

On June 8, with the 6th IDiv guarding the coastline defenses, the 158th RCT, supported by the 1st Platoon, 603rd TCo, began moving west again. About 1,500 yards east of the Tirfoam River, the advance came upon gun emplacements that had been reoccupied by the Japanese. Two tanks came up and immediately began blasting the emplacements with well-placed cannon fire. The next day, when the 158th RCT ran into a line of Japanese bunkers on a slight rise near the far bank of the Tirfoam, the tanks rolled forward again and helped eliminate the positions. By the evening of June 9, the advance was ready to cross the Tirfoam River when it suddenly was told to stop.

For the 158th RCT, combat on New Guinea had come to an end. They were slated to make an invasion of Noemfoor Island, 300 miles northwest of Sarmi. The capture of Lone Tree Hill was left to the 6th IDiv. As the 1st Platoon Shermans waited for the change of infantry, the 2nd and 3rd Platoon tanks of the 603rd TCo were already in action on Biak Island.[28]

CHAPTER FIFTEEN

Bloody Biak

B iak Island rests 180 miles northwest of Wakde, off the New Guinea coast and at the mouth of huge Geelvink Bay. Shaped roughly like an old work boot, with the toe pointing east, most of Biak is covered by tropical rain forest. Dominated by irregular coral terraces and ridgelines, the only flat area on the island is around the southeast corner, on the toe of the boot. Although a high cliff-like ridge dominates the southern shore of Biak, enough land lay between the cliff and the water's edge to enable the Japanese to build three airfields between the settlements of Mokmer and Sorido. Since the Japanese had the beaches leading to these airfields well guarded, the Americans planned to make their invasion a little to the east, near the village of Bosnek.[1]

The soldiers chosen to make the Biak landings were from the 186th and 162nd regiments of the 41st IDiv, supported by numerous other units, including the 2nd and 3rd Platoon tanks of the 603rd TCo. The infantry would be brought over from Hollandia while the two tank platoons would be shipped over from Wakde. By the morning of May 27, naval ships were bombarding the southern shore of Biak and the LVTs were churning their way to the island.[2]

Unfortunately, things went wrong from the beginning. Due to a strong westerly current and a thick dust and smoke screen from the preliminary bombardment, the first soldiers to reach shore, members of the 186th IReg, landed in a mangrove swamp, 3,000 yards west of where they were supposed to be. Following the first wave, the next three waves also came ashore in the swamp. Making the best of a bad situation, the troops pushed through the swamp toward a coastal road that connected Bosnek with the airfields.

When the commanding officer of the 186th IReg realized his men were on the wrong beach, he requested permission to immediately move west to capture the Japanese airfields at Mokmer and Sorido. Instead, he was instructed to head east

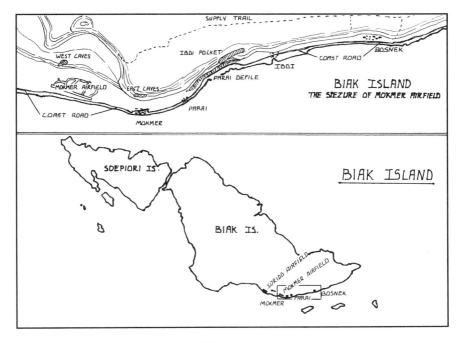

Biak Island

and secure his assigned beachhead. So, at 7:45 A.M., the 186th IReg headed east toward the Bosnek beach instead of west toward the airstrips.[3]

In the ensuing maneuver, the different battalions and companies of the 186th IReg became entangled and confused. Then, to make matters worse, the troops ran into more trouble when they collided with the 162nd IReg and the tanks of the 603rd TCo moving west from the Bosnek beachhead. To get to their assigned position on the eastern flank, the 186th IReg had to pass completely through the 162nd IReg. It was not until noon that the eastern end of the beachhead was secure and the 186th IReg was pushing inland to secure the top of the coral ridgeline.

Once the 186th IReg was out of the way, the 162nd IReg moved west along the coastal road with six tanks from the 603rd TCo in the lead. At 9:30 A.M., the column passed the mangrove swamp where the 186th IReg had landed two hours before. Just 2,000 yards further west, past the village of Ibdi, the men and tanks came upon a geographic feature that was not shown on any pre-invasion maps. Starting just west of the village, and running about 3,000 yards west to the village of Parai, was a vertical cliff wall, 200 feet high and only about 100 yards from the ocean's edge. This wall, soon nicknamed the "Parai defile," limited the movement of the Americans and presented a great tactical advantage to the Japanese. Noted the 41st IDiv historian, "Tall, jungle-covered ridges closed in on our right, beyond the straggling native huts of Ibdi. The ridges became a weathered wall of limestone cliffs, shouldering us into the reefs."[4]

The first troops entered the defile at 11:15 A.M. Spotting a batch of retreating Japanese, they immediately called in naval gunfire. When the firing ceased, five Sherman tanks pushed into the defile. Noted an infantryman, "When 5 tanks rumbled abreast, [we] growled. . . . [The] tanks din and dust made us hike blind." Before long, however, the infantrymen were glad that the tanks were with them. Admitted the 41st IDiv historian, "[We] fought the Japs at 1235, at 1400 [2:00 P.M.], then at 1450 [2:50 P.M.]—at which time our tanks blasted Jap MGs in pillboxes at the cliff base." By three o'clock, the tanks and infantry had pushed through the defile and were in possession of Parai village on the far side. Once there, the GIs dug in for the night.[5]

Around 7:30 A.M. the next day, May 28, the infantrymen moved out without tank support toward Mokmer airfield, about 5,000 yards farther west. From Parai village to Mokmer airfield, the high cliffs that had formed the Parai defile backed slowly away from the ocean to eventually form a high, wide plateau. Advancing without a hitch, the 162nd IReg reached Mokmer village, about halfway between Parai and the airfield, before nine o'clock. Once there, some of the infantry moved up onto the plateau while the rest remained on the coast road and headed directly toward the airdrome. However, when the troops on the coastal road were within 200 yards of the airfield all hell suddenly broke loose.[6]

Japanese infantry, supported by mortars and heavy machine guns, charged out of the airdrome and forced the Americans back 600 yards. As the men retreated, enemy fire poured down on them from caves just below the plateau and from more caves east of the airfield, from an area soon to be labeled the East Caves. The rapid movement of the Japanese drove a wedge between the Americans who had retreated and the men on the plateau, temporarily trapping two companies. Four Sherman tanks from the 3rd Platoon, 603rd TCo rumbled forward and aided in the successful rescue of the trapped men, but not before the Americans had suffered heavy casualties.[7]

Unable to advance, the 162nd IReg hunkered down near Mokmer village as the Japanese began to pound their position with mortar and artillery fire. Col. Harold Haney, commanding officer of 162nd IReg, was with the beleaguered troops and suddenly became fearful of being captured. Climbing inside a 603rd TCo Sherman, he hung on for dear life as the tank raced back to Parai. Recalled the 41st IDiv historian, "The tank gave Haney a jarring ride, with Jap MGs stripping the tank clean [of paint]."[8]

As the Americans hung on, the Japanese launched two unsuccessful frontal attacks. Near 2:00 P.M., during the second attack, a few Japanese Type 95 Ha-Go light tanks armed with a 37mm cannon and 6.5mm machine gun, charged out of the Mokmer airdrome. Three 3rd Platoon, 603rd TCo tanks were still with the infantrymen and opened fire at a range of 1,200 yards. Facing the American tanks and harassed by offshore naval gunfire, the Japanese tanks quickly turned around and fled back toward the airfield.[9]

After some time, Maj. Gen. Horace H. Fuller, commanding officer of the 41st IDiv and in charge of the entire Biak operation, reinforced his endangered troops with the 1st Platoon, 603rd TCo. Shortly thereafter, Japanese patrols cut the road behind the Americans and trapped the reinforced regiment out on a limb. Near 4:00 P.M., General Fuller had seen enough. He ordered his trapped command to fall back to Parai. With tanks in front and rear and spread out down the column, the Americans started eastward. Wrote the 41st IDiv historian, "With tanks at hundred-foot intervals up the road, we formed for retreat—two lines a few feet apart—just like a parade. From the cliff, Jap gunners and mortarmen threw down all they had." In spite of the heavy barrage, the column reached Parai village around 7:00 P.M. The little expedition had cost the 162nd IReg sixteen killed and eighty-seven wounded. The 603rd TCo had three men wounded.[10]

At 7 A.M. on May 29, the Japanese came on again. The first attack was an infantry assault that was stopped far short of the American line, but when the Japanese advanced again an hour later, they were supported by four Ha-Go light tanks. Two Sherman medium tanks of the 1st Platoon, 603rd TCo were waiting. As the Japanese tanks came down the road and passed through a coconut grove, the American tankers opened fire in the only tank-versus-tank battle of the New Guinea campaign. "Each Japanese tank was stopped by one round of 75mm armor-piercing ammunition, while the enemy infantry was literally mowed down by the machine guns and mortars of the [infantry]," wrote historian Robert Ross Smith. "Armor-piercing 75mm shells passed right through the Japanese light tanks, and the Shermans followed with a few rounds of 75mm high explosive, which tore holes in the Japanese vehicles and blew loose their turrets."[11]

A 41st IDiv historian described what S/Sgt. Louis Botta witnessed: "[Sergeant] Botta had not seen two Nip tanks coming at us 500 yards away, but he suddenly saw one of our two waiting tanks revolving its 75mm gun turret. This tank was aptly named 'Murder Inc.,' and it fired and halted the last Jap tank dead in its tracks to block the Parai Road . . . [Botta then] saw 'Murder Inc.' turn its turret and fire again. The second [enemy] tank halted and burned; we saw a half-burned Jap corpse hanging half out of the top hatch door. . . . Botta said that the light Jap tanks looked like Volkswagens as contrasted to our medium General Sherman tanks that seemed like monsters." Although a few 37mm Japanese tank rounds hit the American tanks, they caused no damage.[12]

Thirty minutes later, the stubborn Japanese came on again with three more Ha-Go light tanks leading the way. This time, three 3rd Platoon Shermans were there to meet them. The Japanese and American tanks exchanged gunfire and although the larger Sherman tanks eventually destroyed all three Ha-Go tanks, a lucky shot from an enemy tank created an anxious moment for one American crew. Hit by a 37mm round that locked the Sherman's 75mm cannon at a low elevation, the quick-thinking crewmen backed their tank partway into a shell hole until their gun was level and then blasted the enemy tank into oblivion. With the destruction of their armor support, the Japanese infantry quickly withdrew.[13]

With the loss of seven Japanese tanks in less than one hour, the Japanese lost the incentive for another frontal attack. Instead, they started a mortar and artillery barrage and began circling around to the north, around the American right flank. About noon, the Japanese attacked again and although the American position held, the enemy managed to get behind the GIs again and temporarily cut the coastal road back to Ibdi. Only a spirited attack by two companies of American infantrymen managed to reopen the road.

By noon General Fuller was convinced that two regiments of 41st IDiv troops would not be enough to capture Mokmer airfield. After calling for reinforcements from his 163rd IReg, 41st IDiv, then in the Wakde/Sarmi area, he ordered the 162nd IReg at Parai to fall back to the village of Ibdi. Around 2:00 P.M., the great exodus began, with the tanks of the 3rd Platoon, 603rd TCo in the lead and the tanks of the 1st Platoon, 603rd TCo in the rear. Japanese fire from the East Caves and from the high cliffs near the eastern end of the Parai defile, an area known as the Ibdi pocket, continually harassed the column but the tanks and infantry were safely back around Ibdi by nightfall. Almost immediately, the Japanese moved into the vacated town of Parai.[14] As General Fuller realized, the conquest of Biak was going to be tougher than anyone had imagined.

Over the next two days, while the Americans awaited reinforcements, scouting patrols went out to try to discover a way to outflank the enemy and approach the Mokmer airdrome from the north. On the second day, a patrol discovered a narrow jungle supply trail up on the plateau, running roughly parallel to the coastline and about 500 yards inland from the cliff face. On June 1, after part of the 163rd IReg had arrived, General Fuller began another move against Mokmer airfield.[15]

Utilizing the newly discovered trail, the 186th IReg managed to push its way westward and on June 6 descended upon Mokmer airdrome from the plateau. Although the foot soldiers had an easy time securing the airfield, they would have a hard time trying to keep it.[16]

By 9:30 A.M. on June 7, Japanese mortar and artillery fire was raining down upon the entire Mokmer airfield area. As the 186th IReg hunkered down, 41st IDiv commanders tried to reinforce and resupply the men by boat. In the early afternoon, three 603rd TCo Shermans were put into LCMs and, along with a few supply-laden LCSs (landing craft, support), headed toward the airdrome beach. As the barges approached, however, Japanese soldiers in caves along the water's edge opened fire. Although turned aside, the barges returned near 2:00 P.M. and even though the supply barges were driven off again, the LCMs reached the beach and unloaded the three M4A1 tanks.[17]

Almost immediately the three medium tanks began blasting away at enemy gun emplacements along the beach. When these positions were silenced, the tanks fronted the low ridge north of the airfield and knocked out a Japanese 75mm mountain howitzer and a 20mm field piece. Finally, just before dusk, the three Shermans moved northwest of the airfield and blasted two large Japanese pillboxes.[18]

That same day, General Fuller decided to move most of his 162nd IReg via water from Ibdi to Parai, thus bypassing both the Parai defile and the Ibdi pocket. Once at Parai, some troops would turn west and head toward Mokmer village and the East Caves, eventually linking up with the 186th IReg at Mokmer airfield. Another group would turn east and attack the Parai defile from the west while the few 162nd IReg soldiers left behind at Ibdi would apply pressure on the east end of the defile. If all went well, the attacks would eliminate, or at least contain, the Japanese.

At 2:20 P.M. on June 7, the first infantry-laden LVTs made a landing at Parai and secured a beachhead. At 5:30, six 603rd TCo tanks came ashore to reinforce the foot soldiers. Having arrived so close to nightfall, however, any further movement was out of the question.[19]

On June 8, the 162nd IReg troops and the six tanks at Parai started their move westward against the East Caves. "I always looked upon the presence of tanks as a mixed blessing," said infantryman Francis Catanzaro (162nd IReg, 41st IDiv). "It was comforting to have the additional firepower, but the noise created by the tanks certainly removed any chance of surprising the Japs. Also, the tanks usually drew fire by any Nips within range. . . . It was standard operating procedure for a squad of men to precede the tanks because the Japs had been known to attack tanks and kill the crew members by climbing on the tanks and dropping grenades into open ports or attaching magnetic mines to the hulls of the tanks. Nevertheless, I always thought that the tanks and their crews were in less danger than we were. I would have been much happier if the tanks had been up front leading the column while we protected them from the rear."[20]

The infantry and tanks moved quickly and by noon were within 500 yards of Mokmer village. At this point, however, heavy enemy mortar fire and land mines slowed the advance. As the tanks stopped to let the foot soldiers remove the mines, Japanese mortar fire increased and began impacting around the standing tanks. Unable to move forward, the tanks and infantry pulled back and set up a nighttime defensive perimeter about 1,800 yards short of Mokmer village.[21]

On that same date, some of the 186th IReg troops at Mokmer airdrome began mopping up the last of the Japanese defenders hiding in the caves along the beach. The rest of the regiment, along with the three tanks that had been landed by barge, attempted to clean off the plateau and the ridge lines overlooking the airfield. Sgt. Durand Mandoline of Company B, 186th IReg recalled, "On 8 June, the 3 Shermans went to fight the Jap ridges—with 2 squads of [riflemen] to protect [them] from Nip infantry. The Shermans rolled out 200 yards while scared men ran forward and hit the dirt. The tanks then shot with HMGs [heavy machine guns], and 75s, while scared B men tried to spot Nippo counter-fire. Results of tank fire were not known, but B's men were greatly relieved at orders to return to [the] perimeter." Bombarded throughout the day by Japanese artillery hidden up on the plateau, the Americans eventually moved back to the captured airfield.[22]

On the morning of June 9, the 186th IReg split into three columns to try to silence the enemy artillery pieces atop the plateau. One column, moving northwest, made very little progress, but a second column moving toward the northeast, managed to link up with a detachment from the 163rd IReg that had been moving westward along the jungle supply trail. The third column, assisted by the tanks from the 603rd TCo, moved west along the beach and managed to destroy a few pillboxes and detonate a couple of Japanese ammunition dumps.[23]

To the east, the 162nd IReg and six accompanying Sherman tanks continued to try to get past the East Caves and reach Mokmer airfield. Using a new strategy, some of the tanks were placed aboard LCTs (landing craft, tank) and fired into the caves from offshore. Recalled Navy electrician Tony Grossi, "On the ninth, three

Sherman tanks of the 603rd Tank Company were placed aboard our LCTs and fired their 75mm cannons on the cliffs in the [Parai] defile for an hour. During this gunning attack I was on the port bow .50-caliber machine gun firing/strafing the Jap pocket ashore while the Sherman tanks were each firing about 100 rounds into the Japanese resistance." Near 1:30 P.M., forward patrols from the 162nd IReg finally linked up with the 186th IReg but by nightfall the main bodies of both regiments were still roughly 1,000 yards apart.[24]

On June 10, the 186th IReg went out again to eliminate the Japanese artillery positions hidden inside the caves and up on the plateau. Once again the American tanks fired into the caves from LCTs but the Japanese guns were hard to hit. Hidden inside their caves, the Japanese gunners would roll their guns forward, fire at a target and then roll their guns back to reload. Once reloaded, the entire process was repeated. Because of the skilled way in which these guns were being used, the American tanks were finding it almost impossible to hit the hidden guns.[25]

East of Mokmer airdrome, 603rd TCo tanks were also assisting the 162nd IReg in their move west out of Parai toward Mokmer village. Noted the 41st IDiv historian, "[On] June 10, we sent a security guard with Sherman tanks to Mokmer [village]—6 men atop each tank. No one was hit." Eventually, a solid link was made between the 162nd IReg at Parai and the 186th at Mokmer village and Mokmer airdrome. Still, it would be three whole days before Army trucks could use the coastal road to run supplies from Parai to the airstrip.[26]

Pressured by General MacArthur to get Mokmer airdrome operational, General Fuller sent his infantry and tanks up onto the plateau and westward against a cave area just beyond the airfield known as the West Caves. Throughout June 11, 12 and 13, the Americans continued to push outward and then on June 13, a small artillery liaison plane finally landed on the captured runway. However, an immediate response by the Japanese artillery indicated that the strip was still too dangerous for everyday use. The enemy guns on the plateau had to be eliminated.[27]

Although both the 162nd and 186th Infantry Regiments were beginning to show signs of battle fatigue, the general advance continued. On June 14, as the men were continuing their drive toward the West Caves, General Fuller was relieved of command of the Biak operation. General MacArthur, angered and frustrated that it was taking Fuller so long to capture the three Biak airfields, removed Fuller and replaced him with Lt. Gen. Robert L. Eichelberger. Although General Fuller retained command of the 41st IDiv, he felt that the demotion was unwarranted and on June 18 he left Biak.[28]

On June 15 and 16, the hard-fighting GIs continued to advance toward the West Caves, even throwing back a surprise Japanese counterattack. On June 17, when the 162nd IReg and five supporting tanks circled above the caves, they began taking heavy fire from a Japanese encampment to the northwest. Deciding to eliminate the encampment first, the infantry and tanks managed to circle around behind the enemy position before running into heavy Japanese fire. Eventually, the five tanks from the 1st Platoon, 603rd TCo moved to the front and destroyed a Japanese artillery piece and two machine-gun emplacements. Recalled the 41st IDiv historian, "Worst fire came from cliffs on our right, but tanks blasted out these Japs." Although the main encampment still remained, the 162nd IReg managed to surge forward and grab the high ground above the West Caves before nightfall.[29]

On June 18, General Eichelberger rested his tired troops and brought over the 34th IReg of the 24th IDiv from the Hollandia area. The next day, the 41st IDiv and the 603rd TCo renewed their assaults against the West Caves and the encampment behind it. Simultaneously, the 24th IDiv reinforcements headed westward along the coast toward the remaining two Biak airfields. On June 20, at long last, the two fields fell into American hands.[30]

On the morning of June 21, after a three-day bombardment, the 162nd IReg and the 603rd TCo Shermans renewed their assault against the West Caves. "Flamethrower-rifleman teams cleared [the] Japs from high ground NW, and [Company] C with 2 tanks hit [the] West Entrance," wrote the 41st IDiv historian. "We lobbed grenades into all holes and crevices in reach, shot all Japs we saw. Tank 75s fired into the cave mouth, but coral stalactites blocked off penetration of the caves." Unable to reduce the caves with direct fire, the GIs poured gasoline into the crevices and then ignited it with phosphorus bombs. Noted the historian, "Underground, heated Jap ammo began popping like firecrackers."[31]

During the night, some of the West Caves defenders unsuccessfully tried to break through the encircling American lines. The next morning, when the Americans advanced up to the mouth of the main cave and to two openings in the ground known as North Sump and South Sump, they passed dozens of Japanese corpses. Although the 603rd TCo Shermans tried to help out in the reduction of the two sumps, their efforts proved futile because they could not depress their cannon barrels low enough to fire down into the sumps. Eventually, the entire West Caves complex was neutralized with gasoline and TNT. Over the next few days, soldiers and tankers guarding the mouth of the cave listened to constant explosions of underground caches of ammunition. Finally, on June 27, when a few GIs ventured into the darkness, they discovered "125 more or less whole bodies of dead Japs."[32]

On June 22, even before the West Caves were neutralized, Fifth Air Force P-40 fighter planes began operating from Mokmer airdrome. Noted Army historian Smith, "One of the three fields on Biak was at last operational."[33]

On the plateau above the airstrip, the 186th IReg shoved the Japanese inside the encampment area into a teardrop-shaped defensive position and, after leaving some men behind to contain the Japanese, the rest headed northwest, toward a concentration of Japanese artillery pieces and antiaircraft guns. Over the next two days, the infantry made little headway against stubborn Japanese resistance, but on June 24 two 603rd TCo tanks arrived. The next day, when the tanks and infantry finally overran the position, they captured only one enemy fieldpiece and four wrecked antiaircraft guns that had been disabled by American artillery fire. Somehow, during the night, the Japanese had pulled every other gun out of the area.[34]

With the artillery position gone, the 41st IDiv troops turned back to the teardrop-shaped pocket. Even without the help of tanks, which were halted by the jungle terrain, the pocket fell to the Americans on June 25. A few days later, on

July 4 and 5, the 603rd TCo tanks provided covering fire for engineers working with TNT to seal the entrances to the East Caves. One day later, the East Caves were officially declared secure.[35]

The Ibdi pocket was the last Japanese-held area on Biak. On July 10, the 163rd IReg and a few tanks from the 603rd TCo moved into the Ibdi pocket after it had suffered two straight weeks of naval, artillery and aerial bombardment. What the attackers discovered as they entered the area was a terrain reminiscent of the moon. Huge shell craters dotted the landscape and most of the jungle ground cover had been destroyed. Noted historian Smith, "Tanks fired their 75mm weapons at enemy positions now visible from the northern side of the main ridge." Two days later, the Sherman tanks struck again. Reported the 41st IDiv historian, "About 1705 [5:05 P.M.], two tanks of 603 Tank Co's [1st Platoon] shelled the cliffs, killed four pillboxes, [and] had four possibles." Despite the American firepower, however, the stubborn Japanese continued to hold out.[36]

For a week and a half the Ibdi pocket refused to crumble. Finally, on July 21, the 41st IDiv used a ruse to draw the Japanese into a trap. "At 1030," noted the 41st IDiv historian, "603 Tanks' [1st Platoon] blew up seven pillboxes on the landward side of the cliffs, to make [the] Nips mass for a push from that direction." After giving the Japanese enough time to rush most of their men to the threatened section of the pocket, a squadron of B-24 heavy bombers roared in on July 22 and dropped sixty-four 1,000-pound blockbuster bombs on the area. Later in the day, when the GIs and tanks moved forward, they found hundreds of dead or stunned Japanese. A week later, the Ibdi pocket was just an ugly memory.[37]

Although organized resistance on Biak continued until July 28, General Eichelberger left the island on July 22 to return to Hollandia. In his eyes, once Mokmer airdrome was operational and the West Caves were neutralized, Biak was secure. The Japanese lost 4,700 troops killed and 220 captured defending Biak. For the Americans, more than 400 soldiers had been killed while another 2,150 were wounded. Additionally, more than 7,200 men were incapacitated by disease. At the cost of 9,970 Americans, General MacArthur finally had his Biak airfields.[38]

Sixty miles south of Biak, inside Dutch New Guinea's Geelvink Bay, sits the little island of Noemfoor, measuring only fifteen miles long by twelve miles wide. Since the 41st IDiv was having such a hard time capturing Biak's airfields, General MacArthur decided to invade Noemfoor Island and capture its three airdromes. On July 2, after days of sustained aerial bombardment and an hour of heavy naval bombardment, the independent 158th RCT, direct from Swarmi (see Chapter Thirteen), stormed ashore directly opposite one of Noemfoor's airfields. Coming ashore with the eighth wave were four M4 Sherman tanks from the 1st Platoon, 603rd TCo, also direct from Swarmi. Meeting very little resistance, the infantrymen quickly moved inland while the tanks remained in reserve.[39]

Later in the day, as the beachhead was expanded, the invaders discovered a few occupied caves and emplacements on the eastern flank. In mopping up each "cave, dugout and foxhole," the GIs were assisted by LVT(A) amphibious tanks and the 603rd TCo Shermans. By nightfall, more than 7,000 Americans had landed on Noemfoor and one Japanese airfield had been secured. The cost to the Americans was three dead men.[40]

On July 3, after a Japanese captive gave false information about the number of Japanese defenders on Noemfoor, 1,500 officers and men from the 503rd Parachute IReg made a successful drop onto the island. Although no paratroopers were hit by enemy fire, 128 men were injured because of high winds.[41]

Once on the island, the 503rd Parachute IReg joined the 158th RCT in eliminating all Japanese resistance. By the end of the first week of July, the Americans had all three enemy airfields captured and operational. Although Noemfoor was not officially declared secure until August 31, General MacArthur finally had his staging fields for airplanes covering the further advance along the New Guinea coast.[42] In the meantime, the action had shifted back to the central Pacific and the Mariana Islands.

CHAPTER SIXTEEN

Southern Saipan

Fighting was still going on along the New Guinea coast when three more tank battalions were moved to the Pacific theater. Leaving their tanks behind at Camp Polk, Louisiana, the personnel of the 775th TB were moved to San Francisco and on May 28th, 1944, set sail for New Guinea. For the next three weeks, their ship steamed westward. Finally, on June 20, the battalion was landed near Buna. Moved to a nearby horse racetrack, the men were instructed to begin constructing company kitchens, mess halls, and a chapel.[1] To the men of the 775th TB, it was apparent their stay on New Guinea was bound to be a long one.

The next tank battalion to move to the Pacific Theater was the 716th TB. Activated at Camp Chaffee, Arkansas, the unit was eventually moved to the San Francisco area and on June 1 boarded a ship and steamed under the Golden Gate Bridge. "Thus began a 27-day unescorted voyage on the high seas which ultimately ended at Buna, New Guinea on the 3rd of July," reported the 716th TB historian.

Once at Buna, the tankers began training exercises with the infantry. Noted a 716th TB historian, "Terrain and character of the enemy opposition in the Pacific Theater necessitates a modification of the doctrine of employment of armor as a unit. Primary emphasis is placed upon infantry, with armor in a supporting role. A battalion of tanks is not a separate striking force, but a component of several tank-infantry teams. It was necessary that these tactics be practiced to perfection for a successful completion of future missions."[2]

Close on the heels of the 775th and 716th TBs was the 710th TB. Constituted at Camp North Polk, Louisiana, the battalion headed toward the Pacific Theater from Seattle, Washington on June 14. On June 22, the battalion arrived at Honolulu. Taken to Schofield Barracks, the tankers soon began extensive training at the Unit Jungle Training Center, learning "every phase of jungle life . . . [including] the hardships that the infantryman endures in jungle warfare."[3]

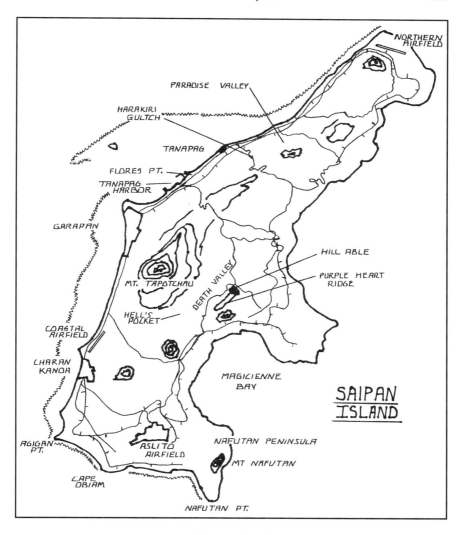

Saipan Island

Having already cracked Japan's outer ring of defense with the seizure of the Gilbert and Marshall islands, the next move in the central Pacific was to try to break through Japan's inner circle. In December 1943, the Joint Chiefs of Staff began planning the capture of the Mariana Islands. Three islands were targeted for invasion: Saipan, Tinian and Guam. As explained by Army historian Capt. Roy Appleman, "Saipan and the other large islands of the southern Marianas were in effect anchored aircraft carriers barring the way to the Philippines and the inner Japanese defenses in the Pacific. The conquest of Saipan would rupture the strong communications from the Japanese homeland extending down through [Japan's inner circle]. The capture of Saipan and its sister islands would provide land bases on which [American] heavy bomber strips could be built within range of Tokyo."[4]

Capture of the Mariana Islands would put the Americans only 1,500 miles east of the Philippines and 1,300 miles southeast of Tokyo. Although Guam was the largest island in the Marianas and a prime objective for Admiral Nimitz, the first island slated for invasion was Saipan because of its excellent airfields and deepwater harbor. About 100 miles north of Guam, Saipan was closer to Tokyo and, when seized, would interfere with any Japanese reinforcing moves toward Guam.[5]

Shaped roughly like a giant anteater, Saipan measured fourteen miles long from head to tail, and five miles wide from backbone to the bottom of the feet. The long head and neck pointed slightly to the northeast, while the feet pointed roughly east. Between the feet lay Magicienne Bay and in the center of the island, just above the forelegs, was Mount Tapotchau, a 1,554-foot peak. Wrote an Army historian, "Unlike the low and generally flat surface of coral islands, the terrain of Saipan presented a confusion of heavily jungled and jagged but low cliff faces, rock outcroppings, sinkholes, and caves often as difficult to see as to walk over and around."[6]

At the center of the western shoreline—the anteater's backbone—was the town of Garapan, and just north of Garapan was Tanapag harbor and a nearby seaplane base. Farther south, near the butt-end of the beast, was the town of Charan Kanoa. Two small landing strips had been built on Saipan, one just north of Charan Kanoa, along the coast, and another along the northern coastline, near the anteater's forehead. Additionally, Aslito airdrome was situated near the top of the Nafutan peninsula, which jutted out to form the hind legs of the anteater.[7]

Admiral Nimitz selected the 2nd and 4th MarDivs, and the 27th IDiv to invade Saipan. The Marines would be aided by their own tanks while the Army would be assisted by the M4 Sherman medium tanks of Company B, 762nd TB and the M5A1 Stuart light tanks of Company D, 762nd TB and Company D, 766th TB. On June 1, the largest transoceanic fleet ever assembled left Hawaii and headed west toward the Mariana Islands.[8]

On June 6, 1944, while Allied forces were landing at Normandy, France, the Marianas invasion fleet steamed across the Pacific.[9] On June 15, D-Day for Saipan, the Navy began a heavy bombardment of the island. Twenty miles to the east, the ships bearing the 27th IDiv and the three tank companies dropped anchor. Selected for a reserve role, the Army units would land on Saipan one day after the initial invasion.[10]

Although the American ships and accompanying planes subjected Saipan to a heavy shelling, the invading Marines met heavy resistance as they moved toward shore. Although Marine Lt. General Holland M. "Howlin' Mad" Smith had wanted the 2nd MarDiv to land north of Charan Kanoa and capture the nearby coastal airstrip, a heavy current drove dozens of amtracs farther north, far away from their intended beach. Fortunately, the 4th MarDiv landed as intended just below Charan Kanoa and began its move south toward Aslito airfield. In spite of all of the problems, however, by nightfall the Marines had captured Charan Kanoa and the coastal airfield and had a significant toehold on Saipan.[11]

Although the Japanese launched a spirited banzai charge during the night, the Marines held on and the next morning began moving inland.[12] Near 3:00 P.M., while the Marines were in motion, the Army's 27th IDiv began splashing ashore directly opposite Charan Kanoa. To make room for the soldiers, the Marines shifted northward, leaving the 27th IDiv to drive southeast across the island toward Aslito airfield. The next day, June 17, the three platoons of M5A1 light tanks of Company D, 766th TB came ashore.[13]

North of the Charan Kanoa, 27th IDiv soldiers began coming ashore at first light but the light Stuart tanks of Company D, 762nd TB did not begin landing until 1:00 P.M. Then, while the foot soldiers turned south to clear the southwestern tip of Saipan, four M5A1 Stuarts belonging to 2nd Lt. John B. Phalon's platoon headed north toward the recently captured coastal airstrip. The 2nd MarDiv, after capturing the strip, had run into a pesky Japanese machine-gun nest and needed the help of armor to knock it out. Using canister and .30 caliber machine-gun fire the tanks quickly silenced the enemy position in the first Army tank combat on Saipan.[14]

By nightfall on June 17, only eleven M5A1 light tanks from Company D, 762nd TB and thirteen from Company D, 766th TB were on Saipan. As the other light tank crews bobbed about in their small landing craft off the west coast of Saipan, waiting for morning light, they were surprised to see the big Navy ships suddenly weigh anchor and disappear. Alerted to an incoming Japanese air raid, the Navy was taking no chances by remaining in an exposed position. Unfortunately, when the ships left, they took with them all of the M4 Sherman medium tanks of Company B and the entire headquarters section of the 762nd TB. Also gone were all the maintenance men and replacement parts for all of the tanks.[15]

At first light on June 18, Lieutenant Phalon took his five light tanks to assist the infantry in clearing Agigan point, near the southwest corner of Saipan. Although sniper fire was a problem throughout the day, the infantrymen and tankers made great headway and cleared the point by nightfall. When darkness fell, the tanks rumbled over to a tank staging area, southeast of Charan Kanoa to replenish their fuel and ammunition.

East of Agigan point, 2nd Lt. Dale H. Sillix's light tank platoon from Company D, 766th TB crossed the island to assist the infantry in trying to clear the southern shore of Saipan. Near Cape Obiam, at the center of the southern shoreline, the advance drew heavy mortar fire, which wounded some infantrymen but left the tanks unscathed. In spite of the shelling, however, the tank-infantry team had moved about 500 yards past Cape Obiam by nightfall.[16]

That same morning, 1st Lt. Willis K. Dorey's light tanks of Company D, 762nd TB set out to support the drive to take Aslito airfield. During the previous day, the infantry had made steady progress against the airfield and at sunup, after four tanks arrived, the GIs renewed their push. Just before noon, the joint tank-infantry team had captured the entire length of the airstrip.[17]

With sunup on June 19, the 27th IDiv renewed its push toward the southeast, southwest and east. Having already helped to clear out Agingan point, Lieutenant Phalon took his M5A1 Stuarts to Cape Obiam. "During the day," reported Captain Appleman, "two machine-gun nests were destroyed in this area. This advance followed the course of the [island sugarcane] railroad a few hundred yards back from the coast."[18]

After the capture of Aslito field, the 27th IDiv troops headed toward Nafutan point, on the far southeast corner of the island. Nafutan point is a short peninsula that constitutes the hind legs of the anteater and is dominated by a high ridgeline that runs north and south down the center. Midway down the ridgeline, at its highest point, was Mount Nafutan. Although there was a low, cultivated plain leading up to the peninsula, the land constituting the hind legs was generally "covered with thick underbrush." Defending this area were about 1,050 Japanese soldiers who had been compressed into the area by the rapid advance of the Americans.[19]

At daybreak on June 19, the platoons of 1st Lt. Louis A. Fleck and 2nd Lt. Gino Ganio, both Companies D, 766th TB, jumped off with the infantry from a point above Aslito airfield. Lieutenant Fleck's tanks knocked out a Japanese 5-inch gun and an enemy machine-gun nest just past the airfield, but when the incoming fire intensified, the tanks and infantry pulled back and called in artillery support. In a move that was oft repeated on Saipan, the tanks evacuated three wounded infantrymen as they pulled back. When the shelling ended, the Americans moved forward again and although three tanks would eventually have their 37mm guns damaged and one tank would have its turret damaged, the advance reached the southern shore of Magicienne Bay by 6:00 P.M.[20]

South of the airfield, the advance eastward was much slower and more hazardous. An infantry-tank assault was supposed to step off at 7:30 A.M. but Lieutenant Dorey's tanks were late in arriving because of their need to resupply, so the infantry left without them. Without tanks, the GIs suffered heavily and were repulsed in their first attempt to take a stretch of level land behind a ridgeline just beyond the airfield. Instrumental in this repulse were several Japanese dual-purpose guns used for either antiaircraft or antipersonnel fire.

When Lieutenant Dorey's tanks finally arrived, the attackers moved forward again. Captain Appleman described what happened:

> The tanks put heavy fire on a cane field and while doing this [Lieutenant Dorey's] tank drew fire from an enemy dual-purpose gun. The muzzle blast of this gun was observed by men in the other tanks and it was destroyed. In the course of this fighting, tank No. 67 exploded a Japanese ammunition dump. The Japanese fire was extremely heavy, small arms and machine gun fire and shrapnel [were] dropping like 'snow drops' . . . The tanks knocked out of action at least three of the estimated seven enemy dual-purpose guns.

In spite of this tank support, the soldiers were forced back again after gaining only a few hundred yards.[21]

During the evening of June 19, 1st Lt. Dudley Williams' platoon of M4 medium Sherman tanks from Company B, 762nd TB finally landed on Saipan. After leaving Saipan on June 17, the tankers had remained at sea while the Navy awaited the outcome of the two-day battle of the Philippine Sea. In the greatest, and last, aircraft carrier battle of the war, the Americans shot down 476 Japanese planes intent on stopping the invasion of the Marianas. Additionally, American planes and submarines sank three carriers and damaged two others, and sank or damaged seven additional Japanese warships. American losses were 76 airmen and 130 planes.[22] Never again would the Japanese Navy pose a real threat to any Allied move in the Pacific.

Coinciding with the arrival of the medium tanks was a change in ammunition for the light tanks. After almost two full days of combat, the Stuart crews had discovered that their armor-piercing shells were almost useless on Saipan. "There were few occasions on Saipan when armor-piercing shells were needed," noted Captain Appleman. "This was due to the fact that seldom was there tank-against-tank fighting, and no steel pillboxes were encountered." Instead, the crews switched to high explosive and canister shells.[23]

On June 20, as the Marines continued to drive eastward, the 27th IDiv continued to attack Nafutan point. While the other Stuart tanks and some of the newly-arriving Shermans assisted in cleaning out the area south of Aslito airfield, Lieutenant Dorey's six light tanks waited to assist the attack against Nafutan point. Although Maj. Gen. Ralph C. Smith, 27th IDiv commander, had ordered the advance to jump off at 10:00 A.M., for various reasons it did not get underway until noon.[24]

Supported by infantry, Lieutenant Dorey lined up with his tank and two other tanks on the right, and two tanks from his platoon and one from 1st Lt. James A. Bullock's platoon on the left. As the advance moved forward against the northern sector of the Nafutan peninsula, it immediately came under heavy Japanese fire. Noted an army historian, "[The] tanks proved to be more of a hindrance than a help since they drew enemy artillery fire into the area of advance." In addition, Lieutenant Dorey's tank was hit with a Japanese 75mm shell, which caused internal injuries to the driver and knocked out the radio system.[25]

Tech 4 Emanuel Mavrikis and Sgt. George B. Lampro spotted the 75mm gun and from only twenty yards away fired a shot that completely demolished the gun. When Lieutenant Dorey discovered his radio was out, he ignored the heavy incoming fire and ran to the rear of another tank. Using the rear-mounted telephone, he calmly called the tank commander and issued instructions to be relayed to the rest of the tanks. Although enemy machine-gun fire swept the area around him, Dorey stuck to the telephone, giving orders and moving his tanks where needed. For his gallantry in action, Lieutenant Dorey was awarded a Silver Star medal. For their actions, Tech 4 Mavrikis and Sergeant Lampro were awarded a Silver Star and Bronze Star, respectively.[26]

By the end of the day the advance had progressed only 2,000 yards, but the tanks had knocked out "[three] dual-purpose gun emplacements, numerous dugouts and trenches, farm houses, and small ammunition dumps." Wrote historian Appleman, "All three [dual-purpose] guns had been silenced the day before by the tanks. Overnight they had been repaired by the Japanese and put back into action.

This experience was repeated constantly during the Saipan struggle. Unless the gun emplacement and the ground were actually occupied, the next day was likely to see the same weapons [wreaking] devastation all over again."[27]

North of the Nafutan peninsula, all three light tank platoons from Company D, 766th TB assisted the 27th IDiv around Magicienne Bay. "This was difficult terrain," noted Appleman. "Here, the infantry were pinned down from enemy fire and made little progress."[28] Fortunately, during the evening of June 20–21, the last two platoons of medium tanks from Company B, 762nd TB landed on Saipan. The Shermans of 2nd Lt. Richard C. Hitchner's platoon came ashore on the evening of June 20 and the mediums of 1st Lt. Jack P. Lansford's platoon arrived very early the next day.[29]

On the morning of June 21, Lieutenant Phalon took his Stuart tanks to assist in the advance along the south shore toward Nafutan point. During the day, the tanks and infantry came up against stiff enemy resistance from caves along a nearby ridgeline, and by the time darkness descended, the advance had gained only 600 yards.[30]

To the north, Lieutenant Dorey moved up with three light tanks to assist the infantry in an advance against a thick sugarcane field on the Nafutan peninsula. At 11:30 A.M., the tanks moved forward, but for some reason the infantry did not. Going back, the tanks moved out a half hour later, but once again the infantry failed to move. Although the tanks managed to kill several Japanese, destroy two small ammunition dumps, and silence one enemy machine gun, they could not maintain the attack without infantry support and had to return to their own lines.[31]

Shortly before 3:00 P.M., Lt. Col. William J. O'Brien, the infantry commander, finally organized his men for an advance. Once again, however, the tanks jumped out in front and the foot soldiers lagged far behind. Unsupported again, Lieutenant Dorey turned his tanks around and headed back toward the infantry. According to the infantrymen, the tanks returned to their own lines "firing as they came." Reported an Army historian, "Colonel O'Brien's frantic efforts to contact the tankers by radio failed, and he finally ran out in the midst of this fire to meet them." Scrambling atop Lieutenant Dorey's tank, O'Brien pounded on the closed hatch with his pistol butt until Dorey opened the hatch. Once the tanks were turned around, the general advance continued.

The Army historian continued, "[M]ost of the men advanced at a dogtrot behind the tanks, keeping up a steady fire to the front. O'Brien continued to ride the tank turret of the lead tank, giving directions to the men inside with his pistol butt and waving the infantrymen forward." Like the advance to the south, the slow movement to the north gained only a few hundred yards on June 21, much to the chagrin of General "Howlin' Mad" Smith of the Marines, who felt the Army was dragging its feet.[32]

By June 21, the 2nd and 4th MarDivs had worked their way across the island from west to east and were getting ready to drive north and attack the central part of Saipan. When the Marines advanced, General Smith wanted the 27th IDiv to be held in reserve. Therefore, during the day, he ordered all of the Army troops, minus one infantry battalion and one light tank company, to assemble behind the two Marine Corps divisions. The one remaining infantry battalion (2nd Bn, 105th IReg) and sixteen tanks of Company D, 762nd TB were now responsible for clearing the entire southern half of Saipan, including the rugged Nafutan peninsula.[33]

On June 23, as the Marines started their attack northward, the 105th IReg and Lieutenant Dorey's tanks were preparing for an advance into the Nafutan valley. The valley itself was situated between a 300-foot ridge and 407-foot Mount Nafutan. Running north-south, the base of the valley varied from 100 to 200 yards wide. Captain Appleman wrote, "On either side rises steep ground, that on the left which looks down the valley toward the Point being cliff-like and studded with caves, that on the right grown over with heavy brush and affording excellent cover for [enemy] gun positions and hideouts."[34]

Shortly after 12:30 P.M., Lieutenant Dorey took his tank No. 66 to the crest of the west ridge of Nafutan valley and spotted a column of Japanese troops moving through a nearby sugarcane field. With a few quick shots, Dorey set the field on fire and then led tanks No. 67 and No. 68 down into the valley to investigate.[35]

Even without infantry support, the three tanks advanced about two-thirds the length of the valley, traveling about one mile. As they went, they intermittently fired into "brush, caves, houses and dugouts," setting at least three small hidden ammunition dumps on fire and knocking out one 75mm and one 47mm gun. As the tanks got deeper into the valley, the enemy became bolder. Three Japanese soldiers climbed atop tank No. 67 and tried to disable the vehicle with hand grenades, but two of the attackers were quickly shot off by machine-gun fire from the other tanks and the third soldier was chased away. Finally, when Japanese 81mm heavy mortar fire began impacting around the tanks, Lieutenant Dorey called off his raid and the three tanks retreated to the northern end of the valley.[36]

After replenishing their ammunition, Lieutenant Dorey and the other two tanks helped the 105th IReg silence a Japanese machine gun that had just wounded seven GIs. Then, while the infantry moved into the valley and eventually up onto Mount Nafutan, the three tanks once again went off on their own, spraying the sides of the Nafutan valley with machine-gun and cannon fire. Although hand-thrown explosives rocked tank No. 67, the vehicle continued to function and rumbled on. The three tanks remained in the valley for at least a half hour before finally being ordered to withdraw. As they did, however, Tech 4 Mavrikis' tank, No. 68, suddenly "ceased to function" and stopped two hundred yards short of his own lines.

Tech 4 Mavrikis was unwilling to abandon the vehicle and "calmly remained in his tank firing upon targets of opportunity." As the 105th IReg troops began to withdraw in front of a scheduled American artillery bombardment, Mavrikis dismounted his tank and supervised the attachment of a tow cable to one of the other tanks. Only after tank No. 68 was safely under tow did the plucky sergeant climb back into his vehicle. For his dedication to duty and unwillingness to abandon his tank, Sergeant Mavrikis was awarded a Bronze Star.[37]

Once all of Lieutenant Dorey's tanks were safely back at command headquarters, they were examined for battle damage. Unbelievably, the only serious damage to any of the tanks was to a bogey wheel on tank No. 68. In turn, it was later discovered that Dorey's tanks had killed at least 200 Japanese infantrymen.[38]

That night, General Holland M. Smith ordered the 105th IReg to begin the next day's advance at sunup, but most of the infantry companies did not move out until midmorning. In the center of the line, Company G, 105th IReg waited until Lieutenant Dorey came up with three light tanks at 11:30 A.M. before starting their advance. Moving rapidly once they got underway, the GIs easily captured the northern end of the ridgeline overlooking the valley and then began moving into the valley itself. When a Japanese machine gun opened fire, however, the advance came to a grinding halt.

Locating the source of the trouble, the infantrymen called on Lieutenant Dorey to assist them. In spite of the apparent danger, Dorey poked his head out of his top hatch and directed the fire of one of his tanks into the enemy position. After a few well-placed 37mm rounds, the Japanese gun fell silent and the infantry advance continued.[39]

Shortly thereafter, the Japanese made a strong counterattack to the right of Company G and Lieutenant Dorey's tanks, causing them to wait two hours before pushing farther ahead. At 4:30, when the advance resumed, the three tanks moved slowly ahead, guided toward possible targets by the infantry. Four enemy machine-gun nests were subsequently knocked out before two dual-purpose guns were spotted by the foot soldiers. Immediately, the adventurous Lieutenant Dorey led his three tanks on an end-around run, slipping "through an opening between huge boulders that barely allowed a light tank to pass." Coming in behind the guns, the tankers fired point-blank into the enemy position, destroying both guns and killing dozens of Japanese soldiers. When an enemy soldier jumped atop one of the tanks, machine-gun bullets from the following tank quickly shot him off. After returning to their own lines, Lieutenant Dorey discovered that one of his tanks had finally received some damage and had to withdraw from the fight.[40]

Unfortunately for the Army troops, their attempt to capture the Nafutan peninsula was making little headway. Every day the Americans pushed forward a little and every night they pulled back to almost the same foxholes that they had occupied the night before. When the Americans pulled back, the Japanese naturally moved back in. On June 25, while Lieutenant Dorey's three tanks were undergoing much needed maintenance, Lieutenant Bullock took three tanks to support the advance of the 105th IReg. To his amazement, he discovered that he had to silence some of the same gun positions that had been silenced by Lieutenant Dorey's tanks the day before.[41]

As Lieutenant Bullock's tanks accompanied the infantry into the Nafutan peninsula, they "became entangled in the undergrowth and rocks and could be of no assistance." In the afternoon, however, the tanks managed to work their way into an area where they could direct their fire into enemy positions and for the next two hours sprayed machine-gun and canister fire into the dense underbrush. Then, around 4:00 P.M., just as the infantry was about to continue its advance, the tankers informed the foot soldiers they were out of ammunition. Without tank support, the infantry canceled its attack and dug in for the night.[42]

Nearby, Lieutenant Phalon's Stuart tanks, fresh from mopping up around Cape Obiam, were helping another company of infantry advance along the Nafutan ridgeline. As Captain Appleman acknowledged, however, "The Japanese positions were in rocks and bad places for tanks to approach." In addition, the Japanese had mined the only available route for tanks, forcing the advance to bog down until the mines were removed. Finally, two tanks moved forward and destroyed two Japanese machine-gun emplacements. The infantry then moved forward again but came under heavy machine-gun fire and had to call for the tanks again.

For a short time, the two tanks moved around firing well-placed shots of canister and machine-gun fire toward the Japanese lines. When the infantrymen finally went forward, they found "six heavy machine guns, several mortars, a wrecked dual-purpose gun, and all types of grenades and ammunition, together with the dead bodies of over a hundred Japanese." Although Captain Appleman claimed that the infantry credited Lieutenant Phalon's tanks with causing all of the damage, the claim is a bit dubious. Still, the combined tank-infantry attack broke the back of the Japanese resistance on the Nafutan peninsula and left the whole ridgeline open to an American advance. The path to Nafutan point and the sea was now open.[43]

On June 26, the 105th IReg pushed toward the sea. One section of Lieutenant Phalon's tanks knocked out a Japanese 75mm pack howitzer and killed twenty-four Imperial soldiers while another section knocked out a machine-gun nest, which had just wounded four GIs. By the end of the day, Phalon's platoon had accounted for four more machine guns and numerous individual snipers. Late in the afternoon, when the tanks returned to battalion headquarters to rearm and refuel, the infantry pushed on. By 4:30 P.M. they had reached the southern end of the Nafutan ridge and dug in for the night.[44]

That night, with the Americans in possession of the western ridge of the Nafutan peninsula, the Japanese decided to quit the Nafutan valley. Breaking into various size groups, an estimated 500 Japanese soldiers slipped through the porous American lines without being detected. As they fled northward, some of the Japanese attacked Aslito airfield and a few Marine Corps positions. Eventually, however, almost all 500 infiltrators were hunted down and killed.[45]

With all able-bodied Imperial soldiers gone from the Nafutan peninsula, the 105th IReg easily swept down the length of the peninsula on June 27 and managed to reach Nafutan Point. Once again, Lieutenant Dorey's platoon of light tanks assisted in the advance. More than 550 Japanese bodies were found strewn about the southern end of the peninsula, causing Captain Appleman to write, "Most of the wounded and sick soldiers unable to travel probably had committed suicide."[46] For all intents and purposes the battle for the Nafutan peninsula was over. Unfortunately, the battle for northern Saipan was just beginning.

CHAPTER SEVENTEEN

The Valley of Death

Marine Corps General Holland M. Smith was not happy with the progress of the 27th IDiv. He believed the Nafutan peninsula could have been captured a lot quicker. In reality, the Army never should have pulled back each night, giving back the ground it had won throughout the day and having to recapture it the next. Still, it was the slow and cautious movement of the soldiers in the center of Saipan that really angered General Smith.[1]

On June 22, the 27th IDiv had moved up to the Marine Corps line that ran across the waist of the anteater. As the troops moved into an area in reserve, the M4 medium tanks of Company B, 762nd TB saw their first action on Saipan. As the 106th IReg moved into its reserve position, it came under heavy machine gun fire. Lieutenant Lansford and his five Sherman tanks were called up and proceeded to knock out four Japanese machine-gun nests. By nightfall, the 27th IDiv and the attached tanks of the 762nd and 766th battalions were ready to assist in the conquest of northern Saipan.[2]

On June 23, the Marines moved out with the 2nd MarDiv on the left, or west, and the 4th MarDiv on the right, or east. The two divisions made good progress throughout the day and when darkness came, the 4th MarDiv was in position to swing farther to its right, hugging the northern shore of Magicienne Bay, and advance into the forelegs of the anteater, into the Kagman peninsula. In doing so, however, the division would lose contact with the 2nd MarDiv troops on their left, so General Holland Smith decided to plug the inevitable gap with the 27th IDiv. On the night of June 22–23, the Army troops moved into position and prepared to enter some of the worst terrain on Saipan.[3]

Facing the 27th IDiv and its supports were areas that came to be known as Death Valley, Hell's Pocket, and Purple Heart Ridge. All three nightmarish areas lay east of Mount Tapotchau, the highest point of Saipan. An Army historian described the areas:

The floor of the valley, less than 1,000 yards in width is dominated along its entire length by the rugged slopes of Mount Tapotchau on the west and a series of hills, the highest about 150 feet above the valley floor, on the east. The eastern hill system was to be called Purple Heart Ridge by the soldiers who fought there. Death Valley, then, was a sort of trough into which the men of the 27th Division were to advance. The valley itself was almost devoid of cover except for a line of trees near the southern end. . . . The cliff on the left was for the most part bare, but above the cliff was wooded ground. The hills on the right were tree-covered. A narrow road—little more than a cowpath—ran up the valley a short distance then branched off, the left branch skirting the cliffs of Mount Tapotchau, the right heading toward . . . the east. . . . Obviously, the terrain was ideally suited for defense.[4]

Before the 27th IDiv moved out on June 23, two of its regiments got tangled together and the entire attack was postponed for almost one hour. This incident, and others, added to Holland Smith's impatience with the Army and General Ralph Smith. Then, when the infantrymen finally got under way, they ran into a wall of Japanese defenses. On the right flank, elements of the 165th IReg came under fire as they worked their way around the northern face of 700-foot Hill Love. Subsequently halted and pinned down, they called for tanks.[5]

Lieutenant Fleck (Company D, 766th TB) sent two of his Stuart tanks to knock out two machine-gun nests "down by the first sharp curve of the road to the right front" while he set off with two other tanks to "search out the ground to the left."

Through some miscommunication, Sgt. Carl E. Green started down the road alone and made good progress until he began taking heavy enemy fire from the front, right front, and rear. Some of the first shots tore off his radio antenna and Sergeant Green could not call for help. More shots wrecked a few of the tank periscopes and when the crew tried to replace them with spares, these too were shot up.

Pressing on, Green's tank eventually ran into a temporary Japanese roadblock with an enemy field piece off to the right. Although the gun was not manned, the Japanese pelted the tank with a couple of Molotov cocktails and set it on fire. Reacting quickly, the tank crew grabbed fire extinguishers and extinguished the flames inside the tank while the driver, Sgt. Joe C. Walsh, pulled the motor fire extinguisher and smothered any flames inside the engine compartment.

By peering out of an undamaged rear periscope, Sergeant Green managed to guide his tank away from the enemy position and turned his tank around. Then, instead of running the enemy gauntlet back to their own lines, the tank slipped down a steep embankment on the left side of the road into a sugarcane field.

As the tank roared across the field, it received a direct hit from a large caliber Japanese gun. The heavy concussion temporarily blinded Sergeant Walsh but the bow gunner, Pvt. Raymond A. Brown, acted as Walsh's eyes and directed the tank across the cane field. After going about one hundred yards, Sergeant Green's tank suddenly came upon Lieutenant Fleck's tank, going in the opposite direction.

Without even stopping, Green's radioless tank passed within two feet of Fleck's tank, got to the end of the cane field, and eventually made it back to friendly lines.[6]

While Sergeant Green's tank was being assaulted, Lieutenant Fleck had run into trouble of his own. Fleck had originally set out with three tanks to check the area to the left of the roadway but after going only a short distance, he decided to go alone since he "did not think the terrain would permit the full section [of tanks] to function satisfactorily." Proceeding into the cane field, Lieutenant Fleck was moving ahead cautiously when the battered and beaten tank of Sergeant Green rushed by. Unable to reach Green because of Green's broken aerial, Fleck pressed on, unaware of the roadblock and the Japanese presence. Angling slightly to his right, Fleck eventually came out of the field and struck the road behind the road- block. Not realizing that he was behind enemy lines, Fleck proceeded northward down the narrow roadway.

Near 3:00 P.M., as the lone tank reached a right-hand curve it came upon two disabled Japanese tanks. Seconds later, Molotov cocktails rained down upon the lone Stuart and set it on fire. Instead of backing straight out of the danger like Ser- geant Green, Lieutenant Fleck's driver attempted to pull a three-point turn in the widest part of the curve. Captain Appleman described what happened next:

> The tank must have been burning fiercely as it attempted to turn around. While the tank motor is running at a good rate of speed it still may be able to draw enough oxygen to permit combustion even though the engine is on fire. In order to shift from reverse to forward in a tank it is necessary to throttle the motor down to an idle. The flames then cut off the air to the motor and the engine stopped. Once stopped, with a fire burning in it, seldom can the engine be started again. In Fleck's tank the engine undoubtedly stopped when the driver slowed the motor to idle in order to shift to forward gear. It then could not be started again.

With a dead engine and the tank in flames, Lieutenant Fleck and his crew decided to abandon the vehicle. Turret gunner PFC Isadore Goldberg was the first out of the tank and managed to reach the safety of a ditch on the left side of the road. Lieutenant Fleck came out second and dropped alongside his tank with a Thompson sub-machine gun. However, when dozens of Japanese soldiers sud- denly rushed toward the tank, Fleck decided to drop the gun and throw up his hands. Seconds later, a Japanese bullet struck him in the back and as he dropped to his hands and knees a half dozen enemy bayonets pierced his body.

As Private Goldberg feigned death in the bottom of the roadside ditch, more than 200 Japanese soldiers swarmed around the tank, bayoneting the driver as he tried to surrender and shooting the bow gunner before he could even get out of the burning tank. After what seemed an eternity, the Japanese finally departed and Private Goldberg rose from the ditch. With his hands damaged from being tram- pled upon by the milling Japanese soldiers, and his left foot injured by shrapnel, Goldberg's progress back to his own lines was extremely slow. Near midnight of

June 23–24, the exhausted and shocked tanker finally gained the safety of a Marine Corps outpost.[7]

Elsewhere along the Army front, progress had been painstakingly slow. On either flank, however, the two Marine Corps divisions had run up against much less resistance and had moved approximately one mile ahead of the Army troops. The cautious and slow advance of the 27th IDiv infuriated Marine General Smith and he sent a blistering dispatch to Army General Smith. He wanted the Army division to push forward at the same rate as the two Marine Corps divisions or heads would roll.[8]

On June 24, Lieutenant Williams led his medium tank platoon over to support Company C, 165th IReg on the right side of the Army line. Somehow the first section of three Sherman tanks, led by Lieutenant Williams, got separated from everyone else and ended up going down the same road that Lieutenant Fleck and Sergeant Green had taken. Lieutenant Williams' tank No. 33 was in the lead, with Sergeant Pusey's tank No. 34 in the middle, and Tech 4 Kuebler's tank No. 35 in the rear. Before long, the three tanks came to the right-hand curve in the road and spotted Lieutenant Fleck's abandoned and still burning Stuart. Nearby lay the mutilated remains of Lieutenant Fleck and two crewmen. In the near distance, Lieutenant Williams noticed the two disabled Japanese tanks but was unaware of their status. Acting defensively, he ordered his driver to skirt around the left side of Fleck's abandoned tank and stop at the foot of a small knoll.

Sergeant Pusey, in the second tank, saw Williams leave the road and followed close behind, coming to a stop when the lead tank did. Sergeant Kuebler saw the first two Shermans swing to the left and come to stop so he ordered his driver to stop in the roadway, some distance behind the other two. At that very instant, the Japanese attacked. Cpl. Howard D. Myers, the gunner in Sergeant Kuebler's tank, recalled "the entire little knoll to the left seemed to move." Hidden Japanese soldiers suddenly sprang to their feet and raced down the knoll toward Lieutenant Williams' lead tank. Almost immediately, Corporal Myers opened fire with his coaxial machine gun. Wrote Captain Appleman, "He swung the gun in a narrow arc . . . and knocked the Japanese down within three or four feet of [William's tank]. He used up sixteen boxes of .30-caliber ammunition, or about 1,400 rounds, at this time, firing as rapidly as possible."

The quick action by Corporal Myers broke the Japanese assault and chased the survivors back over the crest of the knoll. Moving quickly, Lieutenant Williams and Sergeant Pusey backed their Shermans around Lieutenant Fleck's Stuart and then all three tanks turned to the right and headed down a steep grade toward the sugarcane field. As the lead tank descended the embankment, however, the clutch suddenly went out and the driver had to coast the tank down the steep grade. Once at the bottom, Lieutenant Williams fastened a tow cable to Sergeant Pusey's tank and while Sergeant Kuebler's tank stood guard, the stricken vehicle was towed over to a nearby wood line.[9]

It was 11:25 A.M. when the three tanks reached the trees and discovered a detachment of Marines. Somehow, the tanks had entered the 4th MarDiv's zone of control. Thinking their ordeal was over, the tank crew began to relax. As Lieutenant Williams and a Marine stood conversing behind one of the tanks, the Japanese opened up with a heavy artillery barrage. Ignoring the incoming fire, Lieutenant Williams and the Marine continued to chat until a shot suddenly rang out and the Marine dropped dead. Fearing the possibility of a sniper, Williams instantly dove behind Sergeant Pusey's tank.

As Lieutenant Williams looked around, he noticed a Japanese soldier hidden on the opposite side of the tank, trying to wedge a few grenades into the tracks. Climbing onto the rear deck of the tank, Williams tried to get Sergeant Pusey's attention by banging on the closed turret hatch but the crew did not respond. Fortunately, Sergeant Kuebler's crew noticed what was going on and contacted Sergeant Pusey via inter-tank radio. Opening his hatch, Sergeant Pusey initially handed Lieutenant Williams two hand grenades but when the grenades failed to kill the infiltrator, Williams was given a Thompson and despatched the enemy soldier with a burst of gunfire.

Shortly thereafter, the Marine unit received word that Japanese tanks were moving up behind the enemy artillery barrage. Responding quickly, Sergeants Pusey and Kuebler moved their tanks to the edge of the wood line and took up positions beside a few Marine Corps antitank guns. Within ten minutes, the artillery barrage stopped and three Japanese tanks (not five) appeared at the far side of the cane field. Opening fire, the Marine Corps antitank gun and the two Army tanks stopped all three enemy tanks dead in their tracks. Then, with the immediate threat eliminated, Lieutenant Williams and his crew climbed atop the other two tanks and, leaving his disabled tank behind, headed back toward the 165th IReg command post.[10]

On June 24, the 106th IReg, 27th IDiv moved into Death Valley at about 8:00 A.M. By 9:30 A.M., they had traveled no more than fifty yards. Heavy fire rained down upon the men from both sides of the valley, but especially from the cliffs of Mount Tapotchau, which was being assaulted by the 2nd MarDiv. When Marine General Smith got word of the slow advance of the Army troops, he radioed a blistering message to the Army commander. "Advance of fifty yards in one and one-half hours is most unsatisfactory. Start moving at once." The infantry immediately called in the two medium tank platoons of Lieutenants Hitchner and Lansford.[11]

When the tanks arrived, the infantry began moving ahead at a rapid pace and covered another fifty yards before a fusillade of gunfire erupted from their left, from the cliffs of Tapotchau. As the foot soldiers went to ground, three medium tanks commanded by Lieutenant Hitchner moved a few hundred yards out into Death Valley and opened fire against the cliff side. As they fired, however, they received "very heavy antitank gun, mortar, and machine gun fire from the high ground on the left." After one of the Shermans left the area with a load of wounded soldiers clinging to it, Lieutenant Hitchner's tank was hit, and so was Sergeant Wilson's tank, which took a hit in the rear with a high velocity shell that destroyed his engine. In rapid succession, several more rounds hit Hitchner's tank and set it on fire.

Although the Japanese fire continued, Lieutenant Hitchner gave the order to bail out. With the second tank providing covering fire, Hitchner and his crew evacuated their burning tank and eventually made a twenty-yard dash to a small hut in a burned out sugarcane field. As the five men huddled behind the building, they suddenly realized they were only a few hundred yards from the American front line. In an attempt to create a smoke screen for a dash to safety, Lieutenant Hitchner set fire to the hut but all it did was give off a little smoke.

Luckily, at about this time, the tank that had evacuated the wounded returned, along with Lieutenant Lansford and his Sherman. Moving up, the two tanks proceeded to fire smoke shells between the hut and the enemy. However, just before Lieutenant Hitchner's crew could escape, a mortar shell impacted behind the hut and wounded four of the five men. With the two tanks continuing to lay down a smoke screen, Army stretcher teams raced forward and carried two men to safety. A third was placed on the rear deck of one of the tanks and Lieutenant Hitchner, the only man unwounded, and the fourth man walked to safety between the bulk of the two retreating tanks.[12]

Before coming to the rescue of Lieutenant Hitchner and his crew, Lieutenant Lansford and his platoon had run into a little trouble of their own. Two tanks from Lansford's second section had been helping the infantry to the left of the mouth of Death Valley at the very base of the cliffs of Mount Tapotchau. Moving through heavy brush, the tank-infantry advance came to a complete stop when a Japanese 47mm antitank round disabled the 75mm cannon of one of the tanks. Then, in rapid succession, the second tank exploded a mine and was hit five times by antitank shells. Damaged but not disabled, both tanks quickly retired to the rear.

Lieutenant Lansford and his other two tanks had been near the entrance to Death Valley when he was told his second section tanks had retired from the far left flank. With the infantry in front of Mount Tapotchau in dire need of armor, Lansford "borrowed" two tanks from Lieutenant Hitchner's platoon and sent them over to the far left flank.[13]

Shortly thereafter, Lansford received word that Lieutenant Hitchner's crew was in trouble and immediately rushed over to help. After affecting the rescue, Lansford returned to the mouth of Death Valley, where he remained for the rest of the day. In the course of the afternoon, one more medium tank was put out of action when its cannon tube was struck three times by Japanese antitank rounds, another was disabled with a cracked gas tank and a third was lost when its suspension system was shot up. By the end of the day, only two fully functioning Sherman tanks remained out of the ten that had ventured into Death Valley in the morning.[14]

After a full day of fighting, the 27th IDiv had moved no further than the day before. On either flank, however, the Marine divisions had moved ahead another mile. Unable to tolerate the slow movement of the Army troops any longer, Marine Corps General Holland M. Smith relieved Army General Ralph Smith from command and replaced him with Army Maj. Gen. Sanderford Jarman.[15]

Knowing that his every move would be fully scrutinized, Jarman devised a new strategy of attack. According to the plan, the 2nd Bn, 106th IReg with Lieutenant

Williams' two operational medium tanks and the four light tanks of Lieutenant Bullock's platoon would close off the southern end of the valley and hold the defenders in place. At the same time, the 1st Bn and 3rd Bn, 106th IReg, accompanied by the remaining medium tanks of Lieutenants Hitchner and Lansford, would circle around the right flank and close off the northern end of the valley. Then, with both ends of the valley closed off, the 165th IReg would attack westward against the right-hand ridge itself—Purple Heart Ridge. If all went well, the 27th IDiv would squeeze the Japanese inside Death Valley into an ever-shrinking pocket and bring the GIs abreast of the two Marine divisions.[16]

Although June 25 began with the 2nd MarDiv on the left flank overrunning the summit of Mount Tapotchau and the 4th MarDiv on the right completing their occupation of the Kagman peninsula, the 27th IDiv had a hard time executing its flanking move. Hampered by bad roads and heavy opposition, the two 106th IReg flanking battalions ground to a halt after advancing only a few hundred yards.[17]

At the mouth of Death Valley, the 2nd Battalion troops and Lieutenants Williams' and Bullock's tanks were a bit more successful. At 4:30 P.M., after a very heavy artillery barrage, the two medium and four light tanks entered the valley. Although the infantry claimed the tanks "were out of contact with the troops for the rest of the afternoon and operated independently, firing at will at targets of opportunity," the tankers claimed they attempted to make contact with the infantry three separate times with no luck. Each time the tanks rumbled out into the center of Death Valley, fired a few shots, and then went back to look for the infantry.[18]

Whenever the tanks entered the valley they drew heavy enemy fire, especially from the cliffs at the foot of Mount Tapotchau. On the third trip out, Lieutenant Williams' medium tank was hit with an antitank round, causing the turret to lock in place. When another shell went through the engine compartment, Lieutenant Williams decided to withdraw his two Shermans. While the mediums withdrew, the light tanks went out into the valley one more time, still looking for the elusive American infantry. Instead, they found two Japanese tanks. In the following tank-versus-tank action, one American Stuart had a track blown off before both Japanese tanks were destroyed. By the end of the day, the two medium and four light tanks had accounted for two enemy tanks, two antitank guns, and one pillbox.[19]

On June 26, after two more Japanese attempts to reinforce Saipan by water were detected and turned back by the Americans, the 27th IDiv renewed its flanking move. However, instead of having the two battalions from the 106th IReg swing around behind the 165th IReg and its attack against the side of Purple Heart Ridge, the two battalions were ordered to help take the ridge. Although the 106th IReg battalions had no trouble getting onto the southern portion of the ridge, they had a hard time dislodging the Japanese defenders from their caves and outcroppings. Eventually, the American tanks and mobile artillery were brought up and fired point blank into the enemy positions. Whenever the Japanese fled, the American riflemen eagerly picked them off.[20]

By the end of the day, the 106th IReg had still not seized Purple Heart Ridge so General Jarman relieved the regimental commander. The 165th IReg, however, did much better and kept its commander. During the day, two battalions of the

165th IReg and the light tanks of Lieutenant Sillix's platoon from Company D, 766th TB, pushed far ahead of the rest of the 27th IDiv troops until they were almost adjacent to the 4th MarDiv on their right. Since they were so far ahead of the other Army units, the two battalions and Sillix's tanks were temporarily placed under the control of the Marine Corps.[21]

On June 27, aided by mortar and artillery fire, the 2nd Bn, 165th IReg (which was the only battalion of that regiment still attached to the Army), finally managed to capture most of the northern half of Purple Heart Ridge. The only ground that was not taken was a steep hill on the very northern end code-named Hill Able.[22]

Moving up to assist in the attack on Hill Able were a few light tanks of Company D, 766th TB and the medium tanks of Lieutenant Hitchner from Company B, 762nd TB. Fighting in the steep, hilly terrain, one medium tank flipped over, three more tanks threw a track, and one medium and one light were disabled by enemy fire. None of the crewmen were seriously wounded but because of the heavy volume of incoming fire and the rough terrain, all six tanks had to wait until darkness before they could be righted, repaired or recovered.[23]

While Hill Able was being assaulted, the 1st and 3rd Battalions, 106th IReg's pushed westward into Death Valley. Almost immediately, the attackers encountered a steady stream of fire from the cliffs along the base of Mount Tapotchau. When the infantry called for tanks, Lieutenant Williams and his three remaining mediums responded. A Marine Corps historian described what happened next. "Soon after the tanks moved out on their mission, it began to rain. Dust on the tanks turned to mud, vision from within became blurred, and the machines lost direction. Instead of firing on the planned targets, they opened upon men of the 3rd Battalion, 106th Infantry."[24]

Rocked by the fire from their own tanks, the infantry attack stalled until things could be straightened out. Finally, near 12:30 P.M., the infantry began moving again but just like before, they were met by a hail of enemy gunfire. In spite of what had happened before, the infantry immediately called for tanks.[25]

Almost as soon as the tanks arrived, however, the fire from the Tapotchau cliffs slackened. When Lieutenant Williams got out of his tank to talk with an infantry commander, the Japanese opened fire with their artillery. Noted Captain Appleman, "Invariably the Japanese would open fire on a tank man the moment he showed himself."

Scrambling for shelter behind his tank, Lieutenant Williams used hand signals to direct Sergeant Kuebler to move his Sherman tank to the top of a hill to fire at the enemy guns. As Kuebler swung into position, Major Fisher, an infantry officer, ran after the tank and tried to contact the sergeant via the rear-mounted outside telephone. Although Kuebler could hear Fisher pleading with him to fire on the enemy guns that were demoralizing his men, the infantry officer could not hear the tanker's response. While loading the cannon, a shell had become stuck partway into the breech and could not be moved.

For several seconds Major Fisher pleaded with Sergeant Kuebler over the broken phone before realizing the sergeant might not be able to talk back. When he asked the crew if they could hear him, Kuebler's driver raced the engine. Next, one of the crewmen climbed out of the bottom escape hatch and informed Major Fisher of the stuck shell. Finally, Corporal Myers, the gunner, located a block of wood and in spite of the danger of the shell exploding pounded the shell into the chamber. Not knowing what to expect, the men probably uttered a great sigh of relief when the cannon fired without incident. Then, directed by Major Fisher, Sergeant Kuebler's crew fired round after round into the enemy positions, knocking out a dug-in Japanese tank and an enemy machine-gun nest. Near nightfall, the tanks carried sixteen wounded GIs back to the infantry aid station.[26]

While all of this action was taking place, Lieutenant Ganio's platoon from Company D, 766th TB replaced Lieutenant Sillix's tanks that had been placed under Marine Corps control. Advancing into the rough wooded area northwest of Death Valley, with the two battalions of the 165th IReg, the light tanks moved out about twenty-five yards ahead of the infantry to shell a cliff face about 150 yards away. Near 10:00 A.M., a Japanese antitank shell tore through the thin skin of S/Sgt. James N. Linder's Stuart, showering the crew with metal shards. As the men scrambled out of the tank, two more shells set the tank on fire. Unfortunately, Pvt. Martin L. Petosa, the bow gunner, never made it out of the tank. Days later his charred body was recovered from inside the tank.[27]

The next day, June 28, the overall attack was renewed. The two battalions of the 165th IReg, fighting with the 4th MarDiv, continued their northern drive. Eventually, the 4th MarDiv finished clearing out the Kagman peninsula and moved northward and westward to give the infantrymen a hand. As the 4th MarDiv swung westward, the 27th IDiv troops did likewise, finally pinching off the northern end of Death Valley. With the Army troops finally making good ground, a platoon of medium tanks from Company B, 762nd TB and two platoons of light tanks from Company D, 766th TB were sent forward to help. Commented Captain Appleman, "It seemed that all available tanks were thrown into the action in this area. Everywhere about in caves and rocks it seemed there were enemy machine gun nests. Heavy mortar fire was coming from [Hill Able on the northern end of Purple Heart Ridge] and it had been one of the principal factors in checking the advance. The tanks made an effort to locate and destroy these mortars but they were unsuccessful."[28]

By nightfall on June 28–29 the 27th IDiv, with the help of the 4th MarDiv, was holding a backward L-shaped line on Saipan. The long shank of the reversed "L" was being held by the 4th MarDiv and the attached 165th IReg, along with two battalions from the 105th IReg, 27th IDiv that had been sent up from reserve. The bottom of the backward "L" ran along the top of Death Valley and was held by the 1st and 3rd Battalions, 106th IReg. The 2nd Bn, 106th IReg was still fighting around Hell's Pocket, near the mouth of Death Valley, but for all practical purposes, almost all organized resistance inside the valley had been eliminated. The only remaining hot spots were around Hell's Pocket and on Hill Able.[29]

That same date, Maj. Gen. George W. Griner, fresh from Hawaii, replaced General Jarman as commander of the 27th IDiv. After assessing the situation, Griner shifted the 106th IReg to the left to tie it into the 2nd MarDiv and then decided to send the 2nd Bn, 105th IReg, which had seen no action since capturing the Nafutan peninsula, to help in the attacks against Hill Able.[30]

The next day, June 29, while the 27th IDiv attacked Hell's Pocket and Hill Able with renewed vigor, the 4th MarDiv and the attached battalions from the 165th and 105th regiments on the right flank continued to hold the long shank of the "L" as they waited for the Army to finish its work. On the left, elements of the 2nd MarDiv moved up to the city of Garapan, on the far west coast, and then waited for the rest of the division, as well as the 27th IDiv, to come up.[31]

On the morning of June 30, the official fight for Death Valley came to an end with the reduction of Hell's Pocket and the capture of Hill Able. At the northern end of Death Valley, the 105th IReg tried to move north along the long shank of the reversed "L" with nine light tanks from Company D, 766th TB and a medium tank platoon from Company B, 762nd TB. Jumping off at 7:15 A.M., the infantry and tanks moved steadily forward for about two hours until a Japanese dual-purpose gun on a nearby hill opened fire. In a matter of minutes, one medium and one light tank were hit. Although the infantry commander wanted to call in an immediate artillery strike, the American tanks raced recklessly ahead to duel with the gun. More than two hours later, the tanks returned from the front and the artillery barrage was called in.[32]

On the left flank, the 106th IReg spent June 30 waiting for the 105th IReg to catch up with it. As it waited, it discovered the Japanese were still dug into the cliffs at the foot of Mount Tapotchau. In response, a platoon of medium tanks fired at the cliff face and into any visible caves.[33]

Near 2:00 P.M., Lieutenant Bullock's platoon of light tanks from Company D, 762nd TB came up to replace the mediums. By now the infantry was ready to assault the caves but after an advance of only 100 yards ran into heavy Japanese machine-gun fire. Moving out to help, Sgt. John R. Reidy took two light tanks to the top of a ridge to see if he could locate the enemy gun. Instead, he encountered two Japanese medium and one light tank. In the ensuing tank-versus-tank battle, Sergeant Reidy knocked out the light tank and one medium, and damaged the other one before it could quit the field. Then, after the last enemy tank was gone, Reidy returned to his original mission and destroyed the hidden Japanese machine gun. For his courageous actions, Sergeant Reidy was issued a Bronze Star medal.[34]

In the 4th MarDiv sector, the 3rd Bn, 165th IReg, still under Marine Corps control, held the very top of the reversed "L." For all practical purposes, it was the link between the 4th MarDiv and the 27th IDiv. On June 30, five medium tanks led by Capt. Charles S. Ward, commander of Company B, 762nd TB, came up to assist the battalion attack. Having lost a number of tanks and two platoon leaders, Captain Ward "welded the remaining tanks and men of these two platoons into a platoon of his own and fought with and led them as a platoon leader." As the attack stepped off, a Japanese 75mm dual-purpose shell hit and disabled one of the tanks, wounding one crewman. Although Captain Ward looked for a safer route of advance for his four remaining tanks, he found only more dual-purpose guns and eventually was forced to withdraw.[35]

Although the 3rd Bn, 165th IReg was unable to take the hill in front of it, the other 27th IDiv units finally managed to advance well beyond Death Valley. With the 27th IDiv coming on line and closing the gap between the 2nd and 4th MarDivs, the fight for central Saipan came to an end. The conquest of central Saipan had cost the two Marine divisions 2,522 men. The loss for the single Army division was 1,465. Fighting against a stubborn foe in rough terrain had proved costly, but the main Japanese line of resistance on Saipan had been breached.[36] As the Marines and soldiers assembled for the final push toward the northern shore of Saipan, they undoubtedly hoped the going would be easier and a lot less bloody.

CHAPTER EIGHTEEN

Hard Days on Saipan

By the time central Saipan was secure, all of the Army tanks were in dire need of repair. They had been in almost constant combat for seven straight days and among other things had developed problems with their radios and interphone systems. Additionally, by July 1, the different tank companies had "very largely lost their regular platoon groupings." Captain Appleman explained, "The number of knocked out tanks and those in maintenance for major repairs had become so large that it was necessary to put all the operating tanks in a pool and assign a certain number each morning to leaders for particular missions."

On July 1, a platoon of medium tanks under Lieutenant Lansford and some light tanks under Lieutenant Dorey went out to support the 3rd Bn, 105th IReg move along the right side of the 27th IDiv line. While the light tanks waited, Lansford's mediums helped the infantry assault a fortified hill. In the attack, a Japanese tank was knocked out with high-explosive shells at a range of 1,700 yards, but two of Lansford's Shermans flipped over when they tried to go over the hill.[1]

As soon as the mediums came under fire, Lieutenant Dorey's light tanks roared forward. One tank soon retired with a bad generator but the others pushed on. At one point, a Japanese soldier threw a block of picric acid (similar to TNT) at Dorey's command tank but the explosion only rocked the occupants. Darting quickly about the battlefield, the light tanks managed to set an enemy oil dump on fire, destroy two machine gun nests and shoot up "generally a number of caves, houses, and brush-covered areas."[2]

On the far left of the 27th IDiv line, several light tanks under the command of Lieutenant Guffey went out to help the 106th IReg move through a narrow pass and "gain control of a little knoll." Although the Stuarts accomplished their mission, another tank was lost when it threw a track to a Japanese land mine.

With the knoll taken, American artillery fired into the next area of advance while four medium tanks under Captain Ward came up. At 2:00 P.M., when the

An Army or Marine Corps M3A1 Satan flamethrowing tank on Saipan, Summer 1944.

shelling stopped, Captain Ward and his Shermans went out ahead of the infantry. The infantry commander also wanted Lieutenant Guffey to advance his light tanks but according to Captain Appleman, "Lieutenant Guffey protested . . . [saying] that the tanks were in no condition for the task assigned them. The order stood as given, however, and the tanks pressed forward about 800 yards." As Lieutenant Guffey had expected, two of his light tanks soon became victims of Japanese fire. As consolation, Captain Ward's mediums silenced one dual-purpose gun that had been firing on the Americans' advance from a cliff overlooking the pass.[3]

By the morning of July 2, the entire American line was advancing and swinging from right to left like a gate. On the far left side, at the gatepost, the 2nd MarDiv was ordered to advance into Garapan. As one Marine Corps historian called it, Garapan was "the first honest-to-God city under American attack in the Pacific." Laid out with streets, and brick and concrete houses, Garapan had been nearly flattened by naval fire and air attacks. The 2nd MarDiv had reached the outskirts of Garapan on June 24 and had been pounding the city with heavy artillery fire while it waited for the other units to come on line. On July 2, the Marines finally started a slow, cautious advance into the city.[4]

On the opposite side of the American line, the 4th MarDiv also was moving. While its right flank hugged the east coast of Saipan and pushed steadily northward across the narrowing neck of the anteater, its left flank made a steady advance through rolling terrain. By evening, the left flank had advanced more than 1,500 yards.[5]

In the center of the island, the 27th IDiv also made good progress. On the division right flank, the 165th IReg and two platoons of Stuart light tanks made an advance equal to the 4th MarDiv on their immediate right. In the division center, the 105th IReg, with four light tanks and a platoon of medium tanks, had an equally successful day with an advance of almost 1,900 yards.[6]

On the division's far left flank, Lieutenant Bullock's light tanks and Lieutenant Lansford's medium tanks operated with the 106th IReg. While the infantry was going across some rough, hilly terrain, it suddenly came under heavy enemy fire from six Japanese tanks (two medium and four light) dug into camouflaged, stationary positions.

Lieutenant Bullock and his light Stuart tanks swung into action, firing and maneuvering. By the time Lieutenant Lansford came up with three medium tanks, all six Japanese tanks had been silenced, four by the Stuarts and two by the infantry. Since heavy enemy fire continued to come from a number of caves in a nearby hill, Lansford and his mediums poured a steady stream of gunfire into the hillside. After more than one hour, when it appeared as though their fire was having little effect, the tanks withdrew and American artillery took over.

At 4:00 P.M., when the artillery barrage subsided, Lansford's mediums and Bullock's lights bolted forward on a reconnaissance in force. Going down the center of a valley that angled off to the northwest toward the sea, the tanks advanced about 2,500 yards in front of the infantry but encountered only light Japanese machine-gun and mortar fire. Noticing the lack of resistance, the infantry quickly followed the tanks. Before nightfall stopped the advance, the 1st Bn, 106th IReg had moved ahead 1,500 yards.[7]

In this final advance, Lieutenant Bullock once again showed his pluck. When a group of foot soldiers suffered a number of casualties from heavy enemy machine-gun fire, Bullock led his Stuart over to the pinned squad, dismounted, and in the midst of heavy fire helped evacuate three wounded men. Then, "[after] substituting an infantry soldier who thought he knew the position of the [Japanese] gun for a member of his tank crew," Bullock went back out with his tank, located the position and destroyed the machine gun and crew. For his actions, Lieutenant Bullock was awarded a Bronze Star.[8]

By the end of July 2, the left flank of the 2nd MarDiv had captured about one-half of Garapan, while the right flank had moved toward the northwest to take Tanapag harbor. In the center of Saipan, the 27th IDiv was prepared to swing a bit to the left and move in just north of the 2nd MarDiv, threatening Flores Point, a small extension of land jutting out into the ocean. And finally, on the right flank, the 4th MarDiv was ready to continue almost straight north, cutting across the neck of the anteater, which angled slightly to the northeast.[9]

At first light on July 3 the Americans renewed their advance. While the 2nd MarDiv quickly captured the rest of Garapan and continued its advance on Tanapag harbor, and the 4th MarDiv closed off the neck of the anteater, the 27th IDiv began swinging noticeably to its left, toward the sea. On the far right flank and center, the 165th IReg and the 105th IReg, respectively, made noticeable gains, stopping on line with the 4th MarDiv.

On the far left flank of the 27th IDiv line, the 106th IReg moved ahead only about 500 yards, but by the end of the day it was on top of a ridge looking down at Tanapag harbor and Flores point. Earlier, Captain Ward and his M4 Shermans had been sent on an armed reconnaissance over the ridge and had located a large

Japanese motor pool. By the time the reconnaissance was over, Wards tanks had silenced two Japanese tanks, two field pieces, and a large enemy gun that had been firing on the 2nd MarDiv.[10]

Independence Day of 1944 brought a heavy rain to Saipan, which made the roads sticky and the hills slippery. On the left, the 2nd MarDiv completed its conquest of Garapan and Tanapag harbor and moved up to help the 27th IDiv capture Flores Point. On the right, the 4th MarDiv continued to move toward the northwest and the far end of the anteater's head. In the center, the 27th IDiv made its push to the sea.[11]

Starting from a high plateau, the 27th IDiv had to move only 2,000 yards to reach Flores Point and the sea. Near 7:30 A.M., the right side of the division line, consisting of the 165th IReg and a platoon of medium tanks, broke over the edge of the plateau and descended onto the plain in front of Flores Point and the coastal village of Tanapag. Unfortunately, as the tanks started over the summit, they discovered that "the terrain was such that tanks just could not operate in it." The rain-soaked, downward grade was just too steep and the tanks began to lose control. Instead of advancing with the infantrymen, the tanks had to find alternate routes down the incline.[12]

To the left, in the center of the division line, Lieutenant Phalon's light tanks tried to support the foot soldiers of the 105th IReg but ran into the same problem there. Unwilling to have a tank flip over, Phalon led his tanks toward the left, into the zone of the 106th IReg, and followed a shallower incline onto the Tanapag plain.

Once on level ground, the tanks turned back toward the center and got back in front of the 105th IReg, which was still slowly descending from the high plateau. Instead of waiting, Phalon pushed on toward the ocean and began shelling "houses, warehouses, and other structures in the Tanapag area," killing thirty Japanese soldiers and silencing four enemy machine guns.

Shortly thereafter, the foot soldiers, led by a platoon of M4 medium tanks under Lieutenant Lansford, appeared. Apparently, the Shermans had been able to navigate the slippery grade in the center of the division without detouring around it. Once on the Tanapag plain, infantry and tanks rooted out the Japanese from their hiding places and pushed steadily toward the sea. However, just before noon, Lieutenant Phalon's lights and Lieutenant Lansford's mediums broke away from the 105th IReg and moved south to support a planned attack by the 106th IReg against Flores point.

Stepping in to fill the void left by Lansford and Phalon were the medium tanks of Captain Ward. Arriving around 11:00 A.M., Ward's tanks pushed forward with the 105th IReg and helped the infantry overrun a couple of Japanese pillboxes. At 12:30 P.M., the foot soldiers and tanks reached the western shore of Saipan, the first 27th IDiv troops to do so.[13]

On the division's left flank, Lieutenant Dorey's light tanks spent the day fighting beside the infantry of the 106th IReg. After descending from the plateau, the tanks and infantry spent the morning pushing ever closer to Flores Point. Near noon, Lieutenant Lansford's Shermans and Lieutenant Phalon's Stuarts arrived to lend a hand. Almost immediately, the heavier mediums began firing a concentration of "high explosive and shrapnel" against the point. After a half hour, the light tanks joined the mediums and spent the remainder of the hour raking the area with cannon and machine-gun fire. Then, near 1:00 P.M., a coordinated attack went forward with the 2nd MarDiv on the left and the 106th IReg on the right. Preceding the infantry were the tanks of Lieutenants Lansford, Dorey, and Phalon.

Surprisingly, the entire advance met little resistance. The only tank "casualties" occurred when a couple of tanks bogged down in a marshy area near the beach and had to be towed out by other tanks. By 2:30 P.M., Flores Point and a nearby Japanese seaplane base had been overrun.[14] The entire body of the anteater was now in American hands, but the surviving Japanese, although starving, demoralized and exhausted, still controlled the neck and head.

On July 5, the American advance turned northeast and headed toward the nose of the anteater. Since the neck of the anteater was too narrow for three divisions, the 2nd MarDiv dropped back and let the 27th IDiv advance on the left while the 4th MarDiv took the right. While Lieutenant Phalon took several light tanks to fight alongside the 165th IReg in hilly country in the center of Saipan, Lieutenant Bullock led a platoon of light tanks in advance of the 105th IReg, moving along the west coast. Advancing along a coastal road and a parallel island railroad track, Lieutenant Bullock and the infantry silenced a series of Japanese pillboxes and gun emplacements.[15]

About a mile northeast of Flores Point, Lieutenant Bullock and Sergeant Linder turned their tanks inland. As the tanks started across a large field, a lone American soldier suddenly appeared on the far side, running toward the tanks and shouting and waving his arms. Just as the man neared Sergeant Linder's tank, the vehicle rolled over a mine. The explosion killed Sergeant Linder and two other crewmen, badly wounded crewman Pfc. Calvin W. Robinson and flipped the light tank over on its side. Rendered almost senseless, Private Robinson saw light coming through the bottom of the tank and eventually realized he was on his side and the emergency escape hatch had been blown off. As he crawled out the open hatch and dropped into the huge crater created by the explosion, Japanese machine guns opened fire on him.

Once in the hole, Robinson noticed that the soldier who had been running toward the tanks was lying badly wounded in a nearby shell hole. Apparently, the unknown GI, an engineer, had been risking his life to warn the tankers they were entering a Japanese minefield. When Sergeant Linder's tank exploded, the engineer had been no more than fifteen feet away and caught the blast full in the face.[16]

When Lieutenant Bullock and his crew heard the explosion they came to a full stop. Thinking they were being fired on by a Japanese antitank gun, the crew grabbed their machine guns and bailed out into a nearby shell hole. Once there, the men spotted Linder's devastated tank and the wounded Private Robinson, and realized what had happened. In spite of incoming Japanese fire, bow gunner Tech 5 Steve N. Sudovich ran over to help Robinson.

When Sudovich arrived, Private Robinson was still in a daze. According to Captain Appleman, "There were two holes in [Robinson's] right leg, his helmet was crushed, and his face was bleeding and swelling." Sudovich was binding Robinson's wounds when driver Tech 4 Jesus Tijerina arrived to lend a hand. However, once Tijerina saw how badly Robinson was wounded, he decided to go for help. While Sudovich laid down a covering fire with his Thompson, Tijerina rushed off to find a few medics with the 105th IReg.

Within minutes, the infantry started an artillery barrage between the tanks and the Japanese. Forty minutes later, a few medics rushed forward and carried Private Robinson and the wounded engineer to safety. For their gallant effort in helping to rescue Private Robinson and the wounded engineer, both Tech 4 Tijerina and Tech 5 Sudovich were awarded Bronze Stars.[17]

Further inland, in the hilly country northeast of Tanapag, the 165th IReg was stopped at a place nicknamed "Hara-kiri Gulch" near 1:00 P.M. When the call went out for tank support, Lieutenant Phalon sent his Second Section to help out. When the two tanks, commanded by Sergeant Nichter and Sgt. William N. Brown, took a circuitous route to reach the infantry, they ran into trouble. As they came down the steep incline of a sunken road, both crews spotted two disabled Marine Corps tanks at the foot of the road. Warily, they proceeded with caution.[18]

Sergeant Nichter's tank was in the lead and was nearing the two Marine Corps tanks when the sergeant suddenly heard a loud explosion and felt his light tank "rock like a rocking chair." Unknown to the crew, a Japanese soldier crouching inside a spider hole in the embankment beside the road had suddenly dashed out and thrown two magnetic mines atop the tank. The resulting explosions stopped the tank in its tracks, killed the radio, blew the turret hatches open and wounded three of the crew, including Sergeant Nichter. As smoke filled the tank, the crew bailed out.

Sergeant Brown's tank was following close behind Nichter's and the bow gunner quickly fired a burst from his machine gun at the enemy soldier but the man disappeared back into his spider hole. When Brown's tank came abreast of the hole, two magnetic mines were thrown at it. Reported Captain Appleman, "At least one of these mines hit in front of the turret, damaging the radiator. The tank got very hot and carbon monoxide gas began coming inside the crew compartment. Private Donovan, gunner, had seen the Jap who threw these last mines and he swung his turret facing the hole in the road bank and fired [his cannon] into it. There was no further trouble from that enemy position."[19]

In the meantime, Sergeant Nichter's crew had scrambled out of the vehicle. As Japanese machine gun fire from pillboxes and from the two disabled Marine Corps tanks pinged off the armor of their tank, the four crewmen crawled underneath it.

After some time, Lieutenant Phalon arrived with his First Section of three tanks. Having lost radio contact with his second section, Phalon had set out to locate it. Immediately upon arrival, Phalon spotted the smoking ruins of Sergeant Nichter's tank and the idle form of Sergeant Brown's Stuart. Realizing both crews were in trouble, Lieutenant Phalon's three tanks rushed down the hill and quickly managed to silence each enemy position. In the lead, Phalon's command tank raced past the two disabled tanks and then maneuvered to turn around. At that point, a Japanese magnetic mine landed on the rear deck of his tank and exploded.

The explosion did not injure the crew but killed the engine and shattered all of the glass in the periscopes. Before his crew could bail out, Lieutenant Phalon told them to sit tight and calmly instructed his driver to try restarting the engine. Fortunately, the engine roared back to life and the tank completed its turn. Moving forward, Phalon's tank bumped up against Sergeant Nichter's and Phalon's bow gunner and quickly threw open his chassis hatch. Seconds later, two men from Sergeant Nichter's crew climbed inside. At about the same time, another of Nichter's crew crawled out from under the rear of the tank and climbed inside Sergeant Brown's tank.

"In the midst of all this excitement," Captain Appleman wrote, "Sergeant Brown was trying to get his tank turned around." Discovering that the exploding mines had shattered his periscopes, Brown climbed out of his tank and tried directing his driver, Tech 5 LeRoy J. Day, with hand signals. Unknown to Brown, however, Day had been overcome by noxious fumes and had to be revived by the bow gunner, who ventilated the tank by throwing open the driver's hatch. As Day finally began the turning maneuver, Sergeant Brown was shot in the chest. Ignoring the wound, Brown continued to direct Day until the tank was completely turned around and then, as Brown moved back toward his tank, he was shot through the right arm. Unable to get into his own tank, he was helped inside one of the First Section tanks.[20]

With all of his crewmen safely inside the different tanks, Sergeant Nichter finally climbed inside a tank and Lieutenant Phalon gave the order to withdraw. Immediately, the four remaining Stuarts started back up the hill, leaving Sergeant Nichter's smoking and disabled tank behind.[21]

"Two of the tanks had been hit hard," commented historian Appleman, "and they barely made it up the first hill. On the second hill, Phalon's tank, No. 64, failed." At that very instant, however, two medium tanks from Company B, 762nd TB, under the command of Lieutenant Williams, appeared at the top of the hill and came partway down to help their little brothers. While the other light tanks and one of the mediums gave covering fire, the second medium turned around and backed up to Lieutenant Phalon's stalled tank. Sergeant Rustad, Phalon's driver, and Lieutenant Phalon himself then exited their tank under fire and hooked a tow cable to the waiting Sherman. As the two men hustled back to their tank, a bullet creased Rustad's arm and smacked into his chest, breaking his salt tablet container. Scrambling back into their tank, the two caught their breath while their tank was towed to the crest of the hill.

Once safe, Lieutenant Phalon looked back and discovered that the overheating engine on Sergeant Brown's tank, which had been damaged by the explosion of the two mines, had finally quit. The disabled Stuart was still short of the crest of the hill and was in such a position that the remaining medium tank could not get a cable to it. By radio, Phalon ordered the crew to secure all of the hatches and abandon tank. Amidst fairly heavy Japanese fire, Sergeant Brown's three remaining crewmen, and Sergeant Butler from Sergeant Nichter's crew, climbed out and ran for the crest. In mid-stride, Private Donovan suddenly remembered the order to secure all of the hatches and ran back to secure the exit hatch. That done, Donovan turned back around and made it safely back to the other tanks.

Only Sergeant Butler had trouble reaching the crest of the hill. Having suffered a concussion from the mine explosions, Butler temporarily went blind and fell to the ground. Lieutenant Phalon, without hesitation, ran to Butler's side and guided him back to safety. When everyone was finally accounted for, the remaining light and medium tanks fired from the hill top and knocked out two enemy machine gun nests and set one of the enemy-infiltrated Marine Corps tanks on fire. For their actions on July 5, Sergeants Brown and Rustad were awarded a Silver Star and a Bronze Star, respectively.[22]

Although July 5 had been a rough day for Army tanks on Saipan, July 6 would be even worse.

CHAPTER NINETEEN

The End on Saipan

On July 6, while the 4th MarDiv continued its drive toward the northeast, the 27th IDiv received orders to change direction and move straight north, directly toward the coast. In so doing, the division would move through terrain that rose and fell in a series of ravines and gullies and was inundated with Japanese pillboxes, trench lines and machine-gun positions.[1]

On the far left side of the division line, Lieutenant Williams' platoon of medium tanks moved along the main coastal road. At Road Junction 2, where a cross-island road intersected the coastal road, the five tanks were stopped by an infantry commander who believed the coastal road was mined. As a precaution, he sent them to the right, down the cross-island road to a railroad track that paralleled the main road. With Williams in the lead, the five Shermans moved out in single file.

Once on the train tracks, Williams' lead tank "snarled its tread in the steel rails and became immobilized." With minefields on both sides of the track, the other tanks could not pass and were forced to come to a dead stop. Army engineers then tried to clear a path through the minefield but before they could finish, a Japanese antitank gun scored direct hits on the two lead tanks. Although the tankers fired back, they could not move until enough of the mines were removed. Then, finally, tow cables were hooked to the two damaged tanks and they were pulled back out of harm's way.[2]

On the right flank, the 165th IReg tried to skirt the eastern edge of Harakiri Gulch but ran into heavy Japanese small arms fire in an area known as Paradise Valley. Around 11:30 A.M., Captain Ward came up with five medium tanks and was soon leading his tanks down the same hill where Lieutenant Phalon's two sections had run into trouble. As the Shermans descended the hill, they saw Phalon's two abandoned light tanks and the two disabled Marine Corps tanks.

Near the bottom, tank No. 43, the second in line, was hit by antitank fire and began to burn. In an instant, three crewmen evacuated and ran toward Ward's lead tank. As the men ran, a Japanese machine gun opened fire, wounding two of them. In spite of the intense fire, all three men managed to reach Captain Ward's tank and climb inside.

With eight people inside his tank, including two who were seriously wounded, Ward gave instructions for his driver to back around the burning Sherman and get out of there. Unfortunately, as the driver started to execute the maneuver, the vehicle threw a track, which may have detonated a hidden mine. Seconds after the track was thrown, a large explosion rocked the tank and sent it sliding down the hill where it eventually came to rest near Sergeant Nichter's knocked-out Stuart.

Meanwhile, the other two crewmen from burning No. 43 had found refuge behind a nearby tree. Seconds later, they were joined by the crew of the third tank in line, Sergeant Kuebler's, after their tank was engulfed in smoke from the burning tank, which they mistakenly thought was coming from their own. When Kuebler and his men realized their tank was not on fire, they scrambled back inside, taking along the two crewmen from the burning tank.

At this point, S/Sgt. Matthew Watson, commander of the fifth tank in line, backed his tank halfway up the hill and began firing at targets of opportunity. The commander of the fourth tank, Sgt. Dalbert C. Nelson, heard on the radio that Captain Ward had lost a track and immediately moved to the bottom of the hill and into position behind the stricken vehicle so he could tow it out. While Japanese small-arms fire whistled past, Sergeant Nelson leapt out of his tank and began

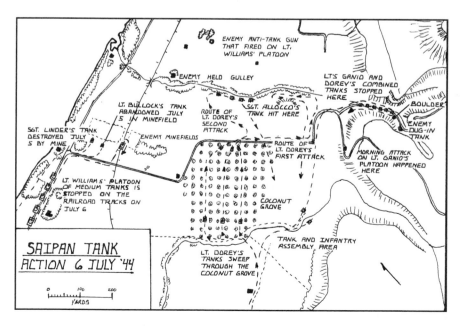

Saipan Tank Action (July 6, 1944)

fastening a tow cable to Captain Ward's tank. Within seconds he was hit in the arm and leg by enemy fire and then an enemy grenade detonated nearby, filling him with shrapnel. Angry now, Nelson pulled out his automatic pistol, looked around "as if he were 'rabbit hunting'" and then collapsed.

When Sergeant Nelson fell, Sergeant Kuebler raced his tank to the rescue. Although already carrying two evacuees, Kuebler moved his tank over to the stricken form of Sergeant Nelson and his crew dragged Nelson inside through the escape hatch. Then, for more than an hour, the four remaining tanks stayed as they were, with three tanks at the foot of the hill and one tank halfway up, firing cannon and machine gun fire at anything that moved.

While the tanks waited, they requested assistance from the 165th IReg. When the foot soldiers reached the top of the hill, however, they began taking heavy fire. Although they could see the Sherman tanks below them, they could not reach them.

Although the mine explosion had destroyed Captain Ward's radio communication, Sergeant Kuebler knew his captain had two injured men inside his tank. Radioing the infantry, Kuebler discovered that two medics were willing to help the wounded if one of the tanks would come back to the top of the hill and get them. Without hesitation, Kuebler turned his tank around and raced up the hill.

Within minutes, Kuebler had exchanged his two evacuees and the wounded Sergeant Nelson for the two medics. After going about halfway back down the hill, he stopped behind Sergeant Watson's tank. When the two medics looked through a tank periscope and saw the heavy Japanese machine gun and rifle fire, they balked at the mission. Instead, Corporal Myers, Kuebler's gunner, volunteered to go. Putting a few morphine syrettes in his pockets, Myers prepared himself for the job. Captain Appleman wrote:

> [Myers] removed the butt strip from his Tommy gun in order to shorten it and lighten it, and loaded two extra clips of ammunition . . . in one of his pockets. Myers then crawled out the escape hatch and wormed his way to the next tank ahead [Sergeant Watson's]. On the way, the clips dropped out of his pocket. . . . Upon reaching [Watson's tank] Myers went up through the escape hatch and got two more clips of ammunition and a drink of water. He then went back out and crawled to the next tank, [burning tank No. 43] the first one to be knocked out as they were going down the road earlier in the day. . . . Myers crawled up into this tank for a moment and found Captain Ward and two men in it.

Unbeknown to anyone atop the hill, Captain Ward and two men had crawled back to the knocked-out tank to use the radio.

When Corporal Myers reached the stricken tank, Ward informed him the two wounded men were both in critical condition. When Myers said he was going to their aid, Ward told him that because of the thrown track, he could only get to the bottom escape hatch by crawling through the suspension system on the good side.

Undaunted, Myers slipped out of No. 43 and crawled toward the disabled command tank. As the other American tanks created a diversion, Myers jumped up and ran the last few feet, reaching the side of the tank safely. While squeezing through the side suspension wheels, Myers got hung up only once when his boot snagged on a bogey wheel, but he quickly kicked himself free and squirmed up inside the Sherman.

"Myers' first impression upon reaching the wounded men was that they were dead," reported Captain Appleman, but after getting a shot of morphine, both men revived somewhat. "Working [the wounded men] out of the escape hatch and through the suspension system was a long and arduous task," wrote Appleman, especially since one of the men was "exceptionally large and heavy." Myers, Captain Ward and his two crewmen worked in pairs and finally got the two wounded men through the suspension. Then, still unseen by the enemy, they began dragging the wounded men back toward the other tanks.

When dragging proved too slow, the rescuers decided to carry the wounded men to safety. Myers and one of Captain Ward's crewmen quickly carried the lighter man to a spot behind a small rise and then rushed back for the heavier man. Working together, the four men carried the wounded tanker all the way to the first able tank. Then Corporal Myers and another crewman rushed back to get the lighter man. Once all six men were safely in among the other tanks, they divided themselves up and climbed up into the bellies of the three remaining able Shermans.

With the rescue complete, the three tanks moved back up the hill and deposited the wounded and evacuees at the aid station. Although Captain Ward had lost two tanks, both crews had been rescued. For their heroic actions on July 6, 1944, Sergeant Nelson and Corporal Myers each were awarded a Silver Star medal.[3]

In the center of the division line, the troops assaulting Hara-kiri Gulch fared a bit better. On the eastern side of the gulch, troops from the 165th IReg made only a little progress but on the western side, the 105th IReg steadily moved ahead. Moving along a tributary ravine, the infantrymen were soon in a position to shoot down into the caves and spider holes in the eastern embankment. At the same time, Lieutenant Ganio's four light tanks were ordered to "work up the trail that ran through the middle of the gulch."

As the four Stuarts rumbled up a heavily wooded hillside, three Japanese soldiers with magnetic mines sprang from hiding and rushed Lieutenant Ganio's tank. In an instant, Ganio's bow gunner shot them down. At the top of the hill, a Japanese soldier exploded a mine on the side of another tank, causing it to throw a track. The four crewmen quickly sought shelter inside the other tanks and then, for the next few hours, the three remaining Stuarts sat atop the hill and fired at enemy machine-gun nests and a few Japanese tanks that appeared on the north side of Hara-kiri Gulch.[4]

Farther to the west, between Hara-kiri Gulch and the western beaches, five light tanks under Lieutenant Dorey were aiding the advance of another portion of the 105th IReg. The infantry started attacking at 7:00 A.M., but soon was pinned down by heavy fire coming from a large coconut grove. Roaring into the grove, Dorey's tanks fired at "two corncrib like structures, surrounding brush, and crude Japanese antiaircraft dugouts," and had the entire area cleared out in ten minutes.

For the next hour, the tanks and infantry moved steadily forward, finding numerous caches of stored enemy equipment. Near 8:15 A.M., the advance reached a cross-island roadway marking the northern edge of the grove.

On orders from the infantry commander, Lieutenant Dorey moved his tanks onto the road and began firing at a cliff line to the far right. Instructed to provide covering fire, Dorey kept his tanks moving and firing, raking the cliff face and shooting up the area as the foot soldiers moved out. Within a short time, an excited infantryman contacted Lieutenant Dorey via the outside telephone and informed him that the Japanese had been located in a heavily fortified enemy gully about 150 yards north of the road. Taking two other tanks with him, Dorey moved up on the flank of the gully and began firing down its entire length. Noted Captain Appleman, "[The Japanese] ran about frantically seeking cover. . . . Numerous casualties were inflicted among the enemy, fires started, and minor explosions caused. Four machine guns were destroyed. The tanks ranged up and down the [gully] engaged in this work until it became evident that the [American] infantry were not going to assault and occupy it." Only then, near 10:00 A.M., did Dorey withdraw his tanks to replenish their ammunition.[5]

After being rearmed, Lieutenant Dorey was given a new mission and took two other tanks over to help Lieutenant Ganio's Stuarts and the 105th IReg make another assault on Hara-kiri Gulch. Near 1:00 P.M., Lieutenant Ganio led all six tanks on a circuitous end around that put them on the northern end of the gulch.

Warned by some waiting infantry that a dug-in enemy tank was watching the roadway, the tanks cautiously rumbled ahead and entered the northern end of Hara-kiri Gulch. Once there, they "put down a barrage on both sides of the canyon, shooting up several caves, enemy positions on rocky ledges, and causing some small ammunition fires and explosions." Lieutenant Ganio's lead tank was about to go around a large boulder, when it was narrowly missed by a shot from a "high-velocity weapon." Figuring they had found the enemy tank, but knowing they had no room to fight and maneuver, the American tanks prudently withdrew.[6]

At 3:30 P.M., when the tanks returned to the infantry, Lieutenant Ganio's three tanks went south for more ammunition and fuel while Lieutenant Dorey's tanks went back to the coconut grove. Apparently, the infantry at the grove finally was ready to attack the enemy-held gully, which by now had been reinforced.

Like before, the tanks moved out and approached the gully from the side, firing shot and shell into the enemy position as they traversed its length. When they reached the far end, the tanks turned around and started back again, continually firing their machine guns and cannon. This time however, a land mine was thrown under the last tank in line, Sergeant Allocco's tank. The resulting explosion knocked the track off, which lodged under the chassis, blocking the bottom escape hatch.

Upon hearing the explosion, Lieutenant Dorey instructed Sergeant Mavrikis to take up a position at the edge of the gully to provide cover fire for the disabled tank while he took his own tank back to see if the infantry was ready to move. When Dorey reached the coconut grove, he explained to the idle infantrymen what had happened and requested help. Following in the path of Lieutenant

Dorey's tank, the GIs rushed up to the edge of the gully and battled the remaining Japanese defenders with rifles, BARs, and hand grenades.

Unfortunately, the infantry assault bogged down about fifty yards short of Sergeant Allocco's tank. Noted Captain Appleman, "After several futile attempts to take the ditch . . . the infantry began to fall back." Lieutenant Dorey, knowing full well now that the rescue of Sergeant Allocco's crew was up to him, raced his tank up beside the disabled vehicle and stopped track-to-track. After repeated attempts to reach Sergeant Allocco by radio, Dorey realized that the radios were not working and threw open his hatch.

With Japanese fire whizzing all around, Dorey shouted for Allocco's crew to abandon their vehicle through the escape hatch and crawl into his. However, the escape hatch on Sergeant Allocco's tank was jammed and in the din of battle, neither crew could communicate with the other.

As the two crews tried desperately to figure out what to do, Japanese soldiers moved up and occupied a nearby cut in the ground. Both Sergeant Mavrikis' crew and Lieutenant Dorey's crew tried to fire down into the cut but they could not depress their weapons low enough. Finally, Lieutenant Dorey grabbed a Thompson sub-machine gun and began popping up out of his top turret, shooting two and three bullet bursts before ducking back down. Next, he threw three or four grenades at the Japanese.

Inside tank No. 73, Sergeant Allocco finally realized that the safest way for his crew to evacuate the tank was through the chassis hatches in front of the driver and bow gunner. But whoever exited on the bow gunner's side, the right side, would come out right next to the gully. Devising a plan, driver Private Proden and bow gunner Pvt. Harry V. Magilton threw open their hatches and Magilton threw two grenades at the Japanese. Proden then scrambled out with his Tommy gun and fired measured bursts at the ditch while Magilton scurried out of the tank with his own machine gun.

Once on the ground, Magilton joined Proden in keeping the Japanese at bay while the cannon gunner came out through the driver's hatch, and Sergeant Allocco came out through the bow gunner hatch. Miraculously, all four crewmen made it out of their tank unscathed. Reported Captain Appleman, "The fire from Sergeant Mavrikis' tank together with the Tommy gun bursts and the grenades Dorey had directed into the gully had kept the Japanese down."

For some reason, the four men did not try to get into Lieutenant Dorey's tank but instead turned and ran toward Sergeant Mavrikis' tank. As Private Proden started to crawl under the tank to come up through the escape hatch the still form of Sergeant Allocco fell across his legs, killed by Japanese fire. Seconds later, Private Magilton fell dead. As quickly as they could, Privates Proden and Stanley crawled up inside tank No. 68.

Once the surviving members from Sergeant Allocco's crew were safely inside his tank, Sergeant Mavrikis backed away from the gulley and headed back to the coconut grove. When Lieutenant Dorey saw Sergeant Mavrikis' tank leave, he too finally turned his tank away from the ditch and headed back to the infantry line.

Once back at the grove, Lieutenant Dorey learned that Sergeant Allocco and Private Magilton had been killed and that their bodies had been left behind. Wanting to confirm their deaths, Dorey left the two survivors behind and along with Sergeant Mavrikis went back to the gully. With Sergeant Mavrikis' tank once again providing covering fire, Dorey straddled his tank over each body and had one of his crewmen reach out through the escape hatch and check for signs of life. To his horror, the crewman discovered that in the short time that the tanks had been away, both bodies had been terribly mutilated by multiple hand grenade blasts.

Although Lieutenant Dorey had lost one tank and two men in the battle for the gully, the infantry later confirmed about 190 Japanese soldiers had been killed, mostly by Lieutenant Dorey's tanks.[7]

Around 4:00 A.M. on July 7, in the midst of a heavy rain, approximately 3,000 Japanese defenders suddenly swept down along the western coast in a banzai charge that burst through the 27th IDiv line and isolated pockets of the 105th IReg.[8] In a desperate attempt to reach some of these troops, two platoons of light tanks under Lieutenants Guffey and Phalon and one platoon of mediums under Lieutenant Lansford were called on for help.

Although the rain had stopped, the night sky was overcast and the tankers had a hard time distinguishing friend from foe. Four hundred yards past Road Junction 2 and the cross-island road, the tanks came upon a narrow bridge that spanned the eastern end of the gully that had been attacked by Lieutenant Dorey's tanks on July 6. Lieutenant Guffey, in the lead tank, and Sergeant Kernoschak, in the second tank, stopped on the north side of the bridge, while a third and fourth tank stopped on the south side. While Guffey tried to make radio contact with the isolated pockets of infantry, Sergeant Hendricks, in the third tank, noticed troop movement in the gully below. Unable to identify the troops as friend or foe, his crew held their fire until a sudden explosion rocked Sergeant Keroschak's tank. Realizing now that the unidentified men were Japanese, and that they had thrown a magnetic mine against Kernoschak's tank, Hendricks' crew swept the gully from side to side with machine gun fire.

The mine explosion tore off one track and ripped open the fuel tank on Kernoschak's tank. When the Japanese began throwing incendiary grenades, Kernoschak's driver managed to pull the damaged tank far enough forward to get away from the spilled fuel and to clear the roadway. For the next fifteen minutes, the four Stuarts fired all around them until Lieutenant Guffey feared they would be overrun. At that point, Guffey ordered Sergeant Kernoschak and his crew to bail out.

Slithering out the escape hatch, the tankers rushed into some thick brush on the west side of the road. There they found four Marines, including one man who was mortally wounded, who had been cut off from their own unit. Banding together, the four tankers and four Marines made their way down to the waterfront and entered a serpentine trench running down the beach. Slipping into the trench, the group was moving cautiously southward when the wounded Marine died. Uncertain of what lay ahead, the seven survivors moved ahead cautiously until the pursuing Japanese caught up with them. In the ensuing firefight, one tanker was killed and another two were wounded before the refugees managed to reach the safety of their own lines.[9]

When Kernoschak's crew fled, Lieutenant Guffey's three remaining tanks stayed around long enough to provide covering fire. Guffey then backed his tank over the bridge and turned around. When Sergeant Hendricks attempted to turn around also, his tank crashed through the roof of an underground Japanese bunker and flipped belly up. As Captain Appleman wrote, "Another tank was out of action and its crew placed in a most dangerous situation."

Although Lieutenant Guffey ordered Sergeant Hendricks and his crew to bail out, the men were afraid to leave the safety of their tank. Instead, they remained inside their upside-down tank when Lieutenant Guffey and the fourth tank withdrew. Fortunately, Sergeant Hendricks discovered that the turret of his upside-down tank would still move so the crew continued to fire canister rounds out of the 37mm gun. In the beginning, most of the Japanese who used the gully to gain access to the beach ignored the tanks, although every now and again a Molotov cocktail was thrown in their direction.

Eventually, however, about 100 Japanese soldiers lined up behind a sword-wielding officer for an assault on the tank. Just as the officer swept his samurai sword forward to propel his men into motion, a well-placed canister round killed the officer and tore a gaping hole in the line. More cannon fire and more machine-gun fire followed and the Japanese line broke and fled toward the beach.[10]

Although Hendricks and his crew had broken the charge, they were running low on ammunition. At that moment, near 7:00 A.M., Lieutenant Lansford arrived with four medium tanks, followed closely by Lieutenant Phalon and a platoon of light tanks. Stopping seventy-five yards short of the upside-down tank, the mediums and lights began laying down a heavy rain of cannon and machine gun fire.

Knowing it was now or never, the trapped crew climbed up and out of the escape hatch, threw a couple of smoke grenades and ran to the nearest medium tank. When they crawled under the Sherman to come up through the escape hatch, they unexpectedly found the hatch still locked. Undaunted, the crew crawled under the next tank, but found their escape hatch locked also. After checking under one more tank, the crew finally gave up and took off down the road on foot. Throughout the entire ordeal, Hendricks' crew had sustained only one injury, when his gunner suffered second degree burns to his right hand while extracting shells from the upside-down cannon.[11]

While Lieutenant Lansford's mediums and Lieutenant Phalon's lights were still firing at the Japanese, a handful of American infantrymen came down the strip of land between the beach and the roadway and warned the tankers they were being pursued by large numbers of Japanese. Seconds later, about twenty Imperial soldiers came into view and were immediately cut down by the informed tankers.

Ten minutes later, however, as Captain Appleman said, "the Japanese started coming down in droves. . . . Some were out in the water swimming or wading in the water up to their necks with only their heads showing, others were coming en masse right down the road, and others were coming through the fields to the right of the road." The tankers immediately opened fire with machine guns, canister, high explosive, and white phosphorous shells.

For the next several hours, the light and medium tanks of the 762nd and 766th TBs stood in a battle line and threw lead at the attacking Japanese. Although most of the Japanese attacks were staged by groups of fewer than thirty men, at one point a group of about 300 Imperial soldiers staged a banzai charge toward the tank line. Standing their ground, the tankers fired fast and furiously, completely shattering the charge before it could get within twenty feet.

Throughout the morning fresh tanks shuttled in and out of the firefight as crews ran out of ammunition and had to pull back to restock. Shortly after noon, after reloading and refueling, Lieutenant Phalon was told to take three other Stuart tanks and report to the 106th IReg, which had moved up from division reserve and was getting ready to advance along the east (right) side of the railroad tracks. When the infantry stepped off, Phalon's four light tanks roared out ahead.

After going about seventy-five-yards, the charging tanks came upon an enemy filled gully—the same gully that had been attacked by Lieutenant Dorey on July 6. Repeating the actions of Lieutenant Dorey's command, Phalon and his Stuarts raced along the southern edge of the gully firing into concentrations of Japanese soldiers. When one tank developed engine trouble, it went to the rear but the others continued on, eventually traversing the entire length of the gully up to Lieutenant Guffey's bridge. After firing canister into a group of enemy soldiers hiding under the bridge, Lieutenant Phalon led all three tanks over the span and then spread them out between the coast and the railroad embankment. Seemingly unstoppable, they continued on.

About 200 yards beyond the bridge, Lieutenant Phalon finally called a halt. He had expected the 106th IReg to follow but when he looked back, his tanks were all alone. Returning to the infantry command post, the three tanks went forward again when the infantry finally stepped off. This time, the GIs took full possession of the gully and soon found four samurai swords under the bodies of dozens of dead Japanese soldiers. In a gesture of good will, the foot soldiers gave two swords to the tankers.[12]

With the gully now in American hands, Lieutenant Phalon's three tanks and the accompanying infantry pushed beyond the ditch and crossed a cane field. At the northern edge of the field, the advance ran up against a number of dug-in enemy positions and began assaulting them one at a time. Surprisingly, hidden inside one of the emplacements were three 4th MarDiv artillerists who frantically waved white handkerchiefs when the Stuart tanks opened fire with their machine guns. Somehow, in the first mad rush of the Japanese banzai charge, some of the Marine artillery positions had been overrun and the artillerists had found shelter in the empty Japanese emplacement. Now, as the 27th IDiv troops began regaining the overrun ground, the Marines came out of hiding.

As the Marine artillerists were taken to the rear on one of Phalon's Stuart tanks, Lieutenant Williams came up with four medium tanks and a few light tanks. Although Lieutenant Phalon and his two tanks were subsequently relieved from the battle, the three tanks soon discovered that they had one more job to do. They had to go to the rescue of Lieutenant Guffey.[13]

In the early afternoon, while Lieutenant Phalon's tanks and the supporting infantry were advancing on the right, another attempt was made to move forward on the left. It was known that about 100 overrun foot soldiers were holed up about 1,600 yards north of the tank battle line, so Lieutenant Lansford was ordered to take his two medium tanks and push down the main roadway for a link-up.

At the same time, Lieutenant Guffey was ordered to move north along the beach with three light tanks to rescue another group of stranded infantrymen. Apparently, while recoiling from the nighttime banzai charge, the GIs had sought refuge on a small reef off of the western shore. When the Japanese followed, they reclaimed a number of their old beach defense positions and began pumping a stream of bullets into the stranded Americans. Lieutenant Guffey was told to rescue what was left of these men.

Before Lieutenant Guffey's light tanks started out, Lieutenant Lansford's two mediums advanced slowly up the road, avoiding swampy ground on either side. Although they saw a number of enemy soldiers, the two crews fired only sporadically, trying to save ammunition. About 3:00 P.M., as the tanks neared a heavily wooded area, dozens of American infantrymen from the lost 105th IReg suddenly rose up from each side of the roadway and ran toward the tanks. A link-up finally had been made with the lost infantry battalion. Although Lieutenant Lansford expected to stay with the found troops he received orders to return to the tank line—his two Shermans were needed to help rescue the men trapped on the reef.[14]

About 4:00 P.M., as Lansford was returning down the road, he received a call from Lieutenant Guffey asking for help. Apparently, Guffey's three tanks had moved north up the beach until they located the men on the reef. Then, taking his three tanks out into the surf, they turned and fired into the re-occupied Japanese beach positions. Unfortunately, the three Stuarts stayed in the water too long and were caught in a rising tide. Within minutes, all three tanks were swamped and Lieutenant Guffey was calling for help.

When Lieutenant Lansford's two tanks arrived they came up behind the enemy positions and systematically began destroying the emplacements with high-explosive shells and machine-gun fire. At the same time, Guffey's stranded crews added a crossfire effect to the fray.

About this time, Lieutenant Phalon arrived with five light tanks. Assessing the situation, Phalon ordered three tanks to help the two Shermans and then took two tanks down to the beach to cover the withdrawal of Guffey's crews. Moving up on the beach opposite Guffey's swamped tanks, the two Stuarts "put heavy canister and machine gun fire" into the Japanese positions while the stranded tankers scrambled out of their tanks and waded to shore.

Although all twelve crewmen made it safely out of the water, one tanker decided to collect souvenirs. As he moved along the beach collecting samurai swords, a Japanese sniper shot him in the head. Lieutenant Phalon saw the man fall and quickly backed his tank opposite the prostrate form. As the body rolled in the surf, Phalon leapt from his tank and rushed to the man's side. Although Phalon picked the man up in his arms and carried him to a nearby aid station, the tanker eventually died. For his gallant actions on July 7, Lieutenant Phalon was awarded a Bronze Star medal.[15]

Near dusk, the stranded 105th IReg soldiers on the reef were finally evacuated by LVTs. During the rest of the night, the Japanese continued to try to move south along the beach and the western coastal road, but the Americans had finally managed to throw a solid defensive line across their path. Included in the line were ten light and medium tanks commanded by Lieutenants Phalon and Williams, respectively. Proclaimed Captain Appleman, "No Japanese actually got through the line that night."[16]

Near daybreak on July 8, four medium tanks under Captain Ward, and seven light tanks commanded by Lieutenant Bullock came forward to "buttress the ten tanks that had stayed on the front line all night." At 10:00 A.M., the 2nd MarDiv moved up and relieved the 27th IDiv and its supporting units. By 2:00 P.M., all of the Army tanks had been relieved. For the men of Companies B and D, 762nd TB and Company D, 766th TB the fight for Saipan was over. On July 9, the 4th MarDiv and the 27th IDiv reached the far northern shore of Saipan. At 4:15 P.M., General Holland M. Smith declared Saipan secure.[17] The first island in the Marianas chain was now firmly in American hands.

In twenty-two days of combat, the 27th IDiv lost 3,674 men killed, wounded and missing, while the 2nd and 4th MarDiv's lost 10,437 men. The three Army tank companies lost eighteen dead, fifty-seven wounded, and six missing. Additionally, the three companies lost a total of seventeen light and five medium tanks and had a number temporarily disabled. Reported Captain Appleman, "Remaining fit for action at the close of the day on [July] 8th . . . were fifteen light tanks and ten medium tanks. This included all the tanks that had been retrieved and repaired during the course of the battle." In an understatement he added, "The service companies and maintenance sections had performed efficiently and well the task of repairing and returning damaged tanks to combat."[18]

On July 10, the 27th IDiv and its attached units were notified to stand by for possible participation in the invasion of Tinian, three and a half miles south of Saipan. One day later, one more medium and three more light tanks were repaired and brought back into action. Over the next two weeks, the men rested and relaxed and tried to prepare themselves for the upcoming fight. Fortunately, the Marine invasion of Tinian on July 25 was so successful that the Army units were never called upon.

On July 30, the 27th IDiv and the tankers from the 762nd and 766th TBs began mopping-up exercises in the northern half of Saipan. Over the next five days, all of the tanks saw various amounts of action as they assisted the infantry in weeding out entrenched Japanese defenders. Finally, on August 4, all three tank companies were released from 27th IDiv command. Three weeks later, on August 25, the combat veterans of the 762nd and 766th TBs put ashore at Pearl Harbor. After eighty-four days away, the battle-hardened tankers were finally back home at Schofield Barracks.[19]

CHAPTER TWENTY

Guam

With Saipan and Tinian captured, the next, and last, major island in the Marianas to be invaded was Guam. Located 105 miles south of Tinian, Guam is shaped like a leaning, upside-down chicken leg, measuring thirty-four miles long and between five and nine miles wide. The largest island in the Marianas, Guam is covered with tropical vegetation, and has "a hilly surface with shoreline cliffs, many caves, and abrupt rises and draws." Although the island had been in Japanese hands only since December 10, 1941, when the Japanese took it from the Americans, they had quickly built up hundreds of defensive positions and had carved out an airfield on Orote peninsula, a rocky promontory off the west cost. Although the Guam garrison of 18,500 Japanese soldiers numbered far less than the garrison on Saipan and had far fewer artillery pieces and tanks, it still was a formidable force.[1]

Selected to conquer Guam were the 3rd MarDiv, the 1st Provisional Marine Brigade (ProvMarBrig), and the Army's 77th IDiv, commanded by Maj. Gen. Andrew G. Bruce. Among the support units attached to the 77th IDiv was the 706th TB, which had been training beside the foot soldiers since its arrival in Hawaii in early April. On July 7, the 706th TB, under the command of Lt. Col. Charles W. Stokes, boarded several transports at Honolulu. Fifteen days and 2,300 miles later, the convoy of attack and transport ships neared Guam.[2]

The attack on Guam began with a sixteen day pre-invasion bombardment by sea and air—the longest of the entire Pacific war.[3] Around 8:00 A.M. on July 21, 1944, the 3rd MarDiv amtracs began churning toward a point almost three miles north of the peninsula. About the same time, the 1st ProvMarBrig moved toward an area about one-half mile south of the peninsula, just below the town of Agat. If everything went well, the 1st ProvMarBrig would pinch off the eastern end of the peninsula and with the 77th IDiv in reserve, would clean out the Orote peninsula.[4]

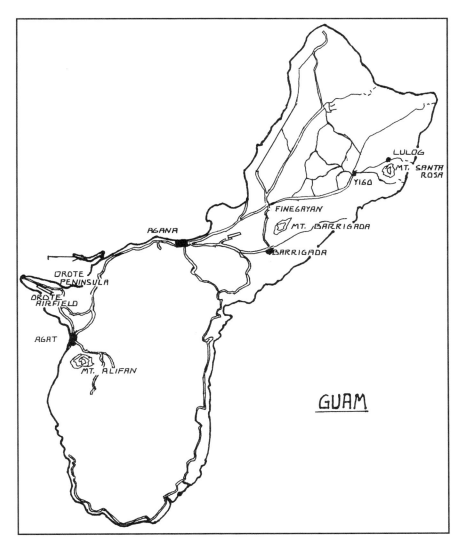

Guam

In spite of the heavy pre-invasion bombardment, the Japanese responded sharply to the invasion and sank a combined twenty-two amtracs. By 9:00 A.M., however, both beachheads were being consolidated and the Marines began landing their own tanks. In the early afternoon, although the 77th IDiv had been designated as a floating reserve, the 305th IReg was ordered ashore. Arriving with the foot soldiers were the company commander's tank and two platoons of M4A1 Sherman medium tanks from Company C, 706th TB. Unfortunately, on the way ashore, the company commander's tank sank into a large unseen shell hole and disappeared under the water. By nightfall, the American troops on both beaches had penetrated about 1,000 yards inland and were each holding a beachhead about 2,000 yards wide.[5]

During the night of July 21–22, the 77th IDiv got its first taste of combat when the Japanese struck with a heavy counterattack. Although the defenses bent, they did not break, and at daylight both the soldiers and the Marines fought their way up a high ridgeline that dominated both beaches. By nightfall, the Marines had captured Mount Alifan in the middle of the ridge, which at 869 feet dominated the southern beach.[6]

The Japanese failed to launch a counterattack on the night of July 22–23 so when daylight came, the Marines and soldiers renewed their attacks. More American troops were brought ashore throughout the next few days, including the Sherman tanks from Companies A and B, and Headquarters and Headquarters Company, 706th TB.[7]

On the night of July 26, the Japanese launched a major counterattack against both the 1st ProvMarBrig, which had cut off the base of the Orote peninsula, and 3rd MarDiv troops holding the northern beachhead. Although the attackers penetrated the Marine lines at a few spots they were eventually thrown back with heavy losses. As Army historian Charles R. Anderson wrote, "When it was over, the American beachhead remained intact, nearly 3,500 enemy lay dead, and the Japanese situation on Guam was hopeless."[8]

On July 27, the rest of the 706th TB finally came ashore. Throughout the day, the Sherman tanks of Company A and the M5 Stuart light tanks of Company D landed on the southern beachhead and assembled near the village of Agat, near the base of the Orote peninsula. Near dark, the last five tanks of Company C (the 3rd Platoon) were brought ashore but remained on the beach rather than roam around in the darkness trying to find their parent unit.[9]

By July 28, the 1st ProvMarBrig had captured about half of the Orote peninsula, but as it neared Orote airfield resistance stiffened. Planning to overpower the defenders, the Marine commander decided to call for armor. While the Marine Corps provided ten Shermans, the Army sent over five Stuarts from Company D, 706th TB under the command of 1st Lt. Charles J. Fuchs, and one M4A1 Sherman tank and one bulldozer tank from Headquarters and Headquarters Company.

At 4:00 P.M., the Marine-led advance started forward. Historian Philip A. Crowl described the combined attack:

> All up and down the line the tanks moved forward cautiously, followed at short distances by the Marine infantrymen. In their zone, the seven Army tanks covered about three hundred yards of front, often firing at ranges of ten to fifteen yards at the reinforced log pillboxes that barred their path. The light tanks of Company D alone expended about 10,000 rounds of .30-caliber ammunition, 100 rounds of high explosive, and twenty rounds of canister. They were credited with the destruction of four pillboxes, numerous dugouts, and about 250 Japanese.[10]

For his part in the action, Lieutenant Fuchs was presented a Bronze Star medal.[11]

In the same advance, the lone Army Sherman knocked out one pillbox and damaged a Japanese 77mm gun. By the end of the day, the 1st ProvMarBrig had reached the near end of the Orote airfield.[12]

The next morning, July 29, the Marines pushed forward again, this time assisted by the seven 706th TB tanks, four Marine Corps mediums and six Army M10 tank destroyers. By 2:00 P.M., the entire airfield was in American hands and the seven Army tanks were ordered to make a dash toward the far western tip of the peninsula, about two miles away. Remarked a 706th TB historian, "After loading the tank decks with infantry, [the] tanks proceeded to [the] tip of [the] peninsula without meeting resistance." Only two live Japanese soldiers were encountered. For all intents and purposes, the Orote peninsula was in American hands.[13]

While the Orote peninsula was under attack, the 77th IDiv slowly began clearing out the southern half of Guam. On July 28, the 77th IDiv troops began a series of reconnaissance patrols into the mountainous southern end of the island. Accompanying the foot soldiers were the M4A1 Sherman tanks of Company B, 706th TB. "Platoons were attached to various patrols and destroyed all shacks that they encountered," noted a battalion historian, "No enemy resistance was met and due to impassable terrain the patrols returned to the bivouac area." Another tank historian added, "[Company B] destroyed houses and grass shacks about 2,500 yards east of the [beachhead]. Platoon Leader . . . burned down (with white phosphorus and HE) four houses along supply road."[14]

Throughout the next five days, as a constant rain fell, the 77th IDiv conducted numerous searches of the southern end of Guam. As a tank battalion historian recalled, "Rain was the predominate feature on Guam at this particular time of the year, and we generally found ourselves slopping around in the mud during the days and involuntarily submitting to a muddy bath in our slit trenches during the nights." By August 2, the southern half of Guam was declared secure and attention shifted to the north.[15]

By the last day of July, the 3rd MarDiv had pushed out of its northern beachhead perimeter and had established a line running across the center of Guam, roughly below the meaty part of the chicken leg. On July 31, the 77th IDiv moved into position on the right side of the line. Together, the two units began a side-by-side, steady advance up the rest of the chicken leg, pushing the Japanese before them.

For their part, the Japanese tried to anchor their remaining defenders around Mount Barrigada, five miles northeast of the Marine beachhead and in the center of the island. The terrain in the northern half of Guam favored the Japanese. Noted one historian, "[The] thickening rain forest opened gaps between [the American] units and ruined alignment, and heavy rains and accompanying mud added to the ensuing communications and logistical confusion." Because of the terrain and weather, the 706th TB tanks were relatively inactive throughout the first few days of the advance.

At 6:30 A.M. on August 2, the Stuart tanks of Company D, 706th TB finally got into action. Capt. Leonard H. Seger took fourteen light tanks out on a reconnaissance of the town of Barrigada, just south of Mount Barrigada and got into the middle of town before drawing "moderate fire." Reportedly, "The tank crews machine-gunned suspected areas and returned to the regiment to report that they had seen only eight Japanese soldiers and a machine gun."[16]

Near 8:00 A.M., the light tanks returned to Barrigada. This time, they passed through the town and at a "Y" road junction went to the left, toward the northwest and the village of Finegayan. About a mile down the road, and just west of Mount Barrigada, the tanks ran into a Japanese roadblock of three trucks and several dozen soldiers. Unleashing a devastating attack, the fourteen Stuarts blasted the roadblock to pieces and killed an estimated thirty-five Japanese soldiers. Then, turning around, the tanks raced back to the road junction near Barrigada.

This time, the fourteen tanks took the right-hand fork toward the northeast and tried to advance around the eastern side of Mount Barrigada. As they moved along, the dense jungle began to close in on them and the road began to narrow. After going a few hundred yards, the lead tank of S/Sgt. Wilbur C. Dennis stalled, effectively blocking the road. Then, with the column halted and Sergeant Dennis' crew trying desperately to restart the engine, the jungle suddenly erupted.

An Army historian reported, "[The Japanese] threw 20mm and machine-gun fire against the sides of the tanks, [and] into the view slits. While their comrades kept up this fire from dugouts, other Japanese crawled forward with grenades, closing in on the tanks. As one enemy tried to climb up on one tank to drop grenades through the openings, the tank behind shot him off." Eventually, the combined fire of the fourteen tanks allowed the Americans to get the upper hand.[17]

With bullets flying all around, Captain Seger maneuvered his tank up behind Sergeant Dennis' tank. Then, in spite of the danger, Captain Seger, Sergeant Dennis and Dennis' driver, Tech 4 Melvin F. Krouth, climbed out of their tanks and attached a tow cable between the two tanks. With the disabled tank in tow, Captain Seger radioed command and asked politely, "Can I come home?" Permission was immediately granted and the fourteen Stuarts were back within the regimental lines by 11:00 A.M. For their courage under fire, Captain Seger, Sergeant Dennis and T4 Krouth all were awarded Bronze Stars.[18]

During the rest of the morning, the 77th IDiv troops tried to take solid possession of Barrigada. Around 1:00 P.M., the light tanks of Company D advanced with the 305th IReg against the east side of Barrigada. Four tanks were on the right and four were on the left.

On the right flank, the tanks and infantry advanced only a short distance before drawing heavy fire. One tank was hit on the left sponson and the left sprocket, and had two connectors shot off, but was able to make it safely back to the American lines. For the time being, all forward movement on the right came to a halt.[19]

On the left, the four tanks under the command of Lieutenant Fuchs and a company of supporting infantry tried to get past a draw. Three tanks and their supporting squads made it safely beyond the draw before the Japanese opened fire, striking the sides of the fourth tank with small arms fire that bounced off and hit a few infantrymen. Although all four tanks returned fire, the surrounding jungle was too dense and the crewmen could not see any targets. Fearing they were drawing fire toward the infantry, the tanks backed up a bit to regroup.

While the tanks were standing idle, 2nd Lt. Edward C. Harper, an infantry commander, volunteered to lead one Stuart into position to knock out a pesky Japanese strong point. Climbing inside Lieutenant Fuchs' tank, *Dirty Detail,* Harper directed the tank to within five yards of the Japanese position. Although American machine-gun bullets ripped into the enemy works, the Japanese returned a heavy counter fire, scoring direct hits on the trailing idler, the drive shaft and the side of the tank. After a short time, Fuchs ordered his tank to withdraw but as the vehicle started moving, the track slipped off the damaged trailing idler and the tank ground to a halt. Fortunately, two medium tanks from the 3rd Platoon, Company C, 706th TB arrived at this time and laid down a heavy covering fire so the stranded crew could abandon tank. Once the crew was safe, the two mediums shot up *Dirty Detail* so it could not be used by the Japanese.[20]

With the Japanese position still intact, Lieutenant Harper decided to try another tank attack, this time using four medium tanks from Company C. Moving out abreast, the tanks rumbled forward and fired a heavy concentration of shells into the suspected Japanese positions. "The fire destroyed some of the enemy's camouflage that had hidden a tank, which the mediums quickly knocked out," reported historian Crowl. "Under protection of the tanks several American wounded who had previously been trapped were evacuated, but by this time it was almost dark, and any hope of following up the attack vanished."[21]

706th TB near Agana on Guam, August 2, 1944. The two lead tanks are composite hull M4 Shermans and have nicknames beginning with "C," "Cognac" and "Cupid," indicating that they belong to Company C. US ARMY

In the gathering darkness, the light tanks of Company D, 706th TB had one more job to do. Barrigada was still in enemy hands and a large number of wounded American soldiers were lying about the town. According to the plan, a group of light tanks would provide covering fire while four Stuarts under the command of 2nd Lt. James M. Ryan and a couple platoons of infantry rushed into town to collect the wounded.

Although the four tanks started forward as scheduled, the supporting infantry went in a different direction. Somehow, both the tanks and the infantry arrived in Barrigada at about the same time and the rescue work began. During this engagement, Lieutenant Ryan "dismounted from his tank amid heavy enemy fire to expedite the evacuation of the wounded and to direct the movement and fire of his tanks, effectively neutralizing the enemy fire." Noted a tank battalion historian, "[The] tanks evacuated 108 wounded." For his heroic actions, Lieutenant Ryan was awarded a Bronze Star. Unfortunately, when the tanks pulled back with the wounded, the supporting infantry was left high and dry.[22]

Almost immediately, another platoon of men from the 307th IReg, and the 1st Platoon Sherman tanks of Company B, 706th TB, moved forward to help extricate their brethren. Heading toward Barrigada, the mediums "moved into assault position firing area fire into [the] dense jungle forward of our infantry, fired on snipers in tree tops, blew up dugouts and six houses and knocked out two machine gun nests." As darkness fell, the rescuers and rescued fell back and left Barrigada in the hands of the enemy. In all, the combined infantry–tank assault had killed another 200 Imperial soldiers.[23]

Near 7:00 A.M. on August 3, after a heavy artillery barrage, the 307th IReg and the 2nd and 3rd Platoons of medium tanks from Company A, 706th TB attacked Barrigada again. Perhaps prompted by the heavy artillery fire, the Japanese had withdrawn from Barrigada and the combined infantry–tank advance soon had the entire village in American hands.

Continuing on, the tanks and foot soldiers quickly pushed around the eastern base of Mount Barrigada until around noon, when they began meeting stiffening resistance. Quickly, a plan was devised to hit the enemy with a heavy artillery barrage and then walk the fire forward as the tanks and infantry advanced behind it. At 1:30 P.M., the artillery opened fire. Five minutes later, the cannon fire moved forward 100 yards and the soldiers and tankers started out. After another five minutes, the barrage moved forward another 100 yards and the infantry and tanks followed.

Although the heavy artillery fire tore through the surrounding jungle, the thick vegetation slowed the forward advance. Noted historian Crowl, "The tropical rain forest had grown so thick that the only way the men could make any progress at all was by reversing the [turrets] on their medium tanks . . . and using the vehicles as trail blazers." Using the tanks as battering rams, the Americans pushed steadily forward. Noted a 706th TB historian, "2nd and 3rd Platoons blazed trail[s] through dense jungle and spear-headed infantry attacks on Mount Barrigada." Around 3:00 P.M., troops from the 307th IReg drove upward and seized the summit of Mount Barrigada.[24]

With Mount Barrigada and the center of the island in American hands, three Shermans from the 1st Platoon, Company A, 706th TB and a squad of infantry from the 307th IReg headed out along a narrow road, the Finegayan Road, in an attempt to establish contact with the 3rd MarDiv on their left. While the Army troops had been advancing at a snail's pace, the Marines had been pushing rapidly ahead, greatly outdistancing the soldiers and creating a wide gap between the two units. The ensuing movement up the Finegayan Road was recorded by a tank battalion historian:

> Tanks with infantry loaded on decks proceeded about 600 yards and encountered a roadblock. The lead tank destroyed the roadblock and advanced about fifty more yards, then struck a concealed land mine which blew off the left track. Other tanks covered the crew while they abandoned the disabled tank. The tanks could not advance due to other land mines and the enemy was too strong for our troops to hold the position. The disabled tank was destroyed and [the] troops returned to [the] bivouac area.[25]

Owing to the difficult terrain, and stiff enemy resistance, the 77th IDiv had gained only one mile of ground by nightfall on August 3, 1944.[26]

On August 4, another attempt was made to make contact with the Marines on the left. At 7:00 A.M., a lone M4A1 Sherman from Company A, 706th TB led a platoon of infantrymen from the 307th IReg along the Finegayan Road. The tank passed by the destroyed Sherman from the day before and about an hour later came upon a Japanese roadblock. Immediately, a request was put in for artillery fire but the request was denied. It was known that Marine Corps personnel were somewhere in the area and the artillery commander was fearful of overshooting and hitting the Marines. Instead, the roadblock would have to be removed by a reinforcement of tanks.

A section of 1st Platoon Shermans from Company A came up and by 10:30 A.M. had forced its way through the initial roadblock and blown its way through another. Moving ahead, the tanks and infantry were advancing cautiously when they suddenly came upon a third roadblock. What happened next was a tragic accident.

"The 3rd Marine Division had been warned of the approach of the Army patrol and was expecting it," historian Crowl wrote "The Army troops, on the other hand, had been told that red smoke grenades would be used as a signal to indicate friendly positions . . . The Marines, recognizing the Army troops, did not fire; the soldiers, not seeing the signal, did." Expecting to see red smoke, the Shermans opened fire. Suddenly, a lone figure came running toward the tanks, waving his arms and holding up an American helmet for everyone to see. "He established that the roadblock was a Marine position," an Army historian wrote, "but before he did so; five Marines had been wounded."[27]

The unfortunate incident finally established contact between the 3rd MarDiv and the 77th IDiv but the contact was short-lived. Almost immediately, the two divisions pushed into dense terrain again. On the left, the Marines met little resistance and surged ahead. On the right, the 77th IDiv had to push over the western slope of Mount Barrigada, which slowed the advance. In the afternoon, the 1st Platoon tanks of Company C, 706th TB moved forward to aid in the strenuous push around the mountain. "[The] medium tanks . . . strained their engines to knock down trees and break trails through the thick vegetation," wrote historian Crowl. In spite of the terrain, by 6:00 P.M., the 77th IDiv reached a cross-island objective line designated by General Bruce. Preparations were then made for the last phase of the conquest of Guam.[28]

By the evening of August 4–5, Marine Lt. Gen. Roy S. Geiger, in overall command on Guam, reached the conclusion that the remaining Japanese were falling back to set up a strong defensive position around Mount Santa Rosa, a bald-faced mountain along the northeast coast. Hoping to deprive the Japanese of the time to dig in, Geiger ordered both his Marine and Army commanders to keep pushing their advance.[29]

Early on the morning of August 5, General Bruce replaced the tired troops of the 307th IReg on the left side of his line with the well-rested 306th IReg, which had been in division reserve since clearing out the mountainous southern end of Guam. Still, the thick jungle and stiffening Japanese resistance slowed the forward movement of the 77th IDiv and its supporting tanks.[30]

To help in the advance, a bulldozer tank from Headquarters and Headquarters Company came forward and began cutting paths through the vegetation. Likewise, tanks from the 1st and 2nd Platoons of Company C, 706th TB also helped break trails. Although some of the 1st Platoon tanks were hit by light machine-gun fire, they received no real damage but managed to inflict "heavy casualties on the enemy."[31]

In the late afternoon, a heavy rain began to fall, which further impeded the movements of the men and tanks. By nightfall, the 77th IDiv was well short of its next objective line. Then, shortly before 2:00 A.M., August 6, the 305th IReg was hit with an unexpected counterattack by two Japanese tanks and a platoon of infantry. Although the soldiers managed to stop the Japanese infantry, both tanks burst through the thin American line.

Tanks from Company C, 706th TB were behind the infantry line but could not fire at the darting Japanese tanks "because friendly troops left their foxholes in the excitement and were running about the area." At one point, one of the enemy tanks collided with an American Sherman. Backing away, the Japanese tank rolled over a jeep, fired into a number of other smaller vehicles and then darted away. After circling around once or twice, the two enemy tanks successfully fled the scene. Left behind were twenty-two dead, forty-seven wounded, and two smashed jeeps. The suddenness of the attack had caught the 305th IReg completely by surprise.[32]

Around daylight on August 6, two platoons of Sherman tanks from Company B and the foot soldiers of the 306th IReg, on the left of the division front, began moving southwest down a narrow jungle road in an attempt to reach Road Junction 363 and reestablish contact with the Marines. Although one tank was lost to a hidden land mine, the column met little resistance and by 9:00 A.M. was at RJ 363.

At this point, a small group of tanks and infantry broke away to continue the advance toward the Marine Corps lines while the main body turned north and pushed up a very narrow, heavily overgrown trail. After an advance of only about 150 yards, the main force ran into a small group of enemy infantry which was instantly attacked. "Encountered machine gun and sniper fire which tanks reduced; approximately fifty enemy dead counted in this area," wrote a tank battalion historian. With the enemy opposition eliminated, the advance to the north continued.

After setting fire to a few native dwellings in a nearby clearing, the tanks and infantry pressed on until the trail came to an end. "[W]ithout reconnaissance, patrol, or guide," reported the tank historian, "[the tanks] took the lead, breaking trail through [the] dense jungle." Around 5 P.M., the trailblazing was halted when a report reached the main column that contact had been made with the 3rd MarDiv.[33]

While part of the 306th IReg was looking for the Marines, another detachment had been moving toward the northeast, down the Finegayan–Yigo road toward Yigo. Accompanying them were four medium tanks from the 3rd Platoon, Company B. Near 8 A.M., a scout spotted an "enemy tank in ambush by the side of the road." The lead tank moved forward to get off a good shot but before he could do so, the enemy opened fire. "The first round flattened a bogie wheel on the American tank," reported Crowl, "but answering fire from the 75mm gun on the Sherman was much more effective. Three rounds set the Japanese [medium] tank aflame, and the Sherman's machine guns and a quick rush by the American infantry took care of the enemy soldiers around the Japanese tank." Sixteen enemy dead were counted.[34]

Picking up the pace, the advance continued on and by 10:00 A.M. the 306th IReg troops had crossed the day's objective line and were only 1,200 yards short of Yigo village. Since any further advance would put the regiment far ahead of any supporting troops, the commander was told to stop and consolidate for the night.[35]

In the 305th IReg sector, on the right of the division front, August 6 was also a day of renewed pursuit. With the coming of daylight, the 305th IReg, supported by the 2nd Platoon Shermans of Company C, 706th TB, pushed into the jungle again. As the men and tanks traveled north up a narrow trail, they ran into an enemy ambush of infantry and two tanks dug in as pillboxes.

As the American infantry spread out, the lead Sherman moved up to engage. As it came within range, a Japanese grenade smacked into the American tank and exploded. The only damage, reported a tank battalion historian, was to the tank commander. Standing exposed in the turret, "the picric acid from [the] grenade changed the color of his hair to reddish-brown."[36]

When it was discovered that neither the American tanks nor the American infantry could get at the dug-in Japanese tanks without exposing themselves, they called in a mortar barrage. When the barrage ended, the Americans went forward and found both enemy tanks had been abandoned.[37]

By noon, the 305th IReg was across the objective line for August 6 and was in contact with the 306th IReg on its left. At this point, it too was halted for the day. The 77th IDiv now had most of its men on the objective line and was preparing for the assault against Mount Santa Rosa, an 870-foot prominence on the left side of the division front that was suspected of being a Japanese strong point.[38]

A spirited all-out attack by both the 77th IDiv and the Marines was planned for August 7. In the center of the island, the 3rd MarDiv, aided by the 1st Prov-MarBrig, would drive toward the sea and take the northern and northwestern end of the island. To their right, the 77th IDiv would assault Mount Santa Rosa and the northeastern edge of Guam. Warships, artillery, and aircraft would aid in softening up the bald top of Mount Santa Rosa.[39]

As envisioned by General Bruce, his division would anchor its right flank on the east coast and pivot the rest of the division like a gate. All three regiments, the entire division, were to move forward during the morning and reach a line of departure facing the mountain. Then, when all of the regiments were on line, the left flank of the division would start the pivot. At the end of the day, the 77th IDiv would be in a position to overrun Mount Santa Rosa and push the defenders into the sea.

During the morning hours of August 7, the 305th, 306th and 307th IRegs moved into position along the designated line of departure. Only the 307th ran into any noteworthy resistance, but a few tanks from Company A, 706th TB quickly silenced the opposition. By 11:00 A.M., the 77th IDiv was ready, so General Bruce set the time of attack for noon.[40]

At 11:38 A.M., artillery and naval gunfire, and a few aerial bombs began tearing into Mount Santa Rosa. As planned, the bombardment would cease at noon and the 77th IDiv would jump forward, spearheaded in the center by ten light tanks of Company D and ten medium tanks of Company C, 706th TB. Driving straight up the Finegayan–Yigo road, the tanks would rush through Yigo and seize some high ground east-northeast of the village. Then, while the tanks stood guard, the 307th IReg would enter Yigo and turn east for their eventual assault on Mount Santa Rosa.[41]

Somehow, Colonel Stokes was never notified of the starting time until 11:55, five minutes before the attack. Instantly, he radioed his tanks to move out. Unfortunately, a battalion from the 307th IReg had started forward without the armor. So, when the light and medium tanks tried to move forward along the Yigo Road, they found the path blocked by the advancing infantry.

Unable to slip through the thick jungle on either side of the road, the M5 Stuarts and M4 Shermans did their best to get through the foot soldiers and past a few A Company tanks, which were moving up in direct support of the infantry. Finally, at 12:20 P.M., the spearheading tanks came out onto an open plain below Yigo behind a group of infantry and fanned out for their advance on the village.

Almost immediately, the tanks and infantry came under fire from the village. The light tanks passed through the infantry and maneuvered toward the right side of Yigo while the medium tanks rumbled through the infantry and drove straight down the road. The light Stuarts, moving quickly, overran a number of dugouts and pillboxes, which were left for the advancing infantry, and then headed straight toward Yigo. Near the southern edge of town, as the tanks came over a slight rise, they were hit with heavy caliber fire from woods to the west. Captain Seger, in command of Company D, quickly called for the mediums.[42]

A few seconds later, an antitank shell hit the left side of Sgt. Joe M. Divin's tank, causing it to stall. Badly wounded in both legs, Sergeant Divin ordered his crew out. An Army historian described what happened next:

> The only means of escape for the other crew members, besides the turret, were the driver and bow-gunner hatches. Owing to the construction of the tank these hatches could not be opened when the turret was traversed off center, as was the case in this situation. Sergeant Divin desperately tried to center the turret, but the mechanism had become damaged by gunfire. His strength ebbing from loss of blood, Divin put a tourniquet on his leg. With a supreme effort, he dragged himself out of the turret hatch onto the rear deck of the tank, leaving the way open for the crew to follow. The tank was now afire and was receiving machine-gun fire from the enemy positions fifty yards away. Divin stayed in this exposed position to direct the escape of his comrades. As they dashed for cover, machine-gun fire struck and killed him.

For his "extraordinary heroism in action," Sergeant Divin was posthumously awarded a Distinguished Service Cross.[43]

Within minutes after Sergeant Divin's tank was hit, 2nd Lt. Ernest W. Pardun's tank was hit three times and burst into flame, killing three crewmen.[44]

The Company C mediums rushed to the rescue but could not locate the Japanese guns because of the dense woods. Only when the Shermans advanced up the slight rise and began taking heavy fire themselves were they able to locate the enemy position. Then, aided by the light tanks of Lieutenant Pardun's platoon, the mediums began slugging it out with the heavy Japanese guns.

In the exchange of fire, two medium tanks were hit and set on fire. "Flames shot out of the bottom [of one tank]," wrote an army historian, "and quickly enveloped the sides. The crew hastily clambered out of it just before the ammunition inside began exploding."[45]

As Cpl. Gerald R. Rowe, a gunner, was exiting the second tank, he noticed that cannoneer Pfc. Emil J. Conrad was seriously wounded and could not help himself. Disregarding his own safety, Rowe started to reenter his tank when he too was severely wounded by Japanese fire. Unable to help Private Conrad now, Rowe crawled out of his tank amidst a "devastating cross fire" and obtained assistance for Private Conrad. For his total disregard for his own safety, Corporal Rowe was presented a Silver Star and a Purple Heart. Private Conrad later died of his wounds, the only tanker from Company C to die on Guam.[46]

In addition to the loss of the two Shermans, Company C lost one more tank to an enemy shell and another that got hung up on a stump. Still, the remaining six Shermans and four light tanks managed to destroy one Japanese antitank gun and two light tanks. Having lost six tanks and thirteen men however, the remaining tanks were ordered to break off their fight along the wood line and head out beyond Yigo to capture the heights northeast of town. As the tanks moved away, the infantry moved in and eventually overran the Japanese wood line position, securing the right flank toward Yigo.[47]

By 2:50 P.M. the tanks had passed through abandoned Yigo and were in position atop the high ground east-northeast of the village. A few minutes later, after securing the village, elements of the 307th IReg came up and relieved the Shermans and Stuarts atop the ridge. As the tanks retired, the infantry advanced another 1,000 yards toward Mount Santa Rosa and then dug in for the night.[48]

On the 77th IDiv's left flank, the infantry and its supporting light and medium tanks had more trouble fighting through the dense jungle than against the Japanese. Noted a tank battalion historian, "Five tanks [moved] abreast covering a 300-yard front with no reconnaissance guide, or patrol ahead of them. They proceeded to break parallel trails through very dense jungle. Tank No. 5 and [a] headquarters tank came upon a platoon of enemy and killed about thirty of them."[49]

During the night, the remaining Japanese attempted a few desperate counterattacks. Each one was thrown aside with minimal damage to the Americans. At sunup on August 8, the 77th IDiv was in motion again. On the right flank, the 305th IReg, which had advanced along the coast on August 7 without tank support, stepped off once again without tanks and encountered only scattered resistance. Moving forward quite easily, they seized their objective zone south-southeast of Mount Santa Rosa well before nightfall.[50]

On the far left of the division line, the 306th IReg set out for the village of Lulog, just north of Mount Santa Rosa. The left side of the regiment advanced down an "improved road" with a few tanks from Company B, 706th TB and made good time. Fearing the regiment was becoming overextended, the men and tanks came to a halt and set up a hasty roadblock. What happened next was a result of faulty communication. "At noon on August 8," reported historian Charles A. Anderson, "the 306th Infantry received and returned fire for two hours before discovering the source: a Marine unit on the division's left flank." Although both sides suffered a few casualties, the lines were straightened out by nightfall.[51]

In the left center, a column of infantry and the 2nd Platoon tanks of Company B pushed steadily forward, harassed only by sniper fire. At one point, the platoon leader made a startling discovery. "His tank knocked down a tall tree," reported a battalion historian, "and a Jap sniper fell out of the tree right on top of [the] commander's hatch, which was open, rolled down in front of the tank and under [the] tank between tracks. Infantry, following tank, completed [the] job of destroying Jap sniper."[52]

On the right center, the 306th IReg moved out with the 3rd Platoon Shermans of Company B and advanced rapidly toward Lulog. As the tanks neared the village, they came under suspicious fire. Noted a tank battalion historian, "[The tanks of Company B] entered area of cross fire from right flank. Liaison plane reported 307th [IReg] with Company A, 706 [TB] in support on right flank." Somehow, the 307th IReg and the Company A tanks had drifted wide of Mount Santa Rosa and had entered Lulog. Fortunately, before anyone was injured, the problem was rectified and the 307th IReg pulled out. As the 306th IReg entered Lulog they found "dead in almost every house." During the 307th IReg's short stay in Lulog, the 1st Platoon Shermans of Company A had "fired at shacks with [high explosive] & .30-caliber. Huts had three or four Japs in each and one had eighteen."[53]

"After leaving Lulog," wrote a 706th TB historian, "the 307th IReg troops and 1st Platoon tanks [of Company A] moved steadily toward the east and by nightfall were on the eastern seashore." In the center and on the right of the 307th IReg zone, the men and the remaining tanks of Company A advanced steadily against Mount Santa Rosa and by 3:00 P.M. the bald summit was in American hands.[54]

While the 77th IDiv had been capturing Mount Santa Rosa and driving to the eastern seaboard, the Marines had been making great gains of their own. On August 8, the 3rd MarDiv had pushed to within a mile and a half of the northern coast while the 1st ProvMarBrig had taken the entire northwestern tip of Guam. As historian Crowl wrote, "That night even Radio Tokyo conceded that nine-tenths of Guam had fallen to American troops."

The next day, the 77th IDiv pushed northward to the sea and cleaned out the area around Mount Santa Rosa. Very little resistance was encountered. In the Marine Corps sectors, the advance encountered only a smattering of half-hearted opposition. On the morning of August 10, General Geiger announced that organized resistance on Guam had ceased.

From the start of the invasion of Guam on July 21 to the end of organized resistance on August 10, the Army suffered 839 casualties, including six tankers killed and twelve wounded. For the Marines, who had borne the brunt of the invasion and the fighting, the casualties numbered 6,716 killed and wounded. For the Japanese, the losses came to roughly 18,500 killed and seventy-seven captured.[55]

As usual, although Guam had been declared secure, the fight continued. On August 10, Sherman tanks from the 1st Platoon, Company B and Stuart tanks from the 2nd Platoon, Company D (both 706th TB) helped the 77th IDiv clear out a pocket of Japanese resistance in a slight depression. "[Three Shermans] took up position on high ground west of depression [while two Shermans] took up position at north end of defile," reported a tank battalion historian. "Then light tank platoon . . . moved north along the east side of depression, clearing out sniper fire and machine-gunning suspected areas. When light tanks had completed mission and reported safe withdrawal, three tanks on high ground to west opened fire with HE and APC [armor-piercing shells] while two remaining tanks moved in from north. When tanks had completed firing . . . infantry moved in at once with flame-throwers and demolitions. About 200 dead were found in the area."[56]

By August 12, the separate elements of the 706th TB were consolidated and moved into an encampment just east of Agat. For the 706th TB, the battle for Guam was over. The men had discovered the extensive tank–infantry training they had gone through with the 77th IDiv in Hawaii had paid off in spades. Both the tankers and the infantry had known what the other was going to do and had worked well together. By having the tanks protect the infantry, and vice versa, casualties among the two branches were minimal.[57]

With Guam conquered, the 706th TB settled in for an extended stay. Unlike many other Pacific tank battalions which were rounded up after a campaign and sent back to Hawaii, the 706th TB would stay in the Marianas to await its next assignment, which was not far off.

CHAPTER TWENTY-ONE

Stepping Stones

W hile the fighting on Guam was still going on, General MacArthur's troops in the southwest Pacific had managed to seize the Vogelkop peninsula on the far northwestern end of New Guinea—without the help of any Army tank battalions. With the Vogelkop in American hands, MacArthur could use its captured Japanese airfields and newly created American airfields to protect his further advances toward the Philippines.[1]

For his next conquest, MacArthur looked at Morotai Island in the Moluccas chain on the far eastern end of the Dutch East Indies. Situated just off the northwestern tip of New Guinea and about halfway between the Vogelkop peninsula and the Philippine Island of Mindanao, an airfield on Morotai would provide an even closer air base for the invasion of the Philippines. Eventually, an invasion was scheduled for September 15, 1944.[2]

The reinforced 31st IDiv, supported by the M4 medium Sherman tanks from Company C, 44th TB, both from the Wakde-Swarmi area of New Guinea, was selected to make the invasion. After the usual preliminary invasion bombardment, the infantry stormed ashore on the beaches of Morotai and ran into more trouble with the "deep mixtures of glutinous clay and mud" than with the Japanese. Although the Americans were subjected to air attacks from nearby Japanese-held islands, they managed to capture Morotai's one enemy airfield and build two new airfields by October 4. That date, Morotai was declared secure at the cost of thirty Americans killed and eighty-five wounded. For the Japanese, the defense of Morotai had cost them 104 killed and another thirteen captured.[3]

With the capture of Morotai, Company C, 44th TB settled in for a long stay of providing protection for the three airfields. In the meantime, General MacArthur went on with planning his invasion of the Philippines while Admiral Nimitz moved against the Palau Islands.

After the fall of both New Guinea and the Mariana Islands, the Joint Chiefs of Staff in Washington sent a communiqué to both General MacArthur and Admiral Nimitz, asking them to consider the "possibilities of expediting the Pacific campaign." The Joint Chiefs suggested the next island they set their sights on should be the strong Japanese naval and air base of Formosa. For MacArthur, that meant abandoning his long sought-after return to the Philippines and for Nimitz, it meant abandoning his plans to invade the Palau group, about 525 miles due east of the Philippines.

In reply, Admiral Nimitz argued that prior to any invasion of Formosa, the Americans would first have to seize forward air bases in either the northern Philippines or in the Palau Islands, or both. Simultaneously, General MacArthur protested that bypassing the Philippines would be morally wrong. It was an election year in 1944, and in a direct meeting with President Roosevelt, MacArthur stated, "American public opinion will condemn you, Mr. President. And it would be justified." In the end, both Nimitz and MacArthur were given the "go-ahead" for their planned invasions.[4]

In early 1944, Admiral Nimitz had made plans to capture the Palau island group on the far western end of the Caroline Islands in order to complete the encirclement and isolation of the strong Japanese garrison at Truk, 1,000 miles to the east. However, once the Marianas were taken, a few Navy commanders argued

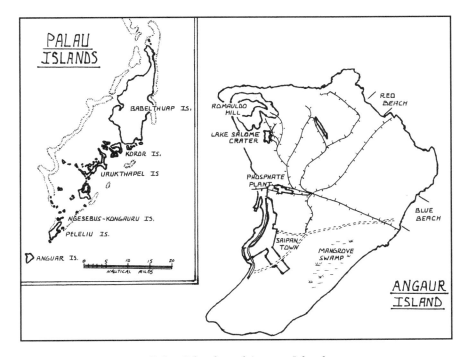

Palau Islands and Angaur Island

that an invasion of the Palaus was unnecessary. Instead, they wanted Nimitz to bypass the Palaus and concentrate on the northern Philippines or Formosa. Unswayed, Admiral Nimitz continued to plan his invasion of the Palaus.[5]

To cripple any air defenses the Japanese had within range of the Palaus, the Third Fleet began a series of devastating air attacks against the Philippine islands of Mindanao and Luzon. When the American fliers met little resistance in the way of Japanese fighter planes, it was suggested that both General MacArthur and Admiral Nimitz should move immediately toward the Philippines. Unfortunately, neither officer was willing to change horses in midstream and the invasion of the Palaus was on.[6]

The Palau Islands had been in Japanese hands since the end of World War I and therefore were thought to be well fortified. However, since most of the Japanese garrison was stationed throughout the northernmost islands, Admiral Nimitz elected to assault two of the southern islands: Peleliu and Angaur. Army historian Charles R. Anderson described both islands:

> Volcanic in origin, each island represented a low profile and rough surface of cliff faces, sinkholes, coral outcroppings, caves, and thick vegetation. Only seven miles long, Peleliu had an airfield in the south; a swamp covered most of the eastern side. Tiny Angaur, only three miles long, lay just six miles away. . . . The Japanese . . . deployed 10,500 troops on Peleliu but only 1,400 on Angaur.[7]

Peleliu was shaped somewhat like a winged helmet, with the front facing west, and the skull and wings reaching back toward the northeast. The thick skull extended back for about 6,500 yards and then tailed off at the base into a series of tiny, dislocated sub-islands that resembled a narrow, trailing ribbon. The wings extended out behind the helmet, reaching back another 4,100 yards, from southwest to northeast. Selected to make the assault on Peleliu was the 1st Marine Division, combat veterans of Guadalcanal.[8]

Tiny Angaur, six miles to the southwest, was shaped like a pork chop, tilted slightly to the northeast. A series of railroad tracks crossed the island and led to a phosphate plant, situated about one-half the way down the west coast of the island and slightly inland from the sea. Just below the plant lay Saipan Town, the only sizable village on the island, and above the plant, at the pointy, northwestern tip, lay Romauldo Hill, rising about 140 feet. Picked to conquer Angaur was the Army's untried 81st Infantry Division, supported by the tanks of the equally green 710th TB.[9]

The 710th TB had been moved to Hawaii in late June where it had been engaged in extensive training. In early August the unit was moved to Guadalcanal and Florida Island to practice a number of "dry run" landings before boarding a pair of transports for the Palaus. "While at sea," the unit historians wrote, "we learned that our objective was to be Angaur Island, in the Palau group. This was a brand new name to us, and unknown to most of the men on board ship. Maps and

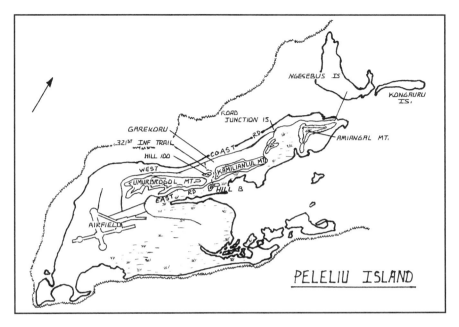

Peleliu Island

documents were brought out and critiques were held daily until every man knew every nook and crevice on the Island. What we didn't know—and were soon to find out—was what laid underground in the caves of the island." On September 15, 1944, the transport arrived off the coast of Angaur.[10]

While the Army units waited, the 1st MarDiv stormed the western beaches of Peleliu, coming in against the front of the helmet. Although the Marines met stiff resistance, they carved out a two-mile long, one-mile deep beachhead by night-fall. Over the next few days, the Marines advanced at a slow but steady pace and by September 20 had managed to capture Peleliu's lone airfield and half the island. From there on, however, they ran into Japanese defenders dug into numerous interlocking caves in the helmet's extending wings. As casualty rates in some units soared above 50 percent, all forward progress halted.[11]

Six miles away, the 81st IDiv went ashore on Angaur on September 17. Taking a calculated risk, Maj. Gen. Paul J. Mueller put his men ashore on two separate beachheads. The 321st IReg moved in against the eastern side of the pork chop (Blue Beach), while the 322nd IReg landed on the northern side (Red Beach). The first troops reached the beaches around 8:30 A.M., meeting extremely light opposition, and at 9:15 A.M. the 710th TB was ordered to bring their tanks ashore.[12]

The first tank company to come ashore was Company B, 710th TB, assigned to assist the 322nd IReg, 81st IDiv on Red Beach. "There was some congestion on the beach," reported Lt. Col. William M. Rodgers, commanding officer of the 710th TB. "One enemy pillbox [was] destroyed by a tank. . . . The tanks were off the beach and inland about 200 yards by 1030. . . . During the remainder of the first day there was no activity except for minor patrols."

To the east, on Blue Beach, the Shermans of Company A, 710th TB were all high and dry by 10:00 A.M. Once again, Colonel Rodgers reported there was "considerable congestion on the beach," which was exacerbated because a tank barrier surrounding the beach had not been breached by preceding bulldozers. By eleven o'clock, however, the bulldozers had completed their job and the tanks moved inland. "The terrain off the beach was flat," Rodgers wrote, "but covered with heavy jungle vegetation which made ground visibility very difficult. . . . The tanks remained just off the beach for the rest of the day and bivouacked [about 100 yards inland] near [a Japanese] radio station for the night."[13]

Near 4:30 P.M., the medium tanks of Company C finally came ashore, landing on Red Beach. "Due to the condition of the beach," Colonel Rodgers noted, "tanks were forced to go ashore in eight feet of water. Waterproofing was damaged on one tank causing the tank to flood with water and putting it out of action for the remainder of the operation." The other seventeen tanks made it safely ashore and spent the night waiting to move inland.[14]

That night, the Japanese tried a spirited banzai attack against the 321st IReg, 81st IDiv on Blue Beach. Coming out of the darkness, some of the Japanese broke through the American line before they were finally stopped and turned away. Instrumental in breaking up the attack were the 81mm mortars of the 710th TBs Provisional Mortar Platoon, a new, interim unit.[15]

At 9:00 A.M. on September 18, the 321st IReg began pushing outward from the eastern beachhead. While elements of the regiment moved north and northwest to establish contact with the 322nd IReg, other elements pushed south. As they did so, they moved out behind the tanks of Company A, 710th TB. "Because of the extremely heavy jungle growth," reported Colonel Rodgers, "it was necessary for the tanks to shoot into the jungle with .30-cal. machine guns and 75 guns, blasting the foliage away to afford visibility. The infantry followed the tanks from twenty-five to fifty yards."

Ernest F. Ciani, a radio operator from the 710th TB Reconnaissance Platoon, was the liaison radioman between the tanks and the infantry. He recalled, "[As] our tanks started moving out a sniper fired at least five shots at me (probably seeing the radio antenna). Someone finally got him, he was up in a tree and was also a bad shot." Coming under direct fire for the first time in his life, Ciani, and many of the other tankers and infantrymen, were understandably scared. "Being scared was one of the things we all felt," he readily acknowledged.[16]

As the tank-infantry teams advanced, they ran into numerous Japanese pillboxes. "These were first fired at by tank 75 guns," Colonel Rodgers wrote. "After placing several rounds in each pillbox, the tank covered the pillbox opening while demolition squads went forward and placed charges. After blowing up the pillboxes, the demolition teams and bulldozers followed the assault and completed the destruction of the pillboxes." Helping the tanks and men throughout the slow advance was the Provisional Mortar Platoon from the 710th TB, which dropped a steady stream of mortars in front of them.[17]

To the north, in the area of the 322nd IReg, the tanks of Company B, 710th TB also found the terrain on Angaur to be almost entirely "impassable." Only the tanks of the 3rd Platoon were able to move forward during the day, rumbling along a railroad bed that cut through the heavy island vegetation. "The tanks blasted suspicious-looking clumps of dense foliage, hit a few caves and bunkers, and fired at some buildings, most of which showed signs of hurried abandonment," reported Army historian Robert Ross Smith. Added Colonel Rodgers, "During this operation the tanks consistently led the infantry by approximately fifty yards. Their fire was directed whenever necessary by the infantry commander through the use of a . . . radio or the sound power telephone on the [rear of the] tanks."[18]

As the 3rd Platoon tanks neared the phosphate plant, one Sherman was hit in the side by a Japanese 77mm round. Then, in quick succession, another shot ricocheted off the turret and another slammed into its rear. Fortunately, the crew was uninjured and there was no permanent damage to the tank. Immediately, the other four tanks stopped and shelled the enemy gun position. "The Japanese gun was located and destroyed by tank fire without further incident," proclaimed Colonel Rodgers. Resuming their advance, the tank–infantry column captured the abandoned phosphate plant without much more trouble.[19]

While a portion of the 322nd IReg was accompanying the tanks moving along the railroad bed, another group was trying to push into the northwestern sector of Angaur. Noted historian Smith, "Angaur's northwestern terrain was honeycombed with natural crevices and covered by tropical trees and thick jungle undergrowth." Unable to make any headway toward Romauldo Hill, and unable to bring up tank support, the infantry advanced only 300 yards before sunset.[20]

At daybreak on September 19, the 321st IReg, near the east coast, began another drive south. Once again, the terrain and heavy Japanese resistance stalled its forward movement. "The 3rd Platoon [Shermans of Company A, 710th TB] . . . at the left flank ran into enemy artillery fire from the vicinity of Rocky Point during the morning," wrote Colonel Rodgers. By late afternoon, however, the 321st IReg and the 3rd Platoon tanks had broken into the Rocky Point defenses and had destroyed the Japanese field piece.[21]

Meanwhile, more soldiers from the 321st IReg clawed their way south and west toward Middle Village, a small settlement near the center of Angaur. At the northern edge of a huge mangrove swamp, which covered a large portion of the pork chop's southern tail, the advance ground to a halt. Instead of sending tanks and infantry through the swamp, Colonel Rodgers suggested he be allowed to send his tanks on an "armed reconnaissance" mission completely around the obstruction. He believed that a column of tanks, carrying infantrymen on their backs, could go down the west side of the swamp, circle underneath it, and come back up the east side, along the coast. Given the green light, Colonel Rodgers selected two platoons of Shermans from Company C, 710th TB and the 1st Platoon Shermans of Company A, 710th TB. Six infantrymen would ride on each tank and the remainder would follow behind on foot, eventually setting up an east–west line across the bottom of the island, just below the swamp.[22]

At 1:30 P.M., the infantry-laden tanks began their circling drive around the swamp. By 5:00 P.M., the column was back at the starting point. "During this movement a great many enemy positions were encountered but [they] were all unoccupied," wrote Colonel Rodgers. With night falling, the two platoons of Company C Shermans moved back below the swamp to help stabilize the new east-west cross-island line, while the 1st Platoon tanks of Company A returned to their company command post west of Rocky Point.[23]

Elsewhere on September 19, the 322nd IReg moved south from the phosphate plant toward Saipan Town. All of the pillboxes and fortifications they encountered pointed out to sea and had been abandoned by the Japanese. By 4:00 P.M., the 322nd IReg had seized an abandoned Saipan Town and made contact with the 321st IReg. At the close of action on September 19, the American troops held all of Angaur except a small 800-yard long, tapering section of the southern tip; a small pocket on the eastern side of the mangrove swamp; and the rugged northwestern end of the island.[24]

At 8:00 A.M. on September 20, the 81st IDiv and its supporting troops began the job of reducing the Japanese-held areas. While the 322nd IReg assaulted the northwestern end of the island, the 321st IReg moved out to capture the southern tip and to eliminate the pocket on the east coast. Assisting in the push south were the mediums of Company C, 710th TB. "[A] general advance was ordered all along the line," noted Colonel Rodgers, "with tanks leading in all cases, shooting down all jungle growth and firing into all possible enemy positions, after which demolition teams and bulldozers completed the destruction of enemy positions." By noon, the entire southern end of the island had been overrun.

Company B/710th TB M4 tanks on Angaur Island, September 20, 1944. US ARMY

Aided by the tanks of Companies A and B, the 321st IReg moved against the small pocket on the eastern side of the mangrove swamp and against the swamp itself. Although the attack through the swamp quickly bogged down, the other attack was more successful and by 3:30 P.M. the eastern pocket had been eliminated. "This completed the operation in the southern half of the island," said Rodgers. In reporting on the actions of his tanks, Colonel Rodgers wrote, "ALL enemy installations were fired upon with 75 and .30-cal. ammunition. The tanks then covered the enemy positions until demolition squads and bulldozers completed the destruction."[25]

To the northwest, the 322nd IReg ran into more trouble as it struggled through the rising terrain around Romauldo Hill. During the morning advance, foot soldiers discovered a Japanese strong point at a large, lake-filled crater at the southeastern base of the hill. Unable to reduce the position on their own, the infantrymen called for armor. Unfortunately, because of the bad terrain, the platoon of Shermans sent over from Company B, 710th TB, was unable to get close to the crater. Without tank support, the infantry backed away and settled in for the night.[26]

While the fighting was still going on, General Mueller decided that since three-quarters of Angaur was now in American hands, he could declare the island secure. At 11:00 A.M. on September 20, 1944, tiny Angaur Island was declared secure.[27] The same could not be said for Peleliu.

On nearby Peleliu Island, the 1st MarDiv was catching hell. Unable to dislodge the Japanese from the mountainous spine of the helmet's wings, the Marines were suffering heavily. On the night of September 20, with Angaur declared secure, the 321st IReg, along with Company A and the Provisional Mortar Platoon from the 710th TB were ordered to prepare for a transfer to Peleliu. The "mopping up" of Angaur would be left to the men of the 322nd IReg, 81st IDiv. Assisting them would be the medium M4 Sherman tanks of Companies B and C, and the light tanks of Company D, which had finally come ashore.[28]

At 8:00 A.M. on September 21, the 322nd IReg and the tanks of Company C, 710th TB began assaulting the crater at the southeastern base of Romauldo Hill. Against stiff resistance, the men and tanks worked their way forward along a narrow-gauge railroad track, taking more than an hour to reach the lip of the crater. Once at the edge, the attackers discovered the only way into the basin was through a crevice-like opening which was blocked by a burning American 75mm SPM halftrack knocked out the day before. The tanks attempted to blow the SPM out of the way, and when this failed a satchel charge was thrown into the vehicle. Instead of demolishing the halftrack, however, the explosion only extinguished the flames. Finally, near noon, a few tankers ran forward under heavy enemy fire, hooked a tow cable to the disabled SPM and a tank pulled the halftrack out of the way.[29]

Historian Smith described what happened next:

Eight tanks, accompanied by a rifle platoon, filed through the railroad cut and out into the bowl. There was scattered small-arms fire from the Japanese, but enemy heavy weapons remained silent as the tanks pushed forward, compelled by the nature of the terrain to follow the narrow-gauge railroad beds. In the bowl the railroad spurs were laid along raised beds from which two tanks slid, one falling twenty feet to overturn and catch fire and the other getting into such a position that it had to be dis-armed and abandoned. Three additional tanks moved about fifty yards into the bowl and halted to provide fire support to [the infantry] who were working along higher ground to the right along the southeast rim. Tank fire was directed mainly into the center of the bowl and towards the high slopes of the north rim. . . . The terrain made coordinated infantry-tank attacks impossible.[30]

During the movement to the crater, Pvt. Oliver C. Ferguson earned a Bronze Star when he volunteered to lead his tank across the very narrow causeway. "Walking in front of the tank," noted his citation, "he was halfway across the dan-gerous area when he was fired on by an enemy machine gun and rifles. With no regard for his own safety, he continued on his mission until the vehicle was com-pletely across."[31]

In assessing the patrol, Colonel Rodgers complained, "No adequate reconnais-sance had been made of the crater area until the tanks reached the . . . end of the [railroad] cut. It was found that the terrain in the crater was impossible for tank operation due to crevices and rock pinnacles." Near 4:00 P.M., both the infantry and tanks had enough and withdrew for the night. Added Colonel Rodgers, "During the time the tanks were in the crater, they received several hits from Japanese guns of 37 or 40mm. No damage was sustained by the tanks and at least one Japanese 37mm gun was knocked out."[32]

On September 22, the tanks and infantry renewed their assault on the crater. This time a two-pronged attack was planned. While the tanks and some support-ing infantry moved up through the railroad defile to attack from the southeast, a group of foot soldiers tried to get at the crater from the south. Unfortunately, the flanking move was stopped by the heavy terrain. In the meantime, three Company C tanks worked their way up to the mouth of the crater but began taking fire from a Japanese 37mm antitank gun, which wounded the commanding officer of Com-pany C. When darkness fell and the three tanks began withdrawing for the night, the second tank in line hit a buried mine or shell and was so badly damaged it could not be removed from the narrow passageway. Since the third tank was com-pletely blocked, the vehicle was abandoned and destroyed in order to keep it out of Japanese hands.[33]

On September 23, the Americans once again attacked the southeastern rim of the crater. At daybreak, while the infantry moved forward, the 710th TB mainte-nance section arrived to remove the stalled tank from the narrow railroad defile. When the tank was finally hauled away, three Shermans from Company C moved through the cut, slipped past the second abandoned tank and added their fire to that of the infantry. Once again, however, the tanks and infantry were unable to get beyond the southeastern rim and around 4:00 P.M., everybody pulled back to their night bivouacs.[34]

After five days of costly attacks, the crater was still in Japanese hands. Because of the terrain, it was almost impossible to bring enough tanks into position to help the infantry. As historian Smith wrote, "A major change in plans seemed to be necessary."

Instead of another direct assault from the south, General Mueller ordered his artillery to pulverize the defenders while part of his infantry swung around to attack from the north. Although the artillery managed to make the center of the crater look like the surface of the moon, the infantry was unable to find a way through the dense jungle. On September 25, after two and a half days of trying, the infantry gave up and General Mueller devised a new plan.

Aerial reconnaissance had indicated that east of the crater the jungle was less dense and the terrain less broken. On the morning of September 25, Army engineers began bulldozing a narrow trail through the jungle from Red Beach to the northeastern edge of the crater. By nightfall, when the job was finished, General Mueller ordered an all-out assault for the next morning.[35]

On September 26, as elements of the 322nd IReg, 81st IDiv drove forward along Bulldozer Trail and moved up to the northern and northeastern rim of the crater, the 2nd Platoon Shermans of Company B tried to follow. Unfortunately, the tankers soon discovered the trail was unsuitable for tanks. Recalled Colonel Rodgers, "The remainder of the day was spent in reconnaissance in an attempt to find a means of placing tanks into the crater from the [northeast] side." With the tanks providing cover, the bulldozers began cutting paths through the thick jungle. By nightfall, the tanks were ready to go.[36]

Early the next morning, September 28, the Shermans moved out. "The 2nd Platoon went into the crater, along Bulldozer Trail," noted Colonel Rodgers, "[but] because of the rough terrain it was impossible for the tanks to move in in any other formation than column." When 2nd Platoon leader 2nd Lt. Frank C. Roundtree attempted to move around another tank, his vehicle got hung up on a rock outcropping. Ignoring the stuck tank, the other tanks fired "at all possible enemy positions on the north and east sides of the crater."[37]

At 2:00 P.M., the tanks had expended all of their ammunition and were preparing to leave when Lieutenant Roundtree and his radio operator were wounded by enemy gunfire and another crewman was fatally wounded. Pvt. James T. O'Connor, an assistant driver in another tank, quickly left the safety of his own tank to attach a tow cable to Roundtree's tank. "Moving through enemy small arms fire," read O'Connor's citation for a Silver Star medal, "he successfully completed his mission and was reentering his tank when he was mortally wounded. Private O'Connor's gallant action made possible the prompt treatment of wounded comrades."[38]

On September 29, the 1st Platoon Shermans replaced the 2nd Platoon tanks in the battle for the crater. Four of the five tanks lined up along the northern edge of the crater and opened fire, "similarly to an artillery barrage." Recalled Colonel Rodgers, "They expended 400 rounds of ammunition in fifty minutes in conjunction with heavy mortar concentration by the [322nd IReg]."

When the barrage ceased, the infantry moved forward and the four tanks retired to replenish their ammunition. "The remaining tank of the Platoon took up a position from which to fire," wrote Rodgers. "This was deemed necessary as it had been found from previous experience that the enemy was reluctant to expose their positions by fire of any kind as long as tanks were present and in position to fire." When the four tanks returned, they supported the infantry until dusk before returning to their company bivouac area.[39]

For the next five days, from September 30 through October 4, the 710th TB mediums returned to the northern and northeastern rim of the crater and fired in support of the infantry. "During this time a large number of caves were shot out," noted Colonel Rodgers. "The results are not obtainable as many of the caves were blown in by demolitions without being inspected; however, several machine guns, one 37, and one 77mm gun definitely were destroyed." Finally, Colonel Rodgers could report, "The only fire remaining in the crater was intermittent sniper fire from around the rim of the crater."[40]

After October 5, the tanks of the 710th TB saw little action. Although an occasional call came in from the infantry, the tankers soon discovered they were seldom needed. Beginning on October 5, the battle for Angaur was an infantry-man's fight.[41]

The infantry resumed the fight for the crater on October 6 while the 710th TB began roving patrols. Four days later, the tanks were ordered to halt their roving and take up stationary positions for a "night defense against [a] possible banzai counterattack." Fortunately, the charge never materialized, and by October 18 the remaining Japanese had been compressed into an area in the northwest corner of the island measuring approximately 100 yards long by fifty yards wide. Three days later, the American infantry overran the pocket. With the possible exception of a few stragglers, all Japanese defenders on Angaur were either dead or captured.[42]

The battle for Angaur cost the Japanese 1,300 men killed and forty-five cap-tured while the Americans lost 264 dead and 1,355 wounded.[43] In the 710th TB, four men had been killed and another nineteen wounded. In tanks permanently lost, the 710th TB lost one Sherman in the surf during the initial invasion and three more in the protracted fight for the crater.[44] Overall, the rookie 81st IDiv and the untried 710th TB had performed admirably.

In his after-action report, Colonel Rodgers praised the work of the Army engineers. He wrote, "The necessity of close cooperation between combat engi-neers and tanks in rough terrain of the type encountered on this island was brought out forcibly. On a number of occasions it would have been impossible for the tanks to support the infantry without prior preparation of tank positions by engineers. The rocky terrain encountered on this island necessitated the use of demolitions and heavy bulldozers to make the terrain passable to tanks. In operat-ing in heavy jungle country it was necessary for the tanks to blast away the foliage with the fire from the 75s. For this purpose it would be better if a canister round were supplied."[45]

In addition to helping the tanks, the Army engineers had begun construction of an airfield near the southern tip of Angaur while the battle of the crater was still in progress. On October 15, twenty-eight days after the initial invasion, a C-47 cargo plane landed on the airstrip. Four days later, the engineers completed two 6,000-foot landing strips.[46] Without much trouble, Admiral Nimitz had a secure airfield for further advances toward Japan. On Peleliu, however, the airfield was nowhere near being usable.

CHAPTER TWENTY-TWO

The Helmet's Wings

On September 23, 1944, the 321st IReg, 81st IDiv left Angaur Island and arrived on Peleliu to assist the battered 1st MarDiv. Near 5:00 P.M., the medium Sherman tanks of Company A, the M10 tank destroyers of the assault gun platoon, and the 81mm mortar teams of the provisional mortar platoon, all 710th TB, arrived to help the infantry. At five o'clock the next morning, the tankers were given their first mission on Peleliu.[1]

Capt. Harold E. Meyer, commanding officer of Company A, was told the 321st IReg was planning to advance north up the West Coast Road, which paralleled the Umurbrogol Mountains that formed the spine of the extended wings of the helmet. The soldiers were told to move forward from a line at the start of the wings, designated the Third Phase Line, until they reached the Fourth Phase Line at the village of Garekoru, situated about one-third of the way up the wings. The commander on Peleliu, Marine Maj. Gen. William H. Rupertus, was hoping to use the fresh Army troops to encircle the Japanese in the Umurbrogol Mountains. The 321st IReg was ordered to move out immediately with the Shermans of Company A in the lead.[2]

Wondering what he was getting his tanks into, Captain Meyer himself went out and inspected the road. "[He] made a reconnaissance of the West Coast Road finding the road very narrow and with limited visibility due to the heavy foliage," reported Colonel Rodgers. "The road was not mined but there were numerous teapot mines a few feet off on either side at intervals of approximately thirty yards. No doubt the Japs had been forced to retreat in a hurry and did not have time to mine the road."

Eventually, Captain Meyer returned to his unit and brought his tanks forward. He moved his entire 3rd Platoon, plus half of the 2nd Platoon, up to Garekora village and placed the 1st Platoon Shermans plus the other half of the 2nd Platoon at a place in the road known as Suicide Curve, just short of Garekora. The tanks on the curve were to act as artillery and "fire on the high ridges east of the West Coast Road."[3]

The movement of the column up the West Coast Road caused a bit of contention with Marine Corps commanders. The Marines had expected the soldiers to move slowly up the road, sweeping through the jungle on both sides and capturing the steep ridges to the right. Instead, when the soldiers found the jungle too thick, they simply filed onto the road and moved ahead at a quicker pace. Exasperated, Marine Corps commanders had to change plans. Noted historians Jim Moran and Gordon L. Rottman, "[The Marines were ordered] to capture the ridges abandoned by [the Army], which they did at some cost—another setback in Army–Marine relations!"[4]

After racing ahead to Garekora, the 321st IReg discovered a semi-hidden trail leading off to the east, behind the northern end of the Umurbrogol Mountains. Nicknamed the "321st Infantry Trail," a detachment of soldiers quickly pushed down the narrow trail and captured most of Hill 100. Overlooking the northern end of the Umurbrogol pocket and the East Road, the seizure of Hill 100 was a strategic coup for the Army.[5]

As the 321st IReg worked to entrap the Umurbrogol defenders in a pocket, a fresh battalion from the 321st was ordered to advance north up the helmet's wings to the Fifth Phase Line. Wrote Colonel Rodgers, "Two columns would be formed, each consisting of the following: three medium tanks, one flamethrower (LVT), two armored LVTs, forty infantrymen, a demolition squad of engineers, and medics." As planned, Column A would move north along the coastline, while Column B traveled northeast up the West Coast Road.[6]

Both columns moved out along their intended routes and met very little resistance. Column A, moving along the beach, destroyed a Japanese 77mm field piece with tank fire from the Company A, 710th TB Shermans and Column B, moving along the West Coast Road, detonated three underground ammunition dumps with tank fire, a flamethrowing LVT, and satchel charges. After going only a short way, however, both columns were ordered to return to Garekora. Instead of using the slow-moving Army troops, General Rupertus had suddenly decided to give the move along the wings to his faster-moving Marine Corps troops.[7]

In the afternoon of September 25, the 5th Marine Regiment, 1st MarDiv, assisted by three Marine Corps tanks and two Army tanks from the 1st section of the 2nd Platoon, Company A, 710th TB, began the drive to the northeast. Moving quickly up West Coast Road, the Marines captured Road Junction 15, where the East Road swerved in to connect with the West Coast Road. A little farther on, the rapidly moving Marines came upon a deserted Japanese radio station. As night fell, the Marines set up night defensive positions on Hill 80, "an isolated terrain feature lying between Kamilianlul Mountain, on the south, and another hill mass named the Amiangal [ridges] located at the northern end of Peleliu."[8]

Before daybreak on September 26, the 321st IReg soldiers stationed near Suicide Curve went forward again, still trying to shove the Japanese off two spiny

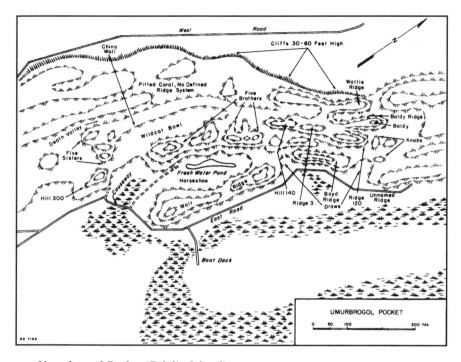

Umurbrogol Pocket (Peleliu Island) FROM BLOODY BEACHES: THE MARINES AT PELELIU
BY BRIG. GEN. GORDON D. GAYLE

ridges dubbed Baldy and Wattie. As before, the mortar platoon, assault gun platoon, and tanks of Company A, 710th TB aided the infantry by acting as mobile
artillery, and once again, the foot soldiers made little progress. At nightfall, the
infantrymen returned to their jumping-off spots along the West Coast Road.[9]

A little to the northeast, around Hill 100, the 2nd Bn, 321st IReg moved out to
attack Hill B from the south and southwest. At the same time, a mobile task force,
commanded by infantry Capt. George C. Neal, began a quick circling run up the
West Coast Road to Road Junction 15, then back down the East road, to assault
Hill B from the north. Known as Task Force Neal, the group consisted of forty-
five infantrymen, one flame-throwing LVT, six armored LVTs, and seven medium
tanks from the 2nd and 3rd Platoon of Company A, 710th TB.[10]

"All personnel and equipment was loaded on either tanks or LVTs," reported
Colonel Rodgers. At 10:00 A.M., Task Force Neal began moving rapidly up the
West Coast Road. "After passing RJ 15," Rodgers wrote, "all infantry personnel
was unloaded and assigned to protect the vehicles. A picked team of twelve men
was assigned to the first tank, to detect any antitank or antipersonnel mines that
might be along the road as well as to pick out and designate tank targets."

Moving "very slowly and cautiously," Task Force Neal inched its way down
East Road, "killing a few Japs that were found hidden along the side of the road."

About 200 yards north of Hill 100, the group linked up with men from the 321st IReg who had managed to circle their way around the southern end of the hill. "The column then moved forward about seventy-five yards where it was stopped by a roadblock consisting of a large tree and boulders piled across the road," wrote Rodgers. When the column halted, an enemy machine gun in a cave on the northern side of Hill 100 suddenly opened fire. "The tanks fired into the cave, neutralizing it," said Colonel Rodgers, "the flamethrower was brought up and used in the assault. The infantry cleared the roadblock and the column moved forward another seventy-five yards where it was stopped by a bomb crater which had destroyed the road."[11]

Unable to get around the huge crater because of impassable terrain on either side, Task Force Neal went into a nighttime defensive perimeter. Recalled Colonel Rodgers, "[A] bulldozer was ordered for the first thing the following morning to repair the road in order that further movement south would be possible."[12]

Meanwhile, the rest of the 321st IReg had captured the rest of Hill 100 and began attacking Hill B from the south and southwest. Although slowed by terrible terrain and a stubborn defense, two companies of soldiers fought their way to the summit, and by nightfall both hills were firmly in American hands. The Umurbrogol pocket was now completely isolated.[13]

To the north, the 5th Marine Regiment, 1st MarDiv stretched out across the island to cut the East Road and sever Peleliu's wings at another spot. The 81st IDiv had cut the island at 321st Infantry Trail and Hills 100 and B, and now the Marines had cut the island 1,500-yards farther north—from the radio station to East Road. Any remaining Japanese on Peleliu were now trapped in three isolated areas: in the Umurbrogol pocket, between 321st Infantry Trail and the 5th Marines; in an area on Kamilianlul Mountain; and between the 5th Marines and the sea, on the Amiangal ridges.[14]

On September 27, the 1st Bn, 321st IReg began moving north along Kamilianlul Mountain. Surprisingly, the men met very little opposition; well before nightfall the entire mountain had been swept clean and the troops were moving forward to make contact with the Marines near RJ 15. About this time, however, the battalion came under heavy fire from a Japanese pillbox located at a sharp bend in the East Road. Tanks were called for but before they could arrive, darkness fell.[15]

At Task Force Neal, the bulldozer arrived at 8:30 A.M. After the crater was filled in, and the tanks and LVTs had been resupplied, the column started south again, hoping to move down to Phase Line X-ray, which cut through the center of the Umurbrogol pocket, before nightfall. After traveling only 100 yards, the task force discovered a Japanese supply cave, which "was set on fire with portable flamethrowers and burned for two days."[16]

While Task Force Neal was traveling down the East Road, two companies of infantry tried to advance to their immediate right through the rough terrain of Umurbrogol Mountain. Almost immediately, the companies came under intense fire from well-concealed Japanese positions and called for assistance from Task

Force Neal. Historian Smith reported, "Direct fire from tanks, which used many white phosphorus shells, and fire from a flame thrower mounted on an LVT . . . helped to reduce many of the enemy positions, but others were inaccessible to such fire or to infantry assault from the low ground along East Road. By late afternoon the intensity of fire on both companies had not appreciably diminished." With the two companies suffering extreme casualties, both units withdrew for the night while Task Force Neal returned to the base of Hill B.[17]

Early on the morning of September 28, two Shermans from Task Force Neal went to help the 1st Bn, 321st IReg. "[The infantry], now supported by two medium tanks and some flamethrowers, struck out against the pillbox at the East Road curve where the advance had halted the previous evening," wrote historian Smith. Resistance was so stubborn, it was eleven o'clock before the pillbox fell. Added Smith, "Minor installations in the same vicinity and some bypassed positions along the base of Kamilianlul Mountain's northern nose continued to give trouble and had to be knocked out one by one in a series of infantry-tank-flamethrower assaults." By nightfall, however, all of the ground between 321st Infantry Trail and Hill 80 had been secured.[18]

Although Task Force Neal officially ceased to exist on September 28 with the removal and replacement of some tanks and infantry, the armored column continued to push south down East Road toward Phase Line X-Ray. At the same time, the 321st IReg renewed its parallel drive down the spine of Umurbrogol Mountain. Although the rugged terrain along the mountainous spine slowed the advance, by late afternoon both the infantry and the armored column had reached Phase Line X-ray. "The column was ordered to remain in its present position for the night," recalled Rodgers. "A perimeter defense was set up by the armored vehicles with the infantrymen digging in and setting up positions under the tanks."[19]

During the two-day advance, Captain Meyer, commander of Company A, 710th TB, earned himself a Silver Star medal. His citation read: "Despite heavy enemy machine-gun and rifle fire directed at his column, he remained in an exposed position on the lead tank in order to more closely supervise all tank action. His personal courage under fire and skillful leadership were largely responsible for a 3,000-yard penetration of enemy-held terrain and the neutralizing of fifteen enemy emplacements."[20]

On September 29, the 321st IReg, 81st IDiv and most of its supporting units were relieved from their duties around the Umurbrogol pocket and replaced by the 1st MarDiv. Only the 710th TB's mortar platoon and assault gun platoon remained in place on Suicide Curve. Relieved from the pocket, the GIs moved north to relieve the Marines on northern Peleliu and on nearby Ngesebus and Kongauru islands. The day before, the Marines had reached the very northern tip of Peleliu, and then had crossed over to Ngesebus and Kongauru. Attacking with a fury, the Marines had all of Kongauru and most of Ngesebus in their hands by the morning of September 29. At that point, the 321st IReg was ordered up to take possession of both islands.[21]

The next day, while most of the Company A, 710th TB Shermans moved into a Marine Corps motor pool near the west end of the Peleliu airstrip, five tanks from the 1st Platoon headed north toward Ngesebus Island.[22]

Although the tanks were guided across a short expanse of water by an LVT, two of the tanks foundered. "The first tank . . ." explained Colonel Rodgers, "following the guide (LVT) ran into a bomb crater underneath the water. The 2nd to be drowned out was pulled back to the shore of Peleliu. . . . Two attempts were made to get [the first] tank out. Being unsuccessful, the guns were disarmed and all portable equipment was removed." The remaining three tanks made the water crossing without difficulty and spent the day cleaning out pockets of Japanese resistance.[23]

On the same date, the naval task force commander declared Peleliu and the surrounding islands "captured and secured." Although it was true that "only some tough mopping-up remained to be done," the Japanese on Peleliu were far from conquered. By the end of September, the Japanese defenders on Peleliu had killed or wounded 5,044 Marines and 279 soldiers. In turn, the Japanese had lost an estimated 9,000 men, mostly killed. Still, intelligence suggested that about 2,500 Japanese soldiers were bottled up in the Umurbrogol pocket. For the Marines and soldiers on Peleliu, the island would never be "captured or secured" until the Umurbrogol pocket was eliminated.[24]

The first day of October the 1st Platoon Shermans of Company A began widening a trail that ran into the northern end of the Umurbrogol pocket. Blasting and crushing down the jungle, the tanks "endeavored to break a trail west through the hills to aid the infantry in their advance." However, as Colonel Rodgers noted, "[They] found the terrain too rugged. . . . A bulldozer and demolition squad was ordered to start building a road."[25]

On the southeastern end of the Umurbrogol pocket, two three-tank sections from the 3rd Platoon went forward to assist the Marines around a 225-foot hill known as Old Baldy, and against five little knobs of land known as the Five Brothers. Over the next few days, the Marines and tanks fought hard but were continually hampered by stiff opposition and "heavy rain, fog, and sickness."[26]

Around October 3, both the 710th TB's mortar platoon and assault gun platoon were relieved from their duty around Suicide Curve and moved north to the area of the Japanese radio station. From there, the M10 tank destroyers helped clean up the helmet's wings. As Colonel Rodgers noted, "Their larger shells and higher velocity, enabled them to destroy targets much more quickly than the tank guns. It became evident that the Japs feared this weapon as the sniper fire always ceased shortly after its guns opened fire."[27]

Two days later, while one of the three-tank sections from the 3rd Platoon was once again advancing with the Marines against Old Baldy, the lead tank had a track blown off. When the next tank in line tried to pass the disabled tank, a sudden explosion rocked that vehicle also. Believing that a hidden Japanese antitank gun was firing at them, the second tank quickly backed away. In spite of a damaged front bogie wheel and a track that was being held together by only one connector, the tank managed to move back about 300 yards.

Fearing that the unseen antitank gun would continue to fire at the disabled first tank, a Marine Corps officer ordered the crew to abandon their vehicle. Only after the men had scrambled to safety was it discovered what had happened. According to Colonel Rodgers, "The crew . . . [had] the following story: [the second] tank had been damaged by a Jap who had run out carrying a satchel charge and laid alongside the tank with the charge beneath his body, committing suicide and causing the damage to the tank." Realizing that there was no danger from antitank guns, the crew decided to retrieve their disabled tank.[28]

Pvt. Billy B. Beasley, acting commander of the abandoned tank, volunteered to go back to retrieve his tank. "Crawling over the exposed area under heavy fire to the damaged vehicle," his Silver Star citation read, "he accomplished the difficult task of maneuvering it to cover, where its repair was then possible." Aided by Marine Corps riflemen, another tank eventually moved forward and helped tow the damaged tank back behind American lines.[29]

On October 8, General Rupertus began a major push against the Umurbrogol pocket. At 7:00 P.M., after an hour-long artillery barrage, four M4 Sherman tanks from the 1st Platoon, Company A entered the Umurbrogol pocket over a causeway that reached across a swamp. Once past the swamp, the tanks turned wide right and headed west toward Mortimer Valley, a slight valley to the east of Five Brothers. Almost immediately two tanks were slightly damaged by a well-concealed Japanese antitank gun, which forced all four tanks to retreat back to the mouth of the causeway.

Regrouping, the four tanks went forward again, this time staying to the right of the causeway mouth and using a high ridge as cover. Coming in from behind the ridge, the tanks managed to surprise the Japanese gun crew and destroy the piece before the crew got off another shot.[30]

Around 10:30 A.M., after the four 1st Platoon tanks were reinforced by two Shermans from the 3rd Platoon, the armor rumbled into Mortimer Valley. Colonel Rodgers described the action:

> As the first tank turned into the mouth of the valley it hit a Jap land mine which blew off its right track. The second, third, and fourth tanks moved around the disabled one and proceeded slowly up the valley, firing on all likely Jap positions. When the second tank reached a position some 100 yards north of the mouth of the valley, it was fired on and hit by a Jap antitank gun. . . . The Jap gun was so cleverly concealed that it was impossible to locate its position. This tank then withdrew from the valley to repair its 75mm gun which had jammed. The third tank moved forward and received three hits from the same Jap gun, but still was unable to locate its position. A radio message was sent to the Marine CP telling them of the condition existing. Their decision was for the tanks to pull out and allow the artillery to work over the suspected area. In backing out

the tanks became bunched and a Jap antitank gun from the Fourth Brother opened up and hit four of them. The tanks returned the fire and retired to a position of cover.[31]

At 2:00 P.M., after another heavy barrage, six more tanks from Company A, 710th TB, and two companies of Marines pushed into Mortimer Valley. Intense enemy fire quickly stopped the Marines, but the tanks kept going. "This time the Jap gun was located and destroyed by tank fire," proclaimed Colonel Rodgers. For the next few hours, the tanks remained in the valley shooting at targets of opportunity. "As the tanks began running out of ammunition during the late afternoon," said historian Smith, "the [Marine] positions in Mortimer Valley became untenable, and under cover of smoke, which the tanks' guns provided, withdrawal was made to the morning line of departure. It was ten days before American troops again attempted to operate in the valley."[32]

During the next week, while the Marines tried to squeeze the pocket from different directions, Company A, 710th TB remained relatively quiet. The 2nd Platoon tanks remained on Ngesebus Island, while the other platoon tanks underwent much needed repairs at the Marine motor park or went out alone or in pairs "on mop-up missions or to suppress local enemy action."[33]

On October 14, with most of the nearby island of Angaur secured, Lieutenant Colonel Rodgers and the 710th TB headquarters moved to Peleliu. Upon inspection of Company A, which had been on Peleliu since September 23, Rodgers discovered, "the morale of the troops [was] high, but they were badly in need of rest." Because of this, he asked for one of the other tank companies to be transferred over from Angaur. While he waited, Colonel Rodgers did a little reshuffling on his own.

The next day, Rodgers replaced the battle-worn 3rd Platoon at the Umurbrogol pocket with the well-rested 2nd Platoon from Ngesebus Island. However, instead of shifting tanks and equipment, he simply shifted personnel. The men of the 3rd Platoon took over the 2nd Platoon tanks on Ngesebus, while the tankers from the 2nd Platoon came down to the northern end of the Umurbrogol pocket and climbed into the tanks of the 3rd Platoon. At the same time, the 81st IDiv began relieving the 1st MarDiv from its activities on Peleliu.[34]

At 3:00 P.M. on October 16, the 321st IReg began pressing in on the northern and eastern sides of the Umurbrogol pocket while the 323rd IReg, fresh from a victory at Ulithi Atoll, 400 miles northeast of the Palaus, pushed in from the west and south. As the infantry moved forward, the 2nd Platoon Shermans of Company A, 710th TB split into two sections. While one section went down a makeshift trail to help capture Hill 140 and Brother No. 1 from the north, the second section moved south down the East Road to a point about midway down the pocket. Here, at a gap between two ridges, a bulldozer began cutting a side road into the northern end of Mortimer Valley. "[The road] eventually proved to be the key to opening up the Jap defensive positions," Colonel Rodgers wrote. As the bulldozer worked, the second section tanks moved onto a nearby small plateau and began working over Hill 140 and Brothers 1 and 2.[35]

Sometime during the afternoon, the first section tanks moved over to the gap after gaining little ground on the makeshift trail. Although the infantry commanders were expecting to make a big push over the new road as soon as possible, progress came to a complete halt when the bulldozer damaged its blade on a Japanese antitank mine. Then, as all of the 2nd Platoon tanks were withdrawing for the night, two of them rolled over hidden mines and lost their treads. "It was evident that these mines were recently put into position by the Japs," noted Rodgers, "as this same ground had been traveled the day before."[36]

By the morning of October 18, however, the road was finally finished. At 9:00 A.M., under covering fire from the infantry, the 2nd Platoon Shermans of Company A, 710th TB moved over the new road between the two eastern ridges and down into the northern half of Mortimer Valley. "The tanks were in column formation to avoid the possibility of more than one tank hitting land mines at a time," recalled Colonel Rodgers. "They fired at numerous caves along the bases of [the eastern ridges] and the Brothers, paying special attention to Brother 1. . . . The tanks stayed in the valley all day supporting the infantry." Aided by tanks and mortar fire, the 321st IReg surged forward and captured the summits of Brothers No. 1, 2 and 3. However, a well-organized Japanese counterattack shoved the Americans off all three and by nightfall the Five Brothers were back in Japanese hands.[37]

That same date, a detachment of Marines from the 1st MarDiv was mopping up an area southwest of the Umurbrogol pocket. Just east of the West Coast Road, it ran into a pesky Japanese cave and called for a tank. A 1st Platoon Sherman commanded by Sgt. John Prehm Jr. went over and reported to Marine Capt. H. W. Jones. Wanting to point out the exact location of the cave, Captain Jones climbed inside the tank and directed it into a little valley beside the road. As the tank was clanking into position, it struck a hidden Japanese aerial bomb and erupted in a "terrific explosion."

The explosion ripped through the thin belly of the tank and tipped it over onto its left side. Sergeant Prehm and PFC Howard Dahms were catapulted out of the tank but the other three crewmen and Captain Jones were killed instantly. Later, Private Dahms died of his wounds, leaving Sergeant Prehm as the sole survivor of the "terrific explosion."[38]

On the morning of October 19, the 1st Platoon Shermans joined the 2nd Platoon tanks in their assault on the northern end of Mortimer Valley. While the 2nd Platoon tanks entered the valley and fired on Brothers 1, 2 and 3, the 1st Platoon tanks moved in and fired on Brother 4 and Old Baldy. Noted Colonel Rodgers, "An uncounted number of Japs were killed by the tanks. One of them was killed trying to place a satchel charge on a track of a LVT flamethrower, that was working with the tanks."[39]

Next day, October 20, as the battered 1st MarDiv continued its withdrawal from Peleliu, overall command was transferred to General Mueller of the 81st IDiv. That same day, three M10 tank destroyers of the 710th TB assault gun platoon moved into Mortimer Valley and continued the bombardment of Old Baldy and a series of smaller hills to the immediate west known as the Five Sisters. Relieved from duty in the valley, the 1st Platoon Shermans moved to the southwest corner of the Umurbrogol pocket, near where Sergeant Prehm's tank had exploded, designated Death Valley.[40]

On one drive into Death Valley, tank commander Pvt. William R. Crowell looked through his periscope and spotted a Japanese soldier with a satchel charge making a suicide charge against another tank. Although heavy small arms and automatic weapons fire filled the air, Crowell threw open his hatch, stood up, and "with deliberate coolness, shot and killed the fanatical enemy with his carbine." Although Crowell earned a Bronze Star for this action, the enemy soldier was not killed until after the explosive had been thrown onto the back of another tank. Immediately, Crowell notified the other tank commander of the situation.[41]

Inside the other tank, tank commander Sgt. Stanley G. Lewandowski heard the warning over his radio headset and immediately threw open his top turret hatch. Spotting the satchel charge, Lewandowski ignored the inherent danger, climbed out of his hatch, and tossed the explosive aside before it exploded. For his "devotion to duty and heroism under fire [in which he] saved his tank and its crew from destruction," Sergeant Lewandowski received a Silver Star medal.[42]

For the next few days, from October 20 through October 26, the 1st Platoon Shermans cooperated with the infantry against Death Valley. Although most of their activities were limited to "short thrusts into enemy territory for reconnaissance purposes," they occasionally ran into trouble. On October 22, as one of the tanks approached the valley, it hit a land mine and lost a track directly in front of a strong enemy cave position, which prevented the crew from escaping and anybody else from giving assistance. "That night," read a letter of commendation for 2nd Lt. Brooke P. Halsey, "Lieutenant Halsey and another officer led another tank crew and a maintenance crew into the valley and replaced the blown track. This action enabled the tank and its crew which had been forced to remain in the disabled tank throughout the afternoon and evening . . . to withdraw from this exposed area without casualties."[43]

Around October 26, the Five Brothers and Hill 140, inside the northern end of Mortimer Valley, were overrun by the infantrymen of the 321st IReg and the 2nd Platoon Shermans of Company A, 710th TB. Then, after turning south and clearing out the rest of the valley up to where the M10 tank destroyers were firing on Old Baldy and the Five Sisters, the battle-worn Shermans were replaced by the 2nd Platoon tanks of Company C, fresh from Angaur.[44]

Beginning on the morning of October 26, elements of Company C, 710th TB began relieving elements of Company A, 710th TB on Peleliu. Although the 3rd Platoon of Company A remained on Ngesebus Island, the 2nd Platoon, engaged against Old Baldy and the Five Sisters, and the 1st Platoon, fighting around Death Valley, were replaced by the 2nd Platoon and 3rd Platoon of Company C, respectively. Left in reserve were the 1st Platoon Shermans of Company C.[45]

From October 26 through November 1, "heavy rains, fog, and accompanying poor visibility" stymied any attacks against the two valleys and the operations changed "from an assault to a siege." During these six days, the 2nd Platoon Shermans of Company C, 710th TB continually fired upon Old Baldy and the Five Sisters while the 3rd Platoon Shermans of Company C, 710th TB managed to advance about 200 yards into Death Valley.

In a harebrained attempt to clear the valley of land mines, about 175 yards of bangalore torpedo tubes were strung together into one long tube and pushed out into the center of the valley by a Company C tank. At the last minute, however, someone realized the folly in such an attempt and called the whole thing off. Still Colonel Rodgers was somewhat fascinated by the idea. "Even though it was never used," he wrote, "the experience gained was well worth the time spent." However, by November 3, Death Valley had been overrun by the infantry and all eyes turned toward the Umurbrogol pocket.[46]

On November 2, the 323rd IReg had finally captured Old Baldy and the Five Sisters, which had caused the Japanese to fall back and concentrate around a narrow draw bordered by Old Baldy and the Five Sisters on the east, and a ridgeline called the China Wall on the west. Beginning on November 7, the 1st Platoon Shermans of Company C, which had been held in reserve, began assaulting the enemy position.

From November 8 through November 13, the medium tanks continued to fight in the draw, now nicknamed "Hell's Pocket." With the aid of a bulldozer, the tanks pushed into terrain labeled "impassable" and met only light resistance. However, every time supporting infantry attempted to occupy the ground, they were met by heavy Japanese small-arms fire. Each night, in an attempt to "keep the Japs from banzaiing out of the draw," the tanks pulled back to the mouth and settled into U-shaped sandbag revetments.[47]

On November 14, three tanks from the 1st Platoon used a bulldozed road to reach the summit of Old Baldy and provided cover fire for the action inside Hell's Pocket. As the tanks fired, a bulldozer entered the mouth of the draw and carved a road along the base of the Five Sisters. "[U]pon completion of the road," said Colonel Rodgers, "an LVT flamethrower, led by two medium tanks [of the 1st Platoon] assaulted the caves in the Sisters." When the caves were cleaned out, the tanks traveled up the pocket, blasting caves and enemy positions as they went. By the time they were through, "a large number of Japs had been killed."[48]

By November 15, the few Japanese defenders still on Peleliu were bottled up in just a few caves. "During the period 16–21 November patrolling continued in all areas, with tanks and LVT-flamethrowers operating throughout," wrote historian Smith. "Engineer flamethrowers and demolition teams, sometimes accompanied by armored bulldozers, followed the tanks and LVTs closely, destroying or sealing all enemy caves which could be reached." By November 23, the few remaining Japanese were contained in a small pocket on top of the China Wall ridgeline.

While the 323rd IReg, 81st IDiv kept pressure on the pocket, Army engineers began building a ramp to the top of the ridge, so that tanks and flamethrowing LVTs could reach the top. On November 26, the armored vehicles climbed the finished ramp and began firing into caves and other suspected enemy positions. Against little opposition, the Americans advanced rapidly. At 11:00 A.M. on November 27, the last cave was closed and the last position was taken. All of Peleliu Island was finally in American hands.[49]

The capture of the Palaus—Peleliu, Angaur, Ngesebus, and Kongauru islands—cost the 81st IDiv 542 killed, and 2,736 wounded. For the 710th TB, the toll was eleven dead and thirty-nine wounded. Because of the effective cooperative training between the tankers and infantrymen prior to combat, the two units worked exceptionally well together throughout the Palau campaign. Noted two 710th TB historians, "Although the battalion never fought as a unit, the elements assigned to other units on Angaur and Peleliu distinguished themselves in combat."

Fighting under adverse conditions that would have taxed the strength of any man, the tankers proved their mettle. "Fighting the enemy was in itself a major task," wrote the two historians, "but we had other things to fight. Sickness was very prevalent throughout the battalion during the operation. At one time, approximately 90 percent of the battalion contracted diarrhea, not a serious illness, but a very disturbing ailment during combat. It was caused largely by the countless millions of flies breeding on the bodies of the dead."

"All these tropical diseases," the two went on, "aided by the intense heat, the deluge of rain, and the strain of combat all tended to make life on the island very miserable. No shelter of any kind was made for approximately a month or more; stretching a poncho, or a tank-tarp between tanks or trees provided the only protection from the sun and rain. Despite all these hardships, the men fared well."[50]

By the middle of November, the entire 710th TB had settled into a bivouac near the eastern shore.[51] Before long, however, the battalion would be on the move again as the Americans had already started the retaking of the Philippines.

CHAPTER TWENTY-THREE

The Return

G eneral MacArthur's long-awaited return to the Philippines was advanced on the Pacific timetable after Admiral Halsey's airmen reported there was little Japanese air opposition over the Philippines. Originally planning to invade the southernmost island of Mindanao on November 15, MacArthur quickly changed the invasion to Leyte Island on October 20 because of Leyte's central location, which would effectively split the Philippines in two and provide MacArthur with a deepwater anchorage in Leyte Gulf. Afterward, Leyte would be "an excellent springboard from which to launch subsequent operations against the Japanese in Formosa or in the rest of the Philippines."[1]

In describing Leyte, historian Charles R. Anderson wrote:

> One of the larger islands of the Philippine archipelago, Leyte extends 110 miles from north to south and ranges between fifteen and fifty miles in width. . . . The interior of the island was dominated by a heavily forested north–south mountain range, separating two sizable valleys. . . . The larger of the two, Leyte Valley extends from the northern coast to the long eastern shore, and . . . contained most of the towns and roadways on the island. Highway 1 ran along the east coast for some forty miles. . . . The roads and lowlands extending inland from Highway 1 provided avenues for tank–infantry operations, as well as a basis for airfield construction.[2]

The other valley, on the western side of the central mountain range, was Ormoc Valley, which was connected to Leyte Valley by Highway 2, "a roundabout and winding road."[3]

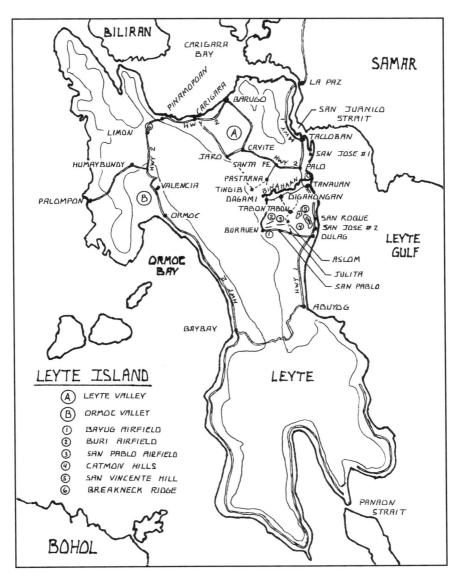

Leyte Island

The conquest of Leyte would happen in three phases. In Phase One, the Americans would seize the small islands east of Leyte to secure Leyte Gulf. In Phase Two, the X and XXIV Corps would land on the eastern coast of Leyte. The X Corps would then "take the city of Tacloban and its airfield . . . secure the strait between Leyte and Samar islands, then push through Leyte Valley to the north coast." At the same time, the XXIV Corps would secure the southern end of Leyte Valley "for air-field and logistical development." Finally, in Phase Three, the II Corps would clear the Japanese out of the mountains to the west of Leyte Valley, capture the coastal city of Ormoc, and take the entire west coast.[4]

To take Leyte, General MacArthur had assembled the greatest fighting force ever created in the Pacific. More than 700 naval vessels, including 157 warships, would carry six different Army divisions and their supporting troops toward Leyte. From MacArthur's own southwest Pacific area would come the 1st Cavalry Division (CDiv) and the 24th IDiv, and from the central Pacific would come the 7th IDiv and the 96th IDiv. In reserve, MacArthur would have the 32nd IDiv from the southwest Pacific, and the 77th IDiv from the central. As historian M. Hamlin Cannon noted, "For the first time ground troops from the central Pacific and southwest Pacific were to join and fight the foe under a common commander." In all, the attacking force, designated the Sixth Army, numbered 202,500 men.[5]

Four infantry divisions would make the initial invasion. X Corps, consisting of the 1st CDiv and the 24th IDiv, both veteran units, would land near Tacloban, near the northeast corner of Leyte. Scheduled to land with the 1st CDiv was the 44th TB, veterans of the New Guinea campaign, while the 603rd Independent Tank Company (TCo), which had seen plenty of action at Biak and along the New Guinea coast, would assist the 24th IDiv.

The 7th IDiv (a veteran unit) and the 96th IDiv (a new unit), were designated XXIV Corps and would touch down fifteen miles south of Tacloban along the center of the east coast. The 767th TB, which had seen action around Kwajalein, would assist the 7th IDiv, while the untested 763rd TB would support the 96th IDiv.[6]

The return to the Philippines began on October 17 when Army rangers seized three small islands off the entrance to Leyte Gulf. Three days later, Navy ships and planes began a four-hour pre-invasion bombardment. Near 9:30 A.M., X Corps began moving against the northern beaches. Preceded by amphibian tanks and flanked by rocket-firing escort ships, the 1st CDiv landed against only slight opposition and quickly captured the town of San Jose No. 2, at the right corner of the beachhead, and a small airfield on a spit of land just north of the beach. Before nightfall, the 1st CDiv had crossed Highway 1 and finally stopped after an advance of about 3,000 yards.[7]

The supporting tanks of the 44th TB (less Company C which was supporting the invasion of Morotai) began coming ashore at 10:30 A.M. The first and second platoon M4 Shermans of Company B landed first and were immediately sent to accompany the advance across Highway 1. The third platoon, along with the light M5A1 Stuart tanks of Company D, landed next and moved off toward the captured airfield. As the tanks pushed north and rumbled over the airstrip, one of the mediums suddenly erupted in flames. "What is believed to be an aerial bomb of considerable size, buried along [the] airstrip completely demolished this vehicle," wrote the 44th TB historian. "The entire crew was seriously wounded."[8]

The two platoons that pushed west soon ran into a vast swamp. Moving north-ward, the tanks eventually found a road running through San Jose No. 2 and then west. "The greatest single factor that hampered employment of tanks in this operation was terrain," commented the battalion historian. "In nearly every instance of tank employment, because of impassable terrain on both sides of the road, the tanks were road bound, and their front limited to the width of the road." By 4:30 P.M., the 3,000-yard objective line had been reached and the tanks and cavalrymen dug in for the night.[9]

Landing just south of the 1st CDiv was the 24th IDiv. Here, the Japanese put up stiff resistance, shelling the invaders with artillery and mortar fire. Although the first five waves made it safely ashore, many of the vessels in the following waves, including the LSTs carrying the tanks of the 603rd TCo, were initially driven off. By 12:15 P.M., however, the Shermans were ashore and helping to lay down cover fire as the 24th IDiv drove across a swampy rice paddy directly behind the beach.[10]

Captain Paul Austin, an infantry commander with the 24th IDiv, remembered the advance:

A [medium] tank came roaring down the beach and he turned into our area and drove the tank right up to . . . our front. Colonel Postelwaite . . . walked up behind the tank, took the telephone [and began] directing fire from the tank. They put a 75mm shell into everything that even looked like it might contain a Jap or a machine gun. He'd fire at two or three targets, then move the tank forward twenty or thirty yards and repeat the process. I knew he destroyed two log pillboxes with shells right into the apertures of them. Colonel Postelwaite moved his front line right up to the edge of a big rice paddy full of water. I saw him talking to the tank and then the gun swung around, to line up on a building across the rice paddy. It put a shell into a small building a few yards away from a house and blew it to pieces. I could see chickens and chicken feathers flying.[11]

Fifteen miles to the south, XXIV Corps began coming ashore near 10 A.M. near the town of San Jose No. 1. The untried 96th IDiv landed on the northern end of the beachhead with instructions to "swing north, neutralize and as soon as possible seize the Catmon hill mass [northwest of San Jose]." Shortly after the first waves of infantry reached shore, the tanks from the virgin 763rd TB came in.

The 763rd TB had been stationed at Oahu until September 15 when it was placed on a ship and started toward Admiral Nimitz' central Pacific. En route, however, the ship was rerouted to the southwest Pacific and the tankers found themselves destined to be a part of the reconquest of the Philippines.[12]

"Tanks were landed in the seventh wave at 1040 [A.M.] 20 October 1944," noted the battalion historian. "Very little enemy resistance was encountered on the beach and the tanks proceeded inland supporting the infantry. The tanks advanced until reaching the swamps a thousand or more yards inland." Similar to the landings of X Corps, the invaders had more trouble with the terrain than with the Japanese.[13]

When Company D, 763rd TB landed on Leyte it came ashore with thirteen regular M5 light tanks and five M3 light tanks that had been converted to flame-throwing tanks. In early 1944, when the M3 was being replaced by the improved M5, the United States began experimenting with the installation of a British Ronson flamethrower in a tank. Replacing the 37mm cannon, the flame gun looked like a stubby cannon and was capable of throwing a stream of flame about 70 yards. The flame gun was supplied from four fuel tanks stored in the hull and pressurized by a cylinder of carbon dioxide stored in the right sponson. Altogether, the 170 gallons of fuel provided two minutes of flame. Because of this extra equipment, the new flamethrowing M3A1 "Satan" had a crew of only two—one driver and one tank commander/gunner. Although the Marines had already used Satan tanks on Saipan and Tinian, the Army Satans would see their first use on Leyte.[14]

South of the 96th IDiv sector, the 767th TB came ashore shortly after the 7th IDiv foot soldiers. The 2nd Platoon tanks from Company A came ashore at 10:15 A.M. opposite the town of Dulag, "and were immediately committed to action." As a 767th TB historian wrote, "Four to five hundred yards inland, the second section was fired upon by a Jap 75mm antitank gun. One hit on No. 18 medium tank penetrated the side and injured three of the crew. No. 17 tank received three hits, one of which froze the 75mm gun; there were no casualties." The heavy Japanese fire caused the advancing tanks and infantry to stop for a while until a few platoons of infantry managed to work their way around both flanks and overrun the positions.[15]

To the left, Company A's 1st Platoon M4 Shermans landed at 10:20 A.M. and proceeded straight toward the town of Dulag. Shortly thereafter, some of the M5

An M4 Sherman on Leyte Island, location unknown, Fall 1944. US ARMY

An M4 Sherman medium tank that was disabled by a hidden land mine near Dulag, Leyte Island, Fall 1944. US ARMY

Stuarts of Company D came up to help and the mediums and lights began "wiping out such opposition as they found." Eventually, the Shermans reached the far western edge of Dulag and were ordered to "advance across Highway 1 and continue across two rice fields." As they started out, an antitank gun hidden inside dense vegetation fired on them. Within minutes, three tanks had been hit, and although none were disabled, one caught fire when the waterproofing material around its 75mm cannon ignited. Acting together, the Company A tanks and the 7th IDiv foot soldiers assaulted the position and were "able to break through the first barriers."[16]

Below and opposite Dulag, the medium tanks of Company B, 767th TB bogged down almost immediately in swampy land behind the beachhead. When one tank tried a different approach, it was hit five times by an enemy antitank gun before the gun was located and destroyed. Even without tank support, the 7th IDiv troops managed to reach Highway 1 before noon and began pushing west along the Dulag–Burauen Highway. By nightfall, the men had pushed about three-quarters of a mile beyond Dulag and had reached the eastern edge of the Dulag airstrip. Although they failed to overrun the strip, they had made good progress and had suffered few casualties.[17]

When October 20 ended, both X and XXIV Corps had carved out beachheads more than one mile deep, although they were ten miles apart. During the day, General MacArthur made his triumphant return to the Philippines. As he came ashore in the 24th IDiv sector he proclaimed, "People of the Philippines, I have returned! By the grace of almighty God, our forces stand again on Philippines soil." In the first twenty-four hours, MacArthur had put ashore nearly 200,000 troops.[18]

That night, the Japanese staged a massive, yet futile, counterattack against the 24th IDiv. When the sun came up on October 21, more than 600 Japanese lay strewn before the American line. Losses among the Americans were minimal.[19]

With the coming of daylight, the 96th IDiv, on the northern end of XXIV Corps, began the conquest attacking northward against the Catmon Hills. By nightfall, part of the division had shifted around the left flank of the hills and was two miles beyond the beachhead while another part, with the light tanks of Company D, 763rd TB, had captured the town of San Roque, about two miles north of Dulag.[20]

South of the 96th IDiv, the 7th IDiv moved forward on October 21 with the objectives of capturing Dulag airfield, Burauen, and Burauen's three nearby airfields. As the 7th IDiv stepped off, the medium tanks of Company C, 767th TB were to the right of the highway, moving through an area inundated with swamps and hedgerows.[21]

Around 9 A.M., the M4 Shermans ran into a series of Japanese 75mm gun emplacements embedded in the hedgerows. Enthusiastically, the battalion historian reported, "the advance was progressing favorably . . . [with] no vehicle or personnel casualties as yet. Several pillboxes had been destroyed." Around 1:40 P.M., while the 1st Platoon tanks of Company C and four M8 self-propelled howitzers were advancing against a few bypassed hedgerow positions, they came

M8 self-propelled howitzers on Leyte Island, Fall 1944. US ARMY

under fire from Japanese 75mm guns. "[One] tank received a hit on the rear track cracking several of the blocks," reported the 767th TB historian. "One M8 received a direct hit and was set on fire. An artillery duel between the tanks, M8s and the Jap field pieces ensued. The Jap guns were destroyed."[22]

Left of the highway, the 184th IReg, with the light M5s of Company D and the medium M4s of Company B, 767th TB, had quickly overrun the Dulag airfield and had moved westward, greatly outdistancing the 32nd IReg. By late afternoon, the column was about two miles beyond Dulag and was told to halt and wait for the slower-moving 32nd IReg to catch up. It wasn't until 6 P.M. that contact was finally reestablished between the two regiments.[23]

At the northern beachhead, the 1st CDiv and the 24th IDiv of X Corps, along with their accompanying independent tank battalions, made good progress on October 21. The 1st CDiv managed to capture Tacloban, the provincial capital of Leyte, while the 24th IDiv retook the town of Palo. The next day, both divisions consolidated their gains and began moving westward, into the eastern foothills of Leyte Valley.[24]

Far to the south, the 96th IDiv of XXIV Corps, spent October 22 fighting around the Catmon Hills. The only real action for any of the Army tank battalions came in the 7th IDiv sector. As the division continued its westward drive along the Dulag–Burauen Highway, four enemy 75mm field pieces opened fire from behind a hedgerow. While American artillery and mortar fire bombarded the position, three tanks from Company C, 767th TB came forward. When the bombardment ceased, the tanks rushed forward and knocked out one Japanese gun and one supporting machine gun. Then, while the tanks provided support, the infantry rushed forward and silenced the other three guns. By nightfall, the 7th IDiv was poised to make a dash down the Dulag–Burauen Highway to seize Burauen and its nearby airfields. Leading the charge would be the 767th TB.[25]

As planned, five Shermans from Headquarters Company would travel straight down the highway. To the left, would be the mediums of Company A, and to the right, the mediums of Company B. The Shermans of Company C would follow in the wake of Headquarters Company, and the light tanks of Company D would tail far behind, escorting advancing supply trucks. All the way to the rear, trying to keep up with the tanks, would be the infantry of 17th IReg, 7th IDiv.[26]

At 8 A.M. on October 23, the flying wedge of tanks jumped off as scheduled. By 9:15, the tanks had overrun three enemy machine guns in the barrio of Julita. When two leading Company A tanks on the left side of the road bogged down in swampy ground, the company commander simply switched his lead platoon and pushed on. At 9:35 A.M., when the column was 3,000 yards west of Julita, one of the lead Headquarters Company tanks hit a concealed mine and lost its right track. Then suddenly, a handful of Japanese soldiers sprang from alongside the road. "Attacking Japs attempted to place a satchel charge on [the] rear deck but [the] Japs were killed and the charge was shot off the deck by machine gun fire from tank in rear," recalled the 767th TB historian. As the crew abandoned the disabled tank, the Flying Wedge pushed on.[27]

An M4 Sherman medium tank that was disabled by a hidden land mine near Dulag, Leyte Island, Fall 1944. US ARMY

Almost an hour and a half after leaving Julita, Company A again ran into swampy ground and was forced to move onto the roadway behind Company C. Near 10:40 A.M., another Headquarters Company tank hit another mine and was disabled. Once again, as the crew bailed out, the Wedge pushed on.

Within ten minutes, the Japanese struck again and another Headquarters Company tank was disabled. "Tank No. 17 hit by a satchel charge on rear deck and caught on fire," reported the historian, "crew abandoned tank through escape hatch." In spite of the loss of three Headquarters tanks, the Flying Wedge reached the village of San Pablo, about two miles east of Burauen, at 11 A.M. and found the village devoid of Japanese. Moving swiftly, Company B moved slightly to the north and captured the San Pablo airfield while the rest of the column fanned out to wait for the Stuart light tanks of Company D to bring up the supply trucks and maintenance vehicles.[28]

By 2 P.M., the Flying Wedge was moving again. Just east of Burauen, Company B again broke away from the main column and seized Bayug airfield against "no enemy resistance." At four o'clock, the main column seized Burauen against only slight sniper fire, but without infantry support the tanks could not hold the town. Around 5 P.M. the tanks began to withdraw. An hour later, the trailing infantrymen finally arrived to occupy San Pablo and the San Pablo airfield as the 767th TB moved back to bivouac just east of Julita.[29]

At 8 A.M. on October 24, the Flying Wedge headed for Burauen again. This time, however, the light tanks of Company D, 767th TB were between the leading mediums of Headquarters Company and the mediums of Company C. At 9:40 Company C broke away from the column and swung north to recapture Bayug airfield. As the main column approached Burauen, the tankers fired at a group of

Japanese seen scurrying back into town. A few minutes later, when the tanks reached the spot where the Japanese had been, the lead tank hit a mine. Damaged but still movable, the tank continued on until the sixth tank in line rolled over another mine near the same spot. Badly damaged and unable to move, the tank blocked the highway until the next Sherman in line towed the disabled vehicle to the side.

Realizing that the fleeing Japanese had been mining the road, the highway tanks simply bypassed the road to the right. As the Wedge drew closer to Burauen, Company B's mediums turned north, circled the town and captured the northern road to Dagami. The rest of the column entered the town, but within minutes, two light tanks exploded hidden mines and blocked the road again. Undeterred, the other light tanks simply went down a side street. As 1st Lt. Frances M. McGuin (Company D, 767th TB) stood behind the two disabled tanks, waving the other light tanks aside, a Japanese sniper shot and killed him.

When the larger M4 Shermans of Company A, 767th TB reached the road-block, they discovered they were too large to use the side streets. Subsequently, Capt. Bruce B. Scott (Company A, 767th TB) climbed out of his tank to try to help untangle the whole mess. Within seconds, however, he became the Japanese sniper's second victim. While the tankers were pulling Captain Scott's body to cover, the 17th IReg arrived to assist in securing the area.[30]

Around 11 A.M., the tanks of Company C, 767th TB reported they had captured both Bayug and Buri airfields but were taking heavy fire from a wooded tree line north of the Buri airfield. As the 2nd Section of the 1st Platoon tried to move around the airstrip, they bogged down in a swamp and had to call for the 1st Section Shermans to tow them out. With enemy shellfire impacting around them, it was discovered that one of the tanks was too badly stuck and had to be abandoned. Unable to hold the airfield without infantry support, Company C withdrew and moved back to Burauen. Later, when the 7th IDiv moved up to the airfield, it too came under the same intense fire and went into a nighttime defensive perimeter.[31]

After Captain Scott's body was recovered from the road junction, the Company A Shermans, the Company D Stuarts, and the 17th IReg foot soldeirs began cleaning out Burauen. Noted historian Cannon, "As the American tanks moved through the barrio, some of the Japanese jumped out of their spider holes and held explosive charges against the tanks in an attempt to destroy them at the cost of their own lives. The assault forces of the 17th [IReg], despite the difficulty of flushing the enemy from the spider holes under the buildings, made steady progress and by 1400 [2 P.M.] had mopped up and secured the town."[32]

With Burauen taken, the tanks and infantry joined Company B north of the town and began the advance toward Dagami, six miles away. Leading the advance were the medium tanks of Company B and the light tanks of Company D but before they had gone even 1,200 yards, a "heavy enemy concentration" was discovered and a number of Japanese soldiers were spotted sowing mines across the road. With swampy ground on either side of the road, a halt was called and the column returned to Burauen.[33]

767th TB M4A1 at Julita, Leyte Island, on Oct. 24, 1944. US ARMY

During the withdrawal, light tank No. 76 bogged down in the swamp to the left and was abandoned by its crew. However, when word reached headquarters that the tank was still operational, light tank No. 73 and a platoon of infantry were sent out to retrieve it. Racing ahead, tank No. 73 reached the disabled tank first, but the crew was unable to hook a tow cable to No. 76 without the suppressive fire of the infantry. Finally, after a half hour of futile attempts, both tank No. 73 and the lost infantry were ordered to return to Burauen. Tank No. 76 was lost for good.[34]

That night, shortly after nightfall, Japanese infiltrators climbed into tank No. 76 and began spraying the 17th IDiv "regimental command post with the tank's 37mm and machine guns, and with four of their own machine guns." Noted historian Cannon, "Fortunately the bullets passed harmlessly over the heads of the troops."[35]

In the 96th IDiv sector, the medium tanks of Company C, 763rd TB, and a platoon of light tanks from Company D, 763rd TB, took a detour on the Dulag–Burauen Highway to avoid the swampy land in their area. After linking back up with the 96th IDiv foot soldiers again, the combined force pushed on toward an important Japanese supply base at Tabontabon until it ran into heavy Japanese fire. Explained historian Cannon, "The tanks and flame throwers flushed the Japanese into the open where they were met by the fire of American riflemen." Although the enemy positions were overrun by 4 P.M., the advance halted an hour later when darkness began to close in.[36]

On October 24, the 1st CDiv made a daring move when it sent a squadron of cavalrymen across the San Juanico Strait to Samar Island. At the same time, a squadron of cavalrymen, accompanied by a platoon of light tanks from Company D, 44th TB, made a spirited sixteen-mile dash up Highway 1 until it terminated at the town of Guintinguian at the northern entrance to San Juanico Strait. With American forces on both sides of the strait, the 1st CDiv was in position to prevent the Japanese from reinforcing Leyte from Samar.[37]

At almost the same time, between October 24 and 25, the Americans and Japanese fought the greatest naval battle in history. In a battle that took place in and around Leyte Gulf, the American Navy succeeded in throwing back an attempt by the Japanese Navy to destroy the American transports and other vessels supporting the Leyte invasion. By the time the battle of Leyte Gulf was over, the Americans had achieved a resounding victory, sinking three Japanese battleships, four aircraft carriers, six heavy cruisers, four light cruisers, ten destroyers, and a number of minor vessels. In contrast, the Americans lost one light aircraft carrier, two escort carriers, four destroyers, and two submarines. Additionally, several American ships had been damaged by Japanese kamikaze planes. By the end of October 25, the Americans were in complete control of the waters around the Philippines.[38]

On the morning of October 25, the 24th IDiv and the 603rd TCo began moving south from San Joaquin. Near noon, the advance reached the Binahaan River just north of Tanauan and a small infantry patrol went into town to reconnoiter. At 2:30 P.M., the patrol met a motorized unit from the 96th IDiv, which also contained light and medium tanks from the 763rd TB. The first link between X Corps and XXIV Corps had been established.[39]

For the 96th IDiv, its arrival at Tanauan began when a platoon of light tanks from Company D, 763rd TB and a section of mediums from Headquarters Company moved north along Highway 1 in support of a motorized engineer platoon. Setting out in the early morning, the motorized column moved along steadily until it found a damaged bridge just below Tanauan. At 2:30 P.M., while engineers were working on the bridge, the patrol from the 24th IDiv suddenly appeared. An hour and a half later, after the bridge was repaired, the column raced through town to the Binahaan River, where solid contact was finally established with the men and tanks from X Corps.[40]

On the far southwestern edge of the 96th IDiv line, Company C, 763rd TB, with the attached platoon of light tanks from Company D, was still supporting the 96th IDiv troops heading northwest toward Tabontabon. On the morning of October 25, the tanks and two battalions of infantry started forward along a secondary roadway. The men and vehicles advanced about one mile until they neared the barrio of Aslom. As historian Cannon wrote, "At Aslom the [tank–infantry group] encountered a strongly fortified position of five gun emplacements and four pillboxes, which the tanks were able to knock out." After going only another 1,500 yards, a halt was called for the night.[41]

For part of the 7th IDiv, October 25 was spent trying to clear the Japanese out of the wood line just north of Buri airfield. Although two platoons of medium tanks from Company C, 767th TB and two platoons of light tanks from Company D, 767th TB tried to assist, four of the medium tanks quickly bogged down in a rice paddy just south of the airstrip and the light tanks found the terrain "impassable." Without tank support, the infantry made only moderate progress and at nightfall the Japanese still held the Buri airfield wood line.[42]

A little to the west, the Sherman tanks of the 2nd Platoon, Company C, 767th TB, carrying a 7th IDiv platoon of supporting infantry on their backs, made a dash north along the Burauen–Dagami Road for about two miles to the barrio of Buri. After destroying a roadblock of "gasoline drums with oil rag fuses," the tanks rammed Buri's grass huts and chased about twenty Japanese soldiers into the open. Noted the 767th TB historian, "The infantry wiped them out." Having gone out on a limb on the dash to Buri, the mobile column finished their dash-and-destroy mission and returned to Burauen just before dark.[43]

In the X Corps zone, the 24th IDiv not only made contact with the 96th IDiv on October 25 but also finally seized Hill C and Hill B and a large portion of the hills that formed the eastern wall of Leyte Valley. To the north, the 1st CDiv reinforced its troops at Guintinguian, thereby strengthening the American presence around the northern end of Leyte Valley.[44]

After capturing Hills B and C, the 24th IDiv moved westward into the center of Leyte Valley. Meeting only slight Japanese resistance, the division, aided by the 603rd TCo tanks, captured the town of Pastrana on October 27 and the small barrios of Cavite and Tingib on October 28. Once at Tingib, the soldiers set up a defensive perimeter and sent out patrols in all directions. On October 30, one of the patrols made contact with the 96th IDiv about four miles south of Pastrana.[45]

In the 1st CDiv sector, different cavalry regiments continued to work westward through the mountainous northern end of Leyte Valley. By October 28, a regiment had moved along the entire northeastern edge of Leyte and was staring into Carigara Bay. During the day, a troop of cavalrymen climbed into landing craft and leapfrogged about ten miles west along the coast to capture Barugo. Although the rest of the cavalrymen tried to advance farther along the coast on Highway 2, strong Japanese opposition stopped them cold.[46]

As October drew to a close, the 24th IDiv, holding the southern end of the X Corps zone, moved southwest and pushed the Japanese out of Jaro. Then, turning northwest up the Leyte Valley Road, the division headed toward Carigara. About the same time, troopers from the 1st CDiv pushed their way into Barugo to relieve the troops who had arrived via landing craft. By October 29, the X Corps was in a position to drive on Carigara with the 1st CDiv from the north and the 24th IDiv from the southwest. The capture of Carigara would put the entire Leyte Valley under American control.[47]

In the XXIV Corps sector, after finally securing the southeastern end of the Catmon Hills, the 96th IDiv began sweeping across the Catmons in a northwesterly direction, toward San Vincente Hill. At the same time, a battalion of infantry and a platoon of light tanks from Company D, 763rd TB began attacking San Vincente Hill from the east. Aided by artillery and mortar fire, and the fact that most of the Japanese had fled to Dagami, the two-pronged attack took control of the entire Catmon Hills by the end of the month.[48]

To the west, a regiment from the 96th IDiv continued its drive toward the Japanese supply base at Tabontabon. "[D]ue to weak bridges and [the] poor condition of [the] road" the infantry had to leave the M4 Sherman tanks of Company C, 763rd TB behind. Although the light tanks from Company D were able to continue on, the weak bridges slowed them down so much they did not reach Tabontabon until October 28, the same date the infantry captured the city.[49]

During that same period, another regiment from the 96th and the medium tanks of Company A, 763rd TB moved up Highway 1 and reached Tanauan on October 27 after meeting only light enemy resistance.[50] Two miles farther, the tanks and infantry "came under fire from 75mm guns, mortars, and machine guns." Noted historian Cannon, "Two hours were required for Company A, 763rd Tank Battalion, and two flamethrowing tanks [from Company D, 763rd TB] to reduce this resistance. Seven pillboxes and three 75mm guns were destroyed and a command post captured."[51]

On October 30, the 96th IDiv and the supporting 763rd TB fought their way into Digahongan and were poised for a strike at the important crossroads town of Dagami, about one and a half miles to the west. To the south, the 7th IDiv, assisted by the medium tanks from Company B, 767th TB, finally captured the Buri airstrip and the northern wood line on October 27.[52]

The day before, October 26, the 17th IReg, 7th IDiv and twelve tanks from Company A, 767th TB moved north out of Burauen toward Dagami. Progress was slow because of "swamps on either side" of the roadway and sporadic enemy fire. At 11 A.M., after advancing only one-half mile, the infantry was held up by Japanese fire from a grass shack until one of the Shermans rammed the structure. Farther along, at the town of Buri, the infantry again was stopped by heavy fire. This time, Company A tanks, plus three tanks from Headquarters Company, rescued the foot soldiers, who were "evacuated by tanks under fire." Having advanced three miles, the column halted for the night.[53]

Early the next morning, the advance resumed. Although there was little enemy opposition, the need to repair wrecked bridges over two deep streams hindered the progress of the column. By nightfall, they were still 2,200 yards short of Dagami. Just before darkness, the Shermans of Company A were replaced by the Shermans of Company C. Little did Company C, 767th TB realize what it would face over the next twenty-four hours.[54]

At 7:30 A.M. on October 28, the 17th IReg and the Company C Shermans set out to eliminate an estimated 1,500 to 2,500 Japanese defenders around Dagami. Almost immediately the advance ran into a "heavy concentration of Jap fire" near a damaged stone bridge and a large swamp. At 9:00 A.M., tank No. 51 hit a land mine, which blew off a track. Under heavy fire, tank No. 54, moved up and under the protective fire from the other Shermans, managed to evacuate the stranded crew.

Dismounting from his command tank, Capt. George J. Duckworth, the commander of Company C, looked over the stone bridge to see if there was any way to get his vehicles over the damaged span. Almost immediately he was shot through both legs and had to be evacuated to the rear. A short while later, 2nd Lt. John E. Unger (Company C, 767th TB) was severely wounded when a tank accidentally crushed one of his legs.[55]

Somehow, three of the Company C tanks and a company of infantry managed to get over a small creek and get north of the bridge. Near 10:15 A.M., as the tanks were traveling along a narrow road bordered by swampland, 1st Lt. James W. Lawrence's lead tank No. 45, hit a mine and lost a track, effectively blocking the forward movement of the other two tanks.

Stranded like sitting ducks, the tanks came under vicious attack by the surrounding Japanese. Almost immediately a satchel charge landed on the rear deck of tank No. 44, completely destroying the "engine and rear armor." Although the crew was unharmed, they could not evacuate the vehicle because of the heavy fire. Less than fifteen minutes later, a Molotov cocktail landed on Lieutenant Lawrence's tank No. 45. The ensuing fire killed three crewmen, including Lieutenant Lawrence, and left the other two severely burned. Luckily, the two wounded crewmen managed to get out of the tank and find refuge in the belly of the third tank, tank No. 48. Unable to proceed any farther, tank No. 48 turned around and raced back to the stone bridge.[56]

Near noon, as the firefight around the damaged bridge intensified, word reached the other Shermans of Company C that the crewmen inside tank No. 44 were still alive. Near 2 P.M., the command post received another message: "C-44 reports large number of Japs around their disabled tank. Appeal for help." While the Army engineers worked hard to repair the bridge, losing three successive bulldozer operators in the process, the tanks laid down close suppressive fire around tank No. 44.

At four o'clock, Company C reported to headquarters that a "large number of Japs killed, but still unable to reach C-44." Two hours later the company reported, "C-44 appeals for help." Near nightfall, the bridge was finally repaired and a few Company C Shermans raced across. Heavy fire was still impacting around the disabled tank as the other tanks drew near but because they approached from the enemy side, they found Lieutenant Lawrence's burning tank No. 45 standing between them and tank No. 44. Appealing for help, two M8 tank destroyers came up and somehow got around the burning tank. Moving alongside tank No. 44, the tank destroyers took the beleaguered crew "into their open turrets." Having finally affected the rescue, the Company C Shermans pumped a few 75mm rounds into tanks No. 44 and 45 and then the whole American force fell back and dug in for the night.[57]

The next day, October 29, the 17th IReg, this time accompanied by the tanks of Company A, 767th TB and a few tanks from Headquarters Company, 767th TB, routed a group of Japanese soldiers who had hidden themselves inside the desecrated graves of an old cemetery and fought their way up to the southern edge of Dagami. At nightfall, the tankers and infantry dug in only 500 yards south of Dagami and at daybreak battled their way into the town. By 10:40 A.M., the important crossroads town of Dagami was finally in American hands.[58]

Far to the south, infantry patrols from the 7th IDiv, escorted by light tanks from Company D, 767th TB, moved out from Burauen and spent the last days of October expanding their hold on Leyte. By October 31, the tanks and infantry had reached La Paz, about seven miles south of Burauen, without meeting any enemy resistance, thus securing the southern flank of XXIV Corps.[59]

Almost fifteen miles northwest of Dagami, in the X Corps zone, the 24th IDiv and the 1st CDiv began their push against Carigara on October 30. As the 24th IDiv and a few 603rd TCo Shermans moved out of Jaro along the Jaro–Carigara Road they ran into stiff Japanese resistance and gained only 700 yards all day.[60]

That night, American artillery carpeted the area and on the morning of October 31, while one infantry battalion attacked the Japanese position, another battalion, along with the 603rd TCo tanks, raced north along the highway toward Carigara. At a river crossing only two miles north of Jaro, the flying column came under heavy mortar and machine-gun fire and the tanks replied. When the Japanese stepped up their fire, the American artillery zeroed in and silenced the opposition.

Pushing on, the column moved only about one mile before running into more trouble at another river crossing. "With all of the troops in a skirmish line," wrote historian Cannon, "the 2nd Battalion, with tanks, moved down the road to attack. When [the infantry] came under fire the tanks went to [their] assistance, and the Japanese then concentrated their fire on the armor." Under such intense fire, the American advance stalled until a couple of self-propelled 105mm howitzers rumbled up and began blasting the enemy positions from close range. Soon, however, one of the howitzers was disabled by a Japanese artillery round and when a 603rd TCo Sherman tried to tow it to safety, it was discovered the howitzer had two broken treads and could not be moved. To "prevent its use to the enemy," the howitzer was destroyed by tank fire.[61]

That night, unbeknownst to the Americans, the Japanese retreated from the area. The next day, November 1, the flying column moved rapidly north and by dusk was only two miles from Carigara. At the same time, the 1st CDiv, which had been sitting at the coastal town of Barugo (only three miles northeast of Carigara) since October 28, had been moving slowly along the coast. By November 1, the 1st CDiv was only one mile west of Carigara.

Under cover of darkness, the Japanese defenders quietly pulled out of Carigara. Near 9 A.M. on November 2, following a heavy rain of artillery, the 24th IDiv moved to the outskirts of town from the south and then waited to hear from the 1st CDiv on their right. Around 10:30, when no word was forthcoming, the 24th IDiv soldiers entered the deserted town.[62]

With the capture of Carigara and Dagami, Leyte Valley and all of northeast Leyte were in American hands. Two of MacArthur's three phases had been reached: the capture of the islands around Leyte Gulf and the capture of Leyte Valley. The only phase that still remained was the capture of Ormoc and the drive to the west coast.

CHAPTER TWENTY-FOUR

The Drive to Ormoc

After the battle of Leyte Gulf, the Japanese believed the American fleet had been crippled and the American troops on Leyte were trapped. Hoping to eliminate the Sixth Army, the Japanese commander in the Philippines began to reinforce Leyte. Between October 23 and November 2, approximately 13,500 soldiers landed on the west coast of Leyte through the port of Ormoc. For the Americans, the capture of Ormoc was a crucial step in the liberation of the Philippines.[1]

The Americans began their conquest of the rest of Leyte on October 29 when the 7th IDiv moved south along Highway 1 and then turned west over the mountainous spine. By November 2, the 7th IDiv was at Baybay on the west coast, poised to drive north toward the port of Ormoc.[2]

On November 4, the 24th IDiv in the north captured Pinamopoan on Highway 2. From Pinamopoan, Highway 2 ran along the coast of Carigara Bay, turned inland, and then went almost thirty miles straight south through dense mountains to Ormoc. With the capture of Pinamopoan, the 24th IDiv was ready to drive over the mountains to Ormoc.[3]

Because of the mountainous terrain south and west of Pinamopoan, very few tanks were used after November 4 in the X Corps Area. After that date, Headquarters Company, and Companies B and D, 44th TB, and the entire 603rd TCo saw no further action on Leyte.[4]

While X Corps was taking care of northern Leyte, XXIV Corps concentrated on southern Leyte. As the 7th IDiv concentrated at Baybay for the drive north to Ormoc, the 96th IDiv set out to capture the central mountains of Leyte. Unfortunately, the weak bridges in the area prevented the 763rd TB from lending full support. Instead, only the light Stuart tanks of Company D were able to accompany the infantrymen.[5]

Near nightfall on November 5, the light tanks finally moved forward to assist the foot soldiers against "a strong enemy force that was entrenched in foxholes and pillboxes." As historian M. Hamlin Cannon noted, "Each of these defensive positions had to be reduced before the advance could continue." In two day's fighting, the tank–infantry assault had accounted for an estimated 115 enemy dead.[6]

On November 7, the assault continued. Wrote historian Cannon, "A large enemy force assaulted the troops at close quarters and tried to destroy the tanks, but when the 382nd [IReg] introduced flamethrowers and supporting machine guns, the attackers fell back in disorder." Noted the 763rd TB historian, "Tanks and Inf. killed 158 Japs, captured two heavy MG and four light MG."[7]

On the night of November 8–9, a typhoon hit Leyte. A flood swept through the 763rd TB bivouac area just east of Dagami. For the next three days most of the tankers tried to "salvage and repair" equipment damaged by the flood. In the middle of November, when the 96th IDiv moved into terrain that was completely impassable to tanks, the entire 763rd TB remained idle in a new bivouac area set up a half mile west of Dagami.[8]

Around the first week in November, General Krueger received word that the Japanese had received heavy reinforcements and was going to make an attempt to break out of the northern end of Ormoc Valley. Acting quickly, Krueger moved the 1st CDiv and the 24th IDiv to the northern part of the valley and brought the 96th IDiv up from the XXIV Corps area to cover the mountainous eastern side. Only the 7th IDiv was left to cover the entire southern half of Leyte.[9]

At the northern end of Ormoc Valley, the 24th IDiv pushed south out of Pinamopoan on November 4. Less than a mile from Pinamopoan, the infantry ran into numerous reinforced Japanese positions, including a ridgeline nicknamed "Breakneck Ridge." Very little tank action occurred until November 7, when two 1st Platoon Shermans of Company A, 44th TB arrived to "reduce hostile automatic weapons [fire] and assist [in the] withdrawal of [a] cut-off infantry platoon" on a spur of Breakneck Ridge. In accomplishing both objectives, the tankers killed "approximately twenty-five enemy" but had one tank severely damaged. As the 44th TB historian explained, "One Jap concealed in [a] foxhole immediately alongside [the] road in tall grass threw two satchel charges at one tank. First failed to detonate, but second exploded on tank's rear deck, ripping up top engine compartment doors, damaging engine severely, but not stopping it. Crew uninjured, so vehicle evacuated under own power."[10]

Over the next two days typhoon rains kept the tanks out of the fight while the infantry continued to attack. Finally, on November 11, the five 2nd Platoon Shermans of Company A, 44th TB advanced over the crest of Breakneck Ridge and rumbled down its reverse slope. Almost immediately, they took "intense automatic weapons fire from enemy machine guns strongly emplaced in [a] ravine to [the] right."

Because of the depth of the ravine, the tankers could not depress their cannons or machine guns low enough to hit the Japanese. Instead, the tanks fired over the heads of the Japanese and pinned them down while the tank commanders lobbed hand grenades and sprayed sub-machine gun fire into the ravine. In all, the 2nd Platoon "killed seventy-five enemy . . . and destroyed or silenced fifteen out of twenty-five automatic weapons." Unfortunately, during the nighttime withdrawal, one Sherman tank became stuck and had to be destroyed, and Capt. Julian Van-Winkle, commanding officer of Company A, was wounded in the hand and side while trying to save the tank.[11]

On the night of November 11–12, American artillery rained down upon Breakneck Ridge and a hill mass known as Little Casino. In the morning, the Sherman tanks from the 1st Platoon of Company A moved forward with the 24th IDiv. The attack began at 7:30 and by noon both positions had been overrun. After capturing the two Japanese strong points, the tanks and infantry continued moving south down Highway 2.[12]

On November 14, as a 3rd Platoon tank led the advance around a bend in the road, a Japanese soldier tossed a satchel charge under it. The explosion blew off one track and jammed the belly escape hatch. With heavy machine-gun fire raining down from the surrounding mountains, the other tanks moved forward to form a screen around the disabled tank so the crew could scramble out of the upper hatches and into another tank. Although the tankers planned to retrieve the damaged tank at a later date, the Japanese infiltrated into the area at night and "completely destroyed it with [a] heavy explosive charge."[13]

On November 15, troops from the 32nd IDiv, which had been brought over from Morotai and Hollandia, began relieving the battle-weary 24th IDiv in the mountains north of Ormoc. On that same date, Company A, 44th TB was transferred to the 32nd IDiv. At noon on November 16, the fresh troops moved upon the town of Limon, located about 1,500 yards south of Breakneck Ridge. Fanning out on either side of Highway 2, the infantry moved through rugged terrain while the M4 Sherman tanks of Company A moved straight down Highway 2. Once again, the rugged, mountainous terrain and stubborn Japanese resistance hampered all forward movement. By November 19, the advance had moved only a few hundred yards.[14]

In a daring move to isolate Limon, elements of the 24th IDiv, which had yet to be relieved, swept around both flanks of the town and captured Kilay Ridge, just below Limon. Then, with the 24th IDiv troops in place, the 32nd IDiv and the Sherman tanks of Company A, 44th TB moved in from the north. Over the next few days, while the 32nd IDiv foot soldiers battled the Japanese for possession of Limon, the Company A Shermans were held in reserve to "repel any Jap tank attack." Finally, on November 24, American artillery destroyed a bridge over the Leyte River just south of town and put an end to any further threat from enemy tanks.[15]

While the 24th and 32nd IDivs were fighting around Limon, the 1st CDiv, without the aid of tanks, moved out of the Carigara area and fought its way through the northeast mountains of Ormoc Valley. Eventually, the cavalrymen linked up with the left flank of the 32nd IDiv near Limon and formed a solid chain around the northern end of Ormoc Valley. At the same time, the 96th IDiv continued its push over the mountainous eastern side of the valley.[16]

"When the [96th IDiv] advanced into the foothills the terrain prevented any further use of medium tanks as support," noted the 763rd TB historian. "It was then decided to use the medium tanks to reinforce division artillery." Beginning

44th TB "Southern Cross," a composite hull M4, near Limon, Leyte, November 28, 1944. US ARMY

on November 20, eight tanks each from Companies A, B and C, 763rd TB were organized into two twelve-tank artillery units stationed around Dagami to aid the 96th IDiv artillery firing into the hills west of the town. With the northern end and eastern side of Ormoc Valley in check, it was up to the 7th IDiv at Baybay in the south to begin the final drive toward Ormoc.[17]

After General Krueger shifted the 96th IDiv to cover the eastern side of Ormoc Valley, the 7th IDiv had been holding the southern end of Leyte all by itself. In mid-November, the 11th Airborne Division (AbnDiv) landed on Leyte and quickly was moved into southern Leyte. On November 22, the 7th IDiv and the light Stuart tanks of Company D, 767th TB, "the only armor on the west coast," began concentrating all their strength at Baybay.[18]

Before the Americans could fully concentrate, however, the Japanese attacked. Beginning on the night of November 22–23, the Japanese repeatedly struck the forward elements of the 7th IDiv along a series of ridgelines just above Baybay. Since the mountainous terrain of the ridges prevented the use of the Company D Stuarts, the battle for the Ridges turned into an infantry slugfest before the Americans came away victorious.[19]

On December 5, the 7th IDiv finally started a major drive north along the western coast toward Ormoc. Making great strides, and assisted by amphibious tanks that fired into Japanese positions along the shoreline, the division moved to within ten miles of Ormoc by December 10. Although the M5 Stuarts of Company D accompanied the foot soldiers every inch of the way, they saw little action.[20]

A few days earlier, however, some of the 767th TB's medium tanks saw plenty of action around their bivouac areas near the town of Burauen. On the evening of

763rd TB "Bushmaster," composite hull M4, is stuck in the mud on Leyte, November 23, 1944. US ARMY

December 6–7, 350 Japanese paratroopers unexpectedly landed on the Buri and San Pablo airstrips and quickly scattered the American Air Corps personnel in all directions. With one platoon of Sherman tanks from Companies A and B stationed just north of Burauen, the 767th TB was ordered to try to recover a stock of American weapons that had been left behind at the Buri airstrip. "Apparently [the attempt] was unsuccessful," noted historian Cannon, "because later in the day the Japanese made 'the best use' of the same arms and ammunition."[21]

For the next four days, hastily-organized service and rear-echelon troops, along with the medium tanks of Companies A, B, and C, 767th TB, kept the Japanese paratroopers in check until front-line soldiers could arrive. Eventually, elements of the 11th AbnDiv and the 38th IDiv, which had just recently arrived on Leyte, wiped out all enemy resistance. Commented historian Anderson, "Although the Japanese destroyed a few American supply dumps and aircraft on the ground and delayed construction projects, their attacks on the airfields failed to have any effect on the overall Leyte campaign."[22]

While the Japanese paratroopers were being eliminated, the Americans tried another gutsy move. On December 7, after a heavy naval bombardment, the 77th IDiv, which had recently arrived from Guam, made an amphibious landing only three and a half miles south of Ormoc and seven miles north of the 7th IDiv. Caught completely by surprise, the Japanese offered almost no resistance as the 77th IDiv surged forward to seize the shattered remains of Ormoc by nightfall on December 10.[23]

South of Ormoc, the 7th IDiv and the light tanks of Company D, 767th TB continued to push northward up Highway 2, fighting their way over a series of ridges and rivers. On the night of December 9–10, the Japanese defenders caught between the advancing 7th IDiv and the 77th IDiv at Ormoc withdrew into the mountains. On the morning of December 11, advance elements of the 7th IDiv met elements of the 77th IDiv near the 77th beachhead. Wrote historian Cannon, "The XXIV Corps was now in undisputed control of the eastern shore of Ormoc Bay and the town of Ormoc."[24]

North of Ormoc, the X Corps troops of the 32nd IDiv and the 1st CDiv were still fighting in the Limon area. Although Limon had been captured on November 21, the Americans soon discovered the Japanese were far from defeated. Entries in the combat diary of Company A, 44th TB attest to the tenacity of the Japanese defenders:

> *1 December.* One section of tanks from 3rd platoon moved north of Limon, fired 93 rounds [high explosive] into pocket of Japs that had infiltrated east of Limon . . . reported 112 Japs killed by tanks . . .
>
> *2 December.* One section of tanks, 2nd platoon . . . [fired] into Jap pocket northeast of Limon. Two hundred Japs reported killed . . .
>
> *3 December.* One section of tanks moved north Limon and fired 100 rounds of area fire at two Jap pockets east of Limon . . .
>
> *4 December.* Fifty-three rounds fired into same pocket as the day before . . .
>
> *5 December.* Section of tanks fired 40 rounds into same pocket as day before . . .

On December 5, the 32nd IDiv renewed its drive south toward Ormoc. Due to the rough, mountainous terrain, a heavy rain forest canopy, and constant rains progress was extremely slow. On December 11, a section of Sherman tanks from the 2nd Platoon, Company A, 44th TB demolished a roadblock south of Limon. Although heavy Japanese machine-gun fire severely wounded a crewman in one of the tanks, the Shermans blasted through the roadblock and continue moving south. Only when they came to a washed-out section of roadway did the two tanks turn and head back to Limon.[25]

From December 12 until December 19, the M4 Shermans of Company A, 44th TB continued to assist the 32nd IDiv in its drive south. On December 18, the tanks were credited with destroying one Japanese tank and two field pieces, and helped cover the evacuation of an antitank platoon that had been pinned down by enemy fire. On December 19, Company A was notified it was "officially relieved" from duty and was to be replaced by Company A, 763rd TB. However, unfavorable road conditions caused by the rain kept the 763rd TB Shermans bogged down at Carigara. In the meantime, the 44th TB men fought on.[26]

"Continued slow advance under heavy enemy small arms fire," noted the 44th TB historian for December 19. "Fired 1000 rounds .30-caliber and 10 rounds 75mm . . ." The next day, as Company A, 44th TB continued to assist in the drive south, the Japanese threw two Molotov cocktails and a few hand grenades at the lead tank. With the tank engulfed in flames, the crew bailed out under a hail of cover fire laid down by the other tanks and some supporting infantry. Three hours later, after the fire had burned itself out, the tank crew climbed back into the charred vehicle, discovered everything was still operational, and withdrew "under [their] own power."[27]

The last action for hard-fighting Company A from the 44th TB came on December 21 when one tank "fired forty-five rounds" and blew up a dug-in Japanese 150mm howitzer. At 12:30 P.M., the medium tanks of Company A, 763rd TB finally arrived at the front and the 44th TB Shermans began the long road back to their tank battalion bivouac area in central Leyte Valley.[28]

The Company A tanks of the 763rd TB were delayed in relieving the 44th TB Shermans because of the poor, rain-soaked roads. Just east of Pinamopoan, the tankers decided to avoid the road altogether and moved out into the waters of Carigara Bay so they could travel along a coral reef. However, the tanks were too heavy for the reef and four broke through and sank. At the same time, two additional tanks bogged down in the mud approaching the beach. With six tanks lost or stranded, the company decided to wait until a causeway could be built around the impassable road.[29]

Five days later, the causeway was completed and the tanks moved into Pinamopoan. On December 21, eight Shermans from Company A, 763rd TB rumbled south down Highway 2 past Limon and at 12:30 P.M. relieved the tanks of Company A, 44th TB. Picking up where the 44th TB had left off, the 763rd TB mediums and the 32nd IDiv fought their way south until they were only eleven miles north of Ormoc. Noted the 763rd TB historian, "Fourteen Jap tanks [were] destroyed in this advance."

That same day, elements of the 1st CDiv, which were advancing on the left flank of the 32nd IDiv, made contact with troops from the 77th IDiv, which had been moving north out of Ormoc. Ironically, with that juncture, the Company A tanks of the 763rd TB, which had taken so long to get to the front, were no longer needed. Noted the battalion historian, "Company A reported mission accomplished."[30]

By December 22, the 77th IDiv had squeezed the remaining Japanese into the mountainous northwest corner of Leyte. Operating with the infantry were the only two active tank companies on the island—Companies A and D of the 706th TB, which had been brought over from Guam with the 77th IDiv.

On December 20, the eighteen Stuart tanks started out overland to meet the infantry at Valencia, seven miles north of Ormoc, while the ten Sherman tanks were loaded aboard two LSMs for shipment to the west coast.

Near 6:45 P.M., as the LSMs were making their way toward Ormoc Bay, a Japanese airplane attacked them. As the 706th TB historian recalled, "Enemy plane flew over through a wall of antiaircraft fire. A round of ammunition fell on one of our tanks, deflected to the deck and splattered." Three tankers were injured. On December 22, the ships completed the circular movement around the southern end of Leyte and landed the ten Shermans at the 77th IDiv beachhead.[31]

In the meantime, the light tanks of Company D, 706th TB had been moving overland toward Valencia. In spite of problems with watery gas and narrow roads, thirteen of the sixteen tanks reached Valencia by 10:00 P.M. on December 20. The next day, nine tanks went forward to engage the enemy but were stopped by a blown bridge. With the help of the 77th IDiv engineers, the tanks were winched across the steep banks of the creek but traveled only a short distance before one of the Stuarts slid off the road and bogged down in a swamp. As the crew evacuated and headed for safety, the other tanks rolled on.[32]

A few miles north of Valencia, the remaining eight tanks turned west and eventually crossed the Togbong River. At 4:00 P.M., the eight light tanks joined the infantry in an assault against entrenched enemy positions. As the attack got under-way, the Japanese opened fire with heavy mortars, hitting three of the light tanks. In one tank, the tank commander had been operating with an open turret hatch and was mortally wounded when a mortar round impacted the turret and sent metal shards through his steel helmet. Although three tanks were out of action, the attack continued until all of the enemy positions were overrun. "Estimated enemy casualties," noted the 706th TB historian, "were one hundred."

On the morning of December 22, a platoon of light tanks and the 77th IDiv foot soldiers moved rapidly toward the barrio of Humaybundy. After advancing only about one and one-half miles, however, the armor was halted by a blown bridge. As the infantry pressed on, the tankers waited all day for the engineers to repair the span.[33]

Early the next morning, after the bridge had been repaired, the five tank crews were informed by the infantry that had gone on ahead "that thirteen bridges were out between [the] tanks and [the] infantry." Throughout the day, progress was very slow. "Fords were impassable because of steep banks and deep narrow streams," recalled the 706th TB historian. In spite of the problems, the tanks reached Humay-bundy and then turned southwest toward Palompon, the last Japanese-held port on Leyte. By nightfall, the tanks had managed to proceed "one and eight-tenths miles and [cross over] four bridges" on the way to Palompon.[34]

In the meantime, five more Company D tanks were selected to make an amphibious move against Palompon with the 77th IDiv. On Christmas Day, the landing craft left Ormoc and executed a perfect, unopposed landing just above the town. Turning quickly southward, the infantry and tanks poured into Palompon and had the town secure by 11:00 A.M. With the seizure of the last Japanese port, General MacArthur announced the end of organized resistance on Leyte, although many Japanese units would continue to fight until New Years Eve.[35]

On New Year's Eve 1944, American troops moving up from Palompon met the American troops moving southwest from Humaybundy. Among the forces that linked up were the two sections of tanks from Company D, 706th TB. Although a few 706th TB mediums would see a bit of action on the Humaybundy-Palompon Road during the first few days of January 1945, most of the tank action on Leyte was over. Although scattered pockets of Japanese soldiers would hold out on Leyte until May 1945, for the many different tank battalions on Leyte, the fight-ing was finally over.[36]

The Leyte campaign cost the Americans 3,504 killed and 12,080 wounded. The Japanese lost an estimated 49,000 men, almost all of them killed. For Japan, the loss of Leyte spelled doom. The Americans now had possession of Leyte's air-fields and a deep-water harbor in the central Philippines from which to carry out attacks throughout the Philippines or intercept Japanese shipping in the Dutch East Indies.[37]

For the five different tank battalions that had seen action on Leyte, the battle had been long and tough. However, while Japanese resistance had been fierce, the tankers had experienced more trouble with the terrain and roadways. "Prior reconnaissance must be made of terrain to definitely determine the practicability of tanks moving over that ground to support the ground action," noted the 763rd TB historian, "and to determine whether routes are available to transport the amounts of fuel and ammunition consumed by an armored unit during combat." Added the 44th TB historian, "Bridges were not strong enough to hold tanks in most instances. . . . Tanks at times were sent out when there was no chance to employ them due to terrain."[38]

On Leyte, the cooperation between the tanks and infantry had been good, but it could have been better. "Very little is known about the use of armor by supported infantry units," wrote the 44th TB historian. "Medium tanks [instead of the light tanks] were used for reconnaissance on occasions. . . . Tanks were sometimes used in a defensive role. This should only be done as a last resort. Tanks are a weapon of opportunity and should not be used until the opportune time. . . . Absolute necessity of assigning infantrymen for close-in defense of each tank when operating in close terrain is not appreciated by some infantry commanders."[39]

The historian for the 763rd TB was just as critical. "While it is recognized that tanks support infantry it must also be recognized that when tanks are spear-heading the assault the infantry must support the tanks. This calls for rigid orders to the infantry that they will support tanks closely and stick to them faithfully. Tanks are prone to draw more enemy fire than the individual soldier and infantry must be trained to remain close to the tank to lend adequate support, but to deploy in such a manner so as to avoid the enemy fire drawn by the tank."[40]

There were still a number of problems to be worked out between the infantry and the tanks, and within each individual tank battalion, but for the most part the overall use of tanks on Leyte had been successful. In spite of bad road conditions and unfriendly terrain, the tanks had performed well whenever and wherever they could get to the front line. And, as a few of the Leyte tank battalions were about to find out, they would get ample opportunity to be at the front line again.

CHAPTER TWENTY-FIVE

Luzon

Even before the Americans had captured all of Leyte, General MacArthur's forces were invading other Philippine Islands. On December 15, 1944, U.S. troops rushed ashore on Mindoro, just south of Luzon, hoping that Mindoro's airfields would be better than the poor, muddy runways of Leyte. Although Japanese kamikaze planes attacked the Navy ships off Mindoro, by December 20, Army engineers had the first captured airfield operational.[1]

The invasion of Luzon took place on January 9, 1945, when American forces stormed ashore at the southern end of Lingayen Gulf. The Sixth Army landed its I Corps troops (6th and 43rd IDivs), on the left, near the town of San Fabian, and its XIV Corps troops (37th and 40th IDivs) on the right, near the barrio of Lingayen. Neither landing was hotly contested and by nightfall the Americans held a beachhead twenty miles long by four miles deep.

The Luzon landings were generally unopposed because Gen. Tomoyuki Yamashita, the Japanese commander, had decided to fight the Americans in the interior. Dividing his men into three groups, Yamashita himself controlled the Shobu group (152,000 men) in northern Luzon. The second group, Shimbu group, (80,000 men) occupied the mountainous region immediately east of Manila, controlling the city's vital watershed area, and the southern half of Luzon, including the Bicol peninsula on Luzon's southeast corner. And finally, Kembu group (30,000 men) was stationed around the Clark Field/Fort Stotsenburg area, Bataan peninsula, and Corregidor Island.[2]

Landing in the I Corps zone on the northern half of the American beachhead was the 716th TB, which came ashore with a distinctive wolf's head battalion insignia painted on the sides of their turrets or hulls. While the medium M4 Shermans of Company A came ashore below San Fabian with the 6th IDiv, the rest of the battalion came ashore to the north with the 43rd IDiv.[3]

Landing with the Shermans of Company A and the 6th IDiv were the medium tanks of Company C, 44th TB. While the rest of the 44th TB was still on Leyte, Company C was sent to Leyte to help augment the 716th TB.[4]

To the south, in the XIV Corps sector, the tanks of the 754th TB were assigned to both the 37th and 40th IDivs. The 754th TB had spent the summer and fall of 1944 on Bougainville before taking a roundabout trip to Luzon. On January 1, 1945, the battalion celebrated the New Year on board a transport ship. Wrote Cpl. Thomas Howard (Company A, 754th TB), "Still alive and it's '45. I hope it's home alive in '45."

As the ships steamed toward the Philippines, the men were kept busy with their tanks and equipment. "The salt air caused havoc with our equipment and it had to be kept constantly clean." Additionally, the men readied their tanks for the upcoming invasion. "We had to waterproof our tanks just in case we have to land them short of the beach," Howard wrote. "A stack was attached to the exhaust section on the rear of the tank so if we go below water, it won't suffocate the engines and stall out our tank."[5]

On January 9, the 37th and 40th IDiv landed on Luzon near the town of Lingayen. In the 37th IDiv sector, the 1st and 2nd Platoons of Company A, 754th TB came ashore at 9:59 A.M. Battered by a rough surf, one of the Shermans drowned out and had to be towed ashore. In the 40th IDiv sector, all of Company B, 754th TB landed around noon without mishap. Almost immediately the tankers from both companies began removing waterproofing kits and cleaning the waterproofing grease from the engines.[6]

The next day, January 10, the infantry expanded its toehold on Luzon against light enemy resistance. During the advance, the 1st Platoon tanks of Company B, 754th TB were called upon for direct fire support in the area of Port Saul on Lingayen Gulf, about seven miles west of Lingayen. "The tanks fired at close range into enemy pillboxes and trenches," noted the battalion historian.[7]

As the infantry spread out over the next few days, the tanks of the 716th and 754th TBs, and Company C, 44th TB had to wait for engineers to rebuild bridges that had been demolished by the Japanese. While waiting, the tankers were overwhelmed by the civilian personnel. "[The Filipinos] beg you blind and pester you for work to do," Corporal Howard confided to his diary. "The women want to wash your clothes and the men want to clean the tanks and guns, carry gas, oil or water. Of course, they want to be paid." Unfortunately, the constant attention had a down side. "One thing about all this is that you have no privacy," Howard continued. "You can't wash or shower without them standing there watching you. Strip naked, take a crap, or urinate, and they follow you and watch. I can't figure it out if it's curiosity or being thankful for our coming and they want to do everything they can to help you."[8]

On January 11, the rest of the 44th TB arrived in Lingayan Gulf fresh from the fighting on Leyte. However, rough seas delayed their departure from the transports and the men spent a few more days aboard the bobbing and weaving vessels before coming ashore near San Fabian.[9]

Company D/44th TB M5A1 lands at Lingayen Gulf, Luzon on January 11, 1945.
US ARMY

Another tank unit that arrived on January 11 was the 775th TB, from New Guinea. Having been on their LSTs since December 22, the men were eager to get off of the ships and did not let the waves deter them. In spite of the rough seas, the entire battalion came ashore and moved into a bivouac area about one mile north of San Fabian. Noted the battalion historian, "Due to the condition of bridges it was necessary to remain in that area from the 11th to the 15th of January."[10]

Beginning around January 12, the I Corps infantry tried to seize the east–west Damortis–Rosario Road but ran into trouble among the low, rolling hills north of San Fabian. On January 15, the M4 Shermans of the Assault Gun Platoon, sporting 105mm howitzers, and the 81mm mortars of Mortar Platoon, both with Headquarters Company, 716th TB, moved east to lay down suppressive fire for the 43rd IDiv's attack against Hill 355, about four miles straight east of San Fabian. At the same time, the Shermans of Company C, plus a platoon from Company B, and the Stuarts of Company D, moved forward to assist the infantry.

According to the 716th TB historian, "[The] terrain proved unfit for tank employment. The tanks failed to gain an approach to Hill 355." Although the tanks managed to "advance into enemy territory, [and] neutralized four pillboxes and killed four Japanese," the tank historian concluded, "Hill 355 was impregnable from this direction."[11]

Discovering that Hill 355 could not be successfully attacked from the east, the 43rd IDiv decided to swing around to the southeast, reach Highway 3, and approach Rosario from the south. Although most of the infantry became bogged down near Manaoag, in an area known as the Hill 200 complex, the 3rd Platoon Shermans of Company C, 716th TB and a handful of foot soldiers managed to break through to the highway on January 17 and then swing north toward Pozorrubio, about nine miles southeast of Rosario. As the tanks advanced along the highway, however, they came under spirited enemy fire. Although they managed to overrun three Japanese mortars and four enemy machine-gun emplacements, the commanding lieutenant was wounded and had to be evacuated the next morning.[12]

On January 18, with the 3rd Platoon staff sergeant in charge, the five Shermans struck out again, assisting the infantry in driving the "fleeing enemy" out of Pozorrubio. Noted the 716th TB historian, "The advance was rapid, the enemy overwhelmed."[13]

On January 18, the 25th IDiv, which had landed in reserve on January 11, and the tanks of Company C, 716th TB moved in below the 43rd IDiv and captured the town of Binalonan, astride Highway 3 and about seven miles below Pozorrubio. The next day, the infantry and tanks, now supplemented by the 1st Platoon Stuarts of Company D, 716th TB moved farther east toward the barrio of San Manuel, six miles away. As the tanks and infantry approached the town, they were hit with machine guns and antitank fire from numerous Japanese tanks dug in as pillboxes. The 716th TB historian reported, "As seen previously, the enemy's use of tanks as pillboxes deprived them of mobility but added additional protection to their very thin armor. Their 47mm guns, fired from concealed positions proved damaging to our tanks." In the ensuing firefight, Company D lost two light tanks and had seven men killed.[14]

From January 20 to January 23, the Americans bombarded the area with artillery. Then, on January 24, the 25th IDiv and the medium tanks of Company C attacked again. "Heavy fighting developed," wrote the 716th TB historian. "With heavy antitank and tank gunfire the Japanese destroyed a medium tank, disabled four more, killed two enlisted men and wounded eight others. We inflicted on the enemy personnel losses of one-hundred and fifty, knocked out numerous gun posi-

Company B/716th TB M4A3 after landing at Lingayen Gulf, Luzon, Philippines, January 1945. US ARMY

An M4A3 Sherman of Company C, 716th TB passes a burning Japanese Type 97 tank on Luzon in the Philippines, January 17, 1945. US ARMY

tions, and silenced mortar fire. Our forces spent the following three days fighting in the town. On 27 January San Manuel was in our hands."[15]

On the southern edge of the I Corps zone, the 6th IDiv and the tanks of Company A, 716th TB began pushing toward the southeast once the 25th IDiv began its drive to the east. As the men and tanks moved toward the barrio of Urdaneta, Filipino guerrillas informed them the Japanese had dug-in tanks positioned along the road in front of the town. On the morning of January 17, the infantry started forward but was soon stalled by a concentration of mortar and machine-gun fire. As three Company A tanks came forward to assist, a few dug-in Japanese tanks suddenly opened fire and set two of the Shermans aflame. The third American tank was struck ten times and had a track blown off but managed to swing off the road before coming to a stop. Then, although the supporting infantry withdrew in the face of another mortar barrage, the tank crew "continued to fire until the enemy tanks were either routed or destroyed." Because of their "cool courage and intrepidity" the entire five man crew was awarded Silver Stars.[16]

Although the first three American tanks had been stopped, more Company A Shermans moved forward. "Two other platoons continued the attack, crushing hostile opposition," noted the tank battalion historian. "[The tanks] destroyed machine guns, tanks, tankettes and killed an undetermined number of personnel. . . . Company A secured the objective [Urdaneta]. . . . The following day, remaining enemy

This M4A3 of 44th TB was destroyed near the Cabaruan Hills on Luzon Island on January 19, 1945 by a Japanese 47mm antitank gun. US ARMY

forces in the town were mopped up. Company A moved across the Agno River to the vicinity of Rosales."[17]

While Urdaneta was being attacked, the 6th IDiv was moving against a series of low hills and valleys a few miles southwest of Urdaneta called the Cabaruan Hills. From January 17 to January 19, the infantry and the medium tanks of Company C, 44th TB infiltrated the area with relative ease. On the night of January 19, Maj. Gen. Edwin D. Patrick, commanding officer of the 6th IDiv, acting under the belief the hill mass would fall easily, moved most of his troops out of the area. Left behind was one battalion of infantry, one company of mortars, and the medium tanks of Company C.

Over the next two days, the advance continued to gain ground but on January 22, the skeleton force was "stopped cold by a tremendous burst of rifle, machine-gun, and light artillery fire." The infantry suffered ten killed and thirty-five wounded, and two tanks were knocked out. Shown the error of his ways, General Patrick sent an infantry battalion back to the Cabaruan Hills and on January 24 the Americans pushed forward again. On January 26, Japanese resistance stiffened and the advance progressed only 150 yards. In the process, the Americans lost another twelve men killed and twelve wounded, and had another Company C, 44th TB medium tank destroyed.

In response, another battalion of infantry and a platoon of tanks from Company A, 716th TB was sent into the hills. On the morning of January 27, the 716th TB tanks spearheaded an attack against the crest of a hill, enabling supporting infantry to move up and seize the objective. The next day, the tanks from both Company A, 716th TB and Company C, 44th TB, along with the light tanks of the 1st Platoon, Company D, 44th TB, which had been brought up from 13th

Armored Group reserve, led the way again. "The attack was launched on a 600-yard front," noted the 44th TB historian. "The tanks moved forward approximately one-half mile ahead of our front lines of infantry, blasting every possible enemy position. This attack lasted for two hours and upon returning to our lines, the tanks were reloaded with ammunition and immediately launched another attack over the same ground. The infantry followed this time at about 200 yards."

By the end of January 29, the entire Cabaruan Hill mass had finally been overrun. "The tankers mopped up concealed 77mm and 47mm antitank guns . . . three knee mortars, several light and heavy machine guns and approximately two-hundred enemy riflemen," crowed the 716th TB historian. In all, about 1,400 Japanese soldiers from the Shobu group had been killed in the Cabaruan Hills. The Americans had eighty killed and 200 wounded.[18]

In the XIV Corps zone, the advance of the 37th and 40th IDivs was almost straight south down Luzon's central plain. Faced with little enemy resistance, the advance moved in leaps and bounds. For once, the accompanying tanks found the paved roads very favorable. "We moved out on the first paved highway I had been on in almost seventeen months," wrote Corporal Howard.[19] In spite of the excellent roads, the tanks still had a hard time keeping up with the infantry. Noted the 754th TB historian:

> This phase of the operation for the tanks . . . was characterized by rapid movements following delays due to their inability to cross the many deep rivers whose bridges had been destroyed by the retreating Japanese. . . . Wherever a bridge was complete and opened for heavy traffic, the tanks made long road marches in an effort to remain in close support of the infantry. This was then, a period of short halts and long marches, of round-the-clock driving, of handling and rehandling of gas, ammunition, and other supplies.[20]

Beginning on January 18, XIV Corps and the supporting tank battalions began their hurry-up-and-wait movements southward. That first day, the tanks of Company A, 754th TB advanced twenty-five miles and jumped ahead of the 37th IDiv foot soldiers. Recalled Corporal Howard, "[At night, we] dug holes and drove our tanks over them for protection." The next day, Company A was at Pura, thirty-seven miles south of Lingayen Gulf, but on January 20 the tanks ran into trouble with bridges and the infantry jumped ahead. By January 23, the tanks had advanced only ten more miles, stopping at the town of Tarlac.[21]

Moving on a parallel road, the 40th IDiv and Company B, 754th TB reached Camiling, twenty-six miles from Lingayen Gulf, on January 20. By January 23, the tanks were rolling into the barrio of Bamban, fifteen miles south of Tarlac and only five miles north of Clark Field and Fort Stotsenburg, the old stomping grounds of the 192nd and 194th TBs.[22]

David Dumbeck was with Headquarters and Headquarters Company, 754th TB at Gerona, only eight miles north of Tarlac, and recalled, "Now with the

Japanese planes all but destroyed, it was a good feeling to know there would be no bombs dropping on us as was the case on the Solomons. Now it was mostly snipers we had to contend with. . . . Any place that looked like a possible ambush site was promptly riddled with bullets and machine-gun fire, cutting everything to shreds. If we ran into a tough entrenchment, we called upon our artillery. . . . With air power on our side and none used against us and the artillery backing us up, we did a good fast job of what we had to contend with northeast of Manila."[23]

While XIV Corps advanced rapidly southward, I Corps continued to slug it out among the rolling foothills of Luzon's mountainous northern region. Having taken Pozorrubio, the 43rd IDiv turned north and advanced up Highway 3 toward Rosario, completely encircling the Japanese on Hill 355. On the afternoon of January 18, the infantry and a few 716th TB tanks began pushing forward up Highway 3. "Two medium and six light tanks spearheaded the continuous fight, literally blowing the way open with 75mm, 37mm and .30-caliber machine-gun fire," stated the 716th TB historian.[24]

Upon reaching a road junction near Sison, about halfway between Pozorrubio and Rosario, the infantry dug in for the night and the tanks were sent back to Pozorrubio since they were drawing enemy mortar and artillery fire. During the night, the infantry withstood a Japanese banzai charge. In the morning, when the two medium and six light tanks returned to Sison, they found the infantry in a "desperate plight." Responding to a calling for more tanks, Lieutenant Colonel Peterson, commanding officer of the 716th TB, personally led the Assault Gun Platoon and the 2nd Platoon light tanks from Company D toward Sison.

Fortunately, the new tanks arrived just as the Japanese launched another banzai charge, this one from the direction of Hill 355. "The tanks of Company D met the Japanese attackers frontally," said the 716th TB historian. "The assault gun platoon met them on the flank and poured 105mm fire into them at ranges varying from fifty to two-hundred yards. The attack was crushed. Very few of the estimated two battalions of Japanese lived to withdraw to Hill 355."[25]

Once the attack had been broken, Japanese artillery and mortars opened fire again and, once again, the tanks were ordered back to Pozorrubio. An M4 Sherman 105mm assault tank, under the command of 1st Lt. Vaughn K. Dissette, was leading the way south when it was hit and burst into flames. Dissette and his crew tried to extinguish the fire but when the Japanese infantry attacked again, they returned to their guns and fought the oncoming enemy until they were out of ammunition.

At this point, Colonel Peterson rushed over and personally ordered Lieutenant Dissette and his crew to abandon the burning vehicle. As the two officers and the crewmen rushed from the tank, an enemy mortar round exploded nearby, mortally wounding Colonel Peterson. In spite of the heavy enemy fire, Dissette and his four fellow crewmen gave Peterson first aid and then carried him to safety. For their "courage and devotion to duty," Lieutenant Dissette and his entire crew were awarded Silver Stars.[26]

By January 22, the 43rd IDiv was ready to take another crack at Hill 355. Advancing up Highway 3 and attacking from the southeast, the infantrymen and the attached medium tanks from the 2nd Platoon, Company B, 716th TB ran into a well-fortified enemy emplacement. Pulling ahead, the tanks attempted to overrun the Japanese positions and force the defenders out into the open. "In one instance," wrote the 716th TB historian, "a 75mm shell uncovered a [Japanese] trench system. Two tanks astride the trench swept its length with enfilading fire, killing a large group of enemy troops."

As the tanks moved into the heart of the position, a Japanese soldier climbed onto the back of one tank and tried "to fire the tank's engines" by stuffing dry grass into the grillwork. He was quickly shot off by another tank's machine gun. Next, Japanese snipers killed one tank commander and seriously wounded the platoon leader. At sunset, with the tanks running low on fuel, the tankers requested permission to return to Pozorrubio. "The infantry commander refused to release the tanks because of the fluid situation," wrote the 716th TB historian.

In order to reinforce the tanks, and despite the growing darkness, Capt. Edward C. Stork (Headquarters and Headquarters Company, 716th TB) immediately moved out of Pozorrubio with his own tank and five 3rd Platoon Shermans of Company B. As Stork's group neared Hill 355, they stumbled onto the east flank of the enemy lines. "Immediately a fire fight began," commented the 716th TB historian. "Tank guns hurled great quantities of 75mm and machine-gun shells while the enemy fired on the six tanks with hidden antitank guns, mortars and machine guns." Although Captain Stork's tank was damaged and forced to withdraw, he quickly mounted another tank and returned to the fight.

Soon, another tank was hit and then another. In all, three tanks were set on fire and one was hit in the 75mm cannon and forced to withdraw. Sgt. Clarence G. Reese, in command of one of the last two tanks, destroyed one Japanese antitank gun and then dismounted from his vehicle to help rescue the crewmen who were bailing out of the burning tanks. As Japanese machine-gun fire impacted around him, he carried a wounded man to safety and then rushed back to help Captain Stork.

Somehow, Captain Stork had become dazed and confused when his second tank was hit and set on fire by a mortar burst. Climbing out of the tank, Stork pulled out his automatic pistol and began walking toward the enemy lines. Sergeant Reese, spotting his captain, raced over and guided Stork back to safety. Then, taking command of the situation, Reese successfully extricated the remaining two tanks from the vicious fight. For his "gallantry in action," Sergeant Reese was promoted to the rank of second lieutenant and presented a Silver Star medal.[27]

Over the next two weeks, the medium tanks from Company B and the light tanks of Company D, both 716th TB, fought beside the 43rd IDiv as they continued their attacks against Hill 355. At the same time, the Assault Gun Platoon and the Mortar Platoon from the 716th TB provided indirect fire support. Spirited attacks were made on January 24, 26 and 27. Each time the tanks and infantry went forward, they inflicted untold damage on the enemy, and each time they pulled back for the night. On January 27, the Japanese defenders began a slow withdrawal so when the Americans went forward again on January 29 they met only token resistance. By February 3, Hill 355 was firmly in American hands. "In summing up," wrote the tank battalion historian, "it is estimated that . . . the 716th Tank Battalion inflicted one thousand personnel casualties on the enemy and destroyed a wealth of [material]."[28]

At the extreme northern flank of the I Corps zone, the 43rd IDiv had been trying to gain control of the ground between Damortis and Rosario since the first few days after the invasion. Near the end of January, two platoons of Stuart light tanks from Company D, 716th TB went north to offer assistance. On January 28, the infantry and tanks finally entered Rosario from the west, finding it abandoned but booby-trapped and mined.[29]

That same date, January 28, the Company C Shermans of the 716th TB crossed the Agno River and pushed eastward along Route 8 with elements of the 25th IDiv. On February 1, the combined force attacked the town of Umingan. While the 3rd Platoon Shermans acted as "a base of fire," concentrating their shells against enemy strong points, the 1st Platoon and some infantry moved against the town from the northwest. Noted historian Robert Ross Smith, "Japanese antitank weapons drove off American tanks that came up Route 8 to support the infantry, while irrigation ditches on both sides of the road prevented the tanks from executing cross-country maneuvers." In the attack, one medium tank was damaged by land mines and another was stopped by Japanese antitank fire. That night, most of the Japanese fled and by the end of February 3, Umingan was completely in American hands.[30]

Pursuing the retreating enemy, the tanks and infantry reached the outskirts of Lupao, about six miles southeast of Umingan, before running into stiffening enemy resistance. The barrio of Lupao formed the top of a Japanese defensive triangle that consisted of Lupao to the north, Munoz, eleven miles straight south, and San Jose, eight miles to the southeast. On January 30, General Krueger, commander of the Sixth Army, had ordered an all-out drive to capture San Jose. If that town could be captured quickly, XIV Corps could then push southward toward the important town of Rizal, about ten miles southeast of San Jose. Once Rizal was in American hands, XIV Corps could push east about twenty-five miles to the coast of Luzon and cut the island in half.[31]

Stationed within the Lupao-Munoz-San Jose triangle were 220 Japanese tanks from the 2nd Tank Division and about 8,000 supporting infantrymen. Since San Jose was a major Japanese supply depot, Shobu Group had good reason to resist the Americans, at least until most of the supplies could be removed to the northern mountains. On February 2, when the advancing 25th IDiv and the tanks of Company C, 716th TB reached Lupao, the Japanese defenders fought back.[32]

"For the next two days [the Americans] battered well-prepared defenses and gun positions," wrote the 716th TB historian. Bitter fighting continued in and around Lupao from February 2 until February 7 as the defenders refused to give up. "On 7 February the tanks fought into the city where they encountered and destroyed nine enemy tanks," proclaimed the tank historian. In return, the Japanese destroyed one Sherman. Finally, on the night of February 7–8, the remaining Japanese, including ten or eleven tanks, tried to break through the encircling American lines and escape into the mountains to the east. While most of the Japanese infantry escaped, only five tanks got away. By noon on February 8, the Americans had cleared out any remaining resistance in Lupao.[33]

At the same time, the town of Munoz at the bottom corner of the triangle came under American attack. On the morning of February 1, the 6th IDiv, along with the medium tanks of Company C, 44th TB and the 1st Platoon light tanks of Company D, 716th TB, moved southeast toward Munoz from the Cabaruan Hills. The 44th TB historian aptly described the difficulties faced by the tankers:

> Tank operations were limited by flat terrain, boggy ground and deep water-filled irrigation ditches. The town of Munoz was fortified with antitank guns, 105[mm] artillery pieces and fifty-seven light and medium tanks, all of which were dug in and with a three-foot thick top of logs and sandbags over them. In addition, numerous alternate positions were available so that the tanks that were in one place one day, would be in an alternate position the next.[34]

Limited by the terrain, the 3rd Platoon Shermans of Company C, 44th TB supported the advance of the 6th IDiv with long-range fire. In this manner, the 3rd Platoon knocked out "six Jap medium tanks, one 105mm artillery piece, four 47mm, and much enemy equipment and personnel." In spite of the good shooting, however, the infantry made little progress in the capture of Munoz and settled in for a short siege.[35]

While Munoz was under siege, two sweeping flanking movements were taking place just south of the town. Beginning on February 1, the 1st IReg, 6th IDiv pushed straight east for about eleven miles until it cut the north–south San Jose–Rizal Road. Then, after brushing aside some slight Japanese resistance, the regiment moved northward and by the afternoon of February 3, was only 1,000 yards south of San Jose.[36]

At the same time, the 63rd IReg, 6th IDiv, accompanied by the 1st and 2nd Platoon tanks of Company C, 44th TB and the light tanks from Company D, 716th TB, moved east below Munoz and then swung sharply north, cutting the Munoz–San Jose Road (Route 5) a mile and a half behind the town. On February 3, the tanks and infantry pushed northeastward along Route 5 toward San Jose and by dusk were at a bridge near Abar, only one mile outside of San Jose. "At the barrio of Abar," noted the 44th TB historian, "the [advance] hit the main defense before San Jose. Here, as in the past, the Jap had placed antitank guns and machine guns in positions covering a water barrier."[37]

On February 4, while the troops from the 1st IReg walked virtually unopposed into San Jose from the south, the column coming in from the west was stopped at the bridge in front of Abar. "In the heavy fighting that followed," recorded the 44th TB historian, "[the tanks] eliminated five 47mm antitank guns, but still were unable to cross the stream due to heavy fire covering the road as it crossed the stream." Forward progress was halted for one day until the tanks finally forced their way across the bridge. "By the use of smoke the second platoon was finally able to pass," continued the tank historian. "After crossing the stream, the second platoon proceeded to eliminate all opposition holding up the advance of the infantry."[38]

While the infantry and medium tanks continued the attack on Abar, the light Stuart tanks of Company D, 716th TB used the cover of descending darkness to move across country to San Jose and link up with the 1st IReg. The next day, February 6, the light M5 Stuarts turned around and attacked Abar from the east with elements of the 1st IReg, while the medium M4 Shermans attacked from the west with the 63rd IReg. With the Japanese trapped between the two pincers, the town soon fell to the Americans. But although both Abar and San Jose were now in American hands, their delay in being captured had given the Japanese just enough time to get most of their supplies out of San Jose and up into the Sierra Madre Mountains along Luzon's east coast.[39]

By the end of the first week in February, the only town of the Lupao–Munoz–San Jose triangle still occupied by the Japanese was Munoz. On February 7, the defenders concluded they had had enough. In the early morning darkness, the Japanese attempted to flee to San Jose up Route 5, apparently unaware that San Jose and most of Route 5 were already in American hands. Moving out in a column of tanks and trucks, the Japanese boldly passed through the American lines until they got to the bivouac area of Company C, 44th TB, which had been established only a few miles northeast of Munoz.

"At about 4:15 in the morning," wrote an Army reporter, "one guard, hearing the sound of an approaching steel-tracked vehicle, alerted the company. Since no shots had been fired by other nearby units, it was believed to be an American tractor or bulldozer, and allowed to pass." As the first Japanese tank and two infantry-laden trucks passed by, someone suddenly shouted, "Hell, that's a Jap tank." The Army reporter recorded what ensued:

> At first it looked as if [the Japanese tank and trucks] were going to get away. In the stygian darkness, C Company's gunnery couldn't be accurate.
>
> Another 200 yards, however, and all three vehicles burst into flame from direct hits. The illumination provided by these burning wrecks enabled the tankers to improve their aim, as three more Nip tanks rounded the corner only to be blown up promptly by C Company's 75s. . . .
>
> Meanwhile, more Japanese tanks pulled into firing position farther up the road, and started shelling the entire C Company area. Although their fire was far from ineffective, one by one they were picked off as the American tankers lined their sights in on the enemy's lurid muzzle blasts. Some gunners searched for targets by spraying machine-gun tracer bul-

lets in a wide arc. When one struck a Jap tank, it would spark as it ricocheted off. The vehicle would then be destroyed by 75 cannon fire.

It was sunup before the last Japanese soldier was either killed or fled the scene. Company C, 44th TB had destroyed one light and ten medium tanks, an artillery prime mover, one carryall, and two trucks. Scattered around the wreckage were 245 Japanese bodies. Company C had one man killed and eleven wounded, and two tanks slightly damaged. By noon on February 7, Munoz was in American hands.[40]

Continuing almost straight east, the 6th IDiv captured Rizal on February 7 against scattered resistance. Pushing eastward, the foot soldiers reached Luzon's east coast at Dingalan Bay on February 11. For all intents and purposes, Luzon had been cut in two.[41]

After the capture of Munoz, Company C, 44th TB went into 6th IDiv reserve. On February 8 and 9, the entire 716th TB was relieved of combat duty and sent to the town of Manaoag for "maintenance and recreation." With the exception of the Assault Gun Platoon, the 716th TB was finished with combat duty on Luzon.[42]

By the end of the third week of January, the 37th and 40th IDivs were on the outskirts of Clark Field and Fort Stotsenburg. Anticipating stiffening Japanese resistance around Clark Field and in the hills and mountains to the west of the airfield, XIV Corps slowed its pace and consolidated around the town of Bamban, five miles north of Clark Field. On January 24, the 40th IDiv moved into the hills west of Bamban and for the first time since landing on Luzon met well-organized resistance from the Kembu Group. The next day, the 40th IDiv extended itself in a north–south line along Highway 3 and attacked westward, capturing a few strategic ridgelines. On January 26, the division began sweeping south toward the Clark Field/Fort Stotsenburg area.[43]

On January 26, one platoon of Shermans from Company B, 754th TB, which had been supporting the southern drive of the 40th IDiv from Lingayan Gulf, moved into the hills west of Bamban and north of Clark Field with the foot soldiers. "The tanks were used all day in assisting the movement of the ground troops," recorded the tank battalion historian. "It was a continuous assault against pillboxes and sniper positions." At nightfall, the tanks returned to Highway 3.[44]

On January 28, part of the 37th IDiv pushed south out of Bamban down Highway 3 until it was opposite Clark Field and then turned west toward the airstrips. Assisted by a platoon of tanks from Company C, 754th TB, the infantry moved steadily forward. Within a short time, the men and tanks overran two runways, but when they continued pushing westward they stumbled into a Japanese minefield. One tank erupted in a ball of flame and although the crew managed to escape, the tank was a total loss. Within minutes, two more Shermans hit mines and were disabled.[45]

The next day, while the medium tanks remained silent, the light M5 tanks of Company D, 754th TB pushed westward again, this time avoiding any Japanese land mines and moving all the way through Clark Field to its border with Fort

Stotsenburg. At 3:00 P.M., four enemy medium tanks suddenly sallied out to engage the American light tanks. "During the ensuing fight," noted the 754th TB historian, "all four enemy tanks were destroyed while our tanks incurred no damage."[46]

By January 31, the 37th IDiv had fought its way into the hills beyond Fort Stotsenburg and was assaulting Top of the World Hill, just west of the old Army base. Assisting in the assault were the medium tanks of Company A, 754th TB. "The terrain was most unfavorable for the use of tanks because of the steep incline," reported the battalion historian, "but the company endeavored to find a route which would take it to a position near the infantry so that it could support their advance with close range fire." Eventually, the tankers discovered a "passable but hazardous route" that took them close to the front lines and allowed them to fire at Japanese pillboxes and other suspected positions.[47]

Elsewhere, a platoon from Company B, 754th TB assisted the 40th IDiv in an attack against Snake Hill, northwest of Clark Field, destroying "two 47mm anti-tank guns and many pillboxes and bunkers," while Companies C and D once again worked with the 37th IDiv around Clark Field and in the foothills to the west.[48]

For the tankers of the 754th TB, the action around Clark Field was extremely trying. As the 754th TB historian noted:

> This was a long and difficult series of operations for the [crews]. Long hours spent in closed tanks produced cases of battle fatigue and heat exhaustion. Tanks were called upon to fight in terrain most unfavorable for their use and in areas covered by land mines and enemy artillery. . . . The principles and lessons learned from long hours of fighting in the jungles of the Solomon Islands had to be forgotten. Established theories and practices gave way to snap decisions and constant hammering against fortified positions. Our only tactics were those of common sense. . . . In spite of all these obvious disadvantages, the tanks performed their missions successfully and earned the praise and commendation of the infantry.[49]

While the fight was going on in the Clark Field/Fort Stotsenburg area, elements of the 37th IDiv had pushed farther south down Highway 3 to capture the town of Angeles. On February 1, the 754th TB moved its bivouac area to Angeles and began readying most of its vehicles for the eventual drive to Manila.[50]

On February 9, after fighting the Kembu Group in the hills west of Clark Field for almost one week, the 40th IDiv made a final drive against Top of the World Hill. Supporting the assault were the medium tanks of Company B, 754th TB, which had discovered that the best ammunition for close-up fighting was an improvised 75mm canister round, made from an artillery round. Moving over "very rugged terrain," the 2nd Platoon managed to outflank a Japanese strong point and take it from the rear. Firing their new ammunition, the tanks knocked out several 40mm and 90mm guns, machine guns, and mortars and killed dozens of Japanese soldiers. At the same time, the 2nd Platoon made a deep penetration on the enemy's left flank and "destroyed several 20mm gun positions before withdrawing."[51]

The next day, Company B, 754th TB was replaced in the Clark Field area by the light tanks of Company D. Instead of continuing the fight in the hills west of Clark Field, Company B was to join the rest of the battalion in capturing Manila.[52]

CHAPTER TWENTY-SIX

Manila

While the fighting was taking place on Luzon's northern plain, General MacArthur made another surprise move by landing two regiments from the 11th Airborne Division (AbnDiv) on a beachhead about forty-five miles southwest of Manila on January 29 and 31. Coming ashore unopposed, the paratroopers raced toward Manila through throngs of cheering Filipinos. The next day, the third regiment dropped by parachute and joined the drive north.

Moving quickly, the paratroopers were within three miles of Manila on February 4 before the surprised Japanese stopped them. Wrote historian Dale Andradé, "The 11th Airborne Division had reached the main Japanese defenses south of the capital and could go no further."[1]

To the north, General MacArthur was becoming more and more exasperated with the XIV Corps as it consolidated around Bamban. Critical of the "lack of drive," MacArthur turned to the 1st CDiv, which had moved southward on the left flank of the infantrymen. On January 30, MacArthur told the cavalrymen, "Go to Manila, go around the Nips, bounce off the Nips, but go to Manila."

At the time, the 1st CDiv was just outside of Cabanatuan on Route 5, about twenty miles south of Munoz and the Japanese triangle. In response to MacArthur's directive, the 1st CDiv commander formed two Flying Columns, each composed of a squadron of cavalry, a company of medium tanks, a 105mm howitzer battery, other supporting troops and enough trucks and halftracks to carry everyone and everything at a high rate of speed. The two companies of tanks selected for the flying columns were Companies A and B, 44th TB.[2]

On the night of January 31–February 1, a provisional reconnaissance squadron composed of a small infantry troop and the Headquarters and Headquarters Company and Company D, 44th TB tanks, bypassed Cabanatuan, crossed the Pampanga River below the town and moved toward the barrio of Gapan on Route 5.

Upon reaching the town, Lt. Col. Tom H. Ross, commanding officer of the 44th TB and in charge of the reconnaissance, led a patrol into Gapan to seize the bridge over the Santa Rosa River.[3]

PFC Harold R. Beeman (Company D, 44th TB), a gunner in the lead light tank which was nicknamed *Destination Tokyo,* recalled, "Lieutenant Colonel Ross and Captain [Charles A.] Kurdle in a jeep . . . moved up the column and crossed the bridge. A second jeep . . . was following. A Japanese machine gun on the river to the right put the second jeep out of commission on the bridge abutment. . . . We heard gunfire in the town of Gapan." Beeman's tank and a second one forded the river and then raced into Gapan to see if they could find Colonel Ross. "We returned to the road and went a block or so when we saw the jeep on a street to our left," recalled Beeman. "We turned and stopped at the mouth of an alley to our left. The jeep was totally shot up."

Jumping out of his tank, Private Beeman ran to a nearby building. "I could see Colonel Ross up against the building," Beeman continued. "He was dead and had been covered by a tipped up bench. His gun and insignia had been taken." Eventually, Private Beeman spotted Captain Kurdle and helped him back to *Destination Tokyo.* "Captain Kurdle had made his way down the alley and into a building. Two Japanese soldiers took his personal items while the captain feigned dead. I radioed for the medical halftrack and we went back across the very narrow bridge. The Japanese machine gun was now on our left; it rattled the side of our tank." In spite of being wounded sixteen times, Captain Kurdle survived his ordeal.[4]

While the Gapan Bridge was being seized, the trucks and halftracks of the Second Flying Column used the covering fire of the tanks of Company B, 44th TB to cross the Pampanga River above Cabanatuan. Moving to the outskirts of town, the infantry ran into about 250 Japanese defenders and eventually called for the Company B tanks. Engaging "in heavy street fighting," the column seized most of Cabanatuan before dusk.[5]

The First Flying Column, led by the medium tanks of Company A, 44th TB, reached Cabanatuan late in the afternoon and relieved the Second Flying Column from further combat. Free to move, the Second Flying Column pushed swiftly down Route 5 with the tanks of Company B in the lead. Passing over the captured bridge at Gapan during the night of February 1–2, the column reached the barrio of Baliuag on the Angat River, about thirty-five miles south of Gapan, near 9:00 A.M. During the day, after establishing contact with a patrol from the 37th IDiv on its right, the Second Flying Column crossed the Angat River just below Baliuag.[6]

The First Flying Column spent most of February 2 mopping up Cabanatuan before the Company A, 44th TB Shermans led the column south down Route 5. In surrounding darkness, the column went through Baliuag and then turned east and entered Bustos. In spite of the darkness, the tanks and trucks were met with heavy sniper fire. After killing five Japanese soldiers and destroying one light machine gun, the First Flying Column pushed on toward Angat, about ten miles away, where it was met by heavy mortar and machine-gun fire. Deciding that the Angat River bridge looked bad, the column turned around and went back to Bustos, arriving there sometime in the early morning hours of February 3. Before finally coming to a halt, the column crossed over the Angat River at Bustos and moved into the small village of Pandii.[7]

At sunup on February 3, the Second Flying Column, which was just below Baliuag, pushed south toward Santa Maria, fifteen miles away, with the Company B, 44th TB Shermans in the lead. Swooping into town, the tanks quickly secured the crossing of the Santa Maria River and then began destroying any Japanese equipment and defenders. After killing 135 Japanese, destroying thirteen trucks and capturing seven more, the tanks pushed on toward Manila. Although it encountered some resistance in Novaliches, the Second Flying Column reached Manila at 5:30 P.M.[8]

Riding inside Capt. Jesse L. Walters' Company B tank, *Battlin' Basic,* was gunner Cpl. John Hencke, who recalled the last few miles to Manila:

> [We] hit a smooth highway. There was a car burning in the middle of it and our driver hit it with the side of the tank, clearing the way for jeeps and trucks. Everybody was buttoned up; there were supposed to be a lot of Japs around. . . . The next thing I can remember is the ringing of bells, church bells out across the fields. Filipinos out there started running toward the road, waving their arms. It was a pleasant sight to see. We were on the outskirts of Manila.[9]

Luzon, Manila. An M4 Sherman passing a burning streetcar. US ARMY

754th TB M4A1 Sherman passes by the capital building in Manila, Luzon, on January 9, 1945. US ARMY

The first tank to enter the city limits was *Yankee,* an M4 Sherman from the 3rd Platoon, Company B, 44th TB, which entered the Philippine capital at 5:30 P.M. on February 3, 1945. The 1st CDiv and the tanks of Company B, 44th TB had beaten both the 37th IDiv and the 11th AbnDiv into Manila.[10]

As the tanks pushed through the streets, happy throngs of liberated people swamped them. "We reached a large, open boulevard," recalled Hencke. "It was like a parade without ticker-tape, the people yelling, hollering, climbing up on the tanks. They were everywhere. Then some Jap snipers fired a few shots and everybody disappeared." As the tanks pressed on, they fired their machine guns at the upper stories and rooftops of the surrounding buildings. While crossing over a trolley car track, the antennae of Captain Walters' *Battlin' Basic* struck the overhead electrical lines and shorted out the radio. "The radio caught fire and we were left without a radio," wrote Corporal Hencke. "The captain pulled over, waved to the other tanks to take their antennae down."

Ahead of the tankers was Santo Tomas Catholic University, which had been turned into an internment camp by the Japanese in 1942. Inside were 3,768 American, English and Dutch civilians who had been captured at the fall of the Philippines. Through hidden radios, the internees had heard of the American invasion of Luzon and as January 1945 came to an end, they kept hearing the song "Hail, Hail, the Gang's All Here." Frances Dyson, an internee, recalled, "This went on hour after hour and we were sure it was some kind of code telling us that the Americans were near at hand." Early on the evening of Sunday, February 3, nine American fighter planes buzzed the walled-in compound and one pilot dropped his goggles, which contained the note: "Roll Out the Barrel. Santa Claus is Coming Sunday or Monday." The internees suddenly realized their salvation was near.[11]

Forewarned that the Japanese might kill all the civilian internees if the Americans reached Manila, Captain Walters led his 3rd Platoon tanks straight down

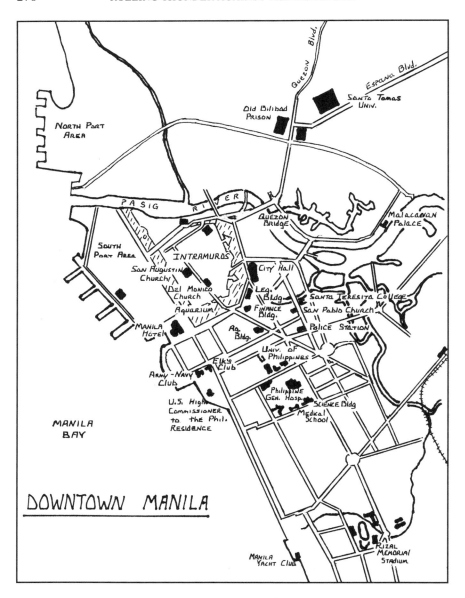

Downtown Manila

Quezon Boulevard toward the Santo Tomas. Inside the university buildings, which had been converted into barracks buildings and living quarters, the prisoners could hear the crackle of machine-gun fire and the nearing clank of the steel tank treads on the cobblestone streets. When the tanks reached the corner of the university compound, they suddenly stopped.[12]

Company B/44th TB enters Santo Tomas University, Manila. US ARMY

"We came to the internment camp. It was already dark," recalled Corporal Hencke. Unsure of where to go, Captain Walters and two crewmen descended from their tank to look around. "It was totally black, and we couldn't see anything," Hencke continued. "I was up in the turret looking around when I saw what looked like a little sparkler fly over the wall into the road by us. At first I thought it might be a fire cracker, but it came to my mind it was a grenade or dynamite." Shouting "Grenade!" Hencke ducked down into the turret as Captain Walters and the others dove safely for cover. Having had enough, Walters and the two crewmen climbed back into the tank and pushed on.[13]

"Where the hell is the front gate?" one of the tankers shouted as the 3rd Platoon Shermans moved onto Espana Boulevard. Finally, after going a few hundred feet, *Battlin' Basic* came up to the main entrance, an iron gate that was chained shut. "Open up," Walters shouted into the darkness but nobody responded. "Open the thing or I'm coming anyway." When his second shout fell upon deaf ears, Walters called down to his driver and crew: "Go on in but don't shoot unless you have to, and be sure they're Japs."[14]

Corporal Hencke was standing beside Captain Walters in the turret and recalled, "We weren't prepared yet; my turret was open, my machine gun still out on the mount. But we didn't think about that. As we began pushing through the gate, I sensed something coming at me. It was a span of concrete over the gate and I just managed to get one side of the turret hatch down. I didn't have time for the machine gun or the other half of the hatch. I managed to get my head and my arm down, though. The concrete cracked the hatch catch, snapped the machine gun off the swivel. I yelled to [our driver] to stop but because our radio was out, he couldn't hear me." In spite of their less than heroic entrance, *Battlin' Basic* was the first tank to enter Santo Tomas internment camp.[15]

Popping up from inside the tank, Hencke turned on a handheld spotlight and shined it into the compound. "What I saw in the circle of light sent chills through me," Hencke remembered. "There was a man about six feet tall, dressed all in white, a flowing robe and a white beard that hung halfway to his navel. In his hand was a staff. I thought I was seeing Saint Peter but after a few seconds I learned he was one of the monks who had come to guide us and show us where the Japs were."[16]

Pushing in behind *Battlin' Basic* were the other tanks of the 3rd Platoon, Company B, 44th TB, commanded by 2nd Lt. Robert E. Lee, a descendant of the famous Civil War general. As the tanks *Georgia Peach, Ole Miss, Block Buster, San Antone* and *Crusader* pushed into the compound, the jubilant internees raced out to greet them. "When the internees realized we were Americans there to free them, they went wild and were all over us," wrote Hencke.[17]

Knowing there were plenty of Japanese soldiers inside the compound, the 3rd Platoon tanks spread out and looked for signs of enemy activity. Although some Japanese were found in a few out-of-the-way places, about sixty Japanese soldiers took 275 internees hostage in the education building and demanded safe conduct out of Santo Tomas University or they would kill all of their prisoners. On February 6, an agreement was finally reached. "They could leave," noted Corporal Hencke, "take their handguns and rifles but no machine guns or grenades. At daybreak, with American soldiers lined up on both sides, the Japs all came down, to

Company B/44th TB, the saviors of the prisoners at Santo Tomas University, pose in front of their composite hull M4 tanks, August 1945. US ARMY

Composite hull M4 medium tanks and a squad of infantry move unflinchingly past the dead body of a Japanese defender in Manila, February 1945. US ARMY

be escorted out through the gate, taken five or six blocks, told there are the front lines, you're on your own."[18]

While the 3rd Platoon was crashing the gate at Santo Tomas University, the 1st Platoon Shermans fought their way through Manila's side streets to the north bank of the Pasig River, which encircled the downtown area of Manila. The tanks and a troop of accompanying cavalrymen moved to Malacanan Palace, the Filipino White House, and quickly seized the grounds. Across the river lay the heart of downtown Manila.[19]

Although General Yamashita regarded Manila as "indefensible," three battalions from the southern Shobu Group and some Japanese marines barricaded themselves inside the strong, earthquake-proof buildings of downtown Manila and destroyed or mined most of the bridges across the Pasig River. On February 4, as the rest of the Second Flying Column troops poured into the northeastern corner of Manila, the Japanese dug in and prepared to fight it out to the last man.[20]

At 8:00 A.M. on February 4, the cavalrymen and the 3rd Platoon tanks tried to make a dash down Quezon Boulevard to seize Quezon Bridge. Knowing their nighttime dash into the city had caught the Japanese by surprise, the men and tankers were hoping another dash might garner them the steel span bridge before the Japanese had a chance to blow it up. Unfortunately, as the column pushed its way down the boulevard it came under heavy fire. Although the tankers claimed they killed eighty-five Japanese soldiers, land mines strewn about the street and steel rails driven into the roadbed prevented any further progress by the Americans. Shortly thereafter, the retreating Japanese destroyed the Quezon Bridge.[21]

As the day wore on, more and more American soldiers entered Manila as the vanguard of the 37th IDiv, which had formed a flying column of its own and had pushed southeast from the Clark Field area, linked up with 1st CDiv troops at Santo Tomas University. Moving farther into the city, the 37th IDiv broke into Old Bilibad prison and rescued about 800 American and Allied prisoners of war and 530 civilian internees.[22]

Moving with the 37th IDiv vanguard were the tanks of Company A, 754th TB. Corporal Howard wrote, "And what a ride it was! We had to keep tight to the tank in front at all times, yet we were traveling as fast as the tank could go relative to the terrain. Went through rice paddies, fields, up hills, through narrow valleys and small barrios, around tight narrow turns, on dirt roads and trails. People rushed out to greet us but we just buzzed on through. Poured on the gas and made Manila's outskirts by dark."[23]

Having reached the city limits, Company A, 754th TB and some soldiers from the 37th IDiv broke into the Balintawak Brewery, where "the vats were full of beer ready for bottling." As Corporal Howard recalled, "The spigots were opened and we filled our five-gallon jerry cans, steel helmets, canteens and cups and anything that would hold beer and took off back to the perimeter. There were so many drunken soldiers that if the Japanese had attacked, they could have walked right over us."[24]

The provisional reconnaissance squadron and the 2nd and 3rd Platoon tanks of Company A, 44th TB reached Manila on February 5 after a few harried firefights. After reaching Santo Tomas University, the provisional reconnaissance squadron was officially disbanded. The next morning, as the tanks extended their hold on the streets around the university, the rest of the 37th IDiv began pouring into the northern part of Manila.[25]

In order to avoid any friendly fire incidents, the city was divided in two, with the 37th IDiv taking the western half of Manila and the 1st CDiv taking the eastern half. As both the 44th and 754th TBs accompanied the foot soldiers into the city, they had to change from jungle warfare tactics to city fighting tactics. The historian for the 754th TB explained:

> For the tanks as well as for the infantry, this was a new type of warfare. Previous to this time, this battalion had not operated against enemy installations in cities. Our tactics were revised and became more flexible to meet the change in conditions. The tanks were used primarily as mobile artillery, firing at strong points at very close range. We encountered an increasing hazard from extensive mine fields. The possible lanes of approach to the enemy installations were channelized by narrow streets over which the infantry was unable to move with any rapidity. Because of the well-fortified enemy installations covering all avenues of approach, mine sappers found it difficult to clear lanes. Their examinations of the

roads were often very cursory and several tanks were damaged on streets, which had been supposedly cleared.[26]

Adding to the confusion of fighting inside a modern city, the Americans had to contend with the fact that the retreating Japanese had set fire to the northern half of Manila before crossing the Pasig River. PFC Sabino L. Goitia, a medic with the 754th TB, wrote in his diary for February 7, "Manila is burning! We are outside the city and can see the smoke and red glare in the distance. Japs are reported burning the city as they retreat."[27]

On February 7, the 1st and 2nd Platoon tanks of Company B, 44th TB advanced without infantry support toward Rosario Heights and the Manila reservoir, just north of Manila, in an attempt to capture the water supply intact. Moving through the streets unsupported, the tanks were attacked with "20mm and 5-inch naval guns and grenadiers with mines and Molotov cocktails." As the tanks rolled along, they blasted enemy pillboxes and bunkers and although one platoon managed to reach the reservoir, it was eventually forced to pull back.

Moving along a different route, a second platoon of five tanks drove to within 500 yards of the reservoir before running into two 5-inch naval guns and a roadway scattered with mines. "Three of the tanks were destroyed and the other two damaged," wrote the 44th TB historian. However, "the two 5-inch guns were knocked out." With six men killed, several wounded, and three tanks destroyed, the two platoons pulled back to safer ground.[28]

While the Company B tanks were trying to secure the reservoir, twelve light tanks of Company D, and five medium tanks from Headquarters and Headquarters Company, 44th TB supported the 1st CDiv in clearing out the subdivision of New Manila, on the far western side of the city. Once the area was secured, the tanks and foot soldiers pushed southward toward the Pasig River in an attempt to encircle Manila. Moving out on four separate streets, the tanks and infantry encountered numerous minefields, snipers, suicide bombers and 20mm fire, but managed to kill a large number of Japanese soldiers. The tanks alone were credited with killing 150 men.[29]

At first light on February 8, the 1st Platoon Shermans from Company A, 44th TB headed south toward the Pasig River. Suddenly, a 5-inch artillery shell slammed into the lead tank. Before the rest of the tanks could maneuver into position, three more artillery rounds smashed through the Sherman's armor, killing four crewmen and completely destroying the tank. After the other tanks knocked out the Japanese fieldpiece, they pushed on, wiping out any other Japanese strong points they encountered. After a short advance, however, the new lead tank rolled over a buried naval depth charge, which "completely demolished" the vehicle. When the tankers discovered that there were more than 150 depth charges buried beneath the road, the remaining tanks pulled back.[30]

Over at the reservoir, six tanks from Company B, 44th TB went forward without infantry support once again and ran into more suicide bombers and Molotov cocktail attacks. Pulling back, the tanks waited for some 1st CDiv infantry to arrive before going forward again. The third time was the charm, however, as the tanks and cavalrymen eventually overran the enemy positions and reached the reservoir at 1:30 P.M. One and one-half hours later, the Manila reservoir was securely in American hands.[31]

On the western side of Manila, Company A, 754th TB and the 37th IDiv had pushed all the way to the north bank of the Pasig River before being stopped by that formidable obstacle. Unable to get across the river, the tankers and infantry took up positions inside the houses along the river bank and waited for landing craft to be brought up.[32]

While in position along the Pasig River, Corporal Howard reported two interesting happenings. "It was observed that objects were floating upstream," he wrote, "and fire was brought to bear on such objects until they turned and traveled their natural way right back to the bay." Later, Corporal Howard and the other tankers spotted a Japanese sniper hidden behind a large billboard. "We decided to pull a tank up, load it with a 75mm canister shell and attempt to remove the sniper. When the tank fired, the billboard sign disintegrated from the shock of 180 stainless steel 3/8-inch pellets tearing through with the force of an artillery shell." Needless to say, the sniping stopped.[33]

In order to protect Manila and its 800,000 civilians, General MacArthur "placed stringent restrictions on U.S. artillery and air support." In spite of this, the battle for Manila left the city in rubble. The retreating Japanese had set the north side of the city on fire and American tanks, mortars and even some artillery fire was used to root the Japanese out of their well-fortified positions inside of, on top of, and even under Manila's downtown buildings. Additionally, when the Japanese defenders finally decided they had had enough in one area, they simply demolished their hideouts and moved on to a new area.[34]

South of Manila, the 11th AbnDiv paratroopers had pushed across the Paranaque River on February 5 but then had run into stiff resistance. For the next seven days, the paratroopers anchored their left flank on Manila Bay and fought their way slowly into the very southern outskirts of the city. At the same time, elements of the division swung to the east and on the evening of February 11 ran into an outpost from the 1st CDiv. The city of Manila was now completely encircled.[35]

On February 7, the 37th IDiv brought up a number of landing craft and sent an amphibious assault across the Pasig River just opposite Malacanan Palace. Once a beachhead had been established, American troops poured across the river. Between February 8 and 10, infantrymen fought their way through the eastern section of Manila until they ran into patrols from the 1st CDiv coming in from the east.[36] Slowly but surely everything was falling into place.

While the 37th IDiv, the 1st CDiv and the 11th AbnDiv were encircling Manila, a special security force was holding the north bank of the Pasig River. Included in this force was Company A, 754th TB. Among the targets fired upon by the Sherman tanks was the Intramuros, an old Spanish walled city within Manila's downtown district. In describing the protection around the Intramuros, historian Gerald Astor wrote, "Great stone blocks piled as high as twenty-five feet and as much as forty feet thick at the bottom surrounded the mostly stone struc-tures." Built to withstand a heavy naval bombardment from Manila Bay, the Intra-muros proved to be a tough nut to crack. "The stone wall was blasted with AP [armor piercing] and HE [high explosive] 75mm shells," wrote Corporal Howard. "That was when we realized the job we had facing us, of trying to break through this wall to get to the Japanese."[37]

As the 754th TB historian recalled, "The platoons [of Company A] were alternated every four hours throughout the day and night in order to keep a con-tinuous rate of fire. The enemy offered heavy mortar and small-arms fire but we sustained no damage during the operation." On February 12, one tank destroyed four enemy assault boats on the Japanese side of the Pasig River and on the morn-ing of February 14, another tank fired into an enemy barge at the river mouth. "The barge burst into flames and was destroyed," noted the 754th TB historian. "It was believed that the barge was loaded with ammunition."[38]

Corporal Howard commented on the living conditions on the north bank of the river. "The state of siege had settled down into a condition where bodies of civilians and Japanese were still strewn over the streets, in gutters, on lawns and in the middle of the pavement," he wrote. "Attempts to remove them were met with sniper fire, so instead of removal, when dusk came, the bodies were covered with quick-lime to hasten their deterioration and to stifle the smell."[39]

The dead bodies, however, attracted millions of flies. "The flies," Corporal Howard recalled years later. "I can still remember the flies; their audible hum in the air, their flitting movements and cloud-like cover, their pestering presence on your clothes, skin, food and on anything and everything you saw. Flitting from the dead bodies on the streets and then to you, was not the most desirous of sanitary conditions. . . . You learned to eat with one hand and constantly wave the other hand and with luck you could get the food into your mouth before it was covered with flies. If you drank anything, you had to look to see if the container was clear of flies or the fluid didn't contain any that had drowned."[40]

In order to help the tankers spot targets of opportunities, Company A, 754th TB set up a number of observation posts in vacated buildings. Ordered not to fire at the Japanese for fear of giving away their positions, the observers only could watch in horror as the enemy soldiers committed numerous act of atrocity on Manila's helpless citizens. Wrote Corporal Howard, "We had to watch while the Japanese soldiers dragged out nuns in their habits and tied them to the flagpole and proceeded to whip them. We had to endure the sight of a group of Japanese soldiers drag Filipino women into the open and rape them. It was hard to hold fire and observe the events. There was no way to describe the emotion of hate of the Japanese and the anguish of not being able to help the women, but orders were orders and we had to comply."[41]

Finally, on February 13, the 1st and 2nd Platoon tanks of Company A, 754th TB crossed the Pasig River on a Bailey bridge and began fighting their way into the heart of Manila's downtown district. "Tanks were used to give protection to the infantry elements advancing toward these heavily fortified buildings," explained

Corporal Howard. "In many instances the 75mm guns had no effect against the thickest stone or reinforced concrete walls of these imposing structures."[42]

The two tank platoons reinforced the 37th IDiv, which had captured a number of buildings, including the two-story Manila police station. A spirited counterattack by the Japanese, however, pushed the infantry out of the police station and forced them to call for tanks. "Under cover of hundreds of rounds from our tanks," reported Corporal Howard, "the infantry . . . were once more in the police station. . . . We lost three tanks in front of the police station." It would take a few more days to capture the building.[43]

The street fighting continued on February 14 when four tanks from the 1st Platoon, Company A, 754th TB assisted in an assault against a downtown structure known as the German Building. After shelling the building for some time, the tanks and infantry moved forward but one tank unexpectedly rolled over a land mine and another was hit with a Molotov cocktail, injuring four crewmen. The infantry surged ahead and managed to enter the German Building but they could not hold it and were soon pushed out. For the next few hours, the two remaining tanks shelled the structure until they ran out of ammunition and were forced to retire.[44]

Throughout February 14, 15 and 16, the Shermans of Company A, 754th TB continued to assist the 37th IDiv in its assaults on Manila's fortified buildings. On February 15, a Japanese airplane dropped a single bomb on the 754th TB command post, killing four men, including the commanding officer of Company A, Capt. Coy "Snake" Rogers, and wounding seven more. On the afternoon of February 16, Company B, 754th TB, which had come to Manila after fighting in the hills around Clark Field, relieved the exhausted tankers of Company A.[45]

As the tanks and men of Company A, 754th TB headed back north across the Pasig River toward a bivouac area, Corporal Howard counted the casualties. "We had started out with seventeen tanks in this company at the time of the landing," he noted, "but now we had eleven that would run but only enough men to man eight using the cooks, mechanics and administrators. We would recruit infantrymen to fill positions of the machine gunner or loader for the 75mm cannon. Although we could never get a volunteer to come back a second time, we were able to get men if we resorted to direct orders from the infantry officers."[46]

That same date, February 16, the Assault Gun Platoon of the 716th TB arrived in Manila. "Because it had the only 105mm guns mounted in the M4 tank," noted the battalion historian, "the Assault Gun Platoon . . . received orders . . . to make an immediate forced march . . . to Manila." Attached to the 37th IDiv, the platoon was told to "make close-in direct assault[s] on the larger fortified buildings, and to knock out pillboxes holding up infantry movements."[47]

While the 716th TB Assault Gun Platoon was getting oriented, the Shermans of Company B, 754th TB continued the fighting through the streets of Manila. On February 17 the 37th IDiv moved farther into the grounds of the University of the Philippines, fighting in the medical and science buildings. "The tanks offered direct fire support to the infantry assault," explained the 754th TB historian. "Two tanks and one recovery vehicle were damaged by enemy antitank mines and one tank was slightly damaged by 47mm antitank gun fire."[48]

On February 18, regiments of the 37th IDiv were shifted around to bring fresh troops to the forefront. After a heavy bombardment by the tanks of Company B, 754th TB and a number of tank destroyers, the fresh infantrymen rushed into the buildings of Santa Teresita College and eliminated the last of the Japanese defenders. And, although the new soldiers were able to fight their way into the police station once again, they still could not hold the building and pulled out before nightfall.[49]

Throughout the next few days the 37th IDiv and the tanks of Company B, 754th TB continued their fight in downtown Manila. The nurses' dormitory at the University of the Philippines was overrun on February 19 after which the tanks moved on to shell City Hall and San Pablo Church and Convent, located two blocks north of the Manila police station. The police station, the church, and the convent were all subjected to a devastating fire from the Sherman tanks, the assault guns, some 105mm SPMs, and various artillery pieces before the infantry rushed the three buildings in the afternoon. Although the church and convent were quickly overrun, the Japanese continued to hold out in the two-story police station, causing the infantry to pull back once again. Finally, on February 20, after more tank and artillery fire pounded the building, the American infantrymen entered the nearly demolished building and cleared out the last Japanese defender.[50]

Throughout February 20 and 21 the American infantry and tanks continued to fight their way through the buildings of the University of the Philippines and the downtown district of Manila. At the same time, the 1st CDiv and the tanks of Company B, 44th TB were cleaning out the southern half of Manila.[51]

The 1st CDiv and Company B, 44th TB began their drive toward Manila Bay on February 14, advancing 700 yards from the Santa Ana district on the southeast side of the city and knocking out two mortars, four machine guns, and numerous bunkers. Although one tank hit a land mine, it quickly was repaired and put back into action. On February 15, although the tanks fought their way across Manila's main north–south thoroughfare, Taft Avenue, and reached Manila Bay, the supporting cavalrymen were held up at numerous Japanese strong points, including Rizal baseball stadium. The next day, three tanks "blasted and battered their way through a cement wall on the east side of the [ball] park, [and] got into the playing field to support the cavalrymen inside," noted historian Robert Ross Smith. By 4:30 P.M., the entire stadium was under American control.[52]

After mopping up the area immediately around the baseball stadium, the 1st CDiv and Company B, 44th TB drove north along Manila Bay on February 19 to join the 37th IDiv and the Assault Gun Platoon of the 716th TB in an attack against the office and residence of the U.S. high commissioner to the Philippines, located along Manila Bay. In the ensuing engagement, two tanks were destroyed, one by antitank fire and one by a Molotov cocktail, and one tank officer was killed. The next morning, after a spirited attack, the cavalrymen successfully overran any remaining Japanese defenders.[53]

With the commissioner's building in American hands, the Company B Shermans and the cavalry troopers moved north. After the tanks knocked out "two forty-foot concrete bunkers and pillboxes," the cavalrymen overran the Army–Navy Club

44th TB and the 1st Cavalry Division troops on the outskirts of Manila. US ARMY

and the Elk's Club buildings. "The third platoon," wrote the 44th TB historian, "lost one tank when it pulled up to a building supposedly occupied by friendly troops and received two satchel charges." Continuing north, the tanks and cavalrymen drove across Burnham Green Park toward the five-story Manila Hotel, which had been the peacetime residence of General MacArthur and his family. Noted the 44th TB historian, "On February 20 this company fired [on] the Manila Hotel after very heavy street fighting."[54]

While the cavalrymen were hugging the shore of Manila Bay, the 37th IDiv troops and the Assault Gun Platoon of the 716th TB were moving up on their right. On February 19, the heavily armed tanks attacked a Manila prison that was being used as an enemy strongpoint. Blasting away at a side wall with their heavy 105mm guns, the six assault tanks routed out about seventy Japanese marines, who were subsequently cut down by infantry fire. The next day, the assault guns pushed almost all of the way to the Pasig River, where they shelled the Manila water works administration building and destroyed three Japanese pillboxes and two machine gun positions. Next, the 105mm M4 Shermans turned their heavy guns around to fire on City Hall.[55]

On February 21, the hard-fighting Shermans of Company B, 44th TB were relieved by the 2nd and 3rd Platoon Shermans of Company A, 754th TB. Before leaving, however, the 44th TB Shermans shelled the Manila Hotel, and the obser-

44th TB entering Rizal Baseball Stadium, south of Manila. US ARMY.

vatory building and University Hall on the grounds of the University of the Philippines. At the same time, the 2nd Platoon tanks of Company A, 754th TB split into two sections and bombarded the Philippine General Hospital and some of the university buildings.[56]

While fighting for the university, Corporal Howard (Company A/754th TB) recalled, "Our goal was to bury [the Japanese] alive if at all possible, use HE shells and ricochet them off the interior walls to spread shrapnel throughout the buildings. Our tanks would shell, move forward, fire again, move forward, fire again, and repeat, repeat, repeat. The tanks would strafe with machine-gun fire while the infantry would assault, evacuate the wounded, and try again to gain an advantage."[57]

Elsewhere, the Assault Gun Platoon of the 716th TB spent the better part of February 21 battering a huge hole in the side of City Hall. Recorded the 716th TB historian, "After two hours of concentrated fire, they blasted a fifteen-foot hole through the east wing of the building and out into the courtyard." Although the infantry surged into the building, the fanatical Japanese defenders quickly threw them out. "The tanks spent the balance of the day," reported the tank historian, "working over strategic parts of the building and destroying the tower to prevent its use as an observation point."[58]

The attack on City Hall continued on February 22 with the assault tanks moving to a position where they could fire on the northeast corner of the building. Noted the 716th TB historian, "Tremendous fire was placed on the target until the entire northeast corner of the four-story building collapsed. . . . The infantry was able to enter, and after six hours of intense room to room combat, secured the City Hall."[59]

That same day, Company B, 44th TB finally retired from the downtown area and pulled back to a bivouac area a few miles north of the Manila reservoir. Replacing the 44th TB Shermans, the 3rd Platoon mediums of Company A, 754th TB moved north toward the Manila Hotel. After receiving harassing fire from a few Japanese machine-gun crews hidden inside a half-sunken ship in Manila Bay, the tankers turned their guns on the ship and quickly set it on fire. Later, after the defenders inside the Manila Hotel were eliminated, the tanks were used to evacuate wounded cavalrymen from in front of the hotel.[60]

By the time the Manila Hotel was captured, the Japanese had been pushed into a pocket of roughly 2,000 square yards consisting of the Intramuros, the south port area, and the legislative, finance, and agriculture buildings just south of the Intramuros. Electing to tackle the old walled city first, artillery and mortars had begun pounding the area on February 17, eventually blasting two large fifty-foot wide breaches through the strong, thick east wall. With two clean breaches blasted through the outer wall, the American artillery rained down a heavy barrage on February 23 in preparation for the final assault.[61]

At 8:20 A.M. on February 23, assault boats carrying the 129th IReg, 37th IDiv left the north bank of the Pasig River while the 3rd Platoon Shermans of Company B, 754th TB fired over their heads into the heart of the Intramuros, firing "continuously at a rate of two rounds per minute per tank." Landing unopposed on the opposite shore, where the Intramuros butted up against the river and was protected only by a low stone seawall, the 129th IReg troops poured into the old walled city while the 145th IReg came through one of the breaches.

As the American infantrymen fanned out through the rubble-strewn streets they met almost no opposition. Eventually, they opened some sealed gates on the east wall to allow some self-propelled guns and the assault tanks from the 716th TB to enter the Intramuros. "In the demolished walled city," commented the 716th TB historian, "the narrow streets were deeply packed with rubble, making impossible tank maneuver and detection of mines." As the tanks and infantry advanced, the Japanese slowly began to recover from the shock of the preliminary artillery barrage. "In the close-in fighting the tanks were forced to use machine guns to knock out hastily prepared positions in crumbling buildings," continued the 716th TB historian. "The heavy guns were used only on strong street intersections."[62]

By noon, the 129th IReg reached the west wall and then spread out north and south, eventually clearing out a strong Japanese position in the northwest corner of the walled city. To the south, the 145th IReg made good progress until it came upon almost 3,000 civilian hostages streaming from San Augustin and Del Monico churches, near the southwest corner of the Intramuros. Released by the Japanese, the civilians were quickly escorted from the area before the American infantrymen, supported by the tanks of the 3rd Platoon, Company B, 754th TB, moved against the two churches. Unable to eliminate the defenders before nightfall, the 145th IReg halted about "two blocks short of the west wall and four short of the southwest corner of the Intramuros."[63]

While the Intramuros assault was taking place, elements of the 37th IDiv, along with the 1st Platoon tanks of Company B, 754th TB, started an attack against the finance building and the legislative building, which overlooked the southeast corner of the Intramuros and allowed the Japanese to fire down into the walled city. At the same time, the 1st CDiv troopers, assisted by the M4 Shermans of Company A, 754th TB, began assaulting the south port area immediately west of the Intramuros.[64]

On February 24, the 145th IReg, assisted by the 3rd Platoon Shermans of Company B, 754th TB and the Assault Gun Platoon, 716th TB, quickly eliminated the Japanese inside San Augustin and Del Monico Churches. By 10:30 A.M. the tanks and soldiers were assaulting the last enemy strongpoint in the walled city, the aquarium, located in a bastion near the center of the south wall. Unable to take the building by frontal assault, the infantrymen discovered an ancient tunnel connecting the bastion to the main section of the Intramuros and came up from below the Japanese. By 5:30 P.M. the last organized resistance inside the Intramuros had been eliminated.[65]

On that same date, Company A, 754th TB and the 1st CDiv cleared out the last Japanese defender in the south port area and were able to advance all the way to the south bank of the Pasig River. Southeast of the Intramuros, the 1st and 2nd Platoon tanks of Company B, 754th TB helped elements of both the 37th IDiv and the 1st CDiv move closer to the finance, legislative, and agriculture buildings. Over the next six days, the tanks of Companies A and B, 754th TB, and the Assault Gun Platoon, 716th TB fired hundreds of rounds into the three buildings. Fighting against a fanatical enemy, the American tanks and artillery blasted the buildings day after day, while the infantry made numerous assaults. On February 28, the legislative building finally fell, and the attackers turned toward the agriculture building.[66]

Working in support of an attack by the 1st CDiv on the five-story agriculture building, the Shermans of Company A, 754th TB alternated their fire with that of a battery of 155mm artillery pieces. On February 28, the artillery fired for one hour, the tanks for the next hour, and then the artillery for a third. Directing their shells against the first floor, the combined fire caused the building to collapse onto itself. Assuming that most of the Japanese defenders were now dead, the cavalrymen moved into the rubble.

Unfortunately, the troopers found clusters of Japanese defenders still alive in the northwest and southeast corners of the building. "A tank mounting a flamethrower thereupon came forward to reduce a pillbox at the southeast corner of the building," wrote historian Smith, "while other tanks lumbered forward to cover all sides of the structure with point-blank 75mm fire." By sunset, the two pockets had been eliminated and on March 1, after the remaining Japanese inside the basement of the agriculture building refused to surrender, the 1st CDiv burned them out with demolition charges and gasoline.[67]

The last bastion of Japanese resistance in Manila, the finance building, was blasted by artillery, SPMs, tank destroyers, and the Sherman tanks of Company B, 754th TB from February 28 until March 2. On March 2, the 37th IDiv was preparing to make a final assault upon the building when three Japanese soldiers came out bearing a white flag. After the American infantrymen relaxed their guard, the enemy soldiers still inside the building opened fire, wounding a number of Americans. "Completely disgusted," noted historian Smith, "the infantry withdrew for a final artillery and tank barrage."[68]

With unaccustomed fury, the artillerymen and tankers blasted huge holes through the five-story structure. "After the tanks [and artillery] had finished their preliminary barrage," said the 754th TB historian, "the infantry was able to enter the building and to capture it." By early March 3, every last defender inside the finance building was dead. "This marked the end of all organized resistance in the city of Manila," proclaimed the 754th TB historian, "and was the last date for the employment of tanks in this area." Late on March 3, 1945, the shattered, rubble-strewn city of Manila was declared secure. After the death of 1,010 Americans, 16,000 Japanese, and an estimated 100,000 Filipino civilians, and the wounding of more than 5,000 Americans, the battle of Manila was finally over.[69]

CHAPTER TWENTY-SEVEN

Corregidor
and Southern Luzon

Even before General MacArthur sent the Flying Columns toward Manila, he made a move to seize Manila Bay, which would enable him to switch his supply lines from Lingayen Gulf. In order to secure the bay, however, MacArthur first had to seize control of Manila, the Bataan peninsula, and the island fortress of Corregidor. On January 29, nearly 35,000 American troops from the 38th IDiv and from the 34th IReg, 24th IDiv landed unopposed just above the Bataan peninsula. Rushed over from Leyte, the XI Corps troops quickly isolated Bataan and in only three weeks overran the entire peninsula and cleared out all organized Japanese resistance.[1]

With Bataan in American hands again, General MacArthur turned toward Corregidor. Shaped like a huge tadpole, the bulbous head of Corregidor pointed west toward the mouth of Manila Bay, while the tail pointed east to Manila. On February 16, the 503rd Parachute Regimental Combat Team (RCT) was air dropped on the high, mountainous head of the island while a battalion of the 34th IReg, 24th IDiv made an amphibious landing on the south side, where the tail met the head. Landing with the infantrymen was the 603rd Independent Tank Company (TCo), brought over from Leyte.[2]

Although the Sherman tanks met little opposition as they came ashore, they stumbled into a hidden Japanese minefield once they reached the beach. In quick succession one M4 Sherman tank and one M7 SPM were destroyed.[3]

While the paratroopers were spreading out on the tadpole's head, the infantrymen and tanks secured the city of San Jose at the base of the head. On February 17, one Sherman tank and two M7 SPMs ran a gauntlet of Japanese fire to bring blood plasma and supplies to the paratroopers. Noted historian General E.M. Flanagan Jr., "They gunned their behemoths past uncleared caves and tunnels from which the Japanese fired a steady beat of small arms against the hulls of the vehicles. Fortunately, the Japanese along that stretch of road had no antitank weapons."

After reaching the paratroopers, the armored crews discovered the paratroopers were dangerously low on water. After evacuating a few seriously wounded troopers down to the beachhead, the tank and the two SPMs turned around and carried water back up to the paratroopers. Whenever the opportunity presented itself, the three vehicles fired "point-blank into a cave or tunnel opening." When the three vehicles finally returned from their second round-trip, someone tried to count the bullet marks on the hulls of the vehicles. "After the count got to two hundred," Flanagan wrote, "he gave up."[4]

With the help of airplanes and ships, the Americans heavily bombed segments of Corregidor before moving the foot soldiers forward. While the paratroopers fought on the head of Corregidor, the infantrymen and the tanks worked to contain the Japanese in Malinta tunnel, just east of San Jose, and to eliminate the defenders on the tail of the island. By February 23, the 503rd Parachute RCT had conquered the mountainous head of Corregidor and turned eastward to help clean out the rest of the island. Two days later, the 34th IReg, 24th IDiv was ordered to Mindoro Island in the southern Philippines. When they left, the 603rd TCo was turned over to the paratroopers.[5]

Working with the paratroopers, the medium tanks helped to systematically reduce enemy strongpoints on Corregidor's narrowing tail. By February 26, the Malinta tunnels had been cleared and the Americans had advanced to within 1,500 yards of the end of Corregidor, where a large number of Japanese were trapped in a tunnel under a small ridge. With paratroopers surrounding the ridgeline, two M4 tanks moved up to the front of the tunnel to blast the entrance. Historian Flanagan described what happened next:

> At about 1105, one of the tanks had fired its main tank gun down into the sloping revetted entrance into the . . . tunnel. Occurring almost simultaneously with the explosion of that shell against the door of the tunnel, a violent underground detonation lifted the top off the ridge . . .
>
> The explosion sent Japanese and paratroopers bodies, arms, legs, and torsos flying into the air. The entire island was shaken as if an earthquake had struck. Both of the 35-ton tanks were tossed into the air like toys, and one of them tumbled end over end for nearly fifty feet down the ridge, trapping the crew inside. Incredibly, rescuers later found that one man inside was still alive. They borrowed an acetylene torch from a Seventh Fleet destroyer and cut open the tank to save him.

The unexpected explosion, probably set off by the entrapped Japanese, killed fifty-four Americans and wounded 145 more.[6]

Over the next six days, the paratroopers eliminated all remaining Japanese opposition on Corregidor. On March 2, the island fortress was declared secure and General MacArthur arrived to once again raise the American flag over "The Rock."[7]

On February 13, Company A, 44th TB was assigned to the 11th AbnDiv, which had been moving toward Manila from the south. When the 1st CDiv and the 37th

IDiv swung around Manila and encircled the city, the 11th AbnDiv and the Company A tanks had been pinched out of line. Turning south, the tanks and infantry traveled down the west coast of Laguna de Bay, a huge three-pronged lake only a few miles southeast of Manila. Noted the 44th TB historian, "The fighting [around this area] was characterized by the open rolling terrain, Japs dug-in in well prepared defenses with artillery, 47mm AT guns, 6-inch mortars and the ever present fanatical Jap with demolition charges or Molotov cocktails." During nine days of action, Company A killed more than 250 Japanese soldiers and knocked out countless bunkers and caves. In the process, the company had only three tanks damaged. On February 23, the tanks moved to Manila Bay for a week of rest.[8]

Although the area immediately around Manila was under American control by the middle of February, General MacArthur and his staff knew the city would never be secure until the rolling hills east of Manila were in American hands. On February 20, XIV Corps began a series of advances into the rough terrain to secure the Wawa dam on the Angat River and the Ipo dam on the Marikina River, both of which supplied water to Manila.

In describing the area over which much of the action would take place, historian Dale Andradé wrote, "Here the coastal plains gave way to rolling mountains

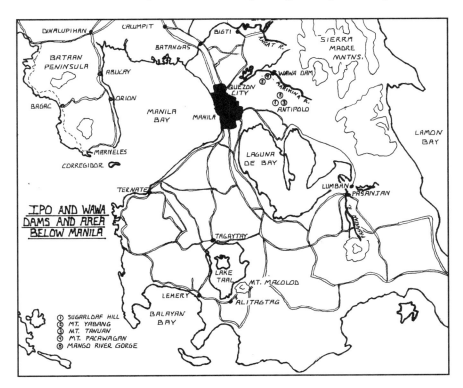

Ipo and Wawa Dams and Area below Manila

and plunging valleys carved by rivers flowing toward the sea. . . . Enemy defensive positions were strung out along a thin line about thirty miles long running from the Ipo dam in the north to the town of Antipolo in the south. The Japanese positions . . . commanded all the high ground east of Manila."[9]

On the afternoon of February 20, the 6th IDiv, aided by the M4 medium tanks of Company C, 44th TB, began moving eastward. The tanks remained in an area northeast of Manila until March 15, aiding in mopping up operations and in attacks against a Japanese defense line about five miles east of the city. In addition to supporting the advancing infantry whenever possible, the tanks fired more than fifty missions in support of the artillery, sometimes at ranges of over 10,000 yards. On March 15, Company C was attached to the 43rd IDiv, which was operating a little more to the south.[10]

Another armored unit to see action east of Manila was the Assault Gun Platoon, 44th TB, which helped establish roadblocks along the eastern approaches to Manila around March 1. On March 4, the 105mm M4 Shermans and infantry were moving eastward on a narrow road when they came under attack. According to the 44th TB historian, "[The] tanks drew 37mm antitank fire which was returned. A Jap satchel charge disabled one of the tanks and it was abandoned. A direct hit on the turret of [another] tank killed the tank commander and the tank was set on fire by Jap white phosphorus grenades." Added another historian, "Nine men were either wounded or suffered burns."

During the action, PFC Deno A. Tufares distinguished himself by going to the rescue of a fellow tanker. According to an Army historian, "[Tufares] was

A composite hull M4 Sherman sits in a firing position just east of Manila on Luzon Island, Spring 1945. US ARMY

loader in the second of two tanks advancing along a curving mountain road. Anti-tank fire hit the leading tank, killing its commander and seriously wounding the gunner." A few seconds later Private Tufares' tank was disabled by a satchel charge. The Army historian wrote, "Tufares was about to crawl to safety, when he noticed the wounded gunner of the lead tank sprawled helplessly in the middle of the road. [Tufares] hurried to his side, despite the vicious zinging of bullets hitting all around, and began to drag his injured companion toward the rear. . . . Inching his way back, [Tufares] was just a few feet short of cover when a Japanese [grenade] rolled a few feet away. Almost instinctively he threw himself upon the wounded man, making a shield of his body. The explosion injured Tufares painfully, but he was still able to drag his unconscious burden back to safety." For his unselfish heroism, Private Tufares was awarded a Silver Star.[11]

The next day, March 5, the Assault Gun Platoon, 44th TB and the cavalrymen headed for the barrio of Antipolo. This time, the tanks blew up bunkers and caves and suffered no damage to themselves. On March 9, however, as the tanks moved forward again, one assault tank rolled over a land mine and caught fire. After two more days of futile fighting with progress measured in yards, the Assault Gun Platoon was recalled to the 44th TB bivouac area at Quezon City. One day later, on March 12, the Americans entered the shattered, abandoned town of Antipolo.[12]

On March 1, while the Assault Gun Platoon was fighting to the east of Manila, one platoon of Shermans from Company A, 44th TB, which was still attached to the 11th AbnDiv, moved south along Manila Bay to support the paratroopers in an attack on the town of Ternate. On March 2, the tanks and a battery of artillery shelled the town for some time prior to the attack. Although the Japanese defenders had buried a number of naval depth charges around Ternate, the tanks managed to avoid the obstacles and overcome a heavy volume of small-arms fire to help capture the town before nightfall.[13]

For four days all of Company A, 44th TB was employed in mopping up around Ternate and then on March 6, the entire company moved southeast, to Tagaytay, a barrio near the northwest corner of Lake Taal. Over the next two weeks, the Company A Shermans supported the 11th AbnDiv troops in the mountainous terrain "overcoming mine fields, 20mm, 40mm, heavy artillery, mortars, machine guns and numerous Jap infantrymen." By March 21, the combined arms had captured the barrio of Lemery, on Balayan Bay on the west coast, and Alitagtag at the bottom of Lake Taal. With Alitagtag in the paratroopers' hands, the reinforced tank platoon retired back to the bivouac area of Company A, 44th TB, which had been set up near Tagaytay.[14]

Shortly after the Assault Gun Platoon/44th TB pulled out of Antipolo on March 11, it was replaced by the Shermans of Company C, 44th TB, where they were attached to the 43rd IDiv. On March 16, the 3rd Platoon was sent about two miles to the southeast to support an infantry attack against Benchmark 7 Hill. According to the 44th TB historian, "This attack was the best coordinated attack that this company has ever participated in, the result being that the enemy was eliminated in short order."[15]

On March 17, the medium tanks of Companies A and B, 754th TB arrived in Antipolo to provide further support to the 43rd IDiv. Noted Corporal Howard of Company A, "The problem with being a bastard battalion is you're available to anyone with a need for your services. It seems the Japanese are acting up in the [area east of Manila] . . . [and] are controlling the water supply for the whole Manila area." In terrain that was deemed "unfavorable but passable," the tanks did whatever they could to assist the infantry. "Because of the terrain," Howard wrote, "mobile artillery is needed, so we have a whole new role to play in this crazy war."[16]

On March 19, Company B, 754th TB helped the infantry grab some high ground in front of Sugarloaf Hill, about three miles northeast of Antipolo. Because of the rough terrain of the hill itself, the tanks were unable to advance with the infantry but continued to give battery support. While moving into position, the tanks had to pass by a number of Japanese-held caves and received heavy small-arms fire. "Once you get in you have to fight your way out," commented Corporal Howard, who also noted that the tanks traveled the road with the turrets facing to the rear, hoping to blast the Japanese caves as they raced past. Unable to get close tank support, the infantry did not capture Sugarloaf Hill until March 27.[17]

On March 21, the Company A Shermans delivered a heavy "artillery barrage" against Mount Tanuan, another promontory just south of Sugarloaf Hill. "The crews' practice paid off," Corporal Howard wrote, "as they were capable of putting the fifth shell in the air before the first one hit and detonated on the side of the mountain. The infantry officers, who were acting as observers, thought the tanks were equipped with automatic cannons."[18]

When the barrage was over, the tanks and infantry started a final assault on Mount Tanuan. "When the advance began," commented the 754th TB historian, "the tanks assisted by firing in close support of our troops. In general, the target area was from twenty to fifty yards in front of the advancing infantry. This was our first experience in delivering fire in such close support of advancing infantry-men. The operation was very successful and the infantry was able to take and secure the objective, at which time the tanks were withdrawn."[19]

On March 22, a Company B, 754th TB Sherman "was completely destroyed by an electrically controlled mine" as it was moving up to support an attack against Mount Yabang, northeast of Sugarloaf. Although the area had been in American hands for days, Japanese infiltrators had planted the mine during the night. "In the vicinity we discovered a storage battery, with two wires leading to the scene of the explosion," noted the 754th TB historian.[20]

While the mediums of Companies A and B, 754th TB were attacking to the east and northeast, Company C, 44th TB and elements of the 43rd IDiv were pushing toward the barrio of Teresa, about two miles southeast of Antipolo. Although hampered by rough terrain, the tanks alone were credited with destroying one 77mm mountain gun, one 37mm antitank gun, three 20mm antiaircraft guns, three 120mm mortars, two Japanese rocket launchers, and seventy-nine Japanese soldiers.[21]

Limited by the terrible terrain, the commanding officer of the 43rd IDiv decided to send Company C, 44th TB and Company B, 754th TB back to Quezon City and keep only Company A, 754th TB in the watershed area. Noted Corporal Howard, "Terrain is still limiting the ability of the tanks for any quick response support of the infantry. We are in an area now where tanks could be used only as mobile artillery support."[22]

Throughout the rest of March, Company A, 754th TB remained in division reserve for the 43rd IDiv as the infantry fought their way to the east coast of Luzon, near Lamon Bay and Laguna de Bay. "The rapid advance of the infantry against decreasing resistance produced no situation where the use of tanks was desired," wrote the 754th TB historian. Added Corporal Howard, "The tanks progressed as far as the terrain allowed and the trails ran out . . . It was terrain for mortars, grenades, and plodding infantry assaults, not tanks." By April 5, the infantry had worked its way around the northwestern point of Laguna de Bay and had moved into the narrow strip of land between Laguna de Bay and Lamon Bay.[23]

On April 5, while the 1st Platoon Shermans of Company A were moving forward to assist the infantry in an attack against Lumban, they ran into an ambush. "The ambush was comprised of one 47mm cannon and a number of machine guns," recalled Corporal Howard. "After receiving glancing hits, No. 1 and No. 2 tanks neutralized the Japanese positions by returning 75mm and 30 caliber machine gun fire." After destroying the Japanese positions, the tanks moved on to Lumban, where they found the American infantry being held up by intense fire coming from a schoolhouse.

Immediately, all four Shermans began shelling the schoolhouse, relieving the infantry so they could sweep through the rest of Lumban. As night approached, the tanks withdrew and set up a perimeter just outside of town. The next morning, the tanks returned and shelled the schoolhouse again. By 10:30 A.M., "all resistance was eliminated" and the infantry were able to occupy the building.[24]

On April 6, an element of the 43rd IDiv made contact with the 1st CDiv near the town of Pagsanjan. A juncture had been made between XI Corps and XIV Corps. Near 7:00 P.M. on April 7, four tanks from the 2nd Platoon, Company A, 754th TB moved up to the Pagsanjan River Bridge to act as bridge guard. For the next thirteen days the tanks remained in place, guarding the span against enemy saboteurs, while the rest of Company A, 754th TB remained inactive.[25]

To the north, Company C, 754th TB and the 6th IDiv began attacking north toward the Wawa dam. On April 3, and for the next two weeks tanks supported the attacks by having one platoon assist the artillery while the other two pressed forward with the infantry.[26]

Because of the hard fighting, a provisional brigade was formed to take over on the left flank of the 6th IDiv. Composed of one regimental combat team from the 1st CDiv and one regimental combat team from the 43rd IDiv, supported by the Shermans of Company B, 754th TB, the formation allowed the 6th IDiv to bunch up a bit and give more power in their forward thrusts. With bald-headed

Brig. Gen. Julian W. Cunningham in command the provisional brigade was designated "Baldy Force."[27]

Beginning on April 7, the tanks of Baldy Force participated in a tank–infantry assault along the two-lane graveled Route 52 that led toward the Wawa dam. Although the enemy was "well dug in, in fortified positions and caves," the tanks blasted the positions and "enabled the infantry to secure the high ground above them."[28]

By April 19 the infantry had pushed its way up to Bigti, about four and one-half miles west of the dam. While supporting the 43rd IDiv, the tanks of the 3rd Platoon fired on "houses, caves, and pillboxes" with excellent results. A few days later, Baldy Force was disbanded and the B Company tanks were reassigned to the 43rd IDiv, which was about to start an eastward drive toward the Ipo dam.

By the first week of May 1945, the infantrymen began pushing into the foot-hills of Luzon's Sierra Madre and the tankers discovered their medium tanks could not follow. Around May 11, the light tanks of Company D, 754th TB replaced the mediums and gave assistance to the infantry in an attack on the northern nose of a hilltop about two miles south of the dam. After helping to seize the objective, the light tanks remained in the area until May 13 and then assisted in another drive into an area northeast of the captured hill. Four days later, on May 17, after American planes "delivered the heaviest concentration of napalm ever used in the southwest Pacific," the 43rd IDiv and Filipino guerrillas raced in and seized Ipo dam

Infantry follow an M4 Sherman tank on Luzon, Spring 1945. US ARMY

intact. After weeks of fighting in terrible mountain terrain, the first objective in the Manila watershed area had been captured.[29]

Just south of the Ipo dam region, in the area of the Wawa dam, elements of the 38th IDiv came out from Manila during the middle of April to reinforce or replace the tired, battered 6th IDiv. On April 21, in one of the first missions in support of the 38th IDiv, the 2nd Platoon tanks of Company C, 754th TB assisted the infantry in a combined assault against Mount Pacawagan, one mile west of Wawa dam. After a devastating artillery and mortar barrage, the tanks and infantry moved forward. Within minutes, however, the lead tank rumbled over a hidden land mine and was badly damaged. Fearful of more hidden mines, the four remaining tanks withdrew and provided long-range, indirect fire for the foot soldiers.[30]

The next day, the 3rd Platoon Shermans supported the infantry in an assault near the Mango River Gorge, at the base of Mount Pacawagan. In spite of terrible terrain, the tanks managed to explode three Japanese ammunition dumps and destroy three enemy tanks that had been dug-in as pillboxes. From April 23 to May 3, Company C, 754th TB saw no further action as the infantry moved into ground that was too rough for tanks. On May 3, Company C's Shermans were relieved from duty and went back to the Manila area for maintenance.[31]

On April 23, the medium M4 Shermans of Company A, 754th TB were attached to the 43rd IDiv and rolled into Antipolo. Working on the right flank of the Manila watershed area, roughly seven miles south and slightly east of Wawa dam, the tanks were used mainly for indirect fire support from the ridges above the Wawa valley. Recalled Corporal Howard, "Foxholes were dug, pillboxes were

An infantry–tank patrol on Luzon, Spring 1945. US ARMY

built, and the tanks were dug in and buried to the turrets so that they looked like a 'Maginot' effect. This would eliminate the silhouette of the tanks on the horizon of the ridge."[32]

On May 2, the Japanese staged a last-ditch desperate attack against the American position across the ridge. "The day started as though normal, then deteriorated," recalled Corporal Howard. "Enemy fire commenced on our positions to button down all of our movements. [The] Japanese then made a frontal assault and were met with a hail of fire. Our 75mm guns were loaded with canister shot which brutalized them." In addition to the fire from the tanks and infantry, the Japanese faced air attacks from American Douglas A-20 Havoc fighter-bombers. "The first wave of A-20s came in from our rear at treetop level and dropped napalm and explosive bombs on the Japanese positions," wrote Howard. "On the second sweep across the lines, the A-20s opened up with their strafing too soon and strafed our lines as well as the enemies. All we could see were tracers tearing through the trees and ricocheting in all directions just over our heads." Fortunately, there were no American casualties and the Japanese attack faltered.[33]

Three days later, on May 5, the American ridgeline was declared "stabilized" and Company A, 754th TB shifted from the 43rd IDiv to the 112th Cavalry RCT.[34]

While Company A, 754th TB was engaged at the southern end of the Wawa dam area, the light tanks of Company D, 754th TB moved into the northern sector. As was becoming the norm, when the infantry moved into rough terrain, only the light M5 Stuart tanks could keep up with them. On May 23, the light tanks were attached to the 38th IDiv and moved to the dam. Four days later, when the 38th IDiv began a wide, sweeping move to the north, the light tanks went with them. As reported, the tanks "destroyed three light machine guns, one heavy machine gun, and one ammunition dump."[35]

The next day, May 28, the advance continued, with the light tanks firing on Japanese cave installations and "all possible enemy positions." Although the infantry managed to push through a narrow gorge and capture the dam, the terrain proved impassable to the light tanks and they were unable to follow.[36]

The capture of both the Ipo and Wawa dams happened because of increased pressure by the American troops. As the infantry and tanks began to encircle the dams, the Japanese decided it was best to withdraw and fight another day. However, as historian Andradé pointed out, "Continued pressure forced the [remaining] Japanese to withdraw deep into the Sierra Madre mountains in eastern Luzon where starvation, disease, and guerrilla attacks eventually decimated their ranks during the remainder of the war." The Japanese defenders from the Manila watershed area were never a factor again.[37]

Far south of the Manila watershed area, Company A, 44th TB continued to support the 11th AbnDiv as it pushed below Lake Taal. For two weeks, from March 26 to April 8, the tanks fought in rough terrain near the southeastern edge of Lake Taal and around the coastal town of Batangas. Around April 3, 1945, Company C, 44th TB, which had landed on Luzon as a separate unit and had been fighting with the 6th and 43rd IDivs in the Manila watershed area, joined the parent organization below Laguna de Bay. "[Company C, 44th TB] completed 77 days of consecutive combat duty," noted the 44th TB historian, "which is believed to be a record for armored units in the southwest Pacific." Commented another battalion historian, "Company C . . . came under battalion control for the first time since 23 June 1944."[38]

On April 5, the light tanks of Company D, 44th TB and the Mortar Platoon, 44th TB were assigned to the 1st CDiv for a sweep around the southern end of Laguna de Bay. After moving unopposed completely around the bottom of the bay, one platoon of the light tanks and the Mortar Platoon shot ahead and secured the barrio of Pagsanjan on the southeast corner of the bay "against small arms and automatic weapons fire." The next day, while the Mortar Platoon fired 242 rounds of 81mm ammunition against the nearby ridges, Company D and the cavalrymen moved further northward and eventually completed the link-up with the 43rd IReg of XI Corps.[39]

As the 43rd IDiv mopped up the area on the east side of the bay above Pagsanjan, the 1st CDiv headed east toward Lamon Bay, and eventually southeast toward the Bicol peninsula. Although the light tanks of Company D and the Mortar Platoon from the 44th TB assisted the cavalry wherever possible, they were constantly hampered by almost impassable mountain roads. On April 6, General MacArthur staged another brilliant maneuver and landed a regimental combat team near the southern end of the Bical peninsula. It began sweeping northward while the 1st CDiv swept southward. Near the middle of May, the last Japanese defender was eliminated from the Bical peninsula.[40]

While Company D and the Mortar Platoon, 44th TB were helping the 1st CDiv clear out the area below Laguna de Bay and the Bicol peninsula, the Company B Shermans were asked to lead an assault by the 11th AbnDiv against Brownie Ridge, near Mount Macolod at the southeastern edge of Taal Lake. Noted the 44th TB historian, "[The] attack on Brownie Ridge . . . proved to be one of the bitterest little battles on the island."

"Brownie Ridge," the historian continued, "was a natural defensive position for the enemy and this natural defense of caves and ridges and ravines was augmented by pillboxes, bunkers, trenches and fox holes in depth—in fact, covering the entire ridge." In fact, the Japanese defensive line resembled a series of four steps leading to the top of the ridge. Although the American paratroopers had made repeated attempts to take the ridge, each assault had failed. Finally, the paratroopers decided to make a "tank–infantry–artillery" attack but before the tanks could move forward, Army engineers had to fill in a 100-foot ravine and construct a roadway through a jumble of trees. "This the engineers did courageously in spite of sniper and mortar fire," admired the 44th TB historian.

At 6:30 A.M. on April 18, after a heavy artillery barrage, the tanks started off with the airborne troops close behind. The lead tank raced up the homemade road and onto the first step, where it immediately drew heavy machine-gun and mortar fire. "Another tank reached the ridge and another," wrote the battalion historian, "all of them answering and soon silencing the Jap guns that could be located."

Minutes later, when the paratroopers reached the ridge they added their firepower to the fight.

"For four complete days of continuous fighting," wrote the 44th TB historian, "the tanks and infantry advanced from position to position finally reaching and controlling the ridge." On April 19 alone, seven tanks fired 313 rounds of 75mm and 10,000 rounds of .30-caliber ammunition against enemy positions. "Every possible position that could hold a Jap or a number of Japs was shelled or sprayed with machine-gun fire, thus enabling the infantry to advance and clean-up." By April 21, Brownie Ridge and Mount Macolod were in American hands. In leading the assault, Company B, 44th TB had one man killed and eighteen wounded.[41]

With the capture of the central hill section near Lake Taal and the seizure of the Bicol peninsula, all of southern Luzon was now under American control.

During the first two weeks of May 1945, all of the scattered units of the 44th TB came together below Laguna de Bay. Anticipating the rainy season, a "semi-permanent camp" was constructed with "bamboo raised floors, sides and frames" and tents for "individuals, mess halls, orderly and supply." Although provided with sixteen new medium tanks as "replacements for those lost during the Luzon campaign," the battalion remained inactive throughout the month of May. In preparation for further activity, however, the 44th TB began installing flamethrower units in nine M4 Shermans, "so each medium tank platoon would have one flamethrower."[42]

For most of the 754th TB, which had been fighting in the Manila watershed area, combat did not come to a close until the end of May, after the Ipo and Wawa dams were captured. As Corporal Howard recalled, "Toward the end of May, during the last week, we were relieved from duty and assigned back to XIV Corps. Orders came to break camp and load all tanks and return to . . . Manila. This was the official end of our operations in Luzon against organized Japanese resistance."[43]

Only the Stuart tanks of Company D, 754th TB remained on active duty, helping elements of the 38th IDiv mop up in the mountainous area east of the twin dams. From June 2 until June 18 the light tanks tried to support the advances of the infantry, but discovered that both the weather and the terrain were against them. As the 754th TB historian noted, "Tanks of little use." On June 23, the light tanks were moved up to northern Luzon, where the Japanese were still hanging on.[44]

CHAPTER TWENTY-EIGHT

Northern Luzon

Beginning on February 11, when Company D, 754th TB replaced Company B, 754th TB in the Clark Field/Fort Stotsenburg area, the light Stuart tanks began aiding the 40th IDiv fight for possession of the rolling hills west of the airfield. All along the front, from Bamban in the north to Fort Stotsenburg and Top of the World Hill in the south, the Company D lights moved into the hills and "destroyed or neutralized enemy positions." West of Bamban, the 3rd Platoon led an advance into the hills but when the infantry failed to secure the position, the tanks withdrew. In the south, in an area west of Top of the World Hill, the 1st Platoon used flanking and frontal assaults to push the Japanese back and "occupy the area."[1]

For the next two weeks the M5 Stuart light tanks went wherever the terrain would allow as they helped the infantry root out the Kembu Group. Commented the 754th TB historian, "[With] combined tank–infantry assault[s] our forces succeeded in destroying the enemy positions and securing the objective." In early March, the tanks and infantry had pushed the Japanese into the mountainous terrain far west of Fort Stotsenburg. "Because the terrain was becoming steeper and less accessible to the tanks," wrote the tank historian, "most of the activities of the company were confined to longer range firing at enemy positions."[2]

On March 12, the light tanks were pulled from the Fort Stotsenburg/Bamban area and eventually sent over to Manila. In May, they assisted the 43rd IDiv in the capture of Ipo dam (See Chapter Twenty-Seven) and then, near the end of June, Company D, 754th TB was attached to the 6th IDiv and moved north to help complete the conquest of northern Luzon.[3]

The major geographic features of northern Luzon consisted of the Sierra Madre on the east coast, the Cordillera Central Mountains near the west coast, and the Caraballo Mountains to the south. In between lay the Cagayan Valley. Known as Luzon's rice bowl, the valley provided the Japanese in northern Luzon with most of their food.[4]

To protect this vital area, General Yamashita's own Shobu Group was stationed in a rough triangle from Baguio on the west, to Bambang on the east and Bontoc to the north. In order to reach any one of the three barrios, the Americans would have to pass over narrow, winding roads through mountainous terrain. Defensively, General Yamashita could not have picked a better geographic location. However, he lacked manpower and was uncertain where the Americans would strike first.[5]

While the American XIV Corps was fighting to capture Manila and XI Corps was conquering Bataan, I Corps had begun probing northward. Stretched out from east to west across the length of the island, I Corps covered an area of more than fifty miles. On the left was the 43rd IDiv, in the center was the 32nd IDiv, and on the right was the 25th IDiv.[6]

Assisting I Corps was the 775th TB, which had landed on Luzon on January 11 as a part of the 13th Armored Group and had been held in reserve. On February 7, when the battalion was attached to I Corps, the different companies spread out to cover the entire front. HQ Company and the 3rd Platoon of Company D (the only platoon of Stuarts to have reached the island so far) were in the 32nd IDiv sector. Company A was with the 43rd IDiv near Pozorrubio, Company B was with the 32nd IDiv at Tayug and Company C was with the 25th IDiv at San Jose.[7]

Using captured Japanese intelligence, General Krueger knew that most of the Shobu Group was within the defensive triangle. In order to break the triangle, General Krueger decided capture both Baguio and Bambang. The 25th IDiv would make a demonstration north up Route 5 while the 32nd IDiv would move northeast through a series of three parallel river valleys and over the Villa Verde Trail through the Caraballo Mountains to connect with Route 5 just below Bambang. At the same time, the 33rd IDiv, which only recently had arrived from Leyte, would be on the left and would push up Route 11 toward Baguio.[8]

The first Japanese pocket that had to be eliminated sat among a ridgeline known as Hills 600–1500, which ran north–south from Rosario to Pozorrubio. On February 19, elements of the 33rd IDiv advanced eastward into the mass of hills and within three days managed to capture the northern and central sections of the mass. However, the southern section continued to hold out. Even with the support of the M4 Shermans of Company A, 775th TB, which fired their 75mm guns "directly into caves and gun positions," the 33rd IDiv made little headway against the southern defenders. Although General Krueger had hoped to clear the entire ridgeline in only a few days, the stubborn defenders held out for almost two weeks. By March 4, when the southern section was finally overrun, General Krueger had been forced to alter his other plans of attack.[9]

While a portion of the 33rd IDiv was assaulting the ridgeline, another portion had been trying to get up Route 11. Although Route 11 was an asphalt, two-lane road, it wound through a steep gorge cut by numerous ravines and crossed over nineteen separate bridges, many of the bridges had been destroyed by the Japanese. As historian Smith wrote, "Tactically, the terrain along Route 11 gave every advantage to the defenders. . . . With a relatively small force, the Japanese could hold up the entire 33rd Division almost indefinitely." Having done just that, General Krueger changed plans again.[10]

Under General Krueger's new plans, the 33rd IDiv would act as a holding force, while the 32nd IDiv would advance through the three river valleys and the Villa Verde Trail, and the 25th IDiv would move up Route 5. Both divisions would aim for Santa Fe, where the Villa Verde Trail came in from the southwest and merged with Route 5.[11]

The 25th IDiv, on the far right flank of I Corps, began probing northward out of San Jose on February 24, moving up Route 5 toward the barrio of Puncan, six miles away. With them went the Company C Shermans, the Assault Gun Platoon and the Mortar Platoon of the 775th TB. While the Company C tanks protected the right flank, the assault guns fired indirect fire against Puncan from a range of 3,700 yards. Although the Japanese held firm for a few days, they eventually retreated when some of the infantrymen worked their way around the Japanese left flank and captured the heights above town. On March 2, the flanking infantry moved unimpeded into Puncan.[12]

By the end of February, the 25th IDiv was seven miles north of San Jose and moving steadily up Route 5. In the center, the 32nd IDiv had encountered only light resistance in two of the three river valleys and only moderate resistance along the Villa Verde Trail. However, in the Arboredo River Valley, the 32nd IDiv ran into stiff resistance. On February 28, the 3rd Platoon Shermans of Company B,

The crew of "Dragon Lady," an M4 of Company C/754th TB on Luzon in the Philippines, February 1945. US ARMY

775th TB moved forward to help knock out some Japanese outposts. "One notable achievement was the reduction of a strong point which had held up the infantry advance for over a week," wrote the 775th TB historian. "In reaching their objective, it was necessary to pass through extremely heavy artillery and machine-gun fire over nearly impassable terrain."[13]

At the beginning of March, the Assault Gun Platoon and Headquarters Company were given "a mission of supporting by direct fire the [25th IDiv] assault on the heavily dug-in positions along Highway 5, just north of Puncan." As the battalion historian explained, "This action included a fight with a Jap 105mm gun, emplaced in a cave thirty feet deep in solid rock." Moving steadily ahead, the infantry and tanks were twelve miles north of Puncan on March 8 and were about to enter Balete Pass, which would lead them through the Caraballo Mountains.[14]

On the far left flank, however, the 33rd IDiv, which was supposed to be acting in a holding capacity, had discovered that Route 3, running north up the west coast, was almost completely free of Japanese soldiers. Surprisingly, patrols from the 33rd IDiv had walked unopposed into the barrio of Agoo and almost five miles beyond. When General Krueger learned of this, he changed plans again, deciding to send most of the 33rd IDiv up the west coast and then turn them east to move over secondary roads toward Baguio. The move would begin on March 7.[15]

In the 25th IDiv sector, the terrain stretching from Putlan north to Balete Pass and on to Santa Fe was none too inviting for infantry and almost impassable for tanks. Heavily wooded ravines and ridges bordered each side of Route 5 as it twisted through a narrow mountain gorge. Knowing full well that the Japanese would have the tactical advantage in defending such terrain, the 25th IDiv split its

"Battle Baby," a composite hull M4 of Company B/775th TB, is led up a steep trail by the company commander, Lt. Jack Belts, Villa Verde Trail, Luzon. US ARMY

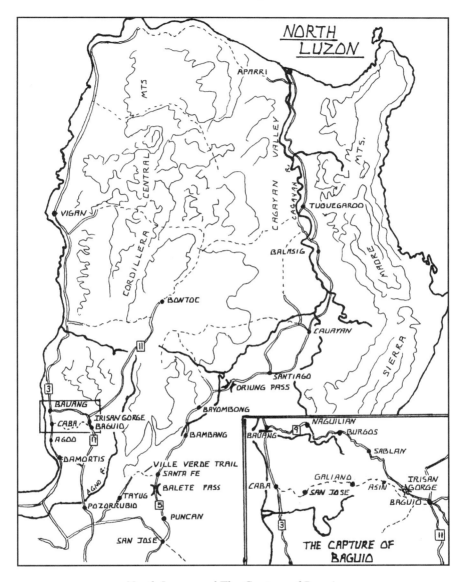

North Luzon and The Capture of Baguio

forces and sent one regiment on a flanking move along a narrow mountain trail while its other two regiments and the 105mm tanks of the Assault Gun Platoon moved forward along Route 5.[16]

"Moving [toward] the opening of Balete Pass . . . [the Assault Gun Platoon] was under daily enemy artillery fire," commented the 775th TB historian. "They remained in firing position covering the junction of Highway 5 with the Villa

Verde Trail . . . at Santa Fe, immediately north of Balete Pass. Missions were assigned almost daily and the platoon was even called upon to fire for the 32nd Infantry Division, then moving eastward across the Villa Verde Trail." At one point, the Assault Gun Platoon fired their guns from "firing positions at Putlan . . . at maximum range, 12,500 yards," a distance of more than seven miles![17]

Far to the northwest, part of the 33rd IDiv and most of Company A, 775th TB continued to exert pressure up Route 11. "The attack to the north[west] on Baguio started the second week of March," recalled the 775th TB historian. "The enemy showed his usual fanaticism and dogged resistance. . . . The drive up [Route 11] was ultimately halted . . . due to efficient enemy demolition of suspension bridges over large rivers and gorges. . . . However, [Company A] saw considerable action along the route of advance before being halted by the previously mentioned obstacles."[18]

While some of the soldiers and tanks were fighting up Route 11, the main body of the 33rd IDiv and a few Company A Shermans and the 2nd Platoon Stuarts of Company D, 775th TB had passed through Agoo on Route 3 to move unopposed into Caba, about seven miles farther north. While some tanks and infantry turned east toward the town of Galiano and eventually Baguio, the rest pushed north toward the barrio of Bauang. For the tanks of Company A, 775th TB, the drive toward Galiano kept them extremely busy. "The three platoons alternated daily, supporting the infantry and affording protection for engineers in building roads," commented the tank battalion historian. "Enemy resistance was intense through the mountainous terrain. By the 30th of March, Galiano was

These 775th TB late composite hull M4s support the 33rd IDiv near Baguio, Luzon on March 8, 1945. US ARMY

entered by the [infantry], being covered by tanks from the 1st and 2nd Platoons. The enemy fled east to Asin."[19]

Bauang, about seven miles north of Caba, fell to the 33rd IDiv and the light tanks of the 2nd Platoon, Company D, 775th TB on March 19. Noted the 775th TB historian, "At Bauang, the platoon leader's tank [was] the first American vehicle to cross the double-span bridge over the Bauang River." The next day, a patrol of foot soldiers met a group of Filipino guerrillas who had been pushing south down Route 3. For all intents and purposes, the entire west coast of Luzon was now in Allied hands.[20]

From Bauang, the 33rd IDiv turned east on Route 9, a two-lane, crushed stone roadway, toward Baguio. "The 2nd Platoon [Shermans of Company A] joined the [infantry] in Bauang and advanced to Naguilian [four miles east]," wrote the 775th TB historian. "Many land mines were encountered while artillery and mortar fire were intense." On March 23, the column entered Naguilian against minor opposition.[21]

While the 33rd IDiv was rapidly advancing up Route 3 and then eastward over a few separate avenues toward Baguio, the 32nd IDiv was still fighting up the Villa Verde Trail. Near the end of the first week in March the infantry and the 3rd Platoon tanks of Company B, 775th TB were stopped by stubborn Japanese defenders at the west end of Salacsac Pass. Because of heavily wooded and steeply mountainous terrain, the tanks were of little use to the infantry. As historian Smith wrote, "In brief, the battle for the Villa Verde Trail became a knockdown, drag-out slug fest. The spectacular could hardly happen—there wasn't room enough."[22]

On March 28, the 1st Platoon Shermans replaced the 3rd Platoon tanks on the Villa Verde Trail. "The [3rd] platoon spent nearly two months in the mountains with their tanks accomplishing unbelievable tasks in climbing 60 degree slopes and building roads," praised the 775th TB historian. Hampered by unseasonable heavy rains and dense fog throughout the first week of April, the 32nd IDiv and the tanks of Company B, 775th TB made very little progress up the Villa Verde Trail until April 17, when the tanks and infantry finally broke through the Salacsac Pass. By that time, the foot soldiers were experiencing low morale and were beginning to show serious signs of battle fatigue.[23]

In the 25th IDiv zone, the infantry, accompanied by the medium tanks of Company C, 775th TB and the 105mm Shermans of the Assault Gun Platoon, were still fighting for control of Balete Pass. Between March 12 and 28, the advance gained only three miles.

In describing the difficulty that was faced by the Company C Shermans, the 775th TB historian wrote:

It was necessary to secure the high ground on each side on [Route 5] before any attempt could be made to go through on the main road. The mountains on either side had some slopes with a gradient as great as 65 degrees up which tanks were bulldozed. . . . Further, these slopes had no paths and it became necessary to 'doze' roads by crashing through the heavy forest vegetation. In order to fire at pillboxes and a gun position, three tanks on one occasion blasted away through the growth making a lane to fire at those positions.

On March 28, the infantry finally captured a prominent feature known as Norton's Knob, which dominated any advance along Route 5. In the final assault, the infantry had been aided by a number of antitank guns and two 105mm Shermans from the Assault Gun Platoon.[24]

Using Norton's Knob as a firebase, the 105mm Shermans pounded away at the Japanese positions closer to Balete Pass, while the 25th IDiv troops pressed forward in a three-pronged attack. Eventually, another flanking move was made to the left, around dominating Mount Myoko. As the infantry pushed around the base of the mountain, they ran into stiff Japanese resistance upon a few hills dubbed The Wart, The Pimple, and Woody Hill. Wrote historian Smith:

By the 15th of April the [infantry] had gained only 250 yards, but had secured The Pimple. This gain had depended in large measure upon tank support. Maneuvering with great difficulty along the slopes of Woody Hill, the tanks—three were now in the forward area—not only provided needed fire support to the infantry but also had a profound psychological effect upon the Japanese, who greeted with consternation the appearance of tanks in such impossible terrain. Not expecting to find tanks along Myoko Ridge, the Japanese had brought no antitank weapons and many Japanese, overcome by surprise as tanks loomed up through the forest, abandoned prepared defenses and fled.[25]

Even with the physical and psychological help of the Sherman tanks of the Assault Gun Platoon and Company C, 775th TB, the 25th IDiv made little progress. From March 28 through April 21, the advance along Route 5 gained only three-quarters of a mile, while the flanking move around Mount Myoko gained one and one-quarter miles. By April 21, the nearest American unit was still almost two miles away from Balete Pass.[26]

Far to the northwest, in the 33rd IDiv sector, the infantry and the accompanying tanks of Companies A and D, 775th TB, continued to push eastward toward Baguio. Although the Americans ran into stiff resistance along other east–west routes, the advance along the Caba–Galiano–Baguio Road and along Route 9 to the north were still going strong. On March 28, the 33rd IDiv captured the town of Burgos on Route 9 and then turned southeast, pushing down toward Baguio from above.[27]

"On March 29," recalled the 775th TB historian, "the [33rd IDiv] started the drive [down] Highway 9 from Burgos toward their objective, Baguio. Elements of [Company D, 775th TB], usually one platoon, were constantly in the point of this advance, clearing the road by fire for the advance of the dismounted infantry. On April 1st, the company was augmented by the attachment of the 2nd Platoon

[Shermans] of Company A, 775th Tank Battalion. Little resistance was encountered until the advance reached Sablan on Highway 9."[28]

During the first week of April, the 37th IDiv replaced the 33rd IDiv along Route 9 and continued pushing southeast toward Baguio. "During the period 11–14 April the [37th IDiv] broke through the Japanese defenses at Sablan in a battle marked by extremely close artillery and medium tank fire," wrote historian Smith.[29]

After taking Sablan, the 37th IDiv and the medium tanks of Company A and Company B (minus the 1st Platoon), and the light tanks of the 1st Platoon of Company D pushed on toward the Irisan Gorge, near where the Caba–Gatiano–Baguio Road made a junction with Route 9. If the 37th IDiv could break through the Japanese defenses at the gorge, they could send some of their troops westward down the Caba–Gatiano–Baguio Road and help elements of the 33rd IDiv.[30]

The 33rd IDiv and the 1st Platoon Shermans of Company A, 775th TB had been fighting along the Caba–Gatiano–Baguio Road since the beginning of April. "It was extremely hazardous, being canalized by high ground on the south and a dry river bed on the north," noted the 775th TB historian. "In addition, vision was limited by heavy shrubs and trees. The tanks fired while on the move and were closely supported by the infantry."

During the nights, after the tanks and infantry had dug in, the tankers employed powerful spotlights to help defend their positions. Recalled the tank battalion historian, "Two men would pull guard and when motion was detected or a noise heard in the tank's assigned zone, the light would be flashed on the area. It temporarily blinded the enemy and made them easy targets for our machine gun and rifle fire."[31]

With the 33rd IDiv stalled at Asin, just two miles west of Route 9, the 37th IDiv attempted to punch its way through the Irisan Gorge and send troops to the

775th TB "Battl'N Virgin," a composite hull M4 of Company B, firing on a Japanese position on Hwy 3 between Banangan and Baguio, April 16, 1945. US ARMY

rescue. On April 17, when a few tanks from the 3rd Platoon, Company B, 775th TB, led the infantry toward the Irisan Gorge bridge, they came under heavy fire where the road made a sharp bend around a hill. "The lead tank rounded a sharp curve and was hit immediately by a round from an antitank gun," reported the 775th TB historian. Almost immediately, the second tank was ordered to back out of the line of fire. The tank battalion historian continued:

> The driver accidentally backed off the road and the tank dropped about 400 feet. The third tank in the column was called up to give support while rescue efforts were made. As blood plasma was being given to one of our wounded, the Japs counterattacked. They bayoneted the wounded, killing him. At the same time two enemy tanks with explosives tied to them, rounded a curve and rammed two of our ranks. A single [American] left in the tank loaded and fired the 75mm gun, knocking out the first enemy tank and then assisted by his platoon leader knocked out the second one.

Facing such determined resistance, the Americans collected their wounded and withdrew to try again.[32]

Over the next few days, the 37th IDiv and their accompanying tank support fought a hard and bitter battle to gain control of the Irisan Gorge. Finally, on April 21, the Japanese were shoved aside and the gorge was taken. Then, while the men and tanks stopped to consolidate their gains, the 33rd IDiv finally began gaining ground along the Caba–Gatiano–Baguio Road.[33]

A bulldozer from the 117th Engineer Battalion is working to remove a composite hull M4, 775th TB, that hit a landmine near Baguio, Luzon, April 22, 1945. US ARMY

Battling eastward toward Baguio, the 33rd IDiv and the tanks of Company A, 775th TB finally forced their way into Asin on April 23. Two days later, the Headquarters section and the 3rd Platoon of Company A, 775th TB rolled into Irisan. The 33rd and 37th IDivs had finally achieved a link-up. The way was now open for a combined assault to the southeast, directly toward Baguio.[34]

Far to the southeast, in the 25th IDiv zone, the foot soldiers, aided by the tanks of Company C, 775th TB, were still trying to force their way through Balete Pass. The 775th TB historian recalled the results of a typical day. "One tank received four direct hits from a 47-mm antitank gun and another received two direct and two glancing hits. A third tank ran over a land mine, which blew the right track apart. A 105mm mortar shell landed to the rear of a fourth tank, destroying both air cleaners. Five pillboxes and one 47mm gun were known to be destroyed during the period and an unknown number of enemy dead were sealed in caves."[35] Stalled by the stubborn defenders and inhospitable ground, the fight for Balete Pass would carry on past the first week in May.

With the 25th IDiv bogged down on Route 5 and the 32nd IDiv stuck on the Villa Verde Trail, it was up to the 33rd and 37th IDivs to capture Baguio. On April 23, as the two American divisions and supporting tanks pressed forward, the 10,000 demoralized Japanese defenders in Baguio began withdrawing in the general direction of Trinidad, about three miles straight north on Route 11.[36]

On April 24, as the 37th IDiv and the tanks of Company B, 775th TB came within sight of Baguio, they encountered the Japanese rear guard. "As the two lead tanks rounded a curve toward the city, an estimated twelve 77mm guns opened up on them," recalled the tank battalion historian. "They moved on, however, after an exchange of rounds and entered the city. There, heavy artillery and machine-gun

775th TB M4 Sherman overlooking Baguio, Luzon Island, on April 27, 1945.

fire was encountered but the first block of the city was secured and the infantry-men came in to support and further secure the city." Added the 775th TB historian quite proudly, "Tanks and crews from this battalion were the first American troops to enter Baguio." Accompanying the Sherman tanks of Company B was a section of light Stuarts from the 1st Platoon of Company D.[37]

Having captured Baguio, the 37th IDiv and the supporting medium tanks of Company B and light tanks of the 1st Platoon of Company D turned north. "A drive was almost immediately commenced toward Trinidad," said the tank battalion historian, "and on April 28, using a three-column attack on that town, moved in with the infantry close behind." Added the 775th TB historian, "The flats south of Trinidad were found to be good light tank country and the [First Platoon] was instrumental in clearing this area of enemy." Having advanced so rapidly, the Americans caught the Japanese in Trinidad by surprise, before they could establish a new line of defense. Once again, the Shobu Group survivors fled to the north and northwest.[38]

On the 25th IDiv front, hard fighting and sweeping flanking moves ultimately paid off as the foot soldiers and the accompanying tanks of Company C, 775th TB finally wrestled control of Balete Pass from the Japanese on May 7. Recalled the 775th TB historian, "In some of the most difficult fighting in the southwest Pacific, over terrain not suited for tank employment, [C] Company slowly pushed with elements of the 25th Division through Balete Pass."[39]

On May 14, the tanks and infantry started a drive to capture Santa Fe, about two and one-half miles above the pass. Almost two weeks later, the town finally fell, but only after most of the Japanese had fled. On May 29, after the tanks and infantry turned west on the Villa Verde Trail from its juncture at Santa Fe, a lead patrol met elements from the 32nd IDiv that had been battling up the trail since early February. The 25th and 32nd IDivs had finally made their link-up.[40]

After the capture of Baguio, the 37th IDiv, which was by far the freshest unit in northern Luzon, "passed through the 25th Infantry Division" and started north up Route 5 toward Appari, on the northern coast of Luzon. Going along would be the Shermans of Company C and the Stuart light tanks of the 3rd Platoon of Company D, 775th TB.[41]

From June 1 through June 4, the 37th IDiv and General Yamashita's Shobu Group fought a "running fight" into the Carabello Mountains at the southern end of Cagayan Valley. "During the first stages of the drive up Highway 5 . . . the light tank platoon and three medium tanks from Company C, were assigned the point of the Division advance," noted the 775th TB historian. Although Japanese artillery and antitank fire destroyed two American tanks and damaged one more, the tankers fought on.[42] The 775th TB historian continued:

> Each day saw the 37th advance ten to twenty miles. It was so rapid that the enemy was helpless and scattered with no semblance of organization. By the 6th of June, Bayombang was taken. On 8 June, heavy opposition was encountered when the tanks leading the column ran into an ambush.

775th TB somewhere on Luzon, Philippines, June 1945. US ARMY

There were no casualties for the 775th tankmen who accounted for a 75mm high-velocity gun and two other field pieces of undetermined caliber. The enemy had thirty-five killed while four surrendered.[43]

On June 8, the Company B Shermans arrived at the front to reinforce the other tanks. Unfortunately, Company B's first encounter in the Carabello Mountains turned into a catastrophe. "At Oriung Pass, en route to Santiago," reported the 775th TB historian, "two disabled tanks with their crews were ambushed by an estimated 200 Japs. A bloody fight ensued but the Company B men were outnumbered and those who were not killed retired. One tank was completely burned out with thermite grenades but the other was salvaged and used in later operations."[44]

In spite of the losses, however, the Americans managed to capture Oriung Pass in three days and by June 13 were on their way again.[45] The 775th TB historian described the advance:

The push through the Oriung Pass completely stunned the enemy as the tanks spearheaded the drive. It was the last natural defense barrier of any importance. With our superior armored might the enemy knew that it would be impossible to stop us on the flat floor of Cagayan Valley. Cordon and Santiago fell on successive days following the penetration of the pass. The advance swung north and met opposition at Balasig, just north of Santiago, but before the day was over our tanks had cracked the defense and moved on to Cauayuan. Only isolated strong points existed from there to Tuguegeraro, important air center in the valley.[46]

On June 23, in a move that was consistent with the daring maneuvers used by the American commanders during the Philippine campaign, the 11th AbnDiv parachuted into the Aparri area. While Filipino guerrillas captured and secured the town, the paratroopers pushed south down Route 5. Around June 26, the paratroopers met the fast-moving column from the 37th IDiv about twenty miles south of Aparri. The whole of Cagayan Valley was now under Allied control.[47]

Although General Yamashita had lost two ends of his defensive triangle with the capture of Baguio and Bambang, and the vital rice fields of the Cagayan Valley, he still had more than 50,000 men on northern Luzon. "Until the end of the war," noted historian Andradé, "Sixth Army forces continued to push Yamashita's men farther into the mountains, taking heavy casualties in the process. . . . By the end of the war, the Japanese were still holding out in the rugged Asin Valley . . . in north central Luzon." For all intents and purposes, however, the fight for northern Luzon ended in June 1945. The Americans and their Filipino allies had won.[48]

On June 30, the Eighth Army relieved the Sixth Army on northern Luzon. Although the Company C M4 Shermans would aid the Eighth Army in its "mopping up activities" in northern Luzon, the rest of the 775th TB were relieved of duty. As the 775th TB historian reported, the tankers were to "commence the prescribed rest and rehabilitation period, preparatory to future operations."[49]

CHAPTER TWENTY-NINE

Clearing the Southern Philippines

While the fighting was still progressing on Luzon, General MacArthur set about to conquer the other islands of the Philippines. After the recapture of Corregidor on March 2, 1945, the northern channel into Manila Bay was open to American shipping, but the Japanese still held three tiny islands in the southern channel. On March 27, MacArthur attempted to seize the first, and largest, island, Caballo.[1]

Only a mile long east–west and about 500 yards wide at its center, Caballo Island was located about a mile south of Corregidor. On the morning of March 27, the 38th IDiv stormed ashore and quickly captured the eastern end of the island. On the western end, the infantry ran into stiff Japanese resistance at Hill 2, where the Japanese were dug into tunnels and mortar pits atop the 250-foot, steeply sided precipice.[2]

On April 2, after several failed attempts to overrun the enemy mortar pits and tunnels, the infantry called for a few tanks from the 754th TB. Three M4 Shermans from the 1st Platoon, Company B were ferried over to Caballo Island but unfortunately, had no better luck. Wrote historian Robert Ross Smith, "From positions near the rim of the pits the tanks were unable to depress their guns sufficiently to do much damage to the Japanese. If the tanks tried to approach from above, they started sliding down Hill 2's slopes into the pits."

The next day, one of the Shermans "fell off a cliff into the ocean and was declared a complete loss." After the loss of that tank, the other two Shermans returned to Manila. Eventually, the infantry dumped 2,500 gallons of diesel fuel into the tunnels and pits and set them on fire. On April 13, Caballo Island was declared secure. One week later, the two smaller islands in the southern channel were also in American hands.[3]

Back on February 6, only three days after the Flying Column entered Manila, General MacArthur set his sights on liberating the islands of the southern Philippines.

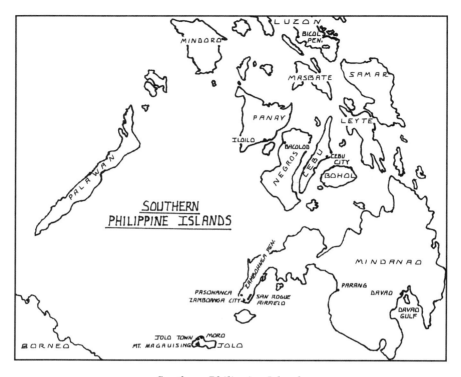

Southern Philippine Islands

The island of Palawan, on the far western side of the Sulu Sea, was seized by a detachment of infantry from the 41st IDiv during the first week of March.[4]

At the same time, the rest of the 41st IDiv was moved to Mindanao and "carried out . . . the seizure of Zamboanga, the large peninsula of Mindanao that extended to the southwest." It was estimated that almost 9,000 Japanese troops defended the peninsula, centered mostly around Zamboanga City on the southern tip. Selected to assist the 41st IDiv was Company A, 716th TB.[5]

After seeing action on Luzon, Company A had been shipped to the island of Mindoro for training alongside the 41st IDiv. Wrote the 716th TB historian, "On 6 March 1945, A Company boarded LCMs and were assembled in an LSD and were ready for the combat operation." On March 10, the M4 Shermans went ashore with the first wave of infantrymen.

Once ashore, the 3rd Platoon and a battalion of infantry from the 163rd IReg turned east and headed toward Zamboanga City. Simultaneously, the 1st Platoon and the 162nd IReg moved to secure the high ground just north of the beachhead. Before the day was over, Company A had "destroyed twelve enemy machine-gun nests and killed approximately sixty Japs."[6]

The next day, the 3rd Platoon spearheaded a drive through Zamboanga City while the 2nd Platoon advanced toward the northeast with the 163rd IReg, overrunning and capturing San Rogue airfield. On this date, the Company A Shermans destroyed "fifteen (15) pillboxes . . . and numerous small arms installations."

Over the next few days, the tanks and infantry continued to push outward from Zamboanga City. As the men and tanks moved forward, a section of a hill in front of them suddenly exploded. "[The Japanese] had mined the hill with large naval torpedoes," noted the 716th TB historian. "The charge was so tremendous that a tank that was sitting 400 yards from the explosion was lifted off the ground." Fortunately, the explosion had been set off prematurely, limiting the number of American casualties.

On March 14, the Company A Shermans split up and moved northwest on parallel roads, destroying a combined twenty-two pillboxes, several small-arms installations, and one 20mm gun. On March 15, the 3rd Platoon assisted in the capture of Pasonanca. "The enemy was driven from the high ground at Pasonanca by heavy, direct fire from tank .30-calibers and 75mm gunfire," said the tank historian.

For the next few days, the 1st Platoon continued to support the infantry attacks around the town of San Rogue while the 2nd and 3rd Platoons supported the troops around Pasonanca. Numerous pillboxes were destroyed and dozens of small-arms emplacements were overrun, all without the loss of a single tank.

On March 17, the 1st Platoon tanks moved up on the southern side of a deep, 500-yard wide valley and began shelling Japanese gun emplacements on the far side. While the infantry worked its way across the floor of the valley, the tanks fired 150 rounds of 75mm shells into the enemy entrenchments. "At the prescribed time," recalled the 716th TB historian, "the tank fire was lifted and the infantry assaulted the Jap positions, overrunning them and seizing the ground."

The assault into the hills north of San Rogue continued on March 18 with the 1st Platoon again assisting in the attacks. At the end of the day, as the tanks were returning to a bivouac area, one of the Shermans ran over a concealed 100-pound aerial bomb buried in the roadway. The resulting explosion blew away the suspension, cracked the motor and blew the bottom of the tank inward, wounding one crewman.[7]

As the infantry pushed farther into the heavily forested interior of the Zamboanga peninsula, it became difficult for the tanks to follow. Recalled historian Smith, "Once American troops entered the peninsula's foothills, tanks could not operate off the bulldozed roads."[8] From March 21 to April 7 the tanks of Company A, 716th TB sat idle around Zamboanga City. During that same period, the 41st IDiv pushed the Japanese steadily northward. Eventually, the demoralized and hungry Japanese filtered into the interior of the peninsula. When the end of the war finally came, only 1,385 Japanese soldiers were still alive in the forested hills of the Zamboanga peninsula.[9]

With the capture of the peninsula, the Americans turned their attention to Jolo Island, off the southern tip of Zamboanga. On April 9, the tanks of Company A, 716th TB and two battalions of the 163rd IReg, 41st IDiv came ashore unopposed on the northwest corner of Jolo. Although the infantry advanced rapidly toward Jolo Town, the tanks were delayed by "heavily mined" roads.

Over the next few days, the 1st Platoon tanks moved north supporting an advance toward the coastal town of Mobo. "Crews from two tanks killed two Japs who were attempting to destroy tanks with pole charges," recorded the tank battalion historian. To the south, the 2nd Platoon advanced rapidly and helped the infantry capture a series of low hills. "The lightning advance was due to [a] road built by [the] tank bulldozer with the infantry following in support of the tanks."

On April 12, the 3rd Platoon assisted the infantry in the area of Mount Magauising, near the southwest corner of Jolo. "Tanks destroyed hostile forces and allowed infantry to move on to objective," noted the 716th TB historian: "[The] tanks were credited with 200 Japs killed in the day's engagement." As the Japanese defenders fled into the rugged, forested mountains and hills of the interior of Jolo, the Shermans of Company A, 716th TB were ferried back to the Zamboanga peninsula. There, they would await their next assignment in the southern Philippines.[10]

Next to face invasion was the sub-island group known as the Visayan Islands, consisting of Panay, Negros, Cebu and Bohol. As historian Lofgren wrote, "While Filipino guerrillas controlled much of the countryside on the four islands, 30,000 Japanese troops held the vital coastal towns, including Cebu City and Iloilo on Panay, the second- and third-largest cities respectively in the Philippines." As MacArthur envisioned it, the two cities would be perfect staging areas for an invasion of Japan. Wrote Lofgren, "The Joint Chiefs of Staff recently had told MacArthur to be prepared to stage twenty-two divisions for the invasion of Japan at Philippine bases by November 1945, with eleven more to follow by the next February."[11]

On March 18, after two weeks of heavy bombardment, the 185th IReg, 40th IDiv came ashore on the southern coast of Panay Island, several miles west of Iloilo. Accompanying the infantrymen were the tanks of Companies C and D, and Headquarters and Service Companies of the 716th TB. When the tanks and infantry came ashore, a large force of Philippine guerrillas, which had managed to capture most of the island already, was there to meet them. The only area still held by the 2,750 Japanese was immediately around Iloilo.[12]

Turning east, the tanks and infantry moved along the coastal road until the vanguard reached the barrio of Molo, just west of Iloilo. On March 19, the advancing infantry, aided by the Assault Gun Platoon from Headquarters Company and the 1st and 2nd Platoons of medium tanks from Company C, found the Japanese dug in behind a heavy concrete wall at the west edge of town. "[The] tanks and assault guns were brought forward to place concentrated fire on the wall," wrote the 716th TB historian. "After thirty minutes of continuous fire, our troops moved forward." Although the infantry suffered a few casualties, the Japanese position was overrun well before noon.

While other tanks were battering the concrete wall, the 3rd Platoon Shermans and a battalion of infantry swung around and came toward Molo from the south. "[There,] our troops received small-arms fire from a group of about forty pillboxes and air raid shelters situated in a grove of coconut palms," explained the 716th TB historian: "Two tanks moved in covered by three tanks and neutralized these positions without casualties." The next day, March 20, the 3rd Platoon Shermans and

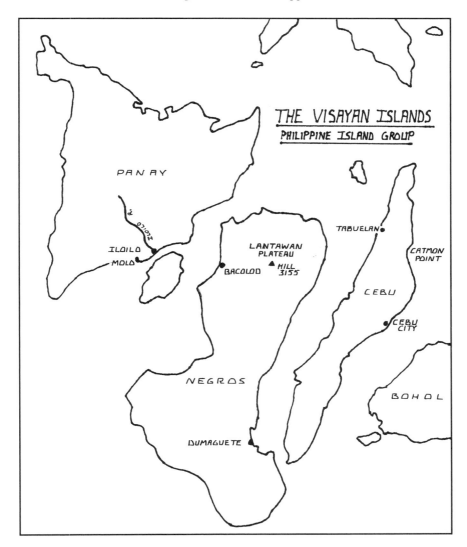

The Visayan Islands

their accompanying infantry pushed into Molo only to discover the Japanese had fled during the night. "[Our] infantry then mounted on the tanks and the column moved rapidly into Iloilo."

While the flanking column was entering Molo, the 1st and 2nd Platoons of Company C, 716th TB and a platoon of infantry moved east and entered Iloilo, finding the city burned out and completely unoccupied. Almost immediately, the light M5 Stuart tanks of Company D, 716th TB, along with the Reconnaissance and Mortar platoons, and a section of infantry, moved north across the Iloilo River to seize the Mandurriao airfield. "In these scattered actions," noted the tank battalion historian, "approximately fifty Japanese were killed and numerous pill-boxes destroyed."

"By 21 March 1945 enemy resistance was scattered and ineffective," wrote the tank historian. As the Japanese fled deeper into the rough interior of Panay, the large M4 Sherman tanks had to give up the chase. On March 23, however, the light Stuart tanks of Company D and a force of infantry discovered a "large pocket of enemy resistance" about ten miles up the Iloilo River from Iloilo. "In the intense firefight forty-four enemy soldiers were killed." Over the next few days, the tanks sat idle as crews readied their vehicles for the next invasion of the Visayan Islands; the invasion of Negros, sixty miles southeast of Panay.[13]

At 9:30 A.M. on March 29, the medium tanks of Company C came ashore on the west coast of Negros and immediately turned north along a coastal road, heading toward the island capital of Bacolod. Fortunately, a 650-foot steel truss bridge over a deep river gorge had already been captured by the 40th IDiv. "The tanks moved north carrying infantrymen from the 2nd Battalion, 185th Infantry for approximately sixteen miles until they reached the Bacolod airport about a mile south of Bacolod," explained the 716th TB historian.[14]

On March 30, the 40th IDiv and the tanks of Companies C and D, 716th TB entered Bacolod and found the city mostly undefended. At one point, however, a suicidal Japanese soldier attacked a Sherman with a satchel pole charge. "The explosion hurled pieces of the Jap's body into the grillwork of a second story window," reported the tank battalion historian. "The tank, undamaged, rolled on."

The next day, April 1, the Company C Shermans and some infantry pushed northeastward from Bacolod while the Company D M5A1 Stuarts and some infantry drove northward along the coast. Over the next few days, the combined tank

Company D, 716th TB M5A1 light tank leads a motorized column of the 40th IDiv on Negros Island, Philippines, March 29, 1945. US ARMY

and infantry columns killed numerous Japanese defenders and knocked out dozens of enemy pillboxes as they pushed deeper into the center of northern Negros.[15]

Although no casualties had been suffered by the tankers thus far, three crewmen and a handful of infantrymen were wounded around April 7 when a flight of U.S. Marine Corps fighter planes strafed the northeast column. Unfortunately, the rapid advance of the Army troops had gone unreported to the Marine Corps fliers.[16]

On the morning of April 9, the 160th IReg and the 3rd Platoon tanks of Company C advanced to a grass-covered, wide-open ridge near the base of Hill 3155, near the exact center of northern Negros. "From 9 April to 3 May the [3rd] platoon moved up daily to fire on heavily entrenched enemy positions on Hill 3155 in a softening up action," reported the 716th TB historian. "During [that time . . .] several Jap guns of large caliber were destroyed and numerous pillboxes [were] destroyed."

Slightly to the north, the 1st Platoon tanks and the 185th IReg moved toward the Lantawan plateau, directly north of Hill 3155. On April 10, the tanks provided covering fire as the foot soldiers moved across a deep ravine to capture an opposing ridgeline. "From 10 until 17 April," noted the tank battalion historian, "the tanks led the infantry in a slow advance over the length of this ridge through heavy mortar and machine-gun fire." By April 18, the assault had reached the far eastern edge of the ridge, where they discovered a Japanese tank trap. "For the next ten days," reported the 716th TB historian, "tanks moved across the tank trap and fired into enemy caves and pillboxes just to the west of the Lantawan plateau."

On April 27, the 1st Platoon Shermans, ably assisted by a section of tanks from the 2nd Platoon and one tank from the 3rd Platoon, spearheaded an infantry attack across the plateau. "The seizure of the Lantawan plateau marked the farthest inland advance of tanks in the 185th Infantry zone of action," wrote the tank historian. "From 28 April until 10 May tanks were employed daily for firing at targets of opportunity from positions on the Lantawan plateau. Enemy caves, pillboxes and dug in emplacements were the principal targets."

North of the plateau, Company C's 2nd Platoon Shermans were supporting the 503rd RCT, which had been brought over to Negros to reinforce the 40th IDiv. For one month, from April 10 to May 10, the M4s helped the paratroopers along a thin, grass-covered ridgeline. "Tank maneuver was restricted to a narrow road running along the ridge because of sharp sides and soft shoulders," recalled the 716th TB historian. "The enemy used great quantities of aerial bombs as mines in this sector." On April 12, one of the Shermans rolled over a concealed aerial bomb. Although the tank received no significant damage, a few of the crewmen were burned by the exploding picric acid.[17]

South of the Lantawan plateau, 3rd Platoon tanks spent the end of April helping the 160th IReg, 40th IDiv get into position to assault Hill 3155. On May 1, the tanks and infantry finally pushed their way around to the northern face of the hill and into a small valley between Hill 3155 and the Lantawan plateau. As the 716th TB historian explained, "Numerous pillboxes and caves were destroyed in this attack which marked the limit of tank advance in the 160th Infantry sector. From this date until June, tanks moved up to firing positions at the base of Hill

3155 firing concentrations in conjunction with artillery . . . and marking air strikes on Hill 3155."[18]

On May 10, both the 1st and 2nd Platoon Shermans were relieved from duty and returned to a bivouac area near the coast. On June 2, the 3rd Platoon joined them. Tank action on Negros had come to an end. In summing up the tank activity, the 716th TB historian wrote, "[Difficult terrain] restricted the tanks to narrow ridges that were never much over 500 yards in length and only fifty to 100 yards wide, flanked by deep and heavily wooded ravines. Fortunately, the ridges were covered with grass and cultivated fields. . . . Whenever possible, terrain permitting, tanks led the attack, accompanied by infantry. . . . Infantry commanders, realizing the tank weaknesses, provided ample infantry protection and mine removing teams where needed."[19]

General MacArthur's next island to assault was Cebu, east of Negros. Although 2,000 Japanese troops were bottled up in northern Cebu by Philippine guerrillas, another 12,500 were concentrated around Cebu City, near the center of the island's east coast. On March 26, 1945, after an hour-long bombardment, two regiments from the Americal Division landed four miles west of Cebu City. Although the beach was heavily mined and several LVTs were destroyed, the M4 Shermans of Company B, 716th TB came ashore without incident.[20]

The next day, the Americans moved unopposed into Cebu City after the Japanese had destroyed much of the town. Over the next few weeks, until the middle of April, the Sherman medium tanks of Company B assisted the foot soldiers in capturing Lahug airfield, two miles northeast of Cebu City, and in the battles that took place among a series of hills to the north. Typically, the big 75mm guns of the tanks were employed to clean out pillboxes, concrete emplacements, and caves.[21]

On April 13, after a regiment of infantry from the Americal Division had made a daring, wide sweeping move behind the Japanese-held hills, the Americans began attacking from two directions at once. While two infantry regiments and the tanks of Company B, 716th TB attacked from the front, another infantry regiment attacked from the rear. Over the next few days, the Americans drove steadily forward and quickly overran one objective after another.[22]

During the strong American push the tanks racked up numerous kills: "Five pillboxes were reduced. . . . Six coral pillboxes were knocked out and the hill was heavily bombarded. . . . Knocked out eight Japanese machine-gun positions holding up the infantry advance." On April 16, the 3rd Platoon tanks of Company B, 716th TB took up a position on a ridge three miles northwest of Lahug airfield and gave fire support to the infantry. By the time the sun set, the tanks had "systematically destroyed fifteen caves, one 90mm mortar, four small mortars, and one 20mm machine gun." As the tank battalion historian wrote, "Twenty active pillboxes were knocked out and an estimated eighty Japs killed. After the tanks had destroyed these positions the infantry moved in."[23]

By the night of April 16–17 the Japanese had had enough. Under the cover of darkness the remaining Japanese began withdrawing to the mountainous northern region of Cebu. Almost immediately the American troops and thousands of Filipino guerrillas started in pursuit. Early on April 21, the tanks joined the pursuit as the

2nd Platoon started in a northeasterly direction astride Highway 1, which ran along the eastern coast of Cebu. "Progress was hindered by twenty abatis road blocks, tank traps nine feet wide and thirteen feet deep flooded with water, and aerial bombs and artillery mines," recorded the 716th TB historian. "An average of eight miles was made against spasmodic opposition from mortars and machine guns."[24]

On April 23, while most of the Americans pushed northward from around Cebu City, elements of the Americal Division and the Shermans of the 3rd Platoon, Company B, 716th TB, boarded landing craft and were carried seventeen miles up the east coast to Catmon Point. The amphibious landing was intended to place a wedge between the retreating Japanese and their counterparts in northern Cebu.[25]

While the fight on Cebu was still in progress, another amphibious move was undertaken, this time against the southeastern tip of Negros Island. On April 26, two battalions of infantry from the Americal Division and the 2nd Platoon tanks of Company B, 716th TB landed near Dumaguete. Almost immediately, they ran into troops from the 40th IDiv, which had invaded Negros on March 29 (see above). After the 40th IDiv and the Company C tanks of the 716th TB had captured Lanta-wan plateau, the men and tanks had rounded the northern tip of Negros and had sped down the east coast almost unopposed. Linking up with the new landing force, the combined groups began eliminating the 1,300 Japanese defenders left on southern Negros. Eventually, the attackers drove the remaining Japanese into an area of "rough, partially jungled hills about ten miles inland" and since the 2nd Platoon tanks could not operate in such terrain, they were shipped back Cebu, and landed at Catmon Point to reinforce the 3rd Platoon.[26]

Back on Cebu, the majority of Japanese continued to retreat over the rough mountains of the interior with the American infantry and Philippine guerrillas in hot pursuit. On April 29, another amphibious landing followed the earlier landing on the east coast at Catmon Point when the 1st Platoon Shermans of Company B, 716th TB and a detachment of infantry from the Americal Division landed on the west coast near Tabuelan, almost squarely opposite Catmon Point. With the two invasion forces pushing inward toward each other, they were in a perfect position to cut off the Japanese retreat from around Cebu City.[27]

For the next week or so, the Company B Shermans had little to do on either coast as the infantry moved farther into the rugged interior of the island. On May 8, tanks helped capture the native village of Lugo but ran into a series of strongly held coconut log roadblocks and tank traps just a little to the north.

On May 9, the 1st Platoon on the west coast and the 3rd Platoon on the east coast both were brought back to Cebu City for rest and recuperation while the 2nd Platoon continued to assist the infantry and engage in "extensive patrol work." On May 29, the 2nd Platoon joined the rest of Company B, 716th TB at Cebu City. As the tank battalion historian wrote, "The campaign was over for Company B."

By June 14, all organized Japanese resistance on Negros was over. On Cebu Island, most of the Japanese defenders had either been eliminated or contained by June 20.[28] With the Visayan Islands firmly under American control, General MacArthur turned his forces back toward the island of Mindanao.

CHAPTER THIRTY

Eastern Mindanao

Although the Americans had managed to capture Mindanao's Zamboanga penin-sula, approximately 43,000 Japanese troops were still on eastern Mindanao. Most of the Japanese were concentrated north of Davao City on the southeastern end of the island, off Davao Bay, and in the north central area.[1]

On April 17, the 24th IDiv, fresh from staging areas on Mindoro Island, landed unopposed on the west coast, near Parang. After linking up with Filipino guerrillas, the Americans pushed southeast along Route 1 and within a few days had penetrated forty-four miles to the southeast to a vital road junction at Kaba-can, which had been captured by a small fleet of riverine gunboats.[2]

On April 20, before the infantrymen reached Kabacan, the Sherman tanks of Company A, 716th TB were ferried over from the Zamboanga peninsula. Two days later, the 31st IDiv, from as far away as Morotai Island and New Guinea, came ashore to reinforce the 24th IDiv. With two divisions on line and a company of tanks to back them up, Lt. Gen. Franklin C. Sibert, the overall commander, stepped up his offensive campaign.[3]

While Company A, 716th TB waited in reserve, the American infantry swept eastward, setting its sights on the coastal city of Davao, on the northwest side of Davao Gulf. On May 3, after running into only slight enemy resistance, the 24th IDiv entered Davao and found the city in shambles. Allied land-based and carrier-based airplanes had pounded the town to rubble.[4]

On May 6, the 31st IDiv started north out of Kabacan on Sayre Highway. As the Americans soon discovered, the "so-called highway . . . [was] something of a fraud." Wrote historian Stephen J. Lofgren, "A thirty-mile stretch had never been completed and dissolved into deep mud whenever it rained—and it rained virtually every day." Six days later, as the soldiers pushed north, the light tanks of Company D, 716th TB, which had been brought over from northern Negros Island, moved up

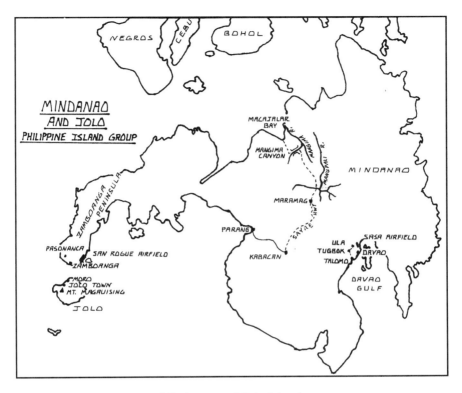

Mindanao and Jolo Islands

to support them. At the same time, a detachment of American infantry was moving south to meet them.[5]

In another daring move, General MacArthur had shipped the 108th IReg, 40th IDiv from Leyte to the northern coast of Mindanao, landing them at Maca-jalar Bay on May 10. Then, while the 31st IDiv moved north up Sayre Highway, the 108th IReg began pushing south down the same highway. As the 716th TB historian wrote, "The action was designed to cut the Jap defenses in two."[6]

Although the bad roads and rough terrain slowed the progress of the Stuart light tanks of Company D, 716th TB, by May 12 they were in the vanguard with the infantry. The 716th TB historian reported on the movements of the tanks once they reached the front line.

> Because of the narrow road, heavy traffic and flimsy bridges, tank move-ments were made slow and dangerous. One light tank and crew fell through a bridge weakened by heavy rain, rolling down a steep embank-ment to the water's edge, injuring one man as well as disabling the tank. Though many derelict vehicles still remained bogged down along the route, all of the [Company D] vehicles successfully completed the move.[7]

On May 15, as the tanks and men moved toward the barrio of Maramag and a nearby airfield, they ran into stiffening Japanese resistance. "This time," wrote the 716th TB historian, "stubborn opposition developed from pillboxes, caves and trenches bordering both sides of the Sayre Highway, and heavy fighting ensued before our troops dislodged the enemy and opened the route for our continued advance." On May 18, the combined tank–infantry force captured another airfield, about twelve miles farther up the trail, and then pushed on for another three or four miles to the Manupali River. Here, the swift, wide, treacherous stream completely halted tank traffic.

Over the next few days, the tankers of Company D waited while engineers built a Bailey bridge, section by section, across the river. "On completion of the bridge," noted the tank battalion historian, "it was discovered that the footings were insufficient to support armored vehicles." Since it was determined that very few Japanese were still active along Sayre Highway, and with a junction with the 108th IReg imminent, the M5 Stuart tanks were sent back south to help guard the area around Davao.[8]

While the 108th IReg was pushing southward, a battalion of soldiers from the Americal Division and the tanks of Company B, 716th TB landed behind them on May 13. Since the 108th IReg had already cleared a good portion of the highway, the tanks quickly moved about ten miles to the front and immediately began "supplying mobile firepower against the enemy's pillboxes and fortified gun positions."

On May 14, the southern advance resumed until it reached Mangima Canyon, about twelve miles south of Macajalar Bay. "When the American infantry reached

716th TB M4 Shermans with the 41st IDiv on Mindanao, Philippines in March 1945. US ARMY

the rim of Mangima Canyon, they stood silhouetted against the sky," recalled the 716th TB historian. "They were easy targets for enemy gunners throughout the canyon. Hostile artillery, mortar, machine-gun and small-arms fire arrested our advance forcing the attackers to retreat."

The rest of the day was spent on a thorough reconnaissance, which revealed the canyon was 800 feet deep and contained the crashing, driving, rain-swollen Mangima River. On May 15, the 108th IReg and the Company B Shermans started the attack against Mangima Canyon. The 716th TB historian described the action:

> Infantry and tanks pushed forward along the highway which bordered the northern rim. Intense artillery, mortar, machine-gun and small-arms fire fell on them immediately. . . . Continually bracketed by enemy artillery, [the] tanks maneuvered on the slippery rain soaked highway, driving forward and sweeping all in front with vicious fire, to capture . . . [a] designated cliff. From this point the tanks covered the first U-turn section of the highway descending to the canyon floor, and placed effective fire on hostile troops who tunneled into rock-hewn crevices below our troops on the north rim. Fanatical Nipponese fired on our forces as they descended the first road section, then retired into their crevices in deep-hewn corridors where heavy tank fire could not dislodge them.[9]

In order to eliminate the Japanese defenders holed up in caves and spider holes dug into the northern side of the canyon, engineers lowered drums of gasoline over the edge and detonated them when they were opposite the enemy positions. "Flames soared into the sky and shot into the rock crevices, but still the enemy survived," lamented the tank historian. During the night, however, most of the Japanese fled to the southern rim of the canyon.

For one solid week the Americans and Japanese slugged it out for possession of Mangima Canyon, while torrential rains soaked the combatants. The Company B tanks continued to lead the way, "destroying rock-hewn pillboxes, sealing caves and entrenchments, and destroying 47mm and 75mm artillery pieces." To fire down into the canyon, tanks often had to move off the road and maneuver into precarious positions which slanted them down toward the canyon bottom. After a few days of heavy fighting, the tanks and infantry finally reached the canyon floor, where they drew incessant firepower from all sides; front, flanks, and rear.

Two bridges across the turbulent Mangima River had to be rebuilt by American engineers while the tanks stood guard, firing into caves and fissures in the cliff walls. When the bridges were completed, and the tanks and infantry crossed over to the southern side, Japanese defenders began a slow withdrawal into the inner mountains of Mindanao, leaving behind selected suicide squads to delay the American advance.

On May 21, the foot soldiers and Sherman tanks finally reached the top of the southern wall, but after only a few miles Sayre Highway completely deteriorated. "[Movement of the tanks was] limited by towering cliffs, sheer walled canyons, and a road which lacked shoulders and base while strewn with rocks and vegetation" reported the 716th TB historian. Halted in their advance, the tanks of Company B, 716th TB were not present when the forward elements of the 108th IReg, 40th IDiv met the vanguard of the 31st IDiv on May 23, about thirty-five miles south of Macajalar Bay. The linkup between the two forces cut the Japanese defenders on eastern Mindanao in two.[10]

While all of the fighting was taking place in central Mindanao, the Sherman tanks of Company A, 716th TB were shuttled to the Davao area from the Zamboanga peninsula to support the 24th IDiv. On May 14, 3rd Platoon, Company A was sent to rescue a company of infantrymen that had been cut off for five hours in an area above Talomo, a barrio about five miles down the coast from Davao. As the tanks approached, they were met by enemy mortar fire from positions well concealed within abaca, or hemp, thickets. Planted in neat rows for easy harvesting, the abaca plants, which resembled banana trees, were at least twenty feet tall. Because of their lack of care during the war some of the older trees had grown a foot thick while dozens of younger plants had sprouted up between the older ones. As historian Smith reported, in the area of the abaca plants, "visibility was virtually nil."[11]

Although the 3rd Platoon Shermans fired 200 75mm rounds into and through the abaca plants, they were unable to suppress the fire of the Japanese mortars and unable to reach the trapped American infantry company. At dawn the next day, the 3rd Platoon tanks moved out again, this time supported by infantry. Pushing steadily forward, the tanks and infantry advanced 1,000 yards and finally reached the beleaguered company, which had been cut off from food and water for thirty-one hours.[12]

On May 23, in another heroic attempt to rescue trapped infantrymen, two tanks from 1st Platoon, Company A set out to rescue two patrols from the 24th IDiv that had run into trouble near Sasa airfield, about five miles above Davao. As the lead tank rumbled over a wooden bridge spanning a deep river, the bridge began to buckle. Although the first tank made it safely across, the second tank remained on the near side. Undaunted, the lead tank continued "alone and unescorted" down the narrow, abaca-lined road until it was suddenly assaulted by enemy rockets, 20mm and machine-gun fire. "By the use of fire and movement, to counter the enemy batteries" recorded the 716th TB historian, "the tank knocked out many enemy positions and exhausted its supply of 75mm ammunition."

Determined to get to the trapped infantrymen, the tank withdrew to the shaky bridge and reloaded its 75mm ammunition from the tank on the near side. Returning to the Japanese gun emplacements, the tank fired another 100 rounds of 75mm shells and so demoralized the enemy that the trapped patrols were able to make it to the road and withdraw behind the safety of the tank. The next day, after replenishing its ammunition once again, the lone tank returned to the area and marked the line of Japanese emplacements with smoke for fighter planes circling overhead. When the air strike ended, the infantry moved in and occupied the destroyed Japanese positions.[13]

About eight miles northwest of Davao, the 3rd Platoon Shermans of Company A were aiding the 24th IDiv in the capture of Tugbok. For several days the American infantry, tanks, and artillery blasted at enemy positions around the town until May 28, when the weakened Japanese defenders pulled out under the cover of darkness. "Our entry into the area revealed the reason for the enemy withdrawal," explained the 716th TB historian. "Enemy casualties left unburied were an estimated battalion."

Over the next few days, fighting became hot and heavy in the area of Tugbok. On June 5, the Assault Gun Platoon and two tanks from Headquarters Company, 716th TB spearheaded an attack against the village of Ula, located about one mile northeast of Tugbok. The big 105mm guns of the assault gun tanks quickly knocked out a pillbox and silenced a few Japanese machine gun emplacements but as the tanks advanced closer to Ula, they became hemmed in by thick abaca fields on either side of the road. Suddenly, a Japanese suicide bomber leaped out of a spider hole in the center of the road and rolled under the lead tank. The ensuing explosion killed the bow gunner and completely destroyed the 35-ton Sherman.

On June 7, another American tank was damaged in the Ula area when a Japanese suicide bomber tossed a box mine under a tank from the 3rd Platoon. As a second tank moved forward to assist the disabled tank, another suicide bomber dashed out to attack the second vehicle. Fortunately, the tank crew spotted the would-be attacker and killed him before he could carry out his mission.

The Assault Gun Platoon was back in action around Ula on June 9 and again on June 10 when it was reported that the Japanese had been "reinforced with heavy weapons." In the ensuing action, the assault guns "disposed of several gun emplacements and silenced [the] remaining heavy guns." Farther up the road, two 3rd Platoon Shermans drove beyond Ula with members of the 24th IDiv and destroyed several enemy pillboxes. When a suicide bomber attempted to destroy one of the tanks with a box mine, he was quickly "dispatched" by the supporting American infantry.[14]

Northeast of Davao, the 1st Platoon Shermans of Company A, 716th TB and the 24th IDiv troops had finally secured the area around Sasa airfield and, like their counterparts around Tugbok and Ula, were steadily pushing westward. On June 7, the Shermans spearheaded an attack about five miles west of the airfield and destroyed several Japanese pillboxes, including one being used as an ammunition dump. "Nips, pillboxes, and all, promptly reported to their ancestors in small pieces," noted the 716th TB historian.

During the morning of June 10, the 1st Platoon M4s wiped out "several enemy pillboxes and dug-in positions" before receiving the call that they were being relieved from front line duty. The 1st Platoon, Company A, 716th TB had been on the front lines for nine straight days without a break.[15]

On the Ula front, the 24th IDiv and two tanks from the 3rd Platoon drove 4,000 yards farther west on June 11, breaching the Japanese defenses in the area. By June 23, the tanks and infantry had reached the foothills of the western mountains. "The battle reached a climax," concluded the 716th TB historian, "when tanks destroyed a large supply dump and several pillboxes. The action subsided quickly and the Nipponese fell back to the mountains."

Within an hour of the ammunition dump explosion the 3rd Platoon tanks were being sent to the rear after running into "impassable mountain terrain." A week later, a few tanks from Company A, 716th TB helped the 41st IDiv, which had been brought over from the Zamboanga peninsula, in an assault against the last few enemy positions east of the mountains. "In a heavy fight, the tankmen destroyed twenty-two pillboxes and caused numerous enemy casualties," recorded the tank battalion historian. "This was the 716th Tank Battalion's farewell to the Japanese conquerors of the Philippines in the Davao sector."[16]

The pursuit by the American foot soldiers gave the retreating Japanese very little time to catch their breath. On June 24, a battalion of infantry from the 31st IDiv landed about sixty-five miles to the east of Macajalar Bay and quickly moved sixty miles inland to threaten the northern flank of the retreating Japanese. On June 30, Lt. Gen. Robert L. Eichelberger, overall commander of the southern Philippines campaign, informed General MacArthur that all organized resistance on Mindanao was over.[17]

The southern Philippine campaign officially ended on July 4, 1945, and the very next day General MacArthur announced to the world that the Philippine campaign had ended. With the seizure of Leyte and Luzon, and the conquest of the southern islands, General MacArthur's promise to return to the Philippines had been fulfilled. In retaking the islands, 10,380 American soldiers had lost their lives and another 36,550 had been wounded. Additionally, perhaps more than 100,000 GIs succumbed to non-battle injuries, mostly diseases. For the Japanese, the cost for the lost campaign was phenomenal. Almost 256,000 Imperial soldiers had been killed or wounded and another 11,745 had been captured.[18]

With the end of the Philippine campaign, General MacArthur turned his sights to his next objective, the eventual invasion of Japan itself. As he did so, he undoubtedly looked at any and all available notes from a savage battle that had taken place on a tiny island just off the southern coast of Japan. The island's name was Okinawa.

CHAPTER THIRTY-ONE

Iceberg

Okinawa had been a Japanese prefecture since 1879, so the Japanese military had more than enough time to fortify every inch of the island. Stretching from the tip of the southernmost island of Japan proper, across the South China Sea to Formosa, the island of Okinawa Shima, as it was officially called, was the largest island of the Ryuku Island chain. Measuring roughly sixty-four miles long, Okinawa slanted northeast to southwest and had a number of peninsulas jutting off in various directions. Although Okinawa measured eighteen miles at its widest point, most of the island was only five miles wide.[1]

About one-third from the southern tip of the island was the Ishikawa isthmus, which nicely separated Okinawa into two distinct regions. Two-thirds of the island north of the isthmus was sparsely populated and covered with rolling hills that branched off from a central ridgeline. Deep ravines and gullies ran between the numerous hills, which terminated at the coast in the form of steep cliffs. Covered with dense pine forests and thick undergrowth, only one "single-track road" ran along the northwest shore.

By contrast, the southern third of the island was densely populated with terrain that featured rolling hills and terraces "cut by ravines and shallow, narrow streams." Underground streams had formed numerous caves throughout the region, providing excellent natural defensive positions. Villages and towns dotting the southern end of Okinawa were surrounded by rice, sugar cane, sweet potato and soybean fields. Numerous single-lane roads crisscrossed the southern end of Okinawa and one two-lane road connected the island's only two real cities, Naha along the western coast and Shuri in the center.[2]

About three and one-half miles west of Okinawa lay the island of Ie Shima. Although only about four miles long and two miles wide, the small flat-topped

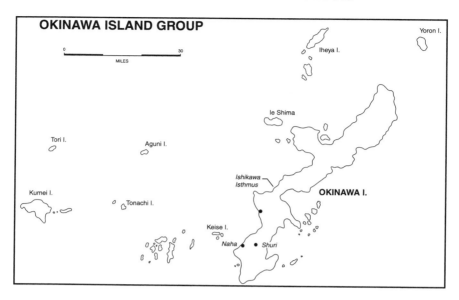

Okinawa Island Group

island with a "sharp pinnacle about 500 feet high at the eastern end" contained three fine runways and dominated northern Okinawa. If captured and controlled, the Americans could use Ie Shima as a base for artillery and airplanes.[3]

American plans for the invasion of Okinawa began in September 1944 when the Joint Chiefs of Staff decided to use Okinawa as a "springboard for the invasion of Japan." The operation, code named Iceberg, was to be a joint Marine Corps–Army venture under the command of Army Lt. Gen. Simon Bolivar Buckner Jr., whose father had been a Confederate general during the Civil War. Buckner's invasion force was designated the U.S. Tenth Army and consisted of three Marine Corps divisions, and five Army divisions, a total of 154,000 men. The force would be conveyed to the island in 430 Navy transports in a flotilla totaling 1,457 ships, the largest such concentration ever assembled in the Pacific.[4]

The assaulting Marines included the veteran 1st and 2nd MarDivs and the newly created 6th MarDiv, which had been formed from veterans of various other Marine Corps units. The 1st and 6th MarDivs would be in the initial invasion, while the 2nd MarDiv would be held in floating reserve.

The Army's 7th and 96th IDivs, fresh from the conquest of Leyte, would land to the right of the Marines, with the 27th IDiv, veterans of the Gilberts, Marshalls and Saipan, in floating reserve. Selected to capture some of the outlying Ryukyu Islands, including Ie Shima, was the 77th IDiv, which had seen action at Guam and Leyte. Overall reserve went to the 81st IDiv, battle-hardened troops of Angaur and Peleliu, who would remain in New Caledonia until needed.[5]

The invasion would take place on the west side of the island, below the Ishikawa isthmus, with the two Marine Corps divisions landing abreast on the left, and the two Army divisions landing abreast on the right. If all went well, the Marines would seal off the Ishikawa isthmus while the two Army divisions would turn south and clear out the southern end of Okinawa. The date of the invasion was set for April 1, 1945.[6]

While Marine Corps tank battalions would support the two Marine divisions, the Army would be supported by its own tanks. The 7th IDiv would be supported by the 711th TB, while the 96th IDiv would be assisted by the 763rd TB. The 711th TB was an untried unit that had been shipped to Leyte from Hawaii. On the other hand, the 763rd TB was a veteran unit, which had seen plenty of action on Leyte.[7]

Held in floating reserve with the 27th IDiv would be the 193rd TB, another veteran unit that had seen action on Makin Island in medium M3 Lee tanks. After returning to Hawaii, the 193rd TB had been refitted and re-equipped with M4 Sherman tanks, including two flamethrowing tanks in each platoon. By the end of March 1945, the reconstituted 193rd TB was ready to go.[8]

Assisting the 77th IDiv in its capture of the outlying islands and Ie Shima would be the 706th TB. A battle-hardened unit, the 706th TB had seen combat on Guam and Leyte. Rested and refitted, the 706th was ready for any upcoming role that came their way.[9]

Near the end of March, U.S. ships, assisted by a British carrier force, bombarded Okinawa and struck at airfields on neighboring islands. On March 25, American ships began pounding Okinawa. Then, between March 26 and March 31, elements of the 77th IDiv began landing on the islands just west of Okinawa, called Kerama Retto. Although the 706th TB was ready to assist, the infantry easily overran the eight islands that made up Kerama Retto without running into much opposition.[10]

At 5:30 A.M. on Easter Sunday, April 1, 1945, a pre-landing barrage rocked the landing site near the town of Hagushi on the central west coast of Okinawa, below the Ishikawa isthmus. Near 8:00 A.M., a line of amphibian tanks started toward the landing beaches, followed by five waves of infantry, and then one wave of LCMs carrying Sherman tanks. Additionally, the LCMs were accompanied by T-6 flotation device tanks from Company B, 711th TB.[11]

A remarkable contraption, the T-6 flotation device allowed a tank to "swim" to shore under its own power. Historian Oscar E. Gilbert described the device:

> The T-6 consisted of six large steel floats attached to the tank, which turned it into a low, turreted raft. Special brackets welded to the front and rear held detachable pontoons, and the smaller non-detachable pontoons were welded to the sponsons [i.e. sides] of the tank. . . .
>
> Propulsion was provided by the churning tracks, which were equipped with special track connectors that incorporated cup-like cleats like those on the tracks of the LVTs. Top speed in the water was only about . . . two miles per hour. The tank commander stood on the deck behind the turret and pulled on two ropes to control the crude rudders.[12]

The floats were attached to the tank by large pins and could be jettisoned once ashore by the flick of a switch in the driver's compartment. As Robert

Clifton (711th TB) wrote, "When on land, the pontoons would be blown off so they could travel on land better." However, first the driver had to blow off the two rear floats, pull forward several yards, blow off the front floats, and then back away from the contraptions. Since the side floats were permanently attached, the floats had to remain in place, adding about eighteen inches to each side of the vehicle. As historian Gilbert noted, "One major problem with the T-6 was its size, which imposed a serious penalty on transport space."[13]

While the 1st and 6th MarDivs landed to the north of Hagushi, the 7th and 96th IDivs landed to the south. The landings met very little opposition since the Japanese planned to defeat the Americans in the interior of the island. Coming in behind the 96th IDiv foot soldiers, M4A1 Shermans of Company B and the M5 Stuarts of Company D, both 763rd TB, immediately started inland and eventually captured some high ground about 3,500 yards from the beach. During the move to the ridge one Sherman rolled over a buried 100-pound aerial bomb and was put out of action. William E. Bonnell (Company B, 763rd TB) was inside the tank and recalled, "When we went onto Okinawa, my tank hit a mine the first day. It blew off a track and pushed the bottom up. The tank was ruined."[14]

A little farther south, the eighteen M4A1 Shermans of Company C, 763rd TB ran into a bit more trouble. While coming ashore, one tank slipped into an unseen shell hole and the driver drowned. Once ashore, the other tanks advanced only about 600 yards before running into an "unfordable river."[15]

On the left of the 96th IDiv, the 7th IDiv assault troops reached shore against light opposition and began driving inland toward the Kadena airfield, just southeast of Hagushi. The first tanks from the 711th TB reached shore at 8:30 A.M. and immediately followed after the foot soldiers. Although hampered by "rough terrain" and hidden land mines, the Company A Shermans drove 4,000 yards inland to assist the infantry in the capture of Kadena airfield.[16]

By 3:30 P.M., all of the 711th TB companies had come ashore and a battalion headquarters was set up near the northeast corner of Kadena airfield. To the right, the 763rd TB had a bit more trouble bringing everybody ashore. At approximately 7:00 P.M. on April 1, a Japanese suicide plane crashed into the ship carrying the service personnel of the 763rd TB, killing a few men, "the first combat casualties of the battalion." Battered and bruised, the 763rd TB would not get Company A or its Headquarters Company and Service Company ashore until the early afternoon of April 3.[17]

On April 2, the 6th MarDiv began probing northward, looking for the enemy, while the 1st MarDiv and the 7th IDiv pushed eastward across the island. Accompanying the men of the 7th IDiv were the tanks of Companies A, B and D, 711th TB. "All companies furnished close support, knocking out enemy strong points as the attack pressed east," reported a 711th TB historian. Although both Companies A and D encountered minefields, no tanks were damaged, and after the mines had been cleared the tanks were able to catch up to and assist their assigned infantry units.[18]

In the 96th IDiv sector on the far right side of the beachhead, the infantry, accompanied by the tanks of the 763rd TB, turned south along the west coast.

"Tanks met heavier resistance as they started south," commented a 763rd TB historian, taking heavy fire from some surrounding ridges and caves. Additionally, the American advance ran into numerous scattered minefields. Noted the 763rd TB historian, "Minefields were indiscriminate and seemingly with no pattern. Mines encountered were the conical beach mines capable of breaking the track and destroying the suspension system."[19]

The next day, the 763rd TB and the 96th IDiv started south again. "[The] assault units are now abreast," wrote the 763rd TB historian. "Heavy sniper and machine-gun fire encountered. Destroyed bridges and mines make progress very slow." In the morning, the M4A1s of Companies B and C and the M5s of Company D assisted the infantry advance. In the afternoon, after the Company A Shermans finally landed, they replaced the Company B tanks.[20]

The 711th TB and the 7th IDiv continued their advance on April 3, reaching the east coast of Okinawa early in the afternoon against light opposition. On April 4, heavy rains carpeted Okinawa and only the light tanks of the 2nd Platoon, Company D, 711th TB saw any real action when they supported an infantry assault to the south, against Castle Hill. Located near the eastern shore of Okinawa, Castle Hill received its name from an old, run down feudal castle that stood atop a central ridge, making it an excellent site for a Japanese observation post.[21]

"The [2nd] platoon arrived at the front lines at 1330 [1:30 P.M.] and took up position thirty yards in front of the infantry," recalled the 711th TB historian. "There was no enemy activity until the infantry started to move, then heavy machine-gun fire was received. Tanks fired on two pillboxes at 400 yards and silenced them, then withdrew at 1930 [7:30 P.M.] to bivouac 200 yards in rear of the front line."[22]

On April 5, when the 7th IDiv moved forward against Castle Hill again, it found the ridge deserted. Pushing rapidly southward, the foot soldiers covered more than two miles until the left flank of their line ran into a Japanese strong point called the Pinnacle, a coral spike that stood atop a 450-foot ridge. While the soldiers prepared themselves for the next day's assault, the 711th TB moved up over muddy, rain-dampened roads.[23]

While the 7th IDiv had been pushing south along the east coast, the 96th IDiv drove down the west coast. On April 4, the 96th IDiv "made sweeping gains," moving almost two miles in one day. Noted the Army historians, "Rapid movement by infantry units supported by tanks reduced the enemy positions." During the rapid advance, Company A, 763rd TB lost two tanks to land mines and one that fell into a huge mud hole, while Company C had one tank slightly damaged by a Japanese 75mm gun.[24]

On April 5, the tanks of the 763rd TB and the men of the 96th IDiv pushed south again. Outside of Uchitomari village the assault ran into heavy fire from Japanese hidden inside ridgeline caves and above-ground tombs. As the Company A Shermans moved forward, two tanks were disabled by 47mm antitank shells. The Company B tanks came up, and along with three 105mm assault gun tanks from the Assault Gun Platoon, 763rd TB, drove forward 600 yards until they reached a large antitank ditch. Finding it impossible to go forward, the vehicles

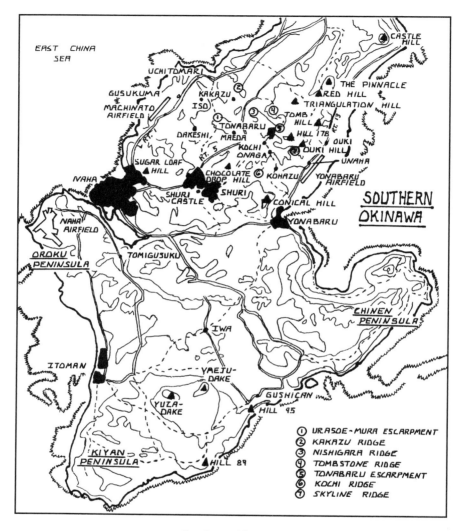

EAST CHINA
SEA

CASTLE
HILL

UCHITOMARI

THE PINNACLE

GUSUKUMA   KAKAZU   ②   RED HILL
                                                    TRIANGULATION HILL
MACHINATO   ISO   TOMB
AIRFIELD   ③ HILL
                    TONABARU   ④   HILL 178
DAKESHI MAEDA   ⑤   OUKI
                        KOCHI   OUKI HILL
                        ONAGA ▲   UNAHA
SUGAR LOAF ▲   ⑥
          HILL   CHOCOLATE ⑥ KOHAZU
IVAHA   DROP HILL   YONABARU
                                              AIRFIELD
          SHURI   SHURI
          CASTLE   CONICAL HILL   SOUTHERN
NAHA   OKINAWA
AIRFIELD   YONABARU

OROKU   TOMIGUSUKU
PENINSULA

                                              CHINEN
                                              PENINSULA

                    IWA

ITOMAN   YAEJU-
                DAKE
                                    GUSHICAN
          YUZA-   HILL 95
          DAKE

KIYAN   HILL 89
PENINSULA

① URASOE-MURA ESCARPMENT
② KAKAZU RIDGE
③ NISHIGARA RIDGE
④ TOMBSTONE RIDGE
⑤ TONABARU ESCARPMENT
⑥ KOCHI RIDGE
⑦ SKYLINE RIDGE

Southern Okinawa

tried to go around the ditch but ran into a minefield and heavy antitank fire. In the ensuing action, another tank was lost to a 47mm antitank gun.[25]

In spite of its losses, the 763rd TB was back again the next day. Although Company A sported only thirteen tanks now, they advanced about 1,000 yards down the center of the island in support of an infantry attack and encountered "machine-gun, mortar and sniper fire, plus mine fields." Noted the 763rd TB historian, "[The] tanks encountered approximately thirty pillboxes and emplacements. Tank fire was concentrated on those in assistance of the infantry." To the right, Company C kept pace with Company A, eliminating possibly three antitank guns and firing into approximately twenty-five caves.[26]

713th FTB on Okinawa Shima, April–June 1945. US ARMY

On April 7, the 713th Flamethrower Tank Battalion [FTB] landed on Okinawa. After arriving in Hawaii in late August 1944, the 713th had trained as a normal tank unit. However, on November 10, 1944, the battalion was "assigned the mission of organizing, equipping and training the only armored flamethrower battalion in the Army." Although flamethrowing tanks had seen action in limited numbers in both the Pacific and European theaters, the 713th TB was to be the first "all flamethrower" tank battalion.[27]

Under their new designation, the 713th FTB gave up its normal Sherman and Stuart tanks and received 54 special flamethrower-equipped M4A1 Shermans. Because of the problems envisioned with keeping the new tanks supplied with napalm and fuel, the light tank company and the battalion mortar platoon were eliminated and most of the personnel were "integrated into Service and Headquarters Company."

The new flamethrowing M4A1 Shermans would utilize the same British Ronson flamethrower gun that had been used in the light M5 Stuart Satan tanks (see Chapter Twenty-Three) but would carry almost twice the flame fuel capacity (300 gallons as compared to 170 gallons). Historian Joseph Morschauser III, described the changes:

> [Internal] turret baskets were ripped out of the tanks and 300-gallon capacity metal containers were fastened to the belly armor. Racks were welded into the right sponsons to hold the big metal bottles of CO_2 gas which was to supply the pressure which pushed the napalm from the gun muzzle. The breeches of the 75mm guns were cut to pieces and tubes for the napalm running from the container under the turret were pushed up the tubes. At the gun muzzle itself an atomizer reduced the napalm to a spray which was in turn set on fire by an electric sparking device.[28]

713th FTB on Okinawa Shima. The two tanks in the foreground are equipped with flamethrowers while the tanks in the background are 105mm Assault Guns from Headquarters and Headquarters Company. US ARMY

Through experimentation, the tankers discovered that the perfect mixture was six percent napalm and ninety-four percent gasoline. "The purpose of the napalm, a soapy, granular substance," wrote historians James and William Belote, "was to absorb the gasoline and cause it to stick, jellylike, to whatever it hit. The result was a frightful [substance], very effective against caves, pillboxes, camouflaged positions—and men. [The flamethrower] was the only weapon from which the Japanese would break and run, abandoning their positions."[29]

The only way the 713th FTB could measure the amount of napalm left in each tank was with an ordinary clock. Through experimentation and research, it was known that the 300-gallon fuel cells gave the tanks approximately ninety seconds of fire. All each crew had to do was time each burst of flame and keep track of the total to know how much time they had remaining before they would have to retire to refuel. "Prior to the [orders to organize as a flamethrower battalion] the armored flamethrower was a new and untried weapon. . . . Very little data were available on the mixing, storage, proper thickness and types of fuel for the new gun." Through trial and error, experimentation and hard research, the battalion was ready to go when ordered to prepare for Operation Iceberg.[30]

While the 713th FTB was disembarking, the 711th TB moved ahead with the 7th IDiv along the eastern side of Okinawa toward "a low, bare hill . . . called Red Hill because of its color." As Army historians noted, "The enemy had made a fortress of the hill by constructing his usual system of caves and connecting tunnels." When an infantry assault failed to dislodge the Japanese, the Americans brought up their armor.[31]

All sixteen tanks from Company C, 711th TB, the five 2nd Platoon light tanks from Company D, 711th TB, and an M8 self-propelled howitzer (a 75mm gun on an M5 light tank chassis), moved forward along a narrow road that wound around the east side of the hill to provide fire support for the infantry. With the light tanks and the M8 howitzer in the lead, the column moved through a valley firing at the "hills on each side covered with caves and pillboxes." Because of the rough terrain, the tanks were forced to travel single file down a road that eventually "wound into the bottom of a deep cut."

When the leading Stuart crews spotted land mines in the road ahead of them, they opened fire with their bow guns and blew up six mines within a few feet of each other. Wrote the tank historian, "After reporting this to the medium tank company commander, he ordered the [light tank] platoon to proceed forward with speed, regardless of the loss of tanks." As the tanks started forward, firing their bow guns at suspected mines, enemy artillery suddenly began raining down around them. "Artillery hit between number one and two tanks and shook up the crews," the tank historian said.

The light tanks, the M8 howitzer, and three Shermans from the 3rd Platoon, Company C, 711th TB reached the bottom of the cut before the tenth tank in line, was destroyed by a hidden land mine. "This cut off the leading tanks from the rest of the column," reported the 711th TB historian. While the Shermans behind the disabled tank sat idle, the light tank platoon and the 3rd Platoon Shermans started up Red Hill ridge.

"After proceeding [past] several caves on a very narrow one way road number one [light] tank hit a mine and blew off the right track," wrote the historian. "The road was now completely blocked [by] number one tank and the turret could not be turned to the rear [because of the steep sides of the road]." As the four remaining Stuarts, the self-propelled howitzer and the three following Shermans came to a dead stop, the Japanese on either side of the road struck.

"No. 4 [light] tank could see the Japs swarming over No. 3 tank but could not fire from its angle," the 711th TB historian said. "[The] Japs placed a satchel charge on number three tank, disabling the tank and injuring the bow gunner." As the crew from No. 3 scrambled out of the tank, they notified the crew of No. 2 that there were Japanese soldiers all around, "putting flaming rags on number two turret." Inside No. 2, the bow gunner spotted some Japanese soldiers trying to set a satchel charge on the rear deck of No. 1 and shot them off.

The crew of the open-topped M8 howitzer, directly behind the five-tank Stuart platoon, responded to the sudden Japanese uprising by firing their Thompson sub-machine guns all around them, killing a few Japanese soldiers who were trying to toss satchel charges into the flaming rags atop No. 2.

Near the end of the line, two of the three medium tanks got into position to give covering fire to the light tanks. "The two tanks held back the enemy," wrote the 711th TB historian, "utilizing all tank weapons and finally hand grenades and small-arms fire, while the crews of the light tanks were evacuated." Under the cover of this heavy firepower, the crews from light tanks No. 1, 2, and 3 scrambled atop No. 4 and 5. Then, although sniper fire rained down upon them, the two remaining light tanks and the open-top M8 howitzer had to wait while the three Shermans turned around. Recalled the 711th TB historian, "The men on these two tanks (Nos. 4 and 5) fired on the enemy snipers with their individual weapons."[32]

Although three light tanks and one medium tank had been lost, the Company C tanks still had some work to do. While the two remaining light tanks and the M8 howitzer returned to the bivouac area, the medium tanks moved around the west slope of Red Hill along an alternate route. "Tanks proceeded at least three miles ahead of supporting infantry and covered the entire valley beyond Red Hill."

During the fight for Red Hill and beyond, the American advance ran into extremely heavy Japanese artillery and mortar fire, forcing the tanks and infantry to employ new tactics. The 711th TB historian explained:

> As the attack on Red Hill continued it was impossible for the infantry to stay with the tanks due to the heavy artillery and mortar fire that was thrown against the tanks. This artillery . . . was primarily intended to separate the infantry from the tanks, so as to enable the "suicide tank destroyer teams" to close with and destroy the tanks. The heavy artillery . . . immediately "put on the shelf" all close in tank–infantry tactics thereby doing away with the tank–infantry team. Tank tactics of platoon covering platoon, section covering section, and even tank covering tank, was resorted to.[33]

A captured Japanese document described exactly how the enemy used its artillery fire to separate troops from tanks. The note read, "The above method of isolating the troops from the tanks with surprise fire followed by close combat tactics is an example in the complete destruction of enemy tanks and will be a great factor in deciding the victories of tank warfare."[34]

Red Hill eventually fell to a flanking infantry and on April 8, the 7th IDiv and the tanks of Company C, 711th TB moved south again. The 3rd Platoon Shermans, with a handful of supporting infantry, moved to an area where they could give cover fire to the infantry moving against Triangulation Hill, about 1,000 yards beyond Red Hill, and Tomb Hill, about 1,000 yards southeast of Triangulation Hill. "Terrain was such that it was impossible for tanks to cover each other as they moved forward." Finally, around noon, two tanks reached an advantageous position and laid withering fire into a few Japanese caves and enemy-held houses, which enabled a trapped 7th IDiv company to withdraw and reorganize. Then, when heavy enemy artillery fire rained down upon the tanks, the 3rd Platoon began to withdraw.

While turning around, the platoon leader's Sherman somehow overturned, completely blocking the road. As Japanese infantry began to attack, the crews from the other tanks grabbed their shovels and dug a path around the disabled vehicle. "At this point," the 711th TB historian wrote, "Japs counterattacked in force, satchel-charged the last tank of the 3rd Platoon, bayoneted two men attempting to evacuate and drove all infantry from [the] vicinity."

Fortunately, the tanks of Company B, 711th TB had been dispatched to relieve Company C and arrived just in time. Machine-gun fire from Company B tanks halted the Japanese assault and prevented any further damage to Company C tanks. However, as the latter company tried to withdraw, the Japanese came on again. "The enemy was counterattacking and [the American] infantry was being pushed back," concluded the 711th TB historian. "As the [Company B] tanks moved into position, heavy mortar fire was received. [The] tanks held off enemy by shrapnel fire and .30-caliber machine-gun fire until [the American] infantry had withdrawn and all casualties were evacuated from the ridge."

Around 2:00 P.M., after the 7th IDiv reorganized, the infantry assaulted Tri-angulation Hill again, this time supported by the 1st and 2nd Platoon Shermans of Company B, 711th TB. "Both platoons preceded the infantry in attack and knocked out several pillboxes as well as killing an estimated 100 enemy infantry." Although rocked by artillery fire, which destroyed two more tanks, the armored vehicles stayed with the infantry until 4:00 P.M., when Triangulation Hill fell to the Americans.[35]

While the April 8 attacks were in progress, another tank battalion, the 193rd TB, landed on Okinawa. Oddly enough, when the battalion came ashore, sixteen tanks sported a device known as a back-scratcher. Explained the 193rd TB histo-rian, "This device consisted of four electrically detonated antipersonnel mines mounted around the turret. These mines could be detonated by push button from the interior of the turret. The purpose of this device was to discourage enemy 'tank hunters' from attacking the tank at close quarters." Once ashore, the 193rd TB went into bivouac near the Hagushi beachhead while the other tank battalions carried on business as usual.[36]

Over the next few days, the 711th TB and the 7th IDiv continued to push southward, capturing such landmarks as Tomb Hill and Tombstone Ridge. On April 10, the town of Ouki was attacked but the entire area was found to be strewn with landmines. Although four regular tanks and one bulldozer tank were dam-aged during the advance, the extraordinary efforts of the 711th TB maintenance section had the tanks up and running again before nightfall.[37]

On the 7th IDiv right flank, near the center of the island, Company B, 711th TB and the 105mm Assault Gun Platoon assisted the infantry in an attack toward Hill 178, about 2,000 yards south of Triangulation Hill. Joining them in the assault were the flamethrowing tanks of 1st Platoon, Company A, 713th FTB. "The flamethrowers supported the standard tanks with [machine-gun] fire as they advanced," wrote the 713th FTB historian. "Two pillboxes were destroyed by 75mm fire [from the 711th TB Shermans], and our tanks destroyed an ammo dump with [.30-caliber] tracer. All tanks were under continuous artillery and mor-tar fire from 0830 [8:30 A.M.] until 1500 [3:00 P.M.]." Although unable to employ their flamethrowers in this first action, each combat crew gained valuable combat experience.

Near 3:00 P.M., when it was time to retire for the night, many of the tanks that had pushed up to the base of Hill 178 discovered that they were stuck in mud. "Due to rain," wrote the 711th TB historian, "tanks had a difficult time pulling out of position. As the tanks withdrew, artillery fire increased and smoke was used to cover the evacuation of the tanks that were stuck." Wrote the 713th FTB historian, "The reserve tanks were called upon to tow the others due to bad hills."[38]

On the west side of Okinawa, the 96th IDiv and the 763rd TB also had been moving steadily southward, trying to keep pace with the 7th IDiv and the 711th TB. Like their brother tankers, the men of the 763rd TB ran into trouble with mine-fields, artillery fire, and mortar fire. In spite of this, however, the tanks continued to accompany the infantry until Mother Nature stepped in and sent a deluge of rain down upon Okinawa. "Terrain and mud limited advance of tanks," noted the 763rd TB historian. Although the armor was ready to help out where needed, it became harder and harder for the tanks to go anywhere.[39]

From April 10 until April 19 there was very little tank action on southern Okinawa. Heavy rains turned the landscape into thick, gooey mud that made it all but impossible for the M4 Shermans and M5 Stuarts of the 711th and 763rd TBs, or the M4 Sherman flamethrowers of the 713th FTB to move. On April 13, during the middle of the storm, word reached Okinawa that President Franklin Delano Roosevelt had died the day before at Warm Springs, Georgia. Vice President Harry S Truman was now president. While most of the soldiers and tankers expressed sorrow over the loss of President Roosevelt, there was still a war to be won. As the infantry continued to inch its way south, the tankers took the opportunity provided by the heavy rains to work on their tanks and ready themselves for a return to combat.[40]

CHAPTER THIRTY-TWO

Hard Days

B y the middle of April 1945, the 1st and 6th MarDivs had cut Okinawa in half and cleared out the Motobu peninsula.[1] At about the same time, on April 16, the Army's 77th IDiv landed on the southern and southwestern coast of Ie Shima, the little island only three and one-half miles west of Okinawa's Motobu peninsula. Meeting little resistance, the foot soldiers pushed inward and quickly overran the three island runways. As on Okinawa, the 3,000 Japanese soldiers and 1,500 armed civilians had elected not to meet the Americans on the beachhead but to fight them in the stone buildings of Ie Town, on the island's southeast corner, or on the cave-pocked 600-foot Iegusugu pinnacle, just north of the town.[2]

On April 17, when the 77th IDiv turned toward Ie Town and the pinnacle, resistance stiffened. In a short while, the commander called for tank support. The 706th TB, which had left Leyte Gulf on March 13 and had been waiting aboard ship, started toward shore opposite Ie Town. "While maneuvering for landing," wrote a 706th TB historian, "the LST hung up on a reef and was unable to beach. Unloading operations, using barges and LCTs, began at 0500 [5:00 A.M.] 18 April."[3]

By the morning of April 19, the 706th TB was safely landed on Ie Shima. At 8:30 A.M. the 2nd and 3rd Platoons, Company A, 706th TB began shelling a number of Japanese caves and pillboxes as the infantry pushed westward through Agarii-Mae Village, just south of Ie Town. The next day, the two platoons stayed with the infantry as they pushed through the eastern outskirts of Ie Town and fought opposite Iegusugu pinnacle.[4]

Company C, 706th TB spent the morning of April 18 "discussing the regrettable death of Ernie Pyle." A much-loved and honored war correspondent, Ernie Pyle had covered the war in Europe until it appeared as though the war there was about played out. Transferring to the Pacific, Pyle had gone ashore on Okinawa to visit the Marines and then had come over to Ie Shima to say hello to the GIs.

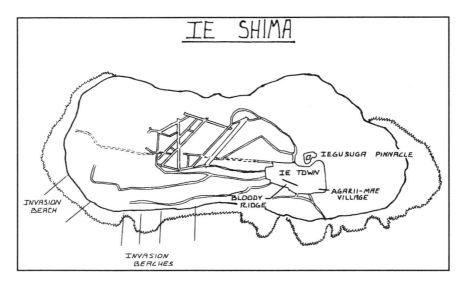

Ie Shima

Ambushed near Ie Town, Ernie Pyle died when a burst of machine gun fire hit him just below the rim of his helmet.[5]

On April 19, Company C, 706th TB and a battalion of infantry from the 77th IDiv tried to fight their way through Agarii-Mae Village toward Bloody Ridge overlooking Ie Town. "The tanks encountered heavy mortar fire and soon the infantry could not stay with them," commented a 706th TB historian: "The tanks stayed up there, however, pouring 75mm and [machine-gun] fire into enemy positions and assisting in evacuating the wounded infantry." Similar to what was happening on Okinawa, a heavy rain made it almost impossible for the tanks to move around. "The company continued the fight on into the afternoon, even when rain and slippery narrow roads further hampered their efforts," wrote another battalion historian. In spite of their tenacity, the Americans were unable to secure the ground in front of Ie Town and had to retire for the night.[6]

By the morning of April 20, the 77th IDiv troops had cleared the northern shore of Ie Shima and had completely circled Ie Town and the Iegusugu pinnacle. Company C, 706th TB once again supported the attack through Agarii-Mae Village toward Bloody Ridge. "A heavy artillery and naval shelling preceded the attack against the steep, strongly defended ridge line," wrote a 706th TB historian. "The third platoon led the way up the ridge, but the company [C] commander's tank was the first to gain the very top of the ridge. Japs were everywhere and heavy mortar fire was directed against us. As soon as all of the tanks were on the ridge line, the third platoon began pounding shells into Jap positions in the valley [i.e. Ie Town] and on the mountainside [i.e. Iegusugu pinnacle] beyond."

After forty-five minutes, the 3rd Platoon tanks ran out of ammunition and were replaced by 2nd Platoon tanks. As the 3rd Platoon was returning to resupply, a satchel charge went off under the lead vehicle, wrecking a track and damaging the engine. Tank No. 2 moved up quickly to furnish protection for the evacuating crew, but "suffered an even worse fate—both tracks blown off and the engine set on fire." As the two crews evacuated the damaged tanks, three Japanese soldiers hiding in a spider hole alongside the road killed one man and wounded two more before they in turn were killed by the remaining crewmen.[7]

On the southwest side of Agarii-Mae, Company B, 706th TB moved into a separate sector between two infantry battalions. At 9:15 A.M., the 1st and 3rd Platoons started forward on a 400-yard front, while the 2nd Platoon followed in reserve. "The advance continued for approximately 600 to 700 yards toward the core of enemy resistance," a 706th TB historian noted, before the tanks encountered heavy Japanese fire. Over the next few hours, the battalion lost one tank to a land mine and another to a satchel charge. Around 2:00 P.M., the infantry on the right flank shifted toward the position held by the tanks. "From this time until nightfall, all platoons were committed to the line in immediate support of the infantry."

The light tanks of Company D, 706th TB and the 105mm assault guns from Headquarters Company saw their first action on Ie Shima on April 20. Circling to the northeast, the 1st Platoon Stuarts, the assault guns and a battalion of infantry assaulted Iegusugu pinnacle. Noted a 706th TB historian, "An estimated sixty Japanese were killed, fifteen pillboxes knocked out, and ten fortified caves sealed in this engagement. A point but fifty yards from the base of [Iegusugu pinnacle] was reached."

During the day's attack, the 1st Platoon leader's tank was destroyed by a land mine and two tank commanders received head wounds from shrapnel when they were caught with their heads poking out of their turret hatches.[8]

By the morning of April 21, the Americans were at the base of the Iegusugu pinnacle and atop Bloody Ridge, and were not far from closing off Ie Town. As the 77th IDiv started forward again, the 706th TB roared along to provide firepower. "The advance was slow but thorough," wrote the tank battalion historian, "and tanks destroyed or neutralized all caves and pillboxes in the sector of advance. . . . The day's advance had carried us to the base of the mountain, the division objective. Further tank operation was limited by rough terrain."[9]

At one point during the advance, the infantry came over a low ridge and was met with heavy machine-gun fire. Immediately the 2nd Platoon Shermans of Company C, 706th TB came up to help. "The tanks moved up swiftly," wrote a 706th TB historian, "and when the Jap spotted them roaring over the ridge and saw the effects of the '75,' they left their positions on the run. The tank gunners didn't miss their chances and were very proud of their bag of fifty Nips."[10]

Before nightfall, the infantry reached the top of the pinnacle and raised an American flag over Ie Shima.

On April 22, while most of the 706th TB assembled at a bivouac area along Ie Shima's southern shore, Company C participated in what would be called "Shermans march to the sea." Aligning their Sherman tanks on a line stretching nearly three-quarters of the way across Ie Shima, the tanks and infantry marched eastward from the base of Iegusugu pinnacle to the eastern coast. "Resistance was not very heavy although widely scattered mines gave the company something to worry about," reported a 706th TB historian. "Luckily, all the tanks completed the mission, but there were a few 'near misses'."[11]

The capture of Ie Shima had cost the 706th TB three men killed and thirty-five wounded. Additionally, the battalion had five tanks destroyed. By the late afternoon of April 24, the entire 706th TB was back aboard their transport ships and by April 28, the entire 706th TB was ashore on Okinawa and sitting in bivouac seven miles east of Hagushi.[12]

On Okinawa the 711th and 763rd TBs, and the 713th FTB waited more than a week for the heavy rain to subside. Recalled Robert Clifton (Company A, 711th TB), "About [the] middle of April we had a lot of rain. Trucks, tanks, and jeeps could not move. Food was dropped in to us by air. [The] men had to stay in their foxholes all night. They couldn't get out because everything that moved at night was supposed to be the enemy. Therefore, sleeping and resting at night was often done in a puddle of water." Optimistically, Clifton added, "At least it was not cold like our troops in Europe had to put up with."[13]

Dean Snow, whose father, Sgt. Milburn Snow, was a member of Company B, 711th TB, recalled, "[My father] told us that at night the tank crews would dig a long trench and park the tank over the top of it. The crew would then sleep in the trench with the tank protecting them from snipers. I seem to recall him saying that the tanks would park in a circle similar to the old west covered wagons."[14]

While the rain came down, the 96th IDiv moved from the western shore of Okinawa to the center, and the 27th IDiv took up their sector along the coast. On April 18, when the rain stopped, American commanders made plans for an all-out assault against the main Japanese defensive line. Built behind a few strong ridges, and stretching from coast to coast across the middle of Okinawa, the line was known as the Shuri defenses. As the Americans lined up for the attack, they had the 7th IDiv on the east coast, the 96th IDiv in the center, and the 27th IDiv on the west.[15]

By the time the Americans moved against the Shuri line, they had developed a new tactic. "The American answer to the enemy's strong and integrated defenses was the tank–infantry team, including the newly developed armored flamethrower, and supported by artillery. . . . Although rockets, napalm, mortars, smoke, aerial bombing, strafing, naval bombardment, and all the others in the array of American weapons were also important," wrote the Army historians, "the tank–infantry team supported by 105s and 155s [artillery] was the chief instrument in the slow approach on Shuri." The historians explained how the teams worked:

> Guns and howitzers battered Japanese cave openings, dugouts, and pill-boxes, forcing enemy gunners back into tunnels for protection and decreasing their fields of fire. Taking advantage of the resulting "dead spaces," infantry and tanks crept up on the most exposed point; the tanks

attacked the position point-blank with cannon, machine guns, and flame, while the infantry prevented Japanese "close-quarters attack troops" carrying explosives from closing in on the tanks. . . .

The tank–infantry team waged the battle. But in the end it was frequently flame and demolition that destroyed the Japanese in their strongholds. General Buckner, with an apt sense for metaphor, called this the "blowtorch and corkscrew" method. Liquid flame was the blowtorch; explosives, the corkscrew.[16]

Although the American assault planned for April 19 would be made along the entire front, the main push would come near the junction of the 27th and 96th IDiv from a battalion of 27th IDiv soldiers and thirty tanks. As planned, the tank-infantry attack would push straight down Route 5 in the center of the island between Nishibaru Ridge on the east and Kakazu Ridge on the west. Once past the ridges, the force would turn west and capture the town of Kakazu, thus splitting the Shuri defenses in two. Picked to spearhead the massive tank attack were the tanks of the 193rd TB, which had been on Okinawa since April 8 but had seen no combat so far.[17]

Company A, 193rd TB would provide eighteen tanks, including six flamethrowing tanks and one 105mm M7 assault gun. The Assault Gun Platoon from Headquarters Company sent over three 105mm M7s while Headquarters Company itself gave up two M4 command tanks. The last five tanks were M4A1 flamethrowing tanks from the 2nd Platoon of Company B, 713th FTB. This would be the first time the 713th FTB would use its flamethrowing tanks in combat.[18]

On the morning of April 19 the entire American line started forward but immediately ran into stiff resistance. In the center, the thirty tanks and their supporting infantry started forward around 7:30 A.M., but an intense artillery and mortar barrage soon halted the infantry. Undaunted, the unsupported tanks continued on.

Two platoons from Company A, 193rd TB, plus one section of flamethrower tanks from the 713th FTB, led the way. Driving straight down Route 5, the tank column headed toward the saddle between the two enemy-held ridges. In a matter of minutes, however, one 193rd TB tank and one 713th FTB tank were lost to hidden land mines.[19]

Continuing down into the saddle, the tanks encountered extreme difficulty, "due to the steep slope of the bypass" and lost another 193rd TB tank when it slipped off the road and overturned. As Army historians wrote, "As the tanks moved down the road in column, a 47mm antitank gun, firing from a covered position to the left on the Nishibaru Ridge [opened fire.]" Two more 193rd TB tanks and two more 713th FTB tanks were hit and disabled before the enemy gun was destroyed by the Assault Gun Platoon.[20]

The remaining tanks hurried south, looking for the "faint track" heading west into Kakazu Village. Unfortunately, they missed it. Continuing south, the column lost another 193rd TB Sherman to antitank fire before turning west down another "faint track," which they mistook for the correct one. Instead of carrying the tanks into the center of Kakazu, however, the track took them into relatively flat ground below the village. As enemy fire continued to rain down upon them, the tanks regrouped and began firing into the rear of Kakazu ridge.

"Discovering that they could not reach the village from this point," wrote the Army historians, "the tanks retraced their way to the main road, turned back, found the right trail, and were in Kakazu shortly after 1000." For the next three hours, the 193rd TB and 713th FTB tanks roamed back and forth throughout the village, blasting enemy fortifications and gun emplacements and burning buildings. At the same time, however, the Japanese were preparing a counterattack.[21]

Attacking with "mines, 47mm Model 1 antitank guns, artillery, and suicide squads," the Japanese wreaked havoc upon the unsupported tanks. "Suicide squads first blinded the tank crews with hand-thrown Model 94 smoke candles," recorded historian Gordon L. Rottman, "kept them buttoned up with Model 97 grenades and small-arms fire, and flung 22-pound satchel charges beneath the tanks. Hand-placed magnetic demolition charges were also used—their one and a half pounds of TNT could penetrate a Sherman tank's side and top armor." Even the electronically detonated back-scratcher devices welded to the sides of some of the 193rd TB tank turrets could not keep the Japanese at bay forever. In all, fourteen more American tanks were destroyed in and around Kakazu. Continued Rottman, "Japanese swarmed over some disabled tanks forcing the hatches open and grenading the crews. Some crewmen dug in under their disabled tanks and held out for two days before returning to American lines."[22]

"At 1330 [1:30 P.M.]," reported Army historians, "since it was now evident that infantry would not be able to reach them, the tanks received orders to return to their own lines. Of the thirty tanks that had maneuvered around the left end of

An M4 medium tank with wooden side panels for protection against magnetic mines on Okinawa Shima, April–May, 1945. US ARMY

Kakazu Ridge in the morning, only eight returned in the afternoon. The loss of twenty-two tanks on 19 April in the Kakazu area was the greatest suffered by American armor on Okinawa in a single engagement."[23] In fact, the loss of twenty-two tanks—eighteen Shermans and assault guns from the 193rd TB and four flamethrowing tanks from the 713th FTB—in a single engagement was the greatest loss of American armor during the entire Pacific war. Concluded the 713th FTB historian, "The tanks must receive support by infantry on a mission of this type."[24]

The only success along the entire American line came on the east coast where the 711th TB and the 3rd Platoon flamethrowers of Company A, 713th FTB aided the 7th IDiv. Moving slightly inland from the ocean, the Americans pushed through Ouki Village and up against Ouki Hill and Skyline Ridge.[25] Somehow, one platoon of Shermans from Company A, 711th TB slipped behind the ridge and began shelling the enemy from the rear. When the Japanese counterattacked, another section of Company A tanks, plus the flamethrowing tanks from the 713th FTB, moved 600 yards beyond Skyline Ridge and repelled the attack.

Farther inland, Company C and the 7th IDiv foot soldiers attacked Hill 178 until they ran into impenetrable terrain. Moving to their left, the tanks took up a position on the western end of Skyline Ridge and began shelling the hill from the flank. "During the next five hours," recalled the 711th TB historian, "the Japs made numerous attempts to crawl up reverse slopes of Skyline Ridge to satchel-charge tanks and all attempts were repulsed by tank machine-gun fire. Artillery and heavy mortar fire fell on the tanks all day causing radiator damage but no losses."[26]

Over the next few days, the Americans ran into the same stubborn resistance whenever they pushed forward. The 711th TB, with elements of the 713th FTB, and the 7th IDiv continued to assault Skyline Ridge, Ouki Hill, Hill 178 and a new enemy position nicknamed "the Rocky Crags." Recalled Robert Clifton (Company A, 711th TB), "Many, many days were fought to secure one hill. . . . Many hills were secured finally by flamethrower tanks and men carrying flamethrowers." On April 24, after days of heavy fighting, the Japanese evacuated Skyline Ridge and Hill 178 and withdrew to a new defensive line.[27]

In the center, the 96th IDiv was faring only slightly better. From April 20 through April 24, the infantry and the supporting tanks from the 763rd TB and 713th FTB slowly inched their way across Tombstone Ridge, and then forward toward Nishibaru Ridge and a heavily fortified escarpment to the east. Utilizing the heavy firepower of the regular tanks and the flamethrowing capabilities of the specially equipped Shermans, the tank–infantry team eventually shoved the Japanese off the ridges and gained valuable real estate. During the attack, however, both the 763rd TB and the 713th FTB suffered the loss of numerous tanks to antitank and artillery fire, land mines, and enemy satchel charges.

William E. Bonnell (Company B, 763rd TB) recalled, "One time my platoon was sent ahead of [the] fighting to fire back on the other side of the hill they were taking. We had just turned and [were] firing back when Japs [suicide bombers] crawled under the rear of two of the tanks with explosives. They set them off under the engine compartment, ruining the engines. The crews got out and into other tanks and we went on back. As we went by the two tanks we saw arms and

legs and other parts of bodies lying there." Fortunately, however, most of the damaged tanks were quickly repaired and put back into action.[28]

On the far west, in the 27th IDiv sector, the tanks and infantry tried to follow
Route 1 toward the town of Gusukuma and the surrounding heights. Numerous
roadblocks and mines, and a few blown bridges, delayed the tanks of the 193rd
TB and the attached elements of the 713th FTB, but the infantry managed to push
ahead and on April 24 they captured the ridges north and east of Gusukuma.

On the left side of the 27th IDiv sector, the tanks and infantry finally captured
Kakazu Ridge and on April 23 the flamethrowing tanks of Company B, 713th
FTB set the town of Iso on fire. The next day, the town of Kakazu followed suit.
At the same time, the 193rd TB tanks supported the advancing infantry by firing
into the mouths of caves and the openings of above-ground tombs. Although the
193rd TB suffered numerous losses to both tanks and personnel during the
advance, none were as costly as the loss of their commanding officer, Lt. Col.
Walter F. Anderson.[29]

On April 21, two platoons of tanks from the 193rd TB and one section of
flamethrowers from Company B, 713th FTB were stalled before Gusukuma by a
blown bridge. Amidst a steady stream of incoming sniper fire, Colonel Anderson
took control and had his tank crews and tank dozer fill in a suitable bypass around
the bridge. Then, Colonel Anderson climbed into his command tank and personally led the column forward. "Approximately one hundred yards past the bypass,"
wrote the 193rd TB historian, "the command tank was hit six or seven times by an
[antitank] gun from the left flank, killing one member of the crew and wounding
three others, including the battalion commander, who managed to get out of the
turret and down to the ground but died a few feet from the tank."[30] Although sad-
dled with the loss of their commanding officer and the earlier loss of so many
tanks on April 19, the 193rd TB fought on.

On April 25, the 27th IDiv troops and the tanks of the 193rd TB and 713th
FTB captured most of Gusukuma and forced the Japanese into a heavily fortified
area northwest of town known as Item pocket. Over the next few days, the Americans attempted to reduce the pocket but ran into stiff resistance. On April 27, as
the 2nd Platoon tanks of Company A, 193rd TB moved around the south side of
Gusukuma, they came under accurate enemy fire. "As they moved through [the
area]," said the 193rd TB historian, "the last two tanks were knocked out, one in
flames, two men were killed instantly, two burned fatally and five others suffered
burns or wounds." The remaining tanks pushed onward and, working diligently
with the infantry, reduced the pocket before nightfall.[31]

With Gusukuma captured and Item pocket gone, the infantry and tanks
turned south again and eventually captured Machinato airfield below Gusukuma.
On May 1, the exhausted, battle-depleted 27th IDiv, which had suffered more than
3,000 casualties since April 1, and the devastated 193rd TB were replaced on the
front lines by the 1st Marine Division, which had finished cleaning up northern
Okinawa. Pulled back to a reserve position, the 193rd TB ceased to exist as a tank
unit. Orders went out for "all serviceable medium tanks [to be] turned over to
other combat units." From May 1 to May 3, the 193rd TB sent sixteen tanks to the

706th TB, eleven tanks to the 711th TB, and fourteen tanks to the 763rd TB. Although personnel from the 193rd TB (including Company D with its M5 light tanks) would remain on Okinawa and perform much needed patrol work, guard duty and mopping-up operations, their medium tanks were never returned to them. The hard-fought Okinawa campaign had been the last for the 193rd TB.[32]

In the center of the island, the 96th IDiv, aided by the tanks of the 763rd TB and Company C, 713th FTB, ran into extremely stiff resistance among the caves and crags of the Urasoe-Mura escarpment, 1,000 yards beyond Kakazu Ridge. On April 26, the tanks and infantry captured the eastern end of the escarpment, over-looking the town of Maeda, with little difficulty but as they crested the escarpment they were subjected to what Army historians termed "reverse-slope defense." As explained, "It was not difficult to occupy the forward slope of the ground, but the crest and reverse slope were forbidden land."[33]

Swinging around the eastern end of the escarpment, a detachment of infantry and tanks reached the town of Maeda on April 26. The next day, when the infantry and tanks looked out into the open fields beyond the town they were surprised to find perhaps 600 Japanese soldiers, "unaccountably exposed." Noted the 763rd TB historian:

> By 1100, tanks were operating along the entire front and having a "Field Day." Initially, the targets for the tanks were small groups of Japs. . . . By fire and movement of the tanks, these small groups were forced over the hill and soon the day's job was evident to the tanks and FT [flame-thrower tanks]. . . . The tanks systematically began flushing the Japs from their numerous holes and were very successful in eliminating great numbers of the Japs. All caves and pillboxes in the advance were fired upon and either closed up or burned out. . . . Of the number of Japs chased out in the open, it is estimated that nearly 300 Japs were annihi-lated by the fire from the tanks and [flamethrowers].[34]

Added the tank battalion historian, "This is the first time that the advancing tanks confronted the enemy in great numbers, especially out in the open, and it indicated that the opposition is being forced back to the rear positions, causing great numbers of the enemy to be exposed."[35]

The slaughter continued on April 28 and 29 as the tanks and infantry flushed more defenders from the Urasoe-Mura escarpment. Company C, 763rd TB and the 3rd Platoon, Company C, 713th FTB attacked a group of caves and ravines on April 29. "[The tanks] flushed out so many Japs," wrote the 763rd TB historian, "that [their] day was completely occupied in the annihilation of over 300 Nips by tank fire and [flamethrower] alone." Added the 713th FTB historian, "Approx 100 Japs were in one cave which was burned. . . . The [infantry] credited tanks with 90 percent of the 290 Japs killed."[36]

On April 30, the tired 96th IDiv and the battle-dented 763rd TB were replaced by the 77th IDiv and the 706th TB, both fresh from Ie Shima. When the 763rd TB pulled back for rest and rehabilitation, it was missing eighteen medium tanks, one light tank, and one 105mm-assault gun tank—an indication of the difficulties of tank warfare during the Okinawa campaign.[37]

Along the east coast, the 7th IDiv and the tanks of the 711th TB, plus elements of the 713th FTB, generally made good progress from April 23 to May 3. On the right side of the 7th IDiv front, tanks and infantry advanced steadily toward Kochi and Kochi Ridge before being forced to halt. Over the next few days, the tanks and infantry gained the top of the ridge and entered the town of Kochi itself but could not eliminate the stubborn defenders in the southern half of the town or beyond.

In the center of the 7th IDiv zone, the 3rd Platoon, Company C, 711th TB and the flamethrower tanks of the 1st Platoon, Company A, 713th FTB, attacked and burned the town of Onaga. By April 29, the tanks had worked their way into the town only to discover it "had been previously leveled by artillery and tank fire." Noted the 711th TB historian, "Tanks moved into the town without infantry cover and proceeded well into the town but had to turn back because of heavy artillery fire. One tank threw a track during the withdrawal and the enemy moved in to destroy the tank, but the dismounted crew beat them off and [got their tank back] to safety."[38]

On the left side of the division line, along the immediate coast, the 7th IDiv and the 711th TB made very little progress from Skyline Ridge as the Japanese rained shot and shell down upon them from 145-foot Conical Hill, which dominated the area. Between Skyline Ridge and Conical Hill were the village of Unaha and the Yonabaru airfield. Rice paddies around Unaha and soft sand along the beach made it difficult for the tanks to go forward in support of the infantry. In fact, on April 28, two tanks and a battalion tank dozer bogged down and on April 29, one tank was disabled by a Japanese mine and three more either overturned or lost their tracks "due to the high crown roads with soft shoulders."[39]

By the evening of May 3 the entire American line had penetrated far inside the Shuri line. On the western flank, the 1st MarDiv had replaced the 27th IDiv and held a position just south of the Machinato airfield straight east toward the Urasoe-Mura escarpment. In the center, the 77th IDiv held the crest of the escarpment and the eastern end of Maeda and then had an outward bulge on the left side of its division line near Route 5. On the east flank, the 7th IDiv held half of Kochi and all of Onaga on the far right and the ground just north of Unaha and Yonabaru airfield on the far left. In the center of their division front, however, a battalion of 7th IDiv foot soldiers held a lodgment about 1,000 yards in front of their line. It was here, and at the 77th IDiv bulge on Route 5, that the Japanese concentrated counterattacks on May 4, 1945.[40]

CHAPTER THIRTY-THREE

The Last Battle

After dusk on May 3, the Japanese sent the "heaviest air assault the Imperial Navy kamikazes had yet launched" against the American ships around Okinawa, sinking two destroyers and two LSMs and damaging countless others. At the same time, a heavy Japanese bombing raid saturated the American rear lines on Okinawa. All of this was, of course, in preparation for a major Japanese counteroffensive against the new American line.[1]

In the early morning hours of May 4, the Japanese shipped several hundred men along both coasts to get behind the American lines "to destroy American tanks and artillery." Fortunately for the Americans, both amphibious flanking moves were discovered before the attackers could land and most of the troops were wiped out. Four hours later, near 4:50 A.M., the Japanese began a thirty-minute artillery barrage against the 7th and 77th IDivs. The Japanese had brought their artillery out of hiding for the assault and had massed them for one of the heaviest barrages ever laid down by the Japanese during the entire Pacific war. At 5:00 A.M., the artillery added smoke to the barrage and 15,000 Japanese soldiers swept forward.[2]

The American 7th and 77th IDivs were hit head-on, with the Japanese attacking down six main avenues. All along the American line, however, the infantry held on and called for artillery support. At Maeda, the infantry and artillery tore apart a thrust by Japanese tanks in the only offensive use of Japanese tanks on Okinawa. At Kochi, the Japanese penetrated into the city, but the American resistance stiffened and forced a halt. At daybreak, American armor and artillery came forward to support the battered infantry line.[3]

While the American artillery tore into the massed Japanese ranks and devastated the exposed Japanese artillery batteries, the tanks of the 711th TB moved in to shore up the 7th IDiv line. "Groups of enemy personnel were observed and

355

destroyed," wrote the 711th TB historian, "concentrated fire was placed on [observation posts], caves, pillboxes, tombs, ravines and gullies."[4]

Near the town of Onaga, the flamethrowing tanks of Company A, 713th FTB supported the 711th TB in repulsing the Japanese that attacked the 7th IDiv lodgment. Reported the 713th FTB historian, "A Jap counterattack developed on the [northeast] side of Onaga and the flamethrowers and standard tanks were called up to assist the infantry. After two hours of firing the attack was repulsed."[5]

Although battered and bruised, the Japanese held onto their precarious forward positions and at nightfall on May 4, renewed their attacks. "At 1930 [7:30 P.M.] heavy enemy artillery fire began to fall in the area and continued to fall throughout the night," noted the 711th TB historian. "The [Assault Gun] Platoon leader counted over two hundred rounds in one concentration." Buoyed by their artillery, about 450 Japanese infantry hit the center of the American line near the junction of the 7th and 77th IDivs and penetrated about one mile to a ridgeline known as the Tanabaru escarpment.[6]

In the 77th IDiv sector itself, the 3rd Platoon Shermans of Company B, 706th TB came up to help shore up the Route 5 bulge and at dawn spotted six Japanese tanks moving into the area. Through a combination of artillery, bazooka and tank fire, six tanks were eventually eliminated. "[The 3rd] platoon knocked out three of the six tanks," bragged the 706th TB historian. "For the remainder of the period, the platoon supported the [infantry in] neutralizing and destroying enemy positions across the front and right flank." By the end of May 5, the Japanese counteroffensive had been broken, although the troops on the Tanabaru escarpment would hold out until May 6. By the time the sun went down on May 6, more than 5,000 Imperial soldiers littered the Okinawan landscape, many more than they could afford to lose.[7]

On May 8, word reached Okinawa that Germany had surrendered and the war in Europe was over. In the Pacific, however, the battles in the Philippines, on Okinawa and elsewhere, continued.[8]

Beginning on May 1, Company B, 713th TB was attached to the 1st MarDiv and began helping the 1st Marine Tank Battalion in cleaning out the area around the Machinato airfield. By May 14, Company B, 713th FTB and the Marines had moved ahead about 1,000 yards. Along the way, the flamethrower tanks found plenty of opportunity to strike at the hidden enemy.

The 713th TB historian remarked on the advance:

May 6— . . . moved out at 1500 [3:00 P.M.] and burned five caves with two loads of napalm. . . . About 200 Japs were driven out, of which fifty were killed by flamethrower and standard tanks.

May 7— . . . moved out and burned caves uncovered by 75mm fire . . . fired 1,200 gals of napalm at caves and area targets . . .

May 9—The flamethrowers moved in to burn two exposed caves. A large number of Japs were forced out of another opening on the reverse slope and [were] killed by Marine tanks and infantry. Four Japs were killed at our end of the tunnel. This action enabled the infantry to advance 600–800 yds.

May 11—1st Platoon . . . attacked caves and dugouts west of Dakeshi at 1100 with all six flamethrowers. About 100 Japs were flushed from the caves, an ammo dump and a 47mm [antitank] gun was [sic] destroyed in this action.[9]

As the Americans moved farther south, the island widened out and the 6th MarDiv came on line between the west coast and the 1st MarDiv. On May 8, the rested 96th IDiv and 763rd TB replaced the tired, battered 7th IDiv and 711th TB along the east coast. Three days later, the U.S. 10th Army Corps began a renewed offensive with the 96th IDiv (with 763rd TB), the 77th IDiv (with 706th TB), the 1st MarDiv (with 1st MTB), and the 6th MarDiv (with 6th MTB), on line from east to west. Supporting all four divisions were the flamethrowing tanks of the 713th FTB.[10]

As the American line started forward, its main objective was the town of Shuri, located in the center of the island, and Naha on the west coast. While the 6th MarDiv drove on Naha, the 1st MarDiv and the 77th IDiv, in the center, moved against Shuri. On the east coast, the 96th IDiv took over the job of capturing Conical Hill and the land south of Kuhazu.[11]

The 96th IDiv, 763rd TB, and Company A, 713th FTB made slow progress against Conical Hill. Soft terrain hampered movement and caused a number of tanks to bog down, but on May 16 infantry and tanks flanked the hill on the east side and entered the outskirts of the big coastal town of Yonabaru. The 1st and 2nd

713th FTB attacking Coral Ridge on Okinawa Shima on May 17, 1945. US ARMY

Platoons, Company B, 763rd TB "had a field day firing at emplacements and numerous Japs in the vicinity," reported the 763rd TB historian. Several land mines in the streets of Yonabaru were exploded by tank machine-gun fire, which led the tankers to believe that the area surrounding the town, including the flat fields to the southwest, were heavily mined.[12]

In the center of Okinawa, the 77th IDiv, plus the tanks of the 706th TB and Company C, 713th FTB, pushed directly toward Shuri. As the medium tanks tackled enemy caves and pillboxes, the light tanks of Company D, 706th TB, and two flamethrowing tanks assaulted Chocolate Drop Hill on May 12 and 13. On May 13, the 706th TB historian reported, "One [flamethrower] tank fired a load of napalm into a large cave causing the cave to blow up with a series of large explosions, indicating that it was probably an enemy ammunition dump."[13]

On May 14, four Stuart tanks of Company D, 706th TB were destroyed by antitank and artillery fire, so on May 15 the Shermans of Companies A and B, 706th TB replaced the light tanks in the assault on Chocolate Drop Hill. Over the next few days, the two medium tank companies lost one tank to an antitank gun, had two tanks blown up by satchel charges, and had a fourth wrecked by a land mine. Numerous tanks were hit by antitank gunfire but continued on unabated.[14]

Eventually, the tanks and infantry worked their way around the flank of Chocolate Drop Hill, taking the enemy from behind. "The tanks fired on targets at the rear

713th FTB composite hull M4 Sherman attacks Japanese cave positions on the southern shore of Okinawa, Shima, April–June, 1945. US ARMY

of the hill and in the valley and ridges [south] of this position," wrote the 706th TB historian. "Caves, dugouts, and other targets were fired upon. One [antitank] gun was destroyed, and one cave completely blew up with a series of explosions proving it to be an ammunition dump." On May 20, the infantry finally overran Chocolate Drop Hill and pushed the American line a few yards farther south.[15]

On the western half of Okinawa, Company B, 713th FTB was still working with the Marines. By May 14, the 1st MarDiv had pushed south of Dakeshi while the 6th MarDiv tried to take Sugar Loaf Hill, just northeast of Naha, against fanatical Japanese defenders. By the time Sugar Loaf was seized, more than 3,000 Marines had been killed or wounded while the Japanese lost "untold thousands."[16]

On May 22, the 6th MarDiv was in the northern suburbs of Naha, the 1st MarDiv and 77th IDiv were west and north of Shuri, respectively, and the 96th IDiv held the eastern slopes of Conical Hill and the coastal town of Yonabaru. As a group of Army historians wrote, "At the end of the third week in May the fighting had penetrated to the inner ring of the Shuri defenses. . . . From 22 to 29 May, [however], except for certain gains on the flanks, there was no appreciable progress against any part of the Japanese inner defense ring. . . . The stalemate was due in large measure to rain, mud and the bogging down of all heavy equipment."[17]

Although occasional rain had drenched both sides during the first six weeks of the Okinawa campaign, torrential rain began falling on May 22. "Mud was to become king," noted the Army historians, "and it was impossible to mount a large-scale attack during this period." Noted the 706th TB historian, "Heavy rains resulting in slippery and muddy terrain precluded the employment of tanks, throughout this period." Unable to move, the tankers used the period to rest their weary bodies and repair their battle-worn vehicles.[18]

Repair and restoration was indeed the first order of business during the last week of May 1945. By May 31, the four Army tank battalions and the one armored flamethrower battalion had 221 tank casualties on Okinawa. "Of this total," the Army historians wrote, "94 tanks, or 43 percent, had been completely destroyed. Enemy mines had destroyed or damaged sixty-four tanks and enemy gunfire 111. Such mishaps as thrown tracks or bogging down in bad terrain had accounted for thirty-eight, of which twenty-five were subsequently destroyed or damaged, mostly by enemy action. The 221 tank casualties constituted about 57 percent of the total number of Army tanks on Okinawa." Included among the total number destroyed were twelve precious flamethrowing tanks from the 713th FTB.[19]

As the rain fell, the center of the American line, just north of Shuri, bogged down, but the two flanks continued to move. Even without tank support, the 6th MarDiv on the west flank continued its drive into Naha only to discover the Japanese had evacuated the shell-flattened coastal town and withdrawn into caves and emplacements in the hills to the immediate east. Turning in pursuit, the Marines pushed their way into the hills and on June 1, after much bitter fighting, laid claim to Naha's high ground.[20]

On the east coast, while the 96th IDiv held the eastern half of Conical Hill, protecting its right flank, a rejuvenated 7th IDiv moved down the coast to Yonabaru and on May 22 and 23 began moving south and west. "[In] spite of heavy rains," wrote the 711th TB historian, "Company C's 1st Platoon [tanks] moved in support of the [infantry]." By nightfall on May 23, two infantry battalions had moved into a position just southwest of Yonabaru and were poised to sweep around behind Shuri. However, the rain changed all that. "The continuing rains had by this time mired the tanks in their assembly areas north of Conical Hill," wrote the Army historians, "and the armor which commanders had counted on to spearhead the drive to the west was unable to function. Heavy assault guns likewise were immobilized. The infantry was on its own."[21]

As soon as the Japanese realized their right flank and rear were in danger, they counterattacked. Although the Japanese were unable to retake Yonabaru, they did manage to stop the American advance. Then, under the cover of the heavy rain, which grounded most of the American airplanes, the Japanese abandoned the Shuri line and began pulling back to previously-prepared positions near the southern tip of Okinawa.[22]

On May 28, the rain slowed enough for the 1st Platoon tanks from Company B, 706th TB to reach the front lines of the 77th IDiv and join an attack against the northwest corner of Shuri. Firing into the town, the tanks "knocked out two enemy [machine-gun] nests, one mortar and one enemy vehicle." Two days later, as the infantry pushed forward against the weakened Japanese defensive line and entered the northern half of Shuri, the tanks fired into numerous caves and silenced one enemy machine gun.[23]

On May 29, a regiment of Marines slipped over the boundary between the 1st MarDiv and the 77th IDiv to capture Shuri Castle, the ancient home of the Ryukyuan kings and the recent headquarters of the Japanese Army. Two days later, the 77th IDiv reached the southern edge of Shuri and declared the town captured. In breaking the Shuri line and capturing the northern half of Okinawa, the American Marines and soldiers had suffered a total of 26,044 killed, wounded, or missing with another 14,000 men listed as non-battle casualties, mostly combat fatigue. For the Japanese, the eight week battle for Okinawa had cost an estimated 50,000 casualties, mostly killed. Still, the fighting went on.[24]

The shape of Okinawa below the Shuri line resembles that of an arrowhead. On the eastern side, just south and east of Yonabaru, one barb forms the Chinen peninsula. On the other side, directly below Naha, the other barb forms the Oroku peninsula. Angling down from both barbs to form the dangerous tip of the arrowhead is the Kiyan peninsula, where most of the remaining Japanese defenders climbed into their previously-constructed emplacements.[25]

On May 29 and May 30, 1945, the 3rd Platoon Shermans of Company A, 711th TB and the 105mm assault guns of the Assault Gun Platoon from Headquarters Company, 711th TB moved about 1,000 yards southwest of Yonabaru and began shelling a series of hills roughly 1,500 yards farther out. By the end of the second day, the tank battalion historian was able to report, "Several hundred rounds of 75mm and thousands of rounds of .30-caliber were fired and the hills were completely neutralized." Oddly enough the historian also noted the lack of Japanese artillery fire, which had plagued the Americans since the beginning of the campaign. "No enemy artillery had been encountered for a week and it seemed as though a large scale withdrawal of heavy weapons had been made following the fall of the Naha-Yonabaru defense line," he wrote.

Over the next few days, the tanks and infantry crept steadily southward, although rain made the roads "almost impassable." On June 2, as the Americans were fighting to clear out the two barbs and assault the deadly arrowhead of southern Okinawa, the 77th IDiv, along with the 706th TB, were relieved from front-line duty. For the remainder of the Okinawa campaign, the fighting would be in the hands of the 1st and 6th MarDivs, the 7th and 96th IDiv, and their attached armor.[26]

While the two Marine divisions worked to clear out the Oroku peninsula and the western half of the southern tip, the two Army divisions moved to capture the Chinen peninsula and the eastern half of the tip. Pushing ahead of their armor, the 7th IDiv cut across the base of the Chinen peninsula and reached the southeast coast of Okinawa on June 3. When part of the 7th IDiv moved into the peninsula itself and found it almost devoid of Japanese troops, General Buckner realized the Japanese were going to make their final stand on the southern tip of the island. Shifting fronts, the 7th IDiv turned and began moving southwest—down toward the arrow point.[27]

Near the center of the island, the 96th IDiv had to advance without support of the 763rd TB because of the rain and the terrain, but by the evening of June 6 the division had captured Iwa town and was in contact with the 7th IDiv advancing down the east coast on its left.[28]

Even as the 7th IDiv pushed southward, Japanese resistance began to stiffen. On June 6, elements of the division reached the town of Gushichan and found the Japanese waiting. The next day, the tanks of Company C, 711th TB braved the mud and standing water and advanced to Gushichan to assist in an attack. While the 3rd Platoon laid down cover fire for a battalion of infantry attacking the town, the 1st and 2nd Platoons moved out with some infantry to neutralize an escarpment to the rear.

"Fire was so coordinated that both of the assault platoons were able to bring [the] fire of the entire company on targets within their respective areas," noted the 711th TB historian. "The terrain caused a change of mission and the Second Platoon moved through the town itself, while the First gave splendid overhead support, and the Third neutralized the escarpments in the rear." Before the end of the day, Gushichan was in American hands.[29]

Although enemy resistance was almost nonexistent on the Chinen peninsula, the 6th MarDiv ran into a detachment of Japanese naval troops that had splintered off from the main Japanese group on the Oroku peninsula. On June 4, the 6th MarDiv executed the last opposed amphibious landing of World War II and came ashore at the northern tip of the Oroku peninsula. Against light opposition, the Marines spread out and quickly overran Naha airfield on the northern end of the peninsula. As twenty-four Marine Corps tanks were quickly shuttled ashore, the 1st Platoon flamethrower tanks of Company B, 713th FTB got ready as reinforcements.[30]

At 6:30 A.M. on June 6, four flamethrowing tanks finally went ashore. For the next two days, however, they remained completely idle. Noted a group of Army historians, "Use of tanks was restricted by mud and the widely scattered mine-fields, which were protected by abundant machine-gun fire." Finally, on June 8, two of the 713th TB flamethrower tanks moved out with the Marines "to burn vil-lages." Reportedly, they killed ten Japanese sailors.[31]

By June 10, the mud on the Oroku peninsula was beginning to harden. The four flamethrowing tanks went forward that day and burned two towns, killing twenty-six Japanese sailors, and the next day moved all the way to the base of the peninsula to burn the town of Tomigusuku as the Marines drove the Japanese Naval Force into a tight pocket along the northern edge of the peninsula. By June 15, the pocket had been eliminated and the Oroku peninsula was declared secure.[32]

Just east of the Oroku peninsula, the 1st MarDiv was having trouble of its own. The Japanese had formed their last defensive line from just below the town of Ito-man on the west coast, through the Yuza-Dake and Yaeju-Dake hill masses in the center of the Kiyan peninsula, to a point on the east coast just south of Gushichan. On June 9, the 1st MarDiv had captured Itoman but when they advanced southward, they ran into strong resistance.[33]

On June 10, the 1st MarDiv, plus their own tanks and tanks from 3rd Platoon, Company B, 713th FTB, attacked and burned a village at the center of the new Japanese line. Over the next few days, the flamethrowers stayed with the 1st Mar-Div and helped burn a number of small villages, caves and trenches, killing a large number of enemy soldiers. During one attack, on June 14, the flame ignition sys-tem failed on one tank and unlit fuel was sprayed across an enemy-held cane field. Within seconds, however, white phosphorus grenades were thrown by the Marines and the entire area erupted in flame.[34]

A composite hull M4, 713th FTB, taking incoming Japanese fire on Okinawa Shima, June 4, 1945. US ARMY

From June 12 to June 15, the 1st MarDiv fought the Japanese for possession of Kunishi Ridge, the westernmost linchpin of the Japanese line, just below Ito-man. Noted the Army historians, "Kunishi Ridge was the scene of the most frantic, bewildering, and costly close-in battle on the southern tip of Okinawa." But while the Marines and their tank units, and the flamethrower tanks of Company B, 713th FTB, were stalled on the western side of the Japanese line, the Army divisions and their supporting tanks were busting through on the east.[35]

While the Company B flamethrowers were fighting with the Marines, the flamethrower tanks from Companies A and C, 713th FTB were assisting the drives of the 96th and 7th IDivs and their attached tank battalions, respectively. The 763rd TB, attached to the 96th IDiv, got into action again on June 7 after the roads began to dry. Moving south from Iwa through slight rising terrain that led up to the Yuza-Dake and Yaeju-Dake hills, the tanks spent the next few days sealing hundreds of Japanese caves. The reports of the 763rd TB historian told the story:

[June 8]—sealed sixty caves . . .

[June 9]—The tanks sealed fifty caves and burned out one village.

[June 11]—Gave direct support to [the infantry] sealing sixty-five caves, and destroying one [antitank] position and one ammunition dump. Tanks fired on several Jap units which were either tanks or prime movers and killed at least twenty-four Japs.

[June 13]—Forty-four caves sealed, one 47mm gun destroyed, one 90mm mortar KO'ed, two [machine guns], one ammo dump and one pill box, all destroyed.[36]

Along the eastern coast, the flamethrowers of Company C, 713th FTB saw frequent action with the 711th TB and the 7th IDiv. After capturing Gushichan, the infantry and tanks continued along the coast and finally ran into the final Japanese defensive line. On June 8, as the Americans sallied forward, the enemy staged a small counterattack. Wrote the 711th TB historian, "The Japs made three attempts to close with [the] tanks, twice were shot off rear decks by covering tanks." He added, "Enemy artillery was periodic in this area and it was evident that another enemy stand was due."[37]

Over the next few days, the 711th TB medium tanks and Company C, 713th FTB stayed around the Gushichan area, firing into the Yaeju-Dake escarpment and at Hill 95 on the coast. On June 10, the flamethrower tanks used a new device to combat Japanese defending two knobs near the northeast end of Hill 95. Although the 7th IDiv soldiers had managed to clear most of the knobs, two well-fortified caves continued to hold out. In response, five flamethrower tanks came up and saturated the knobs with two loads of napalm.

Reported the Army historians, "[Next,] Capt. Tony Niemeyer, 6-foot 4-inch commander of Company C, 713th Armored Flame Thrower Battalion, moved one tank to the base of the two knobs. Then he attached a 200-foot hose, a special piece of equipment for delivering fuel to an area inaccessible to the tank. S/Sgt. Joseph

Frydrych, infantry platoon leader, Captain Niemeyer, and Sgt. Paul E. Schrum [Company C, 713th FTB] dragged the hose onto the high rock and sprayed [flaming] napalm over the two points, forcing out thirty-five or forty enemy soldiers whom the infantrymen killed by rifle or BAR fire." With this new use of flame, the 7th IDiv managed to secure the two pesky knobs and push deeper into the enemy position.[38]

"Niemeyer was active again on the morning of 11 June," continued the Army historians, "when the infantry proceeded against the high end of Hill 95." The infantry had tried an attack against a 170-foot cliff but had been stopped cold. At that point, Captain Niemeyer brought his Company C flamethrower tanks forward and "forced streams of red flame against the portion of the cliff where the infantrymen expected to make the ascent." As the historians explained, "This flame eliminated any threat of close-quarters resistance from caves in the face of the escarpment."

The Army historians continued:

> The next step was to reach the flat top of the hill and secure a toehold on the high ground. At 1100 Niemeyer and a platoon [of infantry] fastened one end of a hose to a flame tank and began dragging the other end up the almost vertical side of the hill. The tanks, artillery, mortars, and machine guns stepped up their rate of fire to keep down enemy interference, the men being as exposed as spiders on a bare wall. This spectacular attack was also slow, and it was forty-five minutes before the men reached a small shelf just below the lip of the escarpment. They stopped here long enough to squirt napalm onto the flat rocks above them in case any Japanese were waiting for them there, then scrambled over the edge and poured flame onto the nearby area. [The infantry] fanned out behind the flame. . . . When the fuel from one tank was exhausted the hose was fitted to another tank.[39]

Throughout the endeavor, the 1st Platoon tanks of Company C, 711th TB provided protection to the flamethrower tanks. "They led the flame tanks the entire length of the escarpment," crowed the 711th TB historian. "This section did splendid work and the terrain negotiated seemed impassable for tank operation. . . . Japs were forced out into the open all day."[40]

Working as a smoothly functioning team, the regular tanks of the 711th TB, the flamethrower tanks of Company C, 713th FTB, and the infantry of the 7th IDiv advanced steadily against the Japanese on Hill 95 and the Yaeju-Dake escarpment over the next few days. Recorded the 711th TB historian:

> [June 11]—Flamethrowers were used throughout the day with the third platoon to flush Japs out of caves. The platoon covered [the] flame tanks and fired 75mm and .30-caliber as Japs ran out into the open.
>
> [June 12]—The Second Platoon, operating in very close support of the infantry, sent one section with flamethrowers into an unnamed town to

the regiment's front. The town was burned and many Japs forced out into the open by flames were killed by tank fire.

On numerous occasions the fire of the company plus attached assault guns was coordinated in large groups of Japs, driven into the open by flame tanks.

By the end of June 13, the tanks and infantry had captured a pass between Hill 95 and the Yaeju-Dake escarpment. When Army engineers widened the pass, all available 711th TB Shermans moved to the top of the escarpment. "The entire battalion," the 711th TB historian wrote, "teamed up in a massing of armor for a perfectly coordinated tank–infantry drive to the southern tip of the island."[41] The final Japanese defensive line had been breached.

"For the remainder of the operation," reported the 711th TB historian, "the tanks had a field day." Once off the high ground that had formed the right side of the Japanese defensive line, the tanks raced toward the cliffs overlooking the Pacific Ocean. "Tanks pushed out front and took targets under fire," wrote the 711th TB historian. "Caves were sealed by tank gun fire; caves, rocky crags, wooded areas and towns were burned by flamethrowing tanks which forced the Japs out into the open to be destroyed by 75mm and machine-gun fire."[42]

Company A/711th TB M4 medium tank with a lost track near Nakaza, Okinawa on June 16, 1945. US ARMY

Near the center of the arrow tip, the 763rd TB and Company A, 713th FTB helped the 96th IDiv push their way past the Yaeju-Dake escarpment. Recalled the Army historians, "The five-day battle for the hills and the fields of coral outcroppings on the surrounding plateau, lasting from 13 to 17 June, was as much like hunting as fighting. It was a battle of massed tanks which operated ahead of the usual infantry support, blasting the coral rocks with shell bursts and almost constant machine-gun fire. The battlefield was perfect for armored flamethrowers, which poured flame into caves and clusters of rocky crags and wooded areas, whether killing Japanese at once or forcing them into lanes of machine-gun fire. In five days the flame tanks of the 713th Armored Flame Thrower Battalion directed more than 37,000 gallons of burning gasoline at the enemy."[43]

As the Americans pierced the Japanese line, light tanks, medium tanks, assault gun tanks and flamethrowing tanks took part in the final push to the sea. Recalled the 711th TB historian, "As the tanks neutralized the hills, towns and crags, with 105mm, 75mm, 37mm, and flame gun fire, the infantry moved in consolidating the positions."[44]

Having captured the Yaeju-Dake escarpment, the 763rd TB and the 96th IDiv rolled on toward the sea. "The enemy, losing practically all of his high ground, made suicide stands from every boulder, clump of grass and anything that afforded concealment," wrote the 763rd TB historian. "All signs of organized resistance vanished at this time and continuous pressure pushed the Japs into a small pocket around Madeera."[45]

In fact, as the Japanese line crumbled, only two pockets held out, one near Madeera, in the very center of the Kiyan peninsula, and one at Hill 89, on the east coast, at the very edge of the line. Unknown to the Americans, the commander of the Japanese forces on Okinawa, Lt. Gen. Mitsuru Ushijima, was inside a cave on Hill 89.[46]

Okinawa Shima, late June 1945. The center tank, a composite hull M4 Sherman, has been hit by Japanese antitank fire, and the other three tanks have come to the rescue. To the right is an M4A3, to the left is another composite hull M4, and the tank nearest the camera is an early M4A3. US ARMY

On the western side of the Japanese line, the 1st and 6th MarDivs finally broke through at Kunishi Ridge on June 17 and began pushing toward the southern tip of Okinawa. On June 18, as General Buckner stood watching the advance of the two Marine Corps divisions, a Japanese artillery shell landed nearby and sent a large shard of coral into his chest. He died ten minutes later. Lt. Gen. Simon Bolivar Buckner was the highest ranking American officer killed in action in World War II.[47]

As the Marines and Army raced for the sea, the 96th IDiv, in the center, was pinched out of line and concentrated on the reduction of the Madeera pocket. At the same time, the 7th IDiv, with the 711th TB and Company C, 713th FTB, turned its attention to Hill 89. "As the tanks and flamethrowers worked their way across the top of Hill 89, burning and blasting their way over treacherous terrain, the Japs started to surrender in large groups," said the 711th TB historian. "At this point the tank-mounted public address systems were put to use by members of the Division language team and large groups were talked out of caves."[48]

As the soldiers and Marines pressed forward, they began to capture hundreds of Japanese soldiers, "an unprecedented accomplishment in the Pacific war." At the same time, thousands of Okinawan citizens began to come out of hiding. However, there were still thousands of Japanese soldiers who refused to lay down their weapons. Recalled the Army historians, "Casualties among the Japanese averaged about a thousand a day during the first half of June, jumped to 2,000 on 9 June, to 3,000 the next day, and reached more than 4,000 on June 21."

Rather than surrender, hundreds of Japanese soldiers either committed suicide by exploding a hand grenade against their chest or by jumping off the high cliffs at the southern edge of Okinawa into the pounding surf and jagged rocks below. Recalled Dean Snow, the son of Sgt. Milburn Snow (Company B, 711th TB), "My father was amazed at the fact that the Japanese would not surrender. He remembered them jumping off the cliffs at the end of the island to avoid capture."[49]

On June 21, the 7th IDiv captured most of Hill 89. During the assault, seven tanks from Company C, 713th FTB used seventeen loads of napalm to burn out a number of caves. That night, with the Americans dug in all around his headquarters, General Ushijima committed hara-kiri.

The next day, June 22, the flamethrower tanks from Company C again went forward with the infantry to burn caves and enemy gun emplacements. "Two of the caves are said to have opened into the Jap Army headquarters," said the 713th FTB historian. "Sergeant Schrum, using the hose attachment, fired ten caves. He was accompanied by an interpreter with a loudspeaker who tried to get the Japs to leave the caves. Only two were taken in this way." At the end of the day, the historian was able to report, "[Company C] expended 4,200 gallons of napalm; 868 Japs were killed."[50]

Although mopping-up operations in the area would continue for days, with the regular tanks of the 711th TB and the flamethrower tanks from Company C, 713th FTB helping out, the battle for Hill 89 was all but over by June 22.[51]

At the Madeera pocket, the 96th IDiv and a unit of Marines from the 1st MarDiv, along with tanks of the 763rd TB and Company A, 713th FTB, began squeezing in on the defenders around June 17. On June 19, the 763rd TB historian reported, "Enemy appears to be making a last-ditch stand and several cases of hara-kari [sic] were observed. The flamethrower tanks were especially active, using 4,500 gallons of [flamethrower] fuel." The next day the assault continued, with the tanks of Company C, 763rd TB alone expending 501 rounds of 75mm ammunition and sealing thirty caves. Again, the flamethrower tanks killed a large number of Japanese, using 4,200 gallons of napalm.[52]

By June 22, most of the Madeera pocket had been overrun, but mopping up in the area would continue until June 26 when the final cave was detonated. On June 22, 1945, Okinawa was declared secure. Eight days later, mopping-up operations were declared complete, and on July 2, the Ryukyus campaign was officially declared a success.[53]

In the 82-day struggle for Okinawa, the United States suffered 49,151 casualties, including those lost aboard ships hit by Japanese kamikaze planes, and in the numerous airplanes that had gone up to protect them. For the Japanese, the defense of Okinawa had cost them approximately 75,000 dead and another 7,400 captured. As historian Gordon L. Rottman noted, "Only the much larger and longer Philippine campaign saw higher casualties in the Pacific Theater than Okinawa." Additionally, it is estimated that over 60,000 Okinawan civilians died during the campaign.[54]

As the Marines, soldiers, and tankers settled into bivouac areas all around Okinawa and began to clean their equipment and get some rest and rehabilitation, American commanders were already eyeing their next major objective—Japan itself. As Robert Clifton (Company A, 711th TB) wrote, "We relaxed and thought about the invasion of Japan as that was the only place left to go."[55]

CHAPTER THIRTY-FOUR

The End

On August 6, 1945, an atomic bomb was dropped on Hiroshima, Japan. More than 92,000 people were killed. Another 37,000 were wounded. Three days later, on August 9, another atomic bomb was detonated over Nagasaki. Over 23,000 more people lost their lives and 43,000 were wounded. Many of the wounded in both cities would die later.

On August 14, 1945, Japan accepted unconditional surrender. World War II was over.[1]

"The night that we heard Japan had surrendered," recalled Robert Clifton (Company A, 711th TB) on Okinawa, "we were watching an outdoor movie. My best friend and I were sitting on a log side by side, and all at once we heard a lot of noise and I told my buddy I bet the war is over. Then it came on the screen that Japan had surrendered. We didn't see the rest of the movie."[2]

All across the Pacific, and indeed throughout the world, there was a celebration that the war was finally over. David C. Dumbeck (Headquarters and Headquarters Company, 754th TB) was on Luzon in the Philippines when the war ended. He wrote, "I was recuperating from yellow jaundice and celebrated the dropping of the atomic bomb. . . . After the bomb was dropped and the Japs surrendered, we knew us guys with more points would be going home."[3]

Another tanker with the 754th TB, PFC Sabino L. Goitia, already had heard about the surrender talks. On August 10, he had written in his journal, "Japan has offered to surrender. Perhaps this is really the end of this damn mess. Lots of shooting in the area. The boys sure feel like celebrating." A month later, after Japan's formal surrender on September 2, 1945, Private Goitia wrote, "Heard about the Army discharging men over 35. Hope I can get home by Christmas."[4]

Cpl. Thomas Howard (Company A, 754th TB) was already in training at Legaspi, Luzon, for the invasion of Japan when his company received news that an atomic bomb had been dropped on Japan. He wrote:

Events started happening, the news rang about a special bomb having been dropped on Japan, an atomic bomb, it was called. We couldn't even fathom the significance. Having watched bombs dropping and exploding and witnessing artillery shellings and the devastation that each could render, it was hard to comprehend the magnitude that the newspapers kept referring to. We jumped for joy. It was all too apparent that the training at Legaspi had great significance to us. Anything that could alter the inevitable, a direct confrontation on the shores of Japan, would be welcomed. The final push was being planned and we were to be a part of it.[5]

Another tank battalion in training on Luzon for the anticipated invasion of Japan was the 44th TB. Donald Mercier (Company C, 44th TB) remembered hearing about the atomic bomb and the surrender of Japan. "The news of the two atomic bombs dropped on Japanese cities gave us the first ray of hope that the end of the war could be coming," he wrote. "We were all prepared for a very costly battle for Americans and Japanese if an invasion took place. When the good news of peace came on 15 August 1945 we were ecstatic. What a relief!!"[6]

At the time of the Japanese surrender, there were fourteen independent tank battalions in the Pacific theater of operations. Three battalions—the 193rd, 711th TBs and the 713th FTB—were on Okinawa. The 767th was in Hawaii and ten battalions were in the Philippines—the 28th, 44th, 706th, 754th, 775th, 779th and 785th TBs on Luzon; the 710th and 763rd on Leyte; and the 716th TB in the southern Philippines. Three of the battalions on Luzon were completely new to the theater and had seen no action at all during World War II.[7]

The 28th TB had been formed at Fort Knox, Kentucky, on December 6, 1943, as an airborne tank battalion. For the next ten months the men trained as airborne tankers, meant to be airdropped with 37mm light M22 Locust tanks alongside airborne infantry. Then, on October 20, 1944, they were redesignated a medium tank battalion and began training with M4 Sherman tanks. In August 1945, the 28th TB set out from California for action in the Pacific but was still at sea when the two atomic bombs were dropped. On September 2, the 28th TB reached Luzon, where it was stationed when Japan officially surrendered.[8]

The 779th TB (Medium) was activated as a separate tank battalion from a reorganization of the 43rd Armored Regiment on November 11, 1943, while the latter was on maneuvers in Tennessee. On July 21, 1945, the battalion set sail for the Pacific, arriving on Luzon on September 3, one day after Japan's formal surrender aboard the battleship *Missouri*.[9]

The 785th TB was activated at Fort Knox on March 1, 1943, as a light tank battalion but was converted to a medium tank battalion on October 22, 1943. In the summer of 1945, the battalion was moved to California and on July 28, 1945, departed San Francisco for Luzon. The transport ship arrived at Manila Bay on September 3 and disembarked two days later.[10]

In mid-August, after the surrender of Japan, the 44th TB changed from "training for combat" to "orientation for occupation duties." Six light tanks and twenty-six medium tanks were received to bring the battalion up to full strength and on August 31 the tankers were alerted for movement to Japan. On September 6, the 44th TB set off in convoy with a number of other vessels carrying American occupation troops toward Tokyo Bay. On September 15, the entire convoy docked in the heart of the Japanese city.

By the time the 44th TB reached Tokyo, thousands of veteran soldiers were being sent home if they had earned enough points through combat. "Men with more than eighty points were on their way home," noted the 44th TB historian, "and men with seventy points or more were being prepared to leave." As veteran tankers were sent home, fresh men from the States, and even infantrymen from the Americal Division, took their place. By the beginning of October, the historian could report that "The battalion was getting accustomed to the idea of being at home in the Tokyo area." Perhaps aiding in this adjustment was the fact that the 44th TB had acquired the use of a Japanese movie studio and could now show movies indoors. "This was an improvement over the method that had been in use," wrote the battalion historian.

In November, the men built a volleyball and basketball court and created a basketball league, "composed of company teams." On Thanksgiving Day, the 44th TB "celebrated the day in Stateside manner with mess halls supplying a dinner consisting of turkey and all the trimmings." On December 24, the last two original officers and the last fifty original enlisted men of the 44th TB were sent back to the United States. "They took with them," lamented the 44th TB historian, "the last of the original core of the 44th."

During the Christmas season, each company had a Christmas tree and decorated their mess halls with "wreaths, bells and tinsel." Christmas dinner consisted of all the trimmings and "every man got about two pounds of turkey." When 1945 slipped into 1946, the 44th TB was still in Tokyo. On May 10, 1946, the battalion finally was deactivated, but by then all of the veteran tankers were already home.[11]

The 706th TB had come to Luzon just prior to Japan's surrender after helping defeat the Japanese on Okinawa and spending the rest of June and the first two weeks of July preparing to move to a new destination. "Regardless of where the destination might be," noted the 706th TB historian, "everyone seemed happy to be leaving Okinawa."

On July 13, the battalion had finally left Okinawa and ten days later landed at Batangas on Luzon. Over the next few weeks, the high-point men began transferring back to the United States while replacements began arriving. On August 14, word was received that the Japanese had offered unconditional surrender and the 706th TB gave a sigh of relief. "This was a day everyone had hoped and prayed for, the end of the war throughout the world," wrote the battalion historian.

In early September, the 706th TB was "alerted for occupation duty in Japan," but the move never came. By the end of September, dozens of high-point men had been sent home, including the battalion commander. In October, the 706th TB was being commanded by a major and by the end of November a captain was in charge. On November 30, 1945, what was left of the 706th TB moved from southern Luzon to Manila. That same date, the 706th TB was inactivated. All men with enough points were sent home while the replacements were transferred to the newly arrived 785th TB.[12]

Another Luzon-based tank battalion was the 754th TB. Noted one battalion historian, "World War II ended with the cessation of hostilities, 15 August 1945, but the battalion continued to function as a unit in the Philippine Islands. . . . Its mission, guarding supplies along the entire length of the Manila Harbor waterfront." Another 754th TB historian added, "The majority of the men who fought with the battalion through the Luzon campaign were returned home during this period [September 1 to December 31, 1945]. Many men were transferred in and out of the unit in compliance with readjustment procedure."[13]

On January 31, 1946, the 754th TB was placed on "inactive status," but in February 1946, the unit was reactivated in Seoul, Korea, absorbing personnel and equipment from the 713th FTB. Almost a year later, the 754th TB was finally deactivated at Seoul on December 31, 1946.[14]

The last tank unit on Luzon was the 775th TB, based near Lingayen Gulf. Reported the battalion historian, "The Luzon campaign had taken its toll of equipment. All of the battalion's tanks were found by ordnance teams to be unserviceable for further combat operations. . . . The unserviceable vehicles were turned in, and new ones were drawn."

Although the war was over, the 775th TB remained active with "camp construction, vehicle maintenance, and training." Recreation came in the form of baseball and basketball games and movies shown three nights a week in a battalion recreation hall. Also, noted the 775th TB historian, "A 'War Exhibit' was maintained at Battalion Headquarters, displaying all types of enemy uniforms and equipment."

On October 12, 1945, 297 enlisted men and twenty-two officers from the 775th TB joined the 37th IDiv for transfer back to the United States. Three days later, the remaining officers and men were transferred to Base X outside of Manila. "The principal duty at Base X was the guarding of various quartermaster depots at widely separated spots throughout the city," wrote the 775th TB historian. On November 29, the 775th TB gathered at Manila Bay for shipment home. At the same time, infantrymen with enough service points were transferred to the 775th TB to bring it up to full strength. "Here," wrote the tank battalion historian, "the unit was processed and embarked at Manila for the United States on 14 December 1945."

"It was discovered that the two millionth man to be returned from the Pacific Theater of Operations was aboard our ship," said the 775th TB historian. "Lots were drawn and the lucky man was S/Sgt. Irving Feldman of Company A, 775th Tank Battalion." On January 3, 1946, the transport ship reached San Francisco and the men were ferried over to Camp Stoneman. Two days later, the 775th TB was deactivated.[15]

On Leyte, the 710th TB began sending their high-point veterans home shortly after the formal Japanese surrender on September 2. Near the end of November, when the battalion was informed the entire unit was going home, it received 538 infantrymen to bring it up to full strength. On Christmas Eve, the men marched twenty-five miles from their bivouac area to Tacloban on the east coast. "From White Beach," noted the 710th TB historian, "troops loaded on barges to board SS Santa Isabel laying at anchor approximately three miles from shore in Leyte Gulf."

Christmas services were held aboard ship and on December 26 the ship finally weighed anchor and steamed eastward toward home. After welcoming the New Year in the middle of the Pacific Ocean, the *Santa Isabel* reached Los Angeles on January 16, 1946. One day later, the 710th TB was deactivated at Camp Anza, California.[16]

Like the 706th TB, the 763rd TB left Okinawa in the summer of 1945 and moved back to its old bivouac site on Leyte to prepare for the invasion of Japan. When word reached the unit that Japan had surrendered, the tankers began counting the days until they could go home. On December 2, 1945, the 763rd TB was deactivated on Leyte Island, Philippines, and the men were sent home.[17]

The last tank battalion to leave the Philippines was the 716th TB. "It was in the Del Monte area of Mindanao, staging for the invasion of the Japanese homeland, that news was received concerning the collapse of the Nipponese empire," wrote the battalion historian. "The 716th had participated in eight amphibious landings and worked with ten infantry divisions." On November 29, the 716th TB boarded the USS *Cavalier* in Macajalar Bay and on December 19 the ship steamed into San Francisco Bay. Deactivation came that same date.[18]

The 713th FTB was on Okinawa in a semi-permanent base camp when it received word Japan had surrendered. "On the 15th of September," recalled the 713th FTB historian, "the battalion was notified that it had been selected for military police duty in Korea." On September 28, the men and flamethrowing tanks were placed aboard two LSTs but were delayed in their embarkation until October 5 because of numerous typhoon warnings. Three days later, a killer typhoon hit Okinawa and destroyed numerous ships and facilities. "The battalion was extremely fortunate in that it was aboard ship and almost at its destination when the typhoon struck Okinawa," recalled the 713th FTB historian, "and as a result we were not affected by it."

On October 10, the 713th FTB landed in Korea and began a long period of occupation and policing. On February 14, 1946, the 713th FTB was finally deactivated at Seoul, Korea.[19]

Two other tank battalions were still on Okinawa when word reached the island the Japanese had surrendered. The personnel of the 193rd TB, which had been stripped of their few remaining tanks in May, had spent the rest of their time on Okinawa patroling and guarding rear-area depots. After the beginning of 1946, the remaining tankers of the battle-hardened 193rd were shipped to San Francisco, arriving on January 18. Three days later, the 193rd TB was deactivated at Camp Stoneman, California.[20]

Unlike the 193rd TB, the 711th TB fought to the bitter end on Okinawa before settling into a semi-permanent bivouac. After January 1, 1946, the battalion embarked aboard a ship and headed east for the United States. On January 18 the ship arrived at Seattle, Washington, and the men were moved to Fort Lawton, Washington. Three days later, the 711th TB was inactivated.[21]

When Japan announced it would accept a formal surrender on August 14, 1945, the 767th TB was stationed at Schofield Barracks, Oahu, Territory of Hawaii. After helping to wrestle Leyte from the Japanese in December 1944, the 767th TB had remained on the island until April 1945. On April 7, the tank battalion was "transferred from station Leyte, less personnel and equipment, to station Oahu." In other words, the name alone was being moved from the Philippines to Hawaii. At the time, the men and tanks of the 767th TB were needed as replacements for the tank battalions fighting on Luzon. While the name of the 767th TB could be spared, the "personnel and equipment" could not.[22]

To implement the "move" of the 767th TB to Hawaii, the phantom unit absorbed the personnel and equipment of the 766th TB, which then was stationed on Oahu. On April 6, 1945, the 766th TB had been deactivated on Oahu. Since its activation in February 1943 only two companies of the 766th TB had seen any action—Company C on Eniwetok in February 1944, and Company D on Saipan in June 1944. On April 7, 1945, when the 767th TB was transferred to Hawaii, it absorbed the men and tanks from the former 766th TB.[23]

To complicate matters, the 762nd TB, which then was stationed on Oahu, was deactivated on April 10, 1945. Like the 766th TB, only two companies of the 762nd TB had seen action in World War II—Companies B and D on Saipan. When the 762nd was inactivated, the personnel and equipment were transferred to the 767th TB to "completely fill" the "new" battalion's ranks and bring it up to strength. So, on August 14, 1945, when the Japanese announced they had accepted unconditional surrender, the 767th TB (constituted from parts of the 762nd and 766th TBs) was at Schofield Barracks, Hawaii.

Near the end of August, the reconstituted 767th TB was notified it was being sent to Japan for occupation duty. On August 29, the battalion boarded a few ships at Pearl Harbor and steamed west toward Japan. On September 27, 1945, the ships arrived at the island of Honshu, Japan. For the next six months, the personnel of the 767th TB performed police and occupation duties on Honshu. On March 31, 1946, the reconstituted unit finally was deactivated in Japan.[24]

With the surrender of Japan, the 28th, 779th and 785th TBs, which all had just arrived on Luzon in late August and early September, were sent home and deactivated at Camp Stoneman, California. In quick order, the 28th TB returned to San Francisco on January 11, 1946, and was deactivated two days later. The 779th TB returned on January 14 and was deactivated on January 16, and the 785th TB steamed under the Golden Gate Bridge on January 17 and was deactivated on January 19.[25]

The U.S. Army formed a total of 118 tank battalions in World War II. Eighteen tank battalions and three independent tank companies saw service in the Pacific Theater. Two battalions, the 192nd and the 194th, ceased to exist after the fall of Bataan in April 1942, although Company B, 194th TB, which had been sent to Alaska in August 1941, was not a part of the surrender and was later redesignated the 602nd Tank Company. In regards to the other two tank companies, the 601st Light TCo was inactive throughout the war but the 603rd TCo saw plenty of combat and had a storied career.[26]

The sixteen other Pacific tank battalions remained active in one form or another until the last active Pacific tank battalion, the 44th TB, was deactivated in Tokyo in May 1946.

Although small in number and often overlooked by the publicity given to the U.S. Marine Corps and their tanks in the Pacific, the Army tank battalions in the Pacific played a vital role in winning the war against Japan.

A part of the war from the very first day, when tankers from the 192nd and 194th TB helped defend Clark Field in the Philippines, until the very end, when the 44th and 767th TB helped occupy Japan, the Army tank battalions saw combat in every form and on dozens of Pacific islands. Fighting in steamy jungles or across coral reefs, through coconut groves or in tall Kunai grass, down muddy, clinging dirt paths or along elegant paved boulevards, the Pacific Army tank battalions gave better than they got and came out of the war holding their heads high.

Fighting against a fanatical enemy who was willing to give his very life to eliminate one American tank, the Army tankers learned to work in tandem with the Army and Marine Corps riflemen. In fighting the Japanese, the Army tank battalions, and all of the other Allied forces in the Pacific, faced an enemy that was arguably more reckless and tenacious than those faced in North Africa, the Mediterranean or northern Europe. Unlike the majority of German and Italian soldiers who knew when to surrender, the average Japanese soldier preferred death to captivity. Against such a fanatical foe, the Army tank battalions had to develop new methods, new tactics and new strategies to ensure success.

Instead of rolling across the countryside in huge armored divisions, as both Allied and Axis tanks did in North Africa or northern Europe, the Pacific tank battalions fought most of their battles in five-tank platoons, or even in sections of platoons. Only when the Americans returned to the Philippines in 1944 were the tank battalions able to work in large numbers, giving mutual support to each other. For the most part, however, the only support the Pacific tanks could rely upon were a few friendly fellow tanks or a few friendly infantrymen.

And, although the Pacific tankers did not have to face German Tiger or Panther tanks, or German 88mm antitank guns, they did have to contend with 37mm, 47mm and 75mm antitank guns that packed a wallop. Additionally, the Pacific tankers had to contend with numerous land mines, including buried aerial bombs that could wreck a tank in a blinding flash. The most fearsome mines, however, were the magnetic mines that stuck to the sides of a tank. In the hands of an enemy who was willing to run up to a tank and die for his emperor, magnetic mines claimed a large number of both light and medium American tanks in the Pacific war.

The marvelous support the Pacific tankers provided to both the Army and the Marine Corps in World War II often is overlooked. But for that matter, so is the role of the Army in the Pacific. When asked who fought the war in the Pacific for America, most people will answer the Navy and the Marines. Few people realize, however, that the Army and the Army Air Force did more fighting in the Pacific than the Marines. Although Admiral Nimitz used primarily Marine units during his island-hopping campaign, his Marine divisions were often bolstered by Army soldiers, cannons and tanks. On the other hand, General MacArthur used primarily Army units for his move across New Guinea and eventually back into the Philippines. Very few, if any, Marine Corps troops saw action in MacArthur's southwest Pacific area.

And right in the middle of the fight, with their armor against the Empire of the Rising Sun, were the men and machines of the Pacific tank battalions.

NOTES

CHAPTER ONE

1. Weaver, James R. N., *Operations of the Provisional Tank Group United States Army Forces in the Far East, 1941–1942,* [hereafter cited as Weaver, *Prov Tank Gp Rpt of Opns],* 16; Morton, *United States Army in World War II, The War in the Pacific—The Fall of the Philippines,* [hereafter cited as *The Fall of the Philippines*] 134–35.
2. Tenney, *My Hitch in Hell,* 23.
3. Proviso East High School, "Biography of 2nd Lt. Ben R. Morin," *192nd Tank Battalion,* http://www.proviso.w-cook. k12.il.us/EAST/Bataan%20Web/Morin.htm [hereafter cited as Proviso East Reports], [accessed Sept. 4, 2001]; Weaver, *Prov Tank Gp Rpt of Opns,* 16.
4. Tenney, *My Hitch in Hell,* 22.
5. Proviso East Reports, "Biography of 2nd Lt. Ben R. Morin," *192nd Tank Battalion;* Hunnicutt, Stuart: *A History of the American Light Tank,* Vol. 1, 5.
6. Proviso East Reports, "Biography of 2nd Lt. Ben R. Morin," *192nd Tank Battalion;* Perret, *The Stuart Light Tank Series,* 9, 14–15.
7. Proviso East Reports, "Biography of 2nd Lt. Ben R. Morin," *192nd Tank Battalion;* Gibson, "Grim Bataan Heroes Find Humor in Beef," *Chicago Herald-American,* July 10, 1942, 1.
8. Ibid.
9. Ibid.
10. Weaver, *Prov Tank Gp Rpt of Opns,* 16; Miller, *The Illustrated Directory of Tanks of the World From World War I to the Present Day,* [hereafter cited as *Directory of Tanks*], 184, 412.
11. Schutt, *Janesville Tankers on Bataan,* 19.
12. Proviso East Reports, "Biography of PFC Henry J. Deckert," *192nd Tank Battalion;* Gibson, "Maywood Cook Wipes Out Jap Nest, Killed," *Chicago Herald-American,* July 11, 1942, 1.
13. Proviso East Reports, "Biography of Staff Sgt. Albert T. Edwards," *192nd Tank Battalion;* Tenney, *My Hitch in Hell,* 24.

14. Tenney, *My Hitch in Hell*, 24; Weaver, *Prov Tank Gp Rpt of Opns*, 16.
15. Proviso East Reports, "Biography of 2nd Lt. Ben R. Morin," *192nd Tank Battalion*.
16. Perret, *There's a War to be Won*, 15–16, 40; Perret, *The Stuart Light Tank Series*, 3; Sawicki, *Tank Battalions of the US Army*, 14; Miller, *Bataan Uncensored*, 10; Stanton, *World War II Order of Battle*, 299.
17. Perret, *There's a War to Be Won*, 40.
18. Ibid., 40–41.
19. Sawicki, *Tank Battalions of the US Army*, 14; Perret, *The Stuart Light Tank Series*, 3; Schutt, *Janesville Tankers on Bataan*, 24–25; Stanton, *World War II Order of Battle*, 299.
20. Poweleit, *Kentucky's Fighting 192nd Light G.H.Q. Tank Battalion*, 2–3; Stanton, *World War II Order of Battle*, 299.
21. Poweleit, *Kentucky's Fighting 192nd Light G.H.Q. Tank Battalion*, 4; Taped interview of Morgan French by Col. Arthur L. Kelley, 1994, http://www.dallas.net/~french/tape1side1.html [hereafter cited as French Interview], [accessed Nov 13, 2000], 1994, Tape 1, Side 1, 1.
22. Stewart Interview, *In the Hands of the Enemy*, http://www.enemyhands.com/bob.html, [hereafter cited as Stewart Interview, *In the Hands of the Enemy*], [accessed Jan 8, 2001], 2; Poweleit, *Kentucky's Fighting 192nd Light G.H.Q. Tank Battalion*, 3, 7.
23. Stanton, *World War II Order of Battle*, 299; Miller, *Bataan Uncensored*, 10; Stanton, *World War II Order of Battle*, 299. Stanton and others have stated that the four General Headquarters Tank Battalions were erected from eighteen scattered National Guard tank companies. However, this author counts only fifteen companies—four each with the 191st, 192nd and 193rd, and three with the 194th.
24. Miller, *Bataan Uncensored*, 14.
25. Ibid., 20.
26. Poweleit, *Kentucky's Fighting 192nd Light G.H.Q.* Tank Battalion, 5.
27. Ibid., 5; Miller, *Bataan Uncensored*, 20.
28. French Interview, 1994, Tape 1, Side 1, 1.
29. Ibid., 2; Poweleit, *Kentucky's Fighting 192nd Light G.H.Q. Tank Battalion*, 5.
30. Miller, *Bataan Uncensored*, 19–20.
31. Ibid., 21–22, 26–27, 40.
32. Each tank company consisted of three platoons with five tanks each, and a company headquarters with two more tanks, a recovery vehicle and numerous service vehicles. Additionally, the battalion headquarters unit had three tanks and numerous service vehicles.
33. Miller, *Bataan Uncensored*, 34, 37, 39.
34. Ibid., 40.
35. Ibid., 41, 42.
36. Perret, *There's A War to Be Won*, 42–45; Tenney, *My Hitch in Hell*, 10.
37. French Interview, 1994, Tape 1, Side 1, 1, 2.
38. Miller, *Bataan Uncensored*, 42–44.
39. Ibid., 45.
40. Ibid., 46–47.
41. Ibid., 46, 48.
42. Schutt, *Janesville Tankers on Bataan*, 48–49.
43. Tenney, *My Hitch in Hell*, 10.
44. Ibid., 11; Poweleit, *Kentucky's Fighting 192nd Light G.H.Q. Tank Battalion*, 17.

45. Schutt, *Janesville Tankers on Bataan,* 50–51.
46. Tenney, *My Hitch in Hell,* 14; Poweleit, *Kentucky's Fighting 192nd Light G.H.Q. Tank Battalion,* 19.
47. Poweleit, *Kentucky's Fighting 192nd Light G.H.Q. Tank Battalion;* Tenney, *My Hitch in Hell,* 17; Ortega Interview, December 21, 2000.
48. Tenney, *My Hitch in Hell,* 17.
49. Poweleit, *Kentucky's Fighting 192nd Light G.H.Q. Tank Battalion,* 22; Schutt, *Janesville Tankers on Bataan,* 67; French Interview, 1994, Tape 1, Side 1, 2.
50. Poweleit, *Kentucky's Fighting 192nd Light G.H.Q. Tank Battalion,* 22–23.
51. Costello, *The Pacific War, 1941–1945,* 100–106; Poweleit, *Kentucky's Fighting 192nd Light G.H.Q. Tank Battalion,* 28–29; Schutt, *Janesville Tankers on Bataan,* 68–69.

CHAPTER TWO

1. Poweleit, *Kentucky's Fighting 192nd Light G.H.Q. Tank Battalion,* 24; Schutt, *Janesville Tankers on Bataan,* 64; Miller, *Bataan Uncensored,* 58; Hunnicutt, *Stuart: A History of the American Light Tank,* 395.
2. Poweleit, *Kentucky's Fighting 192nd Light G.H.Q. Tank Battalion,* 24, 26.
3. Weaver, *Prov Tank Gp Rpt of Opns,* 12–13.
4. Tenney, *My Hitch in Hell,* 19.
5. Schutt, *Janesville Tankers on Bataan,* 68–69.
6. Miller, *Bataan Uncensored,* 50, 62; Poweleit, *Kentucky's Fighting 192nd Light G.H.Q. Tank Battalion,* 26.
7. Poweleit, *Kentucky's Fighting 192nd Light G.H.Q. Tank Battalion,* 27; Miller, *Bataan Uncensored,* 62–63.
8. Knox statement in Knox, *Death March,* 10; Stewart Interview, *In the Hands of the Enemy,* 3.
9. Poweleit, *Kentucky's Fighting 192nd Light G.H.Q. Tank Battalion,* 31; Miller, *Bataan Uncensored,* 64; Tenney, *My Hitch in Hell,* 19; Fitzpatrick, *The Hike into the Sun,* 11.
10. Knox statement in Knox, *Death March,* 10–11.
11. Stewart Interview, *In the Hands of the Enemy,* 2.
12. Salecker, *Fortress Against the Sun,* 34, 35, 36–37.
13. Ibid., 38; Poweleit, *Kentucky's Fighting 192nd Light G.H.Q. Tank Battalion,* 31; Miller, *Bataan Uncensored,* 65.
14. Salecker, *Fortress Against the Sun,* 38; Weaver, *Prov Tank Gp Rpt of Opns,* 13; Fitzpatrick, *The Hike into the Sun,* 12.
15. Ortega Interview, December 21, 2000.
16. Miller, *Bataan Uncensored,* 66–67; French Interview, 1994, Tape 1, Side 1, 5.
17. Knox statement in Knox, *Death March,* 13; Salecker, *Fortress Against the Sun,* 39.
18. Ortega Interview, December 21, 2000; Salecker, *Fortress Against the Sun,* 40; French Interview, 1994, Tape 1, Side 1, 3.
19. French Interview, 1994, Tape 1, Side 1, 3, 6–7; Poweleit, *Kentucky's Fighting 192nd Light G.H.Q. Tank Battalion,* 32. The main parade ground at Fort Knox, Kentucky, is named in honor of Private First Class Brooks, the first armored soldier to be killed in World War II. Although a slight controversy arose because Brooks was of African-American descent, Maj. Gen. Jacob L. Devers, chief of Armored Force, never wavered from his decision to name the parade ground in honor of Brooks. On December 23, 1941, the parade ground was dedicated without a hitch. Poweleit, *Kentucky's Fighting 192nd Light G.H.Q. Tank Battalion,* 206–9.

20. Salecker, *Fortress Against the Sun,* 41.
21. Diaz statement in Knox, *Death March,* 14.
22. French Interview, 1994, Tape 1, Side 1, 2; Ortega Interview, December 21, 2000.
23. Knox statement in Knox, *Death March,* 13–14.
24. Bardowski Interview, December 8, 2000; Poweleit, *Kentucky's Fighting 192nd Light G.H.Q. Tank Battalion,* 32.
25. Ibid.; "Citation for the Bronze Star Medal," Family Papers, Steve Bardowski.
26. Anderson, *A History of the Salinas National Guard Company, 1895–1995,* http://users.dedot.com/mchs/guard.html [accessed Nov 13, 2000], 4; Miller, *Bataan Uncensored,* 67; Sakai, *Samurai!,* 67.
27. Salecker, *Fortress Against the Sun,* 42; Poweleit, *Kentucky's Fighting 192nd Light G.H.Q. Tank Battalion,* 32.
28. Weaver, *Prov Tank Gp Rpt of Opns,* 13; Schutt, *Janesville Tankers on Bataan,* 80.
29. Miller, *Bataan Uncensored,* 71-72.
30. Gibson, "Filipinos Blast Jap Chutists," *Chicago Herald-American,* July 13, 1942, 1.
31. Weaver, *Prov Tank Gp Rpt of Opns,* 14; French Interview, 1994, Tape 1, Side 2, 2.
32. Poweleit, *Kentucky's Fighting 192nd Light G.H.Q. Tank Battalion,* 33; Tenney, *My Hitch in Hell,* 21-2; Rutherford, *The Fall of the Philippines,* 48–55.
33. Rutherford, *The Fall of the Philippines,* 55, 57.
34. Poweleit, *Kentucky's Fighting 192nd Light G.H.Q. Tank Battalion,* 33; Miller, *Bataan Uncensored,* 79.
35. Rutherford, *The Fall of the Philippines,* 57–8; Weaver, *Prov Tank Gp Rpt of Opns,* 14.
36. Miller, *Bataan Uncensored,* 80.
37. Ibid., 80–81.
38. Ibid., 81–82; Fitzpatrick, *The Hike into the Sun,* 16.
39. Fitzpatrick, *The Hike into the Sun,* 16–17.
40. Miller, *Bataan Uncensored,* 82–84.
41. Ibid.; Schutt, *Janesville Tankers on Bataan,* 91–92.
42. DeGroot Interview, *In the Hands of the Enemy,* 1; Gibson, "Grim Bataan Heroes Find Humor in Bombs," *Chicago Herald-American,* July 10, 1942, 1
43. Weaver, *Prov Tank Gp Rpt of Opns,* 8; Anderson, *A History of the Salinas National Guard Company, 1895–1995,* 4.
44. Weaver, *Prov Tank Gp Rpt of Opns,* 15; Rutherford, *Fall of the Philippines,* 63–64; Vader, "Fall of the Philippines," *History of the Second World War,* Pt. 31, 858; Morton, *The Fall of the Philippines,* 125–26.
45. Weaver, *Prov Tank Gp Rpt of Opns,* 15.
46. Poweleit, *Kentucky's Fighting 192nd Light G.H.Q. Tank Battalion,* 37; Schutt, *Janesville Tankers on Bataan,* 94.
47. Schutt, *Janesville Tankers on Bataan,* 95.
48. Ibid., 96; Poweleit, *Kentucky's Fighting 192nd Light G.H.Q. Tank Battalion,* 37.
49. Weaver, *Prov Tank Gp Rpt of Opns,* 15; Rutherford, *Fall of the Philippines,* 64, 66, 68; Morton, *The Fall of the Philippines,* 134.

CHAPTER 3
1. Weaver, *Prov Tank Gp Rpt of Opns* 16; Schutt, *Janesville Tankers on Bataan,* 110.
2. Ibid.
3. Ibid.; Poweleit, *Kentucky's Fighting 192nd Light G.H.Q. Tank Battalion,* 39.
4. Weaver, *Prov Tank Gp Rpt of Opns,* 16; Gibson, "Grim Bataan Heroes Find Humor in Bombings," *Chicago Herald-American,* July 10, 1942, 1.

5. Toland, *But Not in Shame,* 102; Morton, *The Fall of the Philippines,* 135; Schutt, *Janesville Tankers on Bataan,* 100; Weaver, *Prov Tank Gp Rpt of Opns,* 16.

6. Toland, *But Not in Shame,* 102; Morton, *The Fall of the Philippines,* 135.

7. Weaver, *Prov Tank Gp Rpt of Opns,* 16; Morton, *The Fall of the Philippines,* 135.

8. Morton, *The Fall of the Philippines,* 138, 163–64; Zich, *The Rising Sun,* 92.

9. Morton, *The Fall of the Philippines,* 138; Schutt, *Janesville Tankers on Bataan,* 108–110; Weaver, *Prov Tank Gp Rpt of Opns,* 16–17.

10. Morton, *The Fall of the Philippines,* 162–66.

11. Fitzpatrick, *The Hike into the Sun,* 18.

12. Miller, *Bataan Uncensored,* 89; Fitzpatrick, *The Hike into the Sun,* 20.

13. Schutt, *Janesville Tankers on Bataan,* 110–12; Weaver, *Prov Tank Gp Rpt of Opns,* 16–17.

14. Poweleit, *Kentucky's Fighting 192nd Light G.H.Q. Tank Battalion,* 41; Fitzpatrick, *The Hike into the Sun,* 20.

15. Weaver, *Prov Tank Gp Rpt of Opns,* 18; Miller, *Bataan Uncensored,* 96.

16. Miller, *Bataan Uncensored,* 96.

17. Gibson, "Tank Force Saved by Officer's Daring Action," *Chicago Herald-American,* July 14, 1942, 1; Proviso East Reports, "Biography of 1st Sgt. Roger James Heilig," *192nd Tank Battalion.*

18. Miller, *Bataan Uncensored,* 96–97.

19. Morton, *The Fall of the Philippines,* 166, 176; Schutt, *Janesville Tankers on Bataan,* 117.

20. Miller, *Bataan Uncensored,* 97–98; Weaver, *Prov Tank Gp Rpt of Opns,* 18.

21. Weaver, *Prov Tank Gp Rpt of Opns,* 18; Miller, *Bataan Uncensored,* 98; Schutt, *Janesville Tankers on Bataan,* 115–16.

22. Miller, *Bataan Uncensored,* 98–99; Weaver, *Prov Tank Gp Rpt of Opns,* 18; Fitzpatrick, *The Hike into the Sun,* 24.

23. Miller, *Bataan Uncensored,* 99–100

24. Morton, *The Fall of the Philippines,* 177; Miller, *Bataan Uncensored,* 101.

25. Ibid.

26. Miller, *Bataan Uncensored,* 102–3; Morton, *The Fall of the Philippines,* 177.

27. Ibid.; Gibson, "Tank Force Saved by Officer's Daring Action," *Chicago Herald-American,* July 14, 1942, 1; Miller, *Bataan Uncensored,* 108.

28. Miller, *Bataan Uncensored,* 108–9; Fitzpatrick, *The Hike into the Sun,* 25–26.

29. Weaver, *Prov Tank Gp Rpt of Opns,* 19; Miller, *Bataan Uncensored,* 108–9.

30. Ibid.; Gibson, "Tank Force Saved by Officer's Daring Action," *Chicago Herald-American,* July 14, 1942, 1.

31. Miller, *Bataan Uncensored,* 109; Fitzpatrick, *The Hike into the Sun,* 26.

32. Gibson, "Tank Force Saved by Officer's Daring Action," *Chicago Herald-American,* July 14, 1942, 1; Miller, *Bataan Uncensored,* 109.

33. Miller, *Bataan Uncensored,* 117; Morton, *The Fall of the Philippines,* 194; Poweleit, *Kentucky's Fighting 192nd Light G.H.Q. Tank Battalion,* 49; Diaz statement in Knox, *Death March,* 10.

34. Miller, *Bataan Uncensored,* 117–8; Anderson, "Company C, 194th Tank Bn in the Philippines, 1941–42," *Armor,* May–June 1996, 33.

35. Diaz statement in Knox, *Death March,* 10; Weaver, *Prov Tank Gp Rpt of Opns,* 19; Anderson, "Company C, 194th Tank Bn in the Philippines, 1941–42," *Armor,* May–June 1996, 33.

36. Miller, *Bataan Uncensored,* 118; Morton, *The Fall of the Philippines,* 194.

37. Anderson, "Company C, 194th Tank Bn in the Philippines, 1941–42," *Armor,* May–June 1996, 33; Poweleit, *Kentucky's Fighting 192nd Light G.H.Q. Tank Battalion,* 50.
38. Ibid.
39. Miller, *Bataan Uncensored,* 119; Poweleit, *Kentucky's Fighting 192nd Light G.H.Q. Tank Battalion,* 50.
40. Miller, *Bataan Uncensored,* 119–21; Poweleit, *Kentucky's Fighting 192nd Light G.H.Q. Tank Battalion,* 50–51; Anderson, "Company C, 194th Tank Bn in the Philippines, 1941–42," *Armor,* May–June 1996, 33.

CHAPTER FOUR
1. Morton, *The Fall of the Philippines,* 166, 178–79, 180.
2. French Interview, 1994, Tape 1, Side 2, 6; Morton, *The Fall of the Philippines,* 181.
3. Morton, *The Fall of the Philippines,* 181; Miller, *Bataan Uncensored,* 111.
4. Miller, *Bataan Uncensored,* 115.
5. Morton, *The Fall of the Philippines,* 181; Miller, *Bataan Uncensored,* 183; Schutt, *Janesville Tankers on Bataan,* 119; Poweleit, *Kentucky's Fighting 192nd Light G.H.Q. Tank Battalion,* 44.
6. Proviso East Reports, "Biography of Sgt. Raymond P. Mason," *192nd Tank Battalion;* Merrifield, *Report on Personnel of 192nd Tank Battalion Covering the Period 1 December 1941 to 1 November 1945,* 3, 11, 12; Poweleit, *Kentucky's Fighting 192nd Light G.H.Q. Tank Battalion,* 43
7. Poweleit, *Kentucky's Fighting 192nd Light G.H.Q. Tank Battalion,* 44; Morton, *The Fall of the Philippines,* 181.
8. Morton, *The Fall of the Philippines,* 185.
9. Ibid., 185–86.
10. Morton, *The Fall of the Philippines,* 187.
11. Weaver, *Prov Tank Gp Rpt of Opns,* 20; Morton, *The Fall of the Philippines,* 166–67.
12. Hauser statement in Knox, *Death March,* 46; Gentry account in Poweleit, *Kentucky's Fighting 192nd Light G.H.Q. Tank Battalion,* 46.
13. Hauser statement in Knox, *Death March,* 47; Gentry account in Poweleit, *Kentucky's Fighting 192nd Light G.H.Q. Tank Battalion,* 46–47.
14. Gentry account in Poweleit, *Kentucky's Fighting 192nd Light G.H.Q. Tank Battalion,* 47.
15. Ibid.; Hauser statement in Knox, *Death March,* 47.
16. Gentry account in Poweleit, *Kentucky's Fighting 192nd Light G.H.Q. Tank Battalion,* 47–48.
17. Weaver, *Prov Tank Gp Rpt of Opns,* 22; Diaz statement in Knox, *Death March,* 42.
18. Anderson, "Company C, 194th Tank Bn in the Philippines, 1941–42," *Armor,* May–June 1996, 33; Anderson, *A History of the Salinas National Guard Company, 1895–1995,* 5.
19. Weaver, *Prov Tank Gp Rpt of Opns,* 21; Toland, *But Not in Shame,* 154; Fitzpatrick, *The Hike into the Sun,* 30.
20. Miller, *Bataan Uncensored,* 122, 123.
21. Ibid., 117; Gentry account in Poweleit, *Kentucky's Fighting 192nd Light G.H.Q. Tank Battalion,* 48.
22. Schutt, *Janesville Tankers on Bataan,* 127; Weaver, *Prov Tank Gp Rpt of Opns,* 21.
23. Miller, *Bataan Uncensored,* 124.
24. Mattson statement in Knox, *Death March,* 43–4.

25. Schutt, *Janesville Tankers on Bataan,* 128–29; Gentry account in Poweleit, *Kentucky's Fighting 192nd Light G.H.Q. Tank Battalion,* 49; Whitman, *Bataan: Our Last Ditch,* 58.

26. Gentry account in Poweleit, *Kentucky's Fighting 192nd Light G.H.Q. Tank Battalion,* 49.

27. Schutt, *Janesville Tankers on Bataan,* 130; Morton, *The Fall of the Philippines,* 220–21; Whitman, *Bataan: Our Last Ditch,* 63.

28. Morton, *The Fall of the Philippines,* 221; Weaver, *Prov Tank Gp Rpt of Opns,* 22; Miller, *Bataan Uncensored,* 126; Tenney, *My Hitch in Hell,* 25.

29. Miller, *Bataan Uncensored,* 126; Morton, *The Fall of the Philippines,* 221. Miller mistakenly claims the withdrawal order came on January 5.

30. Miller, *Bataan Uncensored,* 128; Weaver, *Prov Tank Gp Rpt of Opns,* 22.

31. Miller, *Bataan Uncensored,* 128; Fitzpatrick, *The Hike into the Sun,* 31.

32. Miller, *Bataan Uncensored,* 126–27.

33. Ibid., 128–29.

34. Ibid.; Whitman, *Bataan: Our Last Ditch,* 66.

35. Miller, *Bataan Uncensored,* 130–31.

36. Schutt, *Janesville Tankers on Bataan,* 134.

37. Ibid.; Miller, *Bataan Uncensored,* 132; Morton, *The Fall of the Philippines,* 223.

38. Miller, *Bataan Uncensored,* 133, 134.

39. Morton, *The Fall of the Philippines,* 223–24; Schutt, *Janesville Tankers on Bataan,* 148.

40. Morton, *The Fall of the Philippines,* 224–25.

41. Whitman, *Bataan: Our Last Ditch,* 6; Miller, *Bataan Uncensored,* 138.

42. Whitman, *Bataan: Our Last Ditch,* 6–7.

43. Costello, *The Pacific War,* 183.

CHAPTER FIVE

1. Morton, *The Fall of the Philippines,* 226; Schutt, *Janesville Tankers on Bataan,* 136–37; Miller, *Bataan Uncensored,* 139–40.

2. Weaver, *Prov Tank Gp Rpt of Opns,* 23; Miller, *Bataan Uncensored,* 140.

3. Miller, *Bataan Uncensored,* 140; Schutt, *Janesville Tankers on Bataan,* 137.

4. Morton, *The Fall of the Philippines,* 245.

5. Schutt, *Janesville Tankers on Bataan,* 148–50.

6. Morton, *The Fall of the Philippines,* 247.

7. Miller, *Bataan Uncensored,* 143; Poweleit, *Kentucky's Fighting 192nd Light G.H.Q. Tank Battalion,* 54–55.

8. Stewart Interview, *In the Hands of the Enemy,* 4; Miller, *Bataan Uncensored,* 144–45.

9. Schutt, *Janesville Tankers on Bataan,* 150.

10. Miller, *Bataan Uncensored,* 1, 7.

11. Weaver, *Prov Tank Gp Rpt of Opns,* 23, 24; Fitzpatrick, *The Hike into the Sun,* 33.

12. Ibid., 24; Schutt, *Janesville Tankers on Bataan,* 154.

13. Poweleit, *Kentucky's Fighting 192nd Light G.H.Q. Tank Battalion,* 56.

14. Morton, *The Fall of the Philippines,* 261, 265.

15. Poweleit, *Kentucky's Fighting 192nd Light G.H.Q. Tank Battalion,* 56. Poweleit states this meeting occurred on January 7, 1942. This is in error, since MacArthur's only visit to Bataan was on January 10.

16. Morton, *The Fall of the Philippines,* 269–71.

17. Ibid., 148; Morton, *The Fall of the Philippines,* 278–80; Weaver, *Prov Tank Gp Rpt of Opns,* 24.

18. Morton, *The Fall of the Philippines,* 275–77, 287.

19. Miller, *Bataan Uncensored,* 146.

20. Morton, *The Fall of the Philippines,* 287–90.

21. Weaver, *Prov Tank Gp Rpt of Opns,* 24; Tenney, *My Hitch in Hell,* 26.

22. Morton, *The Fall of the Philippines,* 281–82.

23. Miller, *Bataan Uncensored,* 148.

24. Weaver, *Prov Tank Gp Rpt of Opns,* 24; Tenney, *My Hitch in Hell,* 26.

25. Weaver, *Prov Tank Gp Rpt of Opns,* 24; Tenney, *My Hitch in Hell,* 27; Miller, *Bataan Uncensored,* 148–49.

26. Ibid.

27. Morton, *The Fall of the Philippines,* 283–85.

28. Ibid., 291; Miller, *Bataan Uncensored,* 153.

29. Morton, *The Fall of the Philippines,* 293; Miller, *Bataan Uncensored,* 156.

30. Morton, *The Fall of the Philippines,* 293; Miller, *Bataan Uncensored,* 156–57; Weaver, *Prov Tank Gp Rpt of Opns,* 25.

31. Miller, *Bataan Uncensored,* 158.

32. Ibid., 159.

33. Weaver, *Prov Tank Gp Rpt of Opns,* 25; Toland, *But Not in Shame,* 183.

34. Weaver, *Prov Tank Gp Rpt of Opns,* 25–26.

35. Tenney, *My Hitch in Hell,* 27.

36. Schutt, *Janesville Tankers on Bataan,* 158; Weaver, *Prov Tank Gp Rpt of Opns,* 26.

37. Miller, *Bataan Uncensored,* 160–61; Fitzpatrick, *The Hike into the Sun,* 39.

38. Weaver, *Prov Tank Gp Rpt of Opns,* 26; Miller, *Bataan Uncensored,* 161.

CHAPTER SIX

1. Morton, *The Fall of the Philippines,* 300–301, 308; Rutherford, *Fall of the Philippines,* 110–11.

2. Morton, *The Fall of the Philippines,* 302–7.

3. Ibid., 313–14.

4. Ibid., 307–10, 315–17; Schutt, *Janesville Tankers on Bataan,* 173

5. Morton, *The Fall of the Philippines,* 338–39.

6. Weaver, *Prov Tank Gp Rpt of Opns,* 27; Miller, *Bataan Uncensored,* 171; Whitman, *Bataan: Our Last Ditch,* 287.

7. Morton, *The Fall of the Philippines,* 318.

8. Whitman, *Bataan: Our Last Ditch,* 357.

9. Ibid.; Schutt, *Janesville Tankers on Bataan,* 188.

10. Morton, *The Fall of the Philippines,* 310; Whitman, *Bataan: Our Last Ditch,* 287; Weaver, *Prov Tank Gp Rpt of Opns,* 27–28.

11. Morton, *The Fall of the Philippines,* 310, 319.

12. Ibid., 320; Tenney, *My Hitch in Hell,* 30; Poweleit, *Kentucky's Fighting 192nd Light G.H.Q. Tank Battalion,* 60. Poweleit incorrectly states this action took place on January 30, 1942. The crew of Private Young's tank included Sgt. Emerson P. Smith and Pvts. Vernon Deck and Sydney M. Ratnor.

13. Tenney, *My Hitch in Hell,* 30; Poweleit, *Kentucky's Fighting 192nd Light G.H.Q. Tank Battalion,* 60.

14. Whitman, *Bataan: Our Last Ditch,* 312, 440.

15. Ibid., 358–9; Morton, *The Fall of the Philippines,* 341.
16. Whitman, *Bataan: Our Last Ditch,* 358, 359.
17. Morton, *The Fall of the Philippines,* 341.
18. Ibid., 320–21; Whitman, *Bataan: Our Last Ditch,* 315.
19. Whitman, *Bataan: Our Last Ditch,* 289–90.
20. Ibid., 290–93.
21. Poweleit, *Kentucky's Fighting 192nd Light G.H.Q. Tank Battalion,* 60.
22. Morton, *The Fall of the Philippines,* 310–12.
23. Knox statement in Knox, *Death March,* 77–78; Poweleit, *Kentucky's Fighting 192nd Light G.H.Q. Tank Battalion,* 60.
24. Knox statement in Knox, *Death March,* 77–78; Whitman, *Bataan: Our Last Ditch,* 315.
25. Whitman, *Bataan: Our Last Ditch,* 359; Ortega Interview, December 21, 2000.
26. Whitman, *Bataan: Our Last Ditch,* 359.
27. Ibid., 362–3; Proviso East Reports, "Biography of 2nd Lt. Edward Garfield Winger" and "Biography of Sergeant Zenon Bardowski," both *192nd Tank Battalion.*
28. Bardowski Interview, December 8, 2000; Bronze Star citation for Sergeant Zenon Bardowski.
29. Ibid.
30. Whitman, *Bataan: Our Last Ditch,* 362.
31. Ibid. 363; Proviso East Reports, "Biography of 2nd Lt. Edward Garfield Winger," *192nd Tank Battalion;* Poweleit, *Kentucky's Fighting 192nd Light G.H.Q. Tank Battalion,* 61–62.
32. Rutherford, *Fall of the Philippines,* 116; Morton, *The Fall of the Philippines,* 342.
33. Whitman, *Bataan: Our Last Ditch,* 364; Morton, *The Fall of the Philippines,* 342.
34. Whitman, *Bataan: Our Last Ditch,* 365; Proviso East Reports, "Biography of Sgt. John Olin Hopple," *192nd Tank Battalion;* Poweleit, *Kentucky's Fighting 192nd Light G.H.Q. Tank Battalion,* 61.
35. Morton, *The Fall of the Philippines,* 322; Whitman, *Bataan: Our Last Ditch,* 315; Poweleit, *Kentucky's Fighting 192nd Light G.H.Q. Tank Battalion,* 61. Poweleit incorrectly states this activity took place on February 2.
36. Morton, *The Fall of the Philippines,* 321–22, 343; Whitman, *Bataan: Our Last Ditch,* 365.
37. Morton, *The Fall of the Philippines,* 322-23, 343; Whitman, *Bataan: Our Last Ditch,* 317–18, 320; Poweleit, *Kentucky's Fighting 192nd Light G.H.Q. Tank Battalion,* 61. Poweleit incorrectly states this activity took place on February 8.
38. Morton, *The Fall of the Philippines,* 343; Proviso East Reports, "Biography of Sgt. John Olin Hopple," *192nd Tank Battalion.*
39. Morton, *The Fall of the Philippines,* 344; Whitman, *Bataan: Our Last Ditch,* 367.
40. Whitman, *Bataan: Our Last Ditch,* 368; Poweleit, *Kentucky's Fighting 192nd Light G.H.Q. Tank Battalion,* 61. Poweleit incorrectly states this activity took place on February 8.
41. Whitman, *Bataan: Our Last Ditch,* 368; Morton, *The Fall of the Philippines,* 345.
42. Morton, *The Fall of the Philippines,* 345–46.
43. Ibid., 345–46; Whitman, Bataan: *Our Last Ditch,* 371.

CHAPTER SEVEN

1. Morton, *The Fall of the Philippines,* 347–48.

2. Ibid., 348.
3. Poweleit, *Kentucky's Fighting 192nd Light G.H.Q. Tank Battalion,* 56, 57, 58, 63, 67.
4. French Interview, 1994, Tape 1, Side 2, 11; Bardowski Interview, December 8, 2000.
5. Ortega Interview, December 21, 2000; Fitzpatrick, *The Hike into the Sun, 49;* Poweleit, *Kentucky's Fighting 192nd Light G.H.Q. Tank Battalion,* 59.
6. Ortega Interview, December 21, 2000; DeGroot Interview, *In the Hands of the Enemy,* 2; French Interview, 1994, Tape 1, Side 2, 11.
7. Miller, *Bataan Uncensored,* 185.
8. Ibid.; DeGroot Interview, *In the Hands of the Enemy,* 2.
9. Tenney, *My Hitch in Hell,* 29–30.
10. Bardowski Interview, December 8, 2000; Miller, *Bataan Uncensored,* 179.
11. Miller, *Bataan Uncensored,* 184.
12. Poweleit, *Kentucky's Fighting 192nd Light G.H.Q. Tank Battalion,* 57, 66.
13. Tenney, *My Hitch in Hell,* 31.
14. Morton, *The Fall of the Philippines,* 258.
15. Tenney, *My Hitch in Hell,* 31; Miller, *Bataan: Uncensored,* 181.
16. Whitman, *Bataan: Our Last Ditch,* 360.
17. Ibid.; Tenney, *My Hitch in Hell,* 31.
18. Bardowski Interview, December 8, 2000.
19. Ortega Interview, December 21, 2000; Whitman, *Bataan: Our Last Ditch,* 360.
20. Schutt, *Janesville Tankers on Bataan,* 199.
21. Miller, *Bataan Uncensored,* 171; Weaver, *Prov Tank Gp Rpt of Opns,* 29.
22. Miller, *Bataan Uncensored,* 175.
23. Schutt, *Janesville Tankers on Bataan,* 200–201; Morton, *The Fall of the Philippines,* 351–52; Ortega speech, San Antonio, Texas, November 19, 1999.
24. Miller, *Bataan Uncensored,* 191.
25. Poweleit, *Kentucky's Fighting 192nd Light G.H.Q. Tank Battalion,* 67.
26. Miller, *Bataan Uncensored,* 191–92.
27. Stewart Interview, *In the Hands of the Enemy,* 5.
28. Ibid.
29. Ortega Interview, December 21, 2000.
30. Schutt, *Janesville Tankers on Bataan,* 212–13; Morton, *The Fall of the Philippines,* 363–65, 405.
31. Weaver, *Prov Tank Gp Rpt of Opns,* 29; Morton, *The Fall of the Philippines,* 409–10.
32. Schutt, *Janesville Tankers on Bataan,* 211–12; Morton, *The Fall of the Philippines,* 409–10.

CHAPTER EIGHT

1. Morton, *The Fall of the Philippines,* 417; Miller, *Bataan Uncensored,* 195.
2. Rutherford, *Fall of the Philippines,* 129, 133; Poweleit, *Kentucky's Fighting 192nd Light G.H.Q. Tank Battalion,* 68–70; Morton, *The Fall of the Philippines,* 421, 424, 431.
3. Morton, *The Fall of the Philippines,* 427.
4. Ibid., 427–29, 432; Miller, *Bataan Uncensored,* 196–97.
5. Morton, *The Fall of the Philippines,* 429–30.
6. Ibid., 431–32, 436; Miller, *Bataan Uncensored,* 198–99; Whitman, *Bataan: Our Last Ditch,* 503–4; Schutt, *Janesville Tankers on Bataan,* 219; Weaver, *Prov Tank Gp Rpt of Opns,* 30.

7. Schutt, *Janesville Tankers on Bataan*, 217–8; Morton, *The Fall of the Philippines,* 438, 441.
8. Morton, *The Fall of the Philippines,* 437–38.
9. Schutt, *Janesville Tankers on Bataan*, 219.
10. Morton, *The Fall of the Philippines,* 442.
11. Ibid.; Whitman, *Bataan: Our Last Ditch,* 522; Miller, *Bataan Uncensored,* 204.
12. Miller, *Bataan Uncensored,* 204.
13. Ibid., 205.
14. Ibid., 205–6; Whitman, *Bataan: Our Last Ditch,* 524–25; Morton, *The Fall of the Philippines,* 442–43; Weaver, *Prov Tank Gp Rpt of Opns,* 30.
15. Morton, *The Fall of the Philippines,* 442–43; Schutt, *Janesville Tankers on Bataan*, 221, 224.
16. Miller, *Bataan Uncensored,* 206–7.
17. Whitman, *Bataan: Our Last Ditch,* 534.
18. Miller, *Bataan Uncensored,* 207–8; Schutt, *Janesville Tankers on Bataan*, 221–22; Morton, *The Fall of the Philippines,* 443–45.
19. Miller, *Bataan Uncensored,* 206.
20. Morton, *The Fall of the Philippines,* 442, 447.
21. Ibid., 450–51; Schutt, *Janesville Tankers on Bataan*, 224.
22. Morton, *The Fall of the Philippines,* 451.
23. Schutt, *Janesville Tankers on Bataan*, 225.
24. Ibid.; DeGroot Interview, *In the Hands of the Enemy,* 2.
25. Schutt, *Janesville Tankers on Bataan*, 225–26.
26. Tenney, *My Hitch in Hell,* 32.
27. Bardowski Interview, December 8, 2000; Whitman, *Bataan: Our Last Ditch,* 569–70.
28. Miller, *Bataan Uncensored,* 208.
29. Ibid.; Poweleit, *Kentucky's Fighting 192nd Light G.H.Q. Tank Battalion,* 70.
30. Tenney, *My Hitch in Hell,* 33; Whitman, *Bataan: Our Last Ditch,* 591.
31. Whitman, *Bataan: Our Last Ditch,* 584–85; Proviso East Reports, "Biography of Pvt. William Edison Burns," *192nd Tank Battalion.*
32. Fitzpatrick, *The Hike into the Sun,* 54.
33. Falconer statement in Knox, *Death March,* 114.
34. French Interview, 1994, Tape 2, Side 1, 7.
35. Miller, *Bataan Uncensored,* 209.
36. Whitman, *Bataan: Our Last Ditch,* 591.
37. Ortega Interview, December 21, 2000; Tenney, *My Hitch in Hell,* 32.
38. Tenney, *My Hitch in Hell,* 33; Ortega speech, San Antonio, Texas, November 19, 1999.
39. Ortega speech, San Antonio, Texas, November 19, 1999.
40. Whitman, *Bataan: Our Last Ditch,* 590.
41. Ibid.
42. Ibid.; Schutt, *Janesville Tankers on Bataan*, 229.
43. Whitman, *Bataan: Our Last Ditch,* 591.
44. French Interview, 1994, Tape 2, Side 1, 8–9.
45. Proviso East Reports, "Biography of Pfc. Frank Goldstein," *192nd Tank Battalion.*
46. Whitman, *Bataan: Our Last Ditch,* 585–88; Proviso East Reports, "Biography of Pvt. William Edison Burns," *192nd Tank Battalion;* Rutherford, *Fall of the Philippines,* 136.

47. Miller, *Bataan Uncensored,* 210.
48. Ibid., 211; Fitzpatrick, *The Hike into the Sun,* 55; Falconer statement in Knox, *Death March,* 114.
49. Tenney, *My Hitch in Hell,* 42–43; Schutt, *Janesville Tankers on Bataan,* 233.
50. Miller, *Bataan Uncensored,* 214–18.
51. Poweleit, *Kentucky's Fighting 192nd Light G.H.Q. Tank Battalion,* 81; Schutt, *Janesville Tankers on Bataan,* 233–34.
52. Toland, *But Not in Shame,* 334–55; Rutherford, *Fall of the Philippines,* 136, 141, 143, 145, 150–51.
53. Tenney, *My Hitch in Hell,* 40; Poweleit, *Kentucky's Fighting 192nd Light G.H.Q. Tank Battalion,* 81.
54. Poweleit, *Kentucky's Fighting 192nd Light G.H.Q. Tank Battalion,* 205.
55. Weaver, *Prov Tank Gp Rpt of Opns,* 32.
56. Poweleit, *Kentucky's Fighting 192nd Light G.H.Q. Tank Battalion,* 204.

CHAPTER NINE
1. "Organizational History of the 193rd Tank Battalion," *Organizational History—193rd Tank Bn, 1 Sept 1940–6 Jan 1946,* 1.
2. Leach statement in Hunnicutt, *Stuart: A History of the American Light Tank,* Volume 1, 5.
3. Ibid.; "Organizational History of the 193rd Tank Battalion," *Organizational History—193rd Tank Bn, 1 Sept 1940–6 Jan 1946,* 11–12.
4. "Organizational History of the 193rd Tank Battalion," *Organizational History—193rd Tank Bn, 1 Sept 1940–6 Jan 1946,* 12; Leach statement in Hunnicutt, *Stuart: A History of the American Light Tank,* Volume 1, 5.
5. "Organizational History of the 193rd Tank Battalion," *Organizational History—193rd Tank Bn, 1 Sept 1940–6 Jan 1946,* 12–13.
6. "Our Proud History," *754th Tank Battalion,* 1.
7. Ibid., 2–4; "HyperWar: History of Task Force 6814 (Americal Division)," <http://www.ibiblio.org/hyperwar/USA/OOB/Americal-history.html> [accessed July 14, 2002]
8. Ibid.
9. "Our Proud History," *754th Tank Battalion,* 5–6.
10. Ibid., 3–5; "History of the 754th Tank Battalion," *History—754th Tank Bn, 1946,* 2; Cronin, *Under the Southern Cross,* 17; "HyperWar: History of Task Force 6814 (Americal Division)," <http://www.ibiblio.org/hyperwar/USA/OOB/Americal-history.html> [accessed July 14, 2002]
11. Dumbeck, *Buddies and Bravery in the South Pacific,* 11; "Our Proud History," *754th Tank Battalion,* 5–6.
12. "Our Proud History," *754th Tank Battalion,* 5–6.
13. Stubbs, *Army Lineage Series, Armor-Cavalry, Part I: Regular Army and Army Reserve,* 62–3; Stanton, *World War II Order of Battle,* 301–2.
14. Stanton, *World War II Order of Battle,* 302; Salecker, *Fortress Against the Sun,* 176; Bonnell to author, February 9, 2001.
15. Nalty, ed., *Pearl Harbor and the War in the Pacific,* 63–71; van Oosten, "Fall of the Dutch East Indies," *History of the Second World War, Part 31,* 849–53; Dunnigan, *Victory at Sea,* 513–21; Salmaggi, *2194 Days of War,* 223–25.
16. Salmaggi, *2194 Days of War,* 225.
17. Dunnigan, *Victory at Sea,* 522; Nalty, ed., *Pearl Harbor and the War in the Pacific,* 79, 81.

18. Salecker, *Fortress Against the Sun,* 171–74, 176–99; Tuleja, "The Miracle of Midway," *World War II,* May, 2002.

19. Costello, *The Pacific War, 1941–1945,* 317–18; Anderson, *The U.S. Army Campaigns of World War II: Papua,* 7.

20. Anderson, *The U.S. Army Campaigns of World War II: Papua,* 20.

21. Salmaggi, *2194 Days of War,* 280; U.S. Government Printing Office, *The U.S. Army Campaigns of World War II: Guadalcanal,* 9.

22. U.S. Government Printing Office, *The U.S. Army Campaigns of World War II: Guadalcanal,* 9, 11, 26.

23. Stanton, *World War II Order of Battle,* 302; "History of the 767th Tank Battalion," *History—754th Tank Bn, YR 44,* 1.

24. Dunnigan, *Victory at Sea,* 543–44, 546, 547, 548.

25. Ibid., 550–54; Drea, *New Guinea,* 8–10; Miller, *United States Army in World War II, The War in the Pacific—Cartwheel: The Reduction of Rabaul,* [hereafter cited as *Cartwheel: The Reduction of Rabaul*], 189–210; Costello, *The Pacific War, 1941–1945,* 410–14.

26. "Our Proud History," *754th Tank Battalion,* 9–10; "History of the 754th Tank Battalion," *History—754th Tank Bn, 1946,* 2–3.

27. Stanton, *World War II Order of Battle,* 296, 299, 301, 303, 346. More specifically, the new tank battalions were formed from a reorganization of the following units:
    706th TB—3rd Bn., 37th Armored Reg., 4th Armored Div.
    710th TB—3rd Bn., 80th Armored Reg., 4th Armored Div.
    711th TB—3rd Bn., 14th Armored Reg., 9th Armored Div.
    713th TB—3rd Bn., 42nd Armored Reg., 11th Armored Div.
    716th TB—3rd Bn., 48th Armored Reg., 14th Armored Div.
    775th TB—1st Bn., 36th Armored Reg., 8th Armored Div.

28. Stubbs, Army Lineage Series—Armor Cavalry, Part I: Regular Army and Army Reserve, 62; Anderson, Richard, "Armor," The United States Army in World War II, http://www.militaryhistoryonline.com/wwii/usarmy/armor.htm, 2.

29. Stubbs, *Army Lineage Series—Armor Cavalry, Part I: Regular Army and Army Reserve,* 62; Stanton, *World War II Order of Battle,* 19.

30. "History of the 706th Tank Battalion," *706th Tank Battalion,* 2, 3.

31. Culver, *Sherman in Action,* 4.

32. "Medium Tank M4 Sherman" <http://afvdb.50megs.com/usa/ m4sherman.html>, [Accessed March 23, 2002], 1–18.

33. Culver, *Sherman in Action,* 5.

34. Ibid., 4–5; "Medium Tank M4 Sherman," 1–18; Miller, *Tanks of the World,* 420.

35. Culver, *Sherman in Action,* 5; "Medium Tank M4 Sherman," 1–18; Gilbert, *Marine Tank Battalions in the Pacific,* 79.

36. Culver, *Sherman in Action,* 5.

37. "716th Tank Battalion Reviews Combat History in Anniversary and Commemoration Parade on Mindanao," History 716th Tank Bn, 20 Sept '43 . . . 24 Sept '45, [hereafter cited as 716th TB Review], 1; "History—716th Tank Battalion, 21 September 1943–19 December 1945," History—716th Tank Bn, 1942–45, 1.

CHAPTER TEN

1. United States Department of War, *The Capture of Makin, 20–23 November, 1943,* [hereafter cited as War Dept., *Capture of Makin*], 4; Crowl, *United States Army in World War II, The War in the Pacific—Seizure of the Gilberts and Marshalls,* [herafter

cited as *Seizure of Gilberts and Marshalls*], 52–53; Newell, *Central Pacific, 7 December 1941–6 December 1943,* 16.

2. Newell, *Central Pacific, 7 December 1941–6 December 1943, The U.S. Army Campaigns of World War II,* 16.

3. Miller, *Directory of Tanks,* 416; "Medium Tank M3 Lee", <http://afvdb.50megs.com/usa/m3lee.html>,[accessed March 23, 2002], 1–2; "M3 Lee Medium tank," <http://www.sos.state.mi.us/history/mag/extra/tanks/m3.html>, 1.

4. "Medium Tank M3 Lee," <http://afvdb.50megs.com/usa/m3lee.html>, [accessed March 23, 2002], 1.

5. "S-3 Journal, 5 September 1943 thru 1 January 44," *193rd Tank Battalion,* 1–2.

6. Ibid., 1.

7. War Dept., *Capture of Makin,* 25; Crowl, *Seizure of Gilberts and Marshalls,* 56.

8. Newell, *Central Pacific, 7 December 1941–6 December 1943, The U.S. Army Campaigns of World War II,* 16; Crowl, *Seizure of Gilberts and Marshalls*], 26–27.

9. War Dept., *Capture of Makin,* 25; "S-3 Journal, 5 September 1943 thru 1 January 44," *193rd Tank Battalion,* 2.

10. War Dept., *Capture of Makin,* 26–29, 32.

11. Ibid., 8–9.

12. The National Historical Society, *United States Army in World War II, The War in the Pacific—Atlas,* 43.

13. Crowl, *Seizure of Gilberts and Marshalls,* 40–42.

14. War Dept., *Capture of Makin,* 31, 34–37, 40; Crowl, *Seizure of Gilberts and Marshalls,* 76; Engle report in "Report of the Makin Operations by the 193rd Tank Battalion, 5 Sept '43–1 Jan '44," *193rd Tank Battalion,* [hereafter cited as "193rd Makin Operations"], 63.

15. Crowl, *Seizure of Gilberts and Marshalls,* 77; Engle report in "193rd Makin Operations", 64.

16. War Dept., *Capture of Makin,* 39; Various reports in "193rd Makin Operations," 63–64, 68–69, 73, 77.

17. War Dept., *Capture of Makin,* 42; Reports of Engle, Rooke and Pruett in "193rd Makin Operations," 63, 69, 77; Crowl, *Seizure of Gilberts and Marshalls,* 79, 94.

18. Ibid., 94–95; Report of Engle, Kulaga and Pruett in "193rd Makin Operations," 63, 68, 77.

19. Crowl, *Seizure of Gilberts and Marshalls,* 81; War Dept., *Capture of Makin,* 35–36, 41, 42, 46, 51, 54–55; Report of Johnson, "193rd Makin Operations," 47; Report of Evans, "193rd Makin Operations," 66.

20. War Dept., *Capture of Makin,* 56; Reports of Johnson and Evans, "193rd Makin Operations," 47, 66.

21. War Dept., *Capture of Makin,* 57; Reports of Brown, Newby and Evans, "193rd Makin Operations," 38, 56, 66.

22. Reports of Edmundson, Erickson, Meyer and Knetter in "193rd Makin Operations," 5, 45, 46, 59.

23. Reports of Gurley, Cline, Coffey and Rowe in Ibid., 42, 43, 51, 52.

24. Reports of Cline and Smarr in Ibid., 43, 53.

25. Reports of Greco, Major and Knetter in Ibid., 50, 58, 59.

26. Reports of Erickson, Johnson, Spenyovics, Greco and Major in Ibid., 45, 47, 49, 50, 58; War Dept., *Capture of Makin,* 71–72.

27. Reports of Erickson, Johnson, Spenyovics, Greco and Major, "193rd Makin Operations," 45, 47, 49, 50, 58; War Dept., *Capture of Makin,* 72; Crowl, *Seizure of Gilberts and Marshalls,* 94.

28. Reports of Erickson, Meyer and Johnson "193rd Makin Operations," 45, 46, 47; Crowl, *Seizure of Gilberts and Marshalls,* 93.

29. War Dept., *Capture of Makin,* 75; Crowl, *Seizure of Gilberts and Marshalls,* 94.

30. Reports of Evans and Willerding, "193rd Makin Operations," 66, 71; Crowl, *Seizure of Gilberts and Marshalls,* 99–100.

31. Reports of Cline and Smarr in "193rd Makin Operations," 43, 53.

32. Numerous reports in Ibid., 5, 42–59, 66, 71, 76; "Headquarters 193rd Tank Battalion, Casualty Report" in Ibid., 31.

33. Reports of Engle, Kulaga, Rooke and McCain in Ibid., 63, 68, 69, 73.

34. Report of Sloane in Ibid., 74.

35. Reports of Rooke and McCain in Ibid., 69, 73.

36. Report of Sloane in Ibid., 74; War Dept., *Capture of Makin,* 99; Crowl, *Seizure of Gilberts and Marshalls,* 111.

37. Reports of Edmundson, Brown, Johnson, Coffey, Smarr, Cline, Viets, Major and Knetter, "193rd Makin Operations," 5, 38, 43, 47, 52, 53, 55, 58, 59.

38. Reports of Pierce, Meyer, Greco, Toole, Erickson, Sorrow, "193rd Makin Operations," 45, 46, 50, 54, 57, 76; Crowl, *Seizure of Gilberts and Marshalls,* 114, 116.

39. Reports of Brown, Smarr and Viets in "193rd Makin Operations," 38, 53, 55.

40. Reports of Evans, Bolt and Pierce in Ibid., 67, 72, 76.

41. Reports of Evans and Sloane in Ibid., 67, 75; Crowl, *Seizure of Gilberts and Marshalls,* 118.

42. Crowl, *Seizure of Gilberts and Marshalls,* 118; Reports of Meyer, Johnson, Greco, Smarr, Engle and Rooke, "193rd Makin Operations," 46, 47, 50, 53, 64, 69.

43. Crowl, *Seizure of Gilberts and Marshalls,* 118–9; War Dept., *Capture of Makin,* 112, 115; Reports of Erickson and Greco, "193rd Makin Operations," 45, 50.

44. Reports of Lawrence and Knetter, "193rd Makin Operations," 40, 59.

45. Reports of Cline, Erickson, Meyer, Spenyovics, Greco, Toole and Sorrow in Ibid., 43, 45, 46, 49, 50, 54, 57.

46. Crowl, *Seizure of Gilberts and Marshalls,* 119, 120–21.

47. Reports of Cline, Erickson, Meyer, Spenyovics, Greco, Toole and Sorrow in "193rd Makin Operations," 43, 45, 46, 49, 50, 54, 57.

48. Ibid.; Crowl, *Seizure of Gilberts and Marshalls,* 119, 120–21.

49. Reports of Erickson, Meyer, Greco and Sorrow in "193rd Makin Operations," 45, 46, 50, 57.

50. Reports of Evans, Willerding and Bolt in Ibid., 67, 71, 72.

51. Report of Sloane in Ibid., 75.

52. Reports of Gurley, Johnson, Smarr and Sorrow, in Ibid., 42, 48, 53, 57; Crowl, *Seizure of Gilberts and Marshalls,* 124.

53. Reports of Tobin and Engle in "193rd Makin Operations," 62, 64.

54. Reports of Lawrence and Holmes in Ibid., 39, 65.

55. Reports of Tobin and Evans in Ibid., 62, 67.

CHAPTER ELEVEN

1. Costello, *The Pacific War, 1941–1945,* 423–24; Dunnigan, *Victory at Sea, World War II in the Pacific,* 557–58; "Our Proud History," *754th Tank Battalion,* 10–11.

2. Dunnigan, *Victory at Sea, World War II in the Pacific,* 560; Miller, *Cartwheel: The Reduction of Rabaul,* 258, 271.

3. "Our Proud History," *754th Tank Battalion,* 10, 11; Dumbeck, *Buddies and Bravery in the South Pacific,* 16.

4. Dumbeck, *Buddies and Bravery in the South Pacific,* 16; Dumbeck, *Memories of Days Gone By,* 257.
5. "Our Proud History," *754th Tank Battalion,* 12; Unknown Tanker, "754th Tank Battalion Narrative," *754th Tank Battalion,* 10.
6. "Our Proud History," *754th Tank Battalion,* 12; Dumbeck, *Buddies and Bravery in the South Pacific,* 17–18; Dumbeck, *Memories of Days Gone By,* 258-59; Dumbeck to author, January 18, 2001, 1.
7. Gailey, *Bougainville, 1943–1945,* 138–39; Sharp & Dunnigan, *The Congressional Medal of Honor,* 306–7.
8. "Our Proud History," *754th Tank Battalion,* 12–13.
9. Ibid., 13; Dumbeck to author, January 18, 2001, 1.
10. Dumbeck to author, January 18, 2001, 1.
11. Zaloga, *Tank Battalions of the Pacific War, 1941–1945,* 22, 23.
12. "Our Proud History," *754th Tank Battalion,* 12–13; Lofgren, *Northern Solomons,* 27.
13. "Our Proud History," *754th Tank Battalion,* 15; Miller, *Cartwheel: The Reduction of Rabaul,* 361–64.
14. "Our Proud History," *754th Tank Battalion,* 14; Miller, *Cartwheel: The Reduction of Rabaul,* 374; Gailey, *Bougainville, 1943–1945,* 163–64.
15. "Our Proud History," *754th Tank Battalion,* 14.
16. Dumbeck, *Buddies and Bravery in the South Pacific,* 18–19.
17. "Our Proud History," *754th Tank Battalion,* 14; Gailey, *Bougainville, 1943–1945,* 164; Frankel, *The 37th Infantry Division in World War II,* 160.
18. "Our Proud History," *754th Tank Battalion,* 15; Gailey, *Bougainville, 1943–1945,* 165.
19. Gailey, *Bougainville, 1943–1945,* 169.
20. Ibid., 177; "Our Proud History," *754th Tank Battalion,* 15–16.
21. Gailey, *Bougainville, 1943–1945,* 177; "Our Proud History," *754th Tank Battalion,* 16.
22. Lofgren, *Northern Solomons,* 32; Frankel, *The 37th Infantry Division in World War II,* 168.
23. "Our Proud History," *754th Tank Battalion,* 16.
24. "1st Cavalry Division," http://www.savethetale.com/Army...201st%20Cavalry%20 Division.html, [accessed January 31, 2001], 2.
25. "44th Tank Battalion Historical Record and History," *History – 44th Tank Battalion, 11 November 1943–30 April 1946,* [hereafter cited as 44th Tank Battalion Historical Record], 1; Stanton, *World War II Order of Battle,* 299. More specifically, the 44th TB was formed from a reorganization of the 44th Armored Reg., 12th Armored Div.

CHAPTER TWELVE

1. Crowl, *Seizure of Gilberts and Marshalls,* 167–68.
2. Ibid., 178; Chapin, *Breaking the Outer Ring: Marine Landings in the Marshall Islands,* 1.
3. "Report of Tank Operations—Flintlock (Kwajalein) Operation, 31 January–6 February, 1944," *767th Tank Battalion* [hereafter cited as Flintlock Report], 1.
4. Flintlock Report, 1; Zaloga, *Tank Battalions of the Pacific War, 1941–1945,* 25.
5. Ibid., 12–13.
6. Ibid., 17.
7. Ibid., 6.
8. Ibid., 15–16; Hunnicutt, *Stuart: A History of the American Light Tank,* 372–73.
9. Flintlock Report, 25, 29; Crowl, *Seizure of Gilberts and Marshalls,* 202–3.
10. Crowl, *Seizure of Gilberts and Marshalls,* 219–21.

11. Ibid., 221–25; Flintlock Report, 26, 58.

12. Crowl, *Seizure of Gilberts and Marshalls,* 230–31.

13. Ibid., 233.

14. Ibid., 236; Flintlock Report, 26–27, 50–51.

15. Crowl, *Seizure of Gilberts and Marshalls,* 236; Flintlock Report, 27, 51.

16. Flintlock Report, 27; The National Historical Society, *United States Army in World War II, The War in the Pacific—Atlas,* 46.

17. Crowl, *Seizure of Gilberts and Marshalls,* 246–49; The National Historical Society, *United States Army in World War II, The War in the Pacific—Atlas,* 46.

18. The National Historical Society, *United States Army in World War II, The War in the Pacific—Atlas,* 46.

19. Ibid., 51.

20. Crowl, *Seizure of Gilberts and Marshalls,* 255–56; The National Historical Society, *United States Army in World War II, The War in the Pacific—Atlas,* 46

21. Crowl, *Seizure of Gilberts and Marshalls,* 256; The National Historical Society, *United States Army in World War II, The War in the Pacific—Atlas,* 46

22. Crowl, *Seizure of Gilberts and Marshalls,* 256–58; Flintlock Report, 28.

23. Flintlock Report, 28–29.

24. Ibid., 29.

25. Ibid., 29; Crowl, *Seizure of Gilberts and Marshalls,* 264.

26. Crowl, *Seizure of Gilberts and Marshalls,* 265.

27. Ibid., 266–67.

28. Ibid.

29. Ibid., 269.

30. Ibid., 271.

31. Ibid., 271–73; Flintlock Report, 30.

32. Crowl, *Seizure of Gilberts and Marshalls,* 273–76.

33. Ibid., 275–76.

34. Ibid., 276–77; Flintlock Report, 30; Crowl, *Seizure of Gilberts and Marshalls,* 280–82.

35. Crowl, *Seizure of Gilberts and Marshalls,* 291–97; Flintlock Report, 29–30.

36. Crowl, *Seizure of Gilberts and Marshalls,* 286; Flintlock Report, 31.

37. Crowl, *Seizure of Gilberts and Marshalls,* 286.

38. Ibid., 287.

39. Ibid.

40. Ibid., 288–89; Flintlock Report, 31.

41. Crowl, *Seizure of Gilberts and Marshalls,* 289.

42. Ibid., 298; Flintlock Report, 31, 55.

43. Crowl, *Seizure of Gilberts and Marshalls,* 300–301; Flintlock Report, 31–32.

44. Crowl, *Seizure of Gilberts and Marshalls,* 300.

45. Ibid., 301; Flintlock Report, 29, 31, 32.

46. Crowl, *Seizure of Gilberts and Marshalls,* 331; Nalty, ed., *Pearl Harbor and the War in the Pacific,* 143–44.

47. Flintlock Report, 53–55.

48. Ibid., 52.

49. Crowl, *Seizure of Gilberts and Marshalls,* 333.

50. Costello, *The Pacific War, 1941–1945,* 451–52.

CHAPTER THIRTEEN

1. Hirrel, *Bismarck Archipelago,* 6–7.

2. Ibid., 17.

3. Ibid., 455.

4. Miller, *Cartwheel: The Reduction of Rabaul,* 316, 321; "United Stated Army, 1940–1945: 1st Cavalry Division," http://www.ibiblio.org/hyperwar/USA/OOB/1-Cavalry.html [Accessed March 24, 2002], 2.

5. Miller, *Cartwheel: The Reduction of Rabaul,* 317, 338–39; Historical Division, War Department, *The Admiralties: Operations of the 1st Cavalry Division, 29 February–18 May 1944,* [hereafter cited as Historical Division, *The Admiralties*], 120.

6. Miller, *Cartwheel: The Reduction of Rabaul,* 342; Historical Division, *The Admiralties,* 80–81.

7. Miller, *Cartwheel: The Reduction of Rabaul,* 317.

8. Historical Division, *The Admiralties,* 84–85.

9. Miller, *Cartwheel: The Reduction of Rabaul,* 344.

10. Ibid.; Historical Division, *The Admiralties,* 89.

11. Historical Division, *The Admiralties,* 90–92.

12. Ibid., 91–92.

13. Miller, *Cartwheel: The Reduction of Rabaul,* 346–47.

14. Historical Division, *The Admiralties,* 93–94.

15. Ibid., 96.

16. Ibid., 103.

17. Ibid., 106–8.

18. Ibid., 108–9.

19. Ibid., 111.

20. Ibid., 113–15.

21. Hirrel, *Bismarck Archipelago,* 25.

22. Ibid.

CHAPTER FOURTEEN

1. 44th TB Historical Record, 1; "Section I: Changes in Organization," *706th Tank Battalion,* 1; "Action Against the Enemy Report, 711th Tank Battalion, Ryukyus Campaign, 1 April to 30 June 1945," *711th Tank Battalion History,* [hereafter cited as 711th TB Ryukyus Report], 3.

2. 711th TB Ryukyus Report, 3.

3. 44th TB Historical Record, 1–2.

4. "Section I: Changes in Organization," *706th Tank Battalion,* 1; "Section III: Stations," *706th Tank Battalion,* 4; "History of the 706th Tank Battalion," *706th Tank Battalion,* [hereafter cited as 706th TB History], 8–9.

5. Smith, *The Approach to the Philippines,* 1,3; Costello, *The Pacific War, 1941–1945,* 456.

6. Drea, *New Guinea, The U.S. Army Campaigns of World War II,* 19, 22.

7. Ibid., 23.

8. Ibid.

9. Smith, *The Approach to the Philippines,* 208–10.

10. Ibid., 208, 211–12.

11. Ibid., 213, 219–21.

12. Ibid., 222–23.

13. Ibid., 224.

14. Ibid., 225.

15. Ibid., 125–26; Westerfield, "F Co., 163rd Infantry: Our Wakde Hell-Hole," in Westerfield, *The Jungleers,* 102.
16. Smith, *The Approach to the Philippines,* 226; Larson, Stanfield and Westerfield, "C Co 163's Coconut Hell on Wakde," in Westerfield, *The Jungleers,* 98.
17. Smith, *The Approach to the Philippines,* 226; Westerfield, "F Co., 163rd Infantry: Our Wakde Hell-Hole," in Westerfield, *The Jungleers,* 102.
18. Smith, *The Approach to the Philippines,* 226–27; Holzimmer, "In Close Country: World War II American Armor Tactics in the Jungles of the Southwest Pacific," *Armor,* July–August 1997, 24.
19. Smith, *The Approach to the Philippines,* 227–28; Holzimmer, "In Close Country: World War II American Armor Tactics in the Jungles of the Southwest Pacific," *Armor,* July–August 1997, 25.
20. Westerfield, "C Co 163's Coconut Hell on Wakde," in Westerfield, *The Jungleers,* 99.
21. Smith, *The Approach to the Philippines,* 230; Holzimmer, "In Close Country: World War II American Armor Tactics in the Jungles of the Southwest Pacific," *Armor,* July–August 1997, 24.
22. Smith, *The Approach to the Philippines,* 230–31; Westerfield, "F Co., 163rd Infantry: Our Wakde Hell-Hole," in Westerfield, *The Jungleers,* 103.
23. Smith, *The Approach to the Philippines,* 231; Larson, Stanfield and Westerfield, "C Co 163's Coconut Hell on Wakde," and Westerfield, "F Co., 163rd Infantry: Our Wakde Hell-Hole," both in Westerfield, *The Jungleers,* 99, 102.
24. Smith, *The Approach to the Philippines,* 231.
25. Ibid., 241–42; Drea, *New Guinea, The U.S. Army Campaigns of World War II,* 24.
26. Smith, *The Approach to the Philippines,* 244–49.
27. Ibid., 249–60.
28. Ibid., 260–62.

CHAPTER FIFTEEN
1. Smith, *The Approach to the Philippines,* 280–82.
2. Ibid., 258, 287, 289.
3. Ibid., 290–91.
4. Ibid., 294–95; Westerfield and Haney, "Col. Haney Forces Parai Defile," in Westerfield, *The Jungleers,* 111.
5. Westerfield and Haney, "Col. Haney Forces Parai Defile," and Westerfield and Brown, "L Co 162 Inf–First Against Mokmer Drome," both in Westerfield, *The Jungleers,* 111, 140.
6. Smith, *The Approach to the Philippines,* 304.
7. Ibid., 304–5; Deacon, "116 Combat Engineers on Biak," in Westerfield, *The Jungleers,* 121.
8. Westerfield and Haney, "Col. Haney Forces the Parai Defile," in Westerfield, *The Jungleers,* 112.
9. Smith, *The Approach to the Philippines,* 305–6.
10. Ibid., 306–7; Westerfield and Brown, "L Co 162 Inf–First Against Mokmer Drome," in Westerfield, *The Jungleers,* 140.
11. Smith, *The Approach to the Philippines,* 309–10.
12. Ibid, 310; Westerfield and Botta, "M Co. 162 Infantry: Machine-gunners in Parai Defile," in Westerfield, *The Jungleers,* 115.
13. Smith, *The Approach to the Philippines,* 310.

14. Ibid., 310–11.

15. Ibid., 313–16.

16. Ibid., 318–19; Westerfield and Brown, "L Co 162 Inf–First Against Mokmer Drome," in Westerfield, *The Jungleers,* 141; Smith, *The Approach to the Philippines,* 320–21; Drea, *New Guinea, The U.S. Army Campaigns of World War II,* 26.

17. Smith, *The Approach to the Philippines,* 324.

18. Ibid.

19. Ibid., 329–30.

20. Catanzaro, *With the 41st Division in the Southwest Pacific: A Foot Soldier's Story,* 75.

21. Smith, *The Approach to the Philippines,* 330.

22. Ibid., 328–29; Mandoline and Westerfield, "Fighting the Mokmer Ridges," in Westerfield, *The Jungleers,* 150.

23. Smith, *The Approach to the Philippines,* 328–29.

24. Ibid., 330; Statement of Tony Grossi in "Sea Stories from LCT Group 24," from ww21ct.org/history/stories/LCT_SEA_STORIES.html,[accessed January 31, 2001], 31.

25. Ibid.

26. Westerfield, "In the Slot on Biak," in Westerfield, *The Jungleers,* 131; Smith, *The Approach to the Philippines,* 382.

27. Smith, *The Approach to the Philippines,* 328–29, 331, 336, 340.

28. Ibid., 337, 343, 344.

29. Ibid., 368; Westerfield, "C Company, 162 Infantry: Ibdi Pocket to West Caves," in Westerfield, *The Jungleers,* 133.

30. Smith, *The Approach to the Philippines,* 368–69, 371–75, 377; Westerfield, "In the Slot on Biak," and "I Company, 186: Our Luck on Biak," both in Westerfield, *The Jungleers,* 132, 163.

31. Westerfield, "C Company, 162 Infantry: Ibdi Pocket to West Caves," in Westerfield, *The Jungleers,* 134.

32. Ibid.; Smith, *The Approach to the Philippines,* 375.

33. Smith, *The Approach to the Philippines,* 375.

34. Ibid., 378; Westerfield, "L Co. 186 Infantry: Night Fighters and Desert Rats," in Westerfield, *The Jungleers,* 168.

35. Smith, *The Approach to the Philippines,* 378, 382–84, 388.

36. Ibid., 388–89; Westerfield, "163 Inf's Third Battalion: Last Days of Ibdi Pocket," in Westerfield, *The Jungleers,* 183.

37. Ibid.

38. Smith, *The Approach to the Philippines,* 392.

39. Smith, *The Approach to the Philippines,* 397–409; Drea, *New Guinea, The U.S. Army Campaigns of World War II,* 26.

40. Smith, *The Approach to the Philippines,* 408–11.

41. Drea, *New Guinea, The U.S. Army Campaigns of World War II,* 26.

42. Smith, *The Approach to the Philippines,* 416–21.

CHAPTER SIXTEEN

1. "Unit History of the 775th Tank Battalion, 1 April '42–4 Jan '46," *775th Tank Battalion,* [hereafter cited as 775th TB History], 2–3.

2. "History—716th Tank Battalion, 21st September 1943–19th December 1945," *History—716th Tank Bn, 1942–45,* 1–2.

3. Camas, "The Story of Our Outfit," in 710th Tank Battalion Association, *History of the 710th Tank Bn,* 1–2.

4. Appleman, "Army Tanks in the Battle for Saipan," *762nd Tank Battalion, 15 June–25 Aug 1944,* [hereafter cited as *Army Tanks on Saipan*], 3, 5–6.

5. Steinberg, *Island Fighting,* 166–67.

6. Ibid., 167; The National Historical Society, *United States Army in World War II, The War in the Pacific—Atlas,* 48; Anderson, *Western Pacific, 15 June 1944–2 September 1945, The U.S. Army Campaigns of World War II,* 8–9.

7. Steinberg, *Island Fighting,* 166–67.

8. Appleman, *Army Tanks on Saipan,* 9.

9. Dunnigan, *Victory at Sea,* 66.

10. Ibid.

11. Steinberg, *Island Fighting,* 167; Crowl, *United States Army in World War II, The War in the Pacific—Campaign in the Marianas,* [hereafter cited as *Campaign in the Marianas*], 81–83.

12. Salmaggi, *2194 Days of War,* 537–38.

13. Appleman, *Army Tanks on Saipan,* 10–11; Anderson, *Western Pacific, 15 June 1944–2 September 1945, The U.S. Army Campaigns of World War II,* 11.

14. Appleman, *Army Tanks on Saipan,* 11.

15. Ibid.

16. Appleman, *Army Tanks on Saipan,* 14.

17. Crowl, *Campaign in the Marianas,* 111-12.

18. Appleman, *Army Tanks on Saipan,* 15.

19. Crowl, *Campaign in the Marianas,* 137.

20. Ibid., 139–40; The National Historical Society, *United States Army in World War II, The War in the Pacific—Atlas,* 48; Appleman, *Army Tanks on Saipan,* 16–17.

21. Appleman, *Army Tanks on Saipan,* 15–16.

22. Crowl, *Campaign in the Marianas,* 441; Salmaggi, *2194 Days of War,* 540; Steinberg, *Island Fighting,* 169–70; Dunnigan, *Victory at Sea, World War II in the Pacific,* 47–50.

23. Appleman, *Army Tanks on Saipan,* 17–18.

24. Ibid., 18; Crowl, *Campaign in the Marianas,* 142–43.

25. Appleman, *Army Tanks on Saipan,* 18; Crowl, *Campaign in the Marianas,* 143.

26. Appleman, *Army Tanks on Saipan,* 18–19; Dorey and Lampro citations, "Silver and Bronze Star Awards," *History, 762nd Tank Battalion, Yr 1944.*

27. Appleman, *Army Tanks on Saipan,* 18–19.

28. Ibid., 19–20; Fischer notation, "Casualty List of Saipan Operation," *History, 762nd Tank Battalion, Yr 1944,* 1.

29. Appleman, *Army Tanks on Saipan,* 20, 23.

30. Ibid.; Crowl, *Campaign in the Marianas,* 145.

31. Appleman, *Army Tanks on Saipan,* 20–21.

32. Crowl, *Campaign in the Marianas,* 146–48.

33. Ibid., 148–49; Appleman, *Army Tanks on Saipan,* 22–23. Although Crowl states only one tank platoon (five tanks) was left behind to mop up the Nafutan peninsula, subsequent events will show that all of the tanks of Company D, 762nd TB aided in the attacks.

34. Appleman, *Army Tanks on Saipan,* 24.

35. Ibid., 25, 26, 27–28; Bishop citation, "Silver and Bronze Star Awards," *History, 762nd Tank Battalion, Yr 1944.*

36. Appleman, *Army Tanks on Saipan*, 26.
37. Ibid., 26–27; Mavrikis citation, "Silver and Bronze Star Awards," *History, 762nd Tank Battalion, Yr 1944*.
38. Appleman, *Army Tanks on Saipan*, 26–27; Crowl, *Campaign in the Marianas*, 153.
39. Appleman, *Army Tanks on Saipan*, 28; Crowl, *Campaign in the Marianas*, 154.
40. Ibid.
41. Appleman, *Army Tanks on Saipan*, 28; Crowl, *Campaign in the Marianas*, 154–55.
42. Crowl, *Campaign in the Marianas*, 155–56.
43. Ibid., 156–57; Appleman, *Army Tanks on Saipan*, 29.
44. Appleman, *Army Tanks on Saipan*, 30; Crowl, *Campaign in the Marianas*, 157.
45. Crowl, *Campaign in the Marianas*, 159.
46. Ibid., 159–61; Appleman, *Army Tanks on Saipan*, 31–32.

CHAPTER SEVENTEEN

1. Crowl, *Campaign in the Marianas*, 160–61; Anderson, *Western Pacific, 15 June 1944–2 September 1945, The U.S. Army Campaigns of World War II*, 14.
2. Appleman, *Army Tanks on Saipan*, 22–23.
3. Crowl, *Campaign in the Marianas*, 169–70.
4. Ibid., 173.
5. Ibid., 170, 172, 175.
6. Appleman, *Army Tanks on Saipan*, 34–35.
7. Ibid., 35–38.
8. Crowl, *Campaign in the Marianas*, 178–79
9. Appleman, *Army Tanks on Saipan*, 40–41.
10. Ibid., 41–43.
11. Crowl, *Campaign in the Marianas*, 184.
12. Appleman, *Army Tanks on Saipan*, 44–46.
13. Ibid., 46; Crowl, *Campaign in the Marianas*, 185.
14. Appleman, *Army Tanks on Saipan*, 46–47.
15. Anderson, *Western Pacific, 15 June 1944–2 September 1945, The U.S. Army Campaigns of World War II*, 14; Crowl, *Campaign in the Marianas*, 191–201.
16. Crowl, *Campaign in the Marianas*, 186–87.
17. Ibid., 207; Appleman, *Army Tanks on Saipan*, 47.
18. Crowl, *Campaign in the Marianas*, 209; Appleman, *Army Tanks on Saipan*, 47.
19. Appleman, *Army Tanks on Saipan*, 48.
20. Crowl, *Campaign in the Marianas*, 214–15.
21. Ibid., 216–17.
22. Ibid., 212.
23. Appleman, *Army Tanks on Saipan*, 51.
24. Ibid., 51; Hoffman, *Saipan: The Beginning of the End*, 171.
25. Ibid.
26. Appleman, *Army Tanks on Saipan*, 51–53.
27. Ibid., 50–51.
28. Ibid., 53–54. The platoon of medium tanks from Company B, 762nd TB belonged to Lieutenant Hitchner but were under the command of 1st Lt. Gordon E. McQuain, who took over when Lieutenant Hitchner was laid up with combat fatigue.
29. Crowl, *Campaign in the Marianas*, 223–25.
30. Ibid., 225.
31. Crowl, *Campaign in the Marianas*, 229–30; Appleman, *Army Tanks on Saipan*, 54–56.

32. Crowl, *Campaign in the Marianas,* 231; Appleman, *Army Tanks on Saipan,* 56–57.
33. Crowl, *Campaign in the Marianas,* 231; Appleman, *Army Tanks on Saipan,* 57.
34. Ibid.; Reidy citation, "Silver and Bronze Star Awards," *History, 762nd Tank Battalion, Yr 1944.*
35. Appleman, *Army Tanks on Saipan,* 57-58; Ward citation, "Silver and Bronze Star Awards," *History, 762nd Tank Battalion, Yr 1944.*
36. Crowl, *Campaign in the Marianas,* 232–33.

CHAPTER EIGHTEEN
1. Appleman, *Army Tanks on Saipan,* 63.
2. Ibid., 63–64.
3. Ibid., 64–65.
4. Johnston, *Follow Me: The Story of the Second Marine Division in World War II,* 212–16.
5. Crowl, *Campaign in the Marianas,* 235–38.
6. Ibid., 236-37; Appleman, *Army Tanks on Saipan,* 66, 67.
7. Appleman, *Army Tanks on Saipan,* 67; Bullock citation,
8. Bullock citation,
9. Crowl, *Campaign in the Marianas,* 236–37.
10. Appleman, *Army Tanks on Saipan,* 69–70.
11. Ibid., 71; Crowl, *Campaign in the Marianas,* 236–37, 242–43.
12. Appleman, *Army Tanks on Saipan,* 72; Crowl, *Campaign in the Marianas,* 242.
13. Appleman, *Army Tanks on Saipan,* 70–71.
14. Ibid.; Crowl, *Campaign in the Marianas,* 242.
15. Appleman, *Army Tanks on Saipan,* 73.
16. Ibid., 74. The tankers never learned the name of the heroic GI who tried to warn them of the minefield, although they later discovered the man had been a member of Company A, 102nd Engineers. It was believed the soldier eventually lost both eyes.
17. Ibid., 74–75; Hoffman, *Saipan: The Beginning of the End,* 209. Hoffman states the tanks were "medium tanks." They were not. They were M5A1 Stuart light tanks.
18. Appleman, *Army Tanks on Saipan,* 76; Crowl, *Campaign in the Marianas,* 246.
19. Appleman, *Army Tanks on Saipan,* 76–77.
20. Ibid., 78; Brown citation, "Silver and Bronze Star Awards," *History, 762nd Tank Battalion, Yr 1944.*
21. Appleman, *Army Tanks on Saipan,* 78.
22. Ibid., 78–80; Phalon and Rustad citations, "Silver and Bronze Star Awards," *History, 762nd Tank Battalion, Yr 1944.*

CHAPTER NINETEEN
1. Crowl, *Campaign in the Marianas,* 251.
2. Ibid., 253; Appleman, *Army Tanks on Saipan,* 82.
3. Appleman, *Army Tanks on Saipan,* 82–88; Nelson and Myers citations, "Silver and Bronze Star Awards," *History, 762nd Tank Battalion, Yr 1944.*
4. Appleman, *Army Tanks on Saipan,* 88; Crowl, *Campaign in the Marianas,* 250.
5. Appleman, *Army Tanks on Saipan,* 89–90; Crowl, *Campaign in the Marianas,* 250–51.
6. Appleman, *Army Tanks on Saipan,* 91.
7. Ibid., 91–8; Detailed map accompanying Appleman, *Army Tanks on Saipan;* Hoffman, *Saipan: The Beginning of the End,* 214; Crowl, *Campaign in the Marianas,* 253–54.

8. Love, *Battle for Saipan*, 33; Crowl, *Campaign in the Marianas*, 258–61; Anderson, Charles R., *Western Pacific, 15 June 1944–2 September 1945, The U.S. Army Campaigns of World War II*, 17.

9. Appleman, *Army Tanks on Saipan*, 101–7.

10. Ibid, 107–9.

11. Ibid., 109–11.

12. Ibid., 112, 114–15; Crowl, *Campaign in the Marianas*, 261.

13. Appleman, *Army Tanks on Saipan*, 113–16.

14. Ibid., 117–19.

15. Ibid., 119–22; Phalon citation, "Silver and Bronze Star Awards," *History, 762nd Tank Battalion, Yr 1944*.

16. Appleman, *Army Tanks on Saipan*, 122–25.

17. Ibid., 125–26.

18. Ibid., 126; "Report of Casualties for Saipan Operation for Headquarters and Headquarters Company," *762nd Tank Battalion, Yr 1944*, 1; "Report of Casualties for Saipan Operation: Company B," *762nd Tank Battalion, Yr 1944*, 1; "Report of Casualties for Saipan Operation: Company D," *762nd Tank Battalion, Yr 1944*, 1; Hoffman, *Saipan: The Beginning of the End*, 269.

19. Ibid., 126–30.

CHAPTER TWENTY

1. Anderson, *Western Pacific, 15 June 1944–2 September 1945, The U.S. Army Campaigns of World War II*, 20.

2. "Section IV: Movement," *706th Tank Battalion*, 1; "Section III: Stations," *706th Tank Battalion*, 4; 706th TB History, 11–12, 16. The 706th TB was transported to Guam on the following vessels; USS *Funston*, USS *Bolivar*, USS *Sheridan*, USS *Comet*, USS *Warhawk*, USS *Monrovia*, and the USS *China Victory*.

3. Costello, *The Pacific War, 1941–1945*, 485.

4. Historical Division, War Department, *Guam: Operations of the 77th Division (21 July–10 August 1944)*, [hereafter cited as War Department, *Guam*], 28, 31.

5. Ibid., 33–37; "Report of Operation on Guam," *706th Tank Battalion*, 1; Anderson, Charles R., *Western Pacific, 15 June 1944–2 September 1945, The U.S. Army Campaigns of World War II*, 21; Costello, *The Pacific War, 1941–1945*, 485.

6. "Report of Operation on Guam," *706th Tank Battalion*, 1; The National Historical Society, *United States Army in World War II, The War in the Pacific—Atlas*, 53; Gailey, *The Liberation of Guam*, 113–7; Anderson, Charles R., *Western Pacific, 15 June 1944–2 September 1945, The U.S. Army Campaigns of World War II*, 21.

7. Anderson, Charles R., *Western Pacific, 15 June 1944–2 September 1945, The U.S. Army Campaigns of World War II*, 21; The National Historical Society, *United States Army in World War II, The War in the Pacific—Atlas*, 53; "Report of Operation on Guam," *706th Tank Battalion*, 2–3.

8. Anderson, Charles R., *Western Pacific, 15 June 1944–2 September 1945, The U.S. Army Campaigns of World War II*, 21, 23; 706th TB History, 22.

9. "Report of Operation on Guam," *706th Tank Battalion*, 2–3; 706th TB History, 19, 22

10. "Report of Operation on Guam," *706th Tank Battalion*, 3; Crowl, *Campaign in the Marianas*, 369; War Department, *Guam*, 44–45.

11. 706th TB History, 55.

12. Ibid., 29; Crowl, *Campaign in the Marianas*, 369–70; "Report of Operation on Guam," *706th Tank Battalion*, 4; War Department, *Guam*, 45.

13. Crowl, *Campaign in the Marianas,* 369–70; "Report of Operation on Guam," *706th Tank Battalion,* 4.

14. Anderson, Charles R., *Western Pacific, 15 June 1944–2 September 1945, The U.S. Army Campaigns of World War II,* 23; Crowl, *Campaign in the Marianas,* 374; "Report of Operation on Guam," *706th Tank Battalion,* 3; 706th TB History, 22.

15. Crowl, *Campaign in the Marianas,* 374–76; 706th TB History, 12.

16. War Department, *Guam,* 80.

17. Ibid., 81.

18. Ibid.; 706th TB History, 54, 55.

19. 706th TB History, 30.

20. Ibid., 30; Crowl, *Campaign in the Marianas,* 386–94; "Report of Operation on Guam," *706th Tank Battalion,* 6.

21. Crowl, *Campaign in the Marianas,* 394; War Department, *Guam,* 92; 706th TB History, 26.

22. "Report of Operation on Guam," *706th Tank Battalion,* 6; Crowl, *Campaign in the Marianas,* 395; 706th TB History, 55.

23. "Report of Operation on Guam," *706th Tank Battalion,* 6; Crowl, *Campaign in the Marianas,* 395–96; War Department, *Guam,* 94–100; 706th TB History, 23.

24. Crowl, *Campaign in the Marianas,* 398–400; "Report of Operation on Guam," *706th Tank Battalion,* 6.

25. "Report of Operation on Guam," *706th Tank Battalion,* 6–7.

26. War Department, *Guam,* 104.

27. "Report of Operation on Guam," *706th Tank Battalion,* 7; Crowl, *Campaign in the Marianas,* 402–3; War Department, *Guam,* 104–5.

28. Crowl, *Campaign in the Marianas,* 403–4; "Report of Operation on Guam," *706th Tank Battalion,* 7.

29. Crowl, *Campaign in the Marianas,* 409.

30. War Department, *Guam,* 107; "Report of Operation on Guam," *706th Tank Battalion,* 8.

31. "Report of Operation on Guam," *706th Tank Battalion,* 7–8.

32. Ibid., 9; Crowl, *Campaign in the Marianas,* 411; War Department, *Guam,* 112.

33. Crowl, *Campaign in the Marianas,* 410, 415; 706th TB History, 8, 23–24.

34. Crowl, *Campaign in the Marianas,* 415; 706th TB History, 8, 24.

35. Ibid.

36. War Department, *Guam,* 114; 706th TB History, 27; Crowl, *Campaign in the Marianas,* 412–13.

37. Crowl, *Campaign in the Marianas,* 412–3.

38. Ibid., 413.

39. Ibid., 418.

40. Ibid., 420–24; 706th TB History, 20.

41. Crowl, *Campaign in the Marianas,* 423; 706th TB History, 31.

42. Crowl, *Campaign in the Marianas,* 423–24; 706th TB History, 31; War Department, *Guam,* 122.

43. War Department, *Guam,* 122–3; "Section IX: Former and Present Members who have Distinguished Themselves in Action," *706th Tank Battalion,* 15.

44. 706th TB History, 31, 32, 36.

45. Crowl, *Campaign in the Marianas,* 423–5; 706th TB History, 27, 31; War Department, *Guam,* 123.

46. 706th TB History, 27, 54, 55–56.

47. Crowl, *Campaign in the Marianas,* 425; 706th TB History, 27, 31, 36.

48. Ibid.

49. Crowl, *Campaign in the Marianas,* 426; 706th TB History, 24.

50. Crowl, *Campaign in the Marianas,* 429.

51. Ibid., 431; 706th TB History, 21; Anderson, *Western Pacific, 15 June 1944–2 September 1945, The U.S. Army Campaigns of World War II,* 24.

52. 706th TB History, 24–25; War Department, *Guam,* 123.

53. 706th TB History, 21, 24.

54. Crowl, *Campaign in the Marianas,* 429–32; 706th TB History, 21.

55. Crowl, *Campaign in the Marianas,* 437; War Department, *Guam,* 133.

56. 706th TB History, 25.

57. Crowl, *Campaign in the Marianas,* 437; War Department, *Guam,* 133.

CHAPTER TWENTY-ONE

1. Smith, *The Approach to the Philippines,* 425–49.

2. Smith, *The Approach to the Philippines,* 450.

3. Ibid., 463, 483–89; 44th TB Historical Record, 2–4; 1st Lt. Elmer F. Balogh nomination in "Nominees for Tank Ace or Other Prestigous Awards," *44th Tank Battalion,* 1; "Historical Report," *Company "B" 44th Tank Battalion, September 1, 1944,* 1; "Men Wounded & Injured in Action and Purple Heart Awards," *History—44th Tank Bn, 11 Nov 1943–30 April 1946,* 1.

4. Costello, *The Pacific War, 1941–1945,* 489–93.

5. Dunnigan, *Victory at Sea,* 67.

6. Costello, *The Pacific War, 1941–1945,* 493–94.

7. Anderson, *Western Pacific, 15 June 1944–2 September 1945, The U.S. Army Campaigns of World War II,* 24.

8. Ibid., 27.

9. Ibid., 25.

10. Camas, "The Story of Our Outfit," in 710th Tank Battalion Association, *History of the 710th Tank Bn,* 2–3; "History of 710 Tank Battalion, 1 January to 31 December 1944 Inclusive" *710th Tank Battalion,* 11.

11. Anderson, *Western Pacific, 15 June 1944–2 September 1945, The U.S. Army Campaigns of World War II,* 25.

12. Ibid., 26; Smith, *The Approach to the Philippines,* 500–1; "Operation Report, Stalemate II, Palau Islands, 710th Tank Battalion," *710th Tank Battalion,* 1–2.

13. "Operation Report, Stalemate II, Palau Islands, 710th Tank Battalion," *710th Tank Battalion,* 1–2.

14. Ibid., 2–3.

15. Smith, *The Approach to the Philippines,* 507.

16. Ciani to author, January 20, 2001, 2.

17. Ibid., 510; "Operation Report, Stalemate II, Palau Islands, 710th Tank Battalion," *710th Tank Battalion,* 3.

18. Ibid.; Smith, *The Approach to the Philippines,* 509.

19. "Operation Report, Stalemate II, Palau Islands, 710th Tank Battalion," *710th Tank Battalion,* 3.

20. Smith, *The Approach to the Philippines,* 509–10.

21. "Operation Report, Stalemate II, Palau Islands, 710th Tank Battalion," *710th Tank Battalion,* 4.

22. Ibid.; Smith, *The Approach to the Philippines,* 512.

23. "Operation Report, Stalemate II, Palau Islands, 710th Tank Battalion," *710th Tank Battalion,* 4.

24. Smith, *The Approach to the Philippines,* 511; The National Historical Society, *United States Army in World War II, The War in the Pacific—Atlas,* 61.
25. "Operation Report, Stalemate II, Palau Islands, 710th Tank Battalion," *710th Tank Battalion,* 5; Smith, *The Approach to the Philippines,* 513.
26. Smith, *The Approach to the Philippines,* 513.
27. Ibid., 515.
28. "Operation Report, Stalemate II, Palau Islands, 710th Tank Battalion," *710th Tank Battalion,* 6; Smith, *The Approach to the Philippines,* 514.
29. "Operation Report, Stalemate II, Palau Islands, 710th Tank Battalion," *710th Tank Battalion,* 6; Smith, *The Approach to the Philippines,* 519.
30. Smith, *The Approach to the Philippines,* 519–21.
31. Ferguson citation in "History—710th Tank Bn, 1 January 1945–31 December 1945" *710th Tank Battalion,* 22.
32. "Operation Report, Stalemate II, Palau Islands, 710th Tank Battalion," *710th Tank Battalion,* 6.
33. Ibid., 6–7; Smith, *The Approach to the Philippines,* 521–22.
34. "Operation Report, Stalemate II, Palau Islands, 710th Tank Battalion," *710th Tank Battalion,* 7; Smith, *The Approach to the Philippines,* 522–23.
35. Smith, *The Approach to the Philippines,* 524–25.
36. Ibid., 525; "Operation Report, Stalemate II, Palau Islands, 710th Tank Battalion," *710th Tank Battalion,* 7.
37. Ibid.
38. "Operation Report, Stalemate II, Palau Islands, 710th Tank Battalion," *710th Tank Battalion,* 7–8; "History of 710 Tank Battalion, 1 January to 31 December 1944 Inclusive" *710th Tank Battalion,* 19.
39. "Operation Report, Stalemate II, Palau Islands, 710th Tank Battalion," *710th Tank Battalion,* 8.
40. Ibid.
41. Smith, *The Approach to the Philippines,* 527, 529.
42. Ibid., 527, 529-530; "Operation Report, Stalemate II, Palau Islands, 710th Tank Battalion," *710th Tank Battalion,* 8; "710th Tank Battalion, S-3 Journal—Angaur Campaign," *710th Tank Battalion,* 2.
43. Smith, *The Approach to the Philippines,* 530.
44. "Operation Report, Stalemate II, Palau Islands, 710th Tank Battalion," *710th Tank Battalion,* 9.
45. Ibid., 10.
46. Smith, *The Approach to the Philippines,* 530

CHAPTER TWENTY-TWO
1. "Headquarters, 710th Tank Battalion, Operation Report on Peleliu Island," *710th Tank Battalion,* 1.
2. Ibid.; Smith, *The Approach to the Philippines,* 536.
3. "Headquarters, 710th Tank Battalion, Operation Report on Peleliu Island," *710th Tank Battalion,* 1–2.
4. Smith, *The Approach to the Philippines,* 537; Moran, *Peleliu 1944: The Forgotten Corner of Hell,* 76.
5. Smith, *The Approach to the Philippines,* 537.
6. Ibid., 539.
7. Ibid.; "Headquarters, 710th Tank Battalion, Operation Report on Peleliu Island," *710th Tank Battalion,* 3. Colonel Rodgers, who was on Angaur, mistakenly reported

this combat patrol took place on September 26. Beginning with that date, the dates listed by Colonel Rodgers are off by two or three days.

8. Smith, *The Approach to the Philippines,* 539; "Headquarters, 710th Tank Battalion, Operation Report on Peleliu Island," *710th Tank Battalion,* 4.

9. Smith, *The Approach to the Philippines,* 541–43; "Headquarters, 710th Tank Battalion, Operation Report on Peleliu Island," *710th Tank Battalion,* 4, 19, 20.

10. Smith, *The Approach to the Philippines,* 542; "Headquarters, 710th Tank Battalion, Operation Report on Peleliu Island," *710th Tank Battalion,* 4–5. Colonel Rodgers reported that Task Force Neal consisted of one flamethrowing LVT, four armored LVTs, and six medium tanks.

11. "Headquarters, 710th Tank Battalion, Operation Report on Peleliu Island," *710th Tank Battalion,* 5.

12. Ibid., 5–6.

13. Smith, *The Approach to the Philippines,* 542.

14. Ibid., 543.

15. Ibid., 544; "Headquarters, 710th Tank Battalion, Operation Report on Peleliu Island," *710th Tank Battalion,* 19, 20.

16. "Headquarters, 710th Tank Battalion, Operation Report on Peleliu Island," *710th Tank Battalion,* 6–7.

17. Smith, *The Approach to the Philippines,* 554–55.

18. Ibid., 545; "Headquarters, 710th Tank Battalion, Operation Report on Peleliu Island," *710th Tank Battalion,* 7.

19. Smith, *The Approach to the Philippines,* 554–55; "Headquarters, 710th Tank Battalion, Operation Report on Peleliu Island," *710th Tank Battalion,* 7.

20. Meyer citation in "History of 710 Tank Battalion, 1 January to 31 December 1944 Inclusive" *710th Tank Battalion,* 20.

21. Smith, *The Approach to the Philippines,* 545; Moran, *Peleliu 1944: The Forgotten Corner of Hell,* 74–75, 79, 81.

22. "Headquarters, 710th Tank Battalion, Operation Report on Peleliu Island," *710th Tank Battalion,* 8.

23. Ibid.

24. Smith, *The Approach to the Philippines,* 549–50.

25. "Headquarters, 710th Tank Battalion, Operation Report on Peleliu Island," *710th Tank Battalion,* 8–9.

26. Ibid.; Smith, *The Approach to the Philippines,* 556.

27. "Headquarters, 710th Tank Battalion, Operation Report on Peleliu Island," *710th Tank Battalion,* 19, 21.

28. Ibid., 9.

29. Beasley citation in "History—710th Tank Bn, 1 January 1945–31 December 1945" *710th Tank Battalion,* 18.

30. "Headquarters, 710th Tank Battalion, Operation Report on Peleliu Island," *710th Tank Battalion,* 10–11; Smith, *The Approach to the Philippines,* 558. At this point in the Operations Report of the 710th Tank Battalion, it appears as though Colonel Rodgers is off by only one day, October 8 actually being October 7.

31. "Headquarters, 710th Tank Battalion, Operation Report on Peleliu Island," *710th Tank Battalion,* 10–11.

32. Ibid., 11; Smith, *The Approach to the Philippines,* 558.

33. "Headquarters, 710th Tank Battalion, Operation Report on Peleliu Island," *710th Tank Battalion,* 12.

34. Ibid.
35. Smith, *The Approach to the Philippines,* 560–61; "Headquarters, 710th Tank Battalion, Operation Report on Peleliu Island," *710th Tank Battalion,* 13. It finally appears as though Colonel Rodgers is correct with the dates in his Operation Report.
36. Ibid., 13–14; Smith, *The Approach to the Philippines,* 563.
37. "Headquarters, 710th Tank Battalion, Operation Report on Peleliu Island," *710th Tank Battalion,* 14; Smith, *The Approach to the Philippines,* 564–65.
38. "Headquarters, 710th Tank Battalion, Operation Report on Peleliu Island," *710th Tank Battalion,* 14; Memorial Plaque, Peleliu Island; "Sherman Tank Memorial Dedication," and "Seabees Help Dedicate WWII Memorial in Palau," provided to author by Ernest J. Ciani.
39. "Headquarters, 710th Tank Battalion, Operation Report on Peleliu Island," *710th Tank Battalion,* 15.
40. Ibid.; "Headquarters, 710th Tank Battalion, Operation Report on Peleliu Island," *710th Tank Battalion,* 15–16.
41. Crowell citation in "History—710th Tank Bn, 1 January 1945–31 December 1945" *710th Tank Battalion,* 17.
42. Lewandowski citation in "History—710th Tank Bn, 1 January 1945–31 December 1945" *710th Tank Battalion,* 17.
43. "Headquarters, 710th Tank Battalion, Operation Report on Peleliu Island," *710th Tank Battalion,* 15–16; Meyer citation in "History of 710 Tank Battalion, 1 January to 31 December 1944 Inclusive" *710th Tank Battalion,* 20–21.
44. "Headquarters, 710th Tank Battalion, Operation Report on Peleliu Island," *710th Tank Battalion,* 15–16.
45. Ibid. 16.
46. Ibid., 16–17; Smith, *The Approach to the Philippines,* 569.
47. Smith, *The Approach to the Philippines,* 566; "Headquarters, 710th Tank Battalion, Operation Report on Peleliu Island," *710th Tank Battalion,* 17–18.
48. "Headquarters, 710th Tank Battalion, Operation Report on Peleliu Island," *710th Tank Battalion,* 18–19.
49. Smith, *The Approach to the Philippines,* 571–72.
50. Camas, "The Story of Our Outfit," in 710th Tank Battalion Association, *History of the 710th Tank Bn,* 4.
51. Ibid.

CHAPTER TWENTY-THREE
1. Cannon, *Leyte: The Return to the Philippines,* 3; Anderson, *Leyte, 17 October–1 July 1945, The U.S. Army Campaigns of World War II,* 7; Smith, *The Approach to the Philippines,* 453.
2. Anderson, *Leyte, 17 October–1 July 1945, The U.S. Army Campaigns of World War II,* 9.
3. Ibid.
4. Ibid., 11–12.
5. Cannon, *Leyte: The Return to the Philippines,* 22, 26; Anderson, *Leyte, 17 October–1 July 1945, The U.S. Army Campaigns of World War II,* 11.
6. 44th Tank Battalion Web site, "Nominees for Tank Ace or Other Prestigious Awards," *44th Tank Battalion,* <http://www.acu.edu/academics/history/12ad/44atbx/personal.htm>, [Accessed June 20, 2000], 1; 44th TB Historical Record, 5; 44th Tank Battalion Web site, "Chronology of the 44th Tank Battalion," *44th Tank Battalion,* <http://www.acu.

edu.academics/history/12ad/44atbx/chron.htm>, [Accessed June 20, 2000], 1; 706th TB History, 56; "Unit Journal, Leyte Operation," *History—767th Tank Bn, YR 44,* 1; "King II Operations Report Against Leyte Island, 763rd Tank Battalion," *763rd Tank Battalion* [hereafter cited as 763rd TB Leyte Report], 1.

7. Cannon, *Leyte: The Return to the Philippines,* 62–63, 65; Anderson, *Leyte, 17 Octo-ber–1 July 1945, The U.S. Army Campaigns of World War II,* 12.

8. "Opn Rpt 44th Tank Bn—Leyte, 2 Oct–31 Dec 44," *44th Tank Battalion,* [Hereafter cited as Leyte Report—44th TB], 1; "Chronology of the 44th Tank Battalion," *44th Tank Battalion,* 1; 44th TB Historical Record, 7.

9. Cannon, *Leyte: The Return to the Philippines,* 65; Leyte Report—44th TB, 4.

10. Cannon, *Leyte: The Return to the Philippines,* 67–70

11. Austin statement in Astor, *Crisis in the Pacific,* 329; Cannon, *Leyte: The Return to the Philippines,* 70–72.

12. "Journal of the 763rd Tank Battalion, From 13 September 1944 to 24 October 1044," *763rd Tank Battalion,* 1.

13. Cannon, *Leyte: The Return to the Philippines,* 72, 74; 763rd TB Leyte Report, 4–5; Barnes, "The U.S. 96th Infantry Division, Part Two," *The Gamers Net: History Remem-bered,* http://www.thegamers.net/articl.../historyrem/96th_inf2/index.asp, 1.

14. Hunnicutt, *Stuart: A History of the American Light Tank,* 372–76.

15. "Unit Journal, Leyte Operation," *History—767th Tank Bn, YR 44,* 43–44; Cannon, *Leyte: The Return to the Philippines,* 77.

16. Cannon, *Leyte: The Return to the Philippines,* 77; "Unit Journal, Leyte Operation," *History—767th Tank Bn, YR 44,* 44.

17. Cannon, *Leyte: The Return to the Philippines,* 78.

18. Ibid.; Anderson, *Leyte, 17 October–1 July 1945, The U.S. Army Campaigns of World War II,* 12; Dunnigan, *Victory at Sea,* 577.

19. Astor, *Crisis in the Pacific,* 342–44, 352; Salmaggi, *2194 Days of War,* 606.

20. Cannon, *Leyte: The Return to the Philippines,* 107–11; 763rd TB Leyte Report, 6.

21. Cannon, *Leyte: The Return to the Philippines,* 128–29; "Unit Journal, Leyte Opera-tion," *History—767th Tank B, YR 44,* 46.

22. Cannon, *Leyte: The Return to the Philippines,* 129; "Unit Journal, Leyte Operation," *History—767th Tank Bn, YR 44,* 47.

23. Cannon, *Leyte: The Return to the Philippines,* 129–30; "Unit Journal, Leyte Opera-tion," *History—767th Tank Bn, YR 44,* 46–47.

24. Cannon, *Leyte: The Return to the Philippines,* 63–64, 148, 159–62; Herndon nomina-tion in 44th Tank Battalion Web site, "Nominees for Tank Ace or Other Prestigious Awards," *44th Tank Battalion,* 2.

25. Cannon, *Leyte: The Return to the Philippines,* 108, 110–11, 130–31; "Unit Journal, Leyte Operation," *History—767th Tank Bn, YR 44,* 49–50.

26. "Unit Journal, Leyte Operation," *History—767th Tank Bn, YR 44,* 49–50.

27. Ibid., 50; Cannon, *Leyte: The Return to the Philippines,* 132.

28. "Unit Journal, Leyte Operation," *History—767th Tank Bn, YR 44,* 50–51.

29. Ibid., 51.

30. "Unit Journal, Leyte Operation," *History—767th Tank Bn, YR 44,* 52, 53, 55.

31. Ibid., 53; Salmaggi, *2194 Days of War,* 614.

32. "Unit Journal, Leyte Operation," *History—767th Tank Bn, YR 44,* 54; Cannon, *Leyte: The Return to the Philippines,* 133.

33. "Unit Journal, Leyte Operation," *History—767th Tank Bn, YR 44,* 54.

34. Ibid.
35. Cannon, *Leyte: The Return to the Philippines,* 138.
36. 763rd TB Leyte Report, 6; Cannon, *Leyte: The Return to the Philippines,* 113.
37. Cannon, *Leyte: The Return to the Philippines,* 155, 157; Salmaggi, *2194 Days of War,* 614; Anderson, *Leyte, 17 October–1 July 1945, The U.S. Army Campaigns of World War II,* 14.
38. Salmaggi, *2194 Days of War,* 608–13; Dunnigan, Victory at Sea, 53–55.
39. Cannon, *Leyte: The Return to the Philippines,* 164; 763rd TB Leyte Report, 6.
40. Cannon, *Leyte: The Return to the Philippines,* 112; 763rd TB Leyte Report, 6.
41. Cannon, *Leyte: The Return to the Philippines,* 114.
42. "Unit Journal, Leyte Operation," *History—767th Tank Bn, YR 44,* 56
43. Ibid.
44. Cannon, *Leyte: The Return to the Philippines,* 165–66, 167.
45. Ibid., 168–72.
46. Ibid., 174–75.
47. Cannon, *Leyte: The Return to the Philippines,* 173, 175.
48. Ibid., 117–20; 763rd TB Leyte Report, 6.
49. Cannon, *Leyte: The Return to the Philippines,* 115–16; 763rd TB Leyte Report, 6.
50. 763rd TB Leyte Report, 5.
51. Cannon, *Leyte: The Return to the Philippines,* 121.
52. Ibid., 122–23, 136–37; "Unit Journal, Leyte Operation," *History—767th Tank Bn, YR 44,* 57, 58.
53. "Unit Journal, Leyte Operation," *History—767th Tank Bn, YR 44,* 57; Cannon, *Leyte: The Return to the Philippines,* 139–40.
54. "Unit Journal, Leyte Operation," *History—767th Tank Bn, YR 44,* 58; Cannon, *Leyte: The Return to the Philippines,* 140–41.
55. "Unit Journal, Leyte Operation," *History—767th Tank Bn, YR 44,* 59.
56. Ibid., 59–60.
57. Ibid., 60; Cannon, *Leyte: The Return to the Philippines,* 142–43.
58. "Unit Journal, Leyte Operation," *History—767th Tank Bn, YR 44,* 62; Cannon, *Leyte: The Return to the Philippines,* 144.
59. "Unit Journal, Leyte Operation," *History—767th Tank Bn, YR 44,* 57–63.
60. Cannon, *Leyte: The Return to the Philippines,* 176.
61. Ibid., 178–79.
62. Ibid., 180–81.

CHAPTER TWENTY-FOUR
1. Cannon, *Leyte: The Return to the Philippines,* 99; Anderson, *Leyte, 17 October–1 July 1945, The U.S. Army Campaigns of World War II,* 19.
2. Cannon, *Leyte: The Return to the Philippines,* 144–45.
3. Ibid., 207–8.
4. Leyte Report—44th TB, 1–3.
5. Cannon, *Leyte: The Return to the Philippines,* 240; "Unit Journal, Leyte Operation," *History—767th Tank Bn, YR 44,* 65–66; "S-3 Periodic Report," *763rd Tank Battalion,* 26.
6. Cannon, *Leyte: The Return to the Philippines,* 242; "S-3 Periodic Report," *763rd Tank Battalion,* 26–28.

7. Cannon, *Leyte: The Return to the Philippines*, 242–43; "S-3 Periodic Report," *763rd Tank Battalion*, 29–30.

8. "S-3 Periodic Report," *763rd Tank Battalion*, 31–42; Cannon, *Leyte: The Return to the Philippines*, 243.

9. Cannon, *Leyte: The Return to the Philippines*, 243.

10. Ibid., 212–13; "Diary Notes of Company A Action—K2 Operation," *44th Tank Battalion*, 1–2.

11. "Diary Notes of Company A Action—K2 Operation," *44th Tank Battalion*, 2.

12. Ibid., 3; Cannon, *Leyte: The Return to the Philippines*, 220.

13. "Diary Notes of Company A Action—K2 Operation," *44th Tank Battalion*, 3–4.

14. Ibid.; Cannon, *Leyte: The Return to the Philippines*, 223–24.

15. "Diary Notes of Company A Action—K2 Operation," *44th Tank Battalion*, 5; Anderson, *Leyte, 17 October–1 July 1945, The U.S. Army Campaigns of World War II*, 23–25.

16. Cannon, *Leyte: The Return to the Philippines*, 235–40.

17. "S-3 Periodic Report," *763rd Tank Battalion*, 42–61; 763rd TB Leyte Report, 8.

18. Anderson, *Leyte, 17 October–1 July 1945, The U.S. Army Campaigns of World War II*, 25–26.

19. Ibid., 26; Cannon, *Leyte: The Return to the Philippines*, 256, 259–60.

20. Anderson, *Leyte, 17 October–1 July 1945, The U.S. Army Campaigns of World War II*, 26–27.

21. Ibid., 27; Cannon, *Leyte: The Return to the Philippines*, 294–303.

22. Anderson, *Leyte, 17 October–1 July 1945, The U.S. Army Campaigns of World War II*, 27; Cannon, *Leyte: The Return to the Philippines*, 297–305.

23. Anderson, *Leyte, 17 October–1 July 1945, The U.S. Army Campaigns of World War II*, 27–28; Salmaggi, *2194 Days of War*, 632; Cannon, *Leyte: The Return to the Philippines*, 285–93.

24. Cannon, *Leyte: The Return to the Philippines*, 293.

25. Ibid., 325; "Diary Notes of Company A Action—K2 Operation," *44th Tank Battalion*, 6–7.

26. "Diary Notes of Company A Action—K2 Operation," *44th Tank Battalion*, 7–8.

27. Ibid., 8.

28. Ibid.

29. Ibid., 62–67; 763rd TB Leyte Report, 5, 14, 15.

30. "S-3 Periodic Report," *763rd Tank Battalion*, 68–75; Anderson, *Leyte, 17 October–1 July 1945, The U.S. Army Campaigns of World War II*, 28.

31. 706th TB History, 61; "Company Reports, 23 Nov–25 Dec 44," *706th Tank Battalion*, 3.

32. "Company Reports, 23 Nov–25 Dec 44," *706th Tank Battalion*, 8–9.

33. Ibid., 10; 706th TB History, 61.

34. 706th TB History, 61; "Company Reports, 23 Nov–25 Dec 44," *706th Tank Battalion*, 11.

35. Cannon, *Leyte: The Return to the Philippines*, 349–51; 706th TB History, 62; Anderson, *Leyte, 17 October–1 July 1945, The U.S. Army Campaigns of World War II*, 30.

36. 706th TB History, 63–64; Anderson, *Leyte, 17 October–1 July 1945, The U.S. Army Campaigns of World War II*, 22, 28–30.

37. Anderson, *Leyte, 17 October–1 July 1945, The U.S. Army Campaigns of World War II*, 30.

38. 763rd TB Leyte Report, 13; Leyte Report—44th TB. 4.

39. Leyte Report—44th TB, 4, 5.

40. 763rd TB Leyte Report, 13–14.

CHAPTER TWENTY-FIVE

1. Andradé, *Luzon, 15 December 1944–4 July 1945,* 5–6; Costello, *The Pacific War, 1941–1945,* 520–21.
2. Andradé, *Luzon, 15 December 1944–4 July 1945,* 7; Salmaggi, *2194 Days of War,* 653–4; Smith, *Triumph in the Philippines,* 78-83.
3. The National Historical Society, *United States Army in World War II, The War in the Pacific—Atlas,* 69; "Narrative History," *716th Tank Battalion,* 2; "716th Tank Battalion Reviews Combat History in Anniversary and Commemoration Parade on Mindanao," *History 716th Tank Bn, 20 Sept '43... 24 Sept '45,* 1; "History—716th Tank Battalion, 21st September 1943–19th December 1945," *History—716th Tank Bn, 1942–45,* 1–2.
4. 44th TB Historical Record, 12, 14.
5. "Operations Report—Battle of Luzon, 9 Jan–30 June '45," *754th Tank Bn,* 7–8; Howard, *All to this End: The Road To and Through the Philippines,* 15–20, 21–23.
6. "Operations Report—Battle of Luzon, 9 Jan–30 June '45," *754th Tank Bn,* 10.
7. Ibid., 11.
8. Ibid., 12-17; Howard, *All to this End: The Road To and Through the Philippines,* 40.
9. 44th TB Historical Record, 13.
10. 775th TB History, 5.
11. "Narrative History," *716th Tank Battalion,* 3; Smith, *Triumph in the Philippines,* 111.
12. Ibid.; Smith, *Triumph in the Philippines,* 111–12.
13. "Narrative History," *716th Tank Battalion,* 3.
14. Ibid., 11.
15. Ibid., 13.
16. Ibid., 9, 30. The men who were awarded a Silver Star for action near Urdaneta on January 17, 1945, were: Sgt. Wilbut G. Shrift, Cpl. Gilbert Thompson, and PFC's William C. Cornette, Sr., Robert P. Karbowski and Pete W. Willhoit.
17. Ibid., 10.
18. Ibid.; 44th TB Historical Record, 14; Smith, *Triumph in the Philippines,* 161–4; "Opn Rpt 44th Tank Bn—Luzon, 3 Jan–30 June 45," *44th Tank Battalion,* [Hereafter cited as Luzon Report—44th TB], 2.
19. Howard, *All to this End: The Road To and Through the Philippines,* 42.
20. "Operations Report—Battle of Luzon, 9 Jan–30 June '45," *754th Tank Bn,* 19.
21. Howard, *All to this End: The Road To and Through the Philippines,* 42, 46, 48, 50.
22. Ibid., 20–25.
23. Dumbeck, *Memories of Days Gone By,* 291.
24. "Narrative History," *716th Tank Battalion,* 4.
25. Ibid.
26. Ibid., 4–5, 25, 26, 28. The men who were awarded Silver Stars for action at Sison on January 19, 1945, were: 1st Lt. Vaughn K. Dissette, Sgt. John R. Chaney, T4 William R. Crouse, Cpl. Henry A. Jerger and PFC Adam Bowman.
27. "Narrative History," *716th Tank Battalion,* 6–7, 27.
28. Ibid., 7–8.
29. Ibid., 11; Smith, *Triumph in the Philippines,* 152–54.
30. "Narrative History," *716th Tank Battalion,* 14; Smith, *Triumph in the Philippines,* 195.
31. "Narrative History," *716th Tank Battalion,* 14; Smith, *Triumph in the Philippines,* 190.
32. Smith, *Triumph in the Philippines,* 190.
33. Ibid., 200; "Narrative History," *716th Tank Battalion,* 14.
34. Luzon Report—44th TB, 2–3.
35. Ibid., 3.

36. Smith, *Triumph in the Philippines,* 196–98.
37. Ibid., 198; Luzon Report—44th TB, 3.
38. Luzon Report—44th TB, 3.
39. Ibid., 3–4; Smith, *Triumph in the Philippines,* 198.
40. Luzon Report—44th TB, 3; "44th Converts 11 Jap Tanks to Flames," *Armored News,* June 25, 1945, 4.
41. Smith, *Triumph in the Philippines,* 201, 214–15.
42. Ibid., 161; "Narrative History," *716th Tank Battalion,* 10, 16, 22.
43. Smith, *Triumph in the Philippines,* 174–77.
44. "Operations Report—Battle of Luzon, 9 Jan–30 June '45," *754th Tank Bn,* 30.
45. Ibid., 31.
46. Ibid., 31, 33.
47. Ibid., 35.
48. Ibid.
49. Ibid., 28.
50. Ibid., 40.
51. Ibid., 41–45.
52. Ibid., 46.

CHAPTER TWENTY-SIX
1. Andradé, *Luzon, 15 December 1944–4 July 1945,* 11–12.
2. Ibid., 11; Luzon Report—44th TB, 6.
3. Luzon Report—44th TB, 6; Smith, *Triumph in the Philippines,* 216.
4. Beeman, Harold. Letter to Rose M. Aiello. August 13, 1994, 1.
5. Luzon Report—44th TB, 6; Smith, *Triumph in the Philippines,* 215.
6. Luzon Report—44th TB, 6; Smith, *Triumph in the Philippines,* 216.
7. Luzon Report—44th TB, 6; 44th TB Historical Record, 16; Map notes—"44th Tank Battalion Action on Flying Column Movement also C Company Action with 6th Infantry Division," *44th Tank Battalion.*
8. Map notes—"44th Tank Battalion Action on Flying Column Movement also C Company Action with 6th Infantry Division," *44th Tank Battalion.*
9. Hencke quoted in Astor, *Crisis in the Pacific,* 513.
10. Astor, *Crisis in the Pacific,* 513.
11. DioGuardi, *Roll Out the Barrel . . . The Tanks Are Coming: The Liberation of the Santo Tomas Internment Camp,* 8, 13, 20; Thomas, "Real People: Remembering Heroism, WW II veteran helped liberate Manila," *The Decatur [Alabama] Daily News,* November 9, 2000, 3.
12. DioGuardi, *Roll Out the Barrel . . . The Tanks Are Coming: The Liberation of the Santo Tomas Internment Camp,* 20; Smith, *Triumph in the Philippines,* 251.
13. Hencke quoted in Astor, *Crisis in the Pacific,* 514; Hencke quoted in Tutt, "World War II Remembered: When MacArthur Returned to Manila," *Houston Chronicle,* July 14, 1995, 4.
14. Checka, "Tank Crashes Prison Gates to Rescue Manila Internees," <http://wae.com/messages/msgs23462.html>, [accessed November 14, 2000].
15. Hencke quoted in Astor, *Crisis in the Pacific,* 514.
16. Ibid., 515.
17. Ibid., 515; Hencke quoted in Tutt, "World War II Remembered: When MacArthur Returned to Manila," *Houston Chronicle,* July 14, 1995, 4; DioGuardi, "Santo Tomas Testament," *VFW Magazine,* March 1988, 34–35.
18. Hencke quoted in Astor, *Crisis in the Pacific,* 516, 518.

19. Luzon Report—44th TB, 7; Map notes—"44th Tank Battalion Action on Flying Column Movement also C Company Action with 6th Infantry Division," *44th Tank Battalion.*

20. Andradé, *Luzon, 15 December 1944–4 July 1945,* 14.

21. Luzon Report—44th TB, 7; Smith, *Triumph in the Philippines,* 252–53.

22. Luzon Report—44th TB, 7; Smith, *Triumph in the Philippines,* 253–54.

23. Howard, *All to this End: The Road To and Through the Philippines,* 72.

24. Ibid., 72–73.

25. Luzon Report—44th TB, 7–8; 44th TB Historical Record, 16.

26. "Operations Report—Battle of Luzon, 9 Jan–30 June '45," *754th Tank Bn,* 42.

27. Kennedy, *A Medic's Journal, PFC Sabino L. Goitia,* http://www.ibiblio.org/hyperwar/USA/pers/sal/Goitia-Jnl.html, [accessed Nov 14, 2000], 7.

28. Luzon Report—44th TB, 8–9; 44th TB Historical Record, 17–18.

29. Luzon Report—44th TB, 9; Map notes—"44th Tank Battalion Action, 'Battle of Manila' February 1945," *44th Tank Battalion.*

30. Luzon Report—44th TB, 9; 44th TB Historical Record, 18.

31. Ibid.

32. Howard, *All to this End: The Road To and Through the Philippines,* 93–4.

33. Ibid., 95, 97.

34. Andradé, *Luzon, 15 December 1944–4 July 1945,* 14, 15.

35. Ibid., 17–18; Smith, *Triumph in the Philippines,* 265–70.

36. Smith, *Triumph in the Philippines,* 259–60, 264.

37. Ibid., 259; Astor, *Crisis in the Pacific,* 549; Howard, *All to this End: The Road To and Through the Philippines,* 106.

38. "Operations Report—Battle of Luzon, 9 Jan–30 June '45," *754th Tank Bn,* 46, 48, 49.

39. Howard quoted in Astor, *Crisis in the Pacific,* 536.

40. Howard, *All to this End: The Road To and Through the Philippines,* 109.

41. Howard quoted in Astor, *Crisis in the Pacific,* 536–37.

42. Howard, *All to this End: The Road To and Through the Philippines,* 110–11.

43. Ibid., 111–12.

44. Ibid., 113; "Operations Report—Battle of Luzon, 9 Jan–30 June '45," *754th Tank Bn,* 50.

45. Howard, *All to this End: The Road To and Through the Philippines,* 125; "Operations Report—Battle of Luzon, 9 Jan–30 June '45," *754th Tank Bn,* 51, 52;

46. Howard, *All to this End: The Road To and Through the Philippines,* 130–31.

47. "Narrative History," *716th Tank Battalion,* 18.

48. "Operations Report—Battle of Luzon, 9 Jan–30 June '45," *754th Tank Bn,* 53; Smith, *Triumph in the Philippines,* 282–83.

49. Smith, *Triumph in the Philippines,* 283.

50. Ibid., 283; "Operations Report—Battle of Luzon, 9 Jan–30 June '45," *754th Tank Bn,* 55, 56.

51. Howard, *All to this End: The Road To and Through the Philippines,* 151; Map notes—"44th Tank Battalion Action, 'Battle of Manila' February 1945," *44th Tank Battalion.*

52. Luzon Report—44th TB, 10; Smith, *Triumph in the Philippines,* 277–78.

53. Luzon Report—44th TB, 10; 44th TB Historical Record, 19.

54. Luzon Report—44th TB, 10.

55. "Narrative History," *716th Tank Battalion,* 18–19.

56. Luzon Report—44th TB, 10; "Operations Report—Battle of Luzon, 9 Jan–30 June '45," *754th Tank Bn,* 58; Howard, *All to this End: The Road To and Through the Philippines,* 151.

57. Howard, *All to this End: The Road To and Through the Philippines,* 152.

58. "Narrative History," *716th Tank Battalion,* 19.

59. Ibid., 19-20.
60. "Operations Report—Battle of Luzon, 9 Jan–30 June '45," *754th Tank Bn,* 58.
61. Smith, *Triumph in the Philippines,* 291–95.
62. Smith, *Triumph in the Philippines,* 297–99; "Narrative History," *716th Tank Battalion,* 20; "Operations Report—Battle of Luzon, 9 Jan–30 June '45," *754th Tank Bn,* 59.
63. Smith, *Triumph in the Philippines,* 299–300.
64. Ibid., 301–2.
65. Ibid., 300.
66. Ibid., 302–4; "Operations Report—Battle of Luzon, 9 Jan–30 June '45," *754th Tank Bn,* 61, 62, 63, 64; "Narrative History," *716th Tank Battalion,* 21–22.
67. Smith, *Triumph in the Philippines,* 305–6; "Operations Report—Battle of Luzon, 9 Jan–30 June '45," *754th Tank Bn,* 63, 64, 65.
68. Smith, *Triumph in the Philippines,* 306.
69. Ibid., 306–7; "Operations Report—Battle of Luzon, 9 Jan–30 June '45," *754th Tank Bn,* 66, 67.

CHAPTER TWENTY-SEVEN

1. Andradé, *Luzon, 15 December 1944–4 July 1945,* 18–19; Smith, *Triumph in the Philippines,* 331–34; "Operations Report—Battle of Luzon, 9 Jan–30 June '45," *754th Tank Bn,* 47, 49, 50, 54, 59, 72.
2. Andradé, *Luzon, 15 December 1944–4 July 1945,* 19–20; Smith, *Triumph in the Philippines,* 342; Flanagan, Jr, *Corregidor: The Rock Force Assault,* 213.
3. Smith, *Triumph in the Philippines,* 342; Flanagan, Jr, *Corregidor: The Rock Force Assault,* 213.
4. Flanagan, Jr, *Corregidor: The Rock Force Assault,* 236.
5. Ibid., 294.
6. Ibid., 294–99.
7. Smith, *Triumph in the Philippines,* 348–49; Andradé, *Luzon, 15 December 1944–4 July 1945,* 20; 44th TB Historical Record, 22.
8. Luzon Report—44th TB, 11; Map note—"44th Tank Battalion Action South of Manila," *44th Tank Battalion.*
9. Andradé, *Luzon, 15 December 1944–4 July 1945,* 21–22.
10. Luzon Report—44th TB, 4–5.
11. "44th Converts 11 Jap Tanks to Flames," *Armored News,* June 25, 1945, 4; 44th TB Historical Record, 30.
12. Luzon Report—44th TB, 11; 44th TB Historical Record, 22; Map notes—"44th Tank Battalion on Flying Column Movement Also C Company Action with 6th Infantry Division," *44th Tank Battalion.*
13. Luzon Report—44th TB, 12.
14. 44th TB Historical Record, 23; Map notes—"44th Tank Battalion Action South of Manila," *44th Tank Battalion.*
15. Luzon Report—44th TB, 5.
16. "Operations Report—Battle of Luzon, 9 Jan–30 June '45," *754th Tank Bn,* 82; Howard, *All to this End: The Road To and Through the Philippines,* 181.
17. "Operations Report—Battle of Luzon, 9 Jan–30 June '45," *754th Tank Bn,* 83, 84; Smith, *Triumph in the Philippines,* 388.
18. "Operations Report—Battle of Luzon, 9 Jan–30 June '45," *754th Tank Bn,* 85; Howard, *All to this End: The Road To and Through the Philippines,* 186.

19. "Operations Report—Battle of Luzon, 9 Jan–30 June '45," *754th Tank Bn,* 85.
20. Ibid., 87.
21. 44th TB Historical Record, 24; Map notes—"44th Tank Battalion Action South of Manila," *44th Tank Battalion.*
22. "Operations Report—Battle of Luzon, 9 Jan–30 June '45," *754th Tank Bn,* 89; 44th TB Historical Record, 24; Map notes—"44th Tank Battalion Action South of Manila," *44th Tank Battalion.*
23. "Operations Report—Battle of Luzon, 9 Jan–30 June '45," *754th Tank Bn,* 102, 103.
24. Ibid., 104.
25. Ibid., 104, 119; Smith, *Triumph in the Philippines,* 434.
26. "Operations Report—Battle of Luzon, 9 Jan–30 June '45," *754th Tank Bn,* 94, 95, 98, 109–18.
27. Smith, *Triumph in the Philippines,* 395–6; "Our Proud History," *754th Tank Battalion,* 26.
28. "Operations Report—Battle of Luzon, 9 Jan–30 June '45," *754th Tank Bn,* 100, 104, 108, 115.
29. "Operations Report—Battle of Luzon, 9 Jan–30 June '45," *754th Tank Bn,* 118, 120–34, 140, 142; Andradé, *Luzon, 15 December 1944–4 July 1945,* 25; Smith, *Triumph in the Philippines,* 405.
30. "Operations Report—Battle of Luzon, 9 Jan–30 June '45," *754th Tank Bn,* 118–20; Smith, *Triumph in the Philippines,* 397.
31. "OperationsReport—Battle of Luzon, 9 Jan–30 June '45," *754th Tank Bn,* 118–20; Smith, *Triumph in the Philippines,* 397.
32. "Operations Report—Battle of Luzon, 9 Jan–30 June '45," *754th Tank Bn,* 121, 122; "Our Proud History," *754th Tank Battalion,* 27.
33. "Operations Report—Battle of Luzon, 9 Jan–30 June '45," *754th Tank Bn,* 122, 123; "Our Proud History," *754th Tank Battalion,* 26; Howard, *All to this End: The Road To and Through the Philippines,* 224.
34. Howard, *All to this End: The Road To and Through the Philippines,* 225.
35. Ibid., 226, 235, 237, 238, 239.
36. "Operations Report—Battle of Luzon, 9 Jan–30 June '45," *754th Tank Bn,* 141, 142, 146.
37. "Our Proud History," *754th Tank Battalion,* 28. 1 Andradé, *Luzon, 15 December 1944–4 July 1945,* 25.
38. Luzon Report—44th TB, 13; Map notes—"44th Tank Battalion Action South of Manila," *44th Tank Battalion*; 44th TB Historical Record, 24.
39. Luzon Report—44th TB, 13; 44th TB Historical Record, 27; Map notes—"44th Tank Battalion Action—Laguna/Tayabas Province," *44th Tank Battalion.*
40. Ibid.; Smith, *Triumph in the Philippines,* 442–45.
41. 44th TB Historical Record, 28–29.
42. 44th TB Historical Record, 31, 32.
43. "Our Proud History," *754th Tank Battalion,* 26, 27; Howard, *All to this End: The Road To and Through the Philippines,* 242.
44. "Our Proud History," *754th Tank Battalion,* 28; "History of the 754th Tank Battalion," *History—754th Tank Bn, 1946,* 22.

CHAPTER TWENTY-EIGHT

1. "Operations Report—Battle of Luzon, 9 Jan–30 June '45," *754th Tank Bn,* 46, 47.

2. Ibid., 48, 49, 50–58, 59, 61–63, 64, 65, 66; Smith, *Triumph in the Philippines,* 206.
3. "Operations Report—Battle of Luzon, 9 Jan–30 June '45," *754th Tank Bn,* 67–132; "History of the 754th Tank Battalion," *History—754th Tank Bn, 1946,* 22; "Our Proud History," *754th Tank Battalion,* 28.
4. Andradé, *Luzon, 15 December 1944–4 July 1945,* 26.
5. Smith, *Triumph in the Philippines,* 453.
6. Ibid., 451; Andradé, *Luzon, 15 December 1944–4 July 1945,* 27.
7. 775th TB History, 4, 6, 8, 10, 12.
8. Smith, *Triumph in the Philippines,* 458–2; 775th TB History, 8
9. 775th TB History, 6; Smith, *Triumph in the Philippines,* 459–60, 471–72.
10. Smith, *Triumph in the Philippines,* 450, 468–70.
11. Ibid., 465, 467, 512.
12. 775th TB History, 5, 10; Smith, *Triumph in the Philippines,* 513.
13. 775th TB History, 8; Smith, *Triumph in the Philippines,* 492–93.
14. 775th TB History, 5; Smith, *Triumph in the Philippines,* 514–16.
15. Smith, *Triumph in the Philippines,* 473–74.
16. Ibid., 516, 518.
17. 775th TB History, 6.
18. Ibid., 6.
19. Ibid., 7; Smith, *Triumph in the Philippines,* 474.
20. Smith, *Triumph in the Philippines,* 466, 474–76.
21. Ibid., 475; 775th TB History, 7, 13.
22. Smith, *Triumph in the Philippines,* 495–98.
23. Ibid., 498-503; 775th TB History, 8.
24. Smith, *Triumph in the Philippines,* 519–22; 775th TB History, 11.
25. Smith, *Triumph in the Philippines,* 525–28.
26. Ibid., 528.
27. Smith, *Triumph in the Philippines,* 477–79.
28. 775th TB History, 14.
29. Smith, *Triumph in the Philippines,* 479–81; 775th TB History, 14.
30. Smith, *Triumph in the Philippines,* 481–82.
31. 775th TB History, 7.
32. Ibid., 8–9.
33. Smith, *Triumph in the Philippines,* 485.
34. Ibid.; 775th TB History, 7.
35. 775th TB History, 11.
36. Smith, *Triumph in the Philippines,* 486.
37. 775th TB History, 9, 14.
38. Smith, *Triumph in the Philippines,* 488; 775th TB History, 7.
39. Smith, *Triumph in the Philippines,* 529–38; 775th TB History, 10.
40. Ibid.
41. Smith, *Triumph in the Philippines,* 561–2; 775th TB History, 11, 12.
42. Smith, *Triumph in the Philippines,* 562; 775th TB History, 13.
43. 775th TB History, 11
44. Ibid., 9.
45. Smith, *Triumph in the Philippines,* 563.
46. 775th TB History, 11–12.
47. Smith, *Triumph in the Philippines,* 569–71.

48. Andradé, *Luzon, 15 December 1944–4 July 1945*, 29.
49. 775th TB History, 6, 8, 10, 12, 14.

CHAPTER TWENTY-NINE
 1. Smith, *Triumph in the Philippines*, 352.
 2. Ibid., 352–53.
 3. Ibid., 353–4; "Operations Report—Battle of Luzon, 9 Jan–30 June '45," *754th Tank Bn*, 98, 99.
 4. Smith, *Triumph in the Philippines*, 587–9; Lofgren, *Southern Philippines, The U.S. Army Campaigns of World War II*, 10–11.
 5. Lofgren, *Southern Philippines, The U.S. Army Campaigns of World War II*, 11; "Narrative History," *716th Tank Battalion*, 16.
 6. "Narrative History," *716th Tank Battalion*, 16.
 7. Ibid., 17–20.
 8. Ibid., 20; Smith, *Triumph in the Philippines*, 596.
 9. "Narrative History," *716th Tank Battalion*, 20; Smith, *Triumph in the Philippines*, 596–97.
10. "Narrative History," *716th Tank Battalion*, 21–22.
11. Lofgren, *Southern Philippines, The U.S. Army Campaigns of World War II*, 13.
12. Ibid., 16; "Narrative History," *716th Tank Battalion*, 2, 6.
13. "Narrative History," *716th Tank Battalion*, 2, 6.
14. Ibid., 2-3, 8; Lofgren, *Southern Philippines, The U.S. Army Campaigns of World War II*, 16–17.
15. "Narrative History," *716th Tank Battalion*, 3, 8, 14.
16. Ibid., 10.
17. Ibid., 12–13.
18. Ibid., 12–13.
19. Ibid., 14.
20. Ibid., 23, 24; Lofgren, *Southern Philippines, The U.S. Army Campaigns of World War II*, 18–19.
21. "Narrative History," *716th Tank Battalion*, 24–25, 26–28, 38; Smith, *Triumph in the Philippines*, 614.
22. Lofgren, *Southern Philippines, The U.S. Army Campaigns of World War II*, 30–1.
23. "Narrative History," *716th Tank Battalion*, 28–29.
24. Ibid., 29–30.
25. Ibid., 30; Smith, *Triumph in the Philippines*, 616. Smith claims the landing at Catmon Point took place on April 20 instead of April 23. I have gone with the latter date.
26. "Narrative History," *716th Tank Battalion*, 30-1; Smith, *Triumph in the Philippines*, 617–18.
27. "Narrative History," *716th Tank Battalion*, 31.
28. Smith, *Triumph in the Philippines*, 617, 618.

CHAPTER THIRTY
 1. Lofgren, *Southern Philippines, The U.S. Army Campaigns of World War II*, 23.
 2. Ibid., 25; Smith, *Triumph in the Philippines*, 623–27.
 3. Smith, *Triumph in the Philippines*, 627; "History—16th Tank Battalion, 21st September 1943–19th December 1945," *History—716th Tank Bn, 1942–45*, 7; "Operations Report 716th Tank Battalion, 15 May–30 June '45," *716th Tank Bn*, 1.

4. Smith, *Triumph in the Philippines,* 627, 628–29; "History—716th Tank Battalion, 21st September 1943–19th December 1945," *History—716th Tank Bn, 1942–45,* 7; "Operations Report" *716th Tank Battalion,* 15 May–30 June '45," *716th Tank Bn,* 1.

5. Smith, *Triumph in the Philippines,* 639–40; "Operations Report 716th Tank Battalion, 15 May–30 June '45," *716th Tank Bn,* 11; Lofgren, *Southern Philippines, The U.S. Army Campaigns of World War II,* 29.

6. Smith, *Triumph in the Philippines,* 625; "History—16th Tank Battalion, 21st September 1943–19th December 1945," *History—716th Tank Bn, 1942–45,* 7.

7. "Operations Report 716th Tank Battalion, 15 May–30 June '45," *716th Tank Bn,* 11.

8. Ibid., 11–12.

9. Ibid., 8–10.

10. Ibid.

11. Ibid., 2; Smith, *Triumph in the Philippines,* 630.

12. "Operations Report 716th Tank Battalion, 15 May–30 June '45," *716th Tank Bn,* 2.

13. Ibid., 1, 3.

14. Ibid., 3–6.

15. Ibid., 5, 6.

16. Ibid., 6-7.

17. Lofgren, *Southern Philippines, The U.S. Army Campaigns of World War II,* 32.

18. Smith, *Triumph in the Philippines,* 652, 692, 694.

CHAPTER THIRTY-ONE

1. Rottman, *Okinawa 1945: The Last Battle,* 12.

2. Ibid., 12–13, 19; Appleman, et al, *Okinawa: The Last Battle,* 9.

3. Appleman, et al, *Okinawa: The Last Battle,* 9, 19.

4. Ibid., 27; Costello, *The Pacific War, 1941–1945,* 554; Alexander, *The Final Campaign: Marines in the Victory of Okinawa,* 5; Astor, *Operation Iceberg,* 189.

5. Alexander, *The Final Campaign: Marines in the Victory of Okinawa,* 5; Appleman, et al, *Okinawa: The Last Battle,* 26–27.

6. Rottman, *Okinawa 1945: The Last Battle,* 28.

7. Gilbert, *Marine Tank Battles in the Pacific,* 279; 711th TB Ryukyus Report, 5; "History—711th Tank Bn, 1 Jan 45–31 Dec 45," *711th Tank Battalion* [hereafter History—711th TB], 1; "Ryukyu's Operation Report Against Okinawa," *763rd Tank Battalion* [hereafter "Okinawa Report," *763rd TB*], 1.

8. "Operations Report, 193rd Tank Bn, Phase I, Nansei Shoto, 1 Jan–30 June '45," *193rd Tank Battalion,* [hereafter Operations Report, *193rd TB*], 1–2.

9. "Ryukyu Operation Report," *706th Tank Battalion,* 1.

10. Rottman, *Okinawa 1945: The Last Battle,* 53–54; Nichols, and Shaw, *Okinawa: Victory in the Pacific,* 38–43; "Ryukyu Operation Report," *706th Tank Battalion,* 1.

11. Rottman, *Okinawa 1945: The Last Battle,* 55–57; Appleman, et al, *Okinawa: The Last Battle,* 68–72; 711th TB Ryukyus Report, 6; "Okinawa Report," *763rd TB,* 3.

12. Gilbert, *Marine Tank Battles in the Pacific,* 280–81.

13. Ibid., 281; Clifton to author, December 13, 2000.

14. Appleman, et al, *Okinawa: The Last Battle,* 72, 74; "Okinawa Report," *763rd TB,* 3; "S-3 Periodic Report [Okinawa]," *763rd Tank Battalion,* 1; Bonnell to author, February 9, 2001.

15. "Okinawa Report," *763rd TB,* 3; "S-3 Periodic Report [Okinawa]," *763rd Tank Battalion,* 1.

16. 711th TB Ryukyus Report, 6; History—711th TB, 1–2.

17. "Okinawa Report," *763rd TB,* 6; History—711th TB, 2.

18. Rottman, *Okinawa 1945: The Last Battle,* 58; 711th TB Ryukyus Report, 6; History—711th TB, 2.

19. "Okinawa Report," *763rd TB,* 6; "S-3 Periodic Report [Okinawa]," *763rd Tank Battalion,* 2.

20. "Okinawa Report," *763rd TB,* 6; "S-3 Periodic Report [Okinawa]," *763rd Tank Battalion,* 3.

21. 711th TB Ryukyus Report, 6; History—711th TB, 3; Appleman, et al, *Okinawa: The Last Battle,* 105.

22. 711th TB Ryukyus Report, 6; History—711th TB, 3.

23. Appleman, et al, *Okinawa: The Last Battle,* 107; History—711th TB, 3.

24. Appleman, et al, *Okinawa: The Last Battle,* 104; "Okinawa Report," *763rd TB,* 6; "S-3 Periodic Report [Okinawa]," *763rd Tank Battalion,* 4.

25. Appleman, et al, *Okinawa: The Last Battle,* 104; "Okinawa Report," *763rd TB,* 6; "S-3 Periodic Report [Okinawa]," *763rd Tank Battalion,* 5.

26. "S-3 Periodic Report [Okinawa]," *763rd Tank Battalion,* 6.

27. "Report After Action, Phase I—Nansei Shoto," *713th Flamethrower Tank Battalion,* [hereafter cited as Report After Action, *713th FTB*], Chapter I, 1–2; Morschauser, Joseph, III, "Blowtorch Battalion," *Armor,* March–April 1960, 31.

28. Morschauser, Joseph, III, "Blowtorch Battalion," *Armor,* March–April 1960, 31–32.

29. Belote, *Typhoon of Steel: The Battle for Okinawa,* 196.

30. Report After Action, *713th FTB,* Chapter I, 1–2, Chapter II, 1, Chapter III, 1; Morschauser, Joseph, III, "Blowtorch Battalion," *Armor,* March–April 1960, 32.

31. Appleman, et al, *Okinawa: The Last Battle,* 104.

32. 711th TB Ryukyus Report, 7–9.

33. Ibid., 9.

34. Appleman, et al, *Okinawa: The Last Battle,* 111.

35. 711th TB Ryukyus Report, 9.

36. "Operations Report, 193rd Tank Bn, Phase I, Nansei Shoto, 1 Jan–30 June '45," *193rd Tank Battalion,* 2.

37. History—711th TB, 7.

38. Ibid., 8; Report After Action, *713th FTB,* Chapter IV, 2.

39. "S-3 Periodic Report [Okinawa]," *763rd Tank Battalion,* 7–10.

40. Ibid., 10–18; 711th TB Ryukyus Report, 10; Report After Action, *713th FTB,* Chapter IV, 2–3; Belote, *Typhoon of Steel: The Battle for Okinawa,* 149–50; Salmaggi, *2194 Days of War,* 710.

CHAPTER THIRTY-TWO

1. Rottman, *Okinawa 1945: The Last Battle,* 64–65.

2. Ibid., 69.

3. "Ryukyu Operation Report," *706th Tank Battalion,* 4–5.

4. Ibid., 6; 706th TB History, 82.

5. "Ryukyu Operation Report," *706th Tank Battalion,*7; Belote, *Typhoon of Steel: The Battle for Okinawa,* 177–78.

6. "Ryukyu Operation Report," *706th Tank Battalion,*7; 706th TB History, 85.

7. "Ryukyu Operation Report," *706th Tank Battalion,*7–8; 706th TB History, 85–86.

8. 706th TB History, 87; "Ryukyu Operation Report," *706th Tank Battalion,* 7–8.

9. 706th TB History, 81, 84.

10. Ibid., 86; "Ryukyu Operation Report," *706th Tank Battalion,* 9.

11. 706th TB History, 81, 83, 84, 86, 88.

12. Ibid., 81, 83, 84, 86, 88, 90–91; "Ryukyu Operation Report," *706th Tank Battalion,* 11.

13. Clifton to author, December 13, 2000, 1.

14. Snow to author, May 3, 2003, 1.

15. The National Historical Society, *United States Army in World War II, The War in the Pacific—Atlas,* 99.

16. Appleman, et al, *Okinawa: The Last Battle,* 255–56.

17. Ibid., 202; Rottman, *Okinawa 1945: The Last Battle,* 72.

18. "Operations Report, 193rd Tank Bn, Phase I, Nansei Shoto, 1 Jan–30 June '45," *193rd Tank Battalion,* 3; Report After Action, *713th FTB,* 3.

19. Rottman, *Okinawa 1945: The Last Battle,* 69; Appleman, et al, *Okinawa: The Last Battle,* 203; "Operations Report, 193rd Tank Bn, Phase I, Nansei Shoto, 1 Jan–30 June '45," *193rd Tank Battalion,* 3.

20. Appleman, et al, *Okinawa: The Last Battle,* 203; "Operations Report, 193rd Tank Bn, Phase I, Nansei Shoto, 1 Jan–30 June '45," *193rd Tank Battalion,* 3–4.

21. Appleman, et al, *Okinawa: The Last Battle,* 203.

22. Ibid.; Rottman, *Okinawa 1945: The Last Battle,* 69.

23. Appleman, et al, *Okinawa: The Last Battle,* 204.

24. Ibid.; "Operations Report, 193rd Tank Bn, Phase I, Nansei Shoto, 1 Jan–30 June '45," *193rd Tank Battalion,* 4; Report After Action, *713th FTB,* Chapter IV, 3.

25. "Operations Report, 193rd Tank Bn, Phase I, Nansei Shoto, 1 Jan–30 June '45," *193rd Tank Battalion,* 5; "After Action Report—193rd Tank Bn, Apr 45," *193rd Tank Battalion,* 3, 5; Report After Action, *713th FTB,* Chapter IV, 3; "S-3 Periodic Report [Okinawa]," *763rd Tank Battalion,* 19a, 19b; "Okinawa Report," *763rd TB,* 7.

26. 711th TB Ryukyus Report, 10–11.

27. History—711th Tank Bn, 9; Appleman, et al, *Okinawa: The Last Battle,* 247.

28. "S-3 Periodic Report [Okinawa]," *763rd Tank Battalion,* 20a-24; Bonnell to author, February 9, 2001, 2–3.

29. "Operations Report, 193rd Tank Bn, Phase I, Nansei Shoto, 1 Jan–0 June '45," *193rd Tank Battalion,* 5–9; "After Action Report—193rd Tank Bn, Apr 45," *193rd Tank Battalion,* 9.

30. "Operations Report, 193rd Tank Bn, Phase I, Nansei Shoto, 1 Jan–30 June '45," *193rd Tank Battalion,* 5–9; "After Action Report—193rd Tank Bn, Apr 45," *193rd Tank Battalion,* 9; Appleman, et al, *Okinawa: The Last Battle,* 211.

31. "Operations Report, 193rd Tank Bn, Phase I, Nansei Shoto, 1 Jan–0 June '45," *193rd Tank Battalion,* 11; Appleman, et al, *Okinawa: The Last Battle,* 218–9.

32. "Operations Report, 193rd Tank Bn, Phase I, Nansei Shoto, 1 Jan–30 June '45," *193rd Tank Battalion,* 10–19; Appleman, et al, *Okinawa: The Last Battle,* 218; Rottman, *Okinawa 1945: The Last Battle,* 72; Costello, *The Pacific War, 1941–1945,* 565.

33. Appleman, et al, *Okinawa: The Last Battle,* 275.

34. "S-3 Periodic Report [Okinawa]," *763rd Tank Battalion,* 27a–27b.

35. Ibid., 27b.

36. Ibid., 29b; Report After Action, *713th FTB,* Chapter IV, 8.

37. Appleman, et al, *Okinawa: The Last Battle,* 265; "Okinawa Report," *763rd TB,* 8; "Ryukyu Operation Report," *706th Tank Battalion,* 8.

38. History—711th Tank Bn, 10–11.

39. Ibid.; Appleman, et al, *Okinawa: The Last Battle,* 272–73.

40. The National Historical Society, *United States Army in World War II, The War in the Pacific—Atlas,* 109.

CHAPTER THIRTY-THREE

1. Costello, *The Pacific War, 1941–1945,* 574.
2. Rottman, *Okinawa 1945: The Last Battle,* 74–75; Appleman, et al, *Okinawa: The Last Battle,* 284–89.
3. Rottman, *Okinawa 1945: The Last Battle,* 74–75; Appleman, et al, *Okinawa: The Last Battle,* 295.
4. Rottman, *Okinawa 1945: The Last Battle,* 74–75; History—711th Tank Bn, 13.
5. Report After Action, *713th FTB,* 10.
6. History—711th Tank Bn, 13; Rottman, *Okinawa 1945: The Last Battle,* 74–5.
7. "Ryukyu Operation Report," *706th Tank Battalion,* 13–14; Appleman, et al, *Okinawa: The Last Battle,* 299–302.
8. Appleman, et al, *Okinawa: The Last Battle,* 300; Salmaggi, *2194 Days of War,* 731.
9. Report After Action, *713th FTB,* Chapter IV, 11–15.
10. Ibid., 14; Rottman, *Okinawa 1945: The Last Battle,* 80.
11. The National Historical Society, *United States Army in World War II, The War in the Pacific—Atlas,* 111.
12. "S-3 Periodic Report [Okinawa]," *763rd Tank Battalion,* 46.
13. "Ryukyu Operation Report," *706th Tank Battalion,* 16, 17.
14. Ibid., 18, 19, 27.
15. Ibid., 19; Appleman, et al, *Okinawa: The Last Battle,* 366.
16. Report After Action, *713th FTB,* Chapter IV, 15, 16; Rottman, *Okinawa 1945: The Last Battle,* 78–79.
17. The National Historical Society, *United States Army in World War II, The War in the Pacific—Atlas,* 116; Appleman, et al, *Okinawa: The Last Battle,* 360.
18. Rottman, *Okinawa 1945: The Last Battle,* 80; Appleman, et al, *Okinawa: The Last Battle,* 360; "Ryukyu Operation Report," *706th Tank Battalion,* 23, 24.
19. Appleman, et al, *Okinawa: The Last Battle,* 386–87.
20. Ibid., 372–77.
21. Ibid., 378; History—711th Tank Bn, 15.
22. Appleman, et al, *Okinawa: The Last Battle,* 378–79, 381, 389.
23. "Ryukyu Operation Report," *706th Tank Battalion,* 24.
24. Appleman, et al, *Okinawa: The Last Battle,* 381–82.
25. The National Historical Society, *United States Army in World War II, The War in the Pacific—Atlas,* 118–19.
26. "Ryukyu Operation Report," *706th Tank Battalion,* 24–5; Appleman, et al, *Okinawa: The Last Battle,* 423.
27. Appleman, et al, *Okinawa: The Last Battle,* 424–25, 427.
28. Ibid., 427, 434.
29. History—711th Tank Bn, 16,
30. Appleman, et al, *Okinawa: The Last Battle,* 431–2; Rottman, *Okinawa 1945: The Last Battle,* 82.
31. Report After Action, *713th FTB,* Chapter IV, 21; Appleman, et al, *Okinawa: The Last Battle,* 432.
32. Report After Action, *713th FTB,* Chapter IV, 22; Appleman, et al, *Okinawa: The Last Battle,* 433–34.
33. Rottman, *Okinawa 1945: The Last Battle,* 83.

34. Report After Action, *713th FTB,* Chapter IV, 23, 24, 25.
35. Appleman, et al, *Okinawa: The Last Battle,* 450–54.
36. "S-3 Periodic Report [Okinawa]," *763rd Tank Battalion,* 68, 69, 70, 71, 72, 73, 74.
37. History—711th Tank Bn, 17.
38. Ibid., 21; Appleman, et al, *Okinawa: The Last Battle,* 441;
39. Appleman, et al, *Okinawa: The Last Battle,* 442.
40. History—711th Tank Bn, 17.
41. Ibid., 17–19; Report After Action, *713th FTB,* Chapter IV, 22.
42. History—711th Tank Bn, 19.
43. Appleman, et al, *Okinawa: The Last Battle,* 456.
44. History—711th Tank Bn, 19.
45. "Okinawa Report," 763rd TB, 9.
46. Rottman, *Okinawa 1945: The Last Battle,* 83, 86–87.
47. Appleman, et al, *Okinawa: The Last Battle,* 461; Gilbert, *Marine Tank Battles in the Pacific,* 315.
48. History—711th Tank Bn, 19.
49. Appleman, et al, *Okinawa: The Last Battle,* 465; Snow to author, May 3, 2003, 1.
50. Report After Action, *713th FTB,* Chapter IV, 33.
51. Ibid., 34, 35, 36, 37; Appleman, et al, *Okinawa: The Last Battle,* 470.
52. "S-3 Periodic Report [Okinawa]," *763rd Tank Battalion,* 80, 81, 82, 83; Belote, *Typhoon of Steel: The Battle for Okinawa,* 309.
53. Appleman, et al, *Okinawa: The Last Battle,* 471–72; Belote, *Typhoon of Steel: The Battle for Okinawa,* 309.
54. Appleman, et al, *Okinawa: The Last Battle,* 473–74; Belote, *Typhoon of Steel: The Battle for Okinawa,* 310; Rottman, *Okinawa 1945: The Last Battle,* 84–5. Rottman contends recent figures show a death toll of 122,000 Okinawan civilians for the Okinawa campaign.
55. "Okinawa Report," 763rd TB, 9; Clifton to author, December 13, 2000, 2.

CHAPTER THIRTY-FOUR

1. Salmaggi, *2194 Days of War,* 744; Nalty, ed., *Pearl Harbor and the War in the Pacific,* 279–83; Costello, *The Pacific War, 1941–1945,* 590–96.
2. Clifton to author, December 13, 2000, 2.
3. Dumbeck, *Memories of Days Gone By,* 300, 301.
4. Goitia, *A Medic's Journal,* 10.
5. Howard, *All to this End: The Road To and Through the Philippines,* 254.
6. Mercier, Donald "Moe," *Story of the 44th Tank Battalion,* 3.
7. Stanton, *World War II Order of Battle,* 298–302.
8. Ibid., 20, 298; "History—28th Tank Bn," *28th Tank Battalion,* 1–6.
9. Stanton, *World War II Order of Battle,* 302; "Military History—779th Tank Battalion, 31 Aug - Sept 45," *779th Tank Battalion,* 1.
10. Stanton, *World War II Order of Battle,* 302; "Historical Data—785th Tank Bn, Mar 43–8 Sept 45," *785th Tank Battalion,* 1.
11. 44th TB Historical Record, 39–44; Stanton, *World War II Order of Battle,* 299.
12. "Ryukyu Operation Report," *706th Tank Battalion,* unnumbered (last seven pages).
13. "History of the 754th Tank Battalion," *History—754th Tank , 1946,* 25; "Our Proud History," *754th Tank Battalion*; 29.
14. "Our Proud History," 754th Tank Battalion, 29; Stanton, World War II Order of Battle, 301.

15. "Chronological History of the 775th Tank Battalion, Part II," *775th Tank Battalion,* 1–2.
16. "History—710th Tank Bn, 1 January 1945–31 December 1945" *710th Tank Battalion,* 14–15; Stanton, World War II Order of Battle, 300.
17. Stanton, World War II Order of Battle, 302.
18. "History—716th Tank Battalion, 21st September 1943–19th December 1945," *History—716th Tank Bn, 1942–45,* 8.
19. "Marches," History, *713th FTB,* 2–3.
20. Stanton, World War II Order of Battle, 299.
21. Ibid., 300.
22. "History of the 767th Tank Battalion," *History—767th Tank Bn, YR 45,* 1.
23. Ibid.
24. Ibid.; Stanton, World War II Order of Battle, 302.
25. Stanton, World War II Order of Battle, 298, 302.
26. Anderson, Richard, "Armor," *The United States Army in World War II,* http://www.militaryhistoryonline.com/wwii/usarmy/armor.htm, [accessed January 8, 2001], 2.

BIBLIOGRAPHY

NEWSPAPERS

"44th Converts 11 Jap Tanks to Flames." *Armored News*, June 25, 1945.

Gibson, Emmett F. "Maywood Cook Wipes Out Jap Nest, Killed." *Chicago Herald-American*, July 11, 1942.

———. "Grim Bataan Heroes Find Humor in Beef." *Chicago Herald-American*, July 10, 1942.

Thomas, Ronnie, "Real People: Remembering Heroism, WW II veteran helped liberate Manila." *The Decatur [Alabama] Daily News*, November 9, 2000.

Tutt, Bob. "World War II Remembered: When MacArthur Returned to Manila." *Houston Chronicle*, July 14, 1995.

PRIMARY AND SECONDARY PUBLISHED MATERIAL

"1st Cavalry Division." http://www.savethetale.com/ Army . . . 201st%20Cavalry%20Division.html (accessed January 2001).

Alexander, Joseph H. *The Final Campaign: Marines in the Victory of Okinawa*. Washington D.C.: Marine Corps Historical Center, 1996.

Anderson, Charles R. *Leyte: The U.S. Army Campaigns of World War II*. Washington, D.C.: United States Government Printing Office, 1994.

———. *Papua: The U.S. Army Campaigns of World War II*. Washington, D.C.: United States Government Printing Office, 1992.

———. *Western Pacific: The U.S. Army Campaigns of World War II* .Washington, D.C.: United States Government Printing Office, 1994.

Anderson, Burton. *A History of the Salinas National Guard Company, 1895–1995*. http://users.dedot.com/mchs/guard.html (accessed Nov 2000).

Anderson, Richard. "Armor," *The United States Army in World War II*. http://www.militaryhistoryonline.com/ wwii/usarmy/armor.htm (accessed July 2000).

Appleman, Roy E, James M. Burns, Russell A. Gugeler, and John Stevens. *Okinawa: The Last Battle*. Washington, D.C.: Center of Military History, United States Army, 1993.

Astor, Gerald. *Crisis in the Pacific*. New York: Dell Publishing, 2002.

―――. *Operation Iceberg: The Invasion and Conquest of Okinawa in World War II*. New
    York: Dell Publishing, 1996.

Barnes, Darwin. "The U.S. 96th Infantry Division, Part Two." *The Gamers Net: History
    Remembered*. http://www.thegamers.net/articl.../historyrem/96th_inf2/index.asp (accessed
    November 2000).

Belote, James and William Belote. *Typhoon of Steel: The Battle for Okinawa*. New York:
    Harper & Row Publishers, 1970.

Camas, Sgt. Joseph G., and Pfc. Julius F. Hoerster. "The Story of Our Outfit." in 710th Tank
    Battalion Association. *History of the 710th Tank Bn*. Private printing, n.d.

Cannon, M. Hamlin. *Leyte: The Return to the Philippines*. Harrisburg, Pa: The National
    Historical Society, 1994.

Catanzaro, Francis B. *With the 41st Division in the Southwest Pacific: A Foot Soldier's Story*.
    Bloomington, Ind.: Indiana University Press, 2002.

Checka, Ernest P. "Tank Crashes Prison Gates to Rescue Manila Internees." http://wae.com/
    messages/msgs23462.html (accessed November 2000).

"Chronology of the 44th Tank Battalion." *44th Tank Battalion*. http://www.acu.edu.academics/
    history/12ad/44atbx/ chron.htm (Accessed June 2000).

Costello, John. *The Pacific War, 1941–1945*. New York: Quill, 1982.

Cronin, Francis D. *Under the Southern Cross: The Saga of the Americal Division*. Washing-
    ton, D.C.: Combat Forces Press, 1951.

Crowl, Philip A. *Campaign in the Marianas*. Washington, D.C.: Center of Military History,
    United States Army, 1993.

―――. and Edmund G. Love. *Seizure of the Gilberts and Marshalls*. Washington, D.C.:
    Center of Military History, United States Army, 1993.

Culver, Bruce. *Sherman in Action*. Carrollton, Texas: Squadron/Signal Publications, 1977.

DioGuardi, Ralph. *Roll Out the Barrel . . . The Tanks Are Coming: The Liberation of the
    Santo Tomas Internment Camp*. Bennington, VT: Merriam Press, 1998.

Drea, Edward J. *New Guinea: The U.S. Army Campaigns of World War II*. Washington,
    D.C.: United States Government Printing Office, 1994.

Dumbeck, Donald C. *Buddies and Bravery in the South Pacific: A Soldier's Tale of World
    War Two*. Private printing, 1991.

―――. *Memories of Days Gone By*. Private printing, 1995.

Dunnigan, James F., and Albert A. Nofi. Victory at Sea. New York: Quill, 1995.

Fitzpatrick, Bernard T., and John A. Sweetster. *The Hike into the Sun: Memoir of an Amer-
    ican Soldier Captured on Bataan in 1942 and Imprisoned by the Japanese Until 1945*.
    Jefferson, N.C.: McFarland & Co. Inc. Pub., 1993.

Flanagan, E.M., Jr. *Corregidor: The Rock Force Assault*. Novato, Calif.: Presidio Press, 1997.

Frankel, Stanley A. *The 37th Infantry Division in World War II*. Washington, D.C.: Infan-
    try Journal Press, 1948.

Gailey, Harry A. *Bougainville, 1943–1945*. Lexington, Ky: University Press of Kentucky,
    1991.

―――.*The Liberation of Guam*. Novato, Calif.: Presidio Press, 1998.

Gilbert, Oscar E. *Marine Tank Battles in the Pacific*. Conshohocken, Pa: Combined Pub-
    lishing, 2001.

Historical Division, War Department. *Guam: Operations of the 77th Division (21 July–
    10 August 1944)*. Washington, D.C.: Center of Military History, United States Army,
    1989.

―――.*The Admiralties: Attack on Manus Island*. Washington, D.C.: Center of Military
    History, United States Army, 1990.

————.*The Capture of Makin, 20–23 November, 1943*. Washington D.C.: Center of Military History, United States Army, 1990.

Hirrel, Leo. *Bismarck Archipelago*. Washington, D.C.: Center of Military History, United States Army, 1998.

Hoffman, Carl W. *Saipan: The Beginning of the End*. Nashville, Tenn.: Battery Press, 1987.

Howard, Thomas. *All to this End: The Road To and Through the Philippines*. Private printing, n.d.

Hunnicutt, H.P. *Stuart: A History of the American Light Tank*, volume 1. Novato, Calif.: Presidio, Press, 1992.

"HyperWar: History of Task Force 6814 (Americal Division)" http://www.ibiblio.org/hyperwar/USA/OOB/Americal-history.html (accessed July 2002).

Johnston, Richard W. *Follow Me: The Story of the Second Marine Division in World War II*. New York: Random House, 1948.

Kennedy, Ellie. *A Medic's Journal, PFC Sabino L. Goitia*. http://www.ibiblio.org/hyperwar/USA/pers/sal/ Goitia-Jnl.html (accessed November 2000).

Knox, Donald. *Death March: The Survivors of Bataan*. San Diego, Calif.: Harcourt Brace & Company, 1983.

Lofgren, Stephen J. *Northern Solomons: The U.S. Army Campaigns of World War II*. Washington, D.C.: United States Government Printing Office, 1994.

————.*Southern Philippines: The U.S. Army Campaigns of World War II*. Washington, D.C.: United States Government Printing Office, 1994.

"M3 Lee Medium tank." http://www.sos.state.mi.us/history/mag/extra/tanks/ m3.html (accessed March 2002).

"Medium Tank M3 Lee." http://afvdb.50megs.com/usa/m3lee.html (accessed March 2002).

"Medium Tank M4 Sherman." http://afvdb.50megs.com/usa/m4sherman.html (accessed March 2002).

Mesko, Jim. *Amtracs in Action*, Pt. One. Carrollton, Texas: Squadron/Signal Publications, 1993.

Miller, Col. E.B. Bataan Uncensored. Long Prairie, Minn.: The Hart Publications, Inc., 1949.

Miller, John, Jr. *Cartwheel: The Reduction of Rabaul*. Washington, D.C.: The Department of the Army, 1959.

Miller, David. *The Illustrated Directory of Tanks of the World From World War I to the Present Day*. London: Salamander Books Limited, 2000.

Morton, Louis. *The Fall of the Philippines*. Washington, D.C.: Center of Military History, United States Army, 1993.

Nalty, Bernard C. ed. *Pearl Harbor and the War in the Pacific*. New York: Smithmark Publishers Inc., 1991.

Newell. *Central Pacific, 7 December 1941–6 December 1943: The U.S. Army Campaigns of World War II*. Washington, D.C.: United States Government Printing Office, 1996.

Nichols, Charles L., Jr., and Henry I. Shaw, Jr. *Okinawa: Victory in the Pacific*. Rutland, Vt.: Charles E. Tuttle, 1966.

"Nominees for Tank Ace or Other Prestigious Awards." *44th Tank Battalion*. http://www.acu.edu/academics/history/12ad/44atbx/ personal.htm (Accessed June 2000).

Perret, Bryan. *The Stuart Light Tank Series*. London: Osprey Publishing, 1980.

Perret, Geoffrey. *There's a War to be Won: The United States Army in World War II*. New York: Random House, 1991.

Poweleit, Alvin C. *Kentucky's Fighting 192nd Light G.H.Q. Tank Battalion*. Newport, Ky: Quality Lithographing Company, 1981.

Proviso East High School, Miscellaneous Biographies. *192nd Tank Battalion*. http://www. proviso.k12.il.us/Bataan%20web/ (accessed January 2001 and February 2002).

Rottman, Gordon L. *Okinawa 1945: The Last Battle*. London: Osprey Publishing, 2002.

Rutherford, Ward. *Fall of the Philippines*. New York: Ballantine books, Inc., 1971.

Sakai, Saburo, with Martin Caidin and Fred Saito. *Samurai!*.Garden City, N.Y.: Nelson Doubleday, Inc., 1978.

Salmaggi, Cesare and Alfredo Pallavisini, compilers. *2194 Days of War*. New York: Windward, 1977.

Salecker, Gene Eric. *Fortress Against the Sun: The B-17 Flying Fortress in the Pacific*. Conshohocken, Pa.: Combined Publishing: 2001.

Sawicki, James A. *Tank Battalions of the US Army*. Dumfries, Va.: Wyvern Publications, 1983.

Sharp & Dunnigan Publications, Incorporated. *The Congressional Medal of Honor*. Chico, CA: Sharp & Dunnigan Publications, Incorporated, 1988.

Smith, Robert Ross. *The Approach to the Philippines, The U.S. Army Campaigns of World War II*. Washington, D.C.: Center of Military History, United States Army, 1993.
————.*Triumph in the Philippines, The U.S. Army Campaigns of World War II*. Washington, D.C.: Center of Military History, United States Army, 1993.

Stanton, Shelby. *World War II Order of Battle*. Novato, CA: Presidio Press, 1984.

Steinberg, Rafael. *Island Fighting*. Alexandria, VA: Time-Life Books, 1978.

Stubbs, Mary Lee and Stanley Russell Connor. *Army Lineage Series, Armor-Cavalry, Part I: Regular Army and Army Reserve*. Washington, D.C.: Office of the Chief of Military History, 1969.

Tenney, Lester I.. *My Hitch in Hell: The Bataan Death March*. London: Brassey's, 1995.

The National Historical Society, ed. *United States Army in World War II Atlas: The War in the Pacific*.

Toland, John. *But Not in Shame: The Six Months After Pearl Harbor*. New York: Random House, 1961.

"United Stated Army, 1940-1945: 1st Cavalry Division." http://www.ibiblio.org/hyperwar/ USA/OOB/1-Cavalry.html (Accessed March 24, 2002).

Weaver, James R.N. *Operations of the Provisional Tank Group United States Army Forces in the Far East, 1941-1942*. http://www.terracom.net/~vfwpost/provisionatank2.htm (accessed November 2000).

Westerfield, Hargis. *The Jungleers: A History of the 41st Infantry Division*. Chelsea, Mich.: Lithocrafters, Inc., 1980.

Whitman, John W. *Bataan: Our Last Ditch*. New York: Hippocrene Books, 1990.

Zaloga, Steven J. *Tank Battalions of the Pacific War, 1941–1945*. Hong Kong: Concord Publications Company, 1995.

Zich, Arthur. *The Rising Sun*. Alexandria, Va.: Time-Life Books, 1997.

UNPUBLISHED TANK BATTALION HISTORIES AND DOCUMENTS

"History—28th Tank BN." *28th Tank Battalion*, ARBN-28-0.1.

"44th Tank Battalion Historical Record and History." *History—44th Tank Battalion, 11 November 1943–30 April 1946*, ARBN 44-0.1.

"Diary Notes of Company 'A' Action—K2 Operation." *44th Tank Battalion*, ARBN 44-0.3.

"Historical Report Company B." *44th Tank Battalion, September 1, 1944*, ARBN 44-0.3.

Map notes—"44th Tank Battalion Action, 'Battle of Manila' February 1945." *44th Tank Battalion*, ARBN 44-0.3.

Map notes—"44th Tank Battalion Action on Flying Column Movement also C Company Action with 6th Infantry Division." *44th Tank Battalion*, ARBN 44-0.3.

Map notes—"44th Tank Battalion Action—Laguna/Tayabas Province." *44th Tank Battalion*, ARBN 44-0.3.

Map notes—"44th Tank Battalion Action South of Manila." *44th Tank Battalion*, ARBN 44-0.3.

"Opn Rpt 44th Tank Bn—Leyte, 2 Oct-31 Dec 44." *44th Tank Battalion*, ARBN-44-0.3.

"Opn Rpt 44th Tank Bn—Luzon, 3 Jan-30 June 45." *44th Tank Battalion*, ARBN-44-0.3.

"Men Wounded & Injured in Action and Purple Heart Awards." *History—44th Tank Bn, 11 Nov 1943–30 April 1946*, ARBN 44-0.1.

"After Action Report—193rd Tank BN, Apr 45." *193rd Tank Battalion*, ARBN-193-0.3.

"Operations Report, 193rd Tank BN, Phase I, Nansei Shoto, 1 Jan–30 June '45." *193rd Tank Battalion*, ARBN-193-0.3.

"Organization History of the 193rd Tank Battalion." *Organizational History—193rd Tank BN, 1 Sept 1940–6 Jan 1946*, ARBN-193-0.1.

"Report of the Makin Operations by the 193rd Tank Battalion, 5 Sept '43–1 Jan '44." *193rd Tank Battalion*, ARBN-193-0.3.

"S-3 Journal, 5 September 1943 thru 1 January 44." *193rd Tank Battalion*, ARBN-193-3.2.

"Company Reports, 23 Nov–25 Dec 44." *706th Tank Battalion*, ARBN-706-0.3.

"History of the 706th Tank Battalion." *706th Tank Battalion*, ARBN-706-0.1.

"Report of Operation on Guam." *706th Tank Battalion*, ARBN-706-0.3.

"Ryukyu Operation Report." *706th Tank Battalion*, ARBN-706-0.3.

"Section I: Changes in Organization." *706th Tank Battalion*, ARBN-706-0.1.

"Section III: Stations." *706th Tank Battalion*, ARBN-706-0.1.

"Section IV: Movement." *706th Tank Battalion*, ARBN-706-0.1.

"Section IX: Former and Present Members who have Distinguished Themselves in Action." *706th Tank Battalion*, ARBN-706-0.1.

"710th Tank Battalion, S-3 Journal—Angaur Campaign." *710th Tank Battalion*, ARBN-710-3.2.

"Headquarters, 710th Tank Battalion, Operations Report on Peleliu Island." *710th Tank Battalion*, ARBN-710-0.3.

"History of 710 Tank Battalion, 1 January to 31 December 1944 Inclusive." *710th Tank Battalion*, ARBN-710-0.1.

"History—710th Tank Bn, 1 January 1945–31 December 1945." *710th Tank Battalion*, ARBN-710-0.1.

"Operation Report, Stalemate II, Palau Islands, 710th Tank Battalion." *710th Tank Battalion*, ARBN-710-0.3.

"Action Against the Enemy Report, 711th Tank Battalion, Ryukyus Campaign, 1 April to 30 June 1945." *711th Tank Battalion History*, ARBN-711-0.3.

"History—711th Tank Bn, 1 Jan 45–31 Dec 45." *711th Tank Battalion*, ARBN-711-0.1.

"History—713th Tank Bn—Armored Flamethrower Provisional, YR—45." *713th Flamethrower Tank Battalion*, ARBN-713-0.3.

"Report After Action, Phase I—Nansei Shoto." *713th Flamethrower Tank Battalion*, ARBN-713-0.3.

"716th Tank Battalion Reviews Combat History in Anniversary and Commemoration Parade on Mindanao." *History—716th Tank Bn, 20 Sept '43 . . . 24 Sept '45*, ARBN-716-0.3.

"History—716th Tank Battalion, 21st September 1943–9th December 1945." *History—716th Tank Bn, 1942–45*.

"Narrative History." *716th Tank Battalion*, ARBN-716-0.3.

"Operations Report 716th Tank Battalion, 15 May-30 June '45." *716th Tank Bn*, ARBN-716-0.3.

"754th Tank Battalion Narrative." *754th Tank Battalion*, ARBN-754-0.3.

"History of the 754th Tank Battalion." *History—754th Tank Bn, 1946*, ARBN-754-0.1.

"Operations Report—Battle of Luzon, 9 Jan–30 June '45." *754th Tank BN*, ARBN-754-0.3.

"Our Proud History." *754th Tank Battalion*, ARBN-754-0.3.

Appleman, Capt. Roy E. "Army Tanks in the Battle for Saipan." *762nd Tank Battalion, 15 June–25 Aug 1944*, ARBN-762-0.3.0.

"Casualty List of Saipan Operation." *History, 762nd Tank Battalion, Yr 1944*,

"Report of Casualties for Saipan Operation for Headquarters and Headquarters Company." *762nd Tank Battalion, Yr 1944*, ARBN-762-0.1.

"Report of Casualties for Saipan Operation: Company B." *762nd Tank Battalion, Yr 1944*, ARBN-762-0.1.

"Report of Casualties for Saipan Operation: Company D." *762nd Tank Battalion, Yr 1944*, ARBN-762-0.1.

"Silver and Bronze Star Awards." *History, 762nd Tank Battalion, Yr 1944*, ARBN-762-0.1.

"Journal of the 763rd Tank Battalion, From 13 September 1944 to 24 October 1044." *763rd Tank Battalion*, ARBN-763-0.3.

"King II Operations Report Against Leyte Island, 763rd Tank Battalion." *763rd Tank Battalion*, ARBN-763-0.3.

"Ryukyu's Operation Report Against Okinawa." *763rd Tank Battalion*, ARBN-763-0.3.

"S-3 Periodic Report [Okinawa]." *Supplemental Action Against the Enemy Report, 26 December 1944 to 10 February 1945, incl., 763rd Tank Battalion*, ARBN-763-3.2.

"History of the 767th Tank Battalion." *History—767th Tank Bn, YR 44*, ARBN-767-0.1.

"History of the 767th Tank Battalion." *History—767th Tank Bn, YR 45*, ARBN-767-0.1.

"Report of Tank Operations—Flintlock (Kwajalein) Operation, 31 January–6 February, 1944." *767th Tank Battalion*, ARBN-767-0.3.

"Unit Journal, Leyte Operation." *History—767th Tank Bn, YR 44*, ARBN-767-0.7.

"Chronological History of the 775th Tank Battalion, Part II," *775th Tank Battalion*, ARBN-775-0.1.

"Unit History of the 775th Tank Battalion, 1 April '42–4 Jan '46." *775th Tank Battalion*, ARBN-775-01.

"Military History—779th Tank Battalion, 31 Aug–Sept 45." *779th Tank Battalion*, ARBN-779-0.1.

"Historical Data—785th Tank Bn, Mar 43–8 Sept 45." *785th Tank Battalion*, ARBN-785-0.1.

JOURNALS AND PERIODICALS

Anderson, Burton. "Company C, 194th Tank Bn in the Philippines, 1941–42." *Armor*, May–June, 1996.

DioGuardi, Ralph. "Santo Tomas Testament." *VFW Magazine*, March, 1988.

Mentor, Lieutenant Colonel John M., and 1st Lieutenant Michael R. Evans. "Remember the Road to Bataan: Training for War in a Resource-Short Environment (Reserve Component)." *Armor*, November–December, 1998.

Morschauser, Joseph, III. "Blowtorch Battalion." *Armor*, March–April, 1960.

Vader, John. "Fall of the Philippines." *History of the Second World War*, Part 31.

van Oosten, F.C. "Fall of the Dutch East Indies." *History of the Second World War*, Part 31.

MISCELLANEOUS

"Citation for the Bronze Star Medal." Family Papers, Steve Bardowski.

Mercier, Donald "Moe." *Story of the 44th Tank Battalion*, typewritten manuscript, 1992.

Ortega, Abel. Speech presented November 19, 1999 at San Antonio, Texas.

Schutt, Donald A. "Janesville Tankers on Bataan." Masters thesis, University of Wisconsin, 1966.

CORRESPONDENCE AND INTERVIEWS

Bardowski, Steve. Interview by author. December 8, 2000.

Beeman, Harold. Letter to Rose M. Aiello. August 13, 1994.

Bonnell, William E. Letter to author. February 9, 2001.

Clifton, Robert. Letters to author. December 13, 2000 and January 7, 2001.

DeGroot, Edward. "Survivor Interviews—Edward DeGroot." *In the Hands of the Enemy*, http://www.enemyhands.com/ed.html (accessed November 2000).

Dumbeck, David C. Letter to author. January 18, 2001.

French, Morgan. Taped interview by Col. Arthur L. Kelley, circa 1994. http://www.dallas.net/~french/tape1side1.html (accessed November 2000).

Ortega, Abel. Interview by author. December 21, 2000.

Snow, Dean. Electronic mail to author. May 3, 2003 and June 8, 2003.

Stewart, Robert. "Survivor Interviews—Robert 'Bob' Stewart." *In the Hands of the Enemy*, http://www.enemyhands.com/bob.html (accessed January 2001).

INDEX

Page numbers in italics indicates illustrations.

Moffitt, Captain, 52, 53
morale, 67, 69
Moran, Jim, 221
Morello, Emil S., 35
  escape of, 36–37
Morin, Ben R., 1, 3, 4, 5, 28
Morschauser, Joseph, III, 339
Morton, Louis, on Luzon action, 38, 39,
  40, 46, 58, 59, 60, 64, 69, 74
Mueller, Paul J., 211, 215, 217, 228
Myers, Howard D., 167, 172, 185–86

Nafutan peninsula, 158–63
Nauru Island, 91
Neal, George C., 222–23
Needham, Robert F., mortal wounding of,
  35
Nelson, Dalbert C., 184–85
New Britain, 129
New Caledonia, 84–85
  terrain, 85
New Georgia Island, 88
New Guinea, 86–87
New Ireland Island, 135
Newby, Jean O., 99
Ngesebus Island, 227
Nichter, Sergeant, 180–82
Niemeyer, Tony, 363–64
Nimitz, Chester W., 86–87, 128, 156
  Palau Islands invasion and, 208–10
  reasons to seize the Marshalls, 116
Noemfoor Island, 152–53

O'Brien, William J., 160
O'Connor, James T., 217
Okinawa, 333–44, 345–54
  Castle Hill, 337
  casualties, 360, 367, 368
  Chinen peninsula, 361
  Chocolate Drop Hill, 358–59
  Hill 89, 366–67
  Hill 95, 363–66
  Hill 178, 343–44
  invasion plans for, 334–35
  island group, map of, *334*
  Item pocket, 352
  Japanese air assault on, 355–68
  Kakazu Ridge, 349–51, 352
  Kiyan peninsula, 362

  Kunishi Ridge, 363
  Machinato airfield, 356–57
  Madeera, 366–67
  Nishibaru Ridge, 349, 351
  Oroku peninsula, 361–62
  Red Hill, 340–42
  Shuri Castle, 360
  Shuri defense line, 348–49
  southern, map of, *338*
  Sugar Loaf Hill, 359
  terrain, 333–34
  Triangulation Hill, 343–44
  Uchitmari, 337–38
  Urasoe-Mura escarpment, 353, 354
  Yaeju-Dake escarpment, 362–63,
    364–65
  Yonabaru escarpment, 357–58, 360–61
191st Tank Battalion, 7
192nd Tank Battalion
  Bataan Peninsula invasion and, 38–47,
    48–56, 58–64, 73–81
  Company B, *22*
  destroying vehicles and weapons, 76
  engaged in Louisiana maneuvers, 10
  formation of, 5–7
  Headquarters Company, 7
  in Lingayen area, 1–5
  Luzon invasion and, 15–26, 27–37
  move north of Clark Field, 25–26
  in Philippines, 11–14
  postwar, 374–75
  training, 8–9
193rd Tank Battalion, 7, 82–83
  Makin Atoll invasion and, 92–106
  Okinawa invasion and, 335–44
  postwar, 373
194th Tank Battalion, 1
  Bataan Peninsula invasion and, 38–47,
    48–56, 71–81
  destroying vehicles and weapons, 76
  formation of, 7–8
  Luzon invasion and, 15–26, 29–37
  move to Manila, 24–25
  in Philippines, 9–11
  postwar, 374–75
  training, 8–9
Operation Cartwheel, 88
Operation Galvanic, 91
Operation Iceberg, 333–44